# COLCHESTER UNITED

## THE OFFICIAL HISTORY

**By Hal Mason**

Published by:

**YORE PUBLICATIONS**

12 The Furrows,
Harefield, Middx.
UB9 6AT.

Printed by:
THE BATH PRESS

ISBN 1 874427 50 X

Published by:
Yore Publications
12 The Furrows, Harefield,
Middx. UB9 6AT.



British Library Cataloguing-in-Publication Data.
A catalogue record for this book
is available from the British Library.

ISBN 1 874427 50 X

## ACKNOWLEDGEMENTS

Many thanks to my daughter Shelley, Mike Thornton, David Johnson and Terry and Tracey Welsh for their help with proof reading.

Also to the following for their assistance with pictures and data without which this book would not have been possible.

Essex County Newspapers, East Anglian Daily Times, Frank Rowland, Bob Curry, John Harrison, Bert. Barlow, Alan Springett, Mike Thornton, David Johnson, Bernard Webber, Bill Bower, Colchester United Football Club, Colchester Borough Library Local Studies and various other footballing friends for information.

Also to James Bowbridge for loan of Layer Road painting to illustrate the cover. To the Directors of Colchester United for permission to title the book the "Official History"

Printed by The Bath Press

**DEDICATION**

My best match.

This book is dedicated
to my dear wife Kathleen

# FOREWORDS

I am delighted and honoured to have been asked by Hal Mason to contribute this foreword to: *"Colchester United - The Official History of The U's"*.

I have known Hal since Jim Smith signed me from Watford in 1973 and we have always got on well together. His depth of knowledge regarding Colchester United is unsurpassed. I remember on one occasion Hal provided me with the most detailed set of season long statistics I have ever seen, and most useful they were too!

This book is a 'labour of love' for Hal and the years of work he has put into it just highlights his dedication to the Club. When I look back at the fourteen or so years at Layer Road as a player, coach and latterly as manager, I remember the happy times and the family atmosphere which made everyone feel part of the 'team'.

I am indebted to Cyril Lea who invited me on to the coaching staff when I finished playing and, ironically I later replaced him as manager. My experience as manager of Colchester United, where I learned to operate on a shoestring budget, have stood me in good stead during my time here at Norwich City.

I may have left Colchester under rather unfortunate circumstances, but that has not affected how I remember the people, staff and supporters of a great Club. No-one was more pleased than me when Colchester regained their League status and it would be great to face Colchester one day in a Premier League match. Who knows!

M.S.G.Walker
Manager - Norwich City Football Club

---

Hal Mason is a legend when it comes to Colchester United F.C., and one can think of no one better qualified to come up with a club history, something I know is close to his heart.

It is a story of soccer romance, of stirring deeds, all synonymous of so many little clubs who have traditions as big and proud as the Carling Premiership members of today.

Hal has been a doyen of the Layer Road Press Box for several decades following on and maintaining the standard set by Fred Draycott, Arthur Wood and Alan Everett - characters all. Hal has had his lighthearted and "hairy" moments. Dealing with a Press Corp army numbering over 40 for the Leeds United F.A. Cup tie was a major highlight!

He is one of the doughty Yorkshire breed, and characteristic of many Northern soccer writers, a talented company alas fast disappearing.

A redoubtable Pressman with an incredible encyclopedic knowledge of players, teams and games. That's why this U's history is so concise and informative, and will be such a welcome new addition to sporting bookshelves.

Bernard Webber

# - CONTENTS -

COLCHESTER UNITED FC
BB

# CHAPTER 1

# In The Beginning When The Amateurs Held Sway

olchester United are one of the youngest clubs in the Football League, for it is only 56 years since the club was launched. However, its antecedents go back 120 years - to October 1873 when the now long defunct Colchester Town Club first appeared on the football map as "The Oysters".

The newspapers of the era gave very little coverage of the game, and it is extremely fortunate that back in 1923, to mark the Town's Silver Jubilee, the late Charles Hedley Clark put pen to paper. Clark was secretary of the club for over 30 years from 1907 onwards. His 39 page book *"Some Reminiscences & Historic Data concerning the Colchester Town Football Club"* is long out of print and quite a rare item.

It is also a valuable reference book, and this - coupled with the extensive notes of the late Fred Draycott, a noted Colchester journalist for over 40 years - makes it possible to record a brief review of the era prior to professional football coming to England's oldest recorded town, in 1937.

Rt. Hon. JAMES ROUND.
First President.
Afterwards a Vice President until his demise.

The Clark book written from first hand knowledge, plus early correspondence and club notices and minutes, is a mine of information. The first team to represent the Town club is recorded and comprised:-

*H. Davey, Don Davey, A. Darken, O. Orpen, I. Bates, A. Griffin, A.G. Gilders, W. Howard and G.F. Wright.*

## EARLY OFFICIALS

The first president of the club was the Rt. Hon. James Round, who was M.P. for Harwich. He held the office for some 20 years and his descendants are still landowners in the Colchester area. Another early committee man was Fred Chaplin. He and the Cant and Orpen families were noted rose growers in the days when Essex was the rose county of England. The Cant business still survives, as does the department store Williams & Griffin, and Frank Wright & Son, butchers, all businesses dating back to members of the original Town team.

The first ground was in Cambridge Road, long built over, and the team colours were blue jerseys and white knickerbockers. By 1879 the club was affiliated to the Football Association. The Cambridge Road playing pitch was almost 200 yards long and it is recorded that a throw in, at that time, had to travel at least six yards.

On the 20th of September 1882, Town were founder members of the Essex F.A. which held its inaugural meeting at the White Hart Hotel in Chelmsford. All the early matches were of a friendly nature against opponents such as Chelmsford, Coggeshell, Braintree and Maldon, plus school teams such as Dedham & Atcham School from Clacton (as an aside Vivian Woodward played for the latter, and also Town, and one of his international caps has a place of honour in Clacton Town's club house).

The 1883 season marked the advent of the Essex Senior Cup, the final resulted Colchester Town 3 Braintree 1. That was the only time that Town won that trophy. In the Colchester team that day were several other players whose families were prominent business people. Goalkeeper Daniell was a scion of the West Bergholt brewing family.

O.E. Lay's name is still perpetuated in the well known Lay & Wheeler wine and spirit merchants. Hector Harris was the son of the headmaste. of the Bluecoat School; while Ernie Goby the winger became a leading racehorse trainer at Epson. Frank Fenner another Town player claimed relationship with the Fenners of Cambridge University Cricket Ground fame. In fact in the early years it was very much a local gentleman & businessmans club.

There is an amazing true story relating to Goby. His father was a funeral undertaker and took a dim view of his son's footballing activities. He forbade him to play in a match at Ipswich and ordered him to accompany the driver of a hearse to a funeral that day. Ernie duly set off on the hearse, but once out of his father's sight he clambered off, collected his bag, hidden under the coffin, and joined the football team at North Station!

About this era the Town colours were changed to chocolate and pink quartered shirts, quite an innovation in these times. While a little later Paul Aggio of musical fame became club captain. Prior to 1890 there was an ongoing argument whether Colchester or a team called Excelsior were the leading club in the town.

In that year a specially convened meeting on the 2nd of September 1890 agreed to merge the two clubs. It was then that the suffix Town was added to the official title, the old club to that date were simply known as 'Colchester'.

## THE MESSAGE STILL APPLIES

Press critics of the time, as today, were not afraid to air their views. Writing of an Essex Cup match in 1895, the scribe in the Essex Telegraph had this to say; *"The Team generally:- talk less, and play with your feet and head, not with your tongues".* These admonitions stand good today – Colchester United in 1992/93 totted up 303 disciplinary points – many for verbals!

By 1895 Colchester Town were competing in the Borough League (still functioning today as the Essex & Suffolk Border League), but time was running out at the Cambridge Road ground. The last match there was in early 1902 for the benefit of a player named "Jim" Holt who had sustained a bad injury. The takings at the gate amounted to £48–0–2d – a quite considerable sum in those days.

NORTH ESSEX LEAGUE.

DIVISION I.

COLCHESTER TOWN v. COLCHESTER CROWN.

REDS RETAIN THE CHAMPIONSHIP.

At Cambridge Road, Colchester. Teams:—

Colchester—Boast, goal; Park and Manning, backs; Downing, Clark, and Orman, half-backs; Leaning, Holt, Moore, Lawton and Gosnell, forwards.

Crown—H. T. Jennings, goal; C. E. Jennings and J. Hawkins, backs; Collins, Lecomber, and Garland, half-backs; Ryder, Cook, Turner, Smith, and Brown, forwards

Referee—Mr. R. A. Cox.

The Crown started well, showing superior smartness, but Holt and Leaning got off, and the latter gave Jennings a warm handful. The Crown retaliated with great vigour, but were grandly checked by Manning, and then pretty play by Orman enabled Colchester to settle down to a stinging attack, with which, however, the defence coped successfully. Again the Crown got away, only to be beaten time after time by Manning, and then once more the Town got close, and Lawton struck the cross-bar. Moore sent in from an off-side position, and from the free kick Brown got clean

*Local Newspaper report – March 1901*

Quite apart from losing the ground to the builders, the Town club were also facing a big challenge from the rising Colchester Crown team who played at Land Lane. Town spent most of the 1902/03 season playing at Reed Hall, and also had a short spell on a ground at the junction of Drury Road and Maldon Road, before finally moving to Albert Road. Gate receipts were meagre and to make matters worse the Crown team had a good season and reached the final of the Essex Senior Cup. The Globe Hotel in North Station Road provided the Town club with headquarters and changing facilities. Training consisted of running a circuit through Berechurch and Layer de la Haye finishing up at the Donkey & Buskins public house for a supper of hot cocoa, cheese, biscuits and pickled onions – the cost met by a "whip round" of those present.

Prominent names at the club in the early days of the century were the Croxford's of the Globe Hotel, Charles Clark (the writer of the book in 1923), the Turrall's of Kelvedon, and Gerald Benham (later to figure prominently in the annals of the club).

By 1908 another move had been made, this time to Sheepen Road. The pitch, prepared by landowner Isaac Lott, was called "The Oval" and officially opened on the 3rd of October 1908. A contemporary record of the first match against the Northamptonshire Regt. records that after the match the Town team *"divested themselves of their red shirts and white nicks and dived into the River Colne which ran adjacent to the pitch to wash off the municipal dust".* The area had once been a rubbish tip!

The 1909/10 season marked yet another – and what proved to be a last – move, to the Layer Road ground; Colchester United's present headquarters. Previously the pitch there had been let to the Army by Arthur Cant the owner. It was described as *"a bleak spot on a cold and rainy day with no cover".*

Colchester Town were fortunate that around that time Alfred Crowther came to the fore. A Yorkshireman who had migrated south – relatives have had a long connection with Halifax Town – and his generosity and contacts enabled the club to erect the long covered stand. Colchester architect Walter Cressall designed and supervised the building work free of charge. Among the subscribers to the cost was one A.A. Gosnell. Albert Gosnell started his career with the Town, signed as a professional for Newcastle United, and played for England against Ireland in 1906. He later played for Spurs and eventually became manager of Norwich City.

## RED LETTER DAY

The 28th of April 1910 was a red letter day at Layer Road, for Arsenal brought their senior side down to mark the opening of the new stand. The Reds won an exciting game 3–2. That was the season too when Colchester Town joined the South Essex League, then a very strong competition. In 1911 Gerald Benham, who had carried out the legal work in connection with the leasing of Layer Road, brought a Luton Town team to play Colchester Town. As far as can be ascertained that was the first occasion an official Town programme was issued at the ground. Later programmes were also issued for exhibition matches against Sheffield United, Derby County, Millwall Athletic and Norwich City.

The 1912/13 season saw Colchester Town champions of the South Essex League, and they also topped the Essex & Suffolk Border League plus the East Anglian League. It was indeed a red letter season.

That team stayed together and were scheduled to visit Sparta Rotterdam when the Great War brought football at Layer Road to an end. The pitch was handed over to the Army as a drill ground.

Seven players were killed in action during the Great War, and a tablet inscribed with their names still hung in the dressing room when Colchester United took over in 1937.

February 1919 saw Colchester Town, with Gerald Benham, William Harper, Alfred Crowther, Fred G. Mills, P.G. Parker and Chas. Clark forming the committee to purchase Layer Road from the Cant family for an undisclosed sum. The cash was raised by issuing five percent debentures and the ground vested in five trustees.

By 1921 the club was looking to progress but were rejected by the Athenian League. A season was spent playing friendlies only, and then a short spell followed in the unlikely surroundings of the Middlesex League with the championship being won at the first attempt.

Two years after their Silver Jubilee in 1925, along with Finchley, Great Western Railway, Hazells (Aylesbury), Hoddesdon Town, Metropolitan Railway and R.A.F. Halton, Colchester Town joined the Spartan League. Of these new entrants only Colchester Town were placed in Division One – a measure of the club's standing in the 1920's.

Though eleven seasons were spent in the Spartan League, Colchester never figured prominently in the competition. Their best season was 1928/29 when they finished fourth, nine points behind the champions Metropolitan Police, with Walthamstow Avenue and Brentwood & Warley in second and third places.

**"INOPPORTUNE TIME TO PROCEED WITH PROFESSIONALISM"**

**Unanimous Resolution of Colchester Town F.C. Executive**

**SCHEME FOR A JUNIOR "NURSERY"**

"The question of professional football was discussed at a meeting of Colchester Town F.C. Executive on Monday evening, and it was decided to issue a statement to the Press to the following effect :— "By a unanimous vote it is resolved that it is inopportune at the present moment to proceed with the scheme for professionalism submitted by Mr. W. E. Knights, a member of the Executive.

"In regard to a nursery, the hon. general secretary (Mr. S. W. Frost) has been in negotiation with a prominent junior club in the town, and providing this [illegible] decides at a general meeting [illegible] week the Colchester club will have a nursery, which should be the means of strengthening the Borderers and the club's playing strength all round, and, what is more important, enable practically a local side to be fielded."

It is understood that the junior club [illegible]

*Newspaper article in 1936*

Changing facilities at Layer Road in those days were in a converted railway carriage, and there was just one tin bath to provide after match ablutions. It was not until the late 1920's that dressing rooms on the present site, under the main stand were provided.

The 1935/36 season saw the Layer Road club transfer to the newly formed Eastern Counties League where they were joined by near neighbours Ipswich Town among others.

That inaugural season saw Harwich & Parkeston and Lowestoft Town finish equal top on 36 points. Colchester Town had a poor season but at least had the honour of staging the Championship play–off. That match ended 3–3 – the one and only time the Eastern Counties League championship has had joint champions.

It was also a season that marked the beginning of the end for Colchester Town. Attendances were poor and although the club started the next campaign, by Christmas 1937 the end had come for "The Oysters".

Had things in the football world in 1937 been different with amateur status not jealously guarded by the F.A., Town could have been alive today. When Colchester United was launched as a professional club the original plan was to continue to also operate the old amateur club, both under one banner.

But the Essex F.A. stepped in, and ruled that a professional and amateur club could not operate under one set of officials. The wheel of fortune was about to turn full circle, for when Colchester and Excelsior merged before the turn of the century the two clubs wanted to name the team Colchester United. That plan had to be scrapped because there was already a minor team named Colchester United in existence. So Colchester Town it had to be, and it was 45 years before the senior club in the town became Colchester United.

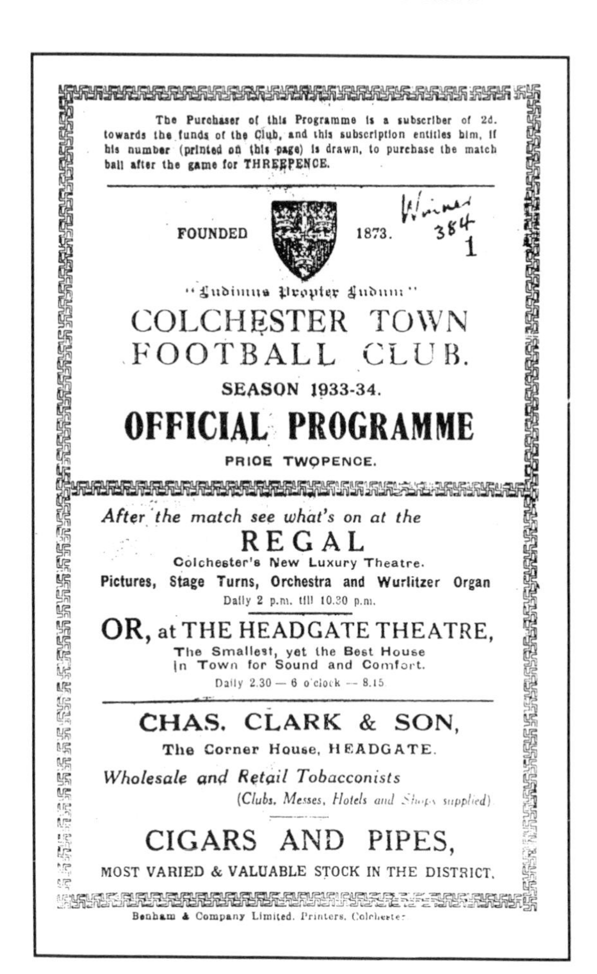

# CHAPTER 2

# The Birth of The U's

*Colchester Town team group of 1931, and two men that became significance with the later U's. Far Left - Charles Clark (of memorial Hall fame), and seated third from left - Ted Fenton.*

*"The local football war is on again".* That was one of Fred Draycott's opening lines in a newspaper article early in 1937. The issue, according to Fred, was whether Colchester Town should continue as an amateur club, or whether the time had come to embark on professionalism. The idea had been mooted in the previous year, and between then and a specially convened meeting held in Colchester Town Hall early in 1937, the issue had been the subject of much correspondence - for and against - in the local Press.

Walter Clark, one of the best known administrators in Essex football circles, and who originally had been opposed to professionalism at Colchester, had joined "The Rebels" and it was largely through his efforts that the Town Hall meeting was convened. Commenting further, Draycott had this to say: *"However sharply divided opinion is, this meeting will at least clear the air and indicate whether or not there is really any substantial backing for a pro-team, or whether it is really the voice of the few".*

Councillor Maurice Pye was the Chairman of the meeting in the Grand Jury Room, and the answer was soon forthcoming. In his opening remarks he stated that a lot of people, *"were not satisfied with the place which the town was occupying in the football world".*

Walter Clark addressing the crowded meeting pointed out that a progressive football club had a catchment area population of almost 200,000. A population more than sufficient to support a professional club. At least 17 clubs in the Football League had far less a population to call on. Looked at from any viewpoint the time was ripe to follow the example of Ipswich Town and venture into a professionally organised club. He mentioned that, *"a substantial measure of financial support had already been promised".* Mr. H.E. Hucklesby in the ensuing discussion told the audience that he had been ashamed... *"to see the deplorable exhibitions witnessed at Layer Road that season"*, and on behalf of the tradesmen in the town said they would be pleased to support the venture.

At the conclusion of the meeting a steering committee comprising Councillor Pye, Mr. Hucklesby, E.J. Markham, B. Myers, A.E. Warner, W. Allen, W. Howard and A.W Martin was elected - with Walter Clark having the brief to call a Town meeting.

It is interesting to note that four of the steering committee, Councillor Pye, Mr. Howard, Mr. Allen and Mr. Myers later became Directors of Colchester United. Bill Allen and Ben Myers in fact served on the Board for over 30 years.

To look back to the end of 1936, Mr. W.R. Knights and 'Spartan' in the Colchester Gazette had outlined the steps needed to float a professional club. A Limited Company with an initial capital of between £3,500 and £4,000 would have to be formed. Assuming entry was gained into the Southern League, the estimated income would be around £5,510. Expenditure would include £400 salary for a manager, players wages of £2,780 and travelling costs of £400. Knights felt it was a viable proposition.

'Spartan' however felt Knights estimated figures would not be realised and wrote: *"Looking at the scheme from a purely financial point of view I venture to suggest that as far as Colchester is concerned it is not possible to run a professional team".* He also rubbished Knights estimate that a professional side would attract gates of 5,000. He wrote: *"Can anyone imagine 4,000 or more people standing out in the driving rain without any cover, for this is what it will mean, as you cannot get 5,000 into the stands".*

In the event time proved both wrong. Knights underestimated the costs, but 'Spartan' was left with egg on his face when ultimately gates soared above the 5,000 mark.

The public meeting at the Albert Hall, chaired by the Mayor Councillor Gerald Benham, on March the 2nd, 1937 attracted a packed audience. Councillor Benham was in fact the man who had organised the purchase of Layer Road by Colchester Town almost 20 years previously.

At the end of a lengthy discussion of the pro's and con's a decision was made to go ahead with the formation of a fully professional team. So March the 2nd, 1937 was undoubtedly the Birth of the U's – although of course at that time the name of the club still had to be decided. It could not be Colchester Town, for the amateur club intended to continue, with the new organisation sharing the Layer Road ground.

Practically the last act of Colchester Town before they finally disbanded at the end of 1937 was to build the Charles Clark Memorial Hall, which was later to be used by Colchester United as a committee and reception room for almost three decades.

The Memorial Hall was in fact much later demolished to make way for the present covered standing area, with offices underneath, at the Layer Road end of the ground. The plaque which was erected to mark the opening of the Hall can still be seen on a wall at the back of the main stand.

The Colchester Town balance sheet showed assets totalling £2,777. These assets were the Layer Road ground, valued at £700, the stand at £1,542 and the Charter Clark Memorial Hall at £293. Councillor W.M. Harper was Chairman and B. Mayers was elected to the committee.

It was agreed that in the 1937/38 season Colchester Town would play in the newly formed Essex Senior League instead of the Eastern Counties League.

The affairs of Colchester United meantime had moved on a pace. There was, of course, no office accommodation at Layer Road in those days, so headquarters – two rooms – were set up in the Salisbury Hotel. Plans were also put in had to improve the banking on two sides of the ground when it was estimated the ground would hold 12,000 to 14,000 spectators.

For the initial season the club, in addition to competing in the Southern League, also took part in the mid-week section of that competition and also entered the Southern League Cup.

Twelve directors joined the Board. They were Maurice Pye, a chairman, a member of the Borough Council and a J.P.; William Allen, later to be the chairman for many years, Leonard Boult, Percy Cook, Leonard Daniell, Councillor William Harper, William Howard, Charles Le Ball, Gilbert Morris, Benjamin Myers and Councillor Ralph Wright.

The share capital was £5,000 divided into 20,000 ordinary shares of five shillings each (25p).

Colchester United also went on the phone, with a similar number to the present one. The company was finally incorporated on August 3rd 1937.

The first game of note was a trial game which took place on August 19, 1937. The line-ups were:-
Probables; *Dunn, Fairchild, Baker, Collins, Leslie, Ritchie, Hodge, Pritchard, Evans, Cheyne, Barraclough.*
Possibles; *Pettitt, Todd, Haley, Fieldus, Ormesher, Thompson, Bennett, Cummings, Smith, Williams, Crisp.*

Probables won 4-0, and nearly 3,000 fans turned up for the match. In the second half Kirk and Mills replaced Fieldus and Cummings; the Essex County Standard reported the teams the other way round. Todd was a former Newcastle United and Burnley player on trial. Davis wanted to sign him but Todd wanted £4 a week – a lot of money in those days. Apparently big wage demands are not peculiar to the present time. Cliff Fairchild who had come to ask for a trial on the day of the match was signed as a professional immediately after the game.

### THE U's KICK-OFF WITH DEFEAT AT YEOVIL

That first season opened with a rail journey to Yeovil. Supporters and players travelled together on a special cheap day rate of 13-6d (67p) return. Yeovil won 3-0, Dave Halliday scoring all three goals. There was early drama in the match, after George Crisp netted after nine minutes. The teams had relined up, the goal having been given, when a linesman walked on and spoke to the referee – who then rescinded his earlier decision – no explanation was ever given.

The teams for this historic match at The Huish were:-
**Yeovil and Petters United:** *Langford, Burges, Kingham, Mann, Bewick, Heward, Whyte, Kirk, Halliday, Attley, Smith.*
**Colchester United:** *Dunn, Fairchild, Wood, Collins, Leslie, Ritchie, (Capt), Hodge, Pritchard, Smith, Cheyne, Crisp*

There was better luck the following Thursday when the first mid-week section game saw the U's win 6-1 at Layer Road against Bath City. Reg Smith scored the club's first hat-trick, Arthur Pritchard got a couple and John Hodge the other one. Mayers replaced Jim Collins who thus can claim the dubious distinction of being the first Colchester player to be dropped.

The first home game in the Southern League found Ipswich Town at Layer Road on September 4, 1937 and the gate receipts were just over £600, a full house. A vociferous crowd witnessed an exciting 3-3 draw. Crisp, Wood andy Cheyne scored for Colchester.

Unknown to most of the spectators at the match there was an outbreak of fire in the stand on the popular side. Colchester Fire Brigade dealt with the outbreak by cutting away one of the steps at the end of the covered stand and using fire extinguishers. At the time work was also going on putting a cover over the previously open Layer Road end and this was completed at the end of September.

The mid-week section match at Bath in October saw a cheap rail ticket organised for travelling fans at 12 shillings (60p) return.

One of the players Syd Fieldus, missed the train but fortunately James Collins was among the fans who made the trip. He came into the side and played, one of the two outings he had in the first team. Ted Davis got a very hostile reception from the Twerton Park devotees who had not forgiven him for leaving Bath City on just two weeks notice!

At Plymouth, a high scoring game was lost 5–4 – in the Argyle goal was a young amateur 'keeper *George Wright* who some 13 years later was to be the U's custodian in the Football League. In October Wolves, then a First Division side managed by Frank Buckley – famous for his monkey gland treatment – paid £250 for *Reg Smith*, a substantial fee in those days. In addition, they agreed to send their full side to play a charity match at Layer Road the following April. On the debit side Davis was thwarted in his bid to sign *Will Prendergast* from Bristol Rovers and *Tweed* a full back who went to Gillingham, both wanted too much money.

In October, *Barraclough, Ritchie* and *Wood* were selected for the Southern League team which beat the Cheshire County League team 7–4 at Sealand Road, Chester.

On November 25th, before a gate of 4,000, *Bill Barraclough* had the dubious honour of becoming the first United player to be sent off. Fred Draycott reported he questioned the referee's parentage! In the same match against Norwich City, goalkeeper *Ronnie Dunn* was concussed, and the U's played the last 30 minutes with only nine men; *Alex Wood* going in goal.

Colchester Town, now with serious financial problems meantime continued to compete in the Essex League, until November. For a match against Crittall Athletic they had a father and son playing in the side.

*"Spud" Cater* – ten years later to be a member of Ted Fenton's Cup giant killing side – played alongside his father *Alf Cater* then 47 years of age. In goal was *Rex Bale*, a youngster on Spurs books as an amateur, who found fame and fortune eventually as one of the star toastmasters in the 50's and 60's era. Both the Caters' incidentally failed to finish the match, each coming off with torn leg muscles.

The Essex County Telegraph of November 24th carried a full report of Colchester United's first annual general meeting.

It was reported the Supporters Club now had 970 members and that the Ground could house 5,000 under cover. The meeting was attended by 337 shareholders and 6,144 shares had been taken up. Trading receipts to that date totalled £3,119 and there was a balance in hand of £1,689. At this meeting the question of running a reserve side was also raised, and a Colchester Town representative reported that that club was on the verge of folding.

## TOWN PACK UP

A month later the Telegraph carried a headline *"Town F.C. is dead. Long live United"*. Financial problems led to the 64 year old amateur club becoming defunct. Three days later on December 15th 1937, Colchester United Reserves secured admission to the Eastern Counties League. Town were later fined £25 for withdrawing from the Essex Senior League, and the remaining five clubs in the competition sought compensation through the Football Association.

There was also a fine for Colchester United for not appearing at Exeter for a Southern League match. Their excuse was that they had missed the train due to fog – the fixture was played three days later – two days after Christmas, when the U's won 3–1, with *Barraclough, Cheyne* and *Crisp* getting the goals. Meantime Chelmsford City, having seen the progress made at Colchester and Ipswich were gearing up for professional football, and in early January 1938 appointed Billy Walker a leading name in the soccer world, as their manager.By Christmas, Colchester had taken 20 points from their first 15 Southern League games, equal on points with Ipswich Town but with a better goal average. They were top of the mid-week section with 12 points from nine games – one point in front of Norwich City Reserves.

## CHRISTMAS DAY DEBUT

On Christmas Day the Reserves team played their first game, with 1,700 fans seeing them beat Ipswich Town Reserves 3–1.

The Colchester team consisted of:– Colchester *Platt, Thompson, Haley, Collins (Capt), Ormesher, Mayes, Simpson, Baker, Fieldus, Cater, Crisp. Fieldus (2),* and *Cater* scored the goals. *Platt*, a 17 year-old 'keeper, was later sold to Arsenal. *Thompson, Haley, Ormesher, Simpson* and *Cater* had joined the club as amateurs from the now defunct Colchester Town.

By the turn of the year the Colchester first team was unbeaten at home, and with a 6–1 win over Barry on New Year's Day, had risen to third in the table with five games in hand on leaders Bristol Rovers Reserves. The News Chronicle of January 6th 1938 carried the following item. *"Barraclough of Colchester United was cautioned and warned that any further complaint against him, if proved, might lead to his permanent suspension from football"*. Barraclough had appeared before an F.A. Disciplinary Committee following his sending off against Norwich City. He had a history of misconduct, and Colchester released him at the end of the season.

In the News of the World the following Sunday Colchester were mentioned in a much more favourable light. Commenting on their highly successful debut in professional football it said:– *"We raise our hats to Mr Ted Davis the best manager in the game, who during the close season was given a day off by his directors, and a £10 note and told to go out and get a team, and to be sure and bring back some change as a supply of oil would be required for the turnstiles"*. Poetic licence no doubt, but it was a fact that the whole Colchester team cost only £30 in signing on fees. There was also a couple of other incidents of interest in January. *Oswald Lewis*, the M.P. for Colchester, bought shares in the club and the St.Botolph's Street Trader's Association set a new trend for the business people of the town by buying £100 of shares.

## GALE DAMAGES STAND

January 1938 also saw something of a minor disaster hit the U's. On the 29th, a severe gale in the early hours of Saturday morning blew the recently erected timber and corrugated roof off the stand at the Layer Road end. Eleven of the 13 sections of the roof were blown into the street and Layer Road was blocked for two days. There was also considerable damage to houses opposite.

February opened with a visit to Portman Road for the Southern League match billed as "The game of the season". There were two special trains and a fleet of coaches from Colchester heading to Ipswich. At the time Ipswich with 26 points from 19 games were one point ahead of Colchester on 25 points from a similar number of games. There were long queues two hours before the kick-off but those who waited were treated to a thriller. A crowd of 23,890 saw the match, Ipswich winning 3–2.

Colchester, through goals from *Pritchard* and *Cheyne* – *Astill* pulling one back for Ipswich – led 2–1 with six minutes to go. But *Perrett* and *Little* netted in a hectic finish to give Ipswich victory by the odd goal in five. *Dunn* in the Colchester goal was at fault for both *Alstill's* and *Little's* goals. The gate receipts amounted to £1,181.

After the match the Colchester Telegraph of Feb 11th prophesied that Ipswich would: *"Walk into the Third Division"* because of their strong financial backing and well appointed ground. A forecast that proved correct. The columnist then went on to ask *"What of Colchester's chances?"*.

*"Simply not running and never will be with their poor financial backing. I can definitely say that a mere 300–odd shareholders and £1,500 or so in Capitol is not nearly enough for league status"*. He added *"There is little public spirit in Colchester. Well it looks like it, doesn't it."*

Talk about damming with faint praise. The team in their first season were laying fourth in the strong Southern League. They had a supporters club with more than 2,000 members who had already contributed a £1,000 towards ground improvements at Layer Road. By now that membership had climbed to 2,085.

The 2,000th member enrolled into the Supporters Club had been William Allen, later to be chairman of the Colchester Board of Directors. He paid 30 shillings (£1–50) for Membership Card No. 2,000 at a supper and smoking concert at the now vanished Cups Hotel. How times have changed. In addition to these regular smoking concerts, the Supporters Club also held monthly whist drivers at Nuthalls Café and organised dances in the Moot Hall.

There was another diversion at the end of the month when a stray dog caused the match against Bristol Rovers to be held up for almost ten minutes. Fred Draycott reported that the dog *"showed more bite than most of the players on the field"* (!)

March saw the first serious injury to a United player. *Prendergast*, who had eventually signed for the club after a long haggle over ten shillings a week, broke his leg playing at Millwall. That proved to be his last game for the club in competitive football, except for a brief wartime re–appearance. That month, a delay on the line due to fog between Brentwood and Liverpool Street, led to the team missing the 11.15am train at Paddington. They were due to play Bristol Rovers at Eastville that day. Manager Ted Davis, not to be beaten, saw the station master at Paddington and got him to arrange for the 11.55 non–stop Paddington to Newport express to stop at Badminton – 18 miles from Eastville. A taxi dash then got them to the ground with 15 minutes to spare before kick–off.

It couldn't happen today – or could it? It was also the occasion of the first benefit match at Layer Road, *Ronnie Dunn* being the recipient. *Dunn*, after six seasons with Crystal Palace, joined the U's on a free transfer. Part of the arrangement required that the London team would send their first team to play, what was in effect a Palace benefit, at Colchester.

The occasion was somewhat marred for *Dunn*, as his father died just before the game. But he had the consolation of the receipts from the gate of 4,000 plus. *Les Williams* scored twice to give Colchester a 2–1 victory.

By the end of March the U's were in fifth place in the Southern League table with 31 points from 25 games; they were unbeaten at Layer Road. The Reserves in the Eastern Counties were also having a reasonable season. Plans were made at the March Board meeting for the April meeting of Wolverhampton Wanderers and Arsenal to play at Layer Road for the Colchester Silver Cup.

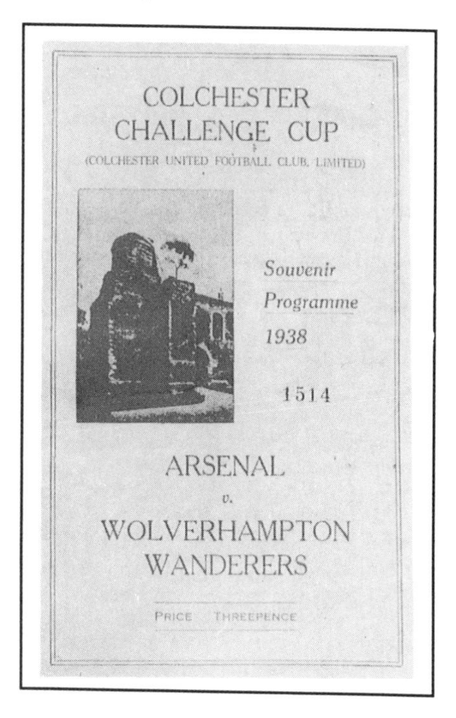


It was announced that seats in the main stand could be booked in advance for 30 and ringside (sounds more like a boxing match) seats for 25. Additional seating was being arranged to provide for a total of 3,000 bookings. The admission to the ground for those wishing to be as far a normal game. Arrangements had also been made for the teams to play each other at golf at Frinton Links and for a civic banquet ball at Colchester Town Hall after the Layer Road match.

Though both Colchester and Ipswich were doing very nicely thank you, at the end of that month came a grim reminder that then, as now, the margin between stability and a hand-to-mouth existence is a very narrow one. Dartford who were due to play Colchester in the Southern League Cup semi-final hoisted distress signals. The directors were reported as paying the wages out of their own pockets, and a public appeal had brought in just £14. Gate receipts were down to £30 a match.

Colchester duly beat Dartford 2-0 in the first leg semi-final *"Tally" Day* and *Jack Hodge* scoring. Then in early April, the Colchester trounced them 8-1 in the second leg at Layer Road, with *Day* getting a hat-trick on that occasion. So just after Easter, in their first season, the U's had progressed to the League Cup Final, were up among the leaders in the Southern League, a close third in the Midweek Section and the Reserves in contention for the Eastern Counties League championship. Not bad going in the first nine months.

On April the 9th, they visited Exeter City Reserves, lost 2-1 and the team were slipping down the table. They had travelled down by train, but the early morning start - they left Colchester before 7 a.m. - had its effect in the second half when they ran out of steam. *Alec Cheyne* was in brilliant form for the U's. He made the goal for *Jack Hodge* to make it 1-1 with eight minutes left. The failure to play to the whistle, *Pollard* looking yards offside, let in City for the winner.

The same week Ipswich Town applied for Football League status. Town were highly unpopular at Layer Road for arranging a friendly fixture with Sunderland for the same night as the Colchester Club game between Wolves and Arsenal fixed for Monday April 25th 1938.

The Essex County Telegraph for the second week in April said; *"All is set for a full - and for the players a trying - programme until the end of the season. Handicapped though they are at present by the absence of the injured Leslie and Prendergast, the players can be relied on to provide a feast of good things for the holidaymakers".*

The first team were at Bath on Good Friday with the reserves playing Harwich & Parkeston at Layer Road. On Easter Saturday the Southern League side were at home to Swindon Town Reserves with the second string away to Cromer. While on Easter Monday it was Bath City at Layer Road with the reserves away to Harwich. On the Tuesday came the Southern League Cup final first leg away to Yeovil & Petters. On Thursday the first team were away to Norwich City Reserves and on Saturday Essex Boys played London Boys at Layer Road. Groundsman "Jack" Duncan later reckoned he worked for 92 hours on the pitch that week - it happened to be wet.

The first team won 3-2 at Bath, beat Swindon Town 7-1 at Layer Road, drew 1-1 with Bath at Colchester, lost the League Cup final first leg 2-1 at Yeovil and lost 5-2 to Norwich City away. Meanwhile the Reserves beat The Shrimpers from Harwich 2-1 at Layer Road, lost 4-1 at Cromer and 3-2 in the return game with Harwich at the Royal Oak.

A crowd of almost 18,000 watched the Colchester Challenge Cup game on Monday April 25th. The Colchester team finished April in a blaze of glory. They beat Yeovil and Petters 3-1 at Layer Road in the Second Leg of the Southern Cup final. *Alec Cheyne* and *Arthur Pritchard* got the goals that gave the U's the Trophy 4-3 on aggregate.

This was Colchester United's first ever trophy - a fine performance in their first season as a professional club.

The month ended with Newport County Reserves being beaten out of sight 8-0 at Layer Road - *Pritchard* establishing a new club record with four goals in the match. Colchester were three up after nine minutes and never looked like conceding a goal. Ipswich meantime were whacking Aldershot Reserves 7-0 and both the East Anglian clubs still had outside championship hopes.

The season finished in May with a 3-2 defeat at Layer Road to Plymouth Argyle Reserves. In the end Colchester finished sixth in the Southern League, second in the Midweek Section, won the League Cup (beating Yeovil in the final) and finished fourth in the Eastern Counties League. They lost just one Southern League game at Layer Road (against Plymouth Argyle Reserves).

In that first season Colchester United's 1st and 2nd teams played 84 matches, won 45, drew 15, lost 24, scored 225 goals and conceded 138.

## A FIRST SEASON TO REMEMBER

*"Brighter and better soccer"* was the call that led to the formation of Colchester United and the demise of Colchester Town. And at the end of the U's first season that call had been answered in no uncertain manner by Manager Ted Davis and his team. They had delivered the goods and put Colchester well and truly on the football map. *"Up the U's"*, then as now, was no empty rallying slogan - though some followers regretted the passing of the nickname "The Oysters", by which Colchester Town had always been known.

The principal goal scorers were:- *Cheyne 37, Pritchard 32, Hodge 23, "Tully" Day 16, Crisp 15, Reg Smith 11.*

The late Fred Draycott of the East Anglian Daily Times wrote, *"The reason the U's had such a notable first season is because they have played together as a team and not as individualists. No one will dispute however, that the scheming of Alec Cheyne in attack, and the third back tactics of George Leslie in the centre of the defence, made them the two key men in a brilliant all round team".*

A crop of injuries notably to Leslie, Wallis, Richie and Barraclough led to a bad patch which wrote finis to their league chances. Ted Davis showed shrewd judgement in his choice of players but could never quite make up his mind on the outside left position. The home crowd appeared to favour the dashing *Crisp*, but in the away games it was the finesse of Barraclough that captured the imagination.

## SEASON'S HIGHLIGHT

Perhaps the highlight of a memorable season was the Colchester Challenge Cup. There were scenes reminiscent of a miniature Wembley when a new ground record was set up - around 18,000 - at Layer Road, when Arsenal met Wolves, and Frank Buckley saw his team win 1-0 over George Allison's Gunners. That match was another example of Ted Davis' eye for making money. Davis had spotted Cliff Fairchild and Reg Smith, two youngsters, in pre-season trials, Smith was sold to Wolves and Fairchild to Arsenal and part of the deal was the Challenge match at Colchester.

The two teams for that game read:–
ARSENAL, *Swindon, Scott, L.Crompton, Grayson, Fields, Collett, Nelson, Jones, Cart, Drury, D.Crompton.*
WOLVES, *Scott, Brown, Robinson, Paton, Cullis, Smalley, Smith, Thompson, Kirkham, Nelson, Ashall.*

Smith played in the Wolves team, but Fairchild was injured and had to miss the game. Thompson scored the only goal of the match after 28 minutes.

Ronnie Dunn the goalkeeper, who had been signed from Crystal Palace, had earlier been a bugler in the army. When Bath City were the first Southern League visitors to Layer Road, Dunn played the post horn gallop as the rest of the team took the field. That was the origination of the Post Horn Gallop tradition. John Ormsher, who was an amateur, at the end of the season left Layer Road to take up a coaching appointment in Hyderabad.

The balance sheet for the first season showed a net profit of £786. The main items of expenditure were to wages and bonuses which cost £3,945.15s 3d., whilst travelling and hotel expenses came to £789.10s 8d. The authorised share capital was £5000 and 994 shares at 25p each had been issued. Cash in hand at the bank was £2275.7s 7d.

## THE U's SECOND SEASON

The supporters club held their annual meeting at the Co–operative Hall on July 28th 1938 with G.M. Brown in the chair. Ald Charles Jolly (who was to serve for almost 40 years) gave the treasurers report. Income amounting to £381.19s 5d. He also revealed supporters had paid £85 for fencing at the Spion Kop end, £29.17s 9d for a half–time scoreboard, donated £200 to the club and brought club badges at a cost of £26.4s 2d. Income from badge sales amounted to £46.7s 0d.

It is interesting to note that of the 18 strong committee, six were ladies. The regular monthly whist drives at Nuthall's Cafe brought in £48.7s 10d, two Smoking concerts £2.12s 11d and a Hot Pot Supper nearly £3.

Meantime Ted Davis had been busy putting together his squad for the 1938/39 season. Of the successful team of 37/38 Bill Barraclough, Jim Collins and Ronnie Dunn were not retained, Alex Wood refused terms. Barraclough joined Doncaster Rovers for £300, the fee going to Chelsea who had retained his Football League registration. Wood who was still on Nottingham Forest's books moved to Chelmsford City for £800. Dunn, who received £204 from his benefit match, and Collins both went into coaching.

The first new signing was Len Astill, who scored one the goals when Ipswich Town beat the U's in the Portman Road match the previous season. Astill was 21 and a rarity among footballers of that era, a non–smoker and a teetotaller. He had joined Ipswich the previous summer but was still on Blackburn Rovers books with a £1,000 fee on his head.

Ipswich had just been elected into the Football League and were thus forced to release Astill or pay Rovers the £1,000 fee. They chose to free Astill who had won England School–boy caps against Scotland and Ireland. Blackburn had paid Wolves £3,000 for Astill as an 18 year–old.

Other new signings included Cecil Allan, an Irish international from Chelsea, who was on the Pensioners transfer list at £2,000. Next to join was 23 year–old striker Ernie Matthews listed by Sheffield Wednesday at £2,500. Ted Davis made an overnight trip to York to get Matthews' signature. A famous professional sprinter, Davis caught up with his man at an athletics meeting, signed him at 9 p.m. and arrived back at 6 a.m. in Colchester the following morning with his man. It was then a trip up to Norwich to recruit the 24 year–old central defender Alf Worton, who had just been released by the Canaries. Davis took George Leslie, a friend of Worton's, to Norwich with him to ensure he got his man.

Behind the scenes Layer Road was being re–turfed and season ticket prices were fixed for the forthcoming season, these went up by 10s 6d to £2.12s 6d. As now, cup matches had to be paid for separately.

At the beginning of August Davis in an interview with the press said *"I am gradually approaching my full complement of players, which will, I anticipate be 20. I am after a first class goalkeeper, my negotiations are complete for a third full back, and there remains now two new half backs and one inside forward of the forceful type. In view of our big programme next season, 60 games in the Southern League and in it's Midweek Section, and 26 in the Easter Counties League – it is essential to have at least 20 professionals. I hope we shall have an increase in our amateur signings".*

He also reported on that occasion that almost 400 season tickets had been applied for, which at the time exceeded the seating capacity at Layer Road.

Ipswich Town, elected to the Football League in place of Gillingham, received a bye to the First Round of the F.A. Cup, Colchester United entering for the first time received an exemption until the Fourth Qualifying Round.

Season 38/39 was also the year in which Chelmsford City were admitted into the Southern League. Other newcomers were Gillingham, Worcester City, Cardiff City Reserves and Arsenal 'A'.

By the beginning of August, Davis had failed to secure another experienced 'keeper and he re–signed Dunn. However, a week later Bill Light, on West Brom's transfer list at £1,500, who had been approached earlier decided to join. Light was to serve Colchester both as a player, and after the war, as trainer. At the time he signed, Davis bought him a drink, and in later years Bill used to recount how that was the only time anyone knew Davis to put his hand in his pocket! A 17 year–old 'keeper Edward Platt, later to play for Arsenal, was also signed. The full staff by the time the new season started was:– Light,Dunn, Platt, Allan, Worton, & Joe Birch who joined from Fulham, Ritchie, Wallis, Baker, Leslie, George Smith, Mayes, Fieldus, Hodge, Pritchard, Thacker, Cheyne, Williams and Crisp (most retained from the previous season), plus Robert Morris, a 25 year old transfer listed by Norwich at £500, and Astill. A total of 21 professionals.

William Kennedy a 6 feet tall centre half joined from South–ampton, he was listed by the Saints at £2,000. He played a couple of trial games but then Hamilton Academicals moved in and paid a transfer fee, and he moved back to his native Lanarkshire.

*August the 27th, versus Gillingham – the first match of the 1938/39 season*

On August the 18th, over 3,000 fans turned up at Layer Road to see the first trial game of the season. A second trial game played two days later attracted an attendance of 3,500. In those trial games Bennett a drummer in the East Surrey Regt., and local lads Thompson, Leach plus Amos all made favourable impressions and were the first signings on amateur forms. Bennett was in fact offered pro. terms but decided to stay in the Army.

A crowd of 8,142 turned up to see the opening Southern League fixture of the 1938/39 season. The visitors were newcomers Gillingham, and the result was a 2–0 win for the U's, with close season signing Ernie Matthews soon making his mark, scoring a brilliant goal. Fed by Cheyne he left two defenders stranded before beating Strong, the former Portsmouth custodian, in the Gills goal. Geo Wallis was the other scorer. The second team opened their Eastern Counties League campaign at The Walks, holding Kings Lynn to a 3–3 draw

Next visitors to Layer Road in the Southern League on Sept the 3rd were Arsenal Reserves. The Gunners included five players with first team experience and also Cliff Fairchild who they had signed from the U's the previous season. The gate this time was 10,129, with goals from Alec Cheyne and Bob Morris giving Colchester a 2–0 win.

The game at Dartford yielded two more points, Cheyne's goal being the only one of the match, where the U's finished with nine men. Matthews was carried off after 30 minutes with torn ligaments, and late in the match Birch had to come off with an ankle injury. Yeovil and Petters United (now Yeovil Town) were the next visitors to Colchester and 7,160 were at Layer Road to see them thrashed 8–1, Arthur Pritchard scored three before half–time. He was only in the side because of the injury to Matthews. Second half scorers were Wallis, Cheyne, Astill and Morris, Gilmour the Yeovil left back contributed an own goal.

By the end of September five of the six Southern League games had been won; eighteen goals had been scored and only three conceded. Two of these were at St James' Park where Exeter City, against the run of play, won 2–1. Pritchard gave Colchester the lead but then two defensive errors allowed Bussey and Bamsey to steal the points for the home club.

Just Prior to the Exeter game there was a ding–dong encounter with Ipswich Town Reserves at Layer Road in the Southern League Cup. Writing about that match the East Anglian scribe had this to say. *"The sooner Saturday's match is forgotten the better it will be for all concerned. It was certainly not good football and as a spectacle it was far from edifying. What was witnessed was degrading and unworthy of the name of sport".*

Harsh words, but tempers flared and Ipswich's Frank Shufflebotham was sent off for a foul on Cheyne after two earlier lectures from the referee. Then left back Gorman limped off at half–time and did not re–appear. So Ipswich played the last half hour with only nine men. Not surprisingly they lost 5–0. The crowd was a bumper 15,700. Astill (the ex–Ipswich player) netted 2.

Meantime down the road at Chelmsford City, the latest newcomers to the professional fold, had made plain their intention of challenging the U's claim that they were the top Essex club outside the Football League. The New Writtle Street directors had secured Billy Walker as manager and signed two well known players in full back Horace Wass from Southport and Jack Landells, a forward from Millwall.

The wave of professionalism apparently sweeping all before it also caused a lot of press speculation as to the future of Crittall Athletic.

In the end Charlie Jones, the former Welsh and Arsenal star felt obliged to issue a statement. This said that the Braintree based works club intended to *"uphold the cause of amateurism"*. This latter remark led to several people pointing out that though Crittall's claimed to be an amateur club, they were able to attract good players by offering them jobs with the company which allowed them to devote most of their time to football!

At the end of September the U's signed inside forward George Merritt from Derby County; Chelmsford also tried to secure his services.

Merritt, prior to joining Derby had scored 49 goals in one season for Margate, and at 21 was hailed as a smart capture by Ted Davis. In the event he never came good at Layer Road and was soon released.

## REPRESENTATIVE HONOURS

There was also news that Alec Cheyne and Len Astill had been selected to represent the Southern League in a match with the Cheshire County League. Also in that side were Cliff Fairchild (Arsenal ex-Colchester), Davidson the Chelmsford goalkeeper and team mate Simon, plus Plunkett and Cassidy from Norwich City, so the team had a strong Eastern Counties flavour.

There were 7,247 spectators when Cardiff City Reserves visited Layer Road for the first time on October 1st 1938. The Ninian Park side included Ernie Blenkinsop the former Sheffield Wednesday and England international full back, Main, who was later to join the U's, and three players who had been capped by Wales.

When the Welshmen led 2–1 at half time they seemed to have the measure of the U's. The second period however, saw Cheyne in dazzling form and the Scottish international laid on goals for Wallis and Pritchard in an exciting finish which Colchester won 3–2. Wallis had also scored the U's opening goal. The Telegraph report said *"A game which ranks among the best – if not the best – seen at Layer Road since professional football came to Layer Road".*

## CIVIC RECEPTION

The Southern League/Cheshire County League representative match was staged at Layer Road in October, with the Southerners winning 4–1. Cheyne scored a goal, Plunkett got two and Holden the other. Astill broke his nose in the match, while Cheyne captained his side.

Before the match Alderman E.A. Blaxill, the Mayor of Colchester, held a Civic Reception at the Town Hall for both teams. Then a tour of historic monuments proceeded luncheon at the now vanished Cups Hotel.

The Reserves were on the rampage again when they destroyed Newmarket Town 7–1 on their own ground. Pritchard and Crisp both scored hat-tricks and Merritt scored his first goal for Colchester. Dunn in goal was seen smoking a cigarette in the second half when he was virtually unemployed!

It was left to Aldershot Reserves to bring the U's back to earth at the end of October when they gained a shock 3–1 win at Layer Road in a Midweek Section fixture.

*"Success eluded the United in this game like an imp of mischief. All the pulsating excitement of a cup tie was crowded into a game where Colchester went full steam ahead, forced 16 corners and to crown it all let the visitors in for three snap goals. The crowd became very angry and hooted loudly as Cheyne and Astill in particular were badly fouled. The referee was booed off the pitch when proceedings closed"*, said Fred Draycott in his report on the game.

In early November came the encounter at Layer Road with Chelmsford City, as visitors for the first time since they turned professional. Although it was only an Easter Counties Cup match not unexpectedly both clubs fielded their full first teams. Sliman, who had replaced Billy Walker, as secretary/manager had Jack Coulter (late of Ireland and Everton), and Eric Keen (the former England International and Derby County player), operating up front.

Landells (ex Millwall) led the attack, and Wass, Tidman and Jones were all experienced ex-Football League professionals in the visitors side.

Layer Road was packed as the U's virtually sewed up the game in the first five minutes. Pritchard headed in from a Morris free kick after three minutes, and two minutes later Wallis ran on to a pass from Astill and glided the ball into the net. The U's played a lot of the second half without Astill, who limped off after being tripped by Pyle.

Five goals on the November the 5th, bonfire night, were put past Norwich City at Carrow Road as the U's surged to second spot in the Southern League table. "C.J.F.'s" note in the Canaries programme said *"Colchester, as most people know, is famous for it's oysters one day it might be famous for it's football. Who Knows!"*. In that Norwich side was a youngster (18 at the time) John Church, who after the war was to become a Layer Road stalwart.

Up north Will Pendergast, who had been released by Colchester in the summer, who, according to Ted Davis had lost the scoring touch, was making history. In the Northern Section he scored in 11 consecutive matches. Previous to joining Colchester he netted 98 goals in 18 months for Bristol Rovers, but he rarely scored during his sojourn at Layer Road.

The U's first venture in the F.A. Cup against Ilford ended in a 4–1 win. But they met their match in the First Round Proper losing 2–1 at Folkestone.

Another well known man in the football circles of the time, Harry Warren, was manager of the Kent side. He had watched the U's play Yeovil and had delegated Longdon to do a man-to-man marking job on Cheyne. The ploy worked and Cheyne hardly saw the ball. The U's were further handicapped when Worton was concussed after heading the soaking heavy ball in the early minutes of the match. Worton remained in a dazed condition throughout the game and went on to the left wing. In the second half Pritchard picked up a new injury and was a virtual passenger for the last half-hour.

Folkestone opening goal was a tragedy for Birch the Colchester right back, since for the second time that season he scored on own goal. This time there was no danger to the U's goal, until Birch won the ball in a tackle on Ashley. He then overhit the back pass to his 'keeper.

With Cheyne and Pritchard marked out of the game it was left to Leslie to pull a goal back for Colchester. The big centre-half, who had been in the Walsall team that beat Arsenal in the F.A. Cup five years earlier, ran through the Folkestone defence to score 10 minutes from the end. He almost snatched an equaliser from an injury time header. The Kent side included W.G. Baker the Welsh Amateur International winger in their side.

There was another seven goals for the free scoring Eastern Counties League side to end November as Gorleston lost 7–1 at Layer Road. By the end of that match the U's two teams had played 35 games, won 25, drawn 3 and lost 7. The goal tally read 106 for 45 against. Two new signings were Will Marriage, a youngster late of Hamilton Road School, and Arthur Higley, who had been with Northfleet the 'Spurs nursery side.

A further seven games were contested in December - three of them Southern League matches - and by the end of 1938 the U's were on 30 points from 18 games. They were fifth in the table, three points behind Guildford City with three games in hand. Also only one point behind Plymouth Argyle, Arsenal and Gillingham and had games in hand on all three.

They were top of the Southern League Midweek Section, 13 points from 8 matches, and the Reserves led the Eastern Counties League with 19 points from 11 outings. The second string had scored an incredible 43 goals and conceded just 12.

During December the Colchester directors were anxiously discussing whether or not to apply for Football League status. Manager Ted Davis advised caution, and pointed out that a number of the players were still on the transfer list of Football League clubs. Therefore if an application for membership was successful, the U's would either have to pay for their services or release then this would mean rebuilding the team.

In the event, although several of the directors were in favour of applying there and then, a decision was taken not to proceed at that time.

The last two matches of 1938 against Charlton Athletic on Boxing Day and Barry Town on New Year's Eve were both won. The first match saw snow having to be cleared off the Layer Road pitch before the Athletic were beaten 2-1. Against Barry, also at Layer Road, a one sided game saw Wallis score a hat-trick before half-time. Hodge and Pritchard also scored to make it 5-1.

An influenza epidemic which laid low five players, a recurrence of Matthews knee injury plus less serious injuries to Cheyne and Wallis meant the postponement of two games scheduled for early January 1939. Manager Davis was busy trying to sign inside right Robert Murray from Bath City and at the same time parting with two players. Ken Mayes whose 18 months contract with the U's had run out, left by mutual consent and joined Chelmsford City. The former Fulham player had failed to get a place in the U's first team and was not happy with Reserves football. Young 'keeper Ted Platt joined Arsenal on loan until the end of the season, his father had been a full back with Bolton Wanderers. Platt had come to Layer Road with Ted Davis a friend of the budding custodian's father. Platt went on to become The Gunners first team 'keeper, although the war years came and went before he made the Highbury team. He also saw service with Portsmouth and Aldershot before retiring from League football in 1955.

Another player who years hence was to be a popular figure at Layer Road, George Fisher, and just 16 at the time, made his debut for Millwall Reserves at The Den on January 9th 1938. George was to play over 300 games for The Lions first team, have a spell at Fulham, before playing 163 League games for Colchester between September 1955 and May 1959. In that game in 1939 George played as a winger, in latter years full back was his position.

The Gillingham programme for the match at Priestfield contained the following notes from W. Harvey, The Gills manager:- *"This afternoon we renew acquaintances with Colchester United - the club which gave us our baptism in the Southern League. I still look back on that game as one of the best I have ever witnessed in any class of football. If this afternoon's encounter is at all in keeping with that, than every reader of these notes will feel well satisfied. Colchester have a very fine team; their record in the league proves that without any words of mine. More over they play real football".*
In the event the U's won the match 3-1. It was the Gills first home defeat of the season and at 3,748, their best gate to date.

**LEAGUE FOOTBALL?**

On 21st January 1939, in view of the speculation still rife in the town on the question of applying for Football League status, the manager Ted Davis writing in the programme for the Newport County match had this to say:- *"Just a reference to various remarks and correspondence to the football League. It has to be remembered that application can be made any time up to May. There can be no advantage in applying so early. One thing, and that only, will give you a case - your records in your league, your attendances and financial backing, naturally ground accommodation - coupled with good friends in the football world.*

*I feel that as far as records go, and financially, and from a ground and every facility with regard to accommodation, dressing rooms etc., there will be no club in a position to put forward a more concrete case than Colchester United. I do not infer that we should be admitted.*

*It needs a tremendous amount of work in preparing your case, canvassing of clubs (which takes up a great deal of time and travel) and a hundred and one other things. I feel certain in my own mind Colchester United will make application".*

Colchester won that game 7-1 and in the next match beat Arsenal Reserves 3-1 in the Southern League Cup. Former U's player Platt (goal) and Fairchild (right back) were in the Gunners team. Just over 10,000 saw that encounter which was much closer than the score-line suggests. Wallis put the U's in front, but Bremner equalised, a goal from Astill and a last minute effort from Pritchard however, carried the day for Colchester.

At the end of January Ted Davis at last managed to secure the services of Murray from Bath City. The inside-forward was still on Manchester United's transfer list with an £800 price tag. He came into the team that beat Folkestone 3-1 in early February. That match was notable for three things. First Wallis with two goals maintained his rich scoring vein - second Joe Birch for the third time that season scored an own goal - third a terrier dog which invaded the pitch and for nearly 10 minutes evaded all attempts to capture it. Finally the dog left the field of it's own accord after using the goal post at the Layer Road end!

There was a 5-1 trouncing for the Reserves at Bury Town. Walker scored three for the Suffolk side. Guildford City with a 1-0 home win also became the first side to beat Colchester in the Midweek Section of the Southern League. A week later the U's lost again, 3-1 away to Tunbridge Wells Rangers.

When March came round the U's were three points clear at the top of the Southern League. Second placed Guildford City on 43 points had played three games more, Gillingham lying third had 41 points with four more matches played. Colchester also led the Midweek Section by one point and the Eastern Counties League with 23 points from 14 games - Bury Town were just one point behind but that was from 18 games played.

All told at all levels Colchester United's record read - 60 games played, 46 won, four drawn, ten lost. An incredible 181 goals scored and 70 conceded. Pritchard 34, Thacker 29, Wallis, Cheyne and Astill all on 17 were the leading scorers. Thacker, kept out of the first team by the brilliance of Pritchard, Cheyne and Wallis, with 23 goals in the Eastern Counties League matches must have felt aggrieved at not getting any first team opportunity.

Light, Worton and Morris were all on 43 appearances and the season still had 10 weeks to run. Hodge 42, Pritchard 41, Birch and Wallis both on 40, Leslie and Astill 35, Smith 34 and Baker 32, emphasised how little the first team squad had changed.

Cheyne on 27 had been unlucky with injuries. The same situation applied in the Eastern Counties League XI where 12 players provided the nucleus of the side week-in, week-out.

A measure of how well the team was playing came on March 4th when after a long, the same day, train journey they beat Plymouth Argyle Reserves 3-0 at Home Park. The Argyle team was made up of entirely first team players but they never got a look in. John Hodge, a former Argyle player had a field day. He scored one of the three goals, laid on the first one for Pritchard and also contributed to that scored by Murray. In the Plymouth goal was George Wright later to come to Layer Road.

## A BUMPER SEASON

The 38/39 season proved to be a bumper one from a Colchester United viewpoint. They won the Southern League championship, were runners-up in the Southern League Midweek Section, and were in the semi-finals of the Southern League Cup which had to be held over to the following season.

The Reserve team won the Easter Counties League, the Miller Shield, and the Colchester Challenge Cup, which again was held over to the following season.

All told the various teams played 101 games. Won 69, drew 12, lost 20, scored 282 goals and conceded 123. Pritchard played in 66 games and scored 51 goals. Morris had a marathon season appearing in 70 games. It has to be remembered too that everyone of the players had a job - part-time in most cases. Yet there is no mention anywhere of any player complaining about the work load. Indeed in the two seasons the U's had been operating four players had already made 100 appearances for the club. Hodge led the way with 111 games, Pritchard was on 106 and Cheyne and Leslie both on 100.

## REJECTED

On May the 23rd 1939 however, there was a setback for the club when the applications for election to the Football League Division Three South were considered. The two bottom clubs Bristol Rovers with 20 points and Walsall with 13 were recommended. Gillingham with 7 votes and Chelmsford City plus Colchester United receiving not a single vote were the unsuccessful applicants.

Walter Clark, a board member, put the case for Colchester but it was obvious that neither the U's nor Chelmsford would receive any support as they had taken on players who were transfer listed by Football League clubs, without consulting the clubs concerned.

Meantime, Ted Davis was looking ahead to the 39/40 season and signing yet another player who was on the books of a Football League club. This time it was Ken Burdett who had refused terms offered by Notts County. Burdett had played 30 Third Division games for the Meadow Lane side in 38/39 and was transfer listed at £1,000. Previously he spent six seasons with Norwich City and assisted the Canaries in getting promotion to Division Two. Burdett also played for Millwall and played for The Lions in an F.A. Cup semi-final. At 27 he was hailed as a fine capture for the U's.

Leaving the club was George Ritchie, who was the U's first skipper. He moved to Portman Road as assistant coach to Ipswich Town.

The full Football League meeting on June the 5th confirmed the voting at the Southern section meeting held on May 23rd. The U's did not bother to attend.

The Southern League annual meeting was held in London the following day. Mr A.J. Darnell, the President, congratulated Colchester United on their achievement in their two seasons in the league. At the meeting it was decided to scrap the Midweek Section. Folkestone (how history repeats itself) resigned and were fined £250 for not tendering their resignation within the prescribed period. Maurice Pye (Colchester United) and F.E. Langton (Chelmsford City) were elected to the Management Committee.

## WAR CLOUDS

Though war clouds were gathering George Law a centre forward released by Norwich City arrived at Layer Road in June. Aged 24, he had been a prolific scorer with the Canaries Reserve team. They put a fee on his head but on appeal the Football League gave him a free transfer.

With the disbanding of the Southern League Midweek Section, Colchester United, Portsmouth, Chelmsford City and Charlton secured admission to the London Midweek League.

There were two more departures from Layer Road in July. Nottingham Forest signed George Crisp and John Hodge joined Hereford United. Incoming was Manningtree born goalkeeper, Walter Brooks. He had three seasons with Fulham before joining Bournemouth, and was on The Cherries transfer list at £1,000.

On July the 11th, Maurice Pye resigned as Chairman and was succeeded by Walter Clark who had been one of the prime movers in the formation of the club. Two weeks later however, the full Board refused to accept Pye's resignation and to smooth ruffled feathers made Clark the first life member of the club.

## STORMY MEETING

The Shareholders Meeting at the end of July was a very stormy affair. There had been a loss of £1,238 on the season. The balance sheet showed a substantial increase in wages, and costly ground and amenity improvement work. The note on the bottom said *"Your directors are now taking steps to reduce expenditure to obviate any further loss in future"*.

Several shareholders said they were not so much querying the loss – they wanted to know what the directors had in mind when they announced: *"Economy will be the future watch-word"*. There was over 2 hours of acrimonious debate and the pitch of excitement was reached when it came to the election of directors. One of the retiring directors was not re-elected and another only after a second vote.

Mr J. Smallwood from the floor moved that the number of directors be a maximum of 12 and a minimum of two, he said 20 was a ridiculous number. He was supported by Mr W. Harding and the resolution was carried by a large majority.

The election of directors followed; Alderman Piper, W. Allen, P.C. Cook and W. Harper, were standing for re-election and there were nominations from Gerald Benham, W.H. Sexton and W.A. Hill. This caused a big argument. Mr Pye in the chair said in the event of a ballot being needed – there were seven nominations for four seats – there would have to be a special meeting. This caused a storm, and finally the majority at the meeting decided the election should be on a show of hands. The voting was Benham 234, Allen 221, Piper 192, Harper and Sexton 86, Cook 56 and Hills 52. On a second vote Harper 109 votes was elected, Sexton with 100 votes joined Hills and Cook as the three rejected candidates. Cook had been one of the founder directors.

It was also mentioned in the chairman's report that the ownership of Layer Road had passed from Colchester Town to Colchester Council as trustees. Mr Pye said *"Every lover of football will, I am sure, welcome this as a move in the right direction, for whatever happens this fine open space will always belong to the town, and be for the benefit of Colcestrians and their love of football"*.

## THE WORLD WAR YEARS

The end of that marvellous 1938/39 season saw the departure from Layer Road of several players who had helped to put the U's on the Southern League map. 'Keeper Ronnie Dunn and Ernie Matthews were given free transfers, and Ken Mayes to Chelmsford City (plus Hodge to Hereford).

In addition to Ken Burdin, George Law and Len Brooks signed in June. Ted Davis added two more players to the staff in July. Bill Main a right-half from Cardiff City and Harry Hawkins from Watford. The later was doomed never to play a game for the club.

On August the 18th 1939, the minutes of the Board meeting reported that there had been discussions with the local reporters regarding press box facilities at Layer Road. Fred Draycott and Arthur Wood were adamant that the facilities – six seats, were inadequate. The Board agreed a further six seats should be made available, and this was undertaken in September. At the same meeting Councillor William Allen successfully moved that military personal in uniform should be admitted at half price. But the meeting rejected a proposal that unemployed persons and ladies should have the same facilities.

## MONEY PROBLEMS

A further meeting at the end of August underlined how little things have changed over the years. Despite the very successful playing season, the club was having problems paying it's way. Messrs. Moss and Sons, who had done building work on the ground over a year before, had written demanding payment in full of their bill in 14 days – or else! The outcome was that six members of the Board chipped in to pay £100 off the amount.

The Builders were asked to accept the remainder at £100 per month. This they agreed to, but the war came along, and they waived the amount still outstanding.

The Press Box extensions were duly carried out by A.W. Hills and cost the princely sum of £4-10-0d. They were not used until 1946.

The directors meeting on September 25th 1939 was a very sombre affair. Mr W.H. Clark, in the chair, reported on the action taken in conjunction with manager Ted Davis upon war being declared. *"All the club's loose property had been packed and an inventory made. The various Trophies won by the club had been deposited at the bank. All players contracts had been suspended and the staff found employment of National importance. Ted Davis had left to return to Bath and trainer James Baker had been paid an extra weeks wages for the work entailed in packing the club's property.*

The running of the club was left in the hands of the chairman W.H. Clark, William Allen, William Harper, Ben Myers and Ald Piper.

Ipswich Town and Plymouth Argyle applied for their share of the Layer Road gate in respect of the Southern League matches played on August the 26th and September the 2nd. Plymouth were also claiming £88.19s expenses. It was decided on November the 6th to advise both clubs that no money was available to settle these claims.

The U's in fact played four Southern League matches before hostilities started. They beat Plymouth Argyle 3–1 at Layer Road, won 5–1 at Carrow Road against Norwich City in the semi-final of the Southern League Cup held over from the previous season, lost 2–1 at home to Chelmsford City and drew 0–0 with Ipswich Town.

There was also a further 14 friendly matches played by the club, before the last match for five years saw Dartford play at Layer Road on December the 30th 1940. The U's won 3–2. Crittall Athletic were played home and away, the game at Braintree ended 1–1 but the visitors triumphed 2–1 at Layer Road. There were three games against Norwich City ( Colchester won 3–1 and drew 2–2 at Layer Road, and won 3–2 in Norfolk). Fulham went down 2–1 at Layer Road, and games against Chelmsford saw one drawn, a 4–0 win for City and in the other, the U's were walloped 6–1 at New Writtle Street. The other game, against the Officers Cadets Training Unit, ended in a 7–0 win for United.

## THE LAST WARTIME TEAM

The last team to play at Layer Road before the U's ceased any wartime playing activity read:–
*Dunn, Birch, Allan, Smith, Leslie, Morris, Rees, Cheyne, Fieldus, Little, Perrett.*

Morris and Fieldus 2 scored in the 3–2 defeat of Dartford. Only two of the players in the game went on to play for the U's after the war. Syd Fieldus, who together with some directors, kept the club ticking over during the war years.

He was for a time acting manager, secretary and player and remained active at the club until 1949. The other player was Cecil Allan. Of the other members of the last team, Stan Rees was a Crittall's player, Jack Little was an ex-Ipswich Town man, and George Perrett ex-Fulham – all the rest had appeared for the U's pre-war. George Leslie of course was a member of the Walsall side that beat Arsenal so sensationally in the F.A. Cup in the 1930's.

## FAMOUS NAMES

Though Colchester United closed down for the duration of the war years at the end of 1939, there was nevertheless a number of games played in Colchester during the period of hostilities, some at Layer Road. Many well known names appeared in those matches which attracted some big attendances.

Players of the calibre of Frank Swift, the England and Manchester City goalkeeper, Tommy Lawton, Ted Fenton who later became the Colchester player-manager, Frank Soo, and Maurice Edleston, to mention but a few, all played from time to time. When the Eastern Command met the South Eastern Command on April the 24th 1943, all proceeds going to charity, Cliff Brittain (Eastern and England), Stan Collins (of Wolves and England fame), Wilf Cooping (Arsenal) and Jimmy Hogan (Sheffield United) were in the S.E. Command team which won 7–4.

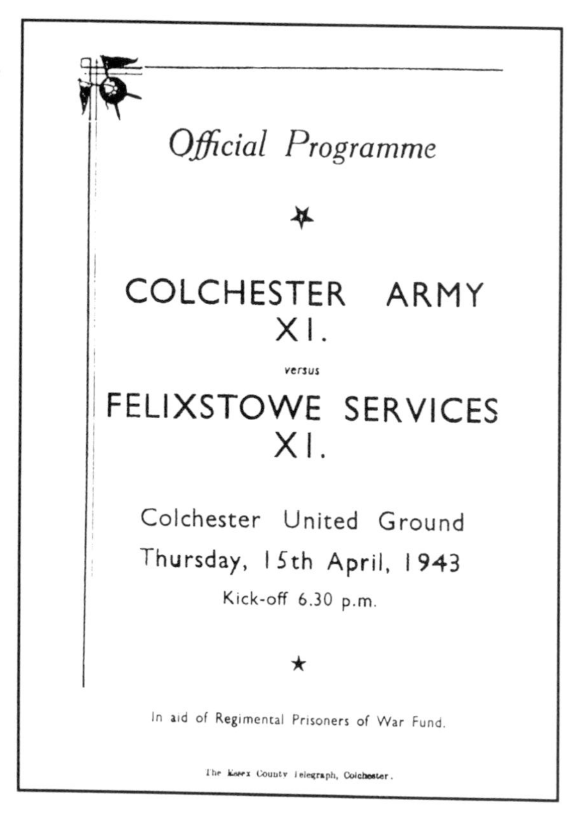


On April the 10th 1944 – when some 4,000 programmes – single sheet on flimsy yellow paper were sold at 2d each – local football enthusiasts had the chance to see an Army XI play an Allied Services team which included internationals from Poland, Czechoslovakia, Belgium, Holland and France. The score finished 4–3 to the Army XI.

The Red Cross Agricultural Fund staged an England v Scotland international game in May 1944 when the England side included Alex Stock, who was later to find fame as a manager.

The top wartime fixture however, was undoubtedly the Colchester Garrison v Combined Services XI match on Dec the 13th 1945 when no less than 14 international players took the field. The programme was a very flimsy blue paper. The last of these war-time games was played on December the 29th 1945, when a Football Challenge Cup put up by the Old Contemptible Association was contested by two army units, before a crowd of some 6,000. Altogether, as far as can be traced, some 22 competitive matches – programmes for which exist – were played, before Southern League Football resumed once again.

During wartime there were eight meetings of the Board of Directors. The ground itself was taken over by the Auxiliary Fire Services, who agreed to keep the pitch and building in order, but the Football Club continued to pay the rent. A cheque for £75 to cover this was sent to the Borough Council on Oct the 13th 1941 – the money was raised by the directors putting their hands in their pockets; a process that was to be repeated several times over the next few years. In Sept 1943 it was reported that Mr Wright, a director, had paid the Fire Insurance on the stands which amounted to £3–8s–6d. By 1944 there were outstanding accounts for £101–5–0d and £41–2–11d in the bank. W.Allen £20, Alderman Piper £10, Mr Le Ball £10, Mr Howard £10 and Mr Myes £10–2–1d contributed in order that the accounts could be paid. At that meeting it was also reported that no football had been played at Layer Road in either 1943 or 1944.

## LAYER ROAD CHARACTERS

At this stage in the history of the club it is an opportune moment to look at some of the early personalities who graced Layer Road.

**Edwin "Ted" Davis**; the first secretary manager has already been mentioned in several earlier chapters. He had a distinguished career as a 'keeper in the Football League before moving to Bath City, initially as player/manager/secretary. Looking back over the years it is interesting to see that Fred Draycott's assessment of him when he arrived at Layer Road was a very accurate one. He said *"Davis is ambitious, knows his way around the football world, and his 10 year record at Bath City speaks for itself. Although he is noted for not putting his hand in his pocket, he is shrewd enough to put together good teams without spending money".*

Those words were amply proved in the two and a bit years he was in charge at Layer Road. It must be said however, that "Ted" was hardly a popular figure in Football League circles as Draycott, in an article tersely remarked: *"Davis' player poaching of professionals in dispute with their clubs hardly enhances Colchester's prospects of election to the Football League".*

Undoubtedly one of his master strokes was signing Scottish international striker Alex Cheyne. The Scot was locked in a dispute with Chelsea, who transfer listed him at £3,000, an enormous figure at the time, and he was over 30. Davis filched him under the noses of several clubs, notably Third Lanark. The 5'–8" inside left proved to be a real crowd pleaser at Layer Road. The war of course finished his career. He later returned to his native Aberdeen.

Another stalwart of those early days was centre–half **George Leslie**. "The cheerful giant" was Arthur Wood's description of him. Leslie was in the Walsall side that caused the FA Cup shock of the 30's by knocking out Arsenal. His great friend Gilbert Alsop, was also in the Saddlers team that day, and was playing for Ipswich Town when Leslie was at Layer Road. Leslie was 26 when Davis turned him away from Guildford City. He played in 46 games during Colchester United's first season. He was appointed club captain in 1939 after undergo–ing a cartilage operation in the summer of that year.

**John Hodge**, a right winger had been the subject of a big offer from Arsenal in 1935. Luton Town, his club, however stuck out for more money and the deal fell through. Hodge, not unnaturally, was unhappy on missing out on a chance to join The Gunners. In the summer of 1937 he refused to re–sign for The Hatters, and Davis, quick off the mark again, brought him to Layer Road. Luton were furious as they had offers for him from both Newcastle United and Crystal Palace.

According to the Colchester boss *"Hodge is my best capture so far"*. He gave yeoman service for two seasons but he was not the easiest of players to control, disliked training, and he moved to Hereford United in the summer of 1939. He was 24 when he joined the U's and like many others the war more or less finished his career, although he did play for Devonshire at junior level after the end of hostilities.

A Woodford man, **Kenny Mayes**, was an inside right who was on Fulham's transfer list at £500 when signed by Colchester. He first made his name as an amateur with Brentwood and Warley and then Barking. He spent two seasons at Craven Cottage and was a regular in the U's team in 1937/38. A loss of form the following season saw him relegated to the U's Reserve team, and in January 1939 he was allowed to join Chelmsford City who were in their first year as a professional club.

**Ronald Victor Dunn** – to give him his full title – was United's first goalkeeper. He instigated The Post Horn Gallop as the U's entry on to the pitch tune. Born in Southall in 1908, he spent several years as a regular in the Army where he learned to play the bugle and the cornet. He was the 'keeper for the British Army team for four seasons. He also represented the Army at cricket and tennis. After leaving the Forces he played for Wealdstone and Hounslow before signing as a pro with Crystal Palace. He spent five seasons at Selhurst Park before joining the U's., being 37 at the time. On the short side for a 'keeper he remained at Layer Road until called up as a reservist in the summer of 1939.

Another steal from a Football League club was left–back **Alexander Wood**. Born in Glasgow, Wood was a naturalised American. He was a member of the Leicester City side that reached the FA Cup semi–final in 1934. Earlier he had won a U.S.A. Cap against Uruguay. A dispute over pay had led him to sign for Nottingham Forest. After making 28 appear–ances for Forest he was transfer listed at £800.

Another ex–Leicester City man **George Thompson Ritchie** came to Layer Road, despite offers from Derby County and Motherwell, when he was given a free transfer after eight seasons at Filbert Street.

A dour Scot, he started his career with Maryhill, then he had three years with Falkirk before moving south. So far as we know the only U's player who could play the bagpipes – *"Not very melodiously"* – according to a programme note of the day. He later joined the coaching staff at Portman Road.

The U's first trainer was large as life **James Baker**, a native Wolverhamptonian, with a voice to match his ample frame. As a player he could operate anywhere in the half back line. In his time Baker had played for his home town club, Port Vale, Coventry City and Bristol City. Baker was a busy man in the opening Southern League season, making over 30 first team appearances.

**Reg Smith** was also an excellent tennis player and was good enough to play in the Wimbledon championships on three occasions. He was recruited from Bristol City. Only 20 at the time, he was only at Layer road for three months, Wolves paying £500 for his services. He finished his Football League career with Tranmere Rovers.

One of three Welshmen among the U's early players, **Arthur Pritchard**, in 1936/37 made a name for himself by scoring 33 goals for Yeovil Town. Only 24 when Davis secured his prolific scorer for the U's in 1938/39, he scored 47 goals in 61 games. He was called up in September 1939 and that was the last heard of him at Layer Road.

Two of the early characters at Layer Road were **Willie Prendergast** and **Bill Barraclough**, who both got into Ted Davis' bad books. Like several other Colchester players over the years they liked a flutter and they were not averse to going missing on race days. Both were also useful golfers and sometimes that got in the way of football. Neither had a long stay at Layer Road. Prendergast before arriving at Colchester in December 1937 had scored 54 goals for Bristol Rovers. Despite his liking for the 'gee–gees' he was a teetotaller and non–smoker, a rarity in footballers in those days.

Other characters of the time included **Roy Morris**, a former Norwich City player who in 1938/39 played in 69 games for Colchester United. Coming away from the last away match of the season, he threw his boots away telling the assembled company: *"They are like me, buggered"*.

There was also **Syd Fieldus**, commercial traveller extra–ordinary (*"You name it I'll get it"*), who for a spell after the war practically ran the club. Also the quiet man **George Crisp**, who it is said never spoke unless spoken to, except for one famous occasion when he was sent off – the wrong man as it happened – and he was heard to protest to the referee.

There were also a couple of players who made history by never appearing for the U's. A certain **Mr Hawkins** from Middlesbrough signed in June 1938 and **James Raven** signed from Bristol Rovers about the same time. Hawkins went back on his word and joined Watford, while Raven, who like Hawkins had been sent his rail fare etc. to report at Layer Road, never put in an appearance at Colchester.

Many other characters flitted across the Layer Road stage in those days. Perhaps the most exotic exit was that of one time Colchester Town amateur **James Ormesher**, who got himself a job as coach to the Nizam of Hyderbad's team in India.

# CHAPTER 3

# Football Returns to Layer Road

With the prospect of Layer Road once again being available to the club, after its compulsory requisitioning during the war years, Walter Clark was deputed to attend a meeting in London to discuss the restart of competitive football. On June the 4th 1945 at a Board meeting in the Pearl Assurance offices in High Street, he stated that he could pilot Colchester United to success and: *"He was sure that he was the only one who could do so".*

This statement caused something of a furore, the Chairman Bill Allen said in view of Mr Clark's remarks he was vacating the chair and suggested Mr Clark might like to take his place. However, after some discussion it was decided to hold the question of the chairmanship over until the Board members attended a meeting.

What went on behind the scenes in the next 10 days or so was not recorded in the minutes. Suffice to say that at the next Board meeting on June the 14th, a letter of resignation from Mr Clark was received in which he gave advancing years as the reason for his decision. (Fred Draycott had a different interpretation. It appeared that Mr Clark had received an offer for his shareholding in the club that was too good to refuse). The upshot was Mr Allen was re-elected to "the chair" and Syd Fieldus was appointed secretary - a move that Mr Clark had not been happy about. Fieldus was given the job of attending a meeting of the Southern League to be held on June the 18th.

The meeting at the Euston Square Hotel decided to restart the competition for the 1945/46 season with the clubs divided into East and West sections, to cut travelling costs. Chelmsford City, Guildford City, Bedford Town, Aldershot and Norwich City had signalled their intention to take part. Fieldus explained however, that with no mandate from the Board, and the directors divided on the issue of starting up again, he had not been in a position to commit the U's one way or the other. There would however, have to be a decision taken by July the 31st, otherwise the club would cease to be members of the Southern League.

After much discussions, and a warning from several members about the financial implications, it was decided to go ahead with plans to take part in the new season. Fieldus was appointed manager with a warning *"there must be no wasteful spending".* The next move was a meeting with the Supporters Club, who were represented by Messrs Jolly, Crocker, Jackson and Richer - all names that were to feature prominently in the annals of the club. It was agreed with the Supporters club that they would produce the necessary funding for an eight page programme and that duplicated sheets giving match details would be sent to all public houses in the Essex area.

President : Oswald Lewis, Esq., M.P.

The club also received a cheque for £100 from the President, O. Lewis, towards the cost of starting up again. The total assets of the club appeared to be just over £300 and there were old debts of around £200.

In August it was agreed prices for the new season would be stand 2/- (10p), ground 1/-, and for pensioners ground 6d (2½p). It was also agreed to hire an Easter National bus for £3-10-0d, to take the team to Chelmsford for a match. In addition to the team the directors, Mr S. Drake (Dedham), Mr C. Scott (Shrub End), Mr Sexton (Boxted) and Mr G. Brown (Colchester) were also invited to be on board.

There was however, another hiccup before the season got under way. The Southern League management committee reversed their decision to run the league in East and West sections and decided that all clubs would compete in one division.

When the board met on the 18th of August, Mr. B Myers questioned whether in view of that happening, the U's could afford to take part. Fieldus, on being asked, estimated the travelling costs would be around £50 per match. The vote could have gone either way until Charles Jolly, on behalf of the Supporter's clubs, pledged his members would raise the money to pay for away travel.

An early season trial game was held and this raised the sum of £17.7s, which was donated to the Essex County Hospital. It was at this stage that a man who was to have a profound influence on the future of the club, came onto the scene. Claude Orrin was on the staff of Fruin Warner, the club's accountants, and was loaned to the U's to act as financial secretary. He later became the club's full time secretary and was the pillar behind the Layer Road scene for some 25 years. Messrs. Drake, Scott, Sexton Brown - mentioned earlier - were also added to the Board.

The first trial game at Layer Road took place on August the 12th 1945, and it is interesting to note the teams who took the field. The Blue and Whites line up was:-
*Light, Beach, Allan, Southam, Jenkins, K.Wallis, R.Saunders, Robinson, Day, Ferguson, Hornby, Canham, Willmott, Robson.* West and Reeves came on in the second half.
Black and Ambers team read:-
*Dawson, Bower, Rose, Titcombe, Kernohan, Mills, Symonds, Northover, Canham, Harman, Sutherly, Dring, Milne, Thompson.* Nutt and Parker also got a run out.

The Blue and Whites won 5-2. Day (2), Ferguson Robinson and Canham (who changed sides at half time) scoring for the Winners, Northover and Canham for the losers. Allan, Light and Day were the only players who had appeared for The U's pre-war.

There were some interesting players in that trial game. Thompson, who was serving with No.1 Holding Battery in Colchester, was a St. Mirren player. Paddy Kernohan was a half back from Derry City, Roy Canham an RAF man from Yorkshire, Ray Dring, a Huddersfield Town goalkeeper, Frank Northover a serving soldier who later played for Colchester Casuals and Titcombe of Swindon Town. Robson was a York City half back, Doug Beach (Luton Town), Jack Ferguson (Southend United) and Willmott, an amateur attached to Barnet. The U's of course, for the first 2 seasons after the war, could call on servicemen stationed at Colchester even though they were registered with other clubs.

## FIRST GAME

The first competitive match was on August the 30th. The Layer Road encounter with Ipswich Town ended 1–1 with Day getting the U's goal. The attendance was 3,525, and the Colchester team read:–
*Light, Bower, Milne, Southam, Jenkins, Nutt, Titcombe, Nelson, Day, Robinson, Hornby.*

Colchester ordered 1500 programmes for this match, but because of paper shortage, Essex Telegraph (the printers), could only produce 1000. Copies of this programme are very rare, few having survived the passage of time.

The game marked the first appearance in Colchester colours of Bill Bower, Ronnie Hornby (a former Wolves player), Jimmy Jenkins ex–Bristol City, Jimmy Southam of West Bromwich Albion, and Bristol Rovers player Nutt. Gate receipts for the match amounted to £203.16s.

The U's played 20 Southern League games and 10 Southern League Cup matches (the cup was run on a points basis that season) during the 1945/46 season. There was one FA Cup tie, and on top of that, there were also 16 friendlies played.

The team line–ups were never the same from one week to another, for with wartime restrictions still applying, clubs were able to register players on the day of the match, irrespective of the fact that a player was on the books of another club.

The U's of course, were able to draw on players posted to service duties in and around Colchester. Altogether, in those 30 Southern League and Cup fixtures, 80 players appeared in the familiar blue and white stripes. Just one, Bill Bower, played in all 30 matches, many played in just one game, and some well known names in the football world had a fleeting acquaintance with Layer Road. Apart from Bower, only seven others reached double figure appearances. Bower was the U's first post war signing, with Syd Fieldus – Honorary manager at the time – securing him from Millwall.

Among the well known names who turned out, were Doug Beach of Sheffield Wednesday and Luton Town fame – he later finished his career with Southend United. Albert Day (Brighton and Hove Albion), who, a year later, joined Ipswich Town making 63 League appearances and scoring 25 goals while at Portman Road. Frank Dudley, just 20 at the time, who later made a name for himself as a forward with Southend United, Leeds United, Southampton and Brentford. Len Duquemin of Tottenham Hotspur fame, Derek Hawksworth (Bradford City) who went on to play over 400 Football League games, including 255 for Sheffield United; a left winger, he was also an England "B" international.

There was also Les Jones of Arsenal and Wales, full back Rod Munroe of Brentford a Scottish international trialist, wing half Dave Nelson then on Arsenal's books and who later played for Fulham, Brentford, Q.P.R. and Crystal Palace. Then too, there was John Robinson, Sheffield Wednesday and an England international, and the one and only Alf Smirke, a Sheffield Wednesday (pre–war), but post–war with Southend, and later still a well known denizen of Football League press boxes.

Playing wise, it was not a particularly good season and the directors were somewhat disappointed by the gates. The home form was not too bad, but scratch teams had to be played on several away games, and there were two–eight goal beatings at Bath City and Yeovil. Arch rivals Chelmsford City won 4–3 in a seven goal thriller at Layer Road, but the U's won their away fixture at New Writtle St. 2–1. That in fact, was their only away league success. The League Cup – sorted out on a home and away league style basis – in the second half of the season yielded 4 wins, 4 draws and just 2 defeats in the 10 games. The U's were unbeaten in the 5 games played at Layer Road. In the FA Cup, Wisbech Town won 5–0 on their Fenland Park pitch.

Strangely enough, while the Board was not too happy at the attendances at Southern League games, some of the 16 friendlies were well supported. Over 5000 to see Harmon and Willmott (an amateur from Barking), give the U's a 2–1 win over an Arsenal X1. There were 4790 to see a Rawcliffe goal earn a 1–1 draw with Brentford, and 5317 to watch a 2–2 draw with Norwich City; Bower (pen) and Fieldus the United marksmen.

Off the field of play and behind the scenes, the U's owed a lot to Major Dai Rees, who acted as a liaison office with the military. He was instrumental in ensuring a regular supply of servicemen to enable a team to be fielded each week. The U's at the time, had only 4 signed players of their own, Bower, Barnard, Hutchings and Fieldus. The Major, who was co–opted on to the board, remained active to something like normality at the end of the 1946–47 season.

Interesting to note, that at a board meeting in October 1945, Ind Coope agreed to pay £35 for an advert on top of the main stand. At the same meeting, a Mr Greenop of Swansea Town applied for the post of secretary/manager. Director Ben Myers said that the time was not opportune to consider the application, and added that there was no doubt that the club could not continue indefinitely relying on Mr Fieldus to do the job on an honorary basis. There was also a minute recording the thanks of the club to the Romans Club for: *"The sound system at Layer Road"*. This was the first mention of a PA system at the ground.

In November 1945, it was reported that Jock Duncan was now free of his Essential Works order duties and able to resume as full time groundsman. The board agreed to that course and asked him as a matter of urgency, to distemper the dressing rooms, paint the water cisterns and scrub and wash the bath and hand basins. He also cleaned the turnstiles and supervised an army fatigue party which was levelling out the top of the Spion Kop (later the Clock End).

In January 1946, by which time Board meetings were being held in the Liberal Club, Mr Richer – the supporters club treasurer – reported that the Xmas draw had exceeded expectations, raising £120–2–6d, and the raffle £32–17–0.

About this time too, a problem arose over centre forward George Barnard. Barnard had been on West Ham's books on amateur forms. He played 4 games for the U's while on National Service at Colchester, and Syd Fieldus persuaded him to sign as a professional in November 1945. Arsenal, not knowing the U's had signed him as a pro, gave notice of approach to West Ham as required by League rules. West Ham then found that Barnard was a Colchester player. The outcome was that Barnard was sold to Arsenal for £500. Ironically, Barnard, who was still in the army, was drafted to the Middle East and disappeared from the football scene.

With the season drawing to a close, Syd Fieldus stressed the urgency of appointing a manager or player/manager for the 1946–47 season, pointing out that his work commitments would not permit him to carry on for another season. The upshot was the appointment of Ted Fenton as secretary/ manager at the end of April. At the same meeting when Fenton's appointment was confirmed, concern was expressed regarding certain articles which had appeared in the local Press. It was agreed that no information, other than team news, would be released to the Press in future, unless approved by Mr W. Allen the chairmen. It was also decided to extend the main stand, Messrs. Cocksedge to prepare the plans for the extension.

## ENTER TED FENTON

Ted Fenton was, of course, no stranger to Layer Road. He had in fact as a teenager, played for the old Colchester Town club in 1931. His stay in the manager's seat was destined to be a very important one in the progress of the U's towards Football League status.

Syd Fieldus, who had given splendid voluntary service as manager/secretary in an honorary capacity, was invited by Fenton to continue as his assistant (unpaid), and did so for that first season under the new management.

Just prior to Fenton arriving at the club, the piece of ground which now is partly occupied by the Sporting U's, was purchased from a Mr Quinnery. Acquiring this land ended a long standing dispute over right of way to the far side of the stadium.

Wartime regulations regarding registration of players still applied. But at the same time, the new manager was busy signing players with an eye to the future. Bower, Fieldus, the two Bobs - Hutchings and Hodgson, Paddy Shiels, Chris Harmon and Ronnie Hornby, had all been retained from the 45/46 season before Fenton's arrival. He soon added to those; Ian Gillespie signed from Ipswich Town, Bob Curry from Gainsborough Trinity, Alf Biggs from Bradford, and a little later, Dennis Hilman from Brighton and Hove Albion. Three others who signed, Wilf Bott from Q.P.R., Jack Finch from Fulham and Stan Gibbs from Charlton, only stayed for a few months before being released.

But that was only the start. In September, Fenton created a sensation by signing Arthur Turner, a striker who had won amateur international honours and was in Charlton Athletic's first team. Not only that, in November, he persuaded Turner to turn professional, something Charlton had tried to do and failed. Turner proved to be an outstanding acquisition and was still at Layer Road when Football League status was secured.

Other arrivals included goalkeeper Harry Wright from Derby County, Frank Stamper, a forward released from the Army, Albert Walker, a left back from West Ham United and Sean Nightingale, an inside forward from Scunthorpe.

Some alarm bells at the wages bill was voiced at the board meeting in September, and at one period there were 28 professionals on the books. But National Service claimed some like Nornby, Hutchings and Shiels, and half a dozen left after just a short stay at the club. That season also marked the first appearance in Colchester United colours of Vic Keeble, of whom, more anon.

The first trial game at Layer Road on August the 24th 1946, attracted 1600 spectators. Mainly, one suspects, to assess the possibilities of a lot of local amateurs who were on view . The possibles won 2–1. Len Carter was, according to Fred Draycott, the player who took the eye. He scored one of The Possibles goals. Sid Smith, a trialist who had played for Dundee United, got the other. The probables goal was scored by Roy Watson, just released by the R.A.F.

Amongst the players were Ron Fenton who was an Orient player, Chiswick a West Ham amateur, Jelly from Colchester Casuals, Leah a serving soldier on South Liverpool's books, Des Knight had played for the Royal Navy, and George Richer from Scottish club Leith Athletic.

The second trial match on August 24th, attracted a gate of 2725, servicemen were admitted free. Ted Fenton himself played in this one, at centre half for the Probables who lost 4–3. Only Nightingale, Sheils, Bell, Jelly, Richer, Thompson, Watson, Cant, Cater, Green and Bell survived from the trial match played 2 days earlier. Some names that were to become very familiar to U's fans were on parade.

## POOR START

So to the first Southern League match of the 46/47 season and a 2–3 defeat from Gloucester City at Layer Road. The U's team on August the 31st 1946 read:-
*Wright, Bower, Sheils, Ross, Fenton, Hutchings, Finch, Cater, Stewart, Curry, S.Smith.*

Curry and Stewart were the scorers. The U's also lost their next 2 games, going down 3–0 at Chelmsford and 3–1 away to Exeter City Reserves. However, things improved after that and they then went through their next 8 Southern League games unbeaten. Although they did lose 4–2 to the old enemy Chelmsford City in a Southern League Cup match at New Writtle Street. Those three early defeats howevei, led to Finch, Bott, Ross and Tobin leaving the club.

Off the field, Major Dai Rees, who had done so much in helping the club to field a team in that difficult 45/46 season, announced that he had been posted away from Colchester. He kept in touch with the club for many years after his departure. Practically, his last gesture was to defray the cost of a new set of goal posts for the club, the cost amounting to 35 guineas (£36–75p). At a board meeting just prior to the stai: of the season, Claude Orrin, in his capacity as honorary treasurer, announced that the police costs for the previous season had been £2. At that same meeting, honorariums of 50 guineas each were presented to Claude Orrin and Syd Fieldus in recognition of their work in starting the club up again after the war.

The club also received a transfer fee of £250 for Frank Rawcliffe from Newport County. Rawcliffe had signed for the U's in March 1946, but declined the terms offered to him at the end of the season. He later played for Swansea Town and Aldershot and altogether, played over 200 Football League games.

In September, a dinner was organised for Major Rees at the Marlborough at Dedham, where he was presented with an inscribed cigarette case, for his services to the club. The club also appointed a Mr Austin at £2-10-0d per week as masseur, to attend on match days and when required during the week.

Fenton at the end of the month, reported that having now sorted out the professionals, he wished to keep the weekly wage bill to £81-10-0d. All the professionals except Sheils, Curry and Gibbs, had jobs and were part-time. He also urged the necessity of employing paid gate men to man the turnstiles on match days. Up to then, the Supporters Club had done the job on a voluntary basis. On behalf of the Supporters Club, Mr Jackson said that his members would be glad to be free of the responsibility, though they would promise the services of four members each match to sell programmes etc.

Arrangements were also put in hand for the visit of Dutch team Zwolle to play a match at Layer Road.

The start of the season also saw the demolition of the stand on the popular side of Layer Road, the later 'Sporting U's' side. The timbers from it were utilised for reconstructing the covered standing end at Layer Road, and on the main stand side, at a cost of £6.

September was also a red letter month for groundsman Jack Duncan. First, his wages were increased by ten shillings a week and the supporters club bought a new motor mower for use on the pitch.

Gate receipts for the first four matches played at Layer Road in the 46/47 season, make interesting reading, the first trial match attracting 1,608 fans (receipts accounting to £55-7s-1d), 2,725 for the second (£97-11-0d). For the opening Southern League match against Gloucester City, the attendance was 6,339, with takings of £375-6-5d and tax paid of £32-1-11d. The 2382 fans who paid to watch the first reserve team match in the Eastern Counties League, contributed £106-10s-8d (tax £7-15-0d).

At the board meeting where the above figures were given, it was reported that all season ticket holders' seats were labelled with their name. Programme sales at the Gloucester City match were 1,500 - a complete sell-out and more could have been sold if the printers had supplied them, but the paper restrictions still made this impossible. Mr Richer, at the meeting, reported that membership of the Supporters Club had now passed the 2,000 mark.

Fenton was certainly not short of ambition, for he reported that he was negotiating with Arsenal for the services of Syd Jones and Eric Bowden, two well known players who were reaching the veteran stage. In the event these overtures came to nothing as both players rejected the chance to come to Layer Road.

The minutes of the October 1946 Board meetings illustrate how things have changed over the years. One minute expressed alarm at the number of bicycles going missing on match days at Layer Road; director Gerald Benham expressed the view that almost a third of the fans cycled to the ground. It was agreed that notices should be displayed disclaiming any club responsibility for bikes left on the ground during matches.

Another entry related to the sale of newspapers on the ground. It was confirmed that no objection be raised providing the vendors paid for admission.

There was also reference to the need to provide terracing behind the far end goal and alarm expressed at the state of the boundary.

At the end of October, the club contacted Colchester Borough Parks Committee regarding the possible purchase of the ground. It was also decided to proceed with erection of the brick wall along the rear of the main stand to prevent people getting in free from the Rainsborrow Road area.

A new departure was the provision of teas in the Director's Room, a new urn was to be purchased; cost of teas not to exceed 1 shilling (5p) per head. Another decision taken was to produce 2,500 programmes of four pages for each first team game. An assurance had been received from the printers that sufficient paper was now available for this to be done.

Playing wise the 1946/47 season was not one of the U's more successful campaigns. They finished eighth in the table with 32 points from 31 games. Gillingham, who won the championship, and Gravesend and Northfleet United, were the only teams to double Colchester - the Gills winning 1-0 at Layer Road and 4-2 at Priestfield. Gravesend won 3-1 at Layer Road and 3-0 at their own ground.

There were some high scoring games at Layer Road. Exeter City Reserves lost 6-1, four goals were scored against Bedford Town and Yeovil, and altogether the U's netted 41 goals in 15 home League matches. On their travels however, things were different. They scored twice at Worcester and Gloucester and four at Cheltenham, but only 10 in the other 12 away matches. The away match with Millwall Reserves was not played, and the Lions failed to complete their fixtures.

The Southern League Cup that season was a two legged affair. Colchester reached the semi-final beating Bedford 7-1 and Chelmsford City 6-5 before losing out 3-2 to Gillingham in a one leg semi-final at Layer Road on June 7th 1947. (The final in which Gillingham beat Yeovil was not played until August).

The semi-final match saw Bill Jeffries make his first team appearance for the U's. It also marked goalkeeper John Jelly's last game for the club. Bill Bower and Len Cater missed just one of the 40 first team matches played.

In the FA Cup, after beating Gothic from Norwich 5-1 in the Fourth Qualifying Round, the U's lost 5-0 at Elm Park to Reading in the first round proper.

Towards the end of the season, on May the 3rd, Vic Keeble - then 16 - was signed on amateur forms. The close season was to see the arrival of 30 year old Bob Allen on a free transfer from Northampton, Harry Bearryman (then aged 22) from Chelsea, Fred Cutting and Aubrey Darmondy from Norwich City, and Frank Rist (the Essex County cricketer) from Charlton Athletic. Players released were Bob Harding - a centre half – Bob Hutchings, former Spurs player Albert Page, Fred Stamper (sold to Hartlepool United), Ron Hornby who was still in the Forces, and 'keeper John Jelly. Fenton also tried to sign Paul Christensen, a half-back from Scandinavia who was serving in the Army at Colchester, but the League refused to accept his registration.

Behind the scenes there were a number of interesting happenings. For example it was agreed that a special carriage on the train journeys for away matches should be laid on for directors and their guests. At Christmas, 24 bottles of wine were distributed to players – the Supporters Club meeting the bill.

At the Board meeting at the end of January 1947, it was agreed to enter into negotiations with the owners of houses in Gladwin Avenue, to purchase 20 feet of their gardens to provide access points to the far end of the ground (after lengthy negotiations this plan was abandoned two years later).

Another minute recorded the fact that agreement had been reached with Detective Inspector Salmon, that in future police would be admitted to the ground on match days without payment! At the same meeting the death of Walter Clark, the man who really got the U's off the ground as a professional club in 1937, was reported; he bequeathed his shares in the U's to the club.

Colchester United were also represented at a meeting called by the Football League to consider the formation of a Fourth Division. Gerald Benham reported that there seemed to be a real prospect of that happening.

The Final Board meeting of the 1946/47 season on June 6th decided that application should be made to enter an "A" team in the Ipswich and District League. No application for membership of the Eastern Counties League was to be made. A trainer was to be appointed at a wage not exceeding £5-10-0d. per week; Jock Kearton got the job later in the month.

### COLCHESTER HIT THE HEADLINES

The 1947/48 season was the one destined to put Colchester firmly on the football map, although it started off pretty quietly. There were 17 professionals on the books, including Vic Keeble who was signed on September 13th 1947.

Claude Orrin who continued as honorary treasurer sounded an early note of warning on the need to watch the finances. The close season with summer wages and expenses in connection with new signings had put the club short of cash flow.

There was a couple of trial games in August, when Keeble soon made his presence felt, by scoring three goals. In the first trial match the Blue and Whites beat the Black and Ambers 3–2 – something of a surprise, since 1,455 fans saw the Reserves beating the probable first team.

A 17 year old goalkeeper, Dennis Blackwell, a King George V Boys Club player, a wing half from Courtaulds, James Speirs, Don Swift who worked at Severalls, Essex county youth player Walter Hymas from Latchingdon all caught the eye. But Keeble was the star of the show according to a contemporary report on the game.

No doubt stung by the reverse in the first trial game, the first team (Probables) thrashed the possibles 5–0 in the second encounter. Keeble (2), Brown, Biggs and Hillman scoring the goals.

Amateur 'keeper Ernest Setchell played in the Probables goal in the first half and then Harry Wright swapped sides with him at half-time. Setchell, according to Fred Draycott, who kept a clean sheet in the first half and only let one in the second, looked the better 'keeper on the day. Len Cater, still an amateur, played in the senior side which included Aubrey Darmody, a new signing from Norwich City. Bob Neville, who was still serving in the Army and Bart Clent, on trial from Fulham, were the pick of the reserve team.

COLCHESTER ANGLO NETHERLANDS SPORTS AND CULTURAL ASSOCIATION
AND
COLCHESTER UNITED FOOTBALL CLUB LTD.

**FOOTBALL TOUR**
**AUGUST 22nd—AUGUST 29th, 1947**

Veotball en Athleticiekvereninging
P. E. C.
Zwolle Holland

COLCHESTER
BARKING
GRAYS
WALTHAMSTOW
LONDON
SOUTHEND

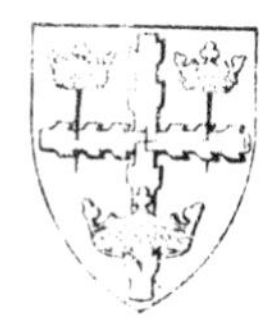

*Presented with the Compliments of The Essex Telegraph Ltd., Colchester.*

On August the 23rd, P.E.C.Zwolle from Holland were at Layer Road. 4,202 turned up to see the Dutch team beaten 3–2, Bob Allen, Bob Curry and Arthur Turner (pen) getting the goals.

Altogether, during the season, the U's played eight friendlies. A gate of 35,000 saw them lose 3–0 to Arsenal at Highbury, and 12,306 to see goals from Fred Cutting and Ted Fenton earn a 2–1 win over Ipswich Town at Layer Road on April the 5th 1948. Charlton Athletic reserves were hammered 6–0 at Colchester, 4,004 were present to see Bob Curry's hat-trick, with Cater, Hillman and Turner scoring the other three. Chelsea reserves were made of sterner stuff with that match ending 1–1 and 4,292 passing through the turnstiles.

There were three matches in an end of season tour of Holland. Zeeburgia were beaten 5–1, the U's lost 2–1 to Sparta in Rotterdam and wound up with a 1–0 win over Zwolle. Those games attracted 36,000 spectators in total.

The other match played was for the Gough Hospital Cup, when Bury Town were beaten 2–1 before a West Suffolk crowd of 3,770.

The Southern League campaign opened with a 5–1 win over Bedford Town at The Eyrie Ground, Keeble scoring three and Cater two. A week later, Gloucester City came to Layer Road. The gate was 11,419 and the U's obliged with an 8–0 victory. The team showed one change to the side that played at Bedford, Alf Page replacing Essex cricketer Frank Rist at centre half. It was Hillman's turn to get three that day, Turner scored two, Biggs, Cater and Curry netted one each.

There was also a 3–0 home win over Chelmsford City in the Southern League Cup, a 0–0 draw at Hereford and a 2–1 victory at New Writtle Street in the second leg of the League Cup. The last Saturday in September however, saw Yeovil bring the U's down to Earth with a 2–0 win on their sloping Huish ground.

By the end of November, the team had played nine League games, won five, drawn two and lost two.

After that early burst of high scores, the U's had done nothing spectacular when FA Cup time came around, but things were to change.

The FA Cup quest started with an unspectacular 3–1 win over local rivals Chelmsford City in the fourth qualifying round. A crowd of 10,396 saw goals from Bob Curry (2) and Arthur Turner put the U's in the first round.

The visitors this time were Banbury Spencer from the Birmingham League. It looked a formality to get through to the second round, but in the event Spencer were unlucky to go away beaten 2–1. With their Harlequin style kit, maybe they dazzled the Colchester players, but they certainly put up a terrific fight. A partisan crowd of 8,574 were screaming for the final whistle with the U's grimly hanging on to the lead. Andy Brown and Curry were the Colchester scorers.

When the second round draw was made, it was Wrexham of the League Division 3 North who drew the short straw. Colchester tuned up for this one in fine style, beating Barry 5–2 down in Wales in a Southern League match. Wrexham at the time, were riding high in the League table and were favourites to win a place in round three. Played on December 13th, it proved to be an unlucky day for the Welshmen. The U's won 1–0, Curry once again being the hero, and getting the only goal before 10,642 spectators. It really was an extraordinary cup–tie. Wrexham were awarded a penalty when their flying winger Bill Tunnicliffe was brought down by Bob Allen. The Clock End goal was a muddy morass and Tunnicliffe, who took the spot kick, slipped as he hit the ball which then trickled slowly into Harry Wright's hands. A short time later, Colchester were awarded a penalty at the Layer Road end – Fenton missed from the spot.

Huddersfield Town of the First Division were next on the FA Cup agenda. But between the Wrexham tie and the Yorkshire club's visit to Layer Road, five more Southern League games were played. The Christmas and New Year results were poor, losing twice to Cheltenham Town and drawing with Gillingham.

A crowd of 16,005 turned up on a cold January day to see Huddersfield, skippered by the great Peter Doherty, put the minnows in their place. That was where Ted Fenton's lucky charm worked the oracle. He had a lucky champagne cork that he acquired at a function in Berlin. Tad always carried it in his shorts and he swore that when it was with him on the field, the team he was playing for had never lost to a side with red in their strip. Huddersfield for this match, had to change into red from their normal blue and white stripes.

Fenton's 'F' Plan, as the newspapers called it, had been devised after he had watched the First Division side in action. The papers were full of it: *"David versus Goliath"*, *"Ted's Plan–the F way"* were just some of the headlines. Even so, every one, including the Colchester supporters, expected Town to win.

*Planning for the Huddersfield Cup match. (Left to right) Kearton (Jun.), Kearton (Sen.–Trainer), Bearryman (Standing), Curry, Fenton, Neville, Rist (standing) and Brown.*

An historic picture. The Huddersfield and Colchester teams before the start of the first "Giant Killing" act in 1948. Colchester (l. to r.) back row: Andy Brown, Ted Fenton, Harry Bearryman, Harry Wright, Bob Allen, 'Digger' Kettle. Front row: Arthur Turner, Dennis Hillman, Bob Curry (Capt.) Fred Cutting, Len Cater. (Courtesy *Colchester Express*)

When the Umbrella Man Harry Fosker, beard and all, led the U's on to the field, the noise was deafening. In the first half Colchester had the edge, with the Huddersfield players seemingly unable to adapt to the tight ground. Fenton marked Doherty out of the game. Then with 70 minutes gone, it happened.

It was Arelight Works electrician "Digger" Kettle who lit the fuse with a run from his own penalty area. On and on he ran until a defender upended him right on the edge of the Huddersfield 18 yard box. Bob Allen hammered the resultant free kick through the defensive wall, Town 'keeper Bob Hesford got a hand to the ball, but it fell to U's skipper Bob Curry, who slammed it into the back of the net. Cheekily, Colchester, far from sitting back, chased the game and for the last 20 minutes, always looked likely to score again.

F.A. Cup: Third Round

*Saturday, January 10th, 1948*

Colchester United

*v.*

Huddersfield Town

Souvenir Programme

PRICE SIXPENCE

At the final whistle, the crowd went mad and the players were carried off the pitch. For the first time in the modern history of the FA Cup, a non-League side had beaten a First Division side.

A 4-0 Southern League Cup win over Bedford Town kept the pot boiling ready for round four, and a home tie with Bradford, who had done a giant killing act themselves, beating mighty Arsenal in round three. Could Colchester do it again?

There were queues for tickets, phone calls from life long supporters who had rarely been seen at Layer Road, all wanting tickets. One in particular, asked for 6 stand seats, and then asked for directions to get to the ground! It was a hectic time coping with all the enquiries.

The day of the match dawned. Layer Road was packed. The Elm trees at the Gladwin Road end were festooned with fans and every corner sardine tight.

This time it wasn't quite so smooth as in the previous matches. Very early on, 23 year old winger Billy Elliot put an angled shot past Harry Wright to give the Park Avenue side the lead. For a time, the crowd was muted, then Bob Curry struck twice in quick succession. First "Spud" Cater crossed from the left, Bradford 'keeper "Chick" Farr was caught in two minds, and Curry got his head to the ball to make it 1-1. The cheers were still echoing around the ground when Curry, with a run down the right, put Fred Cutting through. Curry kept motoring and was there to rocket the return pass into the bottom of the net.

There was pandemonium, but just before half-time, an Elliott shot hit the Colchester bar and George Ainsley smashed in the rebound, 2-2 at the interval. Straight from the restart Colchester had the ball in the net again, but the linesman was flagging for offside against Arthur Turner. The referee, to the chagrin of the crowd who of course, questioned the linesman's eyesight, disallowed the 'goal'.

Just four minutes later however, Turner wrong-footed the Bradford defence by letting a long ball from Cater run for Cutting. He drew Farr out of his goal before blasting home a right foot shot. Curry had the ball in the visitors net again, but once more, Turner had been caught offside. Then, with only three minutes left, only a marvellous save by Wright denied Ainsley an equaliser.

The final whistle went: Colchester United 3 Bradford PA 2, and within seconds the pitch was a seething mass of humanity. Fans climbed down off the stand roof and out of the trees, the noise was unbelievable. The successful team were entertained at the Town Hall by the Mayor, Edward Dansie, and when they appeared on the balcony, the crowd in Colchester High Street went mad.

Sanity returned however, the following Monday, when in the draw for the fifth round, up came Blackpool - Matthews, Mortenson and all - away at Bloomfield Road. The attendances at earlier rounds had swelled the club's coffers nicely.

Apart from the Banbury Spencer game the same 11 players appeared in every tie. In this game Hillman missed the match through injury and Edgar Williams took his place. Williams was from Northampton Town and this was his only Cup outing for the U's.

So there was little doubt that the line up at Blackpool would read:- *Wright, Kettle, Allen, Bearryman, Fenton, Brown, Hillman, Curry, Turner, Cutting and Cater.*

Sandwiched between the Bradford match and the Blackpool game on February the 7th 1948, was an away Southern League match at Torquay. Ted Fenton took the precaution of resting goalkeeper Wright, Curry, himself and Hillman. In came 'keeper John Lamare, Albert Page, Ray Townrow and Frank Rist. The 4,221 spectators at Plainmoor witnessed a 1-1 draw, Cutting scoring the U's goal.

*Harry Fosker – the umbrella man*

*"The peace of Blackpool was shattered before dawn today by thousands of Colchester fans, waving rattles, ringing bells, blowing trumpets and shouting 'Up the U's'. Not since pre-war illumination weekends, has there been such an invasion as stormed our streets from 4 o'clock this morning".*

It was a cold, wet and windy morning, with the early opening breakfast establishments doing a roaring trade, and after opening time, the pubs. But there was no trouble, no vandalism and no gangs of yobbos, a blot on football that erupted many years later.

The Blackpool streets also echoed to Cyril Walker on the accordion, leading the Colchester fans singing *"Up the U's"*, the words and the tune having been adapted by Cyril's brother earlier in the cup run. While cheer leader Harry Fosker and his six blue and white decked minions later had the Saturday morning shoppers in Woolworth's in stitches as their chanting brought business to a temporary halt. It was all good natured fun.

Meanwhile, the build up to the Blackpool match was intense. The reporters from the National Papers haunted Colchester, and the town was decked in blue and white streamers and banners wherever one looked. Colchester's name cropped up on the BBC Twenty Questions programme "Abstract with animal connections" - the question. Jack Train, now long deceased, came up with the answer, "The Fenton Plan", it was all good fun and incredible publicity for the town.

Travelling in those days was not like it is today, although then as now, the trains ran late! The War had been over for almost two years, but there were still many restrictions, including one on petrol with no diesel then. In the 10 days or so before the scheduled date, 52 coaches were booked in Colchester and the surrounding area for the pilgrimage to the Lancashire resort. Tickets had been issued and paid for and all seemed set for the coaches to travel 280 miles to Blackpool, when the men from the ministry put a spoke in the wheels.

Though it was in order for 50 full coaches to make the journey north, no coach would be allowed to travel more than 15 miles without a full pay load. This ruling put the cat amongst the pigeons but despite protests, the Ministry of Fuel and Power was adamant, petrol for 560 miles fine, petrol for thirty miles empty and only partially full, no chance. Just a day before the match, because of this absurd ruling, 40 coaches had to be cancelled, and the monies paid refunded. It was chaos with 10 coaches eventually leaving Colchester, and those left without transport piling into trains to London and then on to Blackpool by rail.

The team of course, travelled North on the day before the match and stayed overnight in Blackpool, guests at the hotel owned by one Stanley Matthews.

The West Lancashire Evening Post on the day of the match, had this to say:-

Meantime, the U's players spent the Friday evening watching a Jessie Matthews show "Maid to Measure", and afterwards went backstage at the theatre where she autographed programmes for each player. Then it was back to the hotel for tea and biscuits and to bed by 11 p.m. Next morning, Matthews himself, assisted by "Spud" Cater, cooked bacon and egg breakfasts. Late arrivals in Blackpool were a party of four, who flew to Blackpool from Boxted Airfield on the Saturday morning. Mike Murayda, an American living in Colchester, piloted the plane, with Mr B. Woolf, Mr K.J.Pecina and Mrs D.G.Woolacombe as passengers.

The match itself saw Blackpool take a fourth minute lead, when Wright misjudged a header from Munro. McIntosh and Mortensen each got two as the First Division club won 5-0. A crowd of 29,500 brought in receipts of £3,200. The Blackpool team read:- Shimwell, Stuart, Johnston, Hayward, Kelly, Matthews, Mortensen, McIntosh, Dick and Munro. Thus ended the F Plan cup run.

### THE ARRIVAL OF CLAUDE ORRIN

The 1947/48 season was a busy one behind the scenes as well as being an exciting one on the field.

It was also where Colchester United made one of their best ever acquisitions to the Layer Road staff. Claude Orrin, was persuaded to accept a full time appointment with the club. Previously Ted Davis, Syd Fieldus in an honorary capacity, and Ted Fenton had been secretary/manager at Layer Road. A full time financial secretary was thus a departure from previous arrangements.

With the growing stature of the club, and the amount of work occasioned by the fabulous F.A. Cup run, it had become obvious that a full time administrator was needed. A full Board meeting on April 6th 1948 were unanimous that Mr Orrin should be invited to fill the post at a wage of £8 per week.

This was one of the best decisions ever made. Claude was to occupy the position for 24 years, and later came to be acknowledged as one of the best and most knowledgeable secretaries in the Football League. Claude, now of course deceased, is remembered and revered by many, many Colchester United supporters and players past and present.

There was also the shock announcement on June the 14th 1948, that Ted Fenton was resigning as manager in order to join West Ham United as assistant manager. At the time the manager was on holiday in Bournemouth, and his departure was the signal for a frantic search for a new boss with the new season looming on the horizon. In the event Jimmy Allen was appointed in July, but more on that later.

In the minutes of the Board meetings of that season there were many interesting pieces that give a good insight into the running of the club 44 years ago.

In those days monies from pre-season practice matches had to be donated to charity. The dispersal from the 1947 practice games was recorded as follows:-
£50 to the Colchester Care of the aged Trust Fund.
£20 to the St. John's Ambulance Association.
£124-3-6d to Essex F.A. Benevolent Fund.
£10 to the Colchester and District Nurses.

In the October minutes a letter from an ex-Italian Prisoner or War - Guiseppe Rebuglio - thanking the club and officials for their hospitality while working on Layer Road was recorded. At another meeting that month Ted Fenton recorded on the problem of drying the players kits and it was agreed to hire a drier from the Colchester Gas Company.

The police, then as now, had a say in ground safety. An inspection of Layer Road by Supt. Phillbrown and Insp. Wisely, accompanied by the Borough Engineer Mr Richardson, revealed one or two danger spots. As a result two new exits had to be provided. One into Gladwin Road, the other at the Layer Road end. The maximum capacity was a matter for decision and it was agreed 16,000 was a reasonable figure. It was also agreed that five new entry points be provided and exit gates opened not sooner than 10 minutes before the end of the game.

In November, director Scott, after some argument, succeeded in securing admission for O.A.P.'s for 6d (2½p). At that same gathering an application by Fulham to undergo cup-tie training at Layer Road was rejected on the advice of Jock Duncan and the groundsman. For F.A. Cup matches it was agreed that visiting teams should be allocated 25 percent of the seats, ie. 265 and that 12 Complimentary tickets be issued for visiting officials.

After Aubrey Darmondy failed to put in an appearance for a reserve match with Norwich City (his former club), his wages were withheld. After hearing Darmondy's explanation the directors however, by a majority vote decided to instruct the treasurer to pay. A number of the board felt he should only be given half-pay. As a result of this case it was decided that in future all players - whether playing or not - should report at noon at Layer Road on match days.

In January 1948, at the suggestion of Syd Fieldus, it was decided that the club would produce a handbook. After much discussion the Supporters Club agreed to finance the project. Alan Everett was approached to prepare the Editorial content. He was the team Sports Editor on the Essex Telegraph, and later the East Anglian Times, for many years.

For the Huddersfield Town F.A. Cup match the Essex County Telegraph agreed to print 8,000 programmes, at a cost of 1d each. Before the match emergency work had to be done strengthening and replacing concrete blocks at the Spion Kop end. (Nothing changes). It was also agreed that three directors, Messrs. Secton, Scott and Wright be available to escort visiting press men to their seats. (Some things do change!).

The profit on programmes sales from the Huddersfield game was later reported to be £150, and the print run for the Bradford game was set at 9,000. Before the Bradford match chairman, "Bill" Allen authorised workmen to come in to shore up the corrugated iron fence at the Gladwin Road end. At a subsequent Board meeting his action was criticised by Alderman Piper who said it had been done without the necessary authority of the Parks Department. Mr Piper also felt that the Board should have acceded to the request from Bradford to increase admission charges for the cup match. The rest of the directors however, disagreed, and endorsed the chairman in his action of turning down the request, and also on the fencing issue.

In February 1948 a rent of £155 per annum for Layer Road was confirmed. In March Mr Allen, the chairman, sent a consignment of Colchester oysters to Leigh Rugby Club. They had asked Colchester for assistance in securing a supply for their Team contesting the Rugby League Cup Final.

The April 1948 meeting of The Board were dismayed to learn that over 1,000 of the 6,000 programmes printed for the game with Ipswich Town had not been sold. (This was the one match programme that did not make a profit for the club).

Later that month it was reported that retaining fees for players should be as follows; full time players £7 winter, £5 summer, part-time players £3 a week winter and summer. Early in May Syd Fieldus terminated his association with the club which extended back to pre-war days.

The retained list was issued at the end of April. The players kept on for season 1948/49 were:- Allen, Brown, Bearryman, Cutting, Curry, Hillman, Keeble, Kettle, Stamper, Turner, Townrow, Wright, Bower, Neville, Walker and Fenton. It was also agreed that Mr Fenton be allowed an expense account of £150 per annum. The final communication of the season was an enquiry from the Ipswich Town manager Scott Duncan for the services of Bob Curry. The proposed offer was rejected.

How times have changed. When the Colchester United directors met on June 22nd 1948 the meeting was held at Silverdene, Lexden Road, the home of chairman "Bill" Allen. The purpose of the meeting was to agree the terms for the players of the 1948/49 season.

Turner's wage perhaps gives a clue as to why Colchester managed to sign him on professional forms when he had turned down a chance to sign as a pro for Charlton Athletic where he had played as an amateur. His Winter/Summer figures were £12/£10 per week compared with other players, many of whom were on much less, the lowest being Walker at £4-10-0/£2.

At the meeting, Lewis Gunary was co-opted on to the Board of Directors. A farmer, Mr Gunary was to serve as a director for over 20 years.

Early in July Claude Orrin was officially confirmed as secretary/treasurer of the club. It was also confirmed that an "A" team had been entered in the Essex and Suffolk Border League and would play on the Garrison No.2 ground. The club also decided to buy a house in Rainsborowe Road. This was to be the first of a number of houses that the club eventually acquired to house staff. The property concerned remained in the U's possession until the 1980's.

### THE NEWCOMERS

Consequent on the departure of Ted Fenton to join West Ham the Board advertised the post of the manager. There were 37 applicants for the job and a short list of four was drawn up for interviews. They were J. Allen, T. Bradshaw, C. Ferguson and G. Turner. Interviews were fixed for Monday July 19th at 7pm at Layer Road. Meeting four days prior to that date the Board agreed the salary to be offered should be £12 per week. The new manager would also share in the match bonus scheme on the same terms as the players. In the event Turner did not turn up for the interview and was ruled out.

Thomas "Tiny" Bradshaw a Scot was 48 but well known in football circles. He first played for Bury moving to Liverpool until World War II. He spent the immediate post war years coaching and was favoured for the job by three of the Colchester directors. Charlie Ferguson was also a Scot with extensive experience with Macclesborough. A classy inside forward he had just hung up his boots – a shin injury ending his playing career.

James Allen, to give him his correct title, had won English International honours. A centre-half, his career started with Poole Town from where he moved to Portsmouth and later to Aston Villa. He was the candidate who got the vote, and commenced at Layer Road from the end of July. Allen was to remain with the club until they attained Football League Status. Ill health ultimately led to his resignation, no doubt aggravated by the fact that Colchester United had a hard time of it in their first two seasons in Division Three South. A departure for the 48/49 season was the decision to make away journeys by coach.

A quotation by Messrs. Chambers & Son of Bures was accepted. Hector Harrington was the driver on some of the early trips.

Pre-war goalkeeper Bill Light was engaged as "A" team coach at £2 per week.

The new manager decided to run two trial games pointing out that having never seen most of the Colchester players his first job was to run the rule over the talent available.

The first match on August the 12th resulted in a 4-0 win for the probable senior team. Turner 2, Curry and Cutting were the scorers, and the attendance was 2,518. Those who were present saw half-a-dozen new signings gracing Layer Road for the first time.

The newcomers who played were Wally Nunn, a 27 year-old centre-half who had been released by Swindon Town. He spent one season at Layer Road refusing the re-engagement terms offered in May 1949, and joined Guildford City.

Winger Stan Foxall was 30 at the time and was on West Ham's books. He became a big favourite at Layer Road and stayed with the club until 1950. When the U's were admitted to the Football League he could no longer play for Colchester as The Hammers held his registration.

Alf "Dusty" Miller was Allen's first signing. He came to United from Plymouth Argyle and at 31 was approaching the veteran stage. At the end of the season he was appointed as coach in place of Jock Kearton, but continued to play for the reserves into the 1950's.

Twenty-four year old Dennis Maffey, a half-back, joined from Ipswich Town. Local man Dick Cullum (later to be signed professionally), George French (in later life a Police Inspector) and goalkeeper Ken Whitehead from Clacton, were with the club on amateur forms.

There were 4470 to view the second trial game, for this match the new manager pitted the first team defence against the first team forwards. The result was an exciting 3-3 draw. Keeble, Foxall and Bob Allen scored for the Blue and Whites, Turner, Cater and Hillman for the Black and Amber.

*Arthur Turner completes his hat-trick (he scored four in total), against Merthyr at Layer Road*

The first Southern League game was away to Cheltenham Town on August the 21st, and resulted in a 1-1 draw - Fred Cutting was the scorer, and the gate was 3,400.

For the opening match at Layer Road, a Southern League Cup tie, 8606 were there to see Exeter City Reserves defeated by 3 goals to 1. Turner penalty, Cutting and Hillman were the scorers. Hillman and Cater came into the side in place of Foxall and Cranfield who were injured at Cheltenham.

There were three big early victories, 4-0 v Kidderminster at Layer Road, 5-1 at Chingford and 6-0 at home to Bradford.

The U's cup run of 1947/48 had earned them exemptions until the First Round and there was great expectations when the club received a home draw against Reading. On November the 27th, 19,072 fans crammed into Layer Road to see the match. An attendance record that has never been, and is never likely to be beaten. But it turned out to be a fiasco. Fog which shrouded the ground before the kick-off got thicker and thicker. The score was 1-1, Bob Curry scoring for Colchester (though few people except the ones behind the Reading goal saw it), then the match was abandoned.

With no floodlights in those days the game had to be restaged in mid-week, on December the 4th. This time 13,371 were at the game looking for another giant- killing feat. Alas! it was not to be, though "Spud" Cater scored twice for the U's the Elm Park side got four and that was that for F.A. Cup dreams.

By the turn of the year Colchester had played 15 Southern League games, six at Layer Road where they were unbeaten, and nine away. Nine games were won, four drawn and they had lost at Chelmsford and Barry. Twenty two points already in the bag and things were looking rosy near the top of the table.

### TWO CUP FINALS IN ONE SEASON

The start of 1949 bought the U's down to earth. The first four games in January producing just two points. A 1-1 draw at Gillingham was followed by a 2-0 loss at Hastings, and a 5-1 drubbing from Dartford. At Layer Road, on January 22nd, a crowd of 7,782 was present when visitors Cheltenham held the U's to a 2-2 draw; there was a lot of barracking.

Manager Jimmy Allen however, stuck by his team,, and his faith in his players was justified by a subsequent 11 match unbeaten run. In that sequence they scored 34 goals and conceded just six.

One strange aspect of the late stages of the campaign was that in a 10 day period the U's played in two Southern League Cup finals. This situation came about since the 47/48 Cup final had not been staged, due to end of season fixture problems.

So it was on the 22nd of April 1949 the U's met Merthyr down in Wales to contest the final for the previous season. They were on the end of a 5-0 beating at Pennydarren Park. They played Merthyr again the following day in a Southern League match and lost that one too, 2-0 the score this time. So the Welsh side had ample revenge for a 5-2 League defeat at Layer Road back in February.

On March the 3rd, Colchester had to travel to Yeovil to contest the 48/49 Cup final. They lost again 3-0 - they can therefore claim some sort of unique record by losing finals for the same cup twice in one season!

In fact towards the end of the campaign they only won two of their last 12 matches. There was a 6-1 defeat at Gloucester, and though they defeated Hereford 4-0 at Layer Road, a crowd of 9,348 saw them lose their last home match 3-2 to Gillingham.

For Arthur Turner it was an eventful season. He scored 34 goals in 36 appearances. Early in the season he scored two in five successive games, but had a lean spell in mid season. He was on song again in a run of nine games which produced 12 goals. This included four against Merthyr on February 26th (this was the third time Turner had scored four in a game; he also produced hat-tricks for the U's on five occasions).

During that 48/49 season, Colchester used 23 players - four of them goalkeepers. Harry Wright was custodian in the first four games and played just one late on, in what was to be his last season at Layer Road. He had been the regular last line of defence for the two previous campaigns.

Local man Ken Whitehead made 39 appearances but his form lapsed towards the end of the season. He was injured in the 4-2 defeat at Worcester and never played for the first team again. Graham Davies made three appearances during which nine goals were conceded, then for the last two matches George Wright appeared on the scene. He was to remain the No.1 choice until 1954.

Few people seem to recall Davis. He had just been released by Watford when Allen brought him on trial to Layer Road. He had won honours for his native Wales as a schoolboy international. Standing well over six foot, he was 28 at the time, and was in fact offered terms at Colchester but declined the offer.

The end of the 48/49 season saw the departure from Layer Road of Frank Stamper, Ray Townrow, Wally Nunn, Norman George, Harry Cranfield, Andy Brown and of course Harry Wright. In addition Peter Hillyard, a centre-half, who made one appearance in the last game of the season, was not kept after an extended trial.

Gillingham, by winning their last game of the campaign at Layer Road took the Southern League championship, with Chelmsford City ending as runners-up. Highest gate at Layer Road in the Southern League was 14,048 for the local derby game with Chelmsford, lowest 4,525 for the visit of Tonbridge for a mid-week match.

The Board minutes for the season shed light on many aspects of the club's activities. For instance in November Claude Orrin reported that the average first team gate was 9,734, and for the Reserves 5,000.

The Reading F.A. Cup match was an all ticket game allocated to the Supporters Club. Prices were stand seats 3/-- (15p), ringside 2/6d. and ground tickets 1/3d - no reduced prices for children.

Just before Christmas the manager reported to the Board that goalkeeper Harry Wright was still on the injured list despite treatment for suspected cartilage trouble. With only Whitehead available he had no suitable first team cover. It was agreed to try secure the services of Len Young from Brighton and Hove Albion. Young had previously been with West Ham and Reading and was a veteran, aged 36. After hearing of the wage Young was asking, the Board decided to take no further action.

Early in the New Year Frank Alexander, a defender from Charlton Athletic, had a two month trial but was not retained. At the time Bob Allen was on the injured list and Colchester were conceding too many goals. Allen's absence had unsettled the defence and it was hoped Alexander would fill the breach.

In January Jock Duncan, then in his tenth season as grounds–man, was given a £1 a week wage increase – his wages went up to £5 per week. This was his first wage increase since 1939.

Director George Brown reported that the club made a profit of £160 from the sale of the Souvenir Programmes for the Reading F.A. Cup match. He also said that the Board's decision to invite all the helpers into the Board Room for a Christmas drink, sausage rolls and mince pies, at the Glou–cester City game on December 25th, had been much appreci–ated.

At another meeting in January the Directors (the manager was not present) discussed the make–up of the first team. Several directors felt that the best use was not being made of the available players. Secretary Orrin however, voiced the view that the directors were treading on dangerous ground and chairman Bill Allen, after complimenting the secretary on his sagacity, ruled the discussion out of order!

In February, after flooding at the Layer Road end of the ground, groundsman Duncan put in a report that in his view the problem was a breakdown in the drainage system (There was trouble at the corner of the ground until recent times despite many attempts to improve the situation).

## WELL IN THE BLACK

At the end of 1948 the share capital of the club amounted to £516–12–6, and the current account at the bank stood at £2,113–13–7 after allowing for current liabilities. The Reading F.A. Cup matches after a share out of the receipts, had brought in £574 for the first game (which was of course abandoned due to fog) and £413 for the second encounter. Receipts for the Southern League Cup match with Chelmsford City were £292 after all expenses had been paid.

Claude Orrin said the club was running with a surplus income over expenditure of £35 to £40 per week. A Good Friday collection for Harry Wright, who was retiring on medical advice, realised £92–14–3. He later moved to live in Kings Lynn.

In April there was severe gale damage to the Layer Road stand at the ground. The roof was blown off across Layer Road and caused damage to properties at the other side of the road. Repairs were estimated to cost £17–11–7, which was covered by insurance and local builders Messrs Moss carried out the repair work. The final Board meeting of that season decided to purchase four further club houses, the cost of each not to exceed £2,000.

The 49/50 season was to be the U's last in the Southern League. They failed to win the championship, but they did win the League Cup. At the end of the season when the Football League was expanded by two clubs, Colchester and Gillingham were elected to the vacancies.

Fifteen of the previous season's players had been offered terms. Wally Nunn, Frank Stamper and Dennis Maffey rejected the terms. Also missing at the start of the new campaign was trainer Jock Kearton, for he had been replaced by Alf Miller who was appointed as coach at £6 a week. For the first time it was agreed the manager should have a car allowance, which was fixed at £1–10–0 (£1–50) a week.

Thanks to a profit of £1,163.7s 3d from the 48/49 season, at the start of the new campaign the club had assets of more than £11,000. It was agreed that a 12 page programme priced at 3d would be issued for all first team matches and that several new features would appear, including a player profile.

Claude Orrin reported all 600 season tickets had been sold, and that the playing staff bill would be £219 a week, exclusive of any bonuses.

The one cloud on the horizon was the fact that the re–con–struction of the Layer Road end was still some way from completion. A shortage of steel was holding up the work. The first programme of the campaign contained a message from the chairman apologising to Layer Road end habitees for the delay.

*The cheque from the Supporters Club, which had an amazing membership of nearly 15,000 – the best in the Country!*

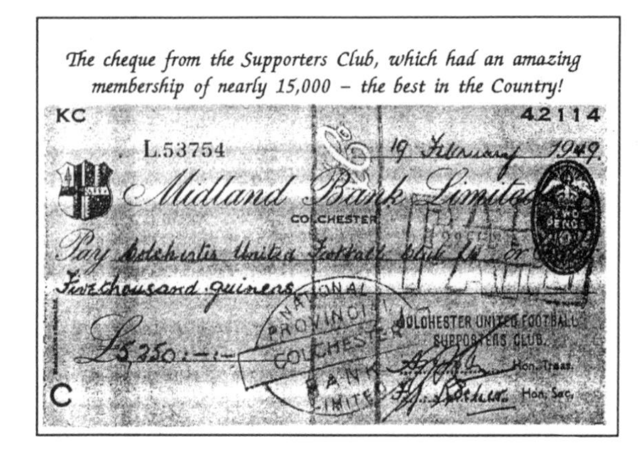


On the 8th of February 1949, Alderman Harper reported that a promising young player – Vic Keeble – had been appren–ticed with a local firm of builders, with an agreement that he was to have time off for matches and for training and ball practice on Tuesday and Thursday mornings.

A donation of £5,250 was handed over to club chairman Bill Allen by the Supporters Club at a buffet and dance held at The Red Lion Hotel on February 19th. The donation was used to pay off the mortgage on the house in Rainsborowe Road. £2,500 was invested in 2½% defence Bonds and £1,000 was deposited in the Trustees Savings Bank.

## TRIAL GAMES

There was the usual couple of trial games in early August with 4,283 fans at the first one and 4,891 at the second, two days later.

New players on view were Doug Beach, a 29 year old defender on Southend United's transfer list at £1,500, Les Burrell a forward released by Ipswich Town, John Fulbrook from Dartford – a former Orient player, 20 year old Jose Gallego who had played for Reading and Southampton, veteran Bill Leyton a defender transfer listed at £4,000 by Bradford, and midfielder John Moore listed by Brentford at £1,000. Reg Stewart (aged 27) a midfielder who was on offer from Sheffield Wednesday at £1,500, Ron Sales a 28 year old who was on Orient's books, and 22 year old John Sharpe who had been released by Southampton, completed the newcomers list.

Of those new players only Beach, Layton and Stewart were to gain regular places. Stewart in fact went on to be the regular occupant of the No.5 shirt until 1956 and proved an outstanding servant to the club. Of the others, Burrell had a job in Brighton and never made the first team, neither did Fulbrook who moved to Gravesend. Gallego played 11 senior games in two years at Layer Road before joining Cambridge United. In a similar period Moore managed 13 matches while Sharpe played one game against Yeovil before being released, as did Sales.

George Wright was the goalkeeper in all 52 first team games. Harry Bearryman, Fred Cutting and Vic Keeble also never missed a match; Reg Stewart and Stan Foxall were absent just once.

For the first Southern League game, 9,897 turned up to see Weymouth lose 3–0 at Layer Road and there was over 9,000 again to see Headington United (now Oxford United) beaten 4–1 a week later. The third match, was away at Gloucester, when Cater replaced Gallego, and where the U's won 3–2. Keeble another 2 and Cutting were the scorers.

Gallego never recaptured his place on a regular basis, and Cater, who replaced him, appeared in just four games before being injured. He had been on United's books since the formation of the club and before that played for Colchester Town. Most of his Layer Road career he played as an amateur. All told he made 117 first team appearances, scored 34 goals, and playing as winger, he provided a goodly number of crosses that led to goals for Curry and Turner. Strangely enough all of his last four senior games were away from home, the last one being at Chelmsford on the 10th of September 1949.

By the turn of the year the U's had lost just three of the 28 games played. Two of these matches were in the Southern League, both away (3–1 at Chingford and 2–0 at Dartford). The other defeat was a surprising 1–0 setback at the now built over Lower Mead Stadium, where Wealdstone won 1–0 in the F.A. Cup Fourth Qualifying Round. That match was the first F.A. Cup-tie to be televised. It was an experimental run for the old Alexandra Palace Studios. The game was on November the 12th when 9,549 spectators crowded into the Wealdstone ground.

Those 28 games up to December the 31st yielded 76 goals, with 27 conceded. Injuries to Bob Allen meant that he made 35 appearances in what was his only season at Layer Road. (He had played in four matches as a guest player in the 45–46 season as a centre forward and scored twice against Worcester City on January the 26th 1946). Bill Bower and Dennis Maffey filled in at number 2 in place of Kettle. Maffey, who was transfer listed after refusing a new contract for the season, played his last game for the club at the end of October against Torquay United Reserves.

The second half of the season started with a resounding 6–1 win over Gloucester City at Layer Road. Yet at the following board meeting, it was stated that members felt an audience of 8,329 was rather disappointing. Indeed, apart from a crowd of 10,130, when Tonbridge visited in the Southern League Cup Semi Final, the gates continued to fall and there was only 7,600 to see Bath City win 4–3 at Layer Road in the last home game of the season. That defeat was in the Southern League Cup Final second leg. Fortunately the U's had won 3–0 in the first leg at Twerton Park, giving them a 6–4 aggregate over the two games.

Two away defeats and two home drawn games in April ruined their chances of achieving a League and Cup double. They lost 1–0 at Yeovil and 5–0 at Merthyr, the latter ending up as champions. A 0–0 draw with Torquay and a 2–2 result against Gravesend led to points being dropped at Layer Road.

The season ended with Merthyr and Colchester both on 71 points, but the Welsh team took the championship with a better goal average. Merthyr, in fact, had also been champions in 1947/48 when Gillingham finished as runners-up. No wonder they felt aggrieved when Colchester and Gillingham were elected to the Football League and they had to stay in the Southern. In fact they went on to take the title in three of the next four seasons – it does in retrospect, all seem somewhat unjust.

Despite the successful season on the field of play, things behind the scenes were not quite so happy. At a Finance Committee meeting in January 1950, it was reported that gates had not matched up to expectations and the club was running at a loss. There was also the matter of a tax demand for £324 for the season.

In April, it was reported that the loss on the season thus far, amounted to £250. There was some discussion regarding the application that had been made for entry into the Football League. Claude Orrin pointed out that with £2,266–12–11 in the club's current account, they were still in a strong financial position. In the event, Colchester became a Football League club in June 1950.

## COMINGS AND GOINGS IN THE SUMMER OF 1950

There was jubilation in June 1950, when the U's secured election to the Football League. There had been three previous abortive attempts to secure a place in Division Three South, as it was known in those days. Colchester and Gillingham were both successful when the League decided to extend both sections of the 3rd Division from 22 to 24 clubs.

The elevation to Football League status however, was to cause a few problems for manager Jimmy Allen. Bill Layton, Reg Stewart, Doug Beach and Ron Sales, all members of the 1949/50 squad, were still on the books of Football League clubs. Layton was listed by Bradford at £4000, Stewart by Sheffield Wednesday at £1,500, Beach by Southend and Sales by Orient at £2,000. In addition, Stan Foxall had received insurance after giving up League Football due to injury. In the event, it was decided Beach and Sales would be allowed to go. Sales joined Hartlepools and Beach returned to non–League football.

In July, a reduced fee of £1,000 was agreed with Wednesday for Stewart, while Bradford accepted £800 for Layton who was 34 at the time. Stewart of course, went on to give sterling service at Layer Road, Layton however, played just eight games before being released; he joined Harwich and Parkeston. Reporting the result of the Stewart and Layton negotiations to the June the 15th Board meeting, Financial Committee Chairman A.W.Sexton intimated that all playing contracts would run to the 31st of July instead of the 5th of May in future seasons.

By the time the Finance Committee met on August the 22nd, Secretary Claude Orrin reported that £9,750 had been spent on the transfer of players. In addition, the club had purchased a house at 23 Canwick Grove, Colchester. The club's bank balance was £1,487–9–8½ (note the precise figure!), and the weekly wage bill amounted to £234. It was further agreed that the manager should have a £3 per week rise, the secretary £2 per week and the trainer £1. Mr Orrin also reported that though the price of season tickets had doubled, sales had increased by almost 40% on the previous season.

**NEW FACES**

During the close season, 10 new professionals were signed. Goalkeeper Bernard Bircham was bought from Grimsby Town. Though he was to be at Layer Road for almost five seasons, the consistency of George Wright restricted his senior team opportunities to just seven games.

A £1,200 fee changed hands for Johnny Church when he joined from Norwich City; Jimmy Elder cost £1,000 from Portsmouth; Johnny Harrison from Aston Villa and Len Jones from Southend both signed for undisclosed fees. Another £1000 signing was Joe McKim from Chelsea, and Joe Locherty was joined for the same sum from Sheffield Wednesday.

Veteran Bill Rochford, he was 37 at the time, arrived on a free transfer from Southampton, but played just two games, against Northampton and Exeter. Bill, who won an FA Cup winners game with Portsmouth, died in 1984 aged 71. Stewart and Layton, mentioned earlier, completed the 10 professional signings. In addition, Dick Cullum later signed as a part time pro. George French, Ron Hunt and Bob Hyde were on amateur forms. Also on Eastern Counties League forms were goalkeeper Tom Collins, Dennis Blackwell, Peter Aitchison – later to become a part time professional – and John McClelland, later to have one League outing for the U's and play for Stoke City, Rochdale and Swindon Town. Ironically, McClelland scored just one goal for Swindon, and that was against Colchester on the 18th of December 1954.

An interesting situation arose in October. Plans were well advanced to buy a further house when secretary Orrin warned they were *"sailing close to the wind"* if they went ahead with the project. Under the club's Articles of Association, they were unable to borrow money in excess of issued share capital. As they only had £450 in hand to avoid contravening the Articles, he advised that it would be best to defer the matter.

Before the season got under way, two practice matches were played at Layer Road. There was a crowd of 4,022 on August the 10th to see The Maroons beat The Stripes 2–1. Hillman (stripes) and Turner (2) for the Maroons got the goals. There were 5,892 present two days later to see the Probables and The Possibles feature in a game where what was ostensibly the first team, lost 3–1 to the Possibles.

It is interesting to look back to see how monetary matters have altered in the past four decades. Terms offered to players for the 1950/51 season look derisory today. Bill Layton £12; Reg Stewart £10, Bob Curry £9 10s; Harry Bearryman £9; while Turner and Wright were on £8 weekly. All told, there were 17 professionals on the playing staff when the season started; all but five had other part time employment.

At the start of the season, secretary Claude Orrin said: *"The financial position of the club is sound, but is lacking as far as liquid cash is concerned".* He urged the directors to consider a new share issue. Mr Jackson of The Supporters Club strongly supported the suggestion – *"The man in the street would prefer to contribute to Share Capital than give a donation",* he declared. In the event, in July 1950, the Share Capital of the company was increased by 20,000, at £1 apiece. The Supporters Club floated a Third Division fund.

A stand season ticket for 1950/51 cost £6–6–0, ground season tickets in the covered stand opposite the main seated stand were £2–5–0. Stand seats were 5s (25p), covered standing 1/6d. For reserve team games, prices were set at 2/– (10p) stand, ground 1/–, (5p.)

Just before the season commenced the Edison Swan Electric Co. produced a scheme for floodlighting at Layer Road. It was eventually turned down, but the U's could have been the first Third Division club with lights. Cooks Publicity Services produced the first Club Handbook for the U's as a Football League Club. The club were provided with 3,000 copies free.

The Board certainly ran a very tight ship in these early days. It was decided for instance that complimentary programmes would not be issued to the Press. There was also an Appeal in early August by the Entertainments Committee director Drake for tea and sugar to be used in the Boardroom.

A proposal to asphalt the pathway from the main entrance up the back of the main stand was turned down – far too expensive at 5–6d (27½p) per square yard.

*Centre–forward Vic Keeble.*
*A Colchester star who appeared for the U's in both the Southern and the Football League.*

# CHAPTER 4

# The Football League

A wintry background to this 1950/51 season (reserve) team line-up:
(Back): Fieldus, Bower, Wright, Walker, Hutchinson, Kettle. (Front): Fenton, Hillman, Curry, Turner, Hodgson, Cater.

Colchester United's first ever Football League game was against Gillingham at the Kent club's Priestfield Stadium on the 19th of August 1950.

There were 19,542 spectators at the match which ended it a 0–0 draw. The U's team read: *George Wright, Albert "Digger" Kettle, Bob Allen, Harry Bearryman, Reg Stewart, Jimmy Elder, Len Jones, Bob Curry, Arthur Turner, Johnny McKim, John Church.* This line-up was in fact retained for the first seven matches.

To take a closer look at that side it is evident that manager Jimmy Allen had assembled a team with a fair amount of experience. In goal Wright had played in the Football League with Plymouth Argyle. He was 30 at the time and he signed for the U's just before the 50/51 season commenced. He was to be the first choice 'keeper until 1954 playing in 151 Football League games before retiring in 1954. Interestingly many years later, in 1963, he applied for the manager's post at Layer Road when Benny Fenton left the club.

"Digger" Kettle, who played at right back, was a local player recruited from Arclight Works. He joined the U's in their Southern League days, and made 23 Football League appearances. He remained at Layer Road until 1954. Bob Allen, at 33, was one of the veterans of the side. He had played League football with Orient, Fulham, Doncaster Rovers and Northampton Town, but did not survive a full season in the U's League side, his last match being against Watford on February 19th 1951.

Harry Bearryman, a cultured wing half recruited from Chelsea, had already played in 102 Southern League games for the U's. He went on to play 186 first team matches in Colchester's colours before leaving to join the Metropolitan Police in 1953.

Centre–half Reg Stewart proved a good investment and went on to appear in 256 first team games. A millwright by trade, he was a nephew of Ernie Blenkinsopp, a celebrated pre–war England international.

Jimmy Elder the wing–half with "the Betty Grable legs" was 22 when signed from Portsmouth in July 1950. A Scot from Perth, he went on to make 199 Football League and 13 Cup appearances in four seasons at Layer Road. His claim to fame was that he never missed a penalty.

Winger Len James started his football career with Barnsley and later played for Plymouth Argyle before joining Chelmsford City. He had a season with Southend United before signing for the U's in July 1950. He was 37 at the time, and spent two seasons with Colchester and made 80 appearances. He was later in the cafe business with Ray Bicknell down the Hythe.

Bob Curry joined the U's in their Southern League days from Gainsborough Trinity. He was a regular in the League side for the first season before joining Clacton as player–manager. He played for Gateshead and Sheffield Wednesday in pre–war days, and scored Colchester's first ever goal in the Football League.

Arthur Turner, surprised the football world, when he chose to turn professional with Colchester rather than with his former club Charlton. He stayed on to play 45 League games in Colchester's colours. Diminutive winger Johnny McKim cost £1,000 from Chelsea on August 1st 1950. He started his career with Port Glasgow Athletic, but never made the Chelsea first team. He scored 42 goals in 137 appearances for Colchester before joining Clacton in 1954. John Church, who wore the No.11 shirt, was another of the manager's good buys.

The home fixture in November was lost 3-2.

Injuries to Church and McKim led to team changes having to be made, for 11 League matches produced just one point out of a possible 22. Kettle, who had been a fixture at right back since the heady days of the Fenton inspired FA Cup run, lost his place to Harrison. Cutting's place was taken by Locherty and he in turn, lost out to Keeble.

In early October, Claude Orrin reported that the average first team gate after six home matches was 13,150, and 3,580 for the reserves in the Eastern Counties League. The run of poor results was reflected in the steady decline in attendances, and gates were down to 9,000 by December.

Born in Lowestoft he had played over 100 games for the Canaries before Norwich sold him to Colchester, and he remained at Layer Road until 1953, when he left to join Critall's. He played 118 League games for Colchester and scored 20 goals.

That first Football League season was a bit confusing for reporters, with Bill Allen as chairman, Jimmy Allen the manager and Bob Allen on the playing staff. Claude Orrin used to recall that he greeted telephone enquiries with the question *"Is it Allen the butcher, Allen the boss or Allen the educated you want"*! Bob Allen was a qualified schoolteacher.

The club minute book for 1950 sheds a lot of interesting light on the week to week goings-on at Layer Road.

In September, the manager reported that injuries to Vic Keeble, newly signed as a professional, Rochford and Layton were causing some concern. In fact for the two veterans, injuries led to them missing most of the season. Rochford who damaged a tendon in training hardly played at all. Layton was also out of action for six weeks. These two players complained that being out of the team meant a £2 a week drop in wages, but the Board ruled they must abide by their contracts.

Ground Committee chairman Richard Wright reported the delays in delivery of materials – expected to be five week late – meant that the new concrete terracing at the Layer Road end on the stand side could not be completed in time for Norwich City's visit on September the 23rd. There were still post war shortages of cement and steel etc. As a result temporary tubular scaffolding was erected just in time to accommodate the 13,843 crowd that attended the match.

That Norwich game saw the U's lose their third game in a row. The team had made a good start to the campaign winning four and drawing three. But the rot set in on September the 13th when they lost 2–0 at Bournemouth. Three days later they went down by a similar margin at Newport. The Canaries won 3–2 at Layer Road and became the first opponents to win a Football League match at Layer Road. Indeed it was not until December that Colchester won another League match. Their sole success between September the 13th and December the 2nd was a 7–1 win at Woodford in the Fourth Qualifying round of the F.A. Cup.

December 1950, saw the U's results improve. After beating Millwall 3–0 at Layer Road, they had a 4–0 home win over Gillingham and drew away with Leyton Orient and Bristol Rovers. On Christmas Day the U's created a surprise by holding Nottingham Forest to a 0–0 draw before a crowd of 17,033 at the Forest Ground. The team travelled to Nottingham by train, 19–6d return each, and the team were back in Colchester just before 9.30p.m.. Next day, Boxing Day, Forest were at Layer Road and won 2–0, the gate being 12,874 (This was the last day when Christmas Day and Boxing Day return games were played).

In the new year, the U's form continued to be erratic. As a result, home gate figures began to slide further. By the end of the season, attendances had dropped to around the 8,000 mark; at the start of the campaign, around 13,000 had been the norm for home fixtures.

In those days the Layer Road directors apparently took a part in team selection. A minute from an October board meeting read:– *"The probable reasons for the present lack of playing success was discussed and various directors expressed their views and opinions. It was felt however, that this was not the time to make drastic alterations and that the manager should be allowed to continue with the team that had played so well in the first four weeks. Any changes to be agreed by the chairman"*. (Does it happen at some clubs today?).

At the same meeting, the report of the Publicity Committee was considered. Programme sales were around 4,000 per match, and director Mr S. Brown said that compared with others' he had seen, he felt that Colchester's compared more than favourably, and was good value for money at 2d.

In October, the Supporters Club paid £2,750 for the purchase of 83b Military Road. The property to be held by four trusties on behalf of the football club. The policy of the club was to provide housing to attract players at Layer Road. At one time in the 50's, the club had seven properties in various parts of the town.

Football was definitely a man's world in those days. When the question of more toilet accommodation was discussed, the board agreed more gents lavatories were needed – there were only two at the time – but felt that there was no call for additional ladies toilets except in the Directors room.

The return at Portman Road also ended in defeat (0-3)

AIR DUEL in the Colchester goal area climaxes a fierce attack by Ipswich; but Colchester left-half, Elder, gets his head to the ball first and heads clear from Ipswich centre-forward, Warne.

Stewart and Bearryman played in all 46 matches, whilst Elder with 45, Jones (41), Church (40), Wright (39), and Turner (36) made regular appearances. Curry led the goalscorers with 16, and Turner netted 15.

## LEAGUE 'FIRSTS'

Vic Keeble scored the U's first hat-trick in the Football League, with all three coming in the first half of the game against Plymouth Argyle on the 17th of March 1951. Keeble also scored three in the Pearson Cup final at Chelmsford on May the 7th. The U's first Football League penalty goal was scored by Bob Allen at Brighton on January the 13th. He had in fact, missed a penalty in the 3-2 defeat by Norwich City in the previous September.

The first own goal scored by a U's man in the Football League was put in by Reg Stewart on the 3rd of February 1951.

Goalkeeper George Wright had his jaw fractured in the 86th minute of the game with Watford on the 10th of February 1951. He had been an ever present in the U's side from August 20th 1949. He was out of action until the end of March, and Bernard Bircham deputised.

By and large, the toll taken by injuries over the season as a whole was comparatively light. McKim picked up an ankle injury on September the 16th against Newport County, and although he played against Northampton two weeks later, the ankle again caused problems and then he was out of action for 16 games. He came back into the side on January the 20th, when, by coincidence, the opposition at Layer Road was provided by Newport County. Vic Keeble missed the early season games due to a back injury sustained in pre season practice games. Church was troubled on and off throughout the season through an ankle injury sustained against Brighton early on in the campaign.

The U's had found the Football League a vastly different proposition to life in the Southern League. After a good start, they were soon brought back down to earth.

When May 1951 came around, their record of Division Three South games played read:-
Played 46, won 14, drawn 12, lost 20, points 40, goals for 63, against 76.

They finished 16th in the final table, 13 points better off than the bottom club Crystal Palace. All told, the first team played 26 games (League/Cup) at Layer Road, with 259,922 passing through the turnstiles to give an average gate of 9,997. Taking League Division Three South games only (23), the average attendance was 10,573. Away from Layer Road, the U's were watched by 359,544 fans - an average of 13,313 per game.

Top home gates of the season were 14,037 against Ipswich Town, 13,843 against Newport County and 13,729 when Norwich City were the visitors. Lowest gate was 6,941 for the visit of Gillingham.

A flying header by Fred Cutting in the home match with Walsall.

At the end of the season, Bob Allen (Bedford), Bob Curry (Clacton), Jose Gallego (Cambridge United), Bill Layton (Harwich and Parkeston), Joe Locherty (Scarborough), John Moore (Staines) and Bill Rochford (retired), all left Layer Road.

**1951/52 - PROBLEMS FOR THE CHAIRMAN**

In June 1951, Bill Allen was re-elected at the annual meeting at the Co-op Hall, and one of his first engagements was to receive a deputation from the National Union of Journalists asking for increased Press box accommodation at Layer Road. In the event, another four seats were provided, and for a time there were two Press boxes, one seating four and the other accommodated six at a pinch. (It wasn't until the 1990's that the Press were provided with a box that did not entail feats of mountaineering to get in and out).

An additional worry for the Chairman was that none of the 50/51 squad of players had signed on for the new season. The players wanted more money, and an amended offer of £12 per week in the playing season and £10 in the close season was eventually made. But it was July before the manager knew who would be staying.

Having finished 16th in this their first season in the Football League, manager Jimmy Allen (now living in Southsea, aged 82) made it clear that there was still a lot to do before the U's could claim to have justified their elevation from the Southern League. Missing from the Layer Road scene was Bob Curry, Bernard Bircham, Dennis Hillman, Bill Layton and Bill Rochford.

Manager Jimmy Allen was given permission to try to sign Rookes, a left back from Portsmouth, with the fee not to exceed £1,000 and Coombs, a 'keeper from Southend, for a fee not of not more than £450. Both players were eventually signed, Phil Rookes went on to make 74 appearances for the club before leaving in 1953 to manage Chichester City. He was later mine host at the Dog and Duck in Portsmouth, had a spell as a beachcomber in Jamaica, and ended up as a postman in Norwich. Frank Coombs played 38 League games in his two seasons at Layer Road. Later, he played for Gravesend, but a broken leg sustained at Headington United ended his career. He became manager for Fieldgate's at The Hythe.

Newcomers in the side when they kicked off at Brighton were, John Church, and Augie Scott together with Phil Rookes. A crowd of 15,000 saw the Albion team run rings round their visitors. As manager Allen said after the game: *"We were lucky to get one"* - the score was 5-1! A very poor start saw just one point collected from the first seven games.

By the end of September, there was concern regarding the poor performances of the team. In the matches played, just two out of eleven had been won and only 8,992 paid to see the match with Plymouth.

Jimmy Allen told a meeting of the board that the staff on the books was not sufficient to give cover when there was a run of injuries. He sought permission to sign three young amateurs as part-time professionals. This was agreed with Wyatt (goalkeeper) and Hyde (centre forward) to be offered £3 per week, in the case of McClelland (midfield) doing his National Service, terms were offered on a match to match basis.

The poor form of the team was also having its effect on the cash situation at Layer Road. Finance director Frank Howard estimated that the club was losing £70 per week. Travelling expenses were also causing concern. To this end, director Harold Moore said he would place a coach at the disposal of the club for day journeys. The Kelvedon based coach proprietor thus saved the club the rail fares previously incurred.

It was also agreed that in future, a director would travel with the team to all away matches - previously it was rare for a member of the board to travel with the team. Mark Gozzett, the landlord of the Castle Public House, was the first director to travel with the team on a Moore's coach. The match was at Port Vale on the 27th of October 1951, which the U's drew 1-1.

After the first disastrous seven games, the next 17 matches produced 23 points, by which time the team were sitting midway in the table. It was a commendable back to the wall recovery, with a crop of injuries and a limited playing staff not helping the situation.

November saw two signings that were to make a significant contribution to the playing side of the club in future years. Ron Hunt and Peter Wright, who were showing outstanding promise in the Eastern Counties League side, were taken on board as full time professionals at £3 per week. Wright had been tapped up by an undisclosed League club to sign for them, hence the decision to register him and Hunt forthwith. Both were destined to give yeoman service at Layer Road over the next decade.

November was also the month in which the club - as opposed to the supporters club - decided to issue badges to officials and players. Five dozen were ordered, costing 7/- each. (These are much sought after now, and are rarely seen).

In December, the EDO club from Haarlem wrote, invited the U's to visit them later in the season. At first, owing to a parlous financial situation at the club, the reaction was to turn down the invitation. However, Claude Orrin pointed out that such a trip could well be a morale booster for the players and suggested EDO should be approached regarding a financial guarantee that the trip would cost the U's nothing. Arrangements were ultimately agreed whereby Colchester received £200 prior to the trip, a further £300 on arrival in Holland, and the Dutch club agreed to pay all accommodation charges for the Colchester party. The Colchester players were to receive winter wages for the trip.

The League 'balance sheet' at the turn of the year read:

| P | W | D | L | F | A |
|---|---|---|---|---|---|
| 24 | 8 | 8 | 8 | 36 | 40 |

Additionally two F.A.Cup matches and one Essex Professional Cup game had been won.

Top scorer was Vic Keeble with 15, which included a spectacular hat-trick against Bristol City at Layer Road. Small wonder that he hit the headlines at that time, and according to the Press three clubs had made enquiries to his availability. The comment in the Green 'Un: *"Be it Newcastle or Ted Fenton's West Ham, whoever wants Vic - even if the club desired to part or the player himself desired to leave - the fee has got to be so attractive that neither the player or the club could turn it down".*

George Wright saves in the Ipswich derby match at Layer Road.
The first U's match under Floodlights was played at Headington.

Fred Draycott went on to say that he felt a fee of £10,000 at the least would have to be tabled before any move could be considered. He recalled that a year earlier, when there was an enquiry for Arthur Turner, a fee of £9,000 had been quoted as the minimum the Board would consider.

Barely a month later, Newcastle United paid £15,000 for Keeble's signature. Claude Orrin in later years loved to relate the story of how the deal was sewn up in a sort of cloak and dagger assignment at a London station on the 12th of February 1952.

A good run in the F.A.Cup once again fuelled interest in the club. Port Vale had been the first visitors to Layer Road; a month earlier a goal from Fred Cutting had earned the U's a 1–1 draw at Hanley. Keeble, Scott and a Jimmy Elder penalty ensured Cup progress, with 10,119 spectators present to see the 3–1 win. What made the victory all the more remarkable was – with the score at 0–0 – the U's winger Len Jones was carried off with a broken leg. No subs in those days.

On December the 15th, Bristol City had come to Colchester for the second round, and obviously mindful of that earlier Keeble hat-trick, had two defenders literally standing on his toes. But the strategy of trying to mark him out of the game failed. Cutting and Scott were given too much room, and the U's were in the third round. The first ever visit to Oakwell, to meet Second Division Barnsley, was the prize.

A special train was laid on for the occasion (the return fare cost £1–25p), which left Colchester at 7.30 a.m., and – notably – arrived on schedule at 1.18 p.m. For Reg Stewart, it was like going home. Sheffield born, he was in his second season down in Essex, having signed for the U's in July 1950; one of the best £1,000's the club ever spent. Despite battling hard Colchester lost 3–0.

The second half of the season started off badly with a 7–0 thrashing (the worst defeat in the League to that time) by Leyton Orient. Later, in April, there were two more heavy defeats – 6–0 at Eastville against Bristol Rovers and 5–0 at Dean Court when Bournemouth, who were below the U's in the table – ran out easy winners. In fact only one away win was recorded in the last 11 matches on foreign territory. Conversely only one of 11 fixtures at Layer Road was lost. The victory that gave most pleasure was the 1–0 success over Ipswich Town. A crowd of 15,175 saw Trevor Rowlands score the only goal. Rowland costs a £1,000 fee from Norwich City in 1950. He was 30 at the time, and was a one time Welsh Schoolboy International. He died in Norwich, aged 51, in 1973.

Two players who continued through the remaining 50's and the early 60's made their debuts; Ron Hunt against Port Vale in March, and Peter Wright at Northampton the same month.

Tenth position in the final table was an improvement on a season earlier. The away form, due to a leaky defence and a shortage of goals after Keeble left kept the team from offering a serious promotion challenge. All told, 55 games were played, Harry Bearryman appearing in every one. Elder, Scott and Stewart were present in 52 matches, and Church with 46 was another regular. Keeble played in 29 games before his transfer, and finished leading scorer with 17 goals.

McKim missed early games but still netted 14 goals in 31 appearances. Rookes, Adam Davidson, Reg Stewart and Turner were also ruled out by injuries early in the season, and at one time there were only ten fully fit players available. Stewart, the club captain, was sent off at The Den, when Colchester drew 1–1 with Millwall in early December, when he was involved in an incident with The Lions player Neary.

The Club fined Stewart £5 and he served a two match suspension, one of which was the 7–0 defeat to Leyton Orient, which he must have been glad to sit out. He was the first Colchester player to be sent off in a Football League match.

The players in unusual 'kit' during the end of season tour in Holland

Fred Cutting scored 10 goals between September and early December, but his scoring dried up and ultimately he was dropped. He played one further game, at Exeter in February, then left to join Great Yarmouth. A real character, he later became a gamekeeper in Norfolk.

Midway through the season, Kevin McCurley cost £750 from Liverpool. He went on to play 237 League and Cup games and score 97 goals in Colchester colours. Yet some wags claimed his shots on the golf course were on a different plane to those on the football pitch!

In May a seven day Dutch tour was undertaken. E.D.O. Haarlem were beaten 4–1 (Grice with two, plus McCurley and Scott were the scorers), and ADO Hague 4–2 (McCurley and Scott grabbing a pair each). The third match against Frisia in Leewarden ended 2–2, Elder and McCurley were the marks-men.

The same eleven players, viz. *Coombs, Harrison, Rookes, Bearryman, Stewart, Elder, Grice, Scott, McCurley, McKim and Church,* were used in all three games. Mike Grice was on trial from Lowestoft Town and signed for Colchester in June.

### OFF THE FIELD

Mr. A.E.Warner, the auditor, told the Finance Committee in October, that a £386–10–9d profit had accrued from the first season in the Football League.

The manager raised the question of installing floodlights, at a meeting in October. He argued that it was vital to get in early with a scheme while various companies were eager to venture into this field, and consequently were offering competitive prices. Edison Swan Electric Co. were invited to inspect and prepare an estimate. Mr.W.K.Howard, the Finance Committee chairman, at a later meeting said it was going to cost at least £500, and that was far too expensive.

In fact the team played a friendly floodlit match on Headington (later Oxford) United's ground on the 13th of February 1952. A gate of over 5,000 attended, and a Jimmy Elder penalty produced the only goal.

Bob Curry, hero of the 1947/48 Cup run defected during the 1951 close season, and went to manage Clacton. One of Layer Road's previously undisclosed secrets – since confirmed by Bob – is that Ted Fenton had got the Board's agreement for Curry to take over as player/manager. In the event Jimmy Allen, a friend of Fenton, was brought in. Curry never saw eye to eye with Allen, particularly over the manner in which Jock Kearton was sacked as trainer.

Director Harold Moore put forward the suggestion that the club should consider the purchase of a coach. He went to the trouble of costing the scheme – purchase, running costs, etc. – but when the matter came up at a meeting, the idea was shelved. Mr. Moore's firm, based at Kelvedon, provided a coach when away trips by rail proved impractical.

At the end of the season, the manager was given a £250 bonus, and secretary Claude Orrin £150, in view of the good financial results. Benefits of £150 each were paid to Kettle and Cutting to mark five years service.

### 1952/53

After that creditable 10th position, Jimmy Allen had high hopes for Colchester's third Football League season. Cutting, Davidson, Moore, Turner and Wilkinson of the previous year's squad had gone. For the opening half-dozen games Allen relied on almost the same team that finished the previous campaign. The one exception was Jones, recovered from his broken leg, who was in the No. 7 shirt in place of the departed Davidson who had returned to Scotland.

Jones however, was soon in the wars again. On September the 6th at Layer Road he hurt his left leg again. It was November before he made his comeback in the Reserves, and in that match he limped off after 10 minutes. He re-appeared briefly in the first team in January and again in March. His last senior game for Colchester was at Selhurst Park on April the 4th 1953.

Stewart, with a troublesome muscle injury missed a couple of early matches, and Rowlands filled in during his absence at number 5, in an unfamiliar role for the Welshman.

The first half dozen matches produced a meagre five goals, and though Stan Edwards scored in his first game for the club, when deputising for McCurley, it soon became apparent that all was not well up front. Keeble had never been adequately replaced, and McKim, apart from two against Reading, was off song and indeed never really recaptured his goalscoring touch. He was sent off in March against Newport County at Layer Road and missed the next 10 games.

The home form up to the turn of the year was not up to the usual standard. Five games were each worth two points, two were lost and four drawn. The 11 away fixtures fulfilled produced seven points. Twenty one points from 22 matches played, and the crowd were starting to get on the players backs, including Jimmy Allen who also came in for some stick.

George Wright, dropped from the side the previous March, regained the goalkeeping spot from Frank Coombs. To try to improve matters the manager ventured into the transfer market. Bert Barlow, who had won an F.A. Cup Winners medal with Portsmouth in 1939, was signed for £1,000 from Leicester City, and he certainly added a touch of class to the side, but unfortunately he had two separate periods on the injury list. The other newcomer was Roy Bicknell from Bristol City. A centre-half, he too was injured, and played only eight games before being ruled out for the season. Edwards was also in the wars with injuries, managing only 19 games, and was released at the end of the season.

Colchester were in luck in the F.A. Cup being drawn against Southern League teams in the first two rounds. Weymouth proved resolute opposition down in Dorset, McKim getting the goal that earned a 1-1 draw and brought The Terras up to Layer Road for a replay. The midweek return brought the worst gate of the season 4,314. Colchester won easily 4-0, helped by an own goal, which added to the two scored by Edwards and one from McKim.

Llanelly in the Second Round on paper looked a pushover. The team from Wales however had other ideas. Colchester were relieved when the final whistle blew with them holding on at 3-2. That tie attracted over 9,000 fans, with the visitors bringing a large contingent who regaled the crowd before the game with a lusty rendition of *"Land of Our Fathers"*. When Rotherham United were held to a 1-1 draw at Millmoor, there were visions of another cup run. McCurley got both the U's goals and really should have had a hat-trick, missing a simple chance - the scoreline in consequence remained at 2-2. It was not to be, for The Millers ran out 2-0 winners at Layer Road. Church had to come off injured - up to that point there was nothing in it -but his loss proved too much of a handicap.

The second part of the League season was a bit of a disaster, for only 17 more points were added to the midway total of 21. Three from bottom was the final position. Aldershot, Coventry City, Northampton Town and Norwich City all won at Layer Road, where five games were drawn, producing the U's worst home record in the League to that date. Only one away game yielded two points, and the last seven matches failed to produce a single win.

Strangely enough the best win of the season came on February the 14th, when Walsall were swamped 6-1 at Layer Road. The two Macs - McCurley and McKim - each scoring a hat-trick.

On May the 5th, 4,164 fans were at Layer Road when Chelsea provided the opposition for Harry Bearryman's testimonial game. The Pensioners, who brought practically their full first team won 2-1. Ausie Scott scored for the U's.

Two matches played after the League season ended brought some crumbs of comfort. On May the 5th West Ham were beaten 3-1 before 6,022 fans at Layer Road in the Essex Professional Cup final. Church (2) and McKim scoring. Two days later Chelmsford City drew 3-3 in the Essex County Cup. The replay at New Writtle Street was not played until a year later, when Colchester won 2-1. The Colchester team that played City at Layer Road in the drawn game included a number of Reserve players. It read: *G. Wright, Kettle, French, Bearryman, Rowlands, R.M. Hunt, Davidson, Elder, McKim, McCurley, Cadman.* Elder, McKim and Andrews were the three marksmen.

Twenty two players were used in League and F.A. Cup games. John Harrison played in all 46 League and five Cup matches, Bearryman appeared in 44 plus 5. McCurley 43 and 5, Rookes 43 and 3, Stewart 40 and 5, plus Scott 38 and 5 were also regulars. In addition Barlow, Church and McKim were automatic choices, but injuries ruled them out of many games. Coombs started the season as first team 'keeper in place of George Wright. In November however, Wright recovered his place and indeed kept it for the 1952/53 season.

Goals were at a premium and McCurley was easily the leading scorer, netting 18 in the League and 3 in Cup ties. McKim, who missed 18 League games through injury, was on target 14 times, getting 13 in League games. Church, 9 in total, was the only other significant contributor. Peter Wright scored in successive end of season games against Millwall and Orient. The one against The Lions was his first in League football.

## OFF THE FIELD

The financial stability of the club was sound, for it now owned six freehold houses and two flats, all free from any mortgage commitments. The Ariel Installation Company – a Colchester firm – offered to install floodlights at the ground free of charge, and the Manager pressed strongly for the offer to be accepted. The Finance Committee after going into the matter refused the offer, Chairman Mr. W.K. Howard reporting that there were hidden terms involved that were not acceptable.

In October, Secretary Claude Orrin reported that the Club needed an 8,500 gate to cover one week's expenses. The club were running at a loss that month, and it was noted that an 8,909 gate for the visit of Bristol Rovers produced receipts of £718–6–3d. Outgoings for that week amounted to £605–8s–1d, and £122–8–2d. had to be paid to Rovers as their guarantee of the match day takings.

By February it was reported that the club had depleted their cash resources by £1,900 since the start of the year. The Secretary warned that if the trend continued the club would face a position later on of having to pay out £3,300 summer wages with no income to meet them.

Rotherham United, no doubt impressed by his performances in the Cup against them, tried to sign Kevin McCurley in March. They refused however to meet the asking fee of £10,000.

In April there was a major disagreement between The Board and Manager Jimmy Allen. Anticipating a loss of £8,000 on the season the Directors wanted to cut the number of full time professionals for the 1953/54 season to about a dozen, and use more part–timers. The Manager was totally opposed to the idea and bluntly told the Directors that the wage bill of £250 a week (season 1952/53) made it almost impossible to assemble a side for Third Division football that had a chance of winning anything.

On May the 2nd, 1953 Allen left after the Supporters Club criticised his style of management. That was the final straw, for he considered he no longer had the support of the Board and that there was a lack of co–operation from the Directors. He tendered his resignation.

## 1953/54 – A DEPRESSING SEASON

For the 1953/54 season, a main stand ticket cost £5–13s–0d., ground enclosure tickets were £2–6s–0d.

On the 4th of June 1953, the Colchester Board had interviewed applicants for the vacant manager's position. Johnny Carey of Manchester United had turned an offer down, and George Hepplewhite (Preston North End) withdrew his application and joined Bradford City. That left three contenders Les Henley (ex Arsenal & Reading), Harry Medhurst (a goalkeeper at the time with Brighton, previously the Chelsea custodian) and Ron Meades (who claimed Cardiff City and Wadebridge Town affiliations).

The post was offered to Meades as player/manager and he accepted. But after just a few days, following enquiries by Arthur Wood, it transpired that he had misled the Colchester Board and he made a hurried departure. He was officially the manager for four days; this was possibly, the record for the shortest tenure of a Football League manager!

At a further Board meeting on June the 16th, Jack Butler the one time Arsenal player, was appointed manager. He had been coach to the Royal Daring Club and the Belgian international team, and also managed Torquay United and Crystal Palace. His salary was £12 per week, plus £5 a week expenses allowance, and a bonus of £3 when the team won and £1 when they drew. He was also housed at a rent of £1–10s–0d. (£1–50) per week.

In July, Alderman Piper resigned as President of the club. He had held office at Layer Road in various capacities since the club's formation in 1937.

It has to be remembered that the club, and manager Jack Butler in particular, were beset by troubles from the very beginning. There was precious little time or hope of doing anything to strengthen the staff when Mr Butler took over the reins. The Meades fiasco caused considerable embarrassment and had brought about a lot of adverse comment among supporters. Then, recurring injuries bedeviled from the start of the campaign. In the circumstances, it was hardly surprising that playing performances were sorely affected. There were other reasons too, for the poor showing.

There was a crying need for good goal scoring forwards, the front runners all lacked height and so a good big one was needed. The overall record highlighted this problem, only 61 goals from 53 matches. The playing statistics for the 1953/54 season were depressing and just about the worst in Colchester's professional history. The full record (including Friendlies) of the League team was as follows:–

| P. | W. | D. | L. | F. | A. |
|---|---|---|---|---|---|
| 53 | 11 | 13 | 29 | 61 | 91 |

Bearing in mind that six of the senior squad were out for long spells through injury and that there was never a time when all the senior players were fit, it was hardly surprising that 26 different players were used.

Lewis played in 51 games, George Wright made 45 appearances in goal. Other leading appearances were, Harrison (44), Elder & Bearryman (41 each), and Scott (40). Despite a long lay off through injury, McCurley top scored with 13 goals, this total included four in the Essex Pro Cup game against West Ham. Barlow (10), was the only other player to reach double figures.

The 23 home League games attracted 176,555 spectators, an average of 7,676 per game. Just under a quarter of a million people watched the U's in action in the League, 247,674 to be exact, with some away gates disappointing. Three home Cup games drew in 12,851 (average 4,283), while three away ties were watched by 13,653 fans (average 4,551).

This season was the last one for Harry Bearryman, one of the pre–League, Cup giant killing side of 1947–48. Harry (now deceased), hung up his boots and joined the Metropolitan Police. Only "Digger" Kettle remained of Ted Fenton's F plan days.

Fred Draycott, writing in the Football Star, had this to say about Bearryman; *"There has been no player who has been more popular with the crowd, or who has rendered finer or more consistent service, for this we all wish him well in his new job. No one will doubt his wisdom in assuring the future, even if he will be missed at Layer Road".*

The one big surprise in the retained list, was the omission of Bert Barlow. Until he missed the match on March the 13th, after sustaining a leg injury at Southend, he had been a regular choice at inside right. To add to the U's woes, Ipswich Town earned promotion to the Second Division and as a result, two lucrative gates were lost the following season. There was a crumb of consolation right at the end of the campaign when silverware, in the shape of the Pearson Cup, came to Layer Road.

With the constant first team calls due to injury, the Reserves in the Eastern Counties League, used 40 players in their competition. "Digger" Kettle made 34 appearances and skippered the side. A player who was destined to play a leading role in future years, Ron Hunt, made a number of appearances. In addition, one Gordon Parker (later to be a director and now chairman of the club), played and scored his one and only goal for the club.

Home gates in the Eastern Counties League totalled 48,522 with an average of 2,310. Arsenal "A", Spurs "A", West Ham "A" and Norwich City "A" all made double visits to Layer Road.

Of the 34 games played, 13 were won, 7 drawn, 14 lost with goals for 60 and against 69. Points total was 33.

From 17th September when they lost 1-0 to Norwich City at Layer Road, the U's went 13 League games without a win; they took just 3 points from those games. Their next win was a 1-0 victory over Leyton Orient on December the 5th.

Seven clubs doubled the U's that season, Norwich City, Ipswich Town, Bristol City, Coventry City Gillingham, Reading and Southend United.

Only two away victories came the U's way, at Exeter City 2-1 in August and against Crystal Palace 1-0 on January the 2nd. Palace were doubled, losing 4-1 at Layer Road on August the 29th.

Snow and ice caused the postponement of the game against Newport County on January the 30th. The match was finally played on the 22nd of April when the U's drew 1-1 at Somerton Park. In fact, between April 22nd and April 29th, four League games, three away and one home, were played.

## OFF THE FIELD

Items from the Board meetings of that season recorded that Ray Stewart and George Wright were granted benefits after completing five years at club. It was reported at both the July and September meetings that Meades, despite several requests, had failed to re-imburse the money advanced to him when he was appointed manager. Tickets for the England-Hungary match at Wembley costing 10/6d each, were bought by the club for 18 players. They saw the Hungarians' historic 6-3 win.

The police had to be called in several times during the season to prevent cycles being parked against the exit gates by fans arriving late at the ground. Because of a lack of heating in the Layer Road office, Board meetings during the winter were held in the Liberal Club. Floodlighting for training purposes was installed in November 1953.

At the end of the season, besides Barlow being given a free transfer, Ron Church (£500), Coombs (£750), Harris (£1,000), Keene & Scott (both at £1,500) were transfer listed.

## 1954/55 - ROCK BOTTOM CAMPAIGN

After successfully applying for re-election, (Colchester United received 45 out of a possible 48 votes), together with Walsall at the end of the previous campaign, there were hopes of better times ahead in the 1954/55 season. It was not to be. Another disastrous time led to the U's finishing rock bottom in Division Three South. Walsall again were their companions in distress.

The close season had seen the departure of old stalwarts such as Bearryman, Church, Barlow and Augie Scott. The new-comers were goalkeeper Jimmy Kirk from Bury, Ron George from Crystal Palace, a defender, midfield man Frank McCourt (a Northern Ireland international) from Manchester City, Paddy Leonard, a forward from Southend and Cliff Birch from Newport County. None of them stayed more than one season at Layer Road. The U's failed to secure the services of 'keeper Pat Welton from Orient during the close season. If he had signed, Percy Ames would almost certainly have never come to Layer Road later in the season.

Overall, manager Butler had a squad of 28 professionals, 16 full time, with the remainder part time or doing National Service.

New offices and boardroom - the site of the present Layer Road offices - were completed in the summer of 1954. In August, a club house, 2 Hamilton Road was sold for £1,475 and the following month, 144 Maldon Road was purchased for £2,250, to be converted into two flats for two players and their families.

The first three League matches all ended in draws, with four of the first fourteen games won and four all square, which was some improvement on the previous season. On August the 28th, Kirk saved a penalty taken by Tom Tilston for Crystal Palace three minutes from the end, to earn the U's a point in a goalless draw at Selhurst Park. At Layer Road against Northampton on September the 4th, Kenny Plant scored in the 40th, 46th and 85th minutes for Colchester. Colchester won 4-1 with Cliff Birch getting the other goal.

Then things fell apart with just three points from 11 encounters. In fact there were eight defeats in a row, followed by three draws before Crystal Palace were beaten 2-0 at Layer Road.

It was reported in November, that a profit of £350 had been made on the previous season. Meanwhile a bid from West Bromwich Albion for Michael Grice was rejected - the board refused to sanction the move. At the shareholders meeting in November, a move to re-appoint Councillor Wright to the board was rejected. Having attained his 70th birthday, he automatically had to retire from the board.

On January the 8th, Kenny Plant's goal gave the U's an unexpected 1-0 win at the Dell. Southampton at the time, had an unbeaten home record and the victory was hailed in the Press as an indication of better times ahead for Colchester.

Indeed, from the next eight fixtures, there were two further wins and four draws, and there seemed to be a hope of avoiding the last two places. That prospect however, went by the board when only two points accrued from the last eight matches. These included a 6–1 hiding at Northampton, where Harrison and Elder both scored own goals, and a 5–3 defeat by Southampton at Layer Road.

The big change was at managerial level when Benny Fenton replaced Butler in March 1955 – but too late to save the club from having to apply for re–election for the second year running. Percy Ames arrived on trial from Spurs and played two games at the end of the season. The first was the defeat at Southampton, and the other at Plainmoor when the U's lost to Torquay United. He became the number one 'keeper the following season.

The 46 games in the Football League yielded just nine victories, one less than in 1953/54. That win against the Saints was one of only two away victories all season. The only team doubled was Norwich City. 24 players were used in the 46 League fixtures. Birch and McCourt (with 12 games apiece), and George (5) were hardly used. Though Kirk and Leonard both made over 30 appearances, they were both allowed to go in the following close season, Kirk having refused to re–sign.

The FA Cup brought an away first round tie with Reading and hopes were high after the team drew 3–3 at Elm Park. They in fact led 2–0 at one time, but then allowed the game to slip and their trio of goals scored by Grice, Birch and McKim was cancelled out due to defensive errors. A crowd of 4,636 turned up for the replay, but despite Jimmy Elder scoring from the penalty spot, the Biscuitmen won 2–1. Strangely enough, Colchester and Reading met three times in a week. The two Cup games were on November the 20th and 25th and the following Saturday (the 27th), Reading won 4–0 at Elm Park in a League encounter.

For the tie at Reading, the team stayed overnight at the Grove Hall Hotel Twyford. Two directors were against the place – *"Far too expensive"*.

Elder's penalty goal in the Cup match came after Plant was scythed down after 38 minutes. The same player later converted two other penalties during the season. Against Brentford in March, he netted after one Ignatius "Paddy" Feehan the Bees 'keeper, kicked Peter Wright. The third was against Gillingham when Plant, according to a "scribe of the day" – *"did a spectacular dive inside the box"*. Elder however, missed an important spot kick on September the 18th at Layer Road. The U's led Bournemouth 2–0 at the time and Elder could have sewn the game up, but he missed, his only serious miss in five seasons. The Cherries hit back and led 3–2 after Dale and Plant scored the U's early goals and only a late strike from Plant rescued a point.

### THE SEASON FACTS

The highest attendance in a game at Layer Road, was when 10,809 paid to see visiting Southend win 4–2. Best away crowd was at Ashton Gate when 18,455 saw Bristol City beat the U's 4–0. All told, in League games, 170,095 passed through the turnstiles, and the average gate was 7,395. In the 23 away games 227,168 spectators attended at an average of 9,876.

During the season, McCourt fractured his right leg at Newport on February 19th, and this was his last game for the club. Bert Hill, fractured a bone in his hand, and missed the last 10 games of the season. John Harrison was out for five matches with a broken thumb.

Manager Jack Butler who had been taken ill at the end of November was granted a month's sick leave. In January, following medical reports, he was given indefinite leave until his contract expired in June 1956. He in fact resigned on January the 18th, and the team was chosen by the directors for the matches between December and March. There were 48 applications for the manager's job – Benny Fenton was the successful applicant.

At the end of the season, Aitchison, Bicknell, Cullum, George, Lewis, Kettle and George Wright were given free transfers. Birch, Elder, Kirk, Leonard and McKim were put on the transfer list. Fenton advised the board that a clear out was needed.

### 1955/56 – FENTON TEAM BUILDING

After the two poor seasons, Benny Fenton had four newcomers in his squad for the new campaign. Percy Ames – signed after two games the previous April – John Fowler (a left back from Bonnyrigg Rose Athletic), who was to give outstanding service, plus Sammy McLeod and Bobby Hill, both from Easthouses Lily. The latter three were the first part of the Tartan invasion that Benny Fenton brought from North of the border. The Fenton raids into Caledonia often caused ripples of embarrassment, and at other times, some hilarious situations. Suffice it to say that from the mid–fifties into the sixties, he was as well known in Scotland as he was in Essex. John Adie from Hearts, refused the chance to join Colchester.

Fraser Allen was co–opted to the board in June. Eric Southernwood, still active with hospital radio, was appointed Supporters club delegate to the board. Arthur Sexton, who had been a director for a decade, resigned from the Board in July. Twenty passes to the ground were issued to the Corporation bus crews bringing "the crowds" to Layer Road on match days. It was stated in a meeting that only about two dozen people came in cars.

There were 14 full time professionals on the staff, and John Henson was the only player who never made the first team. He was also assistant groundsman.

In addition – Trevor Harris, Billy Hunt, Ron Hunt, Sammy McLeod, Peter Wright and Brian Dobson – some of whom stayed to make a major contribution to the future of the U's, were on part time terms. Two 'keepers, George Wright at the end of his League career at 36 was released, and then re–registered, as was John Wright, who was doing his National Service.

The final position in the Southern Section was Colchester's best since they came into the League, although the start had not been particularly promising, with just two wins in the first 10 League matches.

In September, Frank Wright of Bramley Croft Lexden, was co–opted on to the Board in place of Mr Sexton. George Fisher signed from Fulham, to fill a long standing need for a left back.

England amateur international Alf North signed on amateur forms from Briggs Sports. He made one senior appearance.

Following a 2–1 victory over the eventual champions Leyton Orient on September 15th 1955, the U's lost only two of the next twelve League fixtures.

That win for the U's at Layer Road, was something of a surprise, for only a week earlier, they had been thrashed 6–0 at Brisbane Road. The first encounter was something of a disaster for player/manager Fenton. First, he conceded a penalty which was duly converted by Hartburn, then he scored an own goal, deflecting the ball out of Ames reach.

That was the second time six goals were given away in the opening six games, for Southend United beat the U's 6–3 at Root's Hall on the last Saturday in August. Hollis scored four for the Blues.

Fenton's unhappy time continued when a fortnight later, he brought down Norwich City's Hansell, and Coxon's penalty gave the Canaries a point in the 1–1 draw. Hansell in fact, played his only game of the season for City that day. Kevin McCurley scored a hat–trick against Queens Park Rangers on October the 29th, and the U's won the game at Layer Road 4–1, Grice getting the other goal. He repeated the feat on November the 26th when Brighton were the visitors. Albion led 3–0 at one time, until McCurley scored in the 44th, 82nd and 85th minutes to force a 3–3 draw.

The game scheduled for February 4th at Reading, was cancelled due to Elm Park being frozen. It was finally played on the last day of that month and was the first time that Colchester played a League game under floodlights.

Ken Plant on February 18th, scored three against Torquay United. When the U's won that match at Layer Road 3–2, it was the first double of the season, for both teams! On March the 3rd, Plant again scored three, all in the first half, when Swindon were beaten 5–0 at Layer Road.

During the season, player/manager Fenton conceded five penalties. Hartburn (Orient) and Coxon (Norwich), scored from two, Les Graham (Watford) shot yards wide and Ames saved the other two. There were five further penalties against the U's – three of which were converted by Parker (Ipswich), Jackson (Aldershot) and Langley (Brighton). Colchester were awarded just five penalties, Fisher, McCurley and Fenton each netted one, McCurley and Dale missed the other two.

Though the injury situation showed an improvement on the two previous campaigns, Reg Stewart was in the wars a few times, and he sustained a broken nose at Bournemouth in the second match of the season. No substitutes in those days and Reg – a hardy character – played and finished the game. He missed the next match, but was back in action again seven days later when Bournemouth were beaten 1–0 at Layer Road in the return game. Later on, he missed several games with a troublesome thigh injury. George Fisher (shoulder injury), Fenton (knee trouble), Ames (broken finger) and McLeod and Plant with ankle injuries all missed some games , but generally, absences were of a brief duration.

There was one bad accident at Layer Road on November 12th. Fred Monk, the veteran Aldershot full back, broke his right leg in two places after a collision with Grice. The injury finished Monk's career. A one time England Schoolboy international, he made over 200 appearances for Brentford before joining Aldershot.

Fenton of course, was very much the driving force and inspiration behind the improved performances. When the club was definitely safe, he missed the last seven matches of the season and spent most of his time searching for new talent. His influence was missed and those final seven games yielded just five points.

The playing records for the season read:– Played 48, won 18, drawn 11, lost 17, with 76 goals for and 81 against, totalling 47 points.

The club went out of the FA Cup in the first round, losing 2–0 at Torquay. They also lost 2–1 when they met West Ham in the Pearson Cup Final. John Egan, another of Fenton's over the border finds, played in that match and though his name does not appear in official records, he also made one League appearance for the club. He came from Stenhousemuir to Layer Road and later appeared for Halifax Town and Accrington Stanley in the Football League.

In the main, the club relied on just 13 players, though nine others made fleeting appearances. McCurley played in every match and also headed the goalscorers, with 46 in the League and 1 from a Cup game. Peter Wright, who became one of the most sought after wingers, missed just one game. His 46 appearances attracted a posse of scouts, but Wright was not interested in becoming a full time pro. Other leading appearances were :– Ames on 45, McLeod and Fisher with 44, Stewart 43, Harrison 42 and Dale's 41. The majority of goals came from Fowler, McLeod, Fenton, and Dale who each scored 6.

Layer Road's 23 League games brought 175,618 fans through the turnstiles, more than 5,000 up on the previous season, giving an average gate of 7,644. Away from home, 244,449 watched the U's with the average away gate being 10,628. The best attendance was 13,176, which beat by over 3,000, the previous best Layer Road gate. This was for a match against local rivals Ipswich Town on Boxing Day. United exchanged fifty tickets with Ipswich Town in respect of the two games.

Those were the palmy days when Saturday afternoon football was almost a religion. But even then, the elements could adversely affect the numbers passing through the turnstiles. On a bitterly cold snowy day on February the 11th, only 4,811 were at Layer Road for the match. Perhaps it was just as well because Millwall won 2–1, the U's first home set back since the previous September.

On the 17th of March 1956, Grice played his last game in Colchester colours. Five days later, he was sold to West Ham for £10,000. The same day, the Hammers sold Hooper to Wolves for £25,000.

The Reserves won 22 of their Eastern Counties League games, drew five and lost 11, with the biggest victory being a 13–2 thrashing over Biggleswade at Layer Road. Bobby Hill scored 4, Billy Hunt 3 and there were two apiece for Brian Dobson, Bert Hill and Austin Dunne.

For the second string, Russell Blake (31 games), Trevor Harris (35), Bobby Hill (29), Bobby Hunt (32) and Martyn King (8) were to play a prominent role in the senior squad in future years. King in fact, in eight games, scored eight goals, including a hat-trick against Lowestoft, giving prior notice of his future goalscoring ability. Present chairman Gordon Parker, joined Halstead Town, after making five early season appearances. The home match with Sudbury Town was witnessed by 2,779 – the top (reserve) gate of the season. With John Wright, the reserve team 'keeper on National Service, George Wright was re-signed as a part timer.

In February 1956, the Colchester Board discussed the Football League's five point plan for re-organising Division Three. Colchester were in favour of a three section – North, Midland, South – Division Three. (In the event, it was ultimately decided to have a Division Three and a Division Four, to which the U's were opposed).

At the end of the season, the "A" team were withdrawn from the Border League. Five players, Austin Dunne, Billy Hunt, George Wright, Frank McCourt and John Henson were given free transfers. Mike Grice, who had cost just £50 from Lowestoft was transferred to West Ham in March for £1,000.

## 1956/57
## THE SO NEAR AND YET SO FAR SEASON

This was destined to be by far the best in the U's League career. At one time they looked promotion certainties. With just a few games to play, they led the Third Division South table. But then three away defeats, 3–1 at Millwall, 2–1 at Walsall and 4–1 at Swindon, in the space of seven days proved costly. Though they won the final game 2–0 at home to Watford the damage was done and Ipswich Town came up on the rails to take the championship and alter the balance of power in East Anglia, a situation which continues at the present day.

Until that trio of losing games the U's were unbeaten in 20 League matches – still the club record for a Football League sequence without a defeat.

Just to debunk a myth that has grown up, the penalty Benny Fenton missed in the game against Ipswich Town was not what caused the Layer Road boys to miss out on promotion. Nor is the oft repeated story true that Fenton missed deliberately. In fact Roy Bailey the Town 'keeper made a magnificent save – even if he did move before the ball was struck. It was those three away defeats that condemned Colchester to third place behind Ipswich and Torquay.

At the start of the campaign that club had 13 full time pros., and seven on part time forms. There were also nine on amateur forms. The latter included Edgar Rumney, Alan Springett, Tony Miller and Martyn King all later to become familiar names to local football fans. Early in the season, Tommy Williams, a 21 year old amateur with Carshalton Athletic, was signed as a professional. He proved, like most of Fenton's signings, a shrewd recruit and went on to play almost 200 senior games for the club.

The first game of the season saw a derby match with Southend United. The gate was 11,484 and the fans were treated to an exciting encounter which the U's won 3–2. Reg Stewart and Russell Brake, injured in practice games, were both absent. Stewart had a broken toe and close season signing "Chic" Milligan took his place.

U's right-half Bert Hill shapes up to clear – in the Q.P.R. match at Loftus Road in late 1956.

Brake ended up in Black Notley Hospital for a cartilage operation. Les Barrel, a local from Harwich, signed from Lexden Wanderers, came in for Black. Barrell celebrated his debut by scoring, McCurley and Wright got the other two. Southend avenged that early defeat by beating Colchester 4–1 in the F.A. Cup 1st Round on November 17th. That was the fourth season in succession that elimination from the Cup had come in Round One.

September brought three highlights. Southampton, the section leaders at the time, were beaten 3–1 at Layer Road, then in the very next game, bogey team Reading were on the wrong end of a 3–2 result. That was the first time in four seasons that the Elm Park team had lost to Colchester. When the U's won 3–0 under floodlights at Reading the following January, Eddie Smith scoring all three goals in the first half, it was the first time the U's doubled the Biscuitmen. The 6–0 victory over Shrewsbury at Layer Road was the U's biggest win in the League to date. The Shrews 'keeper Russell Crossley was off for most of the game injured.

Cartilage trouble robbed the team of two key players for most of the season. Blake did not make the side until the Walsall match in April. John Harrison played in the two opening games and sustained a knee injury against Crystal Palace. After missing two matches he returned to the side against Southampton only to break down again during the game. Eventually he followed Blake into Black Notley for a cartilage operation. He never played for the club again.

McCurley and Barrell, with muscle problems and Wright and Milligan, all sustained early season injuries. Wright was stretchered off at Northampton on August the 25th early on in the game, but returned in the second half with his head swathed in bandages, even though he was advised no to do so. Later on, he twice had problems with a twisted ankle, yet he only missed three fixtures all season.

(Early 1950's) A happy group celebrate the winning of the Harwich Cup

3–0 away in the final game of the season. All told, in 36 games, they scored 119 goals; they beat Gorleston 10–0, Eynesbury Rovers 9–1, Holbeach 7–2 all at Layer Road. The fans also saw them lose 8–6 to a Spurs side that included half a dozen players with First Division experience. No lack of goals to cheer the faithful. Hardly surprisingly, the gates topped the 3,000 mark.

Benny Fenton was once again hero and villain regarding penalties. Against Crystal Palace (August the 27th), he scored to earn the U's a 3–3 draw. Against Reading, he netted from the spot, again when the U's were two goals down, they eventually won 3–2. Then, on April 13th, his penalty kick earned the U's a 1–1 draw with Aldershot.

Milligan also sustained a hand injury that needed six stitches, at the Dell, the same match in which Harrison had to come off, and for a time the U's were down to nine men. Milligan however, resumed after repairs. Fenton and Smith were also troubled by ankle injuries and had to sit out a number of games as a consequence.

But the biggest blow came in February when Bob Dale, who had not missed a match, was unwell in the match against Ipswich Town. He was thought to be suffering from bronchitis. Two days later, a medical examination found him to be suffering from tuberculosis and he had to retire from the game. Derek Parker was signed from West Ham for £2,500 to reinforce the depleted squad as Milligan was also put out of action by breaking his collarbone during training. Chic Milligan missed the last 12 games.

During the season, gates at Layer Road rose by 38,396 to 214,214, giving an average of 9,309 per match. Away from home, 256,767 paid when Colchester were the visitors, an important point in those days when gate money was shared.

When Ipswich visited Layer Road for the famous 'Fenton Penalty Match', the gate of 18,559 was, by more than 5,000, a new club record for a Football League game. The 21,239 at Dean Court Bournemouth, was the best away gate, beating by 808, the Boxing Day crowd at Ipswich.

In the main, 14 players formed the nucleus of the side. In all, 49 games were played, 46 League, 1 Cup, 1 Pearson Charity and 1 Friendly game. Ames and Plant featured in all 49 encounters, Fisher in 47 and Wright and Fowler, in 46 each.

King, still an amateur, foreshadowed what was to come by scoring twice in his three outings. Ninety goals were scored in the 49 matches. Plant led the way with 26 (24 in the League), Smith came next with 13, including hat-tricks against Palace and Reading.

The Reserves again had a good season in the Eastern Counties League. They won the Championship, pipping Great Yarmouth Town by one point, though they lost to the Norfolk side

On the reverse side, Fenton gave away a goal by deflecting a shot from Wheeler out of Ames reach. In the same game, he atoned by converting a penalty at Torquay. That goal gave the home team a 3–2 lead. Then of course, there was that penalty that Bailey saved in the Ipswich game.

## HAT TRICKS

There were eight hat-tricks during the season. McCurley against Shrewsbury at Layer Road, for the Reserves against Eynesbury Rovers in the Eastern Counties League and four (three in succession) in the same competition against Great Yarmouth. Smith performed the feat twice against Crystal Palace in September and at Reading in January, under the Elm Park floodlights. Brian Dobson (against Eynesbury Rovers), Alan Springett and Sandy McLeod (both against Gorleston) performed the feat for the Reserves.

The championship winning Reserve side had a hard core of about a dozen players. John Wright kept goal in every game, he was unlucky to be at Layer Road when Ames was in possession in the senior side. Ron Hunt also played in every match. Alan Springett missed one, Edgar Rumney two and Les Barrell three. The other regulars were Russell Blake, Trevor Harris and Brian Dobson.

John Maynard (an amateur from Chelmsford), Bert Hill, Tony Miller, McCurley dropped from the first team, David Carter (another amateur), Sammy McLeod and Reg Stewart, were the others who appeared in over half the 36 League games.

Stewart, who joined Colchester for a £1,000 fee from Sheffield Wednesday in June 1950, played in almost 400 games in Colchester colours before leaving in May 1957. Some 268 of those appearances were in the Football League. He was one of Colchester's best ever signings.

When Yugoslavian side Radnicki visited Layer Road in a friendly on December 8th 1956, there was an attendance of 7,103. The visitors won the match 6–2.

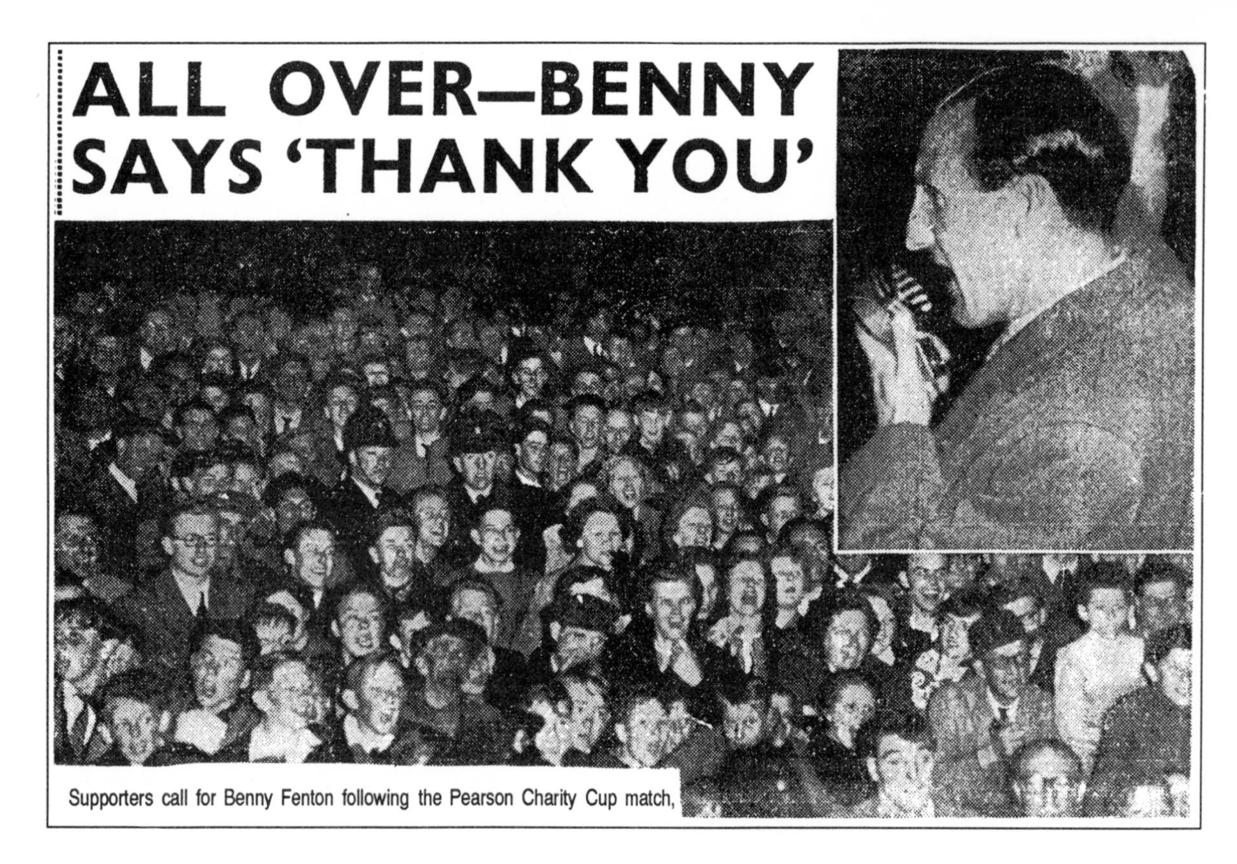
ALL OVER—BENNY SAYS 'THANK YOU'

Supporters call for Benny Fenton following the Pearson Charity Cup match,

**OFF THE FIELD**

Charles "Chic" Milligan, then 25, signed from Ardrossan. A half back, it took three trips to Scotland before his signature was secured at the end of May. Milligan moved into a club house vacated by McCourt.

Director Mark Gozzett, who was mine host at the Castle, arranged for all players to have dinner after a practice match on August 11th. The venue, The George Hotel.

It was reported in September that all eight properties owned by the club, and let to the players, were in good order. The South East corner of the terracing was provided with a cover in the Autumn and early winter of 1956. A buffet – described as "sumptuous" – for the visit of Radnicki, cost £9–2–6d.

In March, it was agreed to build an extension behind the director's box, to provide amenities for directors and visiting officials. That decision meant that the Clark Memorial Hall had to be demolished. The same month, the Supporters Club, who had already donated £3,000 to pay for ground improvements, reported that they still had a balance of £5,000 left.

George Fisher was in the Southern Section team when they played a representative match against the Northern Section.

Following the confirmation of Bob Dale contracting tuberculosis in May, all the players were screened to check that they had not contracted the disease.

**1957/58 – CONFIDENCE AT A HIGH**

After so narrowly missing out on promotion in the previous season, the U's were confidently expected to do well. It was also important to achieve at least the top half position in the table as the Football League had decided to scrap the regionalised Third Division South and North divisions. From the following May, there was to be a Third and a Fourth Division. By July however, things did not look quite as rosy. Of the previous season's staff, Bob Dale and John Harrison had retired from the game, Reg Stewart's long and illustrious career had come to an end and Eddie Smith had joined Queen's Park Rangers. Bobby Hill, Sammy McLeod, Trevor Harris and close season signing John Laidlaw, were all doing their National Service. In fact, with only a dozen full time pros, Fenton himself decided to delay hanging up his boots.

Peter Wright, who had turned down two opportunities to join bigger clubs, (he preferred to stay part–time and continue in his draughtsman's career), Russell Blake, Ron Hunt and Brian Dobson also signed part–time forms. McCurley, who at one time, asked for a move, belatedly agreed terms and Edgar Rumney also joined the staff.

To make matters even more difficult, Bobby Hill and Hunt were both injured in the pre–season trial games and Tommy Williams and "Chic" Milligan were both hurt in the early weeks of the campaign. It was hardly surprising in the circumstances, that early results were very patchy. Only one of the first nine away fixtures yielded maximum points. There was a 7–0 defeat at Reading, at that time the U's record away defeat, they also went down 4–1 at Northampton.

Viewed from any angle, Colchester did not have the best of seasons. The main objective however, to remain in the newly constituted Third Division, was achieved - but only just. A series of injuries at a critical time in the campaign, put things in jeopardy. It needed a 4-2 victory over Southampton at Layer Road in the final game of the season to give the U's the 12th position in Division Three South to make sure of a place among the 24 comprising Division Three.

Two newcomers were added to the squad in November. Neil Langman, a big robust, raw-boned forward from Plymouth Argyle arrived for a fee of £6,750, and John Evans, a playmaker, for £4,000 from Liverpool. Both played a big part in ensuring that important League target, particularly as McCurley lost form and Fenton himself and Bobby Hill were often missing, the manager because of a niggling ankle injury and Hill needed for Service duties. Hamish McNeil, who cost a £600 fee from Bonnyrigg, played in four matches and scored a goal. He scored 23 goals in 24 outings for the Reserves, yet never looked like making the grade at Football League level. Perhaps with hindsight, an extended run with the first team might have paid dividends, and it could be argued that he was one of several Colchester player who, over the years, never had a real opportunity. The same could be said of local player Alan Springett, another prolific scorer for the Reserves. His senior appearance was limited to half a game against Ipswich Town in an end of season testimonial match for Bob Dale, which Colchester lost 1-0.

Sixteen players bore the brunt of the League and Cup games. Ames, who was just about the best goalkeeper in the section, and Fowler appeared in every League game. Fisher and Wright missed just one and Plant two. Plant was leading goalscorer with 22, Wright 16 from the left wing and McCurley 14, also reached double figures.

Plant scored three against Watford on Boxing Day, and McCurley netted three, two of them penalties, against Coventry City on February the 15th at Layer Road. Fenton (2), and Fisher (1), were the other successful spot kick takers. The U's concede six penalties. Reeve (Reading), Corbett (Northampton), Richards (Walsall), Richardson (Aldershot) and Page (Southampton), all beat Ames with spot kicks. Cameron (Q.P.R.) missed, shooting wide after Fisher had handled.

A worrying feature was a significant drop in gates both at Layer Road and on away travels. Attendances at Layer Road amounted to just under 197,000, with an average gate of 8,559 (9,309 in 57/57). Away gates averaged 10,862 (11,163 in 56/57). The biggest home gate amounted to 11,077 for the visit of Norwich City.

In the FA Cup, it was a case of the giant-killers being giant killed. Visitors Wisbech Town, then members of the Midland League, beat Colchester 1-0 at the first hurdle. The Fenland Park side managed by Oscar Hold, had an average age of 34, but at the end of 90 minutes, the Fenman's "Grandads" were worthy winners. The only goal of the game came in the 65th minute when Jesse Pye (the one time England and Wolves centre forward) put a raking left foot shot into the net. An unforgettable minute that captured all the excitement of the FA Cup.

Colchester Reserves brought the only piece of silver to the Layer Road sideboard - they won the Eastern Counties League Cup. The average Layer Road gate to watch the second string was 2,449, with just over 46,500 watching the 18 League and four Cup matches.

**1957/58 FACTS**

On February 8th, when Colchester lost 3-0 at Walsall, they played all the second half with nine men. Bert Hill and "Chic" Milligan had both been hurt in the first half.

Birmingham City had a £10,000 offer for winger Peter Wright rejected. Wright, at 23, elected to continue working as a draughtsman and would not sign as a full time professional.

When Queen's Park Rangers entertained the U's on August the 26th, their left half Archie Andrews was stretchered off after 8 minutes. He returned later, sporting a patch over his right eye. Fifteen minutes later, Pat Woods missed a penalty after Gorge Fisher had handled. Then Bobby Cameron looked to have the ball in the net, but the referee, who was miles behind the play, ruled it had not crossed the line. Cameron however, had his revenge when he scored the only goal of the game with ten minutes to go.

At Layer Road on September the 2nd, it was so gloomy that when the ball went into the Q.P.R. net with 10 seconds remaining on the clock, it was impossible to see from the Press box who got the goal. Peter Wright it transpired, was the scorer. Colchester won 2-1, McCurley got the earlier goal. Bill Finney equalised before Wright's dramatic winner, and Springett, in the Rangers goal, claimed it was so dark that he never saw the match winner.

Away to Bournemouth on the 22nd of September, Percy Ames was knocked out by Dowsett as they tangled for the ball in the Colchester goalmouth. The Cherries centre forward put both the 'keeper and the ball in the net. After treatment for a mouth injury, Ames returned and Dowsett, in another collision with the goalkeeper, limped for the rest of the game. The game ended 1-1, Hamish McNeil scoring for the U's.

One week later, referee Jack Baxter from Royston incurred the displeasure of the Layer Road crowd when the U's were playing Northampton Town. Baxter disallowed a "goal" scored by Peter Wright, and instead gave a free kick for a foul on Wright outside the box. Baxter also booked Benny Fenton and the Cobblers' Ron Patterson - who had a private punch up - plus the visitor's Ray Yeoman for disputing a free kick. Wright later got the only goal as Colchester won 1-0.

A football forum and film show at Colchester's Garrison Theatre featured Benny Fenton, Vic Keeble (who had recently signed for West Ham), and John Bond, who was once on junior terms with the U's. They were besieged by young autograph hunters. Other local football notables on the panel wee "Bill" Dent who presided, Jack Poole, Cyril Sargeant, W.Legget and Sgt. D.Parker.

Colchester United Supporters Club handed over a £4,000 cheque. It was intended to provide extra cover at the Spion Kop End.

**OFF THE FIELD**

A change of heart by the Colchester Board led to Director Ben Myers attending the League AGM in May/June with a mandate to vote for Division 4.

Because of the Dale case, the Board decided that in future, any new signing would be subject to a full medical test. It transpired that Dale had been discharged from the R.A.F. with chest problems some time before he came to Layer Road.

In June, a scheme for covering the Spion Kop corner was approved by the Board. Entrance prices for the season were agreed at £5–15–0 (£5–75) for the main stand, ground £2–7–6d – juniors £1–5–0d. The "Colchester Express" newspaper booked the advertising space on the roof of the main stand at £50 per annum.

Alf Marshall signed from Dagenham Town who were sent a cheque for £25 as a donation. Peter Wright was in the Southern Section team to play the Northern Section. During the season, attempts to sign forward John Shepherd (Millwall), John McNicol (Chelsea) and Len Duquemin ('Spurs), proved abortive. Neil Langman was housed in 75 Layer Road which the club bought for £1,857.

Alderman Harper – associated with the club since it's formation –died shortly after attending his 150th Board meeting in October.

On March the 1st, a collection was held at the ground for the Manchester United disaster fund.

By the end of the season, plans were afoot to provide a bar and tearoom at the ground. The Board were also making arrangements for a brick wall to be erected along the back of the main stand in place of the hedge.

## 1958/59 – CUP RUN PAID FOR FLOODLIGHTS

Looked at from any angle, Colchester had a good season in 1958/59 and certainly it was a big improvement on 12 months earlier. They ended up in fifth place in Division Three and the icing on the cake was a good Cup run after many barren years.

This culminated in Round four when, after the full might of Arsenal had been held at Layer Road, the Gunners, in a fog bound game at Highbury, won the replay before a crowd of almost 63,000.

In the League, the U's at one time, looked sure to finish in the top four, they then lost five matches in succession in and around the Easter period. A series of injuries to key players caused the team to be switched around with fatal consequences.

Before the season started, Benny Fenton at last hung up his boots. He had a staff of 26 overall, with 13 full pros, eight part–timers, and five still on National Service. The only close season departure was Hamish McNeil, who was transferred to Cambridge City. Later on in the campaign, Kenny Plant also left to join Nuneaton.

Newcomers were two more Scots, signed as part timers, after another Fenton foray North of the border. Neither John Roe (2 League games), or Ian Johnstone with a similar number of outings, made much impact at Layer Road.

Six home games were lost and three drawn, with 15 points being surrendered in the process. Had the record at Layer Road been better, they would have given eventual champions Plymouth Argyle a close run.

The U's took three points off the Devonians, winning 2–0 at home and drawing 1–1 at Home Park.

The U's hardly made an auspicious start in the FA Cup. In the first round, Bath City came to Essex and with the one and only Stanley Mortensen in the side, put up a great fight. Plant put Colchester ahead on 15 minutes but City twice came near to equalising. Five minutes from the end, Langman headed a second and deciding goal.

The second round draw brought another Somerset non–League side to Layer Road. Yeovil had beaten Southend United 1–0 in round one, after a draw at Roots Hall. So Colchester should have been forewarned. A crowd of 10,890 turned up to see the game, and Fenton's team took a long time to realise that the Huishmen were no pushovers. In the end, the U's were a shade fortunate to hold on for a 1–1 draw. A replay at Yeovil's infamous sloping ground was not a prospect to relish.

Fenton, who was not amused by the U's display, made his displeasure felt with some gruelling training sessions, and hinted darkly that futures were at stake, before the team sallied forth for the replay.

A record crowd of 10,000 packed into the Huish ground for the replay. Fenton's warnings paid off, and Colchester won 7–1. Neil Langman got four and it is fair to say the U's ran rings round the opposition. Another home draw brought Chesterfield down to Essex in the third round. This was the Derbyshire team's first visit to Layer Road, and they went back to Saltergate beaten 2–0.

A certain Layer Road scribe commenting on the game, said *"The U's had to thank the visitor's young 'keeper for their goals"*. He added that he doubted if the lad would ever make the grade as a custodian. What a gaffe! The goalie making his first team debut that day, was Gordon Banks. First, he fumbled a McLeod shot and left John Evans a simple tap in. Then he was slow responding to a Gordon back pass and Langman got there first to score Colchester's second.

## ARSENAL AT LAYER ROAD

Arsenal came out of the hat for round four and their star team, Tommy Docherty and all, were drawn to visit Essex. Benny Fenton, unlike his brother Ted 12 years earlier, refused to have any special plan.

In the press, he was quoted as follows:– *"We have a playing method that suits us, so that's the one we'll use against Arsenal"*.

The Gunners were expected to win easily. Even so, people queued for half a day beforehand to get tickets for the all ticket encounter. A 16,000 limit was set by the police. The local law were there in force on the day, even bringing a police dog – the first ever – to the ground. In the event, there was no trouble, but what an exciting afternoon.

Vic Groves scored twice early in the second half and it looked like he had wrapped up the game for his side. But then the tank like figure of Langman brushed aside three challenges and hammered the ball past Arsenal's Jack Kelsey to make it 2–1. With a minute left, John Evans struck the ball hard and low into the net to make it 2–2.

The end of the excitement in the F.A.Cup came at Highbury.

The replay on an icy, fog bound Highbury pitch, was farcical from a spectator viewpoint. Some 62,868 fans crowded into the ground, but the vast majority saw little if any of the game, with the floodlights only occasionally penetrating the murk The Gunners won 4–0 – but years afterwards, the argument raged as to whether the ground was fit for play. Still, the money the U's got from the two matches, helped to finance the first Layer Road floodlights.

In the League, the U's doubled Norwich City, Stockport County, Bradford City, Notts County and Newport County. They themselves, were doubled by Hull City, Brentford, Southampton and Mansfield Town. All told, the senior side played a total of 55 games, 14 players were the main core of the side until injuries intervened. Ames once again, featured in all 55 matches. Milligan appeared 53 times, Langman 52, and Wright 51. A total of 20 players were used.

Cyril "Squib" Hammond, a wing half, was a late close season signing from Brighton. Alf Marshall, who had played a few games the previous season, signed from Dagenham on part-time forms. Langman top scored with 20 League and six Cup goals. Evans played in less games but was the next best with 14 League and four Cup goals. Evans and McLeod both scored hat-tricks on October the 4th when Stockport County were beaten 8–2 at Layer Road.

United scored from five of the six penalties they were awarded. Evans converted four and Milligan one, whilst Langman missed the other one.

A total of 178,899 passed through the Layer Road turnstiles – the average gate of 7,778 was down on the previous season. Away from home, attendances totalled 237,519, average 10,326 – also down on 1957/58. The average gate at Reserve home games was 2,380.

The second team, in what was to be their last in the Eastern Counties League for many years, won the championship. They lost in the semi-final of the League Cup to Peterborough, and had to withdraw from the East Anglian Cup because of difficulties with other clubs agreements on dates. McCurley scored 27 goals for the Reserves, 25 in E.C.L. matches, two in Cup games. His tally included three hat-tricks. Martyn King hit five against Biggleswade.

## OFF THE FIELD

Kick off times were altered from 3pm to 3.15 pm on Saturdays.

Kevin McCurley turned down a move to Gateshead – the Tyneside club, then in Division Four, offered £1,000 for his services.

Admission prices for the Arsenal FA Cup match were fixed at 3/- (15p) ground and 6/- and 7/6d stand. Two directors, Scott and Dr. Allen voted against increasing prices and said that it was unfair to the regular supporters. Arsenal took 3,570 tickets for the game, 4,000 were allocated to the Supporters Club for disposal amongst their members. The rest were scheduled to be sold at the Rochdale match on January the 17th, in the event the game was not played as Layer Road was icebound. Nevertheless every ticket was sold and many of the crowd that gathered at the ground, went away disappointed.

At the February Board meeting, a grant of £500 to Benny Fenton and £100 to Claude Orrin was agreed as tangible recognition of their work in the FA Cup run. Work on installing floodlights commenced in March 1959.

A surprise visit by the local Health Inspector to view buffets run by the Supporters Club, led to over £100 having to be spent to conform to hygiene regulations.

The receipts for Southampton's visit on March the 27th, amounted to £936-2-0d., the best of the season for a League match. Jock Duncan, groundsman since the club was started in 1937, was the recipient of £276 following a collection at the Reading match in April.

The floodlights were ready for the start of the new season. Reporting this at the July Board meeting, chairman Allen said that the official opening would be in October with Ipswich providing the opposition. The lights were first used against Norwich City on September 3rd 1959.

CHAPTER 5

# In and out of the Third

1959/60, the second season of the newly constituted Third Division saw Colchester make a bad start, then recover to such an extent that at one time, they had promotion prospects. But they fell back again and had to settle for ninth in the table.

So it was an up and down League campaign. The forwards scored plenty of goals, 83, but a creaky defence, particularly away from home, conceded 74. Only two home games were lost but 15 away defeats and only three wins on foreign soil accounted for the poor return of points away from Layer Road. Nevertheless, ten of the 17 defeats were only by a one goal margin. Accrington Stanley (soon to go out of business), who lost 5–1 at Layer Road in the final game of the season, provided the best win. The heaviest reverses were 4–1 at Grimsby and Shrewsbury.

All told, the first team played 50 matches, 46 in the League, one FA Cup tie and one friendly. Three players, Ames, Fowler and Wright were ever–presents. Parker, Milligan and Hammond each made 47 appearances in total and 43 in the League. 23 players appeared in the first team. In League matches, 97 goals were scored, U's record number for a Football League season at that time. Martyn King topped the scoring chart with 32 goals, including three hat–tricks. His 30 League goals equalled the previous record set up by Kevin McCurley.

Though gates in the country generally fell again, it was quite the opposite at Layer Road, there being a slight increase, in fact 767 more than came through the turnstiles in 1958/59. The overall attendance figures of 179,666 gave an average of 7,810 (well below the 10,000 projected with floodlights in action for the first time). Norwich City again drew the biggest crowd to Layer Road with 13,053 on February the 20th; there were only 5,215 to see Accrington. On opponent's grounds, attendances totalled 215,572 (previous season 257,000).

Fenton retained Ames, Fowler, Parker, Milligan, Hammond, McLeod, Hill, Langman and Rumney and added Trevor Harris and goalkeeper John Wright (previously part–time), as full time professionals. Peter Wright, Roe, Marshall, Ron Hunt, Blake, Johnstone and Tony Millar remained as part–timers. King was just completing his service in the R.A.F. and John Baines was also on National Service. Tommy Millar from Bo'ness and John Laidlaw, still doing National Service, were fresh signings. Bobby Hunt was on amateur forms. Later, Marshall was transfer listed at his own request. Andy Spring–ett was transferred to Chelmsford in November and Brian Dobson moved to Clacton late in the season. Tony Howe from Colchester Casuals, signed as a part–timer in March.

Two local lads who were later to have a distinguished career in League football, made their first team debuts in Colchester colours. Ron Hunt came into the side against Wrexham in October, his brother Bobby had to wait until March when the U's drew 2–2 with York City at Layer Road. He in fact, scored on his debut game – a promise of things to come.

Martyn King was available for almost every game after completing his National Service and soon had the scouts flocking to Layer Road. He was quickly among the goals, scoring 12 in his first eight games, including hat–tricks in two successive games within three days in September. First Port Vale and then Mansfield felt his shooting power. Later in the season he got another three against Norwich City. His first of the trio against the Canaries on February the 20th at Layer Road, was scored after 24 seconds; at the time claimed to be the fastest League goal scored by the U's. Fisher, Evans, McCuskey and Hammond all scored from the penalty spot. Two penalties were awarded against the U's and neither was converted. Angell from Q.P.R. hit the post after Parker had handled and from the other, Ames pulled off a super save from Tighe (Accrington Stanley).

On the serious injury front, Langman tore a knee ligament against Bradford City after 30 minutes of the game at Valley Parade in October. The U's played with ten men for most of the game but drew 0–0. He was out of the side for 13 matches. Fisher missed much of the season with achilles problems, McLeod fractured a toe and Harris broke his ankle.

The Reserves in their first season in the Combination, exceeded expectations by finishing seventh. Of the 38 matches, 18 were won, 7 were drawn and 13 lost. They scored 95 goals and conceded 73.

Twenty six players were used, with 'keeper Jim Wright playing in every game. Apart from him, Howe, Roe, Ron, Hunt, Blake, Miller, Millar, Marshall, Rumney and Evans were the more or less regulars on the team sheet. Blake, with 13, was leading scorer, and King, who appeared in just one game – against Brentford – scored four as the U's won 7–2 at Layer Road in their first Combination game. Bobby Hunt scored a hat–trick against Coventry City Reserves on January the 2nd when the U's won 6–2. The U's obviously had it in for the Coventry second string because they were also 7–2 victors at Highfield Road.

During this season Bobby Hunt joined the club as a part–timer, joining his brother Ron on the staff. Their elder brother Billy was a pro with the club in the early 50's. They provide the only instance of three brothers at the club. Billy never made the first team.

After the euphoria of 1958/59, the U's went out of the FA Cup at the first hurdle. The draw was kind, Queen's Park Rangers at home. At one time Rangers led 3–0, and though McCurley and Peter Wright reduced the deficit, Colchester could not quite recover from giving away those early goals. The attendance was disappointing, 8,866, for more than half were supporters of the London club. By now the post war crowds were dwindling everywhere – in spite of Prime Minister's MacMillan's assertion, *"You've never had it so good"*. Money was getting tighter and counter attractions more varied.

### OFF THE FIELD

With the floodlights ready for use for the new season, it was decided to employ a qualified electrician to be available in case of match day emergencies. M.J.Webster of E.H.Ruddock Ltd was the man appointed.Gate money from the pre–season public practice match of £70–4–6d was divided between a number of charities. Colchester over 65's club received the biggest grant, with £25–4–6d. Gate receipts from the opening League match against Grimsby Town amounted to £955–18–6d, of which the Mariners received £163–1–1d as their share after all expenses were paid. Visiting clubs at that time, were entitled to half the receipts (after Expenses), with a minimum of £100 guarantee.

In December a new deluxe Ford Anglia was purchased for the manager. The first time a brand new vehicle had been acquired by the club. The President of the Football League, Jack Richards, officially switched on the new floodlights. Net gate receipts at the match with Ipswich amounted to £688–16–7d.

The total cost of the new floodlights, as disclosed at the December board meeting was just under £10,000. This was way below the original estimate, mainly due to the director Scott's firm supplying all the materials at cost. The office block at the Town end of the ground, together with a new turnstile, was completed during the season and paid for by the Supporters Club.

The club were in trouble with the Football Combination in January. They took exception to the "Terracite" article in the programme criticising Referees and Linesmen. Frank Rowland - "Terracite" - had his knuckles rapped, albeit gently, over the matter. A doorway in the new Supporters Club building giving direct access to the ground caused some friction. In the end it was bricked up on the orders of the Board.

In April the club gave its support to the Football League regarding the institution of a Football League cup competition.

Colchester Casuals, who at the time acted as a nursery club, were given a grant of £100 towards the cost of financing a reserve team for the 60/61 season.

### 1960/61 - PROBLEMS ON AND OFF THE FIELD

The 60/61 season saw the club again in trouble, both on the field of play, and financially. Nothing quite as disastrous had happened since the club turned professional. It was indeed Colchester United's darkest hour.

The final table for Division Three found the U's 23rd in the table, and together with bottom club Chesterfield they were relegated to Division Four. Looking at the record for the season the stark fact stands out that only 21 points were obtained from the 23 home League games. That, coupled with abysmal away results, just three wins all season, made it the worst campaign playing-wise in the club's history. Only 68 goals were scored, and for the first time over 100 (101 to be precise) were conceded.

Inevitably there were repercussions at the end of the season. Only eight full time professionals were offered terms. Former favourites such as Kevin McCurley, George Fisher, and John Evans were not retained. Neil Langman was first ŏn the transfer list, and Percy Ames looked certain to go until a last minute change of heart by the Board and the player, over terms.

Attendances plummeted, just 113,917 passed through the Layer Road turnstiles, an average gate of 4,954. Away from home the U's attracted some 189,000 spectators, an average of 7,150. The Reserves playing in the Combination drew in 35,125 paying customers at Layer Road, and 19,894 on their travels. Average gates amounting to home 1,760 at home, and 1,046 on their travels. They finished a respectable ninth in the Combination Division Two.

Ames & Fowler both made a total of 51 first team appearances, with Milligan (44), King (43), and Williams (41) behind them. 25 players were used in total. Considering the dreadful season, 27 goals by King was very reasonable. The next highest total was Langman with 15.

The Reserves, consequent on the first team calls, used 32 players. John Wright kept goal in 37 games, whilst Russell Blake and Bert Howe (who lost their places in the senior squad), played in 29 and 27 games respectively. Baines, with 16 headed the list of goalscorers.

The League programme started out fairly well. A 4–0 win over Hull City and a 1–1 draw against Grimsby Town, plus a 4–3 victory over Coventry City followed by a 4–2 success against Barnsley, meant the first four home games yielded seven points. Though two away encounters at Reading and Grimsby both ended in defeat, the margin was only 2–1, and there was quiet optimism at Layer Road.

But complacency was soon shattered by seven defeats in a row and indeed it was not until November that the next League win was recorded. The first away win finally came at Chesterfield in December. The Derbyshire side also lost 4–3 in the last game of the season and the two points from that match enabled Colchester to escape the wooden spoon. The only other double was against Swindon Town.

The poor results after that useful start had a marked effect on attendances. The crowd at Layer Road for the Grimsby match in August was 7,194. By the time the curtain came down with Chesterfield as the visitors, only 3,141 turned up.

"Squib" Hammond put away four penalties early on. Two were for handling offences by Hull City players in the first fixture of the season. Another provided the winning goal when Coventry City were beaten 4–3, the late penalty denied The Bantams a 3–3 draw after they had twice come from behind. The fourth was at Barnsley after the Oakwell centre-half scooped out a shot from Martyn King. William's scored from the spot against Watford on October the 29th when the U's won their first away point in a 2–2 draw at Vicarage Road. Trevor Harris also converted two penalties. One against Chesterfield to give Colchester two consecutive wins away from home. The second was a rather dubious one, after Halifax Town were penalised following Russell Blake's spectacular dive.

Laidlaw, who played well in the two opening wins, had the misfortune to sustain a knee injury in the Grimsby match. This necessitated a cartilage operation and he never played in the first team again.

Peter Wright missed the first 10 games after twisting his knee in one of the pre-season practice games, while Tommy Williams and Edgar Rumney both suffered early season injuries. On January the 14th, Percy Ames, out with a septic knee, missed his first game in four seasons; having made 230 consecutive appearances. Just before he was due to finish his National Service, Martyn King fractured his cheek bone in an R.A.F. match. When Ames missed the Coventry City match John Wright was in goal - his one and only League chance in goal during the season.

McLeod scored a brace of goals, one seen here, in the Layer Road 3-1 victory over Halifax Town.

Two names who were destined to become influential first-teamers at Layer Road in future seasons appeared in the second team line ups - Mick Loughton and Ritchie Griffiths - both local lads.

**OFF THE FIELD**

The Supporters Club still had 17,000 subscribers to their weekly pool.

Stand season tickets were £6-16s-0d (£6-80p). Admission to first team games, ground only, cost 2/6d (12½p) and stand tickets were 4/6d (22½p).

With 15 full time professionals and nine part-time pros, manager Fenton told the Board in July, that there was not a large enough squad - at least four more players were required.

Sports Programmes bought the programme advertising rights for the season. A new seven year lease of Layer Road from Colchester Corporation, to take effect from August the 1st 1961, was agreed.

For the tenth year in succession, the Supporters club bore half of the cost of Christmas gifts to the players. During the season they donated £8,000 to the parent club.

Martyn King signed as a full time professional in January. At the April Board meeting, it was agreed that £14 per week full time wage, plus £3 when in the full first team, and £20 per week, when in the top four, would be the player's remuneration during the 1961-62 season. In May, Michael Foster, a 22 year old winger, signed from Leicester for a nominal fee.

At the final Board meeting of the season, Claude Orrin reported that the club were £3,368 in the red.

Of the newcomers at Layer Road centre-half Peter Casey signed from Queens Park Rangers, and played in 10 senior matches, veteran defender Alan Eagles appeared in 16. Joe Woods, a centre half from Glasgow club St. Roch's, and amateur David Jacobs - a Cambridge blue - never made the League team. All of them left before the next campaign. For once Fenton's signings did not come up trumps.

The one really bright spot of the season came in the Football League cup. On October the 10th a crowd of 9,131 packed into Layer Road when Newcastle United paid their first ever visit to Colchester.

The Magpies were in the First Division, the U's had lost seven of their last eight Division Three games, so not even the most ardent Colchester fan expected the home side to win. But they did, and convincingly 4-1. King 2, Wright and Williams got the goals.

After all expenses were paid, both clubs had £476-1s-10d to boost their finances.

Southampton proved a tougher proposition in the second round when another good gate - 6,264 - saw the Saints win 2-0. But the U's first venture into the League Cup was not unrewarding.

A week after the Southampton tie, 5,571 came through the Layer Road turnstiles to see amateurs Maidenhead United beaten 5-0 in the FA Cup first round. Bobby Hunt and Langman each with two and Williams were the marksmen. Colchester finished with 10 men, King picking up an ankle injury. The U's lost 2-0 at Aldershot in the second round.

On March the 23rd 1961, the final of the Essex Professional Cup, held over from the previous season, saw the U's beat Leyton Orient 4-3 in a game that went to extra time. Bobby Hunt scored three, the last one three minutes from the end of extra time. Langman got the other goal.

During the season, several clubs made enquiries to see if the club would talk transfer terms for Bobby Hunt. Newcastle in fact, offered a five figure sum which was rejected.

**1961/2 STRAIGHT BACK UP**

Following on relegation from the Third Division, Colchester's stay in Division Four proved to be of just one season's duration. They stormed back upstairs at the first attempt winning promotion and finishing second in the table.

After the previous season's debacle ten players were released as Fenton wielded the axe, they were Eagles, Langman, Blake, Carey, Hammond, Laidlaw, Milligan, Parker, Williams and Woods. There was some surprise that Milligan and Williams, both regulars in 60/61, were given free transfers. A fee of £2,500 was asked for Langman and £1,500 for Eagles.

Financially the club were in a bad way and a drastic reduction of the playing staff of 26 was necessary as an economy measure. Only 16 players were on the books when the new season opened. The only new signings of note were Brian Abrey, a wing-half from Chelsea, and Mike Foster a forward from Leicester City.

Early on, gates hovered around the 5,000 mark, although only 4,318 turned up for the opening game when Stockport County were beaten 3-0. During the previous campaign the average first team match at Layer Road was 4,854, a dramatic drop from the 59/60 average of 7,810.

Unbeaten in the first nine League games, the attendance had picked up to 5,961 by the end of September. Thirty-one goals were knocked in during the first eight League matches at Layer Road, that were shared among seven players. The only letdowns in the first three months were the League Cup defeat, 2–1 by Crewe Alexandra, and a 5–0 setback at York.

What helped of course was the fact that the same team was used in the first eleven matches. Indeed only 17 players were used all season. Of those, 21 year old local man Dave Coleman and Colin Lundstrum each played just once. It is worth noting that the regular line-up read:- *Ames, Millar, Fowler, Harris, Abrey, Ron Hunt, Foster, Bobby Hunt, King, Hill and Wright*, played in 35 of the 48 League and Cup matches.

This was the second season of the League Cup, and that home defeat by Crewe cost them the chance of a lucrative tie with Middlesborough in Round 2.

Encouraged by the improved gates Fenton went on another of his forays into Scotland in September. As a result Duncan Forbes and George Ramage arrived, who were signed from Musselburgh and Third Lanark respectively. Forbes did not get a place in the side until the following April, but after that he never looked back, and had a 15 year career ahead of him in League football. He was chief scout with Norwich City at the time of writing.

Accrington's goalie gathers the ball, with Martyn King (he scored a brace in the 3-2 victory) close by.

Accrington Stanley, who failed to see out the season, gave the U's a real fright on their last ever visit to Layer Road, before they were finally beaten 3–2. Later in the season a 4–0 victory at Peel Park gave Colchester the double over the Lancashire club. But the four points were deleted when Stanley resigned from the League and their record was expunged. The loss of those four points probably deprived the club of the championship, Millwall pipping them by one point.

Foster, who scored five goals in the first 10 League games, sustained an injury at Southport that led to him missing five matches. His absence led to Sammy McLeod – he never quite hit it off with the manager – returning to favour, he obliged with two goals, but was soon relegated back to the Reserves.

Six goals were put past Workington, despite heroics by The Reds 'keeper, and a similar number scored against Hartlepools United. By the end of November, with 25 points from 18 League games, and unbeaten at Layer Road, things looked promising. However, in the away results, only three away victories hardly looked promotion form.

The F.A. Cup draw meant a trip to Peterborough. The Posh were riding high in Division Three at the time, and Colchester had lost their last three away matches, but it turned out to be a rip roaring encounter at London Road. Peterborough led 3–0 with 15 minutes left, then goals from Abrey, Wright and Bobby Hunt made it 3–3.

The following Monday night in the replay at Layer Road, Colchester led twice, King and Bobby Hunt scoring, but with less than two minutes left Peterborough made it 2–2. The score remained unchanged after extra time, so it was up to Carrow Road a week later for the second replay.

Martyn King, out injured, was badly missed though McLeod twice came close to scoring, but Posh went through 3–0. The only consolation was the financial rewards for aggregate attendances of almost 39,000 watching the three games.

A home League defeat by Wrexham – the first of the season – proved to be only a temporary hiccup. Immediately after that came a 4–1 win at Stockport, a 5–1 trouncing of Oldham, and a 9–1 walloping of Bradford City. That Layer Road blitz against the Yorkshire club still stands as the U's record win. The only disappointment was that just 4,415 turned up to see that last match of 1961, when Bobby Hunt and King who each scored four, plus Hill, got the goals.

The second half of the season opened with that abortive 4–0 win at Accrington, before the lowest crowd ever at a League match in which Colchester had participated – a paltry 1,411 – on January the 13th. The other nine away matches all came and went without a single victory on foreign soil, and only two points accrued out of a possible 18. Fortunately nine of the home fixtures yielded maximum points, and the other Layer Road match against Rochdale ended 1–1. After losing 1–0 at Aldershot on Good Friday, the penultimate game at Wrexham became a vital one. The Welsh club, Millwall and Colchester were neck and neck for the two promotion places. The crowd of 16,027 at the Racecourse Ground saw a nail biting encounter with a 0–0 draw keeping the U's nose in front of the home team. So to the final fixture – Doncaster Rovers – themselves not quite safe from having to apply for re-election. Urged on by a 6,000 crowd, Bobby Hunt made sure, scoring four in a 5–3 win.

The one discordant note in what had been an exciting season was the serious knee injury Abrey picked up at Rochdale in April. He made one appearance the following season but that match at Spotland was really his swansong.

Bobby Hunt 37, and Martyn King 31, were the scourge of Third Division defenders and accounted for almost two thirds of the U's goals scored. Hunt's 37 goals remains Colchester's highest tally in a League season. (In addition, King with 2 and Hunt both scored in the expunged games against Accrington). Hunt got another two and King one in the Cup matches. Eight players played over 40 League matches, with Ames, Fowler, Ron Hunt and Wright played in every League and Cup game.

## OFF THE FIELD

In October Mr. A.W. Piper who was a Director when the club was formed in 1937 and later Club President for many years, died. A former Mayor and Alderman of the Borough Council he was also one of the Trustees of the Layer Road ground.

In December, when Alderman Charles Jolly was presented with the Freedom of Colchester, the club were represented at the ceremony by several Directors. Alderman Jolly, who lived to be over 90, was the leading light in the Supporters Club, and before that with the defunct Colchester Town Supporters Club.

Peter Benham who had been a Director since 1937, and who had before that played for Colchester Town and been responsible for Town's purchase of the Layer Road ground, became President of the Club in December.

Peter Wright and Ron Hunt, who each completed 10 years with the club, were each given a second benefit.

A £17,000 offer from Newcastle United for Bobby Hunt was rejected. Later in the season Bolton Wanderers and Manchester City both enquired about Hunt but were told he was not for sale; Colchester were over £2,000 in the red at the time.

In March the Supporters Club who earlier in the season had donated £3,750 to the club, gave a further donation of £2,750 to put the finances in the black.

A proposed Charity Match including the T.V. All Stars XI to raise money for the players Benefit Fund was scotched by the Football League, who issued a ruling that the League grounds could not be used for that type of game.

At the Board Meeting in May, Claude Orrin reported that the decision at the April meeting that the team, because of finances, must travel to Crewe on the day of the match, could have cost the club promotion. The game was lost 4–0. It was agreed that the following season no long distance journeys would be made on the day of a match.

Tommy Millar was released in January on compassionate grounds, after his young son was drowned in a garden pool. He was the club's regular right–back at the time, and he and his wife returned to Scotland. Ritchie Griffiths, signed from a local junior club, took over from Millar in the No. 2 shirt.

Despite the club winning promotion, gates only showed a 487 average increase to 5,341 for the First Team. Reserve gates in The Combination averaged 1,254, a decrease of 620 on the previous season.

Ipswich Town won the Division One championship that season, and there was no doubt that their success had a lot to do with Colchester's rather disappointing gates. Considering the fact that overall the League gates fell by 27,979,902, perhaps the U's came out better than most. Millwall, the division's Champions, had average gates of 11,511 for their 22 home League games. Colchester's average was below that of 13 other clubs in Division Four.

To mark winning promotion a celebration dinner, attended by the Directors, Staff, Players and Supporters Club officials, and their wives, was held at the Red Lion Hotel.

## AN ANTI–CLIMAX SEASON

After gaining promotion the previous season, hopes were high for the 1962/63 campaign. Twelve full time and eight part time professionals were retained. Only three players were released – Alf Marshall, Colin Lundstrom and Tony Howe.

Mike Grice was back in the fold from Coventry City, while early in the season Roy McCrohan was recruited from Norwich City, Mike Foster moving to Carrow Road in exchange. In November redheaded Billy Stark was signed from Carlisle United for a reputed £3,750.

The 10th of August 1962 saw the last public pre–season trial match, since from the following season, all such non–competitive matches have been played as Friendlies against a variety of teams. The trial match was between the Probables (in blue and white) and the Possibles (who played in red). The Layer Road attendance was 973, the final score 202, and the teams consisted of:– Probables: *Ames, Griffiths, Harris, Fowler, Forbes, R.M.Hunt, Grice, Hill, King, R.R.Hunt, and Wright.* Possibles: *Ramage, Rumney, Miller, Waylen, Abrey, Brown, Fisher, McLeod, Baines (sub Coleman), Loughton (sub Mansfield) and Mildenhall.* The goalscorers were, Bobby Hunt and Wright, plus Loughton and McLeod.

Things started off reasonably well with seven points, including an early double over Bristol City; a 1–0 win at Layer Road and then a 2–1 victory at Ashton Gate. Four points from three away fixtures looked promising even though a 0–0 home draw with Coventry City was a wee bit disappointing.

Also encouraging were the two home gates 6,824 (versus Bristol City) and 5,781 for the Coventry game. Port Vale however, brought the U's back to earth, winning 4–2 on their own patch and seven days later getting the only goal of the hard fought game at Layer Road.

Unchanged for eight of the previous nine games, Fenton's selection read: *Ames, Griffiths, Fowler, Harris, Forbes, Ron Hunt, Grice, Hill, King, Bobby Hunt, Wright.* That was in the days when clubs played a 2–3–5 formation, with two wingers. How the game has changed! King missed the 1–1 draw at Bournemouth, Baines coming in for what proved to be his only game of the season. King absence was due to his playing in a tennis tournament, with Fenton's permission.

A fine 2–1 away victory over Watford in the League Cup, with the dynamic duo of Bobby Hunt and King the marksmen, looked to be further evidence of a challenge for honours. Any dreams of a run in this cup competition were, however, shortlived. Away to Northampton in Round 2 the U's went down 2–0. In fact it turned out to be a bad year as far as cup matches were concerned. Later, on November the 3rd, Wimbledon (then an amateur side) eliminated Colchester from the F.A. Cup winning 2–1 at Plough Lane. Plenty of red faces that day, for it was bitterly cold, but not half as sharp as Benny's tongue after the game!

By the turn of the year the high hopes of August were fading. From 25 games the points tally was 22 points – hardly promotion form. Port Vale, Millwall, Bradford and Crystal Palace all won at Layer Road. The Lions winning 5–2 with scuffles both inside and outside the ground. There was one very damaging defeat, 6–2 at Peterborough, and a 4–1 reverse at Wrexham.

The in-and-out form continued in the second half of the campaign and a final position of 12th in the table was way below what had been expected. Only 11 home games yielded maximum points, and the away form after the promising start, was not maintained. The defence leaked 93 goals, and only 73 were scored.

Richie Griffiths, a local man from Earls Colne, held the right back position for most of the first half of the season. But after picking up an injury in early December he never regained full fitness. In fact he never made another League appearance after the match at Bradford on December the 15th. Duncan Forbes moved to right back and Keith Rutter, signed for £4,000 from Queens Park Rangers, took over at centre half.

Four players, John Brown (a Scot), Dave Coleman (a local lad), John Baines and Brian Abrey all made just one senior appearance. A loss of form led to Percy Ames giving way to George Ramage for the last 10 games of the season. Ames had made 119 consecutive appearances at the time. Earlier, between February the 18th 1956 and January the 14th 1961, Ames had set a club record by appearing in 236 consecutive games.

One of the fiascos of the season happened three days before Christmas. The game at Highfield Road against Coventry City should never really have started. But mindful that a crowd of over 11,000 (including a large contingent from Colchester) were packed in the ground, the referee decided to start the game. From the outset it was impossible to follow play from the Press Box. Coventry scored twice - wraith like figures emerging from the swirling fog from time to time. At half-time the game was mercifully abandoned.

The hard winter made this the U's last game until February the 16th, when they lost 2-1 to Millwall at The Den. Ten days later it was back to Highfield Road and this time 13,062 fans saw goals from Bobby Hunt earn the U's a 2-2 draw.

The freeze-up left Colchester with 20 League matches to play in March, April and May, and in fact the season was extended. The last match was at Meadow Lane, when Notts County thrashed a full strength U's side 6-0, the worst defeat of the season. Five matches were played in 13 days in May.

Martyn King scored the only hat-trick of the season against Brighton at Layer Road on November the 10th when his side won 4-1. King with 26 League and two Cup goals was leading scorer. Bobby Hunt (for him) had a lean season as he only netted 19 goal in total. No other player reached double figures. Four of Hunt's goals came from penalties, and Coleman netted on his only appearance in the team. All told 20 players were used in League matches. Forbes and Fowler played in every League game, Ron Hunt in 45, Grice 44, King 42 and Peter Wright in 38; they formed the backbone of the side.

On the injury front Ron Hunt missed a number of games with Knee trouble, Bobby Hunt had dental problems, and Martyn King missed three games with a fractured wrist.

The Reserve team in the Football Combination finished next to bottom with 22 points from 34 games. They conceded 111 goals in the process and scored 62. The biggest defeat was 8-1 at Plymouth. The one bright spot was the form of local lad Mick Loughton a part-time pro.

## OFF THE FIELD

Benny Fenton, as ever, was on the trail of three or four players to strengthen his squad. However, he had no luck when he tried to sign Dai Ward the Welsh International forward from Cardiff City, and Eddie Stuart a 30 year old Wolves defender. Ward opted for Watford and Stuart went to Stoke City. Mike Grice returned to Layer Road from Coventry City, the fee being £1,000.

It was agreed to support Cambridge City's application for admission at the Football League A.G.M.

Stand season tickets cost £6-16-6d. - and for the first time for ladies £5-5-0d. Ground only tickets were £3-3-0d., with under 14's paying £1-5-0d. Ground admission was 3/- (15p). and under 14's 1/- (5p).

During the close season Major Peter Benham, who had been associated with the club as Director, President and Legal Adviser, and before that with Colchester Town, died. He had been instrumental in securing Layer Road for Colchester Town in 1911.

Local lad Dave Waylen was signed as a part-time professional. An attempt to sign John Kennedy from Saltcoats Victoria was thwarted when Charlton Athletic secured his signature. In September Roy McCrohan was signed from Norwich City, and Michael Foster went to Carrow Road in part-exchange; the U's also received a cheque for £3,000.

The Financial Accounts for the previous season showed a profit of £909.8s.8d. Gate receipts from the home game with Millwall on September the 29th amounted to £951-7-3d, when the attendance was 7,096. Average attendance for the Third Division games was 5,420 compared with 5,341 the previous season. Reserve team gates slumped from 1,254 in 1962 to 700. The first televised game at Layer Road was on October the 13th 1962, when Anglia T.V. covered the Crystal Palace match.

MARTYN KING

The Board agreed to investigate the possibility of buying some of the new houses being built in Rainsborowe Road. One was eventually purchased from Vaughan's the builders. Club house, No. 34 Gladstone Road was vacated by John Fowler and sold for £1,600. Moore Bros. (Kelvedon) Ltd., who had a contract to supply the team coach, sold out to the Eastern National who continued the contract to the end of the season.

Early in 1963, tentative enquiries were made to secure the services of John Bond from West Ham. A fee of £8,000 however, proved a stumbling block, and the Colchester born player stayed with The Hammers.

## 1963/64 - FENTON GOES, FRANKLIN IN

An undistinguished season summed up the 1963/64 campaign. The League side, after a promising start, slumped to 16th position. In the F.A. Cup they had a good first round victory beating Brighton & Hove Albion 1-0 at the Goldstone Ground. In Round Two however, despite home advantage, they went down to Queens Park Rangers 1-0. In the League Cup they made progress to Round 4, and even then they were very unlucky to lose 1-0 at Workington with Forbes off for most of the game injured.

The Reserves in The Combination looked certain relegation candidates, but four wins, and two draws in the last eight games got them out of trouble.

No players had an ever present record in the League. All told 56 matches were played, League, Cup and two friendlies. Billy Stark appeared in 52 of the matches. Of the other 21 players used McCrohan played in 51, Rutter and Grice 50 each.

King had a League and Cup tally of 23 goals. He also scored four in the two friendlies. Bobby Hunt, before moving to Northampton in February, equalled King's tally of League and Cup goals (and made 38 appearances). Stark scored 19, and Wright 11 (including a League Cup hat-trick).

Bobby Hunt totalled 80 goals in 162 League and Cup games during his stay at Layer Road, including netting one in his debut game against York City in March 1960. He was the U's leading scorer when he left.

League attendances aggregated 120,506 (including an abandoned match with Crystal Palace), an average of 5,208. The all in figure including Cup games was 140,996, an average of 5,422. The top gate was 7,772 against Fulham, although there were two other gates of 7,000 plus. Lowest attendance was 3,263 against Port Vale.

Away from home 247,402 spectators watched the U's, an average of 9,896. The top away gate was the final fixture of the season, a massive 36,901 at Coventry on April the 25th. This was the biggest gate in the whole of the Football League.

Neil Franklin took over from Benny Fenton in December. When Fenton left to manage Orient, the U's had 21 points from 19 games, when the season finished the tally was 43 points. At the end of the campaign, supporters were surprised when George Ramage, Roy McCrohan, Keith Rutter and Peter Wright were transfer listed. All four, McCrohan and Rutter in particular, had been regulars in the first team squad.

It was hinted that part of the reason for the releases was to reduce the summer wage bill. Wright had been a regular choice in the League side since March 1962, and had always refused full professional terms, preferring to continue to pursue his career as a draughtsman.

Peter Wright was a local man, had made 452 appearances and scored 89 goals, a club record at the time. He was 30 when he left and many felt it was a mistake to release him. Another part-timer who left was Ron Hunt, another local man who had joined the club as a junior in 1951. His departure meant that all three Hunt brothers, Billy and Bobby were the other two, had left.

In the Combination 27 players were used in 34 games. Griffiths (33 games) who skippered the side, and two other part-time pros. Dave Waylen (32) and Tony Miller (33) missed only the odd game. Waylen with 14 was the leading scorer, with McColl - who netted 10 - being the only significant contributor to the total of 55 scored. The Reserves for the second season running conceded over 100 goals - 105.

The 17 home Combination games grossed 8,953 an average of only 526 a game. The last game of the season against Mansfield produced just 115.

It could be said that Fenton went out on a winning note. His last match in charge was the F.A. Cup first round match at Brighton. Few of the large Colchester contingent, there were seven coaches and many travelled by car or train, expected the U's to win, but after all it was a day out at the seaside . But win they did, Bobby Hunt scoring the goal, to give Fenton a good send off.

Match day action during the season saw no less than 16 penalties featured in the U's fixtures. The most recorded in a campaign at the time.

On August the 24th, after Ron Hunt handed, Brookes scored for Reading. In September Pythian was successful for Wrexham, and Bobby Hunt scored from the spot against Fulham. During October, Derek Dougan netted for Peterborough, and Bobby Hunt's penalty against Hull City earned the U's a 1-1 draw. In January Hunt scored against Wrexham after he had been felled in the penalty area, while Turner scored from the spot for Luton after McCrohan fouled O'Rourke.

February saw Hunt take what was his last penalty for the club, and he was successful against Oldham. March found George Harris scoring for Watford after Rutter upended McAnearney.

McCrohan, who took over from Hunt as Colchester's penalty taker found the target against Watford on March the 31st, and against Notts. County in April. Finally Ron Allen put away a penalty for Palace after a foul by Rutter, on April the 15th. The other four spot kicks were missed.

There were two hat-tricks. Inevitably Bobby Hunt, against Barnsley, in the opening match of the season at Layer Road, and Peter Wright hit three in a row on November the 4th against Northampton in the League Cup tie. In a friendly against an "All Stars" side at Layer Road King scored three.

Two players Martyn King and Billy Stark were sent off during the season. King and Oldham's Jimmy Frizzell (Oldham) were sent off in the 54th minute of the match at Boundary Park on February the 15th for fighting. Both were suspended for 14 days. Stark was suspended for 7 days and fined five guineas for kicking an opponent during a Charity Cup match against Chelmsford City on April the 27th.

There were two serious injuries during the season. Stark lost two teeth and sustained a mouth injury against Peterborough at Layer Road. He however insisted in playing in the following game with a black and blue face. For good measure he got one of the U's four goals as The Posh lost 4-1. Duncan Forbes was out of action for 14 games after being carried off in the Football League Cup match at Workington.

## OFF THE FIELD

John Brown and Dave Coleman, who had played few senior games, and Trevor Harris were released in May 1963. Brian Abrey had to retire on medical advice. So there were vacancies to fill.

Basic wages for the season were set at £20 in the season and £16 in the summer, for the full-time professionals. There were also various incentive bonuses.

On what proved to be his last Colchester scouting mission in Scotland, Fenton signed John Docherty from Hearts and Tommy McColl from Dennistoun Waverley. Andy Malcolm, a Queens Park Rangers wing-half, turned down a chance to come to Layer Road. Bobbie Hill was transfer listed after turning down the terms offered. In the event however, he spent a further season with the club.

During August the floodlight pylons were repainted, 43 Layer Road was purchased for £2,500, and a new half-time scoreboard was erected at the clock end (Spion Kop) of the ground. "Jock" Duncan, groundsman since the club was formed in 1937, retired and was replaced by Geoff Gasson, on the 14th of March 1964.

In August it was reported in The Press that Benny Fenton was interested in the manager's job at Leyton Orient. Fenton denied there had been any approach. In October, following an approach from Ipswich Town, the Board informed the Portman Road club that they were willing to sell Bobby Hunt for £15,000 plus the registration of Ted Phillips; the deal fell through.

Osborne's of Tollesbury obtained the contract for supplying the team coach for away matches at 2 shillings per mile. Eastern National lost the contract due to a strike.

Ron Hunt received £350 benefit money. The Board also agreed that the joint collection at a future match should be divided between Ron Hunt and Peter Wright, for 10 years service as non-contract players.

Despite denials early in the season, Benny Fenton left to join Leyton Orient in early November. On his departure, he was presented with an inscribed gold watch. Frank O'Farrell, Neil Franklin, Bob Dennison and Arthur Cox were short listed for the vacant manager's post. The salary on offer was £1,650. There were 43 applicants for the post. Franklin was the successful applicant and took over in early December. He joined on a one year contract.

Franklin's first signing was Derek Trevis from Aston Villa. Another Villa player Wilson Briggs turned down the chance to join the U's. First player Franklin transferred was Bobby Hunt to Northampton Town for £20,000.

David Buck and Ivan Thorogood were signed as full professionals and John Mansfield as a part-timer.

## 64/65 - A SEASON OF CHANGE

The big changes at Layer Road included some off the field happenings. Fred Draycott, who had been covering matches at Layer Road since 1920 finally retired. The same year saw another long serving scribe Arthur Wood covering matches for the Essex County Standard for his last season. The Press Box has never been quite the same since. Fred unfortunately died not long afterwards, and at the time of writing Arthur, now over 90, was living in Aberdeen.

Peter Wright had gone to Romford along with Keith Rutter, Tony Miller was with Crittall's and Bobby Fenton had taken George Ramage to Leyton Orient. On medical advice Ron Hunt retired from the game.

New signings included Gareth Salisbury on a free from Luton Town, as was Roy Price, a Newcastle born player from Norwich City. Pat Connolly, a centre-forward from Macclesfield and David Buck, a local who had played in the Youth and Reserve teams - a goalkeeper - signed as a full time pro. Two other players from the previous season's Combination side, Ivan Thorogood and John Mansfield, were added to the staff and Barry Aitchison acquired from Spurs.

Other signings during the season were Tecwyn Jones from Wrexham, who came in October in part-exchange for Martyn King, who moved to the Racecourse Ground. Arthur Longbottom (he changed his name to Langley by deed poll) arrived at the same time from Oxford United, and John Hornsby came from Evenwood Town. Noel Kearney on a month's trial from Ipswich played just three games before being released. Finally towards the end of the season goal-keeper Sandy Kennon signed from Norwich City, and Brian Hall arrived from Mansfield.

By the end of the season only Docherty, Forbes, Fowler and Grice from the Fenton era remained in the first team. Stark and Hill languished in the Reserves. Hardly surprising in view of the wholesale changes in personnel, the team never really got things together, and relegation to Division Four was not unexpected. In just a season and a half Franklin had signed 14 players. Only Aitchison, Hall, Trevis and Kennon stayed to be established first team players. By the end of the campaign calls for the resignation of the manager were heard at Layer Road.

The attendance for the opening match of the season when Carlisle United were the visitors was 4,420, by the end of the season gates generally had slumped to around the 3,000 mark.

Only five of the first 27 games were won, and six drawn. There was something of a goal famine with only 30 scored – King and Hunt had never been adequately replaced. Even more ominously 50 had been conceded.

The second half of the season was even worse, with just four wins in 19 matches, and by Easter the drop was inevitable. After 46 games just 30 points were gleaned, and only Barnsley with 29 points were below them in the table. Port Vale and Luton were also relegated, whilst Carlisle United finished as champions.

In the F.A. Cup the First Round draw was greeted with some relief at Layer Road – Bideford Town of the Western League at home. The previous four League games, two at home, had yielded just two points and at Southend the U's had been hammered 6–2. "A piece of cake" was how many supporters viewed the Cup tie. Bideford however, had other ideas. The Devonians led 3–2 with the clock ticking away, and only a late–late goal from Derek Trevis saved the day. The gallant Bideford side were unlucky not to claim a notable scalp.

It seemed a long way – a seven hour trip in pre–motorway days – down to Devon for the replay. The U's duly won 2–1 but it was close. Connolly and Stark got the goals. Stark – a really nice chap off the field – but with a temperament to match his red hair on it, was very lucky not to get at least a booking. It was another long haul to Devon in Round Two – and a 2–0 defeat by Torquay and Plainmoor.

Earlier in the season Torquay had also accounted for the U's in the League Cup. They won 3–0 at Plainmoor after a 1–1 draw at Layer Road. The West Country was not a happy hunting ground that season.

'Player of the Year' Percy Ames showing his Cup to Mick Loughton, Derek Travis and Billy Stark.

Percy Ames started the season as first choice 'keeper, giving way for 10 games to Alan Buck. Ames then returned and played his final League game at Loftus Road against Q.P.R., before being replaced by Sandy Kennon for the last 10 matches of the season.

Duncan Forbes, who was skipper, played in all 46 League games as did Derek Trevis. All told 24 players were used. Stark, with 13, was the leading scorer, whilst Langley netted 12.

The Reserves in the Combination only won four of their 30 games. They lost 9–0 away to Arsenal, 9–2 at West Ham, 8–2 at Peterborough and 7–1 at Portsmouth, conceding 107 goals all told. Some well known players appeared in these matches, including Sammels, Radford and Tawse (Arsenal), Mel Charles and Ivor Allchurch (Swansea), Tambling and McCalliog (Chelsea)

Bobby Hunt was in the Northampton side when they won 4–0 at Layer Road. When Bristol City won 3–2 at Layer Road on February the 20th the referee Mr. R.A. Paine was pelted with snowballs. As a result Colchester were reported to the F.A., they were let off with a caution, but had to post warning notices at the games against Watford and Southend.

Sandy Kennon and Brian Hall both made their debuts in the game against Watford on March the 6th, 1965. Despite the poor season the Board renewed Franklin's contract for another year.

### OFF THE FIELD

Arthur Neville of Holly Bank, Mistley, was co–opted on to the Board in June.

An attempt to sign John Archer, an inside forward from Bournemouth, came to nothing. On the other hand Barry Aitchison was signed from Spurs. Peter Wright, at that time holder of the record number of appearances for the club, left during the close season. He had made 461 League appear–ances and scored 89 goals. George Ramage moved to Luton Town, Keith Rutter into non–League football and Pat Woods, after one season at Layer Road, emigrated to Australia. Both Ramage and Wright turned down offers from South Coasts, an Australian club.

Ron Andrew the Stoke City centre–half rejected a move South after talks with Franklin. He had been understudy to the U's manager with the Potteries club in earlier times. The new season started with 20 full time professionals, three part–timers and Martyn King on a monthly contract.

The new buffet and bar was opened on October the 31st with Mr. Coveney as manager.

Harry Obeney, ex–Millwall, joined the club on a free transfer in September. He didn't fully recovered from a cartilage operation, never made a League appearance for the U's, and left to join Dover.

David Havell joined the club as assistant to secretary Claude Orrin. Hugh Barr, a forward, and John Mitten a winger, both with Coventry City and on offer, rejected the chance to join the U's.

It was disclosed in November that the club made a profit of more than £25,000 on the 1963/64 season.

Tommy McColl, the promising youngster – one of Fenton's last signings – was transfer listed following dressing room incidents. Tommy Docherty, who felt he could straighten him out, took him to Chelsea for £7,500. He only lasted a month with the Pensioners. Later he emigrated to Australia and years later played for them in the World Cup.

The club had an "A" team in the Essex and Suffolk Border League and a youth team in the Mercia League. Both were new ventures for the U's. John Chandler, later to be physio at Layer Road, was in charge of both teams.

In December, Neil Franklin's contract was extended for a further 12 months. At the time the manager was complaining about the match reports in the local Press, and was generally at loggerheads with them.

In January the chairman "Bill" Allen, who had been ill, said he would not stand for re-election, but eventually he bowed to the wishes of the Board and agreed to serve one more year.

Edgar Rumney was released in January to become player-coach with Sudbury Town. At a Board meeting in April the Board and the Manager agreed to differ on the retained list. Langley and Salisbury (who Franklin wanted to retain) were given free transfers. On the reverse side Aitchison, Hornsby and Stark were added to the retained list, contrary to the manager's wishes. All told 11 players were given free transfers.

Average attendances for home League matches slumped to 3612, compared to over 5,000 the previous season.

## 1965/66 – A YO-YO SEASON

Following their relegation from Division Three, Colchester got away to a good start in the bottom section. They went down 1–0 before an 11,202 crowd away to Port Vale in the opening match, and then had an unbroken run of seven games, which took them into the top four in the table.

Sandy Kennon in goal was in fine form, while Reg Stratton – five goals in that early run – added a cutting edge that had been missing the previous campaign. Ted Phillips heralded his arrival at Layer Road with a brace in the 4–0 defeat of Barnsley at Layer Road on September the 11th. Gates – apart from a midweek Football League Cup match against Exeter City – comfortably topped the 4,000 mark.

There were, however, some early problems. New signings Jackie Bell played in the first three matches, then he was laid low with a mystery illness and thereafter played only four more games all season. Eventually it was found that Bell was suffering from diabetes. His last appearance for the club was at Sincil Bank on the 12th of February, when Lincoln City were beaten 2–0. Released from his contract, he returned to his native county Durham. Diabetes control was not as good then as it is now, otherwise Jackie might have been able to continue playing; he was 26 at the time.

Barry Aitchison, injured against Rochdale in mid-September, was out of action for most of the season with a leg injury that led to his retirement in the close season of 1966.

Defender Ray Price made a piece of U's history at Rochdale on September the 18th. Coming on when Ted Phillips was injured, it was the first time the club used a substitute in the Football League. David Buck was the first sub in a League match at Layer Road. His big day was against Hartlepools on the 16th of October, but it was to be his one and only appearance in first team colours. Brother of goalkeeper Alan Buck, he came on for Reg Stratton, who scored one of the goals in the U's 2–0 win.

At the end of October there was a farcical encounter in the fog at Doncaster. The Belle Vue ground was enveloped in a swirling gloom when play started. It was impossible to see from the Press Box so Peter Hills of the Essex County Standard went behind the Colchester goal. The Writer kept guard behind the net at the other end, and had the dubious satisfaction of seeing Bobby Blackwood appear out of the peasouper to put the ball in the net. The referee, who was nowhere in sight, blew his whistle and called the game off.

The manager insisted on a quick change and then on to the coach for home. Graham Layzell, the driver, had to have people walking in front of the coach to keep his wheels on the road. Luckily after about six miles the fog just vanished. When Colchester travelled North to play the re-arranged game, on a bitterly cold day in December, they lost 2–0 – that's football!

It was a cold-cold Christmas in 1965. After the U's 1–1 draw at home to Chester on December the 27th, it was on to the team coach for a trip to Sealand Road, and the return fixture the next day. Chester won 2–1, and to make matters worse, the heater on the coach packed up for the return journey. It was so cold that Derek Travis, who went to sleep with his head resting on the window, woke up to find his hair frozen to the glass!

All told substitutes (allowed for the first time that season) were used in nine matches. Like Buck, David Laitt replaced Stratton in a later match against Southport for what proved to be his only League outing.

In order, those who appeared in the substitute role were:- Price, Raine, Grice, Buck, Laitt, Mansfield (twice), Raine (twice).

By the end of the year the U's had 31 points from 22 League games. They had also bowed out of both the Football League Cup and the F.A. Cup. In the League Cup First Round the 2-1 win over Exeter brought in just £511-2s-6d. in gate receipts – barely enough to cover expenses.

When Middlesbrough visited in the Second Round a 7,777 crowd paid £1,451-18s-0d. at the turnstiles, a welcome financial boost. The U's lost 4–2, but not before giving the Ayresome Park boys a real fight. In fact the Division Two Teeside club were relegated that season and rubbed shoulders with the U's in Division Three the following campaign.

In the F.A. Cup those perpetual thorns in the United side, Queens Park Rangers, were at Layer Road in early November. The attendance of 6,693 was not quite up to expectations. When the U's led 3–1, Bobby Blackwood scoring two and Brian Hall getting the other, they looked set for Round 3. Rangers, however, hit back and scored another two, so it was down to Loftus Road for a replay, where the homesters won easily, 4–0. The compensations were gate receipts of £1,211 at Layer Road and a similar amount was taken at Loftus Road.

When the New Year came round a sudden swing in form, 18 points from 12 games, once again revived promotion hopes. These matches included a 6–3 win over Bradford at Layer Road, the biggest victory of the season. At Easter Colchester looked to be potential champions and although a 1–0 defeat at Stockport dampened things somewhat, they were still handily placed approaching the end of April. Losing four of their last six games almost cost them promotion. As it was they just sneaked the fourth promotion shot with 58 points. Tranmere Rovers and Luton Town also had 58 points, the U's pipping them both on goal average.

Twenty–three players were used during the season. Brian Hall and Sandy Kennon played in all 46 League matches, Mick Loughton missed just one game, at Chesterfield in early May. Stratton, with 17, was leading goal scorer, followed by Phillips on 13. There were 70 in the 'goals for' column, and 47 were conceded. That was the best defensive record in Division Four.

The Reserves in what was their final season in The Combination finished bottom of Division Two. Their dismal record read:–

| Played | Won | Drawn | Lost | For | Against | Points |
|---|---|---|---|---|---|---|
| 38 | 7 | 9 | 22 | 45 | 94 | 23. |

### OFF THE FIELD

Due to a Football League rule, ground prices for League matches had to be a minimum of 4/– (20p), otherwise prices remained the same for the third year running.

Close season signings included Jackie Bell (Norwich City), Bobby Blackwood (Ipswich Town), Reg. Stratton (Fulham), and David Raine (Doncaster Rovers). Later in August Arthur Kaye arrived from Middlesbrough.

A new look programme was issued priced at sixpence (2½p), production cost were given as 2¼d. (1p) per copy. Programme sellers earned a 1/– in the £ commission (5%).

During the summer, John Anderson was appointed trainer. Bill Light, retired from the position after being with the club as a player pre–war, and had been connected with the club for almost 30 years (Bill died in Colchester in the summer of 1993). A testimonial match for him was held at Layer Road against an International XI.

Season ticket holders when the season commenced numbered a disappointing 116 (Men 42, Women 15 and Old Age Pensioners 59).

Three houses – 25 Hastings Road, 9 De Vere Road and 93 Layer Road were bought at a total price of £11,125.

Colchester United Supporters Club ran a very successful *"United Week"* in the town, as a result season ticket sales rose to 232 (Men 121, Women 30 and Pensioners 81).

In September a swap brought Ted Phillips to Layer Road, with Billy Stark moving to Luton Town. Interestingly both players lasted just one season at their new clubs. Tecwyn Jones moved to Crewe in October, but Peter Kane, who was to be part of an exchange deal declined to come to Layer Road. Instead Peter Bullock was signed from Southend United.

In December, Aberdeen put in a £2,500 offer for Blackwood and Reading enquired about Trevis. Neither of these proposed moves came to fruition.

The Board agreed to support a move by Bristol Rovers for Summer football.

In February Evenwood Town were given a £26–5–0d. donation, consequent on signing John Hornsby from the Northern League club.

Peter Bullock sees his header beat the diving Appleby of Middlesbrough, in the first game of the 1966/67 season

Interesting to note that during the season only eight teams paid more than the minimum £100 guarantee for the visit of the U's. The £341-18-6d., paid by Luton Town as Colchester's share of the League fixture gate at Kenilworth Road, was by far the largest amount received. Colchester paid more than the £100 guarantee to nine visiting clubs £231-19-0d. being the most when Luton were the visitors.

Following considerable discussion it was agreed to withdraw from the Combination and enter the Reserves in the revived London Mid-week League for 1966-67. A proposal that they should return to the Eastern Counties League was rejected.

Average gates for the season were 5148 for the first team, compared to 3612 in the previous year); the reserves, only 304 compared to 409.

At the end of the season Aitchison (who had been out injured for nearly six months), Bell, Phillips, Grice and Hornsly were given free transfers. Three youngsters Barrett, Hughes and Laitt were also released.

**1966/67 - LIKE THE CURATE'S EGG ... GOOD IN PARTS**

After winning promotion the previous season, a dozen or so players remained for 1966/67. Among those who departed was John Fowler who had given sterling service for almost a decade. Brian Hall took over the No.3 shirt, having originally signed from Mansfield as a winger. Mike Grice's second spell at Layer Road had ended, while Ted Phillips left for Malta, the latter had spent just the one season with the U's, played in 33 League games and scored 13 goals.

Newcomers included 24 year-old Ken Hodgson a forward for £4,000 from Bournemouth. Ken gave good service, but his League career ended the following season after he broke his leg in a Reserve team game. John Martin, a 19 year-old winger, from Aston Villa, Denis Mochan from Nottingham Forest and Alan Shires from Southend United.

Middlesbrough newly relegated from Division Two were the first visitors to Layer Road. An encouraging gate of 4,382 witnessed a stirring game with 'Boro just edging it, winning 3-2. Hodgson and Martin were in the line-up, but it was Stratton and Bullock who got the Colchester goals.

The second game was at Loftus Road in the Football League Cup where Queens Park Rangers knocked in five goals. In the match, Bobby Blackwood in an encounter with the Rangers Les Allen, had his jaw fractured. Rodney Marsh scored four of the Rangers goals, although Blackwood had to leave the field before half-time. The player must have become been sick of the sight of Q.P.R.'s Les Allen. A fractured jaw in the second match of the season was bad enough, but he got back in the team again after missing 15 matches, played five games and was back to his best. Then on December the 10th when Q.P.R. visited, and won 3-1 at Layer Road - Allen again fractured his jaw! This time Blackwood missed another nine games before he was fit to resume.

Half-a-dozen unbeaten League games in September were encouraging, Hodgson soon proving his value with seven goals in seven matches. With a settled team Colchester were going well until the end of October.

**GATES: AVERAGE UP TO 6,113**

**AFTER eight League games at Layer Road the average attendance is up to 6,113. A total of 48,905 fans have watched. The last four games give an average gate of 7,400.**

Apart from Raine coming in to replace the injured Blackwood, and Mochan deputising when Shires and Loughton were unfit for a handful of games, the manager saw no reason to alter the shape of the team.

In November however things changed. Four games without a win, including a 4-1 defeat by Peterborough at Layer Road and a 5-0 trouncing at Torquay, raised questions in several areas. After that match at Plainmoor Sandy Kennon replaced Alan Buck in goal and Arthur Kaye was brought back into the team, Shires being left out. Buck in fact had picked the ball out of the net 12 times in three games before he lost his place. The only bright feature of a poor November was progress in the F.A. Cup. Even in that game, on Gainsborough Trinity's Northolme Ground, the team struggled, Hall scoring the only goal of the match, from a free kick.

Another home defeat by Queens Park Rangers and a 4-0 setback at Ayresome Park made it a gloomy pre Christmas period. Things brightened up however, with five points gained from the three holiday period matches. Peter Barlow made history on Boxing Day, when not quite 17, he came into the team in place of the injured Kaye, and became the youngest player to appear in Colchester United's first team. The match was against Bournemouth at Layer Road - the U's winning 2-0. Peter was 16 years of age and still an apprentice; his 17th birthday was not until January the 9th, 1967. Peter's father Bert played for the club in the early fifties, the pair being the only father and son to play for the U's in the Football League, up to that time. The Wrights - Peter and Steve - did so later.

By New Year's Day, 24 League matches had produced 25 points, with 45 goals for an 43 against. Any thoughts of promotion engendered back in October had more or less vanished, unless there was to be a dramatic change in fortunes. The only change however was for the worse, the next seven matches all ended in defeat. The bad run started with a 3-0 beating by Peterborough United in the F.A. Cup Second Round. Franklin got some stick from the Layer Road fans that afternoon from the gate of over 9,000, including many from the well supported Posh.

After Kennon let in seven in the first two matches of the New Year, Buck re-appeared in goal for the next three games. Neither Kennon nor Buck quite fitted the bill and before the season ended the search was on for a new 'keeper.

Seven games yielded only two points between January and May the 13th, when the extended season ended. The pressure was on the manager and there were a number of occasions at Layer Road when supporters voiced their disenchantment. The 25 points gained in the first half of the season were added to by a further 19 from the 22 League games played in the New Year, and the final total of points keeping the club well clear of the relegation places.

Reading's 'keeper Wilkie sprawls desperately as Reg Stratton's header rebounds off the post into the net for United's second. Backing up Stratton is John Martin (No. 11).

Of the four relegated clubs Darlington could feel aggrieved, for they doubled the U's by winning 3–2 at Layer Road, and 4–0 at The Feethams.

Nineteen players were used including Brian Westlake, recruited from Tranmere Rovers in February 1967. A bank clerk by profession he was quite a tearaway in the field. He took over from Hodgson in the No. 9 shirt, and contributed five goals in his 15 games for the club. He is best remembered, by more elderly supporters, for charging a match official with a corner flag after disagreeing with a decision!

Duncan Forbes, John Martin and Reg. Stratton appeared in all 46 League fixtures, Brian Hall and Derek Trevis in 45 and Ken Hodgson in 44. Stratton was top marksman with 24 goals, Hodgson 16 and Bullock 16, of the 86 goals scored.

### OFF THE FIELD

There was the first hint that Secretary Claude Orrin was starting to feel the passage of time, and he told the Board that they should think about a successor. Eventually David Havell came in as Assistant Secretary, he took over from Claude in August 1969.

Geoff Gasson, who had taken over from Jock Duncan a season or two earlier as groundsman, was complimented on the way the pitch looked. A visiting Ipswich director remarked: *"it looks almost like Portman Road's pitch"*. Geoff was quick to retort: *"Yes its good, and your pitch is nearly up to mine"*.

With donations that season the Supporters Club brought up to £150,000 the total money they had given the club in the previous 15 years.

Before the Football League season got under way Colchester made a trip over to the Irish Free State to play in a charity match. Their opponents at Buncrana were Southport, who were managed by Billy Bingham. The U's won 2–0 Peter Bullock getting both the goals. The best parts of the story however happened off the field of play. The hotel at Buncrana where the Southport team stayed later received a very large telephone bill. Enquiries revealed that Mr. Bingham, looking to strengthen his squad, had been busy on the phone looking for likely recruits. To cap it all he ended up signing Eric Redrobe, a player Franklin had on trial for Colchester, and who in fact played for the U's in that Buncrana encounter.

Ernie Adams first appeared on the scene in May 1967 when 2,078 paying customers saw Colchester beat a British Army team 6–3 at Layer Road. Adams on trial from Arsenal at the time was eventually signed in July.

Denis Mochan was given a free by Nottingham Forest in May 1966, and was approached to join Colchester then. He turned down the initial approach as his wife Rose did not want to move from Nottingham. However a change of heart saw Denis move to Layer Road in mid August.

Former groundsman Jock Duncan suffered a stroke in August. He never fully recovered from this illness.

Before the F.A. Cup match at Gainsborough the Colchester team stayed overnight at The Danum in Doncaster. In the match which Colchester won 1-0, Reece Nicholson the Trinity centre-forward was fouled inside the box. Referee Spittle to the astonishment of everyone, including a large contingent of Colchester fans, gave a free-kick outside the area.

The balance sheet for the previous season revealed United had a credit balance of £31,889. This was reported at the Shareholders annual meeting on December the 22nd. There was in fact a trading loss of £22,000. This loss was cancelled out by a £11,446 donation from the Supporters Club and Development Fund proceeds of £14,531, leaving a profit of £3,719.

Duncan Forbes was voted player of the year. The average gate for the season at 6,594 was over a 1,000 more than the previous season's 5,403.

The death of Colchester's most travelled four legged supporter occurred at the end of the season. Whisky was killed in a street accident in Magdalen Street. The dog owned by "Taffy" Richards had been Colchester's mascot for around 16 years and with his master was known on every Third and Fourth Division ground in the country. He also made history when he became the first dog to use Colchester Corporation buses after Mr. Richards fought a council decision to exclude dogs from travelling on their vehicles.

In March, at New Writtle Street, Colchester lost 3-1 to Chelmsford in the Essex Professional Cup semi-final. A crowd of 4,083 watched the game. Franklin's team was booed off the field, by their own supporters, when the final whistle blew.

## 1967/68 BACK TO THE FOURTH

The U's had finished 13th in Division Three in 1967, after winning promotion in '66. Manager Neil Franklin told the annual meeting that he had concentrated on consolidating the position and was looking forward to a promotion push in 1968. Hopes which proved well off target, the U's finishing bottom but one; they were relegated along with Grimsby Town and Scunthorpe.

The unsuccessful season also cost Franklin his job, for at a Board meeting on May the 13th he was relieved of the post. An approach, without success, was made to Tottenham with a view to appointing Dave Mackay as player/manager.

Six players were given free transfers, Kaye, Kennon, Price and Raine who had been first team squad men, a youngster Ball and Charlesworth had never made the senior side.

Bullock, Stratton and Trevis, who were on the retained list refused the initial terms offered. Meantime efforts to sign Stewart Fellows, a half-back from Newcastle United, and Cliff Meyers a forward from Charlton, were rejected. The trio who refused terms eventually signed revised contracts.

Newcomers during the season were custodian Ernie Adams from Queens Park Rangers, Dennis Mochan a full-back from Nottingham Forest, Terry Price a forward - ex-Orient and of course Colchester born - and Peter Barlow, son of Bert Barlow a former U's player who became a full time pro.

The first game of the season, in cricket weather, against Oldham Athletic though goalless looked promising from a U's viewpoint, though the gate was below the 4,000 mark. This was said to be the break even point, by Secretary Claude Orrin at the Press Day at the start of the season. Especially encouraging was the performance of new 'keeper Ernie Adams.

Only three of the first twelve League games were lost. Though in both the away matches, at Tranmere Rovers and Shrewsbury Town, four goals were conceded which raised question marks about the defenders. Four goals were also given away at Brighton when the U's departed the Football League Cup at the first hurdle. Twelve points from a possible 20 was not too bad a record, especially as six of the fixtures were away from home. Loughton broken nose and Martin chipped ankle bone were early casualties.

The Management's reaction to the leakage of 25 goals in those early outings was to move Forbes from right-back to the centre of the defence, leave out Loughton, and bring in Walker at right-back. Forbes retained the No.5 shirt for the rest of the season, Mochan alternated between left and right back, and Hall after starting out on the left wing ultimately took the No. 3 shirt.

In fairness to Loughton it must be said the Manager did not approve when he went part-time. He also had a niggling ligament injury, and broke his nose for a second time against Brighton. He in fact came back into the team in mid-March in midfield, played in the last 13 games, and scored four goals. Despite the defensive switches clean sheets were only recorded in four of the 28 Cup and League games played by the end of the year.

There were groans of anguish in the Layer Road offices when the draw for the F.A. Cup was made - away again on another trip to Plainsmoor. The U's had never found Torquay a particularly happy hunting ground. To make matters worse only a fortnight before the cup tie was due to be played The Gulls had trounced Colchester 5-3 at Layer Road. McKeehnie was injured in that match and Lamont replaced him to become yet another U's player who made just one substitute appearance in the blue and white stripes.

Torquay manager O'Farrell standing on the pitch at snowed-off Plainmoor

The snow arrived early that winter, and it was coming down when the team left Colchester for an overnight stay, en route to Devon. By Friday night, when the supporters coach left, there was a thin white coating, by the time Wiltshire was reached it was blowing a blizzard. Snow drifts, abandoned vehicles, and icy roads made it a hazardous expedition and at the end of it all most Colchester fans arrived in Torquay just in time to find Plainmoor under a thick blanket of snow and the game called off. Star of an otherwise gloomy weekend was one Michael Twiddle – the Club Mascot. "Twiddle" adored his football and it was he who organised the brute force pushing and showing that got the coach to Torquay. He also dispensed a "wee dram" and pork pie to those who had boarded the coach without sustenance!

On the return trip home the coach stopped at a pub near Andover and from the sing-song the locals must have thought the Cup had been won. Hilarious but quite ridiculous.

The Cup game was finally played on December the 12th, when a goal from young Peter Barlow made it 1–1 after 90 minutes. Two goals from Trevis saw the U's through in the replay at Layer Road. That set up an all Essex tie in the Second Round, away to Chelmsford City at New Writtle Street. A crowd of 16,400 turned up for this derby occasion.

He backed his opinion at 100 to 8 and did very nicely – thank you! After the Cup excitement the rest of the season was an anti-climax. Spells of seven and then ten games without a League win plunged the team into the relegation zone. They won none of their last 15 matches, and the drop was inevitable before Peterborough dumped them 5–1 at Layer Road in the last game of the season.

## OFF THE FIELD

A pre-season friendly was arranged with Hapoel from Tel Aviv, which the tourists won 2–1. The other pre-season games resulted in a 3–1 win at Romford, a 2–0 defeat at Luton, and a 3–1 win over Northampton.

Prices for the season were:- Season ticket for men £8.8s.0d. (£8–40p), for women £6., Ground £5. A stand seat cost 7/6d. or 6/–, and ground 5/– (25p). Under 16's at 2/–, and O.A.P. prices remained the same as in 66/67.

In June, Thomas, long time Secretary of the Supporters Club resigned due to ill health. He was replaced by Reg. Casbolt as Secretary. Twenty-six years later Reg. can still be found at Layer Road in charge of the Programme sellers and like Eric Southernwood is actively involved with Hospital Radio.

Johnny Martin (striped shirt) goes close as his shot beats the Chelmsford 'keeper - but hits the post.

Colchester just had the edge, McKechnie and Stratton scoring, to give a 2–0 scoreline, and a home tie with First Division West Bromwich Albion in the Third Round. An all ticket match, 15,981 in Layer Road, and a lovely sunny afternoon. A few yobbos threatened to cause trouble but that was soon sorted out. Stratton's header gave the U's the lead, and the same player had what looked a second goal disallowed. But then a debatable penalty – did Astle dive? The resultant kick made it 1–1 at half-time, and that was the score at the end. But not before high drama in the final minute. John Mansfield slammed the ball in the Throstles net and was celebrating a dramatic winner when the referee disallowed the goal. Later the official said Mansfield controlled the ball with his hand.

Colchester lost the replay 4–0, and West Bromwich went on to win the Cup. Though he was unhappy at the time U's fan Bob Rowland said *"a team as lucky as that will win the Cup"*.

In the close season, Westlake was transferred to Belgium club Royal Daring, the fee being £5,000.

The programme, as the previous season, had the Football League Review as a insert, and it was priced at sixpence (2½p). The print run was 1,000 for the opening League match.

The Football League informed the club in June that a £100 penalty would be payable by the home club for playing on Friday evenings.

Osborne's of Tollesbury retained the contract for supplying the team coach and this was the season when Graham Layzell became the regular driver – a job he still held in 1992/93. In July, the Board decided that any Director retiring because of age should automatically become a vice-president of the club with a seat in the Directors box; there is no trace of the rule being rescinded.

Mick Loughton was released from his contract as a full time professional as he needed to spend more time on the family small holding. He remained with the club as a part-time player. All players' wages were increased by £2 a week in August. The decision came after representations from the senior professionals and was agreed after price increases for season tickets were fixed. Bob Walker, 24, a wing-half from Bournemouth signed on a free transfer.

"Bill" Graver, later to be chairman of the club, and a former Watford Director, was given a Directors Box Season Ticket after making a donation to the club. He had attended a number of matches the previous season.

On October the 3rd, Dr. Fraser Allen and Ben Myers announced their resignation from the Board. Roy Chapman and Eric Allen (son of the former Chairman) replaced them as Directors.

When approached, Millwall asked a fee of £9,000 for Bobby Hunt. While Colchester hesitated over the fee, Ipswich stepped in to sign the former Layer Road favourite.

In November an application was made to enter the Youth Team in the South East Counties League.

To try to strengthen the team, offers were made for Ernie Pythian (Hartlepool) and Keith Webber (Doncaster) - both centre-forwards - but nothing materialised. With Bullock and Hodgson both injured, and along with Stratton on the transfer list, the search for a front runner was a matter of urgency. Eventually Tom McKechnie signed from Bournemouth, and Jim Oliver in January for £2,000 after prolonged negotiations with Brighton.

Gate receipts for the West Bromwich Cup match amounted to £4,975.2s.0d.

At the Board meeting when Mr. Franklin was dismissed, Director Harold Moore said the club had struggled for 4½ years and the time had come to change the Manager. Other Directors said there was little co-operation between the Manager and the players; a lack of method and leadership and public relations were at a low ebb. There was also a further sting in the tail at the end of the season, when long serving Secretary Claude Orrin said he wanted to retire in August.

**1968/69**

Dick Graham had a lot of repair work to do in his first season at Layer Road. Of the team that finished the previous campaign Bobby Blackwood, John Fowler, McKechnie and Alan Shires had departed. Reg Stratton and Peter Bullock refused new contracts.

During the first two months of the season there were many comings and goings at Layer Road. Danny Light cost £4,000 from Crystal Palace, Brian Wood £4,000 from Orient and Brian Gibbs £6,000 from Gillingham. Colin Moughton, who made five first team appearances after coming on two month's trial from Q.P.R., was released.

Duncan Forbes went to Norwich City for £9,000 and a fee of £10,000 took Derek Trevis to Walsall. Then the colourful 'keeper Tony Macedo arrived at Layer Road, first on loan then on contract. He was signed because Alan Buck was ruled out by a cartilage operation and Ernie Adams had refused a new contract and was also unfit. A proposed loan to Oldham fell through because of this, but at the end of the season Adams joined Crewe Alexandra.

Hardly surprisingly it took the team some time to settle down. The first game at Brentford ended in a resounding 4-0 defeat and with new signing Owen Simpson injured. The same squad, except for Simpson, did duty in the second match and performed better, beating Reading 2-1 in the Football League Cup at Layer Road. That however proved to be the only victory in the first seven outings - one game was drawn - and among the defeats was a 1-0 result when Workington eliminated the U's from the League Cup at Layer Road.

September however brought signs of better times ahead, when five League matches produced three wins - one away at Chesterfield. The other two games ended all square 1-1, at Bradford City and at Exeter. Tony Macedo replaced Ernie Adams in goal at the beginning of the month and kept three clean sheets. Despite the improved results a leak of goals was still a cause for concern.

When Gibbs scored a brace in each of the two opening October fixtures there was hope of an improvement in that department. Five matches that month produced seven points - the only disappointment was a 1-0 defeat at Newport where so many chances were missed before the home team won with a sucker goal.

By the end of the year the home League form was looking good and the two Layer Road defeats by Scunthorpe and Doncaster Rovers at the end of August almost forgotten. But not quite, for after amateurs Chesham United were easy 5-0 victims in the F.A. Cup First Round, Exeter City dumped the U's out of the competition by winning 1-0 at Layer Road in a Second Round tie on December the 7th.

In fact due to various factors, mainly severe weather, only two League matches took place in December, but both were won. The team had an enforced rest between Boxing Day and January the 11th due to postponed matches. At that point 24 League games remained to be played. Of the 22 played 11 wins, seven defeats and four draws had produced 26 points - not bad considering the five games in August that yielded just one point.

COLCHESTER UNITED FOOTBALL
CLUB LIMITED

INAUGURAL DINNER DANCE

WEDNESDAY, 2nd APRIL, 1969

THE GEORGE HOTEL
COLCHESTER

Brian Gibbs heads the first goal at Aldershot - the 2-1 victory puts the U's in third place

The second half of the season started with a flourish with four successive wins. Three of them were away from home before the "Old Enemy", Southend United, brought things back to reality winning 3–1 at Roots Hall. By now Graham had got a settled squad which, with the exception of the return of Terry Price to first team duties, changed little until the last game in May. Apart from a 4–0 defeat at Rochdale and that reverse at Southend, the defence, with Macedo Keeping nine clean sheets and only one goal conceded in nine other games, gave little away.

Yet goals 'for' remained a scarce commodity. Apart from the two threes at the beginning of January, the remaining 19 fixtures produced only 20 – and it was perhaps this scarcity of goals that led to the club just missing out in the promotion stakes. The final position was sixth with 52 points, four points adrift of the fourth team Bradford City and Rochdale in third place who went up together with champions Doncaster Rovers and runners up Halifax Town. Of the other clubs only Doncaster managed the double over Dick Graham's side. It was only a poor finish that caused the club to miss out on a quick return to Division Three. The last seven games, four at Layer Road came and went without a single victory. Three home draws and a 1–0 defeat by Swansea Town leaked five points that cost dearly in the end.

Despite conceding six goals in two games at Layer Road in August, only 17 in total appeared in the against column for the 23 home matches. On the other hand the 31 home goals was one of the lowest tallies in Division Four. The 40 goals in the 'against' column for away games also illustrated one of the reasons promotion remained just outside the teams reach.

Twenty seven players were used. Only Brian Hall appeared in all 46 League and 4 Cup games. Dennis Mochan and Danny Light with 42 plus 1, Owen Simpson 41 and 2, Terry Dyson 40 and 2, Macedo 38 and 2 and Brian Gibbs 37 and 1 were the others who missed few matches.

Light with 12 League and 2 Cup goals was the leading scorer, and Gibbs who scored 11 plus Jim Oliver with 9 in the League and one in the Cup, were the only marksmen to get double figures. Of the 12 players selected for the opening game against Brentford, only four – Hall, Simpson, Oliver and Joslyn – were in the line-up for the final League match against Notts County on May the 2nd.

## OFF THE FIELD

Three of the 37 applicants for the vacant managership were interviewed on the 31st of May the 31st 1968.

Dick Graham, then 48, was appointed at a salary of £2,500 plus a club car. He was trainer coach at Walsall and had managed Crystal Palace and Orient. A goalkeeper, his playing career ended because of a back injury sustained playing for Crystal Palace. Tony McShane who had managed Scunthorpe and Chesterfield, and John Quigley the former Nottingham Forest and Huddersfield player – and at that time with Bristol City – were the other two interviewed.

The big news off the field was that the club signed a contract to buy Layer Road from the Corporation. This had been in the air for a couple of years but the deal had been held up due to necessary enquiries into Colchester Corporation's title to the ground. Layer Road was handed over on the demise of Colchester Town in 1937 to the Council as trustees, and it was never satisfactorily explained publicly how they came to be in a position to sell the ground.

In June, Mark Gozzett resigned from the Board of Directors. A retired publican he had been ill for some time and had been a Director for almost 20 years.

Following on the strained relations with the Press in the previous season, The Board decided not to allow reporters to travel on the team coach.

Dick Graham's first signing was Brian Honeywood, who was 19, on a free transfer from Ipswich Town. He also agreed terms with Brentwood for Ian Lawther a Northern Ireland International forward. Lawther however signed for Halifax Town. The player's basic wages were set at £30 per week. It was also agreed that in future the club would not provide housing for young players who married.

In July Mr. Moore finally resigned from the Board. He and Mr. Gozzett were replaced by John Lowe and Jack Rippingale. Later Bill Graver was co-opted. In August the Board made £10,000 available for new players. Graham tried to sign Phil Chisnall from Southend and Charlie Livesey of Brighton, but could not agree terms with either player.

Mick Loughton who had found it impossible to combine working on the family smallholding and professional football, was released from his contract. He continued as a part-timer. Terry Dyson came on a month's trial and was later signed on a one year contract.

## 1969/70 A NEW LOOK TEAM

The 69/70 campaign opened with a trip to Lincoln, and a 3-3 draw at Sincil Bank, with six fresh faces in the U's line up. Graham Smith in goal, Bert Howe, Bobby Howlett, Roy Massey, Steve Pitt and Roy Whittaker all made their debut's. (Massey is still about, working on the Colchester Youth programme, a bad injury bringing an end to his playing career). Smith spent three seasons as first choice 'keeper, but none of the others stayed long. Howlett's career was also wrecked when he broke his leg.

The first ten League games produced 13 points and just one defeat, 3-2 at Darlington. The League Cup First Round at Layer Road ended 1-1, with Brian Gibbs scoring a fine goal. The replay at Elm Park went Colchester's way, with a 3-0 victory, Massey getting an opportunist hat-trick. But the club's joy was only transient, for on September the 3rd, Ipswich Town won the second round tie 4-0. The scoreline flattered the Portman Road side, and two goals came from penalties. Three days later failure to put away chances led to the 3-2 defeat at Darlington, when Dave Bickler and Brian Hall were both out injured for the game at The Feethams. Both were badly missed, and Bobby Howlett playing at centre-half looked what he was - a forward trying to defend! Howlett in fact gave away the penalty that won the game for the Quakers, who up to that match had not scored a goal in five League games. Massey got both the U's goals.

The next game saw Adams the U's former 'keeper almost sneak a point for Crewe. He played a blinder at Layer Road, but Massey did get one past him to make it 1-0, much to the relief of the home fans in the 5,084 crowd. A win at Oldham Athletic's headquarters gave Colchester their first ever points at Boundary Park, and a 1-1 draw at Hartlepool meant that the U's had not lost to the Co. Durham side in their last five encounters.

Scunthorpe brought things down to earth, winning 2-0 at Layer Road. In that match, three players - Massey, Gibbs and Oliver - picked up injuries. As a result they missed the two match away trip to Wales.

Eight goals were conceded there in three days, for it ended 1-4 at Newport, and 2-4 at Wrexham, and the good start to the season was becoming a fading memory.

Another four-two defeat at York followed. Massey, Gibbs and Oliver were still missing, and Graham Smith had joined them on the injured list. The jinx continued at Bootham Crescent when Bickles injured an ankle and missed the next two matches. With the mounting role call of side-lined players, Eddie Presland came on three months loan from Orient, and Terry Dyson - now aged 35 - was recalled from his job of second team supremo to plug one of the gaps.

It was well into November before the injury list was reduced. Five games produced just one drawn game and a quick F.A. Cup exit, 2-1 at Somerton Park, against Newport County. This reverse however was followed by a run of six fixtures in which four were won and two drawn. In the New Year the team were 10th in Division Four, ten points behind leaders Chesterfield.

Bobby Cram became the first major signing of the 70's when he flew in from Canada, having signed from Vancouver Royals. Another encouragement was the return of Roy Massey who had been out of action since October. Unfortunately after just one game he broke down again as his foot injury (though he made several further appearances) ultimately led to him having to quit playing.

There was a frustrating break between Boxing Day, when Notts County were beaten 2-1 at Layer Road, and the second Saturday in January when Hartlepool visited, and somehow escaped with a point in a 1-1 draw. Between these dates there was an abortive trip to The Potteries where thick fog made play impossible at Vale Park.

Ken Jones signed in November, and soon made his mark by scoring five goals in his first nine outings. He then had a purple patch in February and March with ten in eight games. John Martin and Peter Barlow were back at Layer Road when Workington visited. The Reds always seemed to be at their best on visits to Colchester, and this game was no exception - even though the U's won 3-0. There was an element of luck about two of the goals - one from what certainly looked a well offside position.

Chesterfield, still leading the table, were the first visitors in March. The gate was 5,665 - although it looked to be a lot more - and there was a big contingent from the town of the Crooked Spire. They went home disappointed, for the Spireites were demolished 4-1. Jones netted two, he had scored twice against York in the previous game, with Gibbs and Wood (his only goal of the season) getting the other two. In the Chesterfield side was 20 year-old Ernie Moss destined to be a thorn in Colchester's flesh for many seasons.

Also in March, Colchester's Youth team reached the final of the South East Counties League Cup for the first time. They eventually lost to Millwall over the two legs, falling at The Den, after drawing 1-1 at Layer Road. That month however finally ended any promotion hopes. After the win over Chesterfield on March the 2nd, the next four games only yielded two points. Defeats at Exeter, in the return game with Chesterfield, a home draw 1-1 with Brentford, and a similar draw at Workington meant that the April League fixtures were merely a matter of pride.

In fact there was a 3–0 home defeat by Northampton and three away defeats, including a 5–3 reverse at Grimsby in the final game of the season. That match incidentally had been called off on March the 7th when the U's arrived at Cleethorpes to find the game postponed, due to a frozen pitch.

Considering that there had been so many injuries and resultant team changes, a final position of 10th was a reasonable achievement. During the season 23 players were used by the first team. Brian Hall missed just one League game, at Darlington, and he played in all three Cup matches. Smith and Wood each made 43 League appearances, and Gibbs 41. Jones (16 goals) was the leading scorer, and Gibbs netted 14.

**OFF THE FIELD**

At the end of the 1968/69 season, Adams, Buck, Hodgson, Honeywood, Martin, Price and Perryman were given free transfers. Mochan was appointed trainer (replacing John Anderson), and later re–registered as a player.

The 11 players retained were:– Bickles, Brown, Gibbs, Hall, Joslyn, Light, Macedo, Oliver, Simpson, Willis and Wood. Ultimately Macedo and Simpson, refused the terms offered and left. Cook was on amateur forms and working at the club assisting the groundsman. Terry Dyson stayed with the club as second team coach.

In June, Bill Allen resigned from the Board. He had been a member for 27 years, and remained as President of the club. In July Mr. Scott also left the Board of Directors.

In August Macedo was transferred to Durham City for £3,000. With Willis injured in pre–season training, Peter Goy – a former Southend United 'keeper signed on a month's trial as cover. Owen Simpson was transferred to Southend. Roy Massey was the first player to be signed during the close season.

Dave Bickles was sent off in the pre–season friendly at Romford, and as result missed the opening League game due to suspension.

A contract for the purchase of Layer Road from the Borough Council was signed by Chairman Arthur Neville at a Board meeting on September the 17th 1969.

Goy was released after his months trial, and joined Cambridge United. Steven Chapman signed from Crystal Palace, a goalkeeper, he joined the U's on amateur forms.

The Football League inspected the club's books in October and went away happy with what they found. Ex–Police Sargeant "Chalkie" White became the club's Security Officer – he filled this position without taking any remuneration. On November the 28th, Arthur Neville stood down as Chairman, Bill Graver taking his place, on the proposition of Roy Chapman and seconded by Jack Rippingale. Lewis Gunary resigned as vice–chairman at the same meeting and was replaced by Mr. Neville. Mr. Gunary had been a Director for 21 years, and he left the Board in January.

Slater from Orient was signed on loan, and he went back to the O's when his loan period expired. The Brisbane Road club wanted a £5,000 fee.

From December 1969 the players wages were paid through the Bank. Previously it had been paid weekly in cash.

When Mr. Graver was appointed Chairman, he was only a co–opted member of The Board. This was pointed out at the A.G.M. on January the 5th when after discussion he was formally voted on to the Board. At that meeting a motion to approve borrowings of up to £25,000 was carried after it had been explained that as things stood it was not possible to borrow more than the Company's Paid Up Share Capital. At that meeting it was also agreed to play on Friday nights instead of Saturdays whenever possible.

The Football Association granted a £5,000 loan towards the purchase of the ground, which was repayable over 10 years at three percent interest. In January Robert Jackson and Derek Lambeth joined the Board of Directors.

Claude Orrin officially retired on January the 31st. He was presented with a tea maker after the Newport County game. David Havell took over, and at 23 was the youngest Secretary in the League. Later Mr. Orrin received a cocktail cabinet at the Annual dinner.

In February the subject of footballs lost in the gardens surrounding the ground was raised. The Manager mentioned about a dozen had not been returned, and some householders were refusing to return them. This matter still has not been satisfactorily resolved to this day.

Because of financial stringencies notice was given in February of withdrawal of the Youth team from the South East Counties League.

Dick Graham was given a new three year contract. In March apprentices Lindsay Smith and John McLaughlin were singed as professionals.

# CHAPTER 6

# The U's Finest Hour

Three Cups in one year!
In 1971 the Club won the Harwich Charity Cup, The Watney Cup and The Giant-killers Cup.

The 1970/71 season saw Colchester United's finest hour – or should it be hour and a half – when mighty Leeds United found February the 13th distinctly unlucky, as the U's triumphed 3–2 at Layer Road in the F.A. Cup. But that is a story worth a page on its own. Apart from that, what a season it was. Cup drama, the team on a high, and then the disappointment of just missing out on promotion.

It all started off with a couple of pre–season friendlies and a 2–0 defeat of Luton Town, plus a 1–1 draw with Norwich City – the signs were encouraging.

Just under 5,000 turned up for the opening game at Layer Road, when Brian Gibbs scored the only goal of the encounter against Hartlepool. Cambridge United, newcomers that season, proved easy meat in the First Round of the League Cup. Brian Owen marked his debut in the blue and white striped No. 4 jersey with two goals, Jones (2) and Hall got the others, as the visitors were routed 5–0. Owen also scored in the next two League games, and four goals in his first three matches established him as the hero of August.

Dick Graham, who had not been well for some time, had an internal operation in September. The results that month did little to speed his recovery, since four games were lost and there was just one win, at home to Crewe Alexandra 3–1, when Ray Crawford scored all three.

Injuries to 'keeper Graham Smith, Owen and Roy Massey were a handicap. Brian Sherratt made his debut in goal and held the fort for five games while Smith was out.

Birmingham City were lucky to escape from Layer Road with a 1–1 draw in the League Cup, then won the replay 2–1 at St. Andrews before a 17,606 crowd. Colchester actually led 1–0 through a Jones goal until 14 minutes from the end anu left the field to a standing ovation.

October produced four wins, a draw, and a rather unlucky 2–1 defeat at Oldham. At Peterborough, Massey scored in the last minute to give the U's a 2–1 win over the old enemy – The Posh. Aldershot were blitzed 5–2, where the Layer Road faithfuls saw Micky Mahon's famous banana kick corners for the first time.

The 4–0 defeat of Brentford has gone down in United folklore as the "Chic" Brodie match. The Bees goalkeeper had the misfortune to collide with a rather large dog, when both went for a ball on the edge of the penalty area. Brodie had to be carried off, and the sheep dog disappeared into the crowd.

It was a tragedy for Brodie and the Bees, for he never played for them again. As it happened that encounter was Anglia T.V.'s match of the week so the incident is well documented.

In the F.A. Cup Sussex based Ringmer, making their first and so far their only appearance in the First Round, were beaten 3–0 at Layer Road, Crawford getting all the goals. The Second Round of the F.A.Cup found Cambridge United at Layer Road for their second Cup visit of the season. They lost again, 3–0, before a crowd of 7,348, with Garvey, Gilchrist and Jones the scorers. Seven days earlier Colchester had lost 2–1 in a League game at the Abbey Stadium. The Cup win however was achieved at a cost, for Ken Jones picked up an ankle injury and did not play again until March. Brian Owen coming on as substitute for Jones broke his knee cap and never played again that season. Trevor Painter, on loan from Norwich City, came in and played in one match when the U's lost at home to Chester just before Christmas. Dave Simmons and Brian Lewis, hurriedly recruited, both made their debuts at Lincoln on Boxing Day and both scored in the 2–1 win at Sincil Bank.

The New Year was heralded by an unbroken ten game run. A tough 3rd Round F.A. Cup match at Barnet was won through a Mahon goal. But not before a vain trip to Underhill when fog prevented the fixture scheduled for a Saturday afternoon being played. Ironically Colchester was bathed in bright sunshine that January afternoon. The tie was played in midweek under lights.

The Fourth Round tie at Rochdale was a traumatic affair. A large contingent of supporters, around 400, went by special train, "The Oyster Express". "Twiddle" resplendent in top hat, coat and umbrella was early on parade at Spotland. But after Crawford's header gave the U's an early lead the home team equalised and then scored twice in the second half to lead 3–1. With five minutes left many U's fans had left the ground and they missed seeing Brian Lewis and Dave Simmons rescue the situation with dramatic late goals. The U's made no mistake winning the replay 5–0, to earn a plum round five tie with Leeds at Layer Road. The town seethed with excitement.

COLCHESTER UNITED FOOTBALL CLUB LTD.
LAYER ROAD GROUND
COLCHESTER

F.A. CUP 4th ROUND REPLAY

MONDAY, JANUARY 25th 1971

KICK-OFF 7.30 p.m.

**COLCHESTER UNITED**

**V.**

**ROCHDALE**

PRICE SIXPENCE

## THE GLORY DAY

The day Leeds United came to town, was arguably Colchester's biggest day. The gate was pegged at 16,000 and it was really surprising how many "long standing supporters" the club had! Colchester had 12,000 tickets, Leeds 4,000, and they could all have been sold twice over.

It was all hands to the pumps in the Layer Road office with Dave Harvell, Betty Scott and Claude Orrin (he never really retired) up to their neck in it. The writer and Bernard Webber had a hectic time making arrangements for a Press invasion. In fact on the day there were around 30 reporters wanting phones. Extra instruments in the Press Box, plus the loan of most of the private house phones in Layer Road, eventually catered for everyone.

The great day dawned and an hour before kick–off Layer Road was crammed. The Elm trees at the far end of the ground were festooned by viewers who had failed to get a ticket. There were even spectators on the floodlight pylons.

Don Revie brought his strongest side, and Leeds led Division One at the time. Their line–up was:– *Gary Sprake, Paul Reaney, Terry Cooper, Mick Bates, Jack Charlton, Norman Hunter, Peter Lorimer, Alan Clarke. Mick Jones, Johnny Giles and Paul Madeley*, with Rod Belfitt as sub.

At the other end, "Graham's Grandads" – as they were dubbed by the popular Press – lined up:– *Smith, Hall, Cram (the skipper), Gilchrest, Garvey, Kurila, Lewis, Simmons, Mahon, Crawford and Gibbs* – with a very young Michael John Cook on the subs. bench. The average age of the eleven U's men on the pitch was over 30.

After 17 minutes Layer Road erupted when Crawford headed the U's into the lead from a beautifully floated Lewis free kick. Eight minutes later Crawford, challenged by Reaney and Charlton, and on the ground hooked the ball goalwards, it hit the far post and went in the net with Simmons following in to make sure. Leading 2–0 at half–time Simmons set up by the cunning of Lewis made it 3–0, and the crowd went frantic.

With 20 minutes left – and Don Revie going mad on the bench – Leeds scored, when Hunter headed in Lorimers corner. Then ten minutes later Giles netted to make it 3–2. With five minutes left Mick Jones, clear in front of goal, looked certain to equalise. Somehow Graham Smith dived sideways and backwards to hold his shot right on the line, and that was that. How were the mighty fallen.

Colchester 1 Leeds 0

Colchester 2 Leeds 0

Colchester 3 Leeds 0

So nearly 3-3

The tributes flowed, in Dick Graham had £100 and a gallon of Whisky from the Sunday Mirror; Crawford - Evening Standard Player of the month - champagne and an inscribed Table Lighter. The least publicised, but perhaps the outstanding tribute, came from the House of Commons where a motion was passed congratulating the England Cricket Team winning The Ashes and Colchester United on beating Leeds United in the Cup!

February the 13th 1971 – its engraved on my heart, the memory lives on.

Ray Crawford, scorer of two of the goals

### BACK TO THE LEAGUE

Apart from the Leeds epic, the U's were in the middle of a ten match unbeaten League run that revived promotion hopes. It started with the previously mentioned game at Lincoln on Boxing Day, and lasted until the team lost 2–0 at Scunthorpe's Old Showground on March the 16th.

The Cup run came to an end on March the 6th when a crowd of 53,028 saw Everton win 5–0 at Goodison Park. Dick Graham was "Manager of the Month" for February.

There was a real set back in the match at Scunthorpe, for Dave Simmons limped off with what turned out to be a cartilage problem. While recuperating he fell through a glass door badly injuring his arm and was out for the season.

With Lewis breaking his wrist, Sherratt dislocating his shoulder, and Bobby Cram and Jones also missing matches, injuries took their toll and cost the club promotion. They finished sixth in the table.

Crawford was voted player of the year, Steve Leslie – who played a couple of first team games – won three International Youth Caps, and Phil Bloss – now Dick Graham's son-in-law – then a promising youngster was in the team when Barrow were beaten 4–1 at Layer Road and scored a goal on his debut.

Twenty four players were used. Crawford and Gibbs each missed one League game, whilst Garvey and Kurila made 44 appearances each, and Cram 43. Crawford, with 24 in the League, was the leading goalscoring, and next was Gibbs with 11.

### OFF THE FIELD

At the end of the previous season Ron Willis, Brian Wood, Dave Bickles, Jim Oliver, Danny Light, Terry Dyson and Reserve team player Steve Chapman were given free transfers. Dennis Mahon's player registration was cancelled but he stayed with the club as trainer.

Chairman Graver reported in June that the League had given permission for 10 Friday night games during the forthcoming season.

In August, Brian Sherratt was signed as cover for Graham Smith, and John Gilchrist was given a year's contract. In October Roger Joslyn was transferred to Aldershot for £7,300, and Adrian Webster was released to join Hillingdon Borough.

A surplus of £1,000 on the Christmas Draw was reported by Mr. Graver. In March "Bill" Graver resigned from the Board, and Roy Chapman took over as Chairman. Dick Graham, who had tendered his resignation earlier in the month, withdrew it when Mr. Graves stepped down.

The club were awarded the Sunday Mirror Giantkillers Cup following their Cup win over Leeds United. The trophy was presented at a dinner in the George Hotel on March the 8th.

At a Board meeting on April the 6th, the following facts were minuted. *"Deep concern was expressed regarding the nature of outstanding accounts, particularly the fact that they included accounts payable to 12 hotels, and that some accounts dated from as far back as May 1970. It was noted that whilst Board members had been led to believe the club's financial position was satisfactory, the Past Chairman had stated in the Press immediately after his resignation that the position was just the opposite. Furthermore it was noted that the outstanding accounts referred to the Board meeting (by Mr. Graver) on March the 2nd must have been grossly inaccurate and misleading".*

Mr. Neville pointed out that he had repeatedly warned the club was losing £500 a week. During a stormy meeting it emerged that no audited accounts of the Development Association had been submitted for almost two years. It was also revealed that Mr. Graver had promised the players, unbeknown to the Board, a close season tour abroad.

When everything was finally sorted out it was found that £13,808-9-7d was owed for outstanding accounts. There was a £9,755 overdraft, £2,900 owed to Vice-Presidents for loans, and mortgages of approaching £6,000 on two of the club's houses. The club had four other houses free of any mortgage and also owned the Ground.

### 1971/72 A SEASON OF RETRENCHMENT

Before the 1971/72 season started, Roy Chapman – the Chairman – warned that severe financial restraint would have to be exercised. The accounts for the year ending May 1971 revealed a mammoth loss. During the new campaign these restraints, which tried the patience of the supporters, paid dividends, for by the following May the crippling losses had been turned into a profit.

The acute money shortage led to the dispersal of the set of players who beat Leeds, and the decision to release folk heroes like Crawford, Kurila, Garvey, Gilchrist etc., did not go down well with the fans. Nevertheless, winning the Watney Cup in the pre-season Knock-out competition helped to maintain interest and the gates actually went up for the early games.

In August, Colchester beat two Second Division clubs – Luton Town and Carlisle United – at Layer Road and then held West Bromwich Albion to a 4–4 draw at The Hawthorns. Then in a penalty shoot out on that August the 7th day, the youngest player on the field – Phil Bloss – belted in the penalty that won the U's the Watney Cup.

There were 18,487 at that match, and the earlier attendances at Layer Road were 8,186 versus Luton Town and 7,871 for the Carlisle United match.

For the record the results were:-

| | |
|---|---|
| v Luton Town | 1–0 (Lewis penalty) |
| v Carlisle United | 2–0 (Gibbs and Lewis) |
| v West Bromwich A. | 4–4 (Mahon 2, Simmons and Lewis penalty) |

The Watney Cup win was a tremendous tonic. Although the opening League match, at Lincoln yet again was lost, a 3–1 League Cup win over Brentford at Layer Road was another early fillip. Lewis 2 and Mahon got the goals in what was the U's first ever Cup match against The Bees.

Six of the first nine League games were away from home, and these produced just one point. The three matches at Layer Road brought in the maximum six points, and when Crewe were beaten 4–2 the gate topped 6,000. There was also a 4–1 League Cup Second Round win over Second Division Swindon Town, who were managed by Dave Mackay, a one-time contender for the manager's job at Layer Road; Brian Lewis scored a hat-trick.

Cup hopes, as they had done 23 years earlier, ended at Bloomfield Road where Blackpool emerged easy winners in the League Cup Third Round. For this match a party of supporters and manager Dick Graham, flew in a chartered Comet from Stanstead to Squires Gate; it took just 50 minutes. Many others went by train or coach, a journey of over five hours. The Supporters coach arrived back in Colchester at 7 a.m. on Thursday morning, after the tie on Wednesday night. Mike Murayda from Boxted made history in 1948 when he and his friends flew from Colchester to see the F.A. Cup match at Blackpool in a single engine plane.

Brian Owen, who had to give up playing because of injury, went to Wolves and was seconded to the England Youth team trainer. He was at Bisham Abbey when 16 year old Lindsay Smith was called up to train with the England Youth squad.

Colchester United kept up their record of being Aldershot's bogey team when they visited the Recreation Ground. They won 2–0 and that made it five wins and one draw in the last six meetings at the Shots Ground.

Despite four successive wins in the League, a 4–2 defeat at Cambridge and them three draws in a row, the team were only midway in the table by the end of November. Brentford led the way, but what let Colchester down was them only managing to draw in two home games. After beating Southend 1–0 before a 9,807 crowd, the biggest of the season, there was over 6,000 to see first Gillingham and then Brentford pinch a point at Layer Road.

The gate dropped by a thousand after this when Shrewsbury Town were then in town for the F.A. Cup First Round. Not only was the gate disappointing, so was the result – 4–1 to The Shrews. A miserable Saturday all round. It was bitterly cold and Graham Smith was injured after just five minutes and played the rest of the match in considerable pain. This incidentally was Colchester's first defeat at Layer Road in 26 games (Chester were the previous victors, on the 18th of December 1970).

Shrewsbury were also the first team to win a Cup match at Layer Road since Exeter won there 1–0, in December 1968.

By the turn of the year Colchester were still in with a shout in the promotion stakes, but Graham Smith's £10,000 transfer to West Bromwich caused dismay among the fans. In 2½ seasons Smith had played 109 League and Cup games for the club. Barry Smith, a local lad replaced him in goal, and he was the custodian in the next 47 games and looked destined for the top when an injury at Mansfield the following October virtually ended his career.

Chairman Roy Chapman launched a "Floodlight Fund Appeal" after it became obvious that £10,000 would have to be spent to provide new lights in time for next season.

In February the power crisis led to Friday night fixtures having to be transferred to Saturdays. Brian Hall played his 300th League match when Barrow were entertained. The Furness side however, spoilt his celebrations by winning 1–0, and ending Colchester's long unbeaten League match home run of 27 games.

It was Dave Burnside in – on loan from Bristol City – and Ken Jones out – to Margate – in March, as Graham sought to bring some experience into the side, to make a late promotion push. Doncaster Rovers however virtually ended any hopes of going up when they became the second team to win at Layer Road in the space of three weeks. A foggy night at Hartlepool, and a 3–2 defeat made a further stay in Division Four inevitable. Garvey picked up a hand injury, and 16 year old Tony Wingate came on late in the game. He got just two kicks at the ball before the whistle blew. That was to be his one and only bit of Football League action.

Five of the last seven matches were at Layer Road, two of them were lost, and after the high hopes at the start of The Ides of March, things had gone flat.

This was very much a transitional time at Layer Road with a high number of injuries to key players making it difficult to field a settled side. Ten teenagers, including 17 year–old amateur Richard Bourne – who played in two games – appeared in the team. By the end of the season seven players, Graham Smith, John Kurila, John Gilchrist, Ken Jones, Brian Owen and Brian Lewis had gone while Bobby Cram departed in June.

## OFF THE FIELD

With decimal currency coming in earlier in the year there had to be a re–appraisal of admission prices. Season stand tickets were priced at £10, Ground £6. Admission to a match was 50p seated, and 30p to the ground, for adults. There were concessions for O.A.P.'s and Under 16's.

The programme was cut back from 28 pages to 16 pages as an economy measure. Terracite, one of the most popular features in previous seasons, was dropped.

A Spanish summer holiday for the staff, players and their wives cost £1,799.

When Derek Lambeth resigned from the Board only five Directors remained.

A souvenir programme was produced in January when a film of the 1971 Watney Cup Competition was screened at the Cameo Cinema on January the 29th.

After the Borough Council turned down a planning application for a new social club at Layer Road the club appealed and a public enquiry was held in February. The findings went against the club.

John Gilchrist was released to become player/manager of Tunbridge Wells.

Trevor Dodwell joined the Board in April just in time to hear the Chairman Roy Chapman report that the first nine months of the season showed a profit of £787 – a real turn around from the previous season.

When Colchester played Shrewsbury in the F.A. Cup, two of the very few ex–goalkeeper managers in the Football League, Dick Graham and Harry Gregg, were in opposition.

When Colchester travelled to Barrow 34 supporters were on the Supporters Coach organised by Peter Tuckey. A 721 mile round trip to see the U's draw 2–2 at Holker Street.

Roy Massey's testimonial match saw the U's whip Ipswich Town's full strength team 5–2. Brian Lewis scored a hat–trick.

When Colchester won 4–2 at Gresty Road, there were six teenagers in the 12 man U's squad. They were Bloss, Cook, Foley, Leslie, McLaughlin and Lindsay Smith; this is believed to be the youngest ever side fielded in a League game.

A coach load of fans made the 774 miles round trip to Workington in February. The cost was £2 return, how times have changed!

## 1972/73 GRAHAM GOES – SMITH IN

The 72/73 campaign opened with League newcomers Hereford United the visitors to Layer Road. The gate topped the 6,000 mark, and Steve Foley's goal was enough to give the U's the points.

The Colchester team still had Smith in goal, but this time round it was Barrie, Graham having already departed to join West Bromwich Albion. Barrie was joined in the side by two other local lads, Phil Bloss and Foley, while Lindsay Smith and John McLaughlin were still apprentices at Layer Road. It was a very young team that day. Close season signings Stuart Morgan, Bobby Moss, Robert Noble and Steve Wooldridge were also in a new look side. Morgan, who had been a boxer in his younger days, certainly made an impression, especially on the Hereford centre–forward!

Any hopes of progress in the League Cup ended at Priestfield where Gillingham won – a Colchester own goal being the one score of the game.

The first three months of the season hardly augured well. Of the 20 League matches played up to the end of November, only four were won and five drawn – 13 points only and Colchester were too near the bottom for comfort. Gates had also diminished, and there were only 2,676 when Crewe visited in September, with several others were around the 3,500 mark. Funnily enough the Crewe match saw the U's win 5–1 – it turned out to be the top League victory of a somewhat undistinguished season. A hat-trick from Dave Simmons was the feature of the game.

An early season trip to Hartlepool brought home to the Colchester United team how lucky they were to have decent facilities at Layer Road. At the Victoria Ground they had to take it in turns to use a 4' x 5' bath. The Press Box roof that day was held on by ropes that impeded the vision of the game. Shortly afterwards the Hartlepool stand burnt down. Things are a lot different at Hartlepool now – but it always seems to be blowing a gale when Colchester call.

The injury bug struck early. Leslie, after performing well, picked up a nasty ankle injury against Newport, while Brian Hall, after being badly concussed in the same encounter missed the next seven games. In the first five games, five penalties (all converted) were given away. Colchester had one during this time, against Newport, and missed.

Six home games on the trot failed to end in victory and it was some time before anything like a settled team emerged. Wooldridge, who played at right back in the two opening games, was soon discarded with Cook returning. South played just four games, but he like another newcomer – Binks – never succeeded in establishing himself. Both left long before the end of the season.

The sudden departure of Dick Graham in early September (covered elsewhere) catapulted trainer Dennis Mochan into the hot seat as a temporary measure. He was one of the applicants for the manager's job, but Jim Smith was appointed in October. When the new Manager took over the club were firmly entrenched in the bottom four. His second match in charge saw the team win after a 10 match sequence without a victory. Southport were beaten 2–1 at Layer Road with Foley and Thomas getting the goals. Smith himself came on as substitute.

The next game saw Bognor Regis trounced 6–0 in the F.A. Cup First Round. A one-sided tie was seen with Simmons scoring his second hat-trick of the season. When the team won 1–0 at Reading in the next League match it looked as if better times might be ahead. But at the December Board meeting Mr. Smith told the Directors, that after seeing all the players in action, the *"present playing staff"*, stood no chance of keeping clear of the foot of the table. His forbodings proved correct, for the next 20 League encounters produced just three wins. The team finished third from bottom and had to apply for re-election.

One of the early headaches the new boss had to face was recruiting a new 'keeper. Barry Smith played in the game when Jim Smith took over, against Mansfield on October the 28th. After the match it was found that Barry had been playing with a broken wrist. He never made another first team appearance. Des Kelly who played in two matches, to put it kindly – hardly fitted the bill – and John McInally (aged 21), a former Scottish Schoolboy International, signed from Lincoln City after coming to Layer Road on loan.

Joe Hooley took over as trainer-coach in November when Machon, disappointed in his bid for the Manager's job, left Layer Road.

| **Northampton Town**<br>COLOURS<br>**Shirts:** Claret with White Sleeves<br>**Shorts:** Claret with White Trim<br>**Stocking:** White | **BALL SPONSOR**<br>W. A. Salsbury & Co. Ltd.<br>Dulleys Yard, Wellingboro' | **Colchester United**<br>COLOURS<br>**Shirts:** Royal blue with White<br>**Shorts:** Royal blue<br>**Stockings:** White |
|---|---|---|
| JOHN ROBERTS | 1 | JOHN McINALLY |
| DIETMAR BRUCK | 2 | MICKEY COOK |
| JIM BURT | 3 | JOHN McLAUGHLIN |
| STUART ROBERTSON | 4 | BRIAN HALL |
| BILL BAXTER | 5 | BOBBY NOBLE |
| JOHN CLARKE | 6 | STUART MORGAN |
| EAMON ROGERS | 7 | STEVE FOLEY |
| PHILIP NEAL | 8 | DAVE SIMMONS |
| GRAHAM FELTON | 9 | LINDSAY SMITH |
| GORDON RIDDICK | 10 | STEVE LESLIE |
| BOBBY HUNT | 11 | MICK MAHON |
| JOHN HOLD | 12 | PHIL BLOSS |
| **Linesman** (Red Flag)<br>R. RODELL<br>Luton | **Referee**<br>G. E. FLINT<br>Kirkby-in-Ashfield, Notts. | **Linesman** (Orange Flag)<br>K. G. SALMON<br>Barnet |

The line-ups for the League game at Northampton in December. The last full first team appearance of Phil Bloss (Dick Graham's son-in-law), who came in for the injured Simmons. The U's lost 4–0

Another blow was losing the services of Cook for several games after fracturing his cheekbone at Valley Parade. A visit to hospital in Bradford found no fracture, Micky travelled home in considerable pain, and the break was detected in Colchester the following day.

John Mclaughlin, who had established himself at left-back, was called up to join the England Youth squad training at Lilleshall.

The F.A. Cup tie with Bournemouth saw a 0–0 draw at Dean Court, and there was over 7,000 to see the replay at Layer Road when the Cherries won 2–0.

An attempt to sign Bobbie Svarc in December was thwarted when the player's wife declined to move to Colchester. Later a change of heart led to the player signing, but his eight goals failed to rescue the club from the re-election area.

Stan Brown (from Brighton), Ray Harford (ex-Port Vale) and Svarc were all recruited as attempts to strengthen the team were made. Brown became skipper, and Svarc's debut game was in a match at Layer Road when fog obscured most of the action. Typical of Colchester's luck was the game at Aldershot when they had 75 percent of the game, and still lost 2–0. The Shots scored from a dubious penalty, and the inevitable Jack Howarth got the other. Howarth and Fred Binney always seemed to score against Colchester!

In February, McLaughlin, after playing for England Youth against Italy, dislocated his shoulder in a 4–1 defeat at Hereford and Noble came on in his place.

Colchester were also without Morgan that day, suspended after being sent off in the Layer Road game against Darlington.

Graham Taylor (later the England supremo) was The Imps manager when Lincoln City won 2-0 at Layer Road. Taylor at the time was 28 and the youngest manager in the Football League. Jim Smith, McInally, Harford and Svarc were all former Lincoln players. The game was Bobby Roberts first as Colchester's coach, for Hooley had left the club.

A 2-2 Layer Road draw with Reading almost sealed the U's fate in the bottom four. The U's led 2-1 when Bobby Hunt popped up to square matters for the Biscuitmen. Bobby (ten year's earlier Layer Road's favourite son) did the U's no favours, for earlier in the season, on Boxing Day, he scored a brace for Northampton Town when The Cobblers won 4-0.

During the season 26 players were used including Jim Smith and coach Bobby Roberts. Mahon was present for 44 matches and Cook one less. Mahon was the leading League goalscorer, but with only 13, followed by Foley and Svarc, who netted 8 each.

## OFF THE FIELD

At the end of the previous season Dick Graham warned that unless money was forthcoming to strengthen the playing staff it would be difficult to maintain a respectable place in the table.

Dave Burnside, Eric Burgess, Bobby Cram, Brian Garvey, Brian Gibbs, John Gilchrist, Ken Jones, John Kurila, Brian Lewis, Brian Owen, Graham Smith, Charlie Woods and Tony Wingate all left Layer Road before or just after the new season started. When the League matches commenced in August only eight of the previous campaign squad remained with the club.

New floodlights had been installed and the old set were offered to Bilston for £500. They were eventually sold as scrap after Hungerford Town lost interest because of a planning permission delay.

Graham told the Board in June that in future he was looking to sign younger players. During the previous season many problems had been created by older players - *"they seem to be getting even more greedy for money"*, he said.

A new flag pole and a new flag - blue and white bearing the words *"Watney Cup Winners 1971 - Giant Killers Cup Winners 1971"*, were installed at Layer Road.

A cocktail party for all staff and their wives was held at Le Talbooth, Dedham, in July. In early August the Development Association, managed by Vic. Keeble, was selling 28,500 tickets a month.

Essex Telegraph Press printed the programme, it cost 4.98p. and sold at 5p, and included the inserted Football League Review, but only 14 pages compared to 28 previously. Colour was used on some inside pages for the first time.

The question of a new ground came up at several Board meetings, with a suggestion that the club take up an option on land owned by Mr. Lennox, adjoining the by-pass, at £1,000 per acre with the building of a Sports Complex in mind.

During the season Aldershot put in a £7,000 offer for Mahon, Cambridge United offered £8,000 for Leslie, and Shrewsbury enquired if Simmons was available.

Ray Coles was appointed as the club's Physiotherapist in January. Brian Hall, one of the most popular players ever, was given a free transfer in January.

Nan Smith, who had been landlady and almost a mother to 16 players at her home, died in September. Several of them attended her funeral.

Dick Graham, who in 1993 became the father figure at Colchester United Pensioners club, went in early September. He walked out of a Shareholders meeting after Sargeant Frost, a police officer who held just one share in the club, was critical of his style of management. An attempt was made to get him to consider his on the spur of the moment resignation, but to no avail.

## 1973/74 - ON THE UP AGAIN

Jim Smith got the U's back into the Third Division at the end of the 73/74 season. The club finished in third place in the table just three points behind champions Peterborough. Indeed but for a hiccup in the last three games the U's might well have ended up with their first championship.

> *(I will always remember the first game of the season at Barnsley. I travelled up by car, staying overnight in Loughborough, and wore a new pair of shoes that weekend. At Worsborough Bridge just outside Barnsley the car broke down and as I had cut it fine I had to do a rapid walk [I was active in those days] uphill to reach the Oakwell Ground. The new shoes were killing me, and as I limped into the ground what was on the tannoy, but "These Shoes are made for walking"! It was all worthwhile however, a super goal from Bobby Svarc won the game. I really enjoyed my pint in the pub next to the ground at the end, made even more enjoyable because a kind Barnsley fan ran me back to the garage where my recalcitrant car had been patched up)*

It was down to earth the following Wednesday however when Gillingham, for the second season in succession ended any hopes of a run in the Football League Cup. Cook and Svarc got the goals, but at Priestfield the Gills finished the stronger. The best part of that evening was the super fish and chips from the chippie near the ground.

Up to the end of September there was just one League defeat, at Swansea. Twelve points from the first eight games was good going, especially as two of the victories were away from home. Things looked even better when a 12 match undefeated run extended into December, and another 16 points were gathered in. And guess where the fine sequence cane to an end? Priestfield of course, where Gillingham put another four past Mike Walker in the Colchester goal. Mike was in his first season at Layer Road and had 11 clear sheets in the 19 League games played up to that point. At the end of the season the Gills finished second, two points ahead of the U's. They also completed a double - a treble if the Cup tie is included - for they won 2-0 at Layer Road on April the 20th. The two points there clinched the runners up position.

There was a 1–0 defeat at Exeter just before Christmas but Colchester were up among the front runners at the year end with 34 points from 24 matches – almost 1½ points per game, promotion form. The second half of the season started well enough with four straight wins, but then came a sticky patch. The following eight games saw away defeats at Doncaster, Bury, Darlington, Peterborough and Scunthorpe. Swansea and Hartlepool were beaten but Rotherham (on March the 8th) won at Layer Road. That was the first home reverse in the League, and the string of losses put promotion hopes in jeopardy.

Phil Thomas, who had been out injured, and Barry Dyson re-appeared in the squad and these two steadied the boat, along with Paul Taylor a midfield player brought in from Hereford in March.

Taylor in a 12 month spell played for York City, Hereford, Colchester and Southport. He played against Gillingham in the last home game of the season, and years later he managed the Gills. The other, late in the season signing, was Gary Moore from Southend United. He figured in the last 11 games and scored seven very vital goals. He departed at the end of the season joining Chester in the summer.

Bobby Svarc

Twenty three players were used. Harford, Walker and Svarc appeared in all 46 League and both Cup games, Cook played in 44 and 2, Morgan and Thomas in 38 League and the two Cup ties. Steve Foley played in 34 matches until an injury in March brought his season to a premature end. At the time he was being eyed by at least two First Division clubs.

Departures during the season were Micky Mahon to Wimbledon and John McLaughlin to Swindon Town. Barry Dominey made his full debut in the last match of the season.

Bobby Svarc with 25 League and one Cup goal accounted for a third of the 73 League goals; he also scored one in the Football League Cup. No one else reached double figures although Moore's seven in 11 games was a praiseworthy effort.

The top gate was the 10,007 to see the home game with Gillingham – the last League match at Layer Road when points were needed, in case leaders Peterborough slipped up. The Posh however held on to win the championship, they like Gillingham played Colchester three times that season. Both won Cup victories over the U's, and Peterborough took three League points from the two fixtures. On reflection third place for Colchester behind The Posh and The Gills was fair enough.

The Colchester defence conceded only 36 goals, and was the meanest in the division; Walker kept 14 clean sheets.

### OFF THE FIELD

When admission prices were under discussion Director Trevor Dodwell proposed that they should be increased, but at the same time a programme should be issued free to everyone passing through the turnstiles. This was the second time that a similar plan had been put forward. It was finally rejected as impractical.

A supporter, Peter Sharp, who had his spectacles broken by a ball during the match against Reading at the end of the previous season was reimbursed for the cost of the repairs.

First close season signing was Mick Packer from Watford.

### 1974/75: CUP JOY AND SORROW FINANCIAL PROBLEMS

A Centenary match with Ipswich Town the opponents marked the start of proceedings for the 74/75 campaign. (Colchester United in 1937 having taken over the mantle of Colchester Town founded in the 1873/4 season).

A special 10p. programme – with a royal purple cover – was issued for the match at Layer Road on August the 12th 1974. Tommy "Smiler" Dawes refereed the match. Colchester twice led with super goals from Micky Cook and John Froggatt but in the end, a full strength First Division Portman Road side, prevailed. All 2,200 programmes were sold.

Jim Smith was in his second full season as manager, and Colchester were back in Division Three after six seasons in the lower reaches of the League. John Hillier had joined the club – the first Commercial Manager – with Vic Keeble continuing as Development Manager.

New players were John Froggatt from Boston and Jimmy Lindsay from Watford. In fact when the Vicarage Road club visited Layer Road in the first League fixture of the season four of the U's squad were former Watford players – Walker, Packer, Lindsay and Barry Dyson. The match ended 1–1, Steve Leslie having the honour of scoring the club's first goal of the new campaign.

Three days later Oxford, then in Division 2, were knocked out of the League Cup. A Lindsay penalty deciding the issue. That was the start of a remarkable run in the competition that eventually took the U's to a quarter final place.

The first ever visit to Blackburn Rovers ended in a 2–3 defeat at Ewood Park. The highlight, for some of the party who made the trip, was an invitation to see the Rovers magnificent boardroom, a survivor of the days when Blackburn were a power in the land (currently back among the elite again).

A Cook goal was enough to sink Bournemouth in a televised Layer Road game and that was the start of an unbeaten run. During that sequence there was a splendid 2–0 win away to Southend in the League Cup Second Round, with Steve Leslie scoring both goals. The following Saturday he was on target again when Charlton Athletic – their first ever League encounter with the U's – were defeated 3–0 at Layer Road. That was also a game Dave Bunkell will always remember, for he was on the subs bench after being out of action since January the 1st, when he broke his leg at Crewe.

The team were brought down to earth when Walsall won 2–1 at Layer Road, but three points from fixtures with Port Vale away, and Gillingham at home, restored confidence. Carlisle were the visitors in the League Cup third round. That season The Cumbrians surprised the football world by winning a place in Division One. Jim Smith's boys brushed them aside winning far more easily than the 2–0 scoreline would suggest. The occasion was matched by a very flamboyant looking programme, with an orange cover, embellished with an eagle in a blue and white striped shirt. A crowd of 7,842 was present, and all programmes were sold long before the 7.30p.m. kick–off time.

Up to Christmas the U's were able to field a more or less unchanged side. Stuart Morgan and Mike Packer missed a few games through injury, but Dominey, Rowe and Dyson ably deputised when called on. Perhaps the outstanding win was the 2–0 triumph at Deepdale against Preston North End. Ray Harford netted twice, the only goals he got that season.

November found Southampton (in the Second Division) at Layer Road in the Third Round of the League Cup. The Saints had Peter Osgood, Mike Channon, and Bobby Stokes in their team. The conditions were terrible, and Lawrie McMenemy, their Manager, must have thought his team had done the job when they drew 0–0. He was soon disillusioned, since Barry Dominey became the hero of the night for Colchester when he headed in the only goal in the replay at The Dell. Two days prior to that triumph the U's also negotiated the first hurdle in the F.A. Cup with a 1–0 victory at Watford.

At the start of December the team were sitting near the top of the table, and still in both Cup competitions, but it proved something of a disappointing month. Not unexpectedly, on the tight Layer Road pitch, Aston Villa won 2–1 in the F.L.C. Quarter Final. A crowd of 11,871 saw the match. John Froggatt's goal was not enough after a brave fight by the underdogs. Villa went on to win the Trophy, and Ron Saunders admitted they were fortunate to get a result at Colchester. Jim Smith however, was far from amused when Leatherhead, with *"Kelly the Lip"* doing the damage, ousted his team from the F.A. Cup.

Yet when the New Year dawned, at fifth place in the table and just three points behind leaders Blackburn, Colchester were well and truly in the promotion area.

Hopes of Second Division football took a knock with some indifferent form in the first two months of the New Year. Only two games in January and February produced maximum points, both at Layer Road. An injury to Bobby Svarc – he was out of action for three games – led to the goals starting to dry up. At the turn of the year, the U's with 42 goals, were the leading scorers in the Division, and Svarc and Froggatt (what a poaching duo they were) had contributed 25 of them. Phil Thomas, who had been outstanding at right back sustained a ligament injury at Peterborough on December the 28th and did not come back until March. This weakened the defence, indeed the No. 2 shirt was never quite adequately filled for the rest of the season.

Nine of the 13 away fixtures of the second half of the campaign were lost and this poor form ended any hopes of promotion. Home results also suffered, and although only Chesterfield won at Layer Road, three fixtures yielded just three points. The Layer Road matches however, ended on a high note, when champions Blackburn were beaten 2–0, and Bury overcome 3–2, in the final games at home.

Undoubtedly it was the away form that undermined any promotion hopes. Only four wins on foreign soil, and 13 defeats undid the good work at Layer Road where just three matches were lost. Colchester finished eight points short of a promotion place. Perhaps the turning point was in January when Colchester led Swindon 3–0, but the conditions forced referee Les Shapter to abandon the match. Though the re-arranged fixture on March the 4th was won, the team never again played with the same fluency after that cancellation.

Twenty–one players were used. Walker, Cook and Froggatt appeared in all 46 League and 7 Cup games, whilst Lindsay missed just 1 League and 1 Cup game. Svarc scored 24 League and 1 Cup goal, Froggatt netted 16 League and 2 Cup goals. Ian Allinson made his senior debut when he came on as sub. against Preston on April the 19th. Three loan players were used with Danny Cameron and Ian McDonald each appearing in five matches (The Manager would have liked to sign both permanently but could not afford the Sheffield Wednesday and Liverpool asking prices). John Sims with 2 games was the other loanee.

**OFF THE FIELD**

Most of the 1973/4 season's players were retained, and just two signings were made – Froggatt at £2,500 from Boston and Lindsay on a free from Watford. But then, as now, a free transfer was not quite what it seemed, for Lindsay received a signing–on fee of £4,000! Steve Leslie, the subject of a substantial offer from Norwich City declined a move to Carrow Road, and Tottenham were also interested.

Wingate, a young player, who had twice broken his leg playing in the Reserves was released. Paul Aimson, who only played five games after signing from Bournemouth had to retire through injury. Steve Foley, needed a second cartilage operation and missed most of the season. Alex Smith, though retained, was later given a free transfer and joined Halifax.

John Hillier, previously Commercial Manager with Exeter City, joined the club in August in a similar capacity.

New Trainers' boxes – the ones at present in use – were built. Osbourne's provided a newly acquired coach for the teams journeys, at a cost of £2,525 for the season's travelling! In September a loss of £10,539 was reported on the 73/4 season.

Oxford United showed an interest in Svarc but lost interest when a £50,000 fee was mentioned. A shortage of programmes at the Southend United match was caused by a box of that issue being stolen prior to the game.

Stewart Morgan

There was an incident at Gigg Lane on September the 24th in the match with Bury, when the referee sent off Steve Leslie for a bad foul, although Stuart Morgan was clearly the culprit. Subsequently Morgan was censured, relieved of the Captaincy, and fined £10. Leslie was ultimately cleared after a personal hearing by the F.A. and Morgan was suspended for three matches.

Robert Jackson resigned from the Board as Chairman on November the 14th, and Jack Rippingale appointed in his place. Mr. Jackson, whose resignation was said to be due to pressure of work, at a previous meeting had voted against the club accepting a £30,000 loan from the Borough Council.

There was another resignation from the Board when Roy Chapman stepped down in April. Nigel Fitch had joined the Board before Mr. Chapman announced his resignation.

Lee Smelt succeeded Kevin Reakes as junior 'keeper at Layer Road. Loan spells for Ian McDonald from Liverpool and Danny Cameron cost the club £100 a week in wages plus their travel expenses.

The club's accounts were investigated in March by the Football League and it was minuted that *"The Board expressed regret at the disgusting reception and attitude of League vice-president Mr. Bob Lord"*.

The season ended with the club in serious financial difficulties with the Bank asking for a considerable reduction of the £50,000 overdraft.

One important change made in November was the dissolving of Colchester United Supporters Club in its old form. Up to that time it had been the main fundraising organisation for the parent club. With the appointment of a full-time Commercial Manager the Supporters Club were relieved of that role, and the Blue Eagles club was born.

## 1975/76: ROBERTS IN THE HOT SEAT

It was a series of changes at all levels for the 75/76 season. In addition to a new Chairman, Wilf Livingstone the Secretary left in September to return to Barrow, and Betty Scott (previously his assistant) took his place.

Bobby Roberts was the new Manager taking over when Jim Smith moved to Blackburn Rovers.

Of the previous season's players Dyson, Harford, Lindsay, Morgan, and Alex. Smith had gone. Newcomers included Paul Dyer, Terry Anderson, John Williams and, in the New Year, Colin Garwood plus Bobby Gough.

The first ten League games produced just one (2–0) win over Brighton. There was also an early exit from the League Cup, beaten 3–0 by Crystal Palace at Selhurst Park, and 3–2 at Layer Road in the second leg. Roberts himself played in the first match.

By the end of the year only five of the home League games had yielded maximum points. Mansfield, Halifax and Wrexham all went away with victories at Layer Road. Only two fixtures on foreign soil were won, and it was hardly surprising that the U's were only just clear of the relegation zone when the New Year dawned.

For the opening match at Preston in August John O'Donnell (on loan from Cambridge United), Paul Dyer, and Derek Harrison from Torquay were in the line-up. Harrison, a centre-half was injured in his debut game and thereafter made only a handful of appearances. O'Donnell went back to Cambridge, but Dyer (he of the loud voice) went on to become a Layer Road favourite with his never-say-die brand of enthusiasm.

A feature in the early season's programmes dealt with the best watering holes in the Colchester area. Some, alas, are no longer with us, but the display proved a nice little earner advertising wise. It was a pleasure flogging round many of them, and many a quiet pint was enjoyed; that was in pre-breathalyser days!

Dear old Arthur Kates, he died in the early 1990's, after a lifetime of selling draw tickets at Layer Road, was the popular winner of the U's new goal time competition.

When Brighton visited and provided the first League win of the season in September, Peter Taylor, for so long associated with Brian Clough at Forest, was in charge of the Goldstone Club. They had just thrashed Chester 6–0, but the Froggatt – Svarc double act sunk them 2–0 at Layer Road; Colchester lost 1–0 at Chester in their next game. In October, Ray Harford, who had joined Romford after being given a free transfer, returned to Layer Road as coach.

A demoralising 6–1 defeat in a mid-week November game at Chesterfield started a frustrating time which culminated in an exit from the F.A. Cup. A home tie with Dover, a team struggling near the foot of the Southern League table, looked just the job for getting the team back on the rails. The Crabble men had other ideas, for they earned a 3–3 draw at Layer Road, and in the replay in Kent, ran rings round the U's winning 4–1. The one bright spot was a 2–1 win over Sheffield Wednesday in the first ever encounter with the Hillsborough club. Micky Cook chose the occasion to score what proved to be his only goal of the season. It was also his testimonial year.

In January, after 127 consecutive League and Cup games since joining the club, Mike Walker missed three games. Len Bond, on loan, came in, but his stay at Layer Road was brief.

Crystal Palace, managed by the charismatic Malcolm Allison, were clear leaders in January after winning 3–0 at Layer Road. Bobby Gough made his debut but never got a look-in against Palace defender Stewart Jump. The Londoners looked promotion certainties, but eventually had to settle for 5th place in the table.

Colin Garwood was recruited at the end of the month and scored twice in his first match at Layer Road, when newly promoted Cardiff City were beaten 3–2. It was the Bluebirds first visit for a League game. What a perverse team Colchester were, they took points off all three promoted clubs – Hereford, Millwall and Cardiff – yet dropped points when opposed to Halifax, Southend and Aldershot, who all went down with them.

The lowest gate in a League game recorded at the time was recorded on February the 7th, when a meagre 2,626 passed through the turnstiles. Even the faithfuls present on that day probably wished they had stayed at home. The U's lost 3–2 to Chesterfield, who themselves were in the relegation zone, and it was a woeful game.

When Easter came round, Colchester – barring a miracle – were doomed to the drop. Strangely enough they remained undefeated in their last six games (two victories and four draws), and ultimately fell only three points short of safety. Home wins over Southend and away to Grimsby came too late.

During the season 27 players were used. Packer and Walker with 47 total appearances each, Bunkell (45), Froggatt (44), Cook (42), Williams (39) and Leslie (37) were the backbone of the side, in 50 League and Cup games.

A look at the 'goals for' column reveals one of the reasons why the club were relegated. Twenty five at Layer Road, and just sixteen away from home underlined the lack of firepower up front.

Svarc, who was sold in September against the wishes of the Manager, was never adequately replaced. Thirteen players shared the League goals, and Steve Leslie – with just six – topped the scoring; he also netted one of the seven goals in the four Cup games. The defence hardly inspired confidence, for 65 were conceded in the League, and 9 in the four Cup matches.

Highest gate at Layer Road was the 6,240 for the visit of Crystal Palace in January, only two other attendances topped the 4,000 mark. Even the visit of one time League giants Sheffield Wednesday, reduced to Third Division fare, failed to attract the crowds. Just over 3,500 turned up to see that game, and at least half of those were Wednesday fans.

### OFF THE FIELD

Admission charges were:– adults 65p, juniors and senior citizens 25p. Stand seating was £1, and season tickets were £20 for seating, but £17 if bought before June the 30th.

To the ground only the costs were – for adults £12 (£10 if purchased early), and Juniors and Senior Citizens £5 (£4).

John Hillier warned that with the present lottery set up there was no way the club were operating within the Betting and Lotteries Gaming Act. This situation was rectified immediately in order to conform to the rules.

Paul Aimson was granted an ex-gratia payment of £1,000 in settlement of his injury claim against the club. Alan Stephens a 30 year-old defender given a free transfer by Portsmouth was approached with a view to signing. When it was discovered he was on £95 a week at Fratton Park the interest was dropped.

Colchester having won the Mid-Week League the previous season were presented with the awards prior to the Blackburn Rovers match.

The Vice Presidents Club agreed to provide the cash for tip up seats in the main block and the directors box in the Stand. These were the first such seats installed at Layer Road.

The Supporters Club presented a Radio Microphone and provided cash for a new playing strip.

A sponsored walk – the first of its kind organised by the club – raised £1,200 for club funds.

In pre-season trials, Sorrenson (Chelsea) Walsh (Bournemouth), Harrison (Torquay), Dyer (Notts. County) and Stevenson – a Welsh wing-half, appeared. All but Sorrenson were offered terms, Walsh and Stevenson turned them down, but Dyer duly signed.

Bobbie Svarc, despite the Manager opposing the transfer, was sold to Blackburn Rovers – Roberts stating that he was "a steal" at £20,000. Director Stanley Firth said the club had to sell because of the dire financial position.

Steve Dowmen, Ian Allinson and Stewart Bright were re-engaged as apprentices, and all three later became first team players. Allinson, at 18 years old, in fact made his first team debut at Preston on April the 19th 1975, when he came on as sub in place of the injured Jimmy Lindsay.

The new look programme, designed by John Hillier, was an awkward size measuring 9 inches by 6.9 inches. It wouldn't fit in the pocket and was not very popular with the supporters. It is hardly surprising that collectors today will be hard pressed to find one that did not end up folded – the only way to get it in a pocket. An eagle with upraised wings adorned in a blue and white shirt superimposed on a red background adorned the front cover. Sixteen pages, with a team picture of the visitors across the centre pages was an innovation. Unfortunately, after the New Year, most of the teams had changed so much that the photo's were outdated.

Derek Metson was the Promotions Manager working alongside Commercial Manager John Hillier on fund raising for the club. It was reported that from September 1975 up to the start of the following season, commercial activities had led to the club benefiting to the tune of £30,000. However, Vic Keeble – after a difference of opinion with the Chairman – had departed and gone over to work with Chelmsford City. He took some of the agents with him, and his departure was much lamented in many quarters.

The Vice-Presidents Club sponsored the team, at the rate of £10 for every League point gained during the season.

### 1976/77: LAST GASP PROMOTION

Millwall home and away in the League Cup provided an interesting start to the 1976/77 season. Gates were disappointing, but as both matches were played in Cricket Weather – and there was county games in both Essex and Kent – perhaps that was not so unexpected. The two Cup games ended with the teams all square, both winning their home leg by 2–1, and as a result each figured in the draw for the second round, straight knockout, stage.

The Mid-1970's.
Four surviving veterans from the Colchester Town days.
(Back) George Digby and Bill Dent.
(Front) Alf Terroni and Len Cawcutt.

The third encounter was a Layer Road thriller, a pulsating 120 minutes saw the full time score at four apiece – the Lions eventually going through 4–2 on penalties. Colin Garwood was almost in tears at the end of the evening, for he had scored a brilliant hat-trick, finished on the losing side, and missed in the penalty shoot out.

The first seven away League games provided just two points – drawn games at Bournemouth and at Roots Hall with Essex neighbours Southend. Against that a dozen fixtures at Layer Road produced maximum points, which was fortunate, for by the turn of the year the U's were too low in the table for comfort. In spite of that winning home run the first League gate to top the 4,000 mark was not until Boxing Day, when 6,007 turned up to see Aldershot beaten 1–0, Lindsay Smith scoring from a set piece.

The 12 wins at home produced 38 goals, with Hartlepool walloped 6–2 (another Garwood hat-trick), four being put past Torquay, Darlington and Southport and five in the Newport County net. There was progress in the F.A. Cup, although it must be said that a 5,000 plus crowd at the Abbey Stadium felt Cambridge United were very unlucky not to win. The U's managed a draw thanks to a Mick Packer penalty, and 1–1 was the score. Four days later Colchester won the replay 2–0. With over 6,000 in Layer Road, this was 2,000 more than any previous home gate for almost 12 months, and the finances received a much needed boost.

Two bites at the cherry were also needed before Brentford were beaten in the Second Round. The first meeting, on a dreadful Saturday afternoon, proved abortive, with Referee Sewell from Leicestershire calling proceedings off in midstream with neither side scoring. The game should have been staged again three days later, but once again Layer Road was not fit for the tie to proceed. Finally, on December the 20th, The Bees were beaten 3–2 at Layer Road, and Colchester had booked their place for the Third Round tie at Kettering.

One of the features of the early months of the season was the advent of Ian Allinson to first team status. At 19, He had made just three full appearances the previous season, and another up an coming home product – Steve Dowman (18) – were soon dragging the scouts to Layer Road.

When Crewe were beaten 3–2, Colchester kept up a record of never having lost to the Railwaymen at home. They were however, lucky to win that one, a goal from Allinson clinching the points when Alex. looked like getting a point.

Workington made their final visit to Colchester and lost 3–1, despite the heroics of Mike Rogan in goal. The referee in that match was Alan Gunn, the first of his many visits to officiate at Layer Road. The Reds failed to secure re-election at the end of the season but not before they won the return fixture at Borough Park 4–2.

The Youth team went down 9–1 at the Abbey Stadium in October in the F.A. Youth Cup; Andy Loveless scored the consolation goal. It was Cambridge United who also ended the League home run early in the New Year. A crowd of 7,639, a third of them visiting supporters, crowded into Layer Road, and it was the away fans who celebrated as their lads won a tense game 1–0. That was one of only two League defeats on the home pitch, Southend United inflicted the other in March, and also with a 1–0 scoreline.

All told it was a good season for the at home fans – one Cup and two League defeats only. The U's dropped just 8 League points out of a possible 46 at Layer Road

In the F.A.Cup, the tie at Rockingham Road against Kettering was won 3–2. Garwood got a brace, and he was on a purple patch at the time, scoring five goals in four games.

Derby County were the visitors in the F.A. Cup Fourth Round – they made it a memorable first trip, going home with a 1–1 draw. They won the replay 1–0 at the Baseball Ground, with 22,255 at that match. The Rams manager was so impressed with Micky Cook that he tried, unsuccessfully, to tempt him to move to Derby.

In the League it was just as well that the home record was good, for only six away fixtures were won all season. But the 12 points from those games just about enabled Colchester to scrape into third place and promotion in May.

There was in fact a most exciting climax on April the 26th, with five of the six top teams having four games to play and no one assured of going up. Cambridge United led the way with 58 points, with five matches to play, and in the final outcome took seven points from them to win the Championship. Exeter City increased their 26th of April tally of 54 points to 62 taking the maximum eight to take second spot. That left Bradford City, Colchester, Barnsley and Swindon Town contending the last two promotion places. It was the U's who really held the key to the situation, with Barnsley and Bradford City due to visit Layer Road, and they duly won both matches. These four points, plus two from an away win at Southport, earned Colchester the third promotion place, despite losing at Darlington. The last game of the season 2-1 win (with one own goal) over Bradford City was the clincher. City came fourth and Swansea, six points from their last four fixtures, failed by one point to get a move upstairs.

Seventeen players were used, three of them – Stewart Bright, Barry Dominey and Glen Ellis – made just eight appearances between them. Ellis came in when Mike Walker was injured in February. He let in just one goal and Colchester won both games. Steve Foley had a wretched time with injuries and managed only 10 outings. Cook played in all 46 League and 9 Cup games. Walker, Froggatt, L. Smith, Williams, Gough and Garwood all clocked up 50 or more senior appearances.

Bobby Gough, 18 League and 2 Cup, Colin Garwood 16 League and 8 Cup, and Steve Dowman with 12 goals were the leading scorers. Most of Dowman's goals came from – mainly centres – set pieces.

The Reserve team re-entered the Eastern Counties League – named the Magnet and Planet League – for the 1976/77 season. They had left the competition in 1959 to join the Combination, and later transferred to the London Mid-week League. With Ray Bunkell in charge, the very young squad found it hard going against opposing sides of older players. The finished 13th in the 20 strong League. Their record read:- P 40, W 14, D 8, L 18. Goals for 59, against 59. Points 36.

## OFF THE FIELD

During the season Gordon Parker the Vice-Chairman resigned from the Board. Maurice Cadman took over that position, and Harry Piper became a Director.

Vouchers for F.A. Cup Final Tickets were included in the programmes. Six vouchers collected from six home games entitled the person concerned to take part in the May ballot.

The programme was altered from the previous season, Measuring only 4½ by 7 inches, it was much reduced both in size, number of pages (16), and content. The front with a flash of red carried the Eagle motif and a picture with all the Players, Directors and other staff featured. Inside there was very little to read, for it was heavy with advertising, and poor value at 10p. This was reflected in sales, which at times dropped to well below 1,000 a game.

## 1977/78: DIVISION THREE AGAIN

Back in Division Three, Bobby Roberts still had to work on a tight budget with little or no money to spend on players. There were no new players when the fixtures commenced, but during the season three more home-produced youngsters, Russell Cotton, Tony Evans and Steve Wright were blooded in the first team. The departures during the close season were Stewart Bright, Barry Dominey and Lindsay Smith. Bright and Dominey, had graduated from the club's Youth and Reserve teams, but never quite fulfilled their early promise and were given free transfers.

Smith was a different story. He too had grown up at Layer Road and been a regular in the team since January 1972, and had twice previously asked, and been refused, to be transfer listed. When his contract expired in June he rejected a new one. He was loaned out to Charlton and then Millwall, and finally sold to Cambridge United.

Smith's departure led to a reshuffle in the defence with Steve Wignall coming in at left back after signing from Doncaster Rovers in September. He proved to be a bargain buy at £5,000. Mick Packer switched to central defender, with Steve Dowman alongside him, and Micky Cook at right back. With Mike Walker behind them in goal, only 44 goals were conceded in the 46 League games, and the U's – along with Cambridge – boasted the meanest defence in the Division. Unfortunately goals proved hard to come by, otherwise Colchester would have been there or thereabouts for promotion. They finally finished a creditable eighth in the table.

Bobby Gough with 13 League goals was top scorer – he also scored four in Cup games. Colin Garwood overall netted seven League goals, plus five in the nine Cup matches. No other player achieved double figures.

This lack of goals was a cause of concern throughout the season. John Froggatt led the line until into the New Year, but both he and Colin Garwood failed to produce the goods, and both eventually departed – Froggatt to Port Vale and Garwood to Boston. Eddie Rowles, signed in December from Darlington to provide extra firepower, only managed nine goals, scoring three goals before injury sidelined him for the last 11 weeks of the season.

The League fixtures started off well enough with the first three matches producing eight goals with just one conceded, and maximum points. Gough scored in each game and things looked good. Aldershot were also beaten by a 5-2 aggregate in the two legged League Cup First Round. Froggatt got two goals in the 4-1 Layer Road leg victory.

Things looked even better in that competition when a Garwood goal earned a 1-1 draw away to Blackburn Rovers. The replay at Layer Road attracted almost 6,000 spectators to see the U's demolish the Ewood Park side 4-0. The Lancashire team were then in Division Two, and of course Jim Smith was their Manager, which gave an added piquancy to the occasion. Needless to say, though gracious in defeat, Jim was not amused by the result.

A spectacular save Plymouth 'keeper Barron - but the U's still won 3-1 at Layer Road.

Strangely enough just five days before that Cup match Colchester had looked listless when losing their first League match, 1–0 away to Tranmere Rovers.

After that super win over Blackburn the Layer Road gates went on the up and up, and indeed held up well for most of the season.

Unfortunately, following a 3 goal home League win over Plymouth Argyle, the goals started to dry up, and the next three League encounters failed to produce any at all. Indeed, apart from a 3–2 defeat by Port Vale at Layer Road and a 3–1 victory at Carlisle, it was the end of October before there was any sign of any of the forwards recovering their shooting boots. Five other matches in that period failed to produce a single goal.

Meanwhile both the Reserves and the Youth team were banging in the goals. Russell Cotton led the way with a fabulous hat-trick when the Youth team beat Limbury Old Boys 4–2 in the F.A.Youth Cup. The Reserves, with Ray Harford in charge, scored seven in two games, Tony Evans and Phil Hopkins contributing four of them.

In the League Cup third round, Leeds United exacted revenge for that F.A. Cup defeat six years earlier, by dumping the U's 4–0 at Elland Road, with 17,713 at the game. Despite losing four away games in succession, and dropping home points with drawn games against Hereford and Oxford in early December, the U's were seventh in the table – five points behind leaders Wrexham. They had also made progress in the F.A. Cup.

Drawn away to Bournemouth, it took two trips to Dean Court before the tie was finally decided. The first match against the Cherries was drawn 1–1, Steve Leslie being the U's scorer. Three days later at Layer Road there were no goals. The toss of a coin determined a second replay at Bournemouth's headquarters, and this time there was only one team in it. Garwood scored three and Dowman the other, as the U's swept through 4–1. The next hurdle, at Watford, proved too much, and a 2–0 defeat at Vicarage Road ended Cup hopes for the season.

The next 12 League matches produced just one win – and that an unconvincing 2–1 victory at Bradford City. Seven games, five of them at Layer Road, were drawn, and there were away defeats at Shrewsbury, Chester, Preston and Hereford. Only 10 goals were scored in those encounters emphasising yet again the goal famine which afflicted the club, particularly in the second half of the season.

Promotion hopes had faded until three successive home wins, including a spectacular thrashing of Portsmouth in March, left the U's on the fringe of the leading pack. Tony Evans made his debut that month, played in a number of other games and looked a good young prospect, but injury ruled him out towards the end of the season.

It was downhill after that win over Portsmouth, for the goals dried up again. The last 13 League matches produced just 11 more, and three of those were scored in the away win at Port Vale. In six games the U's failed to find the net once.

When Wrexham visited in April the Welsh club, who were Division Three Champions had six internationals in their side. Steve Foley back in the team, after injury ruled him out for most of the first half of the season, scored the goal that enabled the U's to draw 1–1 in a match which provided the best football of the campaign. The campaign ended in May with 1–1 a home draw versus Sheffield Wednesday and 0–0 against Rotherham. The final gate of the season was down to 2,554.

The Reserves in their second season in the Magnet & Planet (Eastern Counties League) finished in eighth position. Steve Wright (son of Peter of the 50's and 60's fame) was the outstanding player in the side, and made his full first team debut against Swindon in April. Another of the 'Stiffs', Russell Cotton, was sub in that match.

## OFF THE FIELD

To sponsor the kit for a player cost £45; first and second strip shirt and shorts £20, boots and socks £15 and training shoes £10. The sponsor for a complete kit received two grandstand tickets, and refreshments in the Directors Lounge, for two matches of their choice.

A new "Three-'n'-Easy" competition was introduced – three chances for 10p. – and a guarantee of £300 in prize money each week.

There was an April highlight for 100 members of the Junior U's – the club run by the local paper, *The Evening Gazette* – who were taken on a special trip to Wembley. They were given a conducted tour of the Stadium, had a run down that famous tunnel, and walked up the steps to the Royal Box. There they posed for photographs, complete with a Cup loaned by the Wembley Stadium authorities for the occasion.

Also in April, Jack Charlton was back at Layer Road for the first time since he was in the Leeds side beaten in that epic Cup match. He came as Manager of Sheffield Wednesday and drew 1–1 in the penultimate match of the season. In the Board Room after the game he joked *"I got a better result today. Last time I was here the tight ground beat us, it looks a bit bigger today and I had warned my lads it was a bit of a furnace to play on".*

The programme for the season found even less favour than the midget issue of 1976/77. This was eight inches long, six inches wide, and awkward to handle, especially on a windy day at Layer Road. It still had a rather constipated looking eagle in blue and white shirt, standing on a football, on a bright red backing on the front. Priced at 15p, a 5p increase on the previous issue, there were 16 pages. To be fair there was a lot of reading inside, though the centre spread of Action Replay photos were not particularly inspiring. The print run varied between 1,500 and 2,000 per game.

*The Colchester Express* sponsored a Miss Colchester United. Julie Hewitt was the lucky lass. Even luckier according to some, was the Chief Steward at Layer Road, the one and only Stan Clough, for he chauffeured her to a variety of functions during the season; with of course the permission of his good lady Elsie Clough who dispensed the hospitality in the Boardroom and Director's lounge for many years.

This was the season when Colchester first encountered the player's agent phenomena. An offer was made for a player, with the permission of the club to whom he was attached. He verbally agreed to the terms offered, but two days later an agent phoned and said before the deal was finalised '£ xxx' would have to be paid to him, as the player was on his books.

In the 23 League games at Layer Road 105,158 passed through the turnstiles. Away from home 120,107 attended the 23 matches in which the U's played.

### 1978/79 – AN EXCITING CUP RUN

By August the only addition to the previous season's squad was Northern Ireland international Pat Sharkey. A midfield player, there was a strong school of thought before he even arrived at Layer Road that the signing was a mistake. He had been playing in the Football League for several seasons after Ipswich Town signed him from Portadown. Town sold him on to Millwall, the Lions in turn transferred him to Mansfield. By the time Colchester recruited him his total number of League appearances only amounted to just 55 in five seasons, and the doubts proved well founded. He was never fully fit and managed just five matches and one substitute appearance in the League, and two Cup games, in his season with the U's.

One of Pat's little foibles was that he liked to wear his International Cap at every opportunity. He also liked his Guiness. A real character off the field.

With Sharkey not filling the bill, either in midfield or up front, Bobby Roberts had to delve into the transfer market. Bobby Hodges and Trevor Lee both arrived early in the campaign. Hodge, 24 at the time, had made 128 League appearances for Exeter City. Lee, a big coloured striker had over 100 games for Millwall under his belt. Both quickly fitted in to the Roberts playing pattern and gave good service to the club.

Charlton Athletic were the first visitors to Layer Road in the League Cup match. They won 3–2 and though Colchester drew 0–0 at The Valley it was the end of the U's aspirations in that competition.

The League programme got off to a somewhat inauspicious start. A 2–2 draw at Layer Road with Swansea City in the opening game was followed by four matches in which the U's failed to get a solitary goal. To make things ever worse they lost 4–0 at Carlisle, the rout starting with a very dubious penalty. The U's were looking the better side when Mike McCartney scored from the spot. After that it was one way traffic as the Brunton Park team rubbed salt in the wound.

Reputations were retrieved somewhat when Chester were beaten 2–1, and Shrewsbury Town 1–0, both games at Layer Road. By October however, it was apparent that, while the defence looked sound enough, there were still shortcomings in midfield and up front. Few chances were being created, and Gough was ploughing a lone furrow up front. It hardly helped that Steve Foley after playing in 11 games spent a month side-lined with a reoccurrence of his knee injury. Steve Wright also missed seven matches, and even when he returned it was December before he was fully fit.

Up to the end of the year Colchester had managed just 20 goals in 20 League games. They had not won a single game on their travels, but at Layer Road they gave little away, until Watford, on the Saturday before Christmas, ended the unbeaten home League record winning 1–0. Ross Jenkins netted the crucial goal for the Hertfordshire team. Any thoughts of a promotion challenge had evaporated and there was a fair amount of barracking at Layer Road, especially when a very poor Bury side were let off the hook when they forced a goalless draw in early December. The gates suffered because of the indifferent form, to under the 3,000 mark. Financial Director Stanley Firth said in November that the gate receipts were in no way covering expenditure, for attendances of 5,000 plus were needed just to cover wages; only three gates all season exceeded that mark.

There was however, progress in the F.A. Cup. In the First Round Oxford United, also in Division Three, were the visitors and the U's won 4–2. Bobby Gough chose the occasion to score three, the only U's hat-trick of the season, Steve Foley got the other goal. Peter Foley and Jason Seacole scored for Oxford.

The Second Round draw brought about a trip to Leatherhead. Memories of that 1–0 defeat at Fetcham Grove five years previously came flooding back. And – believe it or not – Kelly "The Lip" was back at Leatherhead, would he once again prove a fly in the ointment? He did, for he scored again for the Surrey side and caused a few problems. But Bobby Gough got one past John Swannell in the Tanners' goals. The following Tuesday night under the Layer Road lights it was one-sided, with Steve Dowman scoring two in a 4–0 Colchester victory.

The New Year started with further progress in the Cup, a Bobby Hodge special accounting for Darlington in the third round, at The Feethams. By early February Colchester had made further progress, winning 1–0 at Layer Road after being held to a 0–0 draw by Newport County at Somerton Park. Gough once more netted the all important goal.

Even so the Colchester public were not exactly flocking to support their club, although the 7,029 gate was certainly a big improvement on the 3,920 who watched the Leatherhead replay. When the 5th Round draw was made, the U's suddenly found they had more supporters than they knew about! Everybody it seemed had been lifelong fans of the club and expected tickets for the visit of Manchester United. Shades of Leeds United – could Colchester do it again?

The same day as Colchester were winning the replay against Newport, Manchester United were a shade fortunate to beat Fulham in a replay at Old Trafford, Jimmy Greenhoff scoring as they won 1–0. And it was a Greenhoff goal after just three minutes that gave The Reds a 1–0 win at Layer Road on February the 20th.

The Manchester United team of all talents eventually lost to Arsenal in the final, but luck was with them at Layer Road, as Colchester were unfortunate not to get a replay. The visitors team read:– *Bailey, B. Greenhoff, Albiston, McIlroy, McQueen, Buchan, Coppell, J. Greenhoff, Ritchie, Macari, Thomas.*

*(I will never forget that Manchester United game. The worst snowfall for many years was affecting East Anglia. It was a horrendous two hour journey, to travel the 17 miles from my Sudbury home to Layer Road – the trip normally took 25 minutes. In and out of snowdrifts, detours, with the main road blocked by giant drifts, I just made it to Layer Road in time for the 7.30 p.m. kick–off. The return journey took even longer, and was even more hazardous. Even though the U's lost it was definitely a night to remember!)*

Apart from the Cup run the second half of the season was a bit of an anti–climax. Though they did not lose a home League match in the second half of the season, they drew five games at Layer Road, and with the away form continuing to be patchy there was no catching up with the front runners. The campaign however, ended on a high note, with a 5–1 win over Tranmere Rovers at Prenton Park, with Foley and Lee each scoring two.

Eighteen players were used during the season, but only a dozen played regularly. Walker again featured in all 46 League and 9 Cup games, whilst Cook missed just one League and one Cup match. Allinson was in the side for all 55 matches, though in one League encounter he came on as sub. Gough and Wignall both clocked up over 50 appearances.

Sixty League and 13 Cup goals were scored, with Gough (16 League and six Cup goals) as leading marksman. Lee who joined the club in November scored 11, all in the League, but no one else reached double figures.

League gates averaged 3,419, and only Tranmere Rovers with 2,179, had a worse attendance record in the Division.

**OFF THE FIELD**

John Hillier was released from his position as Commercial Manager in October. He had accepted a similar position with Highland League Club, Keith.

The Willhire Tournament raised £3,000 for club funds. Top players on the staff were on £95 a week. Stanley Frith at a Board meeting in August reported a profit of £28,937 on the previous season.

United's *"Three of a Kind"* lottery tickets sales which had been booming suffered a set back when Ind Coope and Greene King ordered that sales in their public Houses must cease. Apparently ticket sales had caused a big drop in one–arm bandit takings in the pubs!

Efforts to strengthen the playing staff – especially in view of the fact that both Steve Wright and Gary Harvey had pelvic problems – were unsuccessful. Offers for Graham Watson (Cambridge United) £12,500, Malcolm Crosby (Aldershot) available at £25,000, John Stone (Darlington) £20,000 and Brian Taylor (Plymouth), proved unsuccessful. Dave Wignall – Steve's brother was not kept, following a trial.

Eddie Keegan took over from Hillier as Commercial Manager with Kitty Watson as his assistant.

A print run of 18,000 programmes was made for the Manchester United Cup Tie, at a cost of £3,750, although only 8,000 were sold at the match. The Writer made the first broadcast from Layer Road with Tim Ewart, now a B.B.C. reporter, the link man in the Orwell Studio. The Broadcasting line for Radio Orwell was installed in the Press Box.

Pat Sharkey was transferred to Peterborough for £8,000 in March. Also during that month, Mr. Firth reported the club were in grave financial problems with an overdraft of over £55,000. There had been a trading loss on that current season, in May the figure was given as £82,142.

Two grants were received from the Football Grounds Improvement Trust. £50,000 in respect of the tarmacing, clubhouse and floodlights for the area that later became the Sporting U's headquarters, plus £2,980, for ground improvements under the provisions of Safety of Sports Ground Act 1975.

**1979/80 – SO NEAR AND YET SO FAR**

So near and yet so far was the story of the 79/80 season. The team hovered among the front runners and by the end of February 1980 they looked a sound bet for promotion to Division Two.

It was a Leap Year and tragically the U's took a leap in the wrong direction. From February the 29th, when they had 13 League matches still to play, only two more fixtures yielded maximum points, and six games were lost. This poor run–in to the end of the season wrecked any hopes of making Division Two. In the final analysis Colchester finished fifth in the table six points adrift of Sheffield Wednesday who won the third promotion place.

The U's made a pre–season trip to Germany to tune up for the final campaign of the 70's. Eight of the younger fans went over to see their favourites in action: Mick Gowlett, Dave Amass, Kim Anderson, Don Bacon, Geoff Jackson, Ken Craig, Bernie Anderson and Tricia Twitchett all came back to Colchester well satisfied with what they had seen, and Ken Craig forecast a successful season.

The pre-season German tour was a big success, where the U's played four matches. Schwarz Wein 2-2 (Gough and Lee), Duisberg S.V. 2-0 (Gough and Wignall), Hamborn 1-2 (Allinson), and the British Army XI 8-1 (Evans, Leslie and Lee 2 each, plus Allinson and Walker).

With the club still unable to afford transfer fees, Bobby Roberts had to rely on the players who had acquitted themselves well in 78/79. Steve Leslie, who only played in four early games in 1978 before breaking his leg, was fit to resume. Eddie Rowles another casualty the previous October returned to the team at the end of August. These two were to be invaluable performers in the season ahead.

Bobby Gough (who netted the second goal) in action during the Watford League Cup-tie

As usual the opening salvoes were fired in the two legged Milk Cup First Round. Hodge from the penalty spot and Gough gave Colchester a 2-0 lead in the home leg against Watford. The return at Vicarage Road was lost 2-1, therefore the U's went through 3-2 on aggregate; Hodge scored the all important goal in the away leg.

Sheffield United, managed by Harry Haslam, were the initial visitors in the League, and the U's first meeting with The Blades. Trevor Lee scored the only goal of the match. Things looked promising with a 2-0 win at Hull, but four days after that Rotherham spoilt things winning 3-0 on their Millmoor Ground.

The League Cup Second Round brought Aston Villa to Layer Road in the 1st leg. A gate of 6,221 was some compensation for the 2-0 defeat. The second leg at Villa Park attracted 19,473 spectators and the U's surpassed themselves by also winning 2-0, Gough and Lee getting the goals. Villa however, won on penalties to put paid to any hopes of further progress.

Sandwiched between the two League Cup games there was a 3-2 defeat at Layer Road by Swindon Town, and when the team lost 3-0 at Chesterfield and only drew 0-0 with Sheffield Wednesday at Layer Road, Larry in the programme was asking where the players were keeping their shooting boots.

He soon got an answer, for an unbeaten run of nine games followed. By the end of October their position in the table was just two points behind leaders Sheffield United - things were looking good. Gates had improved by almost 1,000 on earlier games. By the end of the year an unbeaten record in the 13 games played at Layer Road kept Colchester well in the promotion race - joint top with The Blades. Both teams had 28 points from 22 matches but as an indication of how tight it was at the top, there were ten contestants separated by just five points.

Earlier there had been a rap for Commercial Manager Eddie Keegan for allowing the following comment to appear in the programme, when manager Bobby Roberts was quoted as saying that the players did not like playing at Layer Road because the fans *"bombarded certain players with abuse"*. The Manager and the Board took exception to this and instructed that no comments of that type should appear in future programmes.

The F.A.Cup saw Colchester drawn at home to Plymouth Argyle. As it happened the U's had to travel down to Home Park in search of League points a week previously. They lost 5-2 in that first encounter and when Bobby Saxton's team drew 1-1 at Layer Road on November the 24th it looked as if it would be curtains in the replay in Devonshire three days later. After an overnight stay at The Holiday Inn however, the Colchester boys sprung a surprise, for they won 1-0, when Eddie Rowles was a hero that day netting the only goal.

December dawned with an excellent 2-1 win at Millwall. Steve Foley and former Lion's player Trevor Lee were the marksmen. Colchester's coach driver Graham Layzell missed seeing this one, for the police insisted that he remain with the coach parked outside the ground, for safety reasons.

Progress was made in the F.A. Cup when Bournemouth were beaten 1-0 in the Second Round. Alec Stock, The Cherries manager, saw his star striker Ted McDougall kept firmly in check by Steve Wignall. Eddie Rowles did it again scoring the all important goal.

The New Year saw the end of the Cup run. Reading, a bit of a bogey team to Colchester over the years, won 2-0 at Layer Road in the Third Round. January also saw an end to Colchester's unbeaten home League record with Chesterfield winning 1-0. This was the first home defeat since April Fool's Day 1979 when Shrewsbury took the points.

Blackburn Rovers became the only other team to get a result at Layer Road - 1-0 in March. These two home defeats went a long way towards denying the U's promotion, for both Chesterfield and Blackburn finished in the top four. Other contributory factors were a 3-0 defeat at Hillsborough, since Sheffield Wednesday - 6 points ahead of the U's - finished in third place and were promoted. Five other away fixtures were also lost.

For much of the season the same squad of players did duty, when only 18 players were used. Four of them - Bunkell, Dyer, Harvey and Cotton - played just 13 games between them, while conversely nine played in 40 games or more.

Milk Walker kept up his uninterrupted run in goal. He had not missed a League and Cup game since the 22nd of February, 1977, and all told made 54 appearances during the season.

Steve Leslie also had the maximum tally. The other regulars were Allinson, Dowman, Hodge, Foley, Lee, Packer and Wright. Injuries or illness kept Gough, Rowles and Wright out for a number of games, though all three were automatic choices when fit.

Trevor Lee, 17 League and 1 Cup goal was leading scorer, Bobby Gough (he missed 17 games through injuries) had 10 League and 2 Cup goals to his credit; Eddie Rowles (out for 20 matches) scored 8 League and 2 Cup goals. The average League gate was 3,818, the top crowd being 6,135, against Southend United.

Early in the season Micky Cook broke the Colchester United record for appearances when Aston Villa visited Layer Road in the League Cup on the 28th of August. The record was previously set by Peter Wright in 1965 with 452 appearances.

## OFF THE FIELD

A blueprint for the 1980's for the long term development of Layer Road proposed moving the playing pitch 23 feet towards the Spion Kop end, removing all the terracing from there, and building a new covered stand to ultimately seat 5,000 at the Layer Road end. On the side opposite the grandstand a new stand to incorporate seating and executive boxes was planned.

An architects impression of how the refurbished stadium would look was prepared, but like several previous plans to alter Layer Road it never came to fruition. Maurice Cadman, who was Ground Director at the time said in February that the scheme would cost £320,000 if acted upon. The money was never really available for such a radical scheme.

Martin Bennet, a Foreign Exchange market broker, who resided in Colchester took over from Betty Scott as Secretary in November – a Scot succeeding a Scot – for Betty was an Aberdonian, whilst Martin was born in Edinburgh and for his sins was a Clyde supporter. Betty Scott's resignation as club Secretary came as a result of being involved in a serious road accident earlier in the year, which affected her health. Betty – a popular and efficient Secretary – held the post for four years, first joining the club in 1970 as Dick Graham's Secretary.

At the start of the season the late Eric Pegram formed the Braintree Branch Supporters Club, which for much of the 80's made an outstanding contribution both to the financial well being and also the social side of Colchester United activities. Eric's Christmas parties became the big social occasion for several festive seasons.

Two directors, Trevor Dodwell and Stanley Frith, left the Board at the end of the previous season, whilst Robert Jackson, after a five year absence rejoined the Board on September the 10th.

The general meeting on November the 13th revealed that the 1979/80 season had shown a profit of £3,559.

On the stadium front there was a further development when ASDA (through agents) in April expressed an interest in acquiring Layer Road. The idea was to relocate Colchester United on a site between the River Stour and Colchester North Station. A new 30,000 all under cover stadium would be built for the club at no cost, and rent free in perpetuity.

Seating for 4,500 and under soil heating were other features of the scheme. Looking back it is interesting to note that it was in connection with this scheme that Jonathan Crisp and Eric Johnstone first emerged on the scene. Chairman Jack Rippingale met the pair who were interested in promoting the plan through Marketing Solutions. A £2,000 consultancy fee was mentioned. As will be seen later – despite detailed plans being prepared – the idea was eventually abandoned.

An F.A. Disciplinary Hearing in April fined the club for cushion throwing incidents at the Blackburn Rovers match on March the 8th. Bobby Roberts was also in trouble the same day when he too was fined and cautioned for using abusive language at Plymouth.

Dee Ellwood, later to become club Secretary joined the club as a part–time assistant in the Commercial Department. On the other hand Mrs.Marion Ling, who had been in charge of the bar and the refreshments in the Board Room and Directors Lounge for 12 years retired at the end of the season.

The new look programme, featuring Layer Road Larry on the front cover cost 25p, and the average print run was 2,000.

The extension to provide accommodation for the Vice–President's club – built on to the existing Directors Lounge – was completed during the season. A £2,000, ten year interest free loan from brewers Greene King helped to finance some of the cost. Bobby Roberts budget for the playing staff was set at £95,000 at the start of the season.

Micky Cook had a testimonial match on November the 15th, 1979 when 2,882 were present at Layer Road, with West Bromwich providing the opposition. Gough scored the only goal that night, and Roger Osborne appeared as a guest – his first appearance in a Colchester shirt.

CHAPTER 7

# Back To The Basement

Bobby Hodge's high flying shot is deflected by a Barnsley defender, in the 2-2 early season Layer Road Draw

After two seasons of just missing out in the promotion stakes there were high hopes when the 1980/81 season opened, of making it third time lucky. Things did not however work out that way, and when May came round Colchester were three from bottom and suffered relegation.

Once again they were a hard side to beat at Layer Road, but their away record was abysmal – only two wins on foreign soil – and it was this that led to the return to Division Four. Only ten goals accrued in the 23 away League fixtures. Goals were also hard to come by at Layer Road, 35 in all, and the U's total of 45 in 46 matches was (along with Blackpool's) the worst in the Division. Pre–Season 3,375 fans turned up at Layer Road to see West Ham held to a 1–1 draw. Dennis Longhorn, a close season free transfer signing scored the Colchester goal. In late July/early August the U's competed in the Willhire Cup losing 4–1 at Ipswich, 1–0 to Cambridge United and drawing 1–1 with Norwich City, the latter ties at Layer Road.

Other pre–season attractions were a 1–0 victory for Wolves in Steve Leslie's testimonial game and a 2–0 win over Norwegian visitors Kongsvinger. Alan Hunter and Kevin Beattie were in the Colchester line–up in the Leslie testimonial match.

During the close season, at the end of May, a touring party of 14 United players and officials had a week in Florida. They played one match beating Mirma Americans 1–0. Eddie Rowles had the honour of scoring Colchester's only goal in the United States. There were only 800 at the match.

Dennis Longhorn, Nigel Crouch and Leo Cusenza were the only new faces when Gillingham were the first visitors. The Gills won 2–0 in the League Cup First Round first leg and also won the return at Priestfield 2–1. All these newcomers played in that first game at Layer Road and all three were dropped for the away encounter. Cuzenza never played in the senior side again, Crouch managed just 11 games all season and Longhorn – though he figured in 25 League and Cup games – was in and out of the side.

The first 12 League fixtures yielded 12 points and only 11 goals were scored, and as in the previous season the team did reasonably well at Layer Road. In fact they had a 15 match unbeaten home sequence before losing to Exeter City at the beginning of February. Five of those however only provided one point each from draw games.

It was evident early on that there was a lack of firepower. To remedy this situation Kevin Bremner signed in October from Highland League club Keith for £25,000. He made his first appearance when he came on as sub in the 2–2 draw with Barnsley on October the 11th. From then until the end of the season he never missed a game, and soon became a crowd favourite with his no nonsense approach to the game. It took him time however to find the net, but he ended up with 10 goals.

Gough, troubled by injuries never found any sort of form in what proved to be his farewell season, and his final game was against Exeter City in February. The other striker to leave the fold was Trevor Lee. He was a great character, though Bobby Roberts undoubtedly pulled off a good stroke of business when he transferred him to Gillingham for £90,000 at the end of 1980. Lee had scored a spectacular game against the Gills just prior to his transfer, and presumably it was that which led the Kent side to seek his signature. This was the record fee, at the time, received for the transfer of a Colchester player.

> *I got into hot water over Trevor. He was playing in a match against Rotherham at Layer Road and I was doing a radio commentary on the match. During the game I inadvertently said "Lee is having an off colour game", which did not go down well in certain quarters. Trevor himself, when he heard about it, thought it was a huge joke.*

Considering that the scarcity of goals which put extra pressure on the defence, Walker in goal (an ever present yet again), Wignall and Packer in the middle of the defence and Cook at right back gave little away. The left back position however was never satisfactorily filled, and a study of the goals scored against revealed that almost 70 per cent of them were due to weakness on that flank. In ten of the defeats the margin was only a single goal, and there were 12 games where no goals were conceded.

At the start of April it looked as if Colchester might avoid the drop, for they had 36 points with six games left to play – in the end 41 points proved the safety target. Only three points however came from the last half-dozen fixtures, four of which were away from home. Swindon won 3–0 at the County Ground – a win that ensured their safety. A 0–0 draw at Gillingham kept hopes alive but the 2–0 defeat by Brentford at Layer Road really settled the issue. Though the season ended with Roy McDonough scoring the goal in a 1–0 win over Carlisle United, it was too late to save the day.

McDonough, then 23, was recruited from Chelsea in February and scored on his debut at Layer Road when Burnley were beaten 2–1. Also signed around the same time was Paul Coleman from Millwall, and Roger Osborne (Ipswich). In the last match against Carlisle Tony Adcock made his debut. These four players were to make an impact during the following season.

The F.A. Cup did provide some temporary uplift in a depressing season. Portsmouth were swept aside 3–0 at Layer Road in the First Round. The attendance of 5,837 was at the time the top gate of the season. Opponents in Round 2, Yeovil, brought back memories of epic cup–ties of yesteryear and The Huish men did it again. Wignall of Colchester and Green for Yeovil scored in a 1–1 draw. Four days later, after some hard talking and extra training stints, Lee and Bremner made amends scoring in a 2–0 win down in Somerset.

The best Layer Road crowd of the season, 7,769, was in attendance to see a Poskett goal prove enough to put Watford into the Fourth Round. That goal cost Colchester what would have been a lucrative home tie with Wolves in Round 4.

Twenty–two players were used during the season. Only Walker appeared in all 46 League, and six Cup, games. Allinson, Leslie, Packer and Wignall all appeared in 40 or more games.

Not a single player managed to score double figures in the League. Bremner managed 8 and scored 2 Cup goals, whilst Lee managed 7 plus 2.

The average home gate was 2,688, with only 1,430 at the last home match of the season.

### OFF THE FIELD

A 20 per cent increase across the board in the wages of the playing staff was agreed. It was recorded that this would increase the wage bill by £27,508 over a full year.

Admission charges for the season were: (Stand) £2.50 for bucket seats, £2 bench seats, Ground only £1.30 – juniors and pensioners 80p. Season tickets – Stand £50 and £45. Ground £26, and for senior citizens plus juniors £34 in the Stand and £16 for the Ground only. Stand seating was completed in all blocks by Olympic Seating at a cost of £4,708.

Ray Bunkell, who had been given a free transfer, was appointed Reserve Team Coach.

Steve Wright contracted hepatitis during the close season, and it was the end of December before he played a game.

New showers, in place of baths, were installed in the changing rooms, together with a new hot water system.

The bank overdraft stood at £52,000.

From the start of the season Kitty Watson and Dee Ellwood took over the running of the Board Room and Director's Tearoom drinks and refreshment arrangements, in place of Mrs. Ling. Mrs. Elsie Clough still ran things on Reserve team fixture days.

Steve Foley, the club Captain, signed a new three year contract, and the Board received a letter from him on behalf of the players thanking them for the holiday in Miami.

Just prior to the start of the playing season Steve Dowman, who had refused a new contract, was transferred to Wrexham for £75,000.

Miss Hilary Matheson was appointed, from the 1st of September 1980, as Sports Promoter under the Football and the Community Scheme. This was the forerunner of what later became the Sporting U's.

By the start of the season the Board had cleared the mortgage loan made to it several years earlier by the Football League, and the Deeds of the Ground, which they held, were returned to the club. These were then sent to the Borough Council who became the mortgagees.

The problems of crowd control emerged early in the season partly caused by the fact that at the time it was possible for opposition fans in the Layer Road end to taunt fans still outside the ground. This trouble spot was obviated by sealing the top of the backing wall.

Finance Director Harry Piper reported that in August, Colchester United were in the black to the tune of around £11,000 – the first time for several years. By the end of the season there was a substantial trading loss.

After eight years, Ray Cole was replaced as club physiotherapist. Brian Simpson took over (or one of his assistants when he himself was not available).

During the close season a Frisbee throwing weekend was held at Layer Road, but both that and a proposed car draw flopped. In September questions regarding these were raised, and also with respect to the Commercial Manager's trip to Miami, which cost the club over £350. That Miami venture ended with the players playing just one match in America instead of the three that were scheduled when the visit was sanctioned. There is no record in the club minutes that these matters were ever satisfactorily resolved.

The detailed plans for the development of a 65 acre site costing approx. £16 million with a Football Stadium and ancillaries costing £5 million was unfurled by Mr. Edward Mayhew at a meeting on November the 4th. Mr. Mayhew (it proved to be wishful thinking) estimated that outline planning permission would be given by early February, that site work would commence in September 1981, and the new football stadium would be ready for use in 1984.

In January 1981 Mr. Fitch reported that Royal London were prepared to sponsor the club again in the 81/82 season. A sum of £25,000 to £35,000 was mentioned. In February it was reported by the accountant that the Commercial Department had made a loss of £2,449 from the start of the season up to June 31st. Though advertising revenue of £21,211 had been received, it had been eroded by high running costs.

Dennis Howell, Minister of Sport, officially opened the Football and the Community new pavilion and facilities (later the Sporting U's), on Saturday the 14th of February.

## 1981/82 - ROBERTS GOES

After that poor showing in 1981/82 and relegation, the new season dawned with Hodge a regular in the 80/81 squad having departed, and also the two youngsters - Evans and Harvey who had not lived up to early promise. The big new signing was Roger Osborne from Ipswich Town, Colchester paying out £20,000 for his services. Roger will of course always be remembered as the man who scored the only goal at Wembley, in 1978, when Ipswich won the F.A.Cup. He proved a fine servant for the U's and an inspiration to the young players at the club. John Lyons was to arrive later after signing from Cambridge United, and two former apprentices, Perry Groves and Wayne Ward were promoted to the professional staff.

Pre-season preparations included a trip to Norway where Kongsvinger (2-2), Strommonil (1-0) and Aisn (5-0) were encountered in the ten day tour. Kongsvinger played a return game at Layer Road and won 3-1 towards the end of the season. The last match on May the 19th saw 2,775 attend for Steve Foley's Testimonial match, when Ipswich Town provided the opposition and won 4-0.

Bobby Roberts remained in charge until late on in the campaign when he was replaced by Alan Hunter, who made his debut in the final match of the season at Crewe.

For a change the opening fixture was a League game - a successful trip to Hartlepool. The lads no doubt refreshed by the overnight stay at Thornaby Post House won 3-1 with Bremner getting in the scoring groove with a brace. A Packer penalty accounted for the other goal.

For the second successive season it was Gillingham providing the opposition in the Football League Cup. A super 2-0 win at Layer Road followed by a 1-1 draw at Priestfield saw Colchester through to Round 2. Later, a 6-4 aggregate win over two legs against Cambridge United put the team through to the Third Round. This tie entailed a midweek trip to Prenton Park on a gloomy November night, where a Hutchinson goal saw Tranmere Rovers through to the quarter-finals.

After the initial League victory, the next three away fixtures were all lost, and while the home form was good, it looked as if hopes of a quick return upstairs were premature.

October however proved a good month, the five successive wins -17 goals for and with only two against - revived interest. Gates improved and by the time Wigan Athletic visited on the last day of the month the numbers through the turnstiles had risen to just under 4,000. The Lancashire side upset the applecart by winning 2-1, Coleman's goal for the U's being cancelled out by McMahon and Houghton scoring for the visitors. Even so Colchester were sitting in the leading pack with a quarter of the fixtures played.

Bobby Charlton was a Director of the Springfield Park side at the time and Larry Lloyd was in his first season as player/manager of The Latics. Wigan were so lucky to win that match, and Lloyd said after the game - *"With that sort of luck we should win the Cup"*. It was Wigan's first ever visit to Layer Road. After the game Chairman Maurice Cadman said that while recent attendances had been encouraging, gates of 4,500 plus were needed if the club was to break even.

Behind the scenes, in October, Colin Henson (who was now managing the Reserve team) introduced Rudi Hedman a 16 year-old - later to be a first-teamer, for an initial outing at Thetford.

After that surprise defeat by Wigan there followed an unbroken nine match run which yielded 13 points - just the sort of return to bring promotion hopes very much alive. At the end of January Colchester were third in the table with 43 points from 22 games.

There was also an F.A. Cup run that started with a 2-0 win over Newport County. Steve Leslie, who came on as substitute in place of the injured Roy McDonough, scored the clincher when County looked as if they might cancel out Ian Allinson's early strike. Weather conditions, from a hard frost, delayed the second round tie at Griffin Park. Keith Bowen, later to join the U's was in the Bees side, and Roberts scored for them in the 1-1 draw, with Allinson getting the Colchester goal. A McNichol 'own goal' decided the replay at Layer Road - the Bees actually had the better of the game. They were not unreasonably aggrieved by the 1-0 defeat, especially since Colchester had a plum Third Round draw away to Newcastle United.

What a surprise for The Magpies when Steve Wignall got above their defence to earn Colchester a 1-1 draw at St. James Park. Imre Varadi scored for Newcastle. The replay was a humdinger, when Newcastle finally won 4-3 after extra-time. Allinson put away two penalties, incurred by the visitors over robust tactics, and Cook got the other goal. Waddle (just starting to make a name for himself), Saunders, Brownlie and Varadi ensured progress for the Tyneside team.

Out of the Cup and with 24 League games still to play, promotion beckoned. Alas those 24 fixtures only produced another 29 points, for there was a dramatic slump in form. The goals started to dry up and more were conceded at the other end. At the end of January the goals for tally numbered 48 with 23 conceded. Only 34 were scored and the same number given away in that 24 match run in to the end of the season. John Lyons was signed from Millwall to try bolster the flagging hopes, and long term injuries to Steve Leslie did not help. Allinson and Wignall also missed a number of vital games, and in the end sixth place - 16 points adrift of the fourth promotion spot was a big disappointment.

Bobby Roberts, after a somewhat acrimonious interview with the Chairman Maurice Cadman was dismissed - a sad end to a season that promised so much earlier in the year.

The average home League gate for the season was 2,859, although 14 of the clubs in the Division had a lower average. Sheffield United with an average gate at Bramall Lane of 14,891 were by far the best supported team.

Three players, Walker, Cook and Bremner, played in all 46 League and 10 Cup games. Wignall, McDonough, Wright, Osborne, Adcock and Coleman all made well over 40 appearances. Allinson 21 (6 penalties) League and 5 (3 penalties) Cup goals was the leading scorer. Bremner managed 21 League and 3 Cup goals, and McDonough with 14 League 2 Cup goals, also reached double figures. Tony Adcock, who was soon to figure prominently as a striker, played most of the season as a winger and scored his first League goal against Torquay early in the season, adding five more later on. Why he was never played in the middle was a mystery.

## OFF THE FIELD

There was further discussion on the proposed Colne River Centre during the summer. In answer to a question from the local press, Chairman Jack Rippingale stated: *"That no agreement was in existence between Colchester United and either Land Assets or any of its individuals".*

It also emerged that Colchester Borough Council would require an amendment to the plans with the provision of a new tunnel under the railway line connecting with the existing British Rail ticket office and the widening of roads on the approaches to the proposed complex. It was becoming increasingly apparent that the whole scheme was unlikely to ever get off the drawing board.

The club were actively sponsored both financially and in off the field activities by The Royal London Mutual Insurance Society. One of their senior officials Brian Knights was a regular visitor to Layer Road and often travelled to the away fixtures. No doubt Brian and his wife will remember when another regular fan of those days, Reg. Nelson, booked them in at a Torquay hotel in the honeymoon suite, complete with four poster bed. Mr. Knights car was also suitably decorated.

Martin Smith - nowadays a sports reporter on a National newspaper - Chris Coppin, and Bruce Jackson, with Bernard Webber and the writer, comprised the Layer Road Press corps. Martin upset several people with his slightly astringent style of reporting - but full marks to him for he reported what he saw.

The basic total players' wages the previous season stood at £2,011 a week. The Board agreed that from the start of the 81/82 season a 7% increase costing an additional £145 a week would be given. In addition various bonuses were on offer, including a £5,000 pool bonus if the team won promotion.

The party of 22 players and officials who flew to Norway on August the 14th and returned on August the 21st, cost the club £5,646 including hotel accommodation. Harry Piper was the Director in charge of the party.

The club applied to the Football League to change 19 fixtures, home and away, to Friday floodlight games.

Policing at the ground for the season consisted of one Sergeant and ten constables (times have certainly changed, and it now takes time to count the number of police in attendance these days).

Mrs. Dee Ellwood was officially appointed as official Hostess in the Directors Guest Lounge. Seats giving access to the lounge before each game and at half time for refreshments were priced at £100. But admission to the lounge after the game was by invitation only. Some 25 people had purchased executive box seats by August. Tony Willoughby took over from Hilary Matheson in August at the Sporting U's. Ronald West joined the Board of Directors on August the 24th.

In December it was reported the club were seeking to extend to £100,000, the overdraft facilities at the bank. The possibility of turning the Sporting U's into a charitable organisation was under investigation.

## 1982/83 - HUNTER'S BRIEF STAY

Alan Hunter occupied the hot seat when Colchester played five friendlies in July 1982. Though two of them were against Eastern Counties League opposition, it was felt prudent to use senior players when Bury Town were outclassed 6-0. Felixtowe however proved doughty opposition and only a John Lyons goal separated the teams at Layer Road. Lyons also scored when Southend were beaten 3-1 and Orient 2-0. The other friendly, watched by 3,837 fans was lost 2-1. There were 2,082 spectators for Micky Packer's testimonial game, when West Ham provided the opposition, and Keith Bowen scored the only goal; the match was played at the end of the season.

There was no indication of the traumas to come in what was a happy preparation for the season ahead. Hunter had brought in Cyril Lee as his number two. Charlie Simpson was the club physiotherapist, and Kevin Beattie joined the playing staff. No one could have foreseen that Hunter would decide management was not for him, the tragic death of John Lyons, or that Mike Walker's long reign as 'keeper was approaching its end.

Only two of the first dozen games ended in defeat, both away, at Scunthorpe and Swindon respectively. McDonough scored the first goal of the new campaign when Halifax were beaten 1-0 at Layer Road. The one jarring note was Kevin Bremner's refusal to sign a new contract, he was on the subs bench for that opening match, and replaced McDonough who came off with a slight injury.

Bremner in fact made only 11 full appearances and he had loan spells at Birmingham, Wrexham and Plymouth before being transferred to Millwall for £25,000 in January. His final game for the U's was against Aldershot on December the 28th.

Perry Groves, signed as a pro. the previous May, and just turned 18, played several first team matches, scored twice, and looked very good, only for injury to rule him out for several weeks.

Progress was made in the League Cup with Aldershot beaten 3–0 on aggregate over the two legs. The Shots, after losing 2–0 at The Recreation Ground, made a real fight of it in the return before an Allinson goal finally settled things. It would have been different if Dale Banton had put away a clear cut chance for the visitors early in the game.

Goals from O'Berg and Angus against one from Osborne had sunk Colchester 2–1 at Scunthorpe's Old Showground stadium. After Southampton visited in the League Cup Second Round First Leg, they went away having had slightly the better of exchanges in a 1–1 draw, before a 7,967 crowd. Kevin Beattie made his full debut in that match, having previously come as sub against Blackpool in a League Match.

Kevin Beattie

Referee Malcolm Cotton who officiated at the Bloomfield Road match did his best to ruin the game as a spectacle. Pedantic to excess, he awarded 45 free kicks, 17 offsides, and on eight occasions he booked players, this resulted in very little time for football. The score was 1–1, and the gate a dismal 1,772.

In the Cup replay at The Dell, there were shades of Barry Dominey's dramatic winner in an F.A. Cup replay there almost 10 years earlier, but Colchester failed to come up trumps this time. Goal's from Wallace, Cassells, Armstrong and Moran gave Southampton a 4–2 victory. Allinson from the penalty shot and Lyons scored for United.

Beattie's attempt to resurrect his distinguished career did not last long. He played four full games in the middle of the defence (Hunter left himself out to accommodate his one time Ipswich partner). It was soon apparent however that his leg would not stand up to the rigours of League football.

Though still unbeaten at home in any game, away points were proving elusive, until November the 13th, when Adcock scored his first goal of the season. Allinson got two and McDonough one as the U's beat Tranmere Rovers 4–2 at Prenton Park. Adcock had injury problems in the first half of the season and only managed half–a–dozen appearances.

After that fine win on Merseyside hopes were high for F.A. Cup progress, when Torquay were at Layer Road in the next game. That match brought to an end Mike Walker's long run of consecutive games in goal. Between February the 26th 1977 and January the 1st 1983 he had played in 298 matches, a record unbroken sequence for a Colchester Keeper; he had also played in 40 pre–season friendly/testimonial games. No wonder Bobby Hamilton and Jeff Wood his understudies had moved on! Alec Chamberlain played in the next three League games and also the last match of the season.

John Lyons

Earlier in November, the club had been shaken by the tragic death of John Lyons, who hung himself at his Layer de le Haye home. The following month Steve Leslie broke his leg and missed the rest of the season. What with those incidents and Bremner moving on, little wonder that Alan Hunter decided management was not for him.

When Cyril Lea took over the U's had 36 points from 23 League games and were lagging behind the leaders. The remaining 23 fixtures brought in another 45 points, and in the end Colchester just missed out on a promotion place. What ended their hopes were three defeats in April, and especially the 2–1 loss to Port Vale at Layer Road.

Though they finished in style taking nine points from the last three outings, and scoring eight goals in the process, they ended up a tantalising two points behind fourth placed Scunthorpe. Adcock, who won a regular place in the team in January, scored 18 goals in 24 games, after Cyril Lea changed the playing style. He bought Bowen for £10,000 from Brentford, paired him with Adcock as twin strikers, and both produced the goods.

Allinson once again finished as top scorer with 22 League and 2 Cup goals, six coming from penalties, and Allinson played in all League and Cup games – 50 appearances in all. Adcock appeared in 25 League matches, made four substitute and one cup appearances. His 17 goals from 30 outings gave notice of things to come. McDonough scored eight goals.

This was Roger Osborne's first full season at Layer Road, at the age of 32, and he missed just one League match and played in every Cup tie – 49 outings in all, a tribute to his remarkable fitness. Wignall, Walker, McDonough and Phil Coleman all topped 40 appearances. The average attendance for home League matches was 2,552.

John Schultz joined the Board just before the League fixtures got under way. He was to serve the club well and was particularly involved in the development of the youth policy at Layer Road. Former Chairman Jack Rippingale left the Board at the end of August. A gentleman in every sense of the word, he was remembered also as the driver who put the wind up his passengers – Speedy Gonzalez had nothing on Jack. The writer was his passenger once on a trip to Darlington – never again!

## 1983/84
## FAREWELL TO THREE STALWARTS

The 83/84 season marked the end of an era for three of the finest professionals ever to grace United's colours. Mike Walker and Micky Cook had been fixtures in the team, Cook since 1970, Walker from 1973. Their full record of service on the field is documented elsewhere.

Steve Leslie, like Cook, had been at Layer Road since 1969. That was when he first appeared in a pin striped suit and rolled umbrella to be interviewed by Dick Graham. A studious type – seen reading the Financial Times on the team coach – he played in 375 League and Cup matches for the club. Like Cook, injury forced his retirement.

Walker remained on at Layer Road as player/coach of the Reserve team – he was later to be Manager. Cook came back to the club in 1992 as Community Relations Officer.

Micky Cook

Cyril Lea was in his first full season in charge, and he brought in Stewart Houston from Manchester United as his No.2. Money as ever was tight and apart from Houston the only newcomer of note was Tony Hadley from Southend.

Indeed if Lea had been allowed a bit more money to strengthen his squad early on it could possibly have been a promotion year. As it was eighth in the table was the final position. The team also reached the Third Round of both the Football League/Milk Cup and the F.A. Cup.

The first eight League fixtures produced 12 points – spoiled only by a 2–1 defeat to Tranmere Rovers at Prenton Park. Houston (scoring in his debut game) and Tony Adcock got the season off to a fine start with a 2–0 win at Darlington. But Bristol City took a point from a dull game at Layer Road, devoid both of goals and incident.

Adcock scored six in these early games and it has to be remembered that in the team, besides the red haired striker in his first full campaign, Andy Farrell on his debut in the back four, Alex Chamberlain in goal, and Perry Groves, were all youngsters just edging their way into the senior squad. The two legged First Round Milk Cup games with Reading produced 12 goals, six for each side. The U's progressed on their away goals tally, Adcock scoring three of these goals.

Colchester were away in Round 2 to Swansea City, a Division Two side. It was an Adcock goal again that earned a 1–1 draw at The Vetch Field. The team stayed overnight at Penarth where Alec Chamberlain had an uncomfortable night, his 6'2" frame hardly fitting into a very small bed.

There were away defeats at York and Swindon before the replay with The Swans. The gate at Layer Road for the first time that season topped 5,000, and there was a great atmosphere when that man Adcock knocked in the goal on 40 minutes that dumped the Welsh team. He got the better of Emlyn Hughes before netting; but for Jimmy Rimmer making a fabulous save, he would have had another in the second half.

Lea's first signing of the season was Ian Phillips, a 25 year old left back, and a one time Ipswich Town apprentice. Shortly afterwards Jeff Hull, recovered after a long injury lay off, returned to the side and this pair added strength to what had earlier been a vulnerable left flank.

By mid–October, Colchester's three teams had played 30 games between them with just six defeats. The first team were sitting in fifth place, Colin Henson's Reserve Team led the Eastern Counties League, and Roy Massey's Youth Team had lost just one Border League and Cup game. Against Ipswich in the Southern Junior Floodlit Cup, the lad who did the damage in that 2–1 defeat was Jason Dozzell, who of course went on the bigger and better things as his career blossomed.

Mike Walker, who in his senior days had hardly a blemish on his record sheet was sent off, for clattering an opponent in an Eastern Floodlight Competition game at Heybridge Swifts. This dismissal was something of a sensation at the time.

Two home wins against Crewe and Reading, and a 3–3 draw at Doncaster in the League, put the players in good heart for the visit of Manchester United in the Milk Cup 3rd Round. Adcock scored four goals in those three matches and was obviously on song.

The Reds with Ron Atkinson manager, brought a talent laden team to Layer Road for the tie. The previous season Colchester's balance sheet showed wages and salaries cost the club £244,000.

In the Manchester side was Bryan Robson – the fee paid for him from West Brom. would have paid the U's wage bill for the next six seasons. Old Trafford games were bringing in about £50,000 a match, Colchester's 23 home games just about totalled that in 1982/83. It was therefore very much a 'Rich v Poor' meeting. For Steve Leslie it was a match to savour, as it marked his 450th game for the U's in League and Cup matches.

Ron Atkinson was no stranger to Layer Road since he had been there with Oxford in his playing days, and also during his stint as Manager of Cambridge United, when he was a pretty regular visitor.

A crowd of 13,031 packed in Layer Road for the tie. The U's lost 2–0 but were by no means outclassed by a Manchester side which read:– *Bailey, Duxbury, Albiston, Wilkins, Moran, McQueen, Robson, Moses, Stapleton, Whiteside (Macari) Graham.* Tom Bune was the referee, and McQueen and Moses got the goals. The Colchester team included six players – *Chamberlain, Cook, Farrell, Leslie, Adcock and Groves* – who could claim to be home produced.

Shortly after that epic, it was down to Torquay. Yes – It was Plainmoor yet again in the F.A. Cup! Keith Bowen scored both goals as Colchester avenged their defeat there in the first round the previous season. A week later the Gulls had their revenge. Was it walking up that steep hill from the Oreston House Hotel that tired the troops, for they looked listless, and lost 2–1, in a League game.

However, in the next home match the U's trounced Hartlepool 6–0, and were in good heart when it was Wealdstone of the Alliance at Layer Road – their first ever visit – for the F.A. Cup Round 2. Bowen scored three on this occasion, and Houston the other, to see Colchester through 4–0.

On the last day of the old year a workman inadvertently led to a wasted journey down to Hereford. The home side were leading 1–0 after 68 minutes when the Edgar Street floodlights went out. It transpired that a workman making an excavation outside the ground had cut the power cable. Still there was a bright side – when the fixture was replayed on April the 4th, the U's got a point, in a 1–1 draw.

From a League points angle the second half of the season was not over productive. But there was more Cup action before the curtain rang down on an eventful nine months. A Houston own goal led to a Third Round exit from the F.A. Cup, losing 1–0 to Charlton of the Second Division before a rather disappointing 6,296 crowd.

The introduction of the Associate Members Cup caused a heavy programme load in the last 10 games of the season. Eighteen games were played between March the 1st and May the 11th, when the extended season finally ended.

The A.M.C., eventually won by Bournemouth, was hardly a success. Colchester had two home ties, beating Wimbledon 2–1, and losing 2–0 to Southend. Only 1,888 were at the Dons game and 2,841 to see the Blues encounter.

As ever Colchester proved hard to beat at Layer Road, they had not lost in 22 home League fixtures when York City ended the run, winning 3–1 in March; York won the Championship with a record 101 points.

Tranmere were successful at Layer Road in the next home game, and two reverses in succession at Layer Road caused consternation.

The Reserves finished third in the Eastern Counties League with an unbeaten 14 match run to end the season. Micky Cook, who had been injured, played in the last but one game at Clacton, his final appearance in Colchester colours.

Twenty players were used during the season, with Chamberlain playing in all 56 Cup and League games. Bowen appeared in all 46 League matches, and missed one of the 10 Cup encounters; Houston, Hadley and Adcock all made over 50 appearances.

Adcock, his first full season in the team, with 26 was the leading scorer in the League, and grabbed 7 in Cup matches. Bowen got 12 in the League and 8 in the Cup. The average gate for League matches was 2,220.

Eight players who were all products of Colchester's youth team appeared during the season. Cook of course was an established member of the team, as was Leslie. Groves and Adcock became regulars in the senior squad, and Andy Farrell laid claim to a permanent place the following season. For John Taylor and Craig Oldfield – both of whom were prominent in the Reserves – it ended in disappointment when they were released at the end of the campaign. Taylor re-emerged later and starred for Cambridge United and Bristol Rovers, whilst Oldfield was still banging in the goals at non-League level in 1992. Rudi Hedman had the misfortune to get glandular fever but recovered well to claim a place in the 1985/86 squad.

During the close season Ian Allinson left the club in not the happiest of circumstances. The player claimed freedom of contract on what was a technicality, and after three lengthy F.A. hearings he was given a free transfer. Before the last, Allinson was all set to join Fulham, but immediately after the last hearing he joined Arsenal. In fact a Director of the Highbury club was on the panel which gave him a free.

Allinson had played in every match the previous season and scored 24 goals. Not only was he missed as player, but the club lost what should have been a substantial transfer fee.

(An amusing incident at Elm Park before the Second Leg of the Milk Cup can be related). The writer, who had undertaken the Radio commentary on the First Leg at Layer Road, was having a quiet drink with fellow scribe Peter Jones. Two Reading fans on the same table were chatting together. One of them said: *"I couldn't get to Colchester but I listened on the Radio, some bloody Yorkshireman on, couldn't understand what he said"* !

This was the first season where the home team retained all the gate receipts.

### 1984/85 – OLD FAVOURITES MOVE ON

There were three new faces in the 12 who did duty for the U's in the opening match of the 84/85 season, when Southend provided a derby day opener.

Keith Day, signed from Aveley, and Daryl Godbold released by Norwich City, both figured in the defence. An ex-Portman

Road player Russell Irving was on the bench and came on in place of Adcock ten minutes from time. Adcock scored all Colchester's goals in a 3–3 draw. In fact he started in majestic fashion scoring 12 goals in the opening dozen League matches. Noel Parkinson was the only other close season signing.

When the coach left Layer Road for the first away match at Scunthorpe, there was an unfamiliar look about things. Missing was Cook from the second seat back on the nearside, his 'pew' for so long. Further back across the centre aisle the Liverpudlian tones of Steve Wignall were heard no more. While at the rear there was no Steve Leslie displaying his holey socks with feet up on the table – darning was not one of his strong points! Graham Layzell – now re–christened Fletch – was still at the wheel. The passage of time grinds relentlessly on.

An early setback was a 2–0 Milk Cup defeat by Gillingham at Layer Road. The U's had much the better of the game, they had 12 corners against The Gills two, but just could not get the ball in the net. Mark Weatherley converted two of the three clear cut chances that fell to the visitors. As the U's had earlier lost 3–2 at Priestfield there was to be no repetition of the 83/84 run.

It was amazing how many times Colchester and Gillingham clashed in Cup matches in the early 80's. Two League Cup meetings in 1980, two in the same competition the next year, two more meetings in 1984, and an F.A. Cup Second Round encounter the same year. They also played the Gills in the Freight Rover Cup.

Colchester won the Cannon Fourth Division Goal Scoring award for August/September. The U's and Bury had both hit 15 in the period, but the U's took the award by scoring more away goals than the Lancashire club. The sad thing was that the goal scoring feat had little impact at the Layer Road turnstiles, with under 2,000 at every game.

Two home defeats in October, one against Halifax who were rock bottom of the table, did little towards attracting more paying customers, though there were two good away wins at Chester and Darlington.

When Exeter won 4–3 at Layer Road it was the first time in ten years since four had been conceded at Layer Road – previously Hereford had won 4–1 on January the 24th, 1975.

Hopes that the F.A. Cup would rekindle interest were high after a 2–2 First Round draw at Southend. Irving scored after three minutes at Roots Hall and Houston on 21. The replay on November the 25th went Colchester's way, 3–0. Bowen and Adcock scored and Glen Pennyfather contributed an own goal. But that was as far as Colchester went in the competition, for Gillingham again proved too good and won the Second Round tie at Priestfield 5–0, with David Shearer, Tony Cascarino and Dave Mehmet leading the Colchester defence a merry dance.

Prior to the F.A. Cup tie, six out of the 17 League games played had been lost, and with 28 points the U's were in a mid–table position. A 2–1 defeat at Swindon followed the Cup exit. Later, with Phillips, Houston and Hull out with long term injuries, things were looking very dicey indeed. Houston returned to the team in the New Year, but Hull never played another first eleven game that season. Houston's shoulder that he dislocated caused problems again later, and Phillips with a hairline fracture of the femur missed nine games.

Rudi Hedman, who made four appearances the previous season, and Russell Irving, got an extended run as a result of those injuries to others. Both held their places for the rest of the season. Hedman missed the early games though glandular fever.

The other bonuses were the performances of Keith Day, who stepped straight into the side and made the centre–half role his own, and Andy Farrell (19 at the time) who came in at right back. Late on in the campaign Simon Burman took over from the injured Phillips.

A 12 match undefeated run from Christmas time to early March got the team back in a challenging position on the fringe of the promotion race. They took 25 points from the ten League games played. Another confidence booster was a 4–2 win over the old enemy Gillingham in the Freight Rover Cup first round. The U's drew 2–2 at Priestfield and an Adcock brace made it 2–0 at Layer Road.

Match action versus Hereford (Boxing Day 1984)

Keith Bowen and Ian Phillips both compete for this high cross supported by Parkinson and Adcock.

With 53 points in the bag and 19 League games still to play, Cyril Lea – by now confirmed as manager after his caretaker capacity – blooded Tony English in February. With so many injuries still plaguing the club he came in on the left flank, either in midfield or at left back, in place of Phillips.

Stockport County ended the unbroken League run, winning 1–0 at Edgeley Park, that ended as a tragedy for Chamberlain. He kept Colchester in the game only to put the ball in his own net, for what proved to be the only goal.

Chamberlain, 11 days later, played his 100th game for the club against Darlington, as did Keith Bowen. Irving (he scored four goals in three games) got one for Colchester. Carl Airey and long serving David McLean both netted however, as The Quakers won 2–1 at Layer Road. This defeat and losing away games at Hereford, Hartlepool and Aldershot cost Colchester a promotion place. All three away setbacks were by just a single goal. In the final count Colchester finished seventh, 10 points adrift of the fourth promotion place.

In the Freight Rover Trophy a visit to Fellows Park proved beyond their capabilities, in the Second Round, with Childs scoring the only goal before 4,108 fans.

In retrospect a lengthy injury list was probably what put paid to a move back into Division Three. In addition to the previously mentioned absences of Houston, Hull and Phillips, Osborne (a key figure in midfield) missed four games in April, being a victim of a flu epidemic going the rounds at the time. Paul Shinners signed on loan from Gillingham in April, after being booked in his first game, picked up an injury and missed part of one game and the whole of another.

On the plus side home produced youngsters Rudi Hedman, Simon Burman, Tony English and Stuart Youngman, all sampled League football. With Adcock, Farrell and Groves, all former apprentices having become established first–teamers, it was apparent that Colchester's youth policy was paying off. Chamberlain was proving a worthy successor to Walker, and by the end of the season had made 111 consecutive appearances, and was once again an ever present (54 games) in the side. Keith Day missed just 1 League and 1 Cup game, making 52 appearances in all. Groves missed two matches, due to suspension after being sent off at Darlington. Parkinson missed two early League and 1 Cup games, whilst Phillips, Farrell, Osborne and Irving all played in 45 or more matches.

Tony Adcock, with 24 League and 1 Cup goal, was by some distance the leading marksman. Keith Bowman 17 (3 penalties) in the League and one in the Cup, came second. Perry Groves scored 11 and Russell Irving 10.

The average home League gate was 144 down on 1983/84 at 2,220, but it was still better than that of nine other clubs in Division Four.

### ENTER MR. CRISP

The 2nd of May 1985 will always be remembered as the day when Millionaire business man Jonathan Crisp reappeared on the Layer Road scene.

He made a successful £150,000 takeover bid which was given approval at an Extraordinary meeting of the club's shareholders. He purchased £75,000 of the club's shares which gave him a controlling interest. The other half of his investment was in the form of a six–year loan, serving as a mortgage on the U's property.

Crisp, 39 at the time, joined the Board and brought with him one of his employees, former Ipswich journalist Eric Johnstone, who also became a Director. Although born in South Africa, Crisp had East Anglian links, and had also been interested in Ipswich Town, but not in any official capacity. At one time he also looked likely to join the Reading Board.

He told the shareholders on that fateful night that the money he was putting in would:

Remove the burden of back debts and the expense of servicing them.
Remove the necessity to sell assets, i.e. the club's promising young players.
Create security for the existing staff.
Help to improve the ground and give better facilities to the fans.

He also stated his aim of guiding the U's to the Second Division of the Football League in five years. How far Mr. Crisp was successful in those worthy aims unfolds over the happenings of the next five seasons.

At the time Colchester, in common with many other clubs, were in low water, and Chairman Maurice Cadman said unless new money came in there was a distinct chance of the club folding; at the time the U's were in the red to the tune of just over £140,000.

*"Exciting new era for the U's"*, said the headlines. Yes, there was certainly plenty to talk and write about during the seasons ahead. Excitement yes – but eventually the club ended up in The Conference and were saddled with massive debts.

There can be no doubt that Jonathan Crisp rescued the club in crisis, and that his intentions were to really put the U's on the map. No one should doubt that he also felt that he could lead the club to new horizons and that at the start his heart and soul went into his new found interest. But like many others who have put money into football clubs, and felt that as successful business men they could apply their methods to the task in hand, Mr. Crisp found that it was not quite as easy as that. Again in common with many others, once he became Chairman, he soon made it evident that he wanted his own men round him.

There were blushing cheeks at Layer Road when Newmarket Town visited Layer Road on January the 21st for an Eastern Counties match. The Jockeys 'keeper, when his track suit trousers lost elasticity, had to do a bare faced change behind the Layer Road goal. He got three new fans from some young lady spectators in the Stand!

Ton Cheney the groundsman died early in 1984. He was 63 years old, and had been tending the pitch at Layer Road for 10 years.

Adcock scored the quickest goal of the season, when he netted after 11 seconds in the game with Aldershot at Layer Road on December the 27th. There had been other changes at Board level in the close season of 1984 well in advance of Mr. Crisp's arrival. Ron West, a wealthy local business man had quit, and Gordon Parker after several years absence, returned to the Board.

## 1985/86 - TOP SCORING TEAM

The 85/86 season saw the U's finish a creditable sixth in the Fourth Division. It was also a campaign of big chances both on and off the field. Maurice Cadman was Chairman and Cyril Lea manager when the fixtures got underway in August. When the last ball was kicked in May, Jonathan Crisp was in the chair and Mike Walker was caretaker/manager.

The average League gate, at 2,076, was 251 up on the previous season. Ten fourth division clubs were worse off, and only 11 teams in the section increased their support.

The team in fact played some attractive football, and with 88 goals were the top scoring side in the division. With 51 of the strikes coming at Layer Road, and just 22 goals conceded at home, there was no lack of entertainment for home supporters.

John Reeves, recruited from Fulham, was the only new face in the line-up when Stockport County provided the opening day opposition at Layer Road. With various other summer attractions, the gate, not surprisingly, was well under 2,000. It was also an 11 a.m. kick-off. Perry Groves had to come off injured - Reeves coming on as sub - and goals from Adcock, Day and Osborne ensured a 3-1 win.

The gate was even lower for the mid-week Milk Cup-tie, with Millwall, only 1,430. Though Keith Bowen got a brace, The Lions won 3-2 - two of the Millwall goals came from Steve Lovell penalties. Colchester lost 4-1 in the second leg at the Den, and that was the end of interest in that competition. Interestingly Paul Hinshelwood was in the No. 2 shirt for Millwall in both games, he came to the U's later on.

Up to the end of September nine games, four away, produced 21 points. All five home games were won, and there were away wins at Prenton Park and Brisbane Road.

Adcock was once more knocking goals in regularly, eight at the end of September, including a hat-trick against Cambridge United, whilst Bowen with three League and three Cup goals was also on song.

There were three player milestones in those early encounters. Roger Osborne made his 300th Football League appearances against Cambridge. The next match away to Orient marked Adcock's 150th game for Colchester, then against Port Vale, Ian Phillips clocked up his 250th League game.

October was not quite as good a month. Losing 2-0 at home to Northampton Town and drawing the other two matches at Layer Road, was a bit of a let down after the earlier home successes. A 4-2 victory at Southend was a triumph for Groves who smashed in three. In this match at Roots Hall, Keith Day dislocated his shoulder for the second time.

Refurbishment of the Layer Road end of the Ground - Summer 1985

He suffered this injury to the same shoulder at Burnley on October the 1st. This second dislocation led to him missing the next four games.

November was a black month – there were defeats at Hereford and Chester plus a home defeat by Rochdale, also a swift F.A. Cup exit at Wycombe. Day was sadly missed from a defence that conceded 12 goals in those four encounters. It was Rochdale's first ever win at Layer Road. Robin Turner and Tom English made their debuts in that game. English came on as sub in place of Turner, but neither player exactly shone.

In the Cup match at Wycombe, Colchester never got to grips with the Loakes Park slope, and goals from Read and West put The Swans into the Second Round. Kirk Game deputised for the injured Day at centre half against Rochdale and at Wycombe. A big lad he looked a real prospect but never quite lived up to his early promise.

> *Though I was at the match at Deepdale when Colchester lost 3–2 to Preston North End I only saw three of the goals. I suffered a black-out, while broadcasting, in the Press Box and can only remember being carted out and being revived by the Preston club doctor. One thing I will never forget was Cyril Lea's kindness and concern for my welfare. I have never forgotten that, or the support given to me by everyone on the coach on the long night journey home.*

Severe weather restricted the December programme to three games, a win, a draw and a defeat. Trevor Whymark played in a couple of matches, but at 35 the one-time Ipswich Town player was obviously not up to Division Four helter-skelter. The 4–2 success over Wrexham at Layer Road on December the 20th was a welcome relief, it came after six defeats in a row.

Some lost ground was made up in January. Simon Burman was given an extended run in the team, but Andy Farrell, Stuart Houston and Keith Day all missed matches through injury. Day dislocated his shoulder again at Swindon on New Year's Day, he had it put back, but it came out of joint once more in the following match with Hereford. He had to have it pinned and did not appear again until April. Terry Baker, a one time West Ham apprentice, replaced Day in the squad. He remained in the Number 5 shirt for the rest of the season.

For the last two months of the campaign injuries, illness and loss of form by one or two players posed problems. Adcock ill for the last 13 games, Noel Parkinson missed all the matches in April and May, and like Turner was completely out of touch.

Crisp dropped a bombshell on April the 9th when he sacked Cyril Lea, and Houston left at the same time. The Manager and the Chairman had not seen eye to eye for some time and it was said that matters came to a head over the signing of a player against the Manager's wishes. Whatever the reason, Mike Walker was asked to stand in. His first four games in charge produced two away draws, and two home wins, with 13 goals for, 4 against, and 8 points.

In the four successive home games Tom English scored three against Preston, not to be outdone his brother Tony also scored three against Peterborough.

The last away game at Cambridge, was a stormy encounter, which Colchester won 3–1. The referee, Gilbert Napthine from Loughborough, booked eight players. Brothers Tom and Tony English were sent off and Andy Farrell was booked. A well known Cambridge journalist who was reporting the game, dropped a classic in his match summary. He had earlier been at Fenners for the opening of the cricket season and had obviously wined and dined well. In his summary he stated: *"Referee Napthaline inflamed the situation by producing his book at every opportunity".*

In the Freight Rover Trophy, Colchester beat Southend 4–1, Groves scoring a hat-trick against The Blues for the second time in the season. However Colchester lost 2–1 to Northampton and failed to qualify for the Southern Section Quarter Final.

During the season 22 players were used. Alec Chamberlain played in all 46 League and five Cup matches. Tony English with 45 and 5, Groves 43 and 5, Phillips 37 and 3, Houston 36 and 5, plus Hedman 39 and 5, were the others with 40 or more appearances.

Adcock scored 15 goals in 33 League games and 1 Cup goal. Groves 12 League and 3 Cup, Tom English 11 (3 penalties) and Tony English 10 (all in the League), were the other main marksmen.

Though Cyril Lea was not everyone's cup of tea, the fact remains that he performed miracles during his stay at Layer Road. The following season the team continued to perform well. But looking back it has to be said that the slide in playing fortunes began when Cyril, and then Mike Walker, were dismissed by Chairman Crisp, at a time when the playing record was satisfactory.

## OFF THE FIELD

The programme for the season once again was not too popular with supporters. An awkward size that did not fit into the pocket without folding, and what was described in one paper as "a garish front"; blue background with a diagonal stripe across the centre carrying an action shot in an anaemic looking red tint. It was priced 30p.

Inside, on Page 3, there was an innovation with head and shoulder pictures of all the Directors plus Antony Buck Q.C. M.P. the club patron, Roy Chapman the president, and Martin Bennet – club Secretary – in a white circle on a blue background.

John Myatt, the B.B.C. "Look East" sports reporter contributed a column in each programme.

## 1986/87 – A BUSY BUILD UP

With Mike Walker confirmed as manager the 1986/87 campaign opened with a whole series of pre-season warm up games. Sixteen in all were played involving the senior squad, the reserves and the youth team. Altogether 43 different players were used with Walker taking an early opportunity to see the talent available at all levels.

Scott Young, then still a Y.T.S. boy, scored eight goals, appearing in the squad at all three levels – easily the leading scorer. Highlight of these warming up games was a visit to

Arsenal, and though the team lost 4–0 it was an experience, for none of the lads had ever played against The Gunners previously.

The season opened with a 3–1 defeat at Lincoln, a 1–1 home draw with Exeter in the League, and a goalless Littlewoods Cup draw with Peterborough at Layer Road. In those early matches Sean Norman made his senior debut and Scott Young and Mark Radford were blooded in the Cup match with Peterborough.

Perry Groves

The other big news items were the sale of Perry Groves to Arsenal, the signing of two experienced players – Paul Hinshelwood and Nick Chatterton – and Tony Adcock breaking his arm in training. Perry Groves who was transfer listed at his own request joined Colchester as a trainee. He made his senior debut just nine days before his 17th birthday on the 17th of March 1982, played a total of 155 League and 28 Cup games, and scored 32 goals before joining Arsenal. It was a really eventful September.

Losing the second leg by 2–0 at Peterborough meant a quick exit from the Littlewoods Cup. The Posh, not for the first time, seemed to have the Indian sign over the U's. They beat them again, 3–1, in the League at the end of September. There were however three successive wins at the beginning of the month, though Walker was not too pleased with the defence that leaked 14 goals in those early matches.

October produced 13 points from seven League games and there was a noticeable tightening up of the defence with Andy Farrell returning to the side. Adcock no sooner returned after recovering from a broken arm than he was struck down by a mystery virus. He was out of action until the end of November.

Stephen Grenfell, a 20 year–old, arrived at Layer Road on loan from Spurs (he was later recruited on a permanent basis), and went straight into the side against Wolves. The attendance for that match, which ended in a fine 3–0 win, was more than double the early gates, at 4,741.

In spite of a formidable injury list, and the early departure of Groves, the U's were in fourth place in early December though well adrift of runaway leaders Northampton who had only lost one game. Progress was also made in the F.A. Cup, Bishops Stortford held the team to a 1–1 draw on their home ground, but lost 2–0 in the replay.

The draw for the Freight Rover Trophy brought Peterborough United to Layer Road yet again. It was third time unlucky for Posh, a 2–0 win was sweet revenge after the two earlier meetings had gone the visitors way. There was however to be no F.A. Cup run. Early in December there was an abortive trip to Aldershot. The Shots, with Steve Wignall in their ranks, winning 3–2. Five days later it was also goodbye to the Freight Rover Trophy – following another trip to the Recreation Ground. This time the Shots won again, 4–2. Richard Wilkins in the Colchester team for his first full game scored both the goals, having joined the club from Haverhill Rovers.

A New Year's Day trip was made to Northampton, when it poured with rain – and there was little shelter for observers – saw Colchester lose a real thriller by the odd goal in five. Hinshelwood made his 400th Football League appearance that day.

The visit to Exeter City on January the 17th caused some major headaches. Heavy snowfalls on the previous two days meant that Osborne's Coaches were unable to get the team coach from Tollesbury to Colchester. Martin Bennet finally managed to locate a coach that could get to Layer Road, and the team travelled down on the day previous to the match. All the players, and the manager, who lived outside Colchester had problems getting to Layer Road. The journey itself was a nightmare. To make things worse Colchester lost 2–0.

By January Colchester's casualty list had assumed frightening proportions. Chatterton, Reeves, Simon Burman, were still missing with long term injuries, Robin Turner retired through injury. Adcock missed 10 games, Tom English had been side lined twice. Mike Ferguson with back trouble, Richard Wilkins hamstring, and six of the Reserves were walking wounded. Only Alec Chamberlain had appeared in every match.

The Christmas period saw several milestones reached. Tom English made his 150th League appearance, spread over five different clubs. His brother Tony made his 100th League and Cup appearances all with Colchester, whilst skipper Ian Phillips celebrated his 300th League match – 134 of them with Colchester. Andy Farrell also made his 100th League appearance just before the holiday period. To complete the celebrations the new signing from Hartlepool – Simon Lowe – had his 24th birthday.

History was made on the 21st of February 1987. It was exactly 10 years since any player, other than the then manager Mike Walker or Alec Chamberlain, appeared in goal for the U's. A wonderful sequence and believed to be a Football League record.

A circular sent out by Colchester United to all the other Football League clubs, marked confidential, which invited offers for any of Colchester United's players, was leaked to the Press. The leak was finally traced to Robert Jobson, who worked on a local free paper. He was the son of the Southend United Chairman Vic Jobson, and a statement was made saying that the leak certainly did not emanate from the Roots Hall club.

By the end of February it was apparent that Colchester's promotion hopes were fading. The casualty list and the resultant changes to the team, had taken its toll. Keith Bowen who had a serious car accident before the season started never recovered fitness and had to call it a day. Winston White was signed in early March, but it was really too late to get up among the leading pack and the automatic promotion spots.

March, April and early May however saw a revival in fortunes, with 25 points from the last 14 games, which led to Colchester finishing in fifth place and qualifying for the play-offs. A very creditable achievement considering all the trials and tribulations during a long arduous campaign.

The introduction of the end of season play-offs finalised the promotion and relegation places, and also automatic promotion and relegation between the Football League and the Conference became a reality. In the play off semi-finals Wolverhampton Wanderers won 2-0 at Layer Road, and though the U's held them 0-0 at Molineux, it was once again a question of near but not near enough. Aldershot beat Wolves in the final to clinch the third promotion place.

Chamberlain kept goal in all 46 League and five Cup games. Hedman 38 and 6 sub League appearances, Day 38, Adcock 33 and 2 subs. and Phillips 33 were the other regulars, when not ruled out through injury.

Adcock scored 11 League and two Cup goals, and Tom English with 9 League and 3 Cup goals, were the only marksmen to reach double figures. The remaining goals were shared by 15 players, plus two own goals.

In League and Cup games 24 players were used. The average gate for the 23 League matches was 2,740, an increase of 413 on the previous season. Sixteen Fourth Division clubs had lower average gates so the U's were at least just holding their own, although gate receipts were in no way covering running costs.

### OFF THE FIELD

The programme for the 86/87 season had several interesting features. First a brand new cover design was commissioned by the Chairman, showing the club shield printed over a background of a serene looking blue sky and wispy clouds. Match details were in black on a yellow oblong enclosed by a red line at the base, and the price was 50p. On the orders of the Chairman no list of officials, as customary, was included, only the name of the programme editor and the printer in a panel on Page One.

Before the season got under way the club launched Appeal 86, a scheme where Mr. Crisp matched £1 for every £1 donation made by supporters. New Director David Johnson also chipped in with 50p. per £1 given.

A nice touch, just before the season got under way, was an invitation from The Mayor of Colchester, Bob Russell, to the Directors and Staff to a reception in the Mayor's Parlour. The then Mayor was (and still is) a committed United fan - a real terrace man behind the top end goal.

There was also a very successful "Meet the U's night" at Layer Road when over 300 attended. Manager Mike Walker and Secretary Martin Bennet answered a wide range of questions, the event finishing off with a match between the first team and the reserves.

Steve Foley returned to the club in August to assist Roy Massey with the Reserve team. Colin Henson continued in charge of the Reserves. Bertie Mee and Financial Consultant Stuart Timperley were co-opted by Mr. Crisp as advisors to the Board.

Retired pensioner Harold Pitt was complimented in the programme on the cleanliness of the stands and terraces. He came in voluntarily three days a week to tidy up. He continued to do this into the nineties.

Frank Carson

Comedian Frank Carson was appointed a Director in October; another new recruit at Layer Road was Sandra Howe, she joined the club as Commercial Manager.

Shoulder injuries to John Reeves and Nick Chatterton depleted Milk Walker's squad, both were ruled out for many weeks. On a more cheerful note Lee Hunter, Allan's son was capped by Northern Ireland at youth level.

The writer did a cost survey of advertising board, and programme space. The average charge for ground boards, from 22 Third and Fourth Division Clubs, came to £11 per foot, for a minimum size 20 foot by 3 foot board, i.e. £220. Average cost of producing such a board, including sign-writing, came to £90. Most clubs had an arrangement with an established sign-writing firm. Colchester were the most expensive, with Orient at £14 a foot coming second. Rochdale and Crewe at £8 a foot were the cheapest. Average cost of a one page advertisement in the programme was £250, and a half page cost £195.

### 1987/88 - DRASTIC CHANGES

Golden Jubilee Year dawned with Mike Walker in the manager's chair, David Barnard as Chief Executive and Dee Ellwood promoted to secretary.

Martin Bennet the secretary, to the regret of many, had gone the previous May. He, like others before him and several later on, had not seen eye to eye with the chairman. Mr Crisp once again indicating that he wanted his own team, so much for the staff security he promised when he joined the Board.

Before the Jubilee season was very old further changes were in the offing. In July, David Barnard joined the club as Chief Executive, previously at Fulham, he had applied for the post, after learning from Colin Henson during the Zeebrugge Youth Tournament in Holland, that there was a vacancy at Layer Road.

A jubilant Richard Wilkins and Dale Tempest ran out in triumph as Tempest's goal gives the U's a 2-0 lead in the F.A Cup game with Tamworth.

Mike Walker won the Manager of the Month award for October, things looked to be going swimmingly. Then came the bombshell! On Sunday November the 1st, Walker took the team down to Burnham Ramblers for a match to mark the official opening of the Essex Senior League club's palatial new ground. Everyone was in high spirits and enjoyed the festivities. That evening the manager had a meeting arranged with Mr Crisp. He went along fully expecting to discuss progress and possibly a new and improved contract. What exactly went on at the meeting has never been made clear. The chairman said the manager resigned, Walker and his coach Alan Hunter maintained they were sacked.

In any event it soon became apparent that the Board had decided on a change of management before the meeting took place. How else could it have happened that within a very short space of time Roger Brown was appointed, and was in fact in charge the following Saturday when Tamworth visited in the F.A. Cup First Round.

By one of those quirks of fate the new manager was a Tamworth man, who had come into League football late after a career in engineering. He played for Bournemouth, Norwich City and Fulham and at the time of his appointment was managing Poole Town. His brother was the Tamworth manager. The first month of his incumbency went well enough. Tamworth were beaten 3–0, and though there was a 1–0 defeat by Wolves at Layer Road, another eight points accrued from the other four League games.

December was even better, for League games plus a second round F.A.Cup–tie were all won, and Brown was Manager of the Month. The programme for the match with Scunthorpe United on New Year's Day contained a League table showing Colchester second in Division Four, just one point behind leaders Wolves. Scunthorpe won that game 3–0, and that was the start of an 11 match run without a single win.

In January and February nine League games produced just two points, there was also a 2–0 F.A. Cup defeat at Plymouth, and Notts County won 3–2 at Layer Road in the Sherpa Van Trophy.

By mid–March, though there was a 2–1 win at Swansea, the team were only midway in the table and any hopes of promotion had evaporated. There was some improvement in fortunes in the last 13 matches, and four wins plus four draws enabled a respectable, if disappointing, final position of ninth to be attained.

The whole season only produced 47 League goals, the lowest total for a campaign in the 50 years history of the club. A total of 31 players were used. Richard Wilkins appeared in all 46 League games, and in 8 cup matches. Other League appearances included Tempest with 44, English 43, Hedman 41, White 40 and Greenfell 39. English, Hedman, Hinshelwood and White turned out in all 9 cup–ties, Grenfell in 8 and Tempest in 7.

Tempest 11, Wilkins 9, Chatterton 7 (6 pens) and White 7 accounted for 34 of the 47 League goals scored. White 4, Tempest 3, Wilkins 3, Chatterton 2 (1 pen) and Norman shared the 12 cup goals.

The average home gate was 3,141. At the end of the season Colchester had played in the Football League a total of 1,746 League matches, of which 652 had been won, 461 drawn, and 633 lost. During this time 2,539 goals had been scored and 2,526 conceded.

### OFF THE FIELD

From the Football Trust £13,500 for Closed Circuit Television, and a further £4,500 for Football in the Community was granted. Also £2,291 towards police charges were received from the previous 86/87 season.

Early in the season Norcros Estates became club sponsors.

Shortly afterwards, David Brimacombe was appointed Sales and Marketing Director, he previously held a similar position with Coral Racing Ltd.

### THE MIDNIGHT MOLAR

Team coach driver extraordinaire Graham Layzell has been ferrying the Colchester team for around 25 years. Nicknamed "Grimble" by Ray Bunkell, and later "Fletch" (as in T.V's. "Porridge"), he has had his moments.

Staying at the Broadfield Hotel at Rochdale, he had the misfortune to be stricken with raging toothache during the night. Hotelier Terry Sutcliffe organised a visit to a dentist just before midnight. Graham was duly conveyed to the surgery only to find the power had been switched off. Nothing daunted the dentist, using manual power – while a couple of sturdy lads held Graham in the chair - extracted the offending molar, right on the stroke of midnight. Bernie Dixson, now chief scout at Leyton Orient, then the U's first aid man, resuscitated the patient!

**1988/89**
**RECORD DEFEAT HERALDS CHANGES**

New players at Layer Road were goalkeeper John Grace (ex Tolka Rovers), Eamonn Collins (from Portsmouth), and Dave Barnett from Windsor & Eton.

There were early indications that all was not well on the playing front. After struggling to beat York City 1-0 in the opening match at Layer Road,and a goal-less draw at Tranmere Rovers, Doncaster Rovers won 1-0 at Colchester. In these matches the strike force of Tempest and Swindlehurst made little impression.

The York game saw Barnett set off for a second bookable offence and he was yellow carded again at Prenton Park in the following match.

A 2-2 draw at Wrexham followed by a 3-1 win over visiting Scarborough perked things up a little. But support was melting, for there were only just over 1,400 at the latter match and less than 5,000 in total passed through the turnstiles for the first three home games.

A disastrous spell followed, only one of the next five games producing a favourable result - at Carlisle where Tempest and Swindlehurst scored. Sendall pulled one back for the Cumbrians who had not won a game at the time. Lincoln won 3-1 and Scunthorpe 2-1 at Layer Road, and there was a 2-0 defeat at Burnley.

The final blow as far as Roger Brown was concerned came on Saturday October the 15th, when the U's crashed 8-0 to Leyton Orient at Brisbane Road. This remains as Colchester's biggest ever defeat. On the team coach a disconsolate manager announced his intention to quit, and he tendered his resignation to the chairman that night. It had all been a bit of a sickener for Roger with little going right for him during his 12 months in charge.

Steve Foley again stepped into the breach as temporary manager when Brown departed. His task was an unenviable one, for morale was low and at the end of the year from 11 games just three points had accrued. Strangely things were different on the F.A.Cup front. A goal from Mario Walsh settling the first round tie against Fulham at Craven Cottage. But when Swansea City drew 2-2 at Layer Road on December the 10th, few gave the team any chance in the replay at the Vetch Field. Rudi Hedman, Richard Wilkins and Walsh against all odds scored, as a rejuvenated looking Colchester side stormed to a famous 3-1 victory. It must have been the Mumbles air that did the trick, as the team stayed there overnight, and they won hands down.

Though nothing seemed to be going right on the League front it appeared that Foley could get the players to raise their game in cup matches. In addition to progress in the F.A.Cup, first Lincoln City and then Southend United were beaten in the Sherpa Van Trophy. The 2-1 win at Sincil Bank was mainly due to the work of Tony Kelly who ran the midfield and Mario Walsh who scored both goals. There were only 993 paying fans when Southend were entertained at Layer Road (both these were preliminary round ties). Swindlehurst and Tempest scored for the U's and Young for The Blues, to produce a 2-1 Colchester win.

So, although the League position was precarious at the end of 1988, the U's still had a live interest in the F.A. Cup and the Sherpa Van Trophy. After a surprise 3-0 victory at Shrewsbury Town in the F.A.Cup, the U's were drawn to play Sheffield United at Brammall Lane in the 4th round. A shock 3-3 draw resulted, Hicks, Hill and Hetzke netting for Colchester. The best attendance for a long time, 7,638, came to Layer Road for the replay, but there was no further shock, for the Yorkshire team won 2-0. Despite an encouraging start in the Sherpa Van Trophy, no honours came in this competition.

As the season wore on, a disastrous drop out of the Football League loomed. The first 20 games of 1989 produced just four victories. But when all looked lost, an amazing end of season string of five consecutive wins lifted the team to third from bottom. Hardly a successful season, but none the less a final eight points clear of relegated Darlington.

**OFF THE FIELD**

The annual shareholders meeting in the 1988 close season proved to be a very stormy affair. Mr Crisp, the chairman, came in for a great deal of flak after a loss of £150,612 was reported for the year ending May 1988.

Robert Jackson drew attention to the fact that the annual meeting seemed to get later and later each year, this one being just three days within the legal limit. If the pattern continued the next meeting would be in September 1989, and shareholders would be denied an opportunity to comment on any apparent mismanagement by the present board of directors.

Mr Crisp tartly observed that as long as the meeting was held within the legal limit he could not see the validity of the arguments. He disliked the suggestion of *"apparent mismanagement"*, especially as it came from the former chairman of the club.

Earlier he had said to Mr Jackson: *"If I walked away, would you put up the money to keep the club going?*

*The reality is that if I had not come in there would be no club".* Mr Crisp also stated that enough people had tried to stop him joining the Board in the first place, and he was becoming increasingly aggravated by some of the unwarranted criticism that was being levelled at the management of the club.

On the prospects of the long talked about new ground the chairman said that, *"with the fairest of winds three months could see the question of a new location solved. When that was done a new ground could be built within two years".* (Four years later the project was still at square one and Layer Road had been updated at a cost of around £85,000!) After telling the shareholders that a 15,000 average gate was needed to balance revenue and ground receipts (at the time the ground capacity was limited to 5,000 for safety reasons at the time), the acrimonious meeting was closed.

A Colchester United Ladies football team was formed, however, most football fans in the town have forgotten that there was a Colchester Woman's Team back in the mid-sixties.

## 1989/90
## OUT OF THE LEAGUE AFTER 40 YEARS

Jock Wallace took his squad to Scotland for a pre-season tune up. There were matches against Partick Thistle, Raith Rovers, Cumnock Juniors and Stranraer.

Partick won 2-1 at Firhill with Robert Scott (back in his native land) scoring for the U's. Two bad defensive errors led to Gallagher and Peetler scoring for Thistle. At Starks Park against Raith Rovers, 1,500 spectators saw a seven goal thriller. Rovers led 1-0, then a three goal blitz saw Scott (2) and Allinson make it 1-3. Raith pulled back to 2-3 and there were further goals from Bennett and another for Rovers before play ended with a final score of 4-3 to Colchester. Stranraer were hammered 5-0 at Stair Park. The last match at Cumnock was more like a war than a football match. Chris Roll scored to enable the U's pleased to get away with a 1-1 draw. This was Colchester's first venture north of the Border and was a big success.

Gary Brooke, the former Spurs and Norwich player was with the party for a trial run, but was not retained. Chris Roll, a U's apprentice played in two games but the Norfolk lad never made a first team appearance for the club when he got back home.

John Grace, the only 'keeper in the Colchester party was injured in the game at Stranraer, and Jock Wallace borrowed Colin Hunter - a Dunfermline Athletic custodian - for the game at Stranraer. One friendly was played at Layer Road, when a crowd of 3,309 gathered at Layer Road for the visit of First Division Chelsea. The Pensioners won 3-1. The start of the new season was not particularly inspiring. Five of the first six fixtures fulfilled, resulted in draws. There was a 4-0 home win over Maidstone United, and away defeats at Grimsby (where new 'keeper Grace was at fault for three of the four goals) and 1-0 at Carlisle.

A 12 game run followed without a single victory, and between September the 26th and Boxing Day just two points were collected. By the end of the year the U's were bottom of Division Four.

Southend United won 6-4 on aggregate in the two legged Littlewoods Cup First Round. In the F.A. Cup a goal from Gary Bennett eliminated Brentford in the First Round, but the joy was short lived. Having won at Griffin Park, Third Division Birmingham City at home proved to too big a hurdle. One time Ipswich Town man Nigel Gleghorn scored both goals as City won 2-0.

Jock Wallace who was a very sick man had to stand down for health reasons, he was made a Director of the club but took practically no part in the affairs of the club after Christmas. Mick Mills the former Ipswich and England player took over in his place.

The new man, left with a mountain to climb, could do little to stop the rot. The team won eight matches and drew three others under his stewardship. The 27 points gleaned however were never going to be enough to escape the drop. At the end they trailed Halifax Town by six points, and 40 years of League football at Layer Road came to an end.

## OFF THE FIELD

Steve Hetzke played in the pre-season friendly against Chelsea and that proved to his last game for the club. Problems with his right knee and Achilles tendon compelled him to retire after a seventh operation. He was 34 at the time, he left Layer Road to join Chesterfield as coach.

Alan Ball quit at the end of October and joined Stoke City as coach, where Mick Mills was the Manager. Two weeks, later Mills was sacked by Stoke, Ball got the manager's job at the Victoria Ground, and Mills - after a brief spell out of the game - took over from Jock Wallace as manager at Layer Road. Mills brought with him Sammy Chung who had been with him as coach at Stoke. When Colchester failed to avoid relegation, both men left in May 1990.

One of Jock Wallace's sharpest deals was signing Paul McGee from Bohemians in Dublin. McGee spent just three weeks at Layer Road before he was sold to Wimbledon for £75,000, with three additional payments of £25,000 due if the player made a certain number of appearances for The Dons. In fact the U's received a further £25,000 after McGee played 10 games for them. This made the total fee received £100,000. Trevor Lea at £90,000 is quoted in the reference books as the biggest fee the U's received for a player. Which sum is right?

Steve Restarick will always remember his 18th birthday, for he scored four goals as Colchester blasted Hitchin Town 8-0 in an Eastern Junior Cup-Tie to mark the occasion. At the time Steve had knocked in 14 goals in 10 youth team games. He was one of number of young players who many felt did not get a fair break at Layer Road.

When the U's lost to Exeter City on November the 1st, it was their seventh League defeat in a row. Fortunately they drew at Burnley in the next game, and this stopped the all time record of eight successive League defeats (between the 9th of October and the 14th of December 1954) being equalled.

At the start of the season it was rumoured that Colchester were £750,000 in the red. Even so the fans were asking why none of the £250,000 received in transfer fees for McGee, Hill and Walton had not been available to buy new players?

Jock Wallace's signings of Tom English, Billy Gilbert and Trevor Morgan were criticised as "cheap alternatives". Mr. Crisp when asked, 'why Mark Blake', who had been impressive while on loan from Bournemouth replied: *"What Bank Manager is going to sanction a further £150,000 deal in our financial position?"*.

## THE GM VAUXHALL CONFERENCE FIELD AND PASTURES NEW

When Colchester lost their League status in 1990 it looked a complete disaster for football in the town. Two years later when the club returned to the Football League there were those who questioned whether it would not have been better for the future well being of the U's to have stayed in The Conference.

Far from it being two years in the wilderness, a rejuvenated Colchester United re-appeared in top circles with interest re-kindled in an organisation that in the late eighties made survival questionable.

New fields and pastures, newly found friends and two of the most successful (from a playing viewpoint) seasons, since Southern League days, got the Layer Road turnstiles clicking again. Unfortunately still not enough to guarantee future viability.

A constantly changing scene, in the backroom, as well as on the pitch, made the U's news - and gained exposure that was mostly favourable - after years in the doldrums. It saw the end of Jonathan Crisp's controversial years as Chairman and controlling shareholder. Also a time of many changes in personnel and a long overdue facelift for Layer Road. Many more came through the turnstiles and altogether the atmosphere was better after the cleansing influences of life in the Conference.

Mr Crisp stayed on as chairman for the first year of the new experience, finally conceding in the summer of 1991 that it was time to go. He admitted that he left having failed to fulfil the targets he set himself when he joined the Board of Directors in 1985. Certainly the U's had never looked like achieving the Second Division status he aimed for.

His pledge of security for the staff, made in his first speech when he was elected to the Board, was hardly borne out by the many subsequent comings and goings. Over and above that the club debts were well over the £1 million mark and Layer Road had been sold back to the Borough Council. The club were in the red for around £¼ million when he took over and owned the ground, valued at one time before the building recession set in at around £3 million.

It was a sad ending to Crisp's stewardship which started with so much hope, and a genuine desire to put the club on the map, and ended when the U's failed to get back into the League at the first attempt.

## A TIME OF COMINGS AND GOINGS

Mr Crisp's reign as chairman of the club was an era of many comings and goings. During his six years at the helm the club had six managers. Cyril Lea, Mike Walker, Roger Brown, Jock Wallace, Mick Mills and Ian Atkins, with Steve Foley twice filling in on a caretaker basis.

Martin Bennet was secretary until he was replaced by David Barnard (chief executive). Eric Johnstone, originally came in as a director, then became football secretary, and he in turn was replaced in that capacity by Dee Ellwood. Mrs. Ellwood remained in that capacity when Peter Day succeeded David Barnard, who moved to Wimbledon. When Mr. Day left to join Swindon Town, Trevor Spall became Executive Director with Mrs. Ellwood continuing as football secretary. She in turn was replaced by Sue Smith shortly before Mr Crisp left the Board.

On the commercial front, when the new chairman took over, there were three employees in that department Mrs. Ellwood, Mrs. Kitty Watson and Cyril Harvey. Eddie Keegan (who had been Commercial Manager) had just relinquished his position as commercial consultant. There was also one voluntary helper who worked full time. Then Sandra Howe, David Brimacombe, Gerry Carter, Nick Chatterton, Paul Mariner (briefly), and Diane Duffett came and went. All those before Marie Partner appeared on the scene.

There was also a change of groundsman, David Blacknell (now stadium manager) replaced Alan Power.

On the accounting side Tony Coker was followed by a number of people on a part time-basis. Mike Thew became company secretary, whilst Bertie Mee and various other people flitted briefly across the Layer Road stage.

The two things that stand out from the period were that the staff security promised in Mr Crisp's initial statement when he joined the Board was hardly realised by subsequent events. Secondly, several of the newcomers drafted in failed to live up to the faith put in them by Crisp when they were appointed.

The chronicles of seasons 1990/91 and 91/92 follow, and during that time many players came, and many went. The Board had an entirely different make up when League football returned. Colchester built up a travelling following that was the envy of many clubs (except for the small hooligan element), and many who had deserted Layer Road came back into the fold.

Practically Mr Crisp's last act in control was to axe some long serving staff. Dee Ellwood and Kitty Watson had given years of unstinting service to the club in various capacities. Diane Duffett of the Commercial Department was also made redundant as was the assistant groundsman. These were said to be a cost cutting exercise, a sad statement of affairs considering earlier the chairman went on record as saying the staff salaries at Layer Road were too low, and that he himself had raised them.

With James Bowdidge as chairman in the 91/92 season - he acquired Mr Crisp's shares for what was said to be a nominal sum - there was an openness and 'glasnost' at Layer Road after five years of factfinding had proved difficult for the Press. It was a season when the sun shone and everything appeared to be coming right, plus a Wembley appearance, which was attended by over 20,000 Colchester wellwishers to bring down the curtain on two memorable seasons.

The U's were on the march once more.

## 1990/91 - INTO THE UNKNOWN

The descent into the Conference was viewed with considerable trepidation by many of the U's fans. In the event, after just a few games, they found it was a refreshing change – viewing new grounds, getting friendly receptions on their travels, and seeing a surprisingly high standard of play.

Ian Atkins was in charge and had Steve Foley as coach. Colchester also had another advantage, for they were the only team using a full time professional staff. That fact had a counter productive side, for they were the team all the others wanted to beat. Every game was in effect played with a Cup-tie atmosphere – fortunately the team seemed to thrive on that scenario.

The fact that things did not work out quite as planned – a quick return to the Football League was the prime objective – could not detract from what was the best entertainment for years.

For the first match in the new sphere, at Yeovil, a crowd of 4,169 turned up to see how Colchester coped at the brand new Huish Park ground. Atkins himself, Morrys Scott, Mark Yates and Nicky Smith were all making their debut in Colchester colours. To the delight of the home club's fans, goals from Peter Conning and Mickey Spencer gave Yeovil the points. The next six games, three were drawn, showed that it was going to take Colchester time to adjust to Conference football.

Merthyr Town, opponents of long ago in Southern League days, were the first visitors to Layer Road. There were just over 2,000 at the game, a 3–1 win was the result, with on loan Mark Yates scoring along with Eammon Collins and Gary Bennett.

Mario Walsh, arrived back at Layer Road, and in his first game following his return scored two in the 4–0 win over Northwich Victoria. The £25,000 fee looked well spent. The next new arrivals, Warren Donald and Laurie Ryan (on loan from Cambridge) plus Mark Rees (on trial), signed on shortly afterwards. The two latter only had brief stays, Rees leaving to play in Luxembourg.

By the time the team travelled to Runcorn at the end of September Walsh had found the net seven times in five matches and Colchester were on the march. The one discordant note was the behaviour of a small band of Colchester louts throwing seats about at the Bath City game. The same lot had disgraced themselves at Layer Road by jeering the Sutton United keeper as he was stretchered off.

Macclesfield however spoilt the party mood on October the 6th, when one time Burnley player Darren Heesom scored direct from a corner – 10 minutes from time – to sink the U's on their first visit to the quaintly named Moss Rose ground.

The team soon recovered their poise however winning the next four matches before taking on Kettering Town. Kettering with 13 wins and two draws in the first three months of the season were firmly ensconced at the top of the table. They lost their first Conference match the week before Colchester's visit, going down 5–1 at Wycombe. Chelmsford City also knocked them out of the F.A. Cup, winning 2–1 at Kettering, in a replay, after being held to a 0–0 draw at home.

A crowd of 5,020, including around 1,000 from Colchester, packed in to Rockingham Road, and the home fans went wild when Doug. Keast scored the only goal of the game.

Colchester performed better than The Poppies in the F.A. Cup. On the Saturday after that meeting at Kettering they knocked out Reading 2–1 in a First Round tie at Layer Road. An Atkins penalty at the start of the second half, and a Neale Marmon special on the hour did the trick. The second round saw Leyton Orient draw 0–0 at Colchester and win 4–1 in the replay at Brisbane Road. In that match Martin Grainger was shown the red card. He did not get another first team game until February.

In the battle for Conference points the U's twice came from behind to draw when Wycombe visited Layer Road. Mike Masters, the big American, made his Colchester debut that day, for all of six minutes, replacing Walsh who took a knock in scoring Colchester's second equaliser.

● *U's attacking against Witton in the first-half - Gary Bennett in a far post heading duel*

Another debutant was Shaun Elliott from Sunderland – he had been on trial at Blackpool – Colchester lost 3–0 that afternoon at Merthyr. By the end of 1990 Kettering led the Conference by a street and carried the look of champions. The transfer of Andy Hunt to Newcastle for £150,000, Kevin Shoemake moving on, and the loss of Keith Walwyn with a heart complaint, eventually proved too big a handicap. The Poppies eventually finished fourth.

The sporting Press seemed to take it as read that The Poppies, who had only lost one game, would win the championship. Colchester though had shown on New Year's Day that they had other ideas when they went to Underhill and beat Barnet 3–1.

Masters who came on as substitute scored one of the goals, Bennett and Walsh got the other two. Between January the 1st and March the 25th Colchester remained unbeaten in Conference matches. The games for points were interspersed with F.A. Trophy and Bob Lord Cup matches. In the Trophy, Windsor and Eton, Runcorn and Wivenhoe Town were safely accounted for, but Witton Albion (then in the Northern Premier League) put paid to the U's hopes at Layer Road in Round Four.

In fact in two weeks at the end of March the form book went out of the window and there was a worrying wobble. Apart from the defeat by Witton, the team lost 1-0 on their first visit to Wycombe's new Adams Park ground. Even worse Yeovil completed the double by winning 1-0 at Layer Road on the last day of the month. In the run in those two defeats proved expensive. Kettering's lead had been whittled away, but Barnet were coming up on the rails and on the last Saturday of the season the Bees were crowned champions with 87 points to Colchester's 85.

At one time on the final Saturday, Barnet were behind in their match, whilst Colchester were winning 2-0 against Kidderminster. If only..... but the Underhill boys recovered and for the U's it meant a second season in the conference. Barnet, who won the Championship by two points, with Colchester second, could claim with some justification that they were deserving winners. They drew 0-0 at Layer Road in a game spoilt by a gale force wind, and won 3-1 at Underhill when Tony English, a flu victim, missed his first game of the season.

What really ensured another season's stay in the Conference for the U's was dropping seven points in April. They drew with Altrincham at Layer Road, had a goalless draw at Kidderminster, and then lost 2-0 away to Telford United. Two successive defeats in March, 1-0 at Wycombe's impressive new Adams Park stadium, and a 1-0 setback when Yeovil won 1-0 at Layer Road (doubling the U's), did not help much either. In that latter game Colchester missed chance after chance. Paul Batty (well known to Colchester in League days) with his only shot on goal, in the 90 minutes, put a 30 yard screamer out of Barrett's reach into the net.

A total of 25 players appeared in Conference games. Four made over 40 appearances - Bennett in goal with 42, player/manager Atkins 41, Daniels 40, and English with 39+1 as sub. The 68 goals were shared by 13 players. Walsh netted 17, Bennett 9, McDonough 8, and Atkins and English managing 7, were the main contributors.

**OFF THE FIELD**

Nick Chatterton, who after retiring from playing worked in the Commercial Department at Layer Road, left in August. He took up an appointment at Sudbury Kingfisher Pool, a leisure centre run by former U's player Mick Packer.

When Merthyr Town became the first Conference team to visit Layer Road on August the 25th, it was almost 40 years to the day from when Colchester played their first Football League home game. That was against Bristol Rovers on August the 26th 1950. Chairman Crisp, in the Chairman's view, in the programme said Colchester were: *"The Liverpool of the Conference, the only fully professional side"*.

At the end of October, Barnet were even money, Kettering 7-4 and Colchester 100-30 to win the championship. At the time Kettering were 12 points in front of the U's in third place, Barnet were second, six points behind the leaders. Colchester had games in hand on both clubs.

Mike Masters became Colchester's first ever American signing when he came on trial for a month in November. A 6'3" giant he became a popular figure at Layer Road.

Paul Wilkin and Ken Craig, two exiled U's fans, started a newsletter *"U.F.O."* ("U's from 'Ome") - a title dreamed up by the Evening Gazette's, Neil Thomas. Paul and Ken, living in Peterborough, thought it a good idea to keep Colchester supporters living away from Essex informed of the goings on at Layer Road. It is still going strong.

Holimarine Holiday Parks - Pennant Holidays were the clubs sponsors that season. During the season 63,068 passed through the turnstiles for the 21 Conference games. The average attendance of 3,003 was the highest in the competition, the biggest crowd being 7,221 against Altrincham on March the 20th.

Trevor Spall after a year as Executive Director left the club to return to school teaching. Sue Smith was promoted to Football Secretary on his departure.

Tom English visits a young fan in hospital.

Leeworthy and Hedman look on as a cheque is presented to the 'Buy a Player' appeal

There was a new chairman - James Bowdidge - when the U's second season in the Conference got under way. Jonathan Crisp after six years involvement stepped down during the close season, no doubt a poorer and wiser man, after his dream of getting Colchester up and among the football elite in five years had faded away.

The F.A.Trophy 1st Leg semi-final versus Macclesfield at Layer Road was won 3-1. Roy McDonough scored the third from the penalty spot.

Ian Atkins, after his season as player-manager, and the narrow failure to jump back into the Football League at the first attempt, decided to move on.

As in the previous campaign the 1991/92 season provided plenty of drama and excitement with promotion back to the Football League, and the F.A. Trophy triumph at Wembley a wonderful climax to nine months of suspense.

August and September saw the on the field results not entirely satisfactory. Three of the four home games were won easily enough, but Farnborough Town, newly promoted to the Conference, provided an early shock winning 3-2 at Layer Road. Defensive mistakes cost the U's dearly in that game. Farnborough led 2-1 at half time, and then in the second half - though Scott Barrett saved a penalty - another defensive clanger left the visitors leading 3-1. For the last 20 minutes of the game the Farnborough goal was under constant siege, Collins made it 3-2 but that was the final score.

Previous to that setback Roy McDonough scored all four goals as Colchester won 4-2 at Slough. McDonough naturally wanted the match ball from the Slough game as a souvenir. His wife Jackie, the U's lottery manager, had to buy it (at a cost of £30), as Slough were not prepared to donate the ball.

After that defeat by Farnborough, on September the 10th, Colchester were unbeaten in The Conference until they lost to Redbridge Forest 2-1 on Boxing Day. When the New Year dawned Colchester led the table and it looked as if a two horse race for the championship was developing. Wycombe Wanderers in second place were six points behind but had three games in hand.

Wycombe in fact lost 3-0 at Layer Road in early December when a crowd of over 5,000 saw the Chairboys swept aside, with Steve McGavin at his elusive best - he scored a couple of top drawer goals - and the Colchester defence made sure the points stayed at home.

Just under a fortnight later, under the Layer Road floodlights, the scoreline read Colchester United 2 Wycombe Wanderers 6. That was in a Bob Lord Trophy match and it was the general opinion that this was a game that was unimportant in the eyes of the U's management. Half-a-dozen youngsters (several apprentices) played while Wanderers turned out a full strength side.

In the F.A. Cup Colchester had to play in the last qualifying Round for the first time since 1950. Burton Albion were beaten 5-0 in October, McGavin (two - including a penalty), McDonough, Kinsella and Steve Restarick got the goals; it was the latter's first senior outing. The First Round brought Exeter City to Layer Road, complete with Alan Ball their manager and Scott Daniels, who had been sold to the Grecians during the previous summer. Only superb goalkeeping by Kevin Miller - and two glaring misses by Gary Bennett - saved the visitors, they also had Williams sent off. The game was televised by B.B.C. Match of the Day cameras with John Motson doing the commentating, but there were no goals to report. The replay at St. James Park also ended 0-0 after extra time. In the following penalty shoot out Exeter won 4-2.

In the second half of the season just two of the 20 Conference fixtures were lost. The first was at Merthyr on January the 4th, and the last a surprise 4-1 hammering at Welling on February the 15th.

Wycombe were still right on Colchester's tail at Easter. Both teams had 75 points, the U's leading on goal difference but the Wanderers had a game in hand. By the end of April it was still neck and neck, both teams on 84 points, both with four game left. Colchester had a sticky game at Macclesfield, where they eventually shared eight goals.

The Silkmen in their previous game had helped Colchester's cause by beating Wycombe at their Moss Rose ground. Colchester looked to have the championship sewn up when they led Macclesfield 2-0, the home team however hit back to lead 3-2. McDonough made it 3-3, only for Lambert to bring the game to 4-3, before English scored to make it 4-4.

Meantime Wycombe, after being held 2-2 at Gateshead, snatched a late goal to win 3-2. Level pegging again at the top with 88 points each. Colchester had two home games left, whilst Wycombe had one home and one away, but the U's superior goal difference kept them in the lead.

The Wanderers duly won at Yeovil and at home to Witton, whilst Colchester wound up beating Kettering 3-0 and Barrow 5-0 to make certain of going up.

But that was not quite the end of the season's long tussle, for the U's had booked a Wembley place in the F.A. Trophy final.

During the New Year Colchester had worked their way through four rounds of the F.A. Trophy and then beaten Macclesfield in a two-legged semi-final to win a place in the Wembley final on Sunday May the 10th. Witton Albion, who had knocked the U's out of the competition the previous season, provided the opposition.

Colchester, with goals from Masters, Smith, and McGavin won 3-1, but for many the enjoyment of the triumph was marred by what was a thoroughly bad tempered encounter. Referee K.P. Barratt hardly helped with some inconsistent refereeing. He sent off Jason Cook - the first player to walk in a Trophy final - and yellow carded two Colchester and four Witton players. What the referee failed to do was impose his authority early on, and as a result things got out of hand.

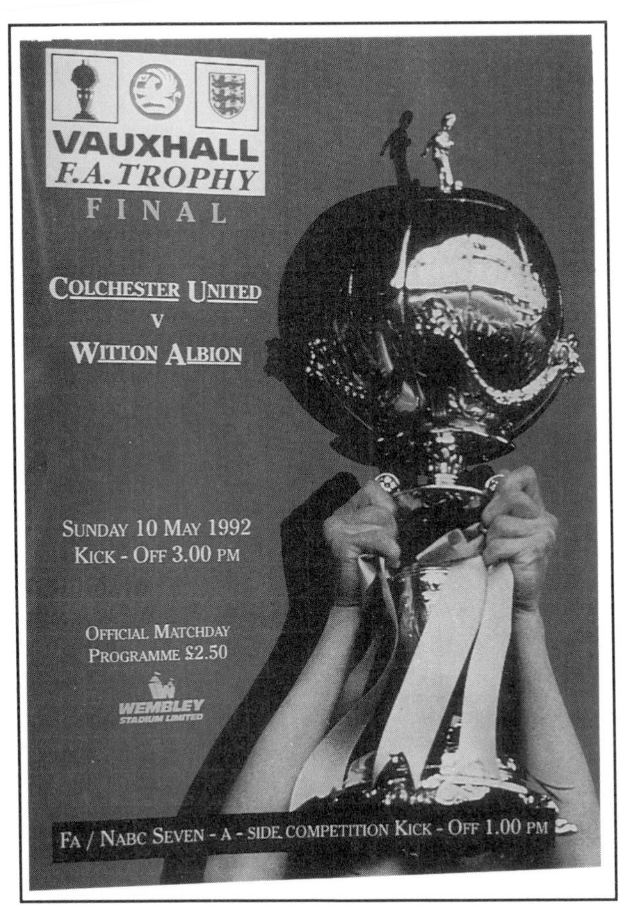


When Colchester won 2-1 at Wycombe on September the 28th, one of the most extra-ordinary goals of all time gave the U's the points. It was 1-1 with the game just in injury time when Colchester keeper Scott Barrett heaved an enormous goal kick downfield, the ball bounced over the head of the Wycombe centre half,past bemused keeper Paul Hyde, and into the net.

Peter Heard, a businessman based in London, but a Colcestrian, and former referee, joined the Board as did Colchester solicitor Peter Powell.

A new look programme priced at £1 printed by Acorn Press appeared of the scene. Unfortunately the firm went out of business during the season. 'Better Design' took over the artwork and setting, with 'Five Castles Press' doing the printing.

### OFF THE FIELD

James Bowdidge, the new Chairman, was the grandson of Harold Moore, a former Colchester United Director and Chairman in the 1950's and 60's. He had strong links with Layer Road right from his childhood days. His plan was to make the U's very much more of a community club and float a new share issue to encourage Colcestrians to buy into, and take an active involvement, in Layer Road affairs.

David Johnson and Gordon Parker left the Board. With the departure of Mr.Crisp, Robert Jackson returned as a Director, and John Worsp, previously an Associate director, joined the main board. Another innovation instituted by Mr. Bowdidge was the setting up of a Board of Management. It had 14 members and included representatives with interests in the month to month operation of the club. It only survived the one season, but during that time performed a useful function at a time of rapid change.

Roy McDonough's four goal spree at Slough was the sixth time a Colchester player scored a quartet of goals. The other four goal men were Neil Langman (11th of December 1958), Bobby Hunt twice in the 1961-62 season and Martyn King (also in the 61-62 season), and Bobby Svarc during 1973-74. No player has managed five in a match. McDonough should have achieved this, but missed a sitter in the Slough game!

Cook through being sent off was not given a Trophy winners medal, but Eammon Collins who was an unused sub gave cook his medal - a very generous and sporting gesture.

*(It was to be my last season of taking an active part in Layer Road affairs. Having past three score years and ten some considerable time previously it was time to call time. I trust that my readers will get as much enjoyment from this book as I have done from my long innings at Layer Road)*

### 1992/93 - UP THE U's!

So we come to the last chapter in the continuing saga of the U's. No doubt in the years ahead, scribes of the future will update the history. In the meantime what better way to finish than with Colchester United safely back in the Football League. A return made possible by a wonderful last season in The Conference, champions and F.A. Trophy winners. A return also tinged with regrets at leaving so many new found friends from two years in top grade Non-League football. Looking back it was perhaps a blessing in disguise to be relegated back in 1990. It gave time to regroup, take a new look at the problems of running the club, and - let's face it - it attracted fans back to Layer Road.

Due to the re-organisation of the Football League in 1992, the U's found themselves in Division Three for the first time since 1981. Still the basement division of course! They finished 10th in the table, four points adrift of the play-off positions.

One of the remarkable features of the campaign was the fact that no less than five goalkeepers were used, four of them on loan, and the fifth - a former apprentice - who had just signed as a full professional. Paul Newell (Orient) 14 League games,

Ron Green 4, Carl Emberson (Millwall) 13, Barber (Peter-borough) 10, and Nathan Munson 1 (he played in the last game at Wrexham) were the men between the sticks.

Roy McDonough, who successfully steered the team back into the Football League fold was, it must be said, something of a surprise choice; first as player/coach, and then the player/manager. During his first spell at Layer Road, big Roy was very much one of the lads, and got into hot water on more than one occasion.

He is still today a very outgoing, ebullient personality, and apt to make rash statements at times. Yet it must be said that in the twilight of his career he led from the front. And, like him or not, he can point to the fact that he has scored goals, encouraged those around him on the field, and most important, established a rapport with the supporters, especially the younger ones. Time however is against him as a player, and really he should now be thinking ahead towards completing his education as a manager. Not a easy transformation to make, and made more difficult by the fact that finances prohibit the club carrying a big playing staff.

It took a long time to establish a pattern, and assemble a more or less settled squad, back in the 'big time'. Only Nicky Smith and Paul Roberts played in all 42 League games. Mark Kinsella (38), Mark Bennett (38), McGavin (37), Cook (34), English (33) and Grainger (31) were other regulars. McDonough himself appeared in 25 games and scored nine of the 67 League goals (3 from the penalty spot). Steve McGavin 9 and Bennett 8 were the other main contributors. The fact that 16 different players' names appeared on the scoresheet serves to illustrate how much the team personnel changed over the months.

During the season apart – from the changes in the goalkeeping role – Warren Donald, Darren Oxbrow, Dean Martin, and Julian Hazel were all tried out and discarded for a variety of reasons. On the credit side, Simon Betts, and Paul Abrahams got extended opportunities and both looked good future prospects. Four other products of the club's youth scheme – Andy Partner, Scott Ridgers, Paul Flowers and Nathan Munson – were drafted into the senior squad late in the season.

The performances on the field are too fresh in the recent memory of Layer Road addicts to need much comment. Considering that only a couple of the regular players cost a fee it was a highly creditable return to League Football. It was a dodgy start, just two home wins in the first eight League games, 16 goals given away, and only eight scored.

At one time the team were bottom of the table, but things gradually improved. Steve McGavin, out of sorts early on, returned to something like the form he is capable of, and the introduction of Peter Crawley in the middle of the defence tightened things up at the back. The final position of tenth owed a lot to the decision of the manager to leave himself out and give Paul Abrahams an extended run late on. The youngster repaid the manager's faith by scoring six goals in his ten games.

Paul Roberts, in his 31st year, was the most consistent player and his experience was invaluable in a defence, which, after early hiccups, gave little away. Apart from one match at Crewe, where Barber had seven put past him, and a 5–2 walloping at Rochdale, there was not a lot wrong with the rearguard in the latter stages of the season.

On the Cup front there was an early exit from the Coca Cola competition. Brighton were a shade lucky to draw 1–1 at Layer Road in the first leg and again had fortune on their side when Dean Wilkins got the only goal in the return. Barry Lloyd admitted that his side had the rub of the green to progress 2–1 on aggregate over the two legs.

In the F.A. Cup, Slough Town – beaten 4–0 – posed few problems in the First Round at Layer Road. A 1–1 draw against old cup foes Gillingham at Priestfield gave promise of further progress in the Layer Road replay. It was not to be, for the Gills won 4–2 and went on to lose to Huddersfield in Round 3.

One worrying feature was the club's disciplinary record – 303 points accumulated in the season. Chairman Gordon Parker seriously concerned by the mounting total introduced a stiff fines system, rightly so for too many players were getting booked for silly things – too much mouth – yellow cards for dissent were all too frequent. The record led to the Chairman and Manager being called before a Disciplinary Commission, a suspended fine hopefully will lead to the bookings being considerably reduced in future.

The big question for the future – can the family team of Gordon Parker (Chairman) and Roy McDonough (son-in-Law) achieve that once promised land of Division Two? Will the present Board be able to get the club on a viable financial keel? Will a new ground ever materialise?

*(I have personally enjoyed my years at Layer Road, and would be sorry if what is – despite its short-comings – a ground of character, disappears. It will probably see my time out).*

What better way to conclude than quoting the club song – not often heard these days:–

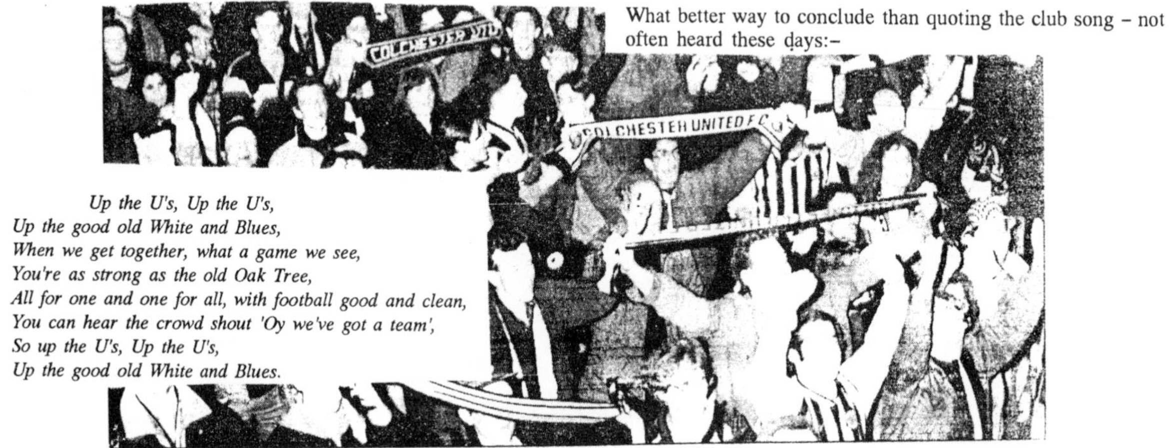

*Up the U's, Up the U's,*
*Up the good old White and Blues,*
*When we get together, what a game we see,*
*You're as strong as the old Oak Tree,*
*All for one and one for all, with football good and clean,*
*You can hear the crowd shout 'Oy we've got a team',*
*So up the U's, Up the U's,*
*Up the good old White and Blues.*

**The supporters of Colchester United see their loyalty rewarded**

# CHAPTER 8

# THESE WHO HAVE ALSO SERVED

Over the years many characters have adorned the Layer Road scene, some briefly, others for almost a lifetime. These notes are intended as a tribute to a few who stand out either in my memory, or of my predecessor, the late Fred Draycott.

It is quite impossible in the space available to include everyone, and as a result I trust those not mentioned will excuse the omission. They can rest assured they are not forgotten – they also served and did the club proud.

I must give pride of place to four journalists from the early years without whose notes and articles this book would not have been possible. **Fred Draycott, Arthur Wood, Allan Everett** and **Sammy Crump** (Colchester Town), were all newsmen and outstanding football scribes. Their articles are models of honest reporting from the days when football was a game to be enjoyed – especially on Saturday afternoon.

At the time of writing Messrs Everett and Wood, though getting on in years, are still with us. The other Layer Road scribe I must mention is **Bernard Webber**. Bernard and I have enjoyed, endured, laughed, and at times almost cried together in the Layer Road Press Box for over three decades. I still don't know whether his first love is Colchester United or Essex County Cricket Club.

**Frank Rowland** who wrote that marvellous book *"Giant-killers"* some 20 years ago, has been a Layer Road man for over 50 years. Though now almost blind, accompanied by his son Bob, he still gets along to the matches. (I gratefully acknowledge his help with many reminiscences and titbits). Fred Draycott also kindly passed on to me The Colchester Town Jubilee book of 1924, which he helped Charles Clark to compile. That too has been a real quarry of information on the Colchester Town era.

**Howard Walker, Robin Frost, Derek Drew, Tony Garnett, Bruce Jackson, Martin Smith, Peter James** and latterly **Francis Ponder, Neil Manning** and **Carl Marston** are other journalists whose names are imprinted in the annals of the U's. There was also, some years ago, an excellent series of Colchester players' pen pictures, by **Dick Barton** in the local paper.

There have been many long serving stewards at Layer Road over the years. To mention just the odd one or two to represent a band of stalwarts who in fair weather and foul have done sterling work. **Stan Clough,** was chief steward for many seasons until his untimely death, and to choose just one other as standard bearer – how about **Charlie Warren** with well over 40 years to his name. Still about at Layer Road.

Among the many directors who have served on The Board, pride of place must go to **William "Bill" Allen**. A master butcher in the town, he was one of the original directors back in 1937, later became Chairman, and eventually President of the club. He took an active interest in Layer Road affairs for well over 30 years. His son **Eric Allen,** who joined the Board in the 60's, continued the family interest. "Bill" Allen was Chairman in the 1950/51 season when the club joined the Football League, in the years after that he twice bailed the club out when finances were strained.

Charlie Warren

**Ben Myers,** also one of the founder directors, continued in office until the late 60's. Ben was an authority on churches. Along with **Peter Hills,** I was once given a conducted tour of Wakefield Cathedral by Mr. Myers. He really made church architecture most interesting, though we missed the coach, we got to Halifax in the end.

A succession of other Chairmen, **Harold Moore, Arthur Neville, Bill Graver** all now deceased, **Roy Chapman, Robert Jackson, Jack Rippingale, Maurice Cadman** etc., all did their stint, often under adverse circumstances. **Jonathan Crisp** and **James Bowbridge** are mentioned elsewhere in the text and so is present incumbent **Gordon Parker,** who can claim one distinction in common with **Robert Jackson,** they have both served three separate spells on the Board.

Gordon Parker

The doyen of the secretaries who have served the club, undoubtedly **Claude Orrin** who held office for well over 20 years. A Chartered Accountant by profession, Claude really was Colchester United in the late 50's and 60's. Behind the scenes his word was law. Since then **David Harvell, Wilf Livingstone, Betty Scott, Martin Bennet, Dee Ellwood,** and now **Sue Smith** have occupied the secretarial chair. In latter years too there were three chief executives in the genial **David Barnard, Peter Day,** and **Trevor Spall**.

Nor must one forget a succession of tea ladies – **Elsie Clough, Lilian Ling, Dee Ellwood, Kitty Watson, Yvonne Stone,** and the present girls who look after the liquid needs in the Directors room and lounge.

Betty Scott

Martin Bennet

Tony Spall

Elsie Clough

Sue Smith

Lillian Ling

Three Smiths have given devoted service in varying capacities. **Ron Smith** as cashier on match days, turnstile operator, youth and reserve team – all the jobs no one else wanted – and all on a voluntary basis for around 30 years. Finally he stepped down after being taken too much for granted. **Brian Smith,** tannoy man extraordinaire, Supporters Club ex-Chairman, still to be found at Layer Road on matchdays, another voluntary man worth his weight in gold. **Doug Smith,** was part-time accounts man for many years. You had to account for the last half-penny with Doug, and a receipt to prove it – a great character. **Reg Casbolt, Chris Dowsett** (and his late father before him), **Eric Southernwood,** all happily still round and about, have tackled a variety of tasks in their time and still do.

Nor must one forget the late **Joe Osborne,** and now his sons **George & Barry,** who between them have for around 30 years made sure the teams travelled in comfort. I personally travelled something like 18,000 miles a season in the team bus for longer than I care to remember. Most of the time with **Graham Layzell** as driver – like me, sometime laundry man, fish and chip collector, conveyor of injured players to hospital and collector of players from obscure addresses. It's been great fun, most of the time, except when I was landed with a very large brunette (very tight one too) in my hotel room one night. Thanks lads.

**Vic Keeble,** after his playing days finished was a very successful fund raiser while operating the Commercial Department for many years. He was aided and abetted, at one time, by another of the playing greats of former years **Bobby Hunt**.

Later there was **John Hillier,** the controversial **Eddie Keegan** – he had some brilliant ideas programme wise – Layer Road Larry, etc. – with Dee Ellwood and Kitty Watson running the office side of things. Canvassing and Sportsman's dinner organising thrown in for good measure. Although for me the best article ever in the programme, were Frank Rowland's *Terracite* contributions. Near the knuckle at times, but always a good and at times hilarious read. Well done Frank.

And what about **Harry Fosker,** the Umbrella man of Southern League days; **"Taffy" Richards** with his dog **Whisky,** and **Twiddell** of Football League times. Mascots of this type would not be allowed today, but in their time they brought colour and laughter to Layer Road, and on football grounds all over the country. Characters all, the like of which we shall not see again. **Steve Foley, Micky Cook, Terry Price, Ray Massey** all former players are still very much part of the Colchester United scene. Nor must we forget trainers of the past like **Jock Kearton, "Dusty" Miller, Bill Light** and **John Anderson**.

And what about **John Schultz,** a man who as a director, and later on various projects for the club – especially on the youth side – has and still is doing sterling work. **Tony** and **Margaret Willoughby** who have made such a resounding success of the Sporting U's and who ran the club shop for many years will unfortunately be moving on when they eventually have the new Ormiston Trust sports area at Monkwick. I only hope that the attendances at Layer Road, especially among the supporters of tomorrow, do not go down when they move their project elsewhere. On the physiotherapy side **John Chandler** (also one time youth team manager), **Ray Coles,** and now **Brian Owen,** spring to mind. Then there was **Bernie Dixson** who had a spell with the magic sponge. But undoubtedly the top man of them all, **Charlie Simpson,** who is sadly missed. Charlie a fellow Yorkshireman, was not only an expert at his job he was also a shrewd assessor of character, it was no good trying to pull the wool over his eyes – he soon picked out the lead swingers. He eventually became a director, with his death one of the legends of the football world passed on. I have left until last the groundsmen. The canny **Jock Duncan, Geoff Gasson, Tom Cheney** and some others with a shorter tenure in office.

I think however it is fair to say that the present incumbent – grandly termed Stadium Manager these days – **David Blacknell** must surely have got the Layer Road pitch and surrounds looking the best ever. A beautiful playing area, bright and cleaned up, the old ground has certainly had a new look since David arrived on the scene.

One last set of characters – which like the small band of yobs still seem to infiltrate – the fox family who dig up parts of his hallowed turf. The yobs the club can do without, the fox David would like to give it and its progeny the brush off!

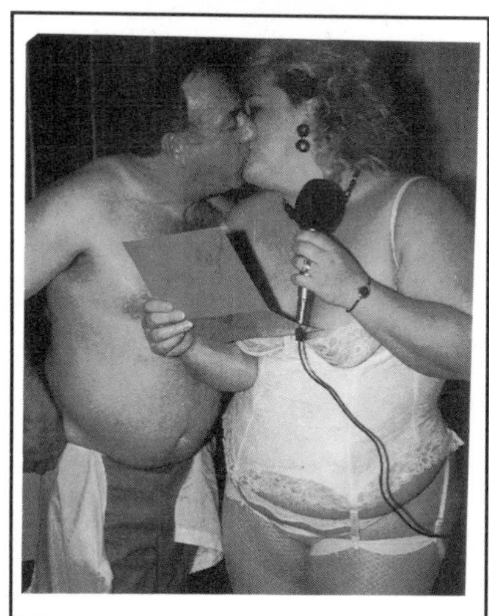

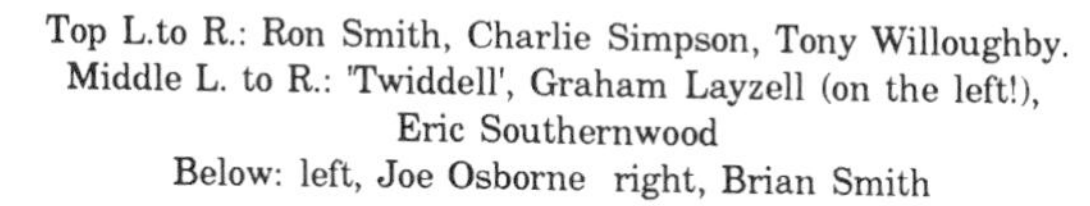

Top L.to R.: Ron Smith, Charlie Simpson, Tony Willoughby.
Middle L. to R.: 'Twiddell', Graham Layzell (on the left!),
Eric Southernwood
Below: left, Joe Osborne right, Brian Smith

# CHAPTER 9

# The Supporters Club and Hospital Radio

The football commentary service as it now exists in Colchester, was initiated by Colchester United Football Supporters Club ("CUFSC"). Many current supporters may not be too familiar with the history of this organisation and a brief outline of its achievements is fitting within the U's history.

The organisation was formed on the 9th of September 1937 as Colchester Town and United Football Supporters Club, the reference to the former amateur Colchester Town being dropped by the end of the 1938/39 season. In common with most similar organisations it became dormant during the Second World War. The balance in hand in May 1940 was £7–12–9d. (£7–64p.), which remained unchanged until the Club was revived in 1945, subsequent to which many thousands of pounds were raised for Colchester United. The money was applied in financing projects, which ranged from the acquisition of houses to accommodate players, to the erection of covered accommodation at the ground; the installation of floodlights, etc., as well as in straight cash donations to the Football Club. This club was dissolved on the 19th of November 1975, by which time the style of supporters' organisations required by most Football League clubs had changed.

In 1953, CUFSC first began to look towards an extension of an arrangement whereby scores at Layer Road were telephoned to local hospitals for the benefit of the patients. Near neighbours Ipswich, had by that time installed the necessary equipment, and were relaying commentaries from Portman Road to their local hospitals. Friendly rivalry decreed that anything "Town" did, U's could do as well, if not better!

The first commentary from Layer Road was relayed in January or February 1953, the commentators being drawn from four Supporters Club volunteers, none of whom had any previous experience of broadcasting. Currently the commentary team is headed by one of the founder–members, and the son of another founder member. There thus remains a very strong link with the past as far back as the establishment of the service, which is relayed over B.T. (formerly G.P.O.) landlines.

One aspect which has changed a number of times, is the location of the commentary point. Originally this was sited at a small lectern style table immediately above the tunnel access to the dressing rooms. But within a season or so the position was moved to the rear of the main stand, close by the Press box. On occasions the commentators were displaced by Pressmen when there was a shortage of space – for fixtures such as big F.A.Cup–ties, which attracted extra interest. On those occasions, the commentators would revert to their previous positions above the tunnel.

In either position however there was space only for 2 commentators, who shared one microphone, with the personnel changing at half–time. The next move was to the so–called popular side of the ground at a commentary position within the then CUFSC offices and committee room, which current supporters will recognise as the premises of the members bar. The window in that room, set at an angle from the main wall of the building, and jutting out more or less directly above the corner flag, was a specially designed feature. This was introduced by the local architects who were engaged for the project, and was completed in 1962. The development also included the construction of a new turnstile block – the total costs being funded by CUFSC.

For the first time the entire commentary team of four could, if necessary, be accommodated in one place, but still served by one – albeit improved design – microphone. This made it necessary to hand over the mike to a colleague if one wished to invite comment on a specific incident, or in the event of a situation arising which required an exchange of views. Despite sufficient room, each half of the match was invariably covered by two pairings, the order of commentary more often than not being dictated by whatever other voluntary tasks a particular individual was performing at the ground on matchdays.

Current devotees of Layer Road will be familiar with the existing commentary box which is situated on the roof of the Main Stand, in a structure which is shared with the football club's Public Address Personnel. This gives an unrivalled view of the pitch, but the steep climb up the ladder to gain access to the commentary box probably limits the age to which commentators can continue operating! By the time of the 1962 move to the CUFSC committee room, the service had been extended from the Essex County Hospital, to then include the Military Hospital in the Colchester Garrison and Black Notley Hospital. This remained the position until Christmas 1963, when a new organisation entitled *"Colchester Hospitals Broadcasting Service"* was formed under the joint sponsorship of CUFSC and Colchester Community Fund, in association with 'King Cole's Kittens'.

For many years CUFSC had hosted a reception for the Colchester Carnival Queen, and the visiting Queens participating in the annual Carnival Procession, including of course their own Colchester United Football Queen. The Carnival Queen was invariably chaperoned by representatives of the Colchester Community Fund, some of whom began to take an interest in the link to the local hospitals. They viewed the prospect of making use of that link to broadcast to patients, on occasions other than match days, with programmes of music, including record requests.

Many aspects of the proposals by the Community Fund, which although generally welcomed, required consideration and debate by the Officers and Committee of CUFSC. Not the least of the problems was the difficulty of accommodating another organisation in premises which were in constant use for social and fund raising activities in support of Colchester United. This included regular committee and sub-committee meetings, which were responsible for such matters as ground maintenance and improvements, the operation of 2 refreshment bars, fund raising competitions, social functions, away travel, etc.

For these reasons, initial broadcasts by the Colchester Broadcasting Service were necessarily restricted to a 'Family Favourite' style programme for two hours on a Sunday morning. Even this had its drawbacks for CUFSC, since Sunday was a busy day in the routines associated with the major fund raising projects that were in vogue from time to time. Eventually, broadcasting from the CUFSC committee room was also permitted on one evening a week (plus Sunday), but when demand extended to other weekdays it became clear that Colchester Hospital Broadcasting Service would have to set up it's own studio. Under the new arrangements established late in 1965, the commentary point at the Layer Road ground remained, albeit with the commentary being relayed to hospitals via the new studio (which changed its name to "Radio Colchester"), instead of direct from the stadium to patients.

Following the move from Layer Road, Radio Colchester considerably extended their network, and at its peak, St. Mary's, Myland, Severalls and Maternity Hospitals in Colchester and St. Michaels plus William Julian Courtould Hospitals in Braintree also received Soccer commentaries, a total of 9 hospitals.

Inevitably further changes occurred following medical services rationalisation in the 1970's – Colchester Military Hospital closed, the status of the two Braintree Hospitals changed to geriatric and were eventually disconnected, and more recently, first Myland, and later St. Mary's Hospitals in Colchester were closed. The soccer commentary currently reaches Colchester General, Essex County, Severalls and Maternity Hospitals.

The opportunity has arisen from time to time to relay commentaries from other grounds on the occasion of Colchester United's away fixtures. Additionally, but not so frequently, invitations have been extended to the Colchester commentary team to send a representative to share the presentation from such matches. Equally of course visiting teams to Layer Road have sought to share in the presentation of the commentary, and have a temporary link set up to the hospitals in their own area. The most significant example of an exchange visit was probably a cup-tie with West Bromwich Albion, who sent a representative to the first match at Layer Road, and Colchester were given the opportunity to share the commentary from the Hawthorns. A temporary receiver was also set up in the CUFSC committee room, so that the members unable to travel to the match could follow the fortunes of the team by listening in. This arrangement in fact gave rise to some amusement, when it was disclosed that some of the Committee members listening had been unable to recognise the voice of their own commentator!

There have of course been many epic encounters at Layer Road over such a long period of time, particularly in the principle Cup competitions. Aston Villa, Manchester United, Newcastle and Fulham in their heyday, are some of the names which immediately spring to mind. However, one commentator's three highlights over the past 40 years :-

1970
F.A. Cup Tie versus Leeds United – this match took place at a time when Leeds were at the pinnacle of their power in the First Division, and paraded a glittering array of stars in what on paper was to be a very uneven contest versus a side nicknamed as "Graham's Grandads". The atmosphere was electric from the start increasing to something akin to frenzy as the U's went into the lead with their opponents pulling back two goals towards full time. The match was a commentator's dream with a full house lending atmosphere via the sound effects microphone, and adding to the David & Goliath encounter that unfolded. A special recording was made of this commentary, and within one week – with the aid of the Colchester Hospitals Broadcasting Service whose Chairman had the necessary contacts – 1,000 records were produced ready for sale at the League fixture versus Newport County on the following Saturday. At that time, the Welshmen were bottom of Division IV and arguably gave United greater difficulty than Leeds! Needless to say there was great demand for the discs, and no doubt these remain treasured possessions of many supporters.

1991
The final match of the first season in the Vauxhall Conference – the League had become a two horse race by the end. The U's had to win to stand any chance of taking the title, but this was conditional upon Barnet failing to win their last fixture. United went about their task purposefully, spurred on at various stages by reactions in the crowd from those with radios who were listening in to the proceedings at Barnet. Here again was drama which was self motivating for the commentators, concluding with the utter despair of the players and spectators when it was realised that Barnet, having first gone behind in their match, finally emerged as the victors.

1992
Again the destiny of the Vauxhall Conference Championship was unresolved until the final fixture, the contenders for honours on this occasion being Wycombe. There was however, the visit to Wembley still to come, and it proved possible to arrange a link to the Hospital Radio Colchester Studio and thus relay a commentary for the benefit of any United Supporters, and others, unfortunate enough to be hospitalised at the time. Presenting a commentary from Wembley Stadium, with all the advantages of modern technology and instant replay facility via T.V. monitors was an experienced denied to most. The added spice of the U's going for, and achieving the double, again provided the perfect script for a commentator to enjoy.

Hopefully some readers of this 'Hospital Radio History' will become sufficiently interested to come forward to try their hand at commentating, and thus help to ensure the future of the service for the benefit of hospital patients.

(Article by Eric Southernwood)

# CHAPTER 10

## STATISTICAL MISCELLANY

**Colchester United have met 82 different teams in their Football League career.**
**Figures taken up to and including the 1992/93 season (Football League matches only):**

Most Meetings:
Exeter City and Southend United have each been played in 54 matches.
Least Meetings:
Barnet, Bolton Wanderers, Fulham, Maidstone United, Middlesbrough, Nottingham Forest and Wigan Athletic have each been played in only 2 matches.

Never Beaten:
Barnet, Fulham, Middlesbrough, Nottingham Forest, Rotherham United, and Wigan Athletic.
Undefeated Against:
Accrington Stanley.

Most Goals Scored Versus:
Southend United – 86 (average 1.593 per game)
Most Goals Conceded Versus:
Southend United – 94 (average 1.741

Most Victories Versus:
Crewe Alexandra – 24 in 36 games (66.67% success rate)
Most Defeats Versus:
Exeter City, Peterborough United, and Southend United – 22 each.
Most Home Victories Versus:
Aldershot, Crewe Alexandra and Torquay United – 14
Most Home Defeats Versus:
Southend United – 9 (33.33%)
Most Away Victories Versus:
Crewe Alexandra – 10 (55.55% success rate)
Most Away Defeats Versus:
Peterborough United – 16 (66.66%)
Most Homes Drawn Games Versus:
Gillingham – 11 (47.83%)
Most Away Drawn Games Versus:
Stockport County and A.F.C.Bournemouth

Most Goals in one game:
10 on two occasions.
9–1 versus Bradford City (30th of December 1961)
8–2 versus Stockport County (4th of October 1958)
(9 goals scored once, 8 goals scored once, 6 goals scored nine times)
(8 goals conceded once, 7 goals conceded five times, 6 goals conceded eleven times)
180 goals have been scored in the fixtures versus Southend United (average 3.33 per game)

Matches Failed To Score A Goal:
477 in 1880 games (25.37%)
Matches Not Conceded A Goal:
472 in 1880 games (25.11%):

## Seasons 1950/51 to 1992/93
### Top Goalscorers

| Div | Season | Leading Goalscorer | Gls/Total | Gls/Leag | Gls/Cup | App/Lge | App/Cup |
|---|---|---|---|---|---|---|---|
| 3S | 50/51 | Arthur Turner | 15 | 12 | 2 | 36 | 2 |
| 3S | 51/52 | Vic Keeble | 17 | 16 | 1 | 25 | 3 |
| 3S | 52/53 | Kevin McCurley | 19 | 16 | 3 | 42 | 5 |
| 3S | 53/54 | Bert Barlow | 10 | 0 | 0 | 32 | 2 |
| 3S | 54/55 | Kenny Plant | 13 | 13 | 0 | 40 | 2 |
| 3S | 55/56 | Kevin McCurley | 29 | 29 | 0 | 46 | 1 |
| 3S | 56/57 | Kenny Plant | 24 | 24 | 0 | 46 | 1 |
| 3S | 57/58 | Kenny Plant | 19 | 19 | 0 | 44 | 1 |
| 3 | 58/59 | Neil Langman | 27 | 20 | 7 | 44 | 6 |
| 3 | 59/60 | Martyn King | 30 | 30 | 0 | 39 | 1 |
| 3 | 60/61 | Martyn King | 25 | 23 | 2 | 38 | 3 |
| 4 | 61/62 | Bobby Hunt | 39 | 37 | 2 | 43 | 4 |
| 3 | 62/63 | Martyn King | 28 | 26 | 2 | 42 | 2 |
| 3 | 63/64 | Bobby Hunt | 23 | 20 | 3 | 33 | 5 |
| 3 | 64/65 | Arthur Langley/Billy Stark | 13 | 12/12 | 1/1 | 33/28 | 3/2 |
| 4 | 65/66 | Reg Stratton | 20 | 17 | 3 | 37 | 2 |
| 3 | 66/67 | Reg Stratton | 24 | 24 | 0 | 26 | 3 |
| 3 | 67/68 | Reg Stratton | 11 | 9 | 2 | 29 | 4 |
| 4 | 68/69 | Danny Light | 14 | 12 | 2 | 42 | 2 |
| 4 | 69/70 | Ken Jones | 16 | 16 | 0 | 28 | 0 |
| 4 | 70/71 | Ray Crawford | 31 | 24 | 7 | 45 | 10 |
| 4 | 71/72 | Brian Lewis | 20 | 15 | 5 | 29 | 4 |
| 4 | 72/73 | Micky Mahon | 12 | 12 | 0 | 44 | 4 |
| 4 | 73/74 | Bobby Svarc | 26 | 25 | 1 | 46 | 2 |
| 3 | 74/75 | Bobby Svarc | 25 | 24 | 1 | 42 | 8 |
| 3 | 75/76 | Steve Leslie | 7 | 6 | 1 | 36 | 2 |
| 3 | 76/77 | Colin Garwood | 24 | 16 | 8 | 40 | 9 |
| 3 | 77/78 | Bobby Gough | 17 | 13 | 4 | 42 | 9 |
| 4 | 78/79 | Bobby Gough | 22 | 16 | 6 | 42 | 8 |
| 4 | 79/80 | Trevor Lee | 18 | 17 | 1 | 43 | 4 |
| 4 | 80/81 | Kevin Bremner | 10 | 8 | 2 | 33 | 4 |
| 4 | 81/82 | Ian Allinson | 25 | 21 | 4 | 41 | 10 |
| 4 | 82/83 | Ian Allinson | 24 | 22 | 2 | 46 | 5 |
| 4 | 83/84 | Tony Adcock | 31 | 26 | 5 | 41 | 8 |
| 4 | 84/85 | Tony Adcock | 25 | 24 | 1 | 27 | 5 |
| 4 | 85/86 | Tony Adcock | 15 | 15 | 0 | 33 | 3 |
| 4 | 86/87 | Tony Adcock | 13 | 12 | 1 | 33 | 5 |
| 4 | 87/88 | Dale Tempest | 12 | 11 | 1 | 44 | 3 |
| 4 | 88/89 | Mario Walsh | 12 | 9 | 3 | 24 | 6 |
| 4 | 89/90 | Trevor Morgan | 12 | 12 | 0 | 31 | 2 |
| VC | 90/91 | Mario Walsh | 18 | 17 | 1 | 31 | 6 |
| VC | 91/92 | Roy McDonough | 29 | 26 | 3 | 40 | 11 |
| 3* | 92/93 | Steve McGavin/Gary Bennett | 10 | 9/8 | 1/2 | 37/38 | 5/5 |

* Old Fourth Division revised to 'Third Division'.

# CHAPTER 11

# The Players

## THE FOOTBALL LEAGUE PLAYERS 1950/51 to 1989/90

| Players | Years | Appearances Lge.u | Cup | Total | Goals Lge. | Cup | Date of Birth | Pos. | Former Club | Succeeding Club |
|---|---|---|---|---|---|---|---|---|---|---|
| Abrey Brian | 61–62 | 38 | 0 | 38 | 2 | 0 | 25/4/39 | CH | Chelsea | Retired Injury |
| Adams Ernie | 67–68 | 48 | 0 | 48 | 0 | 0 | 17/1/48 | G | Arsenal | Crewe Alex. |
| Adcock Tony | 81–87 | 212 | 37 | 249 | 98 | 12 | 27/3/63 | F | Apprentice | Manchester City |
| Aimson Paul | 73–74 | 4 | 1 | 5 | 2 | 0 | 3/8/43 | F | Bournemouth | Retired Injury |
| Aitchison Barry | 64–65 | 49 | 5 | 54 | 7 | 0 | 15/11/37 | W | Tottenham | Cambridge City |
| Aitchison Peter | 51–54 | 18 | 0 | 18 | 2 | 0 | 19/9/31 | W | Local Juniors | Sittingborne |
| Allen Robert | 50–51 | 29 | 2 | 31 | 1 | 0 | 11/10/16 | FB | Northampton | Brentford |
| Allinson Ian | 73–83\88–90 | 346 | 90 | 436 | 79 | 12 | 1/10/57 | F | Luton | Arsenal |
| Ames Percy | 55–64 | 397 | 26 | 423 | 0 | 0 | 13/12/31 | G | Tottenham | Romford |
| Anderson Terry | 74–76 | 19 | 2 | 21 | 0 | 0 | 13/3/44 | W | Bournemouth | Scunthorpe |
| Angell Darren | 1987 | 1 | 0 | 1 | 0 | 0 | 9/1/67 | D | Portsmouth loan | Portsmouth |
| Baines John | 60–62 | 4 | 0 | 4 | 0 | 0 | 25/9/37 | F | Colchester Cas. | Lexden Wan |
| Baker Terry | 85–88 | 55 | 9 | 64 | 11 | 0 | 3/11/65 | D | Billericay | Billericay |
| Barlow Bert | 52–54 | 60 | 7 | 67 | 16 | 1 | 22/7/16 | F | Leicester City | Crittalls |
| Barlow Peter | 66–68 | 21 | 2 | 23 | 5 | 0 | 9/1/50 | F | Apprentice | Workington |
| Barnett David | 88–89 | 20 | 12 | 32 | 0 | 0 | 16/4/67 | HB | Windsor Eaton | Non League |
| Barrell Les | 53–57 | 4 | 0 | 4 | 1 | 0 | 30/8/32 | F | Lexden Wan | Clacton |
| Bearryman Harry | 47–54 | 174 | 12 | 186 | 3 | 0 | 26/9/24 | W | Chelsea | Met Police |
| Beattie Kevin | 82–83 | 4 | 1 | 5 | 0 | 0 | 18/2/53 | CH | Ret'd from Inj | Middlesbrough |
| Bedford Kevin | 88–89 | 26 | 9 | 35 | 0 | 0 | 26/12/68 | F | Wimbledon | Non League |
| Bell Jackie | 65–66 | 7 | 0 | 7 | 0 | 0 | 17/10/39 | WH | Norwich | Grinford Town |
| Bennett Gary | 88–92 | 83 | 0 | 83 | 25 | 0 | 13/11/70 | FB | Tottenham | Braintree |
| Benstead Graham | 1987 | 18 | 1 | 19 | 0 | 0 | 20/8/63 | G | Norwich | On loan |
| Bickles Dave | 68–70 | 67 | 5 | 72 | 3 | 0 | 6/4/44 | CH | Crystal Palace | Romford |
| Bicknell Roy | 52–54 | 25 | 4 | 29 | 0 | 0 | 19/2/26 | CH | Bristol City | Clacton |
| Binks Martin | 72–73 | 10 | 0 | 10 | 0 | 0 | 12/9/53 | HB | Orient | Cambridge Utd |
| Birch Cliff | 54–55 | 12 | 1 | 13 | 3 | 1 | 1/9/28 | W | Newport County | Welsh N.League |
| Bircham Bernard | 50–51 | 7 | 0 | 7 | 0 | 0 | 31/8/24 | G | Grimsby | Non League |
| Blackwood Bobby | 65–68 | 105 | 10 | 115 | 7 | 2 | 20/8/34 | IF | Ipswich | PM Hawick |
| Blake Russell | 55–61 | 57 | 5 | 62 | 8 | 0 | 24/7/35 | F | Local | Sudbury |
| Bloss Phil | 69–72 | 34 | 4 | 38 | 2 | 0 | 16/1/53 | M | Apprentcie | West Brom |
| Bond Len | 1976 | 3 | 0 | 3 | 0 | 0 | 12/2/54 | G | Bristol City | On loan |
| Bourne Richard | 71–73 | 4 | 0 | 4 | 0 | 0 | 9/12/54 | FB | Local | Bath City |
| Bowen Keith | 83–86 | 116 | 17 | 133 | 38 | 10 | 26/2/58 | F | Brentford | Retired |
| Bremner Kevin | 80–83 | 95 | 15 | 110 | 30 | 5 | 7/10/57 | F | Keith | Millwall |
| Bright Stewart | 75–77 | 25 | 0 | 25 | 0 | 0 | 13/10/57 | RB | Apprentice | Chelmsford |
| Brown John | 61–63 | 1 | 2 | 3 | 0 | 0 | 6/3/40 | HB | Dunbar Utd | Stenhousemuir |
| Brown Micky | 67–70 | 52 | 6 | 58 | 12 | 0 | 11/4/44 | F | Luton | Non League |
| Brown Stan | 72–73 | 23 | 0 | 23 | 0 | 0 | 15/9/41 | WH | Fulham | Retired |
| Buck Alan | 64–69 | 38 | 3 | 41 | 0 | 0 | 25/8/46 | G | Local | Poole Town |
| Buck David | 1964 | 1 | 0 | 1 | 0 | 0 | 25/8/48 | WH | Local | Non League |
| Bullock Peter | 65–68 | 94 | 7 | 101 | 33 | 0 | 17/11/41 | IF | Southend | Exeter |
| Bunkell Ray | 73–80 | 129 | 19 | 148 | 9 | 1 | 18/9/49 | WH | Swindon | Retired |
| Burgess Eric | 70–72 | 51 | 3 | 54 | 9 | 0 | 27/10/44 | WH | Plymouth | Non League |
| Burman Simon | 83–86 | 20 | 0 | 20 | 0 | 0 | 26/11/65 | D | Apprentice | Weymouth |
| Burnside David | 1972 | 13 | 0 | 13 | 0 | 0 | 10/12/39 | IF | Bristol City | Retired |
| Cameron Danny | 1975 | 5 | 0 | 5 | 0 | 0 | 9/11/53 | D | Sheff Wed | Loan |
| Carey Peter | 60–61 | 10 | 0 | 10 | 0 | 0 | 11/4/33 | WH | Q.P.R. | Aldershot |
| Cartwright Steve | 1988 | 10 | 0 | 10 | 0 | 0 | 8/1/65 | FB | Tamworth | Tamworth |
| Chaberlain Alec | 83–87 | 188 | 13 | 201 | 0 | 0 | 20/6/64 | G | Ipswich | Everton |
| Chatterton Nick | 1986 | 50 | 9 | 59 | 8 | 2 | 18/5/54 | M | Millwall | Retired |

| Players | Years | Appearances Lge.u | Cup | Total | Goals Lge. | Cup | Date of Birth | Pos. | Former Club | Succeeding Club |
|---|---|---|---|---|---|---|---|---|---|---|
| Church John | 50–54 | 118 | 11 | 129 | 21 | 1 | 17/9/19 | W | Norwich | Crittals |
| Coleman David | 61–63 | 2 | 1 | 3 | 1 | 0 | 27/3/42 | F | Stanway | Clacton |
| Coleman David | 1988 | 6 | 6 | 12 | 1 | 0 | 8/4/67 | LB | Bournemouth | Loan |
| Coleman Phil | 81–84 | 86 | 16 | 104 | 6 | 0 | 8/9/60 | D | Millwall | Aldershot |
| Connolly Pat | 64–65 | 21 | 4 | 25 | 6 | 1 | 27/7/41 | F | Macclesfield | Altrincham |
| Cook Michael | 69–84 | 614 | 81 | 695 | 22 | 3 | 9/4/51 | RB | Orient | Retired |
| Coombe Mark | 1988 | 0 | 2 | 2 | 0 | 0 | 17/9/68 | G | Bristol City | Torquay |
| Coombs Frank | 51–54 | 38 | 0 | 38 | 0 | 0 | 24/4/25 | G | Southend | Gravesend |
| Cotton Russell | 76–82 | 35 | 1 | 36 | 1 | 0 | 4/4/60 | WH | Apprentice | Denmark |
| Cram Bobby | 70–72 | 100 | 12 | 112 | 4 | 0 | 19/11/39 | WH | Vancouver W | Canada |
| Crawford Ray | 70–71 | 45 | 10 | 55 | 24 | 7 | 13/7/36 | CF | Charlton | Durban City |
| Crouch Nigel | 80–81 | 10 | 1 | 11 | 0 | 0 | 24/11/58 | D | Ipswich | Harwich |
| Cullum Arthur | 50–54 | 2 | 0 | 2 | 1 | 0 | 28/1/31 | F | Local | Sittingborne |
| Cutting Fred | 49–52 | 29 | 3 | 32 | 13 | 2 | 4/12/21 | IF | Norwich | Yarmouth |
| Cusenza Leo | 80–81 | 0 | 1 | 1 | 0 | 0 | 20/2/63 | F | Non League | Harlow |
| Curry Bob | 46–51 | 32 | 2 | 34 | 14 | 2 | 2/11/18 | F | Gainsborough | Clacton |
| Dale Bob | 53–57 | 127 | 1 | 128 | 11 | 0 | 31/10/33 | IF | Bury | Retired |
| Daniels Scott | 88–90 | 113 | 14 | 127 | 1 | 0 | 22/11/69 | CH | Local | Exeter City |
| Davidson Alan | 51–52 | 19 | 2 | 21 | 0 | 1 | 28/11/29 | M | Sheff Wed | Carnoustie |
| Day Keith | 84–87 | 114 | 16 | 130 | 12 | 0 | 29/11/62 | CH | Aveley | Orient |
| Dennis Alan | 69–71 | 5 | 0 | 5 | 0 | 0 | 22/12/51 | HB | Local | Dover |
| Dobson Brian | 55–59 | 22 | 1 | 22 | 0 | 0 | 1/3/34 | D | Local | Clacton |
| Docherty John | 63–65 | 76 | 8 | 84 | 2 | 0 | 28/2/35 | HB | Hearts | Chelmsford |
| Dominey Barry | 73–77 | 71 | 9 | 80 | 3 | 2 | 21/10/55 | CH | Enfield WHC | Dorchester |
| Dowman Steve | 74–80 | 155 | 30 | 185 | 22 | 5 | 15/4/58 | CH | Apprentice | Wrexham |
| Dunne Austin | 53–54 | 1 | 0 | 1 | 0 | 0 | 31/7/54 | HB | Limerick | Tonbridge |
| Dyer Paul | 75–80 | 144 | 22 | 166 | 4 | 0 | 24/1/53 | D | Notts County | Gravesend |
| Dyson Barry | 73–75 | 43 | 3 | 46 | 7 | 0 | 6/9/42 | IF | Orient | Retired |
| Dyson Terry | 68–70 | 56 | 2 | 58 | 4 | 0 | 29/11/34 | OL | Fulham | Guilford |
| Eagles Alan | 1961 | 16 | 0 | 16 | 1 | 0 | 6/9/33 | FB | Orient | Q.P.R. |
| Edwards Stan | 52–53 | 16 | 3 | 19 | 5 | 2 | 17/10/33 | CF | Chelsea | Orient |
| Elder Jimmy | 50–55 | 199 | 13 | 212 | 15 | 2 | 5/3/28 | WH | Portsmouth | Non League |
| Ellis Glen | 76–77 | 2 | 0 | 2 | 0 | 0 | 3/10/57 | G | Ipswich | Lowestoft |
| English Anthony | 84– | 255 | 26 | 281 | 36 | 0 | 19/10/66 | D\M | Coventry City | |
| English Tom | 84–87 | 60 | 7 | 67 | 20 | 3 | 18/10/61 | F | Plymouth | Wealdstone |
| Evans John | 57–60 | 56 | 4 | 60 | 22 | 2 | 28/8/29 | F | Liverpool | Non League |
| Evans Tony | 77–81 | 32 | 2 | 34 | 2 | 0 | 30/8/58 | F | Apprentice | Non League |
| Farrell Andy | 83–87 | 105 | 24 | 129 | 4 | 0 | 7/10/65 | D | Apprentice | Burnley |
| Farrell Sean | 1988 | 9 | 0 | 9 | 1 | 0 | 28/2/69 | F | Luton Loan | Luton |
| Fenton Benny | 55–58 | 104 | 2 | 106 | 14 | 0 | 28/10/18 | WH | Charlton | Retired |
| Ferguson Mike | 86–87 | 26 | 3 | 29 | 11 | 0 | 3/10/54 | F | Brighton | Wealdstone |
| Fisher George | 55–60 | 163 | 9 | 172 | 6 | 0 | 19/6/25 | RB | Fulham | Non League |
| Foley Steve | 69–72 | 284 | 30 | 314 | 54 | 2 | 21/6/53 | F | Apprentice | Retired Injury |
| Forbes Duncan | 61–68 | 270 | 26 | 296 | 2 | 0 | 19/6/41 | CH | Musselburgh | Norwich City |
| Forrest Craig | 1986 | 11 | 0 | 11 | 0 | 0 | 20/9/67 | G | Ipswich Loan | Ipswich |
| Foster Mike | 61–62 | 36 | 4 | 40 | 9 | 0 | 3/2/39 | W | Leicester | Norwich |
| Fowler John | 55–68 | 415 | 27 | 442 | 5 | 0 | 17/10/33 | LB | Bonnyrigg RA | Heybridge |
| French George | 50–55 | 3 | 0 | 3 | 0 | 0 | 10/11/26 | D | Amateur | Parkside |
| Froggatt John | 74–78 | 155 | 29 | 184 | 29 | 6 | 13/12/45 | F | Boston | Port Vale |
| Gallego Joe | 49–51 | 4 | 0 | 4 | 0 | 0 | 8/4/29 | LW | Southampton | Cambridge Utd |
| Game Kirk | 85–86 | 25 | 8 | 33 | 0 | 0 | 22/10/66 | D | Southend | Chelmsford |
| Garvey Brian | 70–72 | 77 | 13 | 90 | 1 | 1 | 3/7/37 | WH | Watford | Romford |
| Garwood Colin | 76–78 | 87 | 18 | 105 | 27 | 13 | 29/6/49 | F | Huddersfield | Portsmouth |
| George Ron | 54–55 | 6 | 2 | 8 | 0 | 0 | 14/8/22 | RB | Crystal P | Sudbury |

| Players | Years | Appearances Lge.u | Cup | Total | Goals Lge. | Cup | Date of Birth | Pos. | Former Club | Succeeding Club |
|---|---|---|---|---|---|---|---|---|---|---|
| Gibbs Brian | 68–72 | 157 | 28 | 185 | 41 | 0 | 6/10/36 | F | Gillingham | Retired |
| Gilchrist John | 70–72 | 41 | 13 | 54 | 2 | 1 | 5/9/39 | D | Fulham | Tonbridge |
| Godbold Daryl | 84–85 | 7 | 3 | 10 | 1 | 0 | 5/9/64 | D | Norwich | Retired |
| Gough Bobby | 76–81 | 197 | 34 | 231 | 65 | 15 | 20/7/49 | F | Southport | Chelmsford |
| Gorman Keith | 1981 | 3 | 0 | 3 | 0 | 0 | 13/10/66 | F | Ipswich | Loan |
| Grenfell Stephen | 85–86 | 64 | 12 | 76 | 1 | 1 | 27/10/66 | L\HB | Tottenham | Non League |
| Grice Mike | 52–56\62–66 | 246 | 17 | 263 | 28 | 2 | 3/11/31 | W | Lowestoft\Coventry | West Ham\Lowestoft |
| Griffiths Ritchie | 61–65 | 48 | 5 | 53 | 0 | 0 | 21/3/42 | RB | Cor Casuals | Police |
| Groves Perry | 81–86 | 157 | 23 | 180 | 26 | 6 | 19/4/65 | W | Apprentice | Arsenal |
| Hall Brian | 65–73 | 328 | 33 | 361 | 29 | 9 | 9/3/39 | LB | Mansfield | Local League |
| Hammond Cyril | 58–60 | 95 | 5 | 100 | 5 | 0 | 10/10/27 | WH | Charlton | Severalls |
| Harford Ray | 73–75 | 107 | 10 | 117 | 4 | 1 | 1/6/45 | CH | Port Vale | Non League |
| Harris Tom | 53–54 | 3 | 0 | 3 | 0 | 0 | 8/11/24 | F | Orient | Tonbridge |
| Harris Trevor | 53–63 | 100 | 10 | 110 | 6 | 0 | 6/2/36 | WH | Wilson MS | Local League |
| Harrison Derek | 75–76 | 7 | 1 | 8 | 0 | 0 | 9/2/50 | HB | Torquay | Non League |
| Harrison John | 50–56 | 233 | 12 | 245 | 1 | 0 | 27/9/27 | RB | Aston Villa | Retired |
| Harvey Gary | 77–81 | 6 | 0 | 6 | 2 | 0 | 19/11/61 | F | Apprentice | Non League |
| Hedman Rudi | 83–89 | 176 | 27 | 203 | 9 | 1 | 16/11/65 | D | Col. Youth | Crystal Palace |
| Hetzke Steve | 88–89 | 23 | 8 | 31 | 2 | 0 | 3/6/55 | D\M | Chester | Reading |
| Hicks Stuart | 88–90 | 64 | 9 | 73 | 0 | 1 | 30/5/67 | D | Wisbech | Reading |
| Hill Bert | 52–58 | 105 | 3 | 108 | 3 | 0 | 8/3/30 | WH | Chelsea | Dartford |
| Hill Bobby | 55–65 | 238 | 17 | 255 | 21 | 1 | 9/6/38 | IF | Easthouses Lily | Bury Town |
| Hill Colin | 87–89 | 69 | 13 | 82 | 0 | 1 | 12/11/63 | D/M | Maritimo | Sheffield United |
| Hillman Dennis | 48–51 | 4 | 0 | 4 | 0 | 0 | 27/11/18 | RW | Brighton | Gillingham |
| Hinshelwood Paul | 86–88 | 83 | 15 | 98 | 6 | 0 | 14/8/56 | D | Millwall | Non League |
| Hodge Bobby | 78–81 | 92 | 19 | 111 | 14 | 2 | 30/4/54 | M | Exeter | Norway |
| Hodgson Ken | 66–68 | 56 | 4 | 60 | 19 | 0 | 19/1/42 | F | Bournemouth | Poole |
| Hornsby John | 64–66 | 12 | 1 | 13 | 1 | 0 | 3/8/45 | F | Evenwood Town | Ferryhill Ath. |
| Honeywood Brian | 68–69 | 18 | 3 | 21 | 0 | 0 | 8/5/49 | F | Ipswich | Chelmsford |
| Houston Stewart | 86–87 | 88 | 19 | 107 | 5 | 3 | 20/8/49 | CH | Man Utd | Plymouth |
| Howe Anthony | 57–58\1960 | 10 | 0 | 10 | 2 | 0 | 14/2/39 | OL | Colchester Cas | Southend |
| Howe Bert | 69–70 | 29 | 1 | 30 | 1 | 0 | 16/11/38 | FB | Orient | Romford |
| Howlett Bobby | 69–70 | 16 | 2 | 18 | 0 | 0 | 12/12/48 | FB | Southend | Non League |
| Hubbick Dave | 84–86 | 24 | 4 | 28 | 2 | 0 | 16/3/60 | F | Wimbledon | Sudbury |
| Hull Jeff | 82–85 | 79 | 12 | 91 | 10 | 0 | 25/8/60 | M | Local | Retired |
| Hunt Billy | 52–56 | 1 | 0 | 1 | 0 | 0 | 25/11/34 | WH | Local | Sudbury |
| Hunt Bobby | 59–64 | 151 | 13 | 164 | 90 | 9 | 1/10/42 | CF | School | Northampton |
| Hunt Ron | 51–64 | 177 | 10 | 187 | 3 | 0 | 26/9/33 | WH | School | Retired |
| Hunter Alan | 82–83 | 19 | 4 | 23 | 0 | 0 | 30/6/46 | CH | Ipswich | Retired |
| Hunter Lee | 1988 | 9 | 0 | 9 | 0 | 0 | 5/10/69 | D | Apprentice | Wivenhoe Town |
| Irving Russell | 84–86 | 50 | 12 | 62 | 7 | 1 | 4/1/64 | F | Ipswich | Stowmarket |
| Johnstone Ian | 58–60 | 2 | 0 | 2 | 0 | 0 | 2/3/39 | F | Ormiston Prim | Clacton |
| Jones Ken | 69–72 | 77 | 7 | 84 | 22 | 5 | 9/2/41 | IF | Millwall | Margate |
| Jones Len | 50–53 | 71 | 3 | 74 | 3 | 1 | 9/6/13 | OR | Southend | Ipswich |
| Jones Tecwyn | 64–66 | 28 | 1 | 29 | 0 | 0 | 3/1/30 | WH | Wrexham | Crewe |
| Joslyn Roger | 1968 | 99 | 6 | 105 | 4 | 0 | 7/5/50 | M | Apprentice | Aldershot |
| Kaye Arthur | 65–67 | 50 | 7 | 57 | 2 | 0 | 9/3/33 | OR | Middlesbrough | Retired |
| Keane Tommy | 87–88 | 16 | 2 | 18 | 0 | 0 | 16/9/68 | F | Bournemouth | Galway Utd. |
| Kearney Noel | 64–65 | 3 | 0 | 3 | 0 | 0 | 7/10/42 | F | Ipswich | Chelmsford |
| Keeble Vic | 49–52 | 46 | 3 | 49 | 23 | 1 | 25/6/30 | CF | Col. Casuals | Newcastle |
| Keeley Glen | 1988 | 4 | 0 | 4 | 0 | 0 | 1/9/54 | CH | Oldham Loan | Oldham |
| Keene Doug | 53–54 | 22 | 2 | 24 | 1 | 0 | 30/8/28 | OL | Brighton | Dartford |
| Keith Adrian | 82–83 | 4 | 0 | 4 | 0 | 0 | 11/12/62 | D | West Ham | Haverhill Rovers |

| Players | Years | Appearances Lge.u | Cup | Total | Goals Lge. | Cup | Date of Birth | Pos. | Former Club | Succeeding Club |
|---|---|---|---|---|---|---|---|---|---|---|
| Kelly Des | 72–73 | 1 | 1 | 2 | 0 | 0 | 1/11/50 | G | Norwich | Lowestoft |
| Kennon Neil(Sandy) | 65–67 | 77 | 6 | 83 | 0 | 0 | 28/11/33 | G | Norwich | Lowestoft |
| Kettle Albert(Digger) | 46–55 | 23 | 1 | 24 | 0 | 0 | 3/6/22 | RB | Arclight Sports | Sudbury |
| King Martyn | 58–64 | 211 | 16 | 227 | 132 | 0 | 23/8/37 | F | Pegasus | Wrexham |
| Kirk Jimmy | 54–55 | 32 | 0 | 32 | 0 | 0 | 12/11/25 | G | Bury | Torquay |
| Kurila John | 70–71 | 53 | 11 | 64 | 4 | 0 | 10/4/41 | WH | Southend | Lincoln |
| Laidlaw John | 57–60 | 41 | 1 | 42 | 1 | 0 | 5/7/36 | HB | Easthouses Lily | Clacton |
| Laitt David | 65–66 | 1 | 0 | 1 | 0 | 0 | 1/11/46 | HB | Apprentice | Local Club |
| Lake Trevor | 87–88 | 0 | 1 | 1 | 0 | 0 | 2/1/68 | G | West Ham | Stanway Rovers |
| Langley Arthur | 64–65 | 33 | 3 | 36 | 12 | 1 | 30/1/33 | IF | Oxford Utd | Scarborough |
| Langman Neil | 57–61 | 128 | 21 | 149 | 51 | 9 | 31/2/32 | S | Plymouth | Bath City |
| Layton Bill | 49–51 | 7 | 1 | 8 | 0 | 1 | 13/1/15 | IF | Bradford | Retired |
| Lamont David | 66–68 | 1 | 0 | 1 | 0 | 0 | 2/4/49 | M | Apprentice | Local |
| Lee Trevor | 78–81 | 95 | 17 | 112 | 35 | 4 | 3/7/54 | F | Millwall | Gillingham |
| Leonard Paddy | 54–55 | 34 | 0 | 34 | 5 | 0 | 25/7/29 | F | Southend | Tonbridge |
| Leslie Steve | 71–84 | 433 | 71 | 504 | 40 | 0 | 4/9/52 | F\M | Amateur | Chelmsford |
| Lewis Brian | 70–72 | 46 | 8 | 54 | 17 | 7 | 26/1/43 | F | Oxford Utd | Portsmouth |
| Lewis Fred | 53–55 | 85 | 4 | 89 | 4 | 0 | 27/7/23 | LB | Chelsea | Headington |
| Light Danny | 68–70 | 67 | 6 | 73 | 17 | 2 | 10/7/48 | F | Crystal P | Guildford |
| Lindsay Jimmy | 74–75 | 45 | 6 | 51 | 6 | 1 | 12/7/49 | M | Watford | Hereford |
| Linford John | 1983 | 7 | 0 | 7 | 0 | 0 | 6/2/57 | F | Ipswich Loan | Ipswich |
| Locherty Joe | 50–51 | 10 | 1 | 11 | 1 | 0 | 5/9/25 | F | Sheff Wed | Scarborough |
| Longhorn Dennis | 80–83 | 71 | 7 | 78 | 0 | 0 | 12/9/50 | M | Aldershot | Chelmsford |
| Loughton Mick | 61–68 | 122 | 11 | 133 | 7 | 0 | 8/12/42 | CH | Casuals | Chelmsford |
| Lowe Simon | 1987 | 36 | 3 | 39 | 8 | 0 | 26/12/62 | F | Hartlepool | Scarborough |
| Lundstrum Colin | 61–62 | 1 | 0 | 1 | 0 | 0 | 9/10/38 | F | Ipswich | Clacton |
| Lyons John | 1982 | 30 | 4 | 34 | 9 | 1 | 8/11/56 | F | Cambridge Utd | Deceased |
| Macedo Tony | 68–69 | 38 | 2 | 40 | 0 | 0 | 22/2/38 | G | Fulham | Durban |
| McAllister Tom | 1989 | 20 | 1 | 21 | 0 | 0 | 10/12/52 | G | West Ham | Loan |
| McClelland John | 51–52 | 0 | 1 | 1 | 0 | 0 | 11/8/30 | F | Local | Stoke |
| McColl Tommy | 63–64 | 11 | 1 | 12 | 2 | 0 | 19/9/45 | F | Dennistown | Chelsea |
| McCourt Frank | 54–55 | 12 | 0 | 12 | 0 | 0 | 9/12/25 | WH | Man City | Poole |
| McCrohan Roy | 62–64 | 76 | 6 | 82 | 4 | 0 | 22/9/30 | WH | Norwich | Bristol Rovers |
| McCurley Kevin | 52–60 | 224 | 13 | 237 | 94 | 6 | 2/4/26 | F | Liverpool | Oldham |
| McDonald Ian | 74–75 | 5 | 0 | 5 | 2 | 0 | 10/5/53 | F\M | Liverpool | Loan |
| McDonough Roy | 81–83/92– | 118 | 15 | 133 | 22 | 2 | 16/10/58 | F | Chelsea | Southend |
| McGee Paul | 1989 | 3 | 1 | 4 | 0 | 0 | 17/5/68 | W | Bohemians | Wimbledon |
| McInally John | 72–73 | 27 | 2 | 29 | 0 | 0 | 26/9/51 | G | Lincoln | Braintree |
| McKechnie Tommy | 67–68 | 23 | 4 | 27 | 5 | 1 | 9/2/40 | F | Bournemouth | Bury Town |
| McKim Johnny | 50–55 | 129 | 7 | 136 | 45 | 1 | 22/1/26 | F | Chelsea | Clacton |
| McLaughlin John | 72–74 | 68 | 6 | 74 | 2 | 0 | 29/10/54 | D | Apprentice | Swindon |
| McLeod Sammy | 55–62 | 150 | 12 | 162 | 21 | 2 | 4/1/34 | F | Easthouses Lily | Romford |
| McNeil Hamish | 57–58 | 2 | 0 | 2 | 1 | 0 | 16/11/34 | F | Bonnyrigg Rose | Cambridge City |
| Mahon Micky | 70–74 | 143 | 16 | 159 | 25 | 5 | 17/9/44 | W | York City | Wimbledon |
| Mansfield John | 64–68 | 34 | 8 | 42 | 3 | 0 | 13/9/46 | F | Local | Brentwood |
| Martin John | 66–69 | 78 | 11 | 89 | 11 | 0 | 4/12/46 | F | Aston Villa | Workington |
| Marshall Alf | 57–60 | 29 | 0 | 29 | 0 | 0 | 21/5/33 | D | Dagenham | Clacton |
| Massey Roy | 1969 | 33 | 5 | 38 | 11 | 4 | 10/9/43 | F | Orient | Retired |
| Milligan Chic | 56–61 | 183 | 13 | 196 | 3 | 0 | 26/7/30 | CH | Ardrossan | Non League |
| Mills Robbie | 72–74 | 20 | 6 | 26 | 0 | 0 | 16/3/55 | F | Apprentice | Chelmsford City |
| Millar Tommy | 59–62 | 48 | 7 | 55 | 4 | 0 | 3/12/38 | D | Bo'ness | Raith Rovers |
| Miller Tony | 58–64 | 1 | 0 | 1 | 0 | 0 | 26/10/37 | F | Local | Local |
| Mochan Dennis | 66–70 | 115 | 8 | 123 | 2 | 0 | 12/12/35 | RB | Nottm Forest | Club Trainer |
| Moore Gary | 1974 | 11 | 0 | 11 | 7 | 0 | 4/11/45 | CF | Southend | Chester |

| Players | Years | Appearances Lge.u | Cup | Total | Goals Lge. | Cup | Date of Birth | Pos. | Former Club | Succeeding Club |
|---|---|---|---|---|---|---|---|---|---|---|
| Moore John | 50–51 | 2 | 0 | 2 | 0 | 0 | 25/9/23 | M | Brentford | Staines |
| Morgan Stuart | 72–75 | 81 | 7 | 88 | 10 | 1 | 23/9/49 | CH | Reading | Bournemouth |
| Moss Bobby | 72–73 | 18 | 1 | 19 | 3 | 0 | 13/2/52 | F | Orient | Non League |
| Moughton Bobby | 68–69 | 4 | 1 | 5 | 0 | 0 | 30/12/47 | M | Q.P.R. | Bedford |
| Noble Alf | 55–66 | 1 | 0 | 1 | 0 | 0 | 18/9/24 | F | Briggs | Leytonstone |
| Noble Bobbie | 72–73 | 27 | 4 | 31 | 0 | 0 | 25/5/49 | D | Barrow | Southport |
| Norman Sean | 86–87 | 21 | 2 | 23 | 0 | 0 | 27/11/66 | D | Lowestoft | Wycombe Wand |
| O'Donnell John | 1975 | 1 | 0 | 1 | 0 | 0 | 21/3/54 | D | Cambridge Utd | Cambridge Utd |
| O'Rourke Ken | 68–69 | 1 | 1 | 2 | 0 | 0 | 8/12/49 | F | Ipswich | Bedford |
| Oldfield Craig | 83–85 | 4 | 0 | 4 | 0 | 0 | 24/11/63 | F | Apprentice | Bury Town |
| Oliver Jim | 68–70 | 74 | 5 | 79 | 10 | 1 | 3/12/41 | RW | Brighton | Kings Lynn |
| Osborne Roger | 81–86 | 206 | 29 | 237 | 9 | 0 | 9/3/50 | M | Ipswich | Sudbury |
| Owen Brian | 70–72 | 13 | 5 | 18 | 2 | 2 | 2/11/44 | W | Watford | Wolves |
| Packer Mick | 73–83 | 342 | 45 | 387 | 21 | 3 | 20/4/58 | D | Watford | Wivenhoe |
| Painter Trevor | 1970 | 1 | 0 | 1 | 0 | 0 | 2/7/49 | F | Norwich | Kings Lynn |
| Parker Derek | 57–61 | 129 | 8 | 137 | 1 | 0 | 23/6/26 | WH | West Ham | Stowmarket |
| Parkinson Noel | 84–86 | 80 | 12 | 92 | 13 | 0 | 16/11/59 | M | Scunthorpe | Retired |
| Perryman Gerry | 68–69 | 2 | 1 | 3 | 0 | 0 | 3/10/47 | D | Northampton | Corby |
| Phillips Ian | 83–86 | 151 | 11 | 162 | 10 | 0 | 23/4/59 | LB | Northampton | Aldershot |
| Phillips Ted | 65–66 | 38 | 2 | 40 | 13 | 0 | 21/8/33 | F | Luton | Floriana(Malta) |
| Pitt Steve | 1969 | 6 | 1 | 7 | 0 | 0 | 1/8/48 | F | Tottenham | Stevenage |
| Plant Ken | 54–59 | 188 | 7 | 195 | 82 | 2 | 15/8/25 | CF | Bury | Nuneaton |
| Presland Eddie | 1969 | 5 | 1 | 6 | 0 | 0 | 27/3/43 | D | Crystal P | Loan |
| Price Ray | 64–67 | 17 | 0 | 17 | 0 | 0 | 18/5/44 | RB | Norwich | Non League |
| Price Terry | 67–69 | 57 | 7 | 64 | 5 | 1 | 11/10/45 | F | Orient | Non League |
| Radford Mark | 87–90 | 64 | 8 | 72 | 0 | 0 | 20/12/68 | M | Apprentice | Bury Town |
| Raine David | 65–67 | 49 | 4 | 53 | 0 | 0 | 28/3/37 | D | Doncaster | Burton Albion |
| Ramage George | 61–64 | 38 | 4 | 42 | 0 | 0 | 28/3/37 | G | Third Lanark | Orient |
| Ray John | 87–88 | 1 | 0 | 1 | 0 | 0 | 21/11/68 | CH | YTS | Non League |
| Reeves John | 86–88 | 43 | 8 | 51 | 0 | 0 | 8/7/63 | M | Fulham | Cornard United |
| Roberts Bobbie | 1973 | 2 | 0 | 2 | 0 | 0 | 2/9/40 | M | Coventry | Manager |
| Rochford Bill | 50–51 | 2 | 0 | 2 | 0 | 0 | 23/5/13 | FB | Southampton | Retired |
| Roe John | 58–60 | 2 | 0 | 2 | 0 | 0 | 7/1/38 | RB | West Calder | Dunfermline |
| Rookes Phil | 51–53 | 68 | 6 | 74 | 0 | 0 | 23/4/19 | LB | Portsmouth | Chichester |
| Rowan Barry | 68–69 | 2 | 1 | 3 | 0 | 0 | 24/4/42 | W | Middlesbrough | Reading |
| Rooke Rodney | 1988 | 4 | 2 | 6 | 0 | 0 | 7/4/70 | D | Apprentice | Non League |
| Rowe Colwyn | 73–75 | 4 | 8 | 12 | 2 | 0 | 22/3/56 | W | Ipswich | Gillingham |
| Rowlands Trevor | 50–53 | 46 | 0 | 46 | 5 | 0 | 2/2/22 | W\D | Norwich | Yarmouth |
| Rowles Eddie | 77–82 | 86 | 18 | 104 | 17 | 3 | 10/3/51 | F | Darlington | Retired |
| Rumney Edgar | 57–65 | 50 | 2 | 52 | 0 | 0 | 15/9/36 | D | Local | Local |
| Rutter Keith | 63–64 | 63 | 5 | 68 | 0 | 0 | 10/9/31 | CH | Q.P.R. | Romford |
| Salisbury Gareth | 64–65 | 15 | 2 | 17 | 2 | 1 | 11/3/41 | F | Luton | Chesterfield |
| Scott Augie | 51–54 | 120 | 7 | 127 | 10 | 2 | 19/2/21 | W | Southampton | Cheltenham |
| Scott Robert | 89–90 | 37 | 4 | 41 | 8 | 2 | 13/1/64 | F | Whitburn | East Fife |
| Sharkey Pat | 1978 | 6 | 2 | 8 | 0 | 0 | 26/8/53 | M | Mansfield | Peterborough |
| Shinners Paul | 1985 | 6 | 0 | 6 | 1 | 0 | 8/1/59 | F | Gillingham | Loan |
| Shires Alan | 66–68 | 22 | 2 | 24 | 3 | 0 | 29/6/48 | F | Southend | Pegasus |
| Sherratt Brian | 70–71 | 9 | 0 | 9 | 0 | 0 | 29/3/44 | G | Gainsborough T | Oxford City |
| Silvester Peter | 1973 | 4 | 0 | 4 | 0 | 0 | 19/2/48 | F | Norwich City | Loan |
| Simmons Dave | 70–73 | 59 | 9 | 68 | 11 | 6 | 24/10/48 | F | Walsall | Cambridge |
| Simpson Owen | 68–69 | 43 | 2 | 45 | 4 | 0 | 18/9/43 | Ut | Orient | Southend |
| Sims John | 1975 | 3 | 0 | 3 | 0 | 0 | 14/8/52 | G | Derby County | Loan |
| Slater Mal | 69–70 | 4 | 0 | 4 | 0 | 0 | 22/10/39 | F | Orient | Inverness Cal |

| Players | Years | Appearances Lge.u | Cup | Total | Goals Lge. | Cup | Date of Birth | Pos. | Former Club | Succeeding Club |
|---|---|---|---|---|---|---|---|---|---|---|
| Smith Alex | 73–75 | 53 | 4 | 57 | 1 | 0 | 11/5/47 | D | Southend | Halifax |
| Smith Barrie | 71–73 | 48 | 1 | 49 | 0 | 0 | 3/3/53 | G | Local | Sunderland |
| Smith Eddie | 56–57 | 35 | 1 | 36 | 13 | 0 | 23/3/39 | CF | Northampton | Q.P.R. |
| Smith Gary | 87–88 | 11 | 1 | 12 | 0 | 0 | 3/12/68 | D | Fulham | Wycombe W. |
| Smith Graham | 69–72 | 95 | 17 | 112 | 0 | 0 | 2/11/47 | G | Notts County | West Brom |
| Smith Jim | 72–73 | 8 | 1 | 9 | 0 | 0 | 17/10/40 | M | Boston | Blackburn Rvrs |
| Smith Lindsay | 71–76 | 212 | 16 | 228 | 12 | 5 | 18/9/54 | W\D | Apprentice | Cambridge |
| South John | 72–73 | 4 | 0 | 4 | 0 | 0 | 30/11/52 | CH | Orient | Non League |
| Stafford Clive | 1989 | 33 | 2 | 35 | 0 | 0 | 4/4/63 | D | Diss Town | Exeter City |
| Stark Billy | 62–65 | 96 | 6 | 102 | 31 | 3 | 27/5/37 | F | Carlisle | Luton |
| Stewart Reg | 50–57 | 255 | 13 | 268 | 2 | 0 | 30/10/25 | CH | Sheff Wed | Clacton |
| Stratton Reg | 65–68 | 112 | 9 | 121 | 49 | 5 | 10/7/39 | CF | Fulham | Vancouver R |
| Svarc Bobbie | 72–75 | 116 | 12 | 128 | 59 | 4 | 8/2/46 | CF | Boston | Blackburn |
| Swindlehurst David | 88–89 | 12 | 6 | 18 | 5 | 1 | 6/1/56 | F | Non League | Retired |
| Taylor John | 82–84 | 1 | 0 | 1 | 0 | 0 | 24/10/64 | F | Apprentice | Sudbury Town |
| Taylor Les | 88–90 | 52 | 5 | 57 | 1 | 0 | 4/12/56 | M | Reading | Retired |
| Taylor Paul | 1974 | 9 | 0 | 9 | 0 | 0 | 3/12/49 | M | Hereford | Southport |
| Telford Billy | 1976 | 2 | 0 | 2 | 0 | 0 | 5/3/56 | F | Peterborough | Loan |
| Tempest Dale | 87–89 | 44 | 7 | 51 | 0 | 0 | 30/12/63 | F | Lockeren | Hong Kong |
| Thomas Phil | 72–76 | 108 | 14 | 122 | 8 | 0 | 14/12/52 | IF | Bournemouth | Non League |
| Trevis Derek | 64–65 | 197 | 18 | 215 | 12 | 3 | 9/9/42 | IF | Aston Villa | Walsall |
| Turner Arthur | 46–52 | 45 | 2 | 47 | 14 | 2 | 23/1/22 | F | Charlton | Headington |
| Turner Robin | 85–86 | 11 | 3 | 13 | 0 | 0 | 10/9/55 | F | Swansea City | Retired |
| Walker Bob | 1967 | 17 | 2 | 19 | 0 | 0 | 23/7/42 | D | Margate | Salisbury |
| Walker Mike | 73–87 | 451 | 71 | 522 | 0 | 0 | 28/11/45 | G | Watford | Coach |
| Ward Wayne | 81–83 | 20 | 8 | 28 | 0 | 0 | 28/4/64 | D | Apprentice | Wivenhoe |
| Warner John | 89–90 | 17 | 1 | 18 | 3 | 0 | 20/11/61 | F | Burnham | Dagenham |
| Walton Mark | 1987 | 40 | 7 | 47 | 0 | 0 | 1/6/69 | G | Luton | Norwich City |
| Walsh Mario | 1987 | 13 | 4 | 17 | 2 | 0 | 19/1/66 | F | Torquay | Southend |
| Westlake Brian | 1966 | 15 | 0 | 15 | 5 | 0 | 19/9/43 | CF | Tranmere R | Royal Daring(B) |
| White Winston | 1988 | 55 | 7 | 62 | 0 | 0 | 26/10/58 | W | Bury | Burnley |
| Whittaker Ray | 69–71 | 45 | 5 | 50 | 7 | 0 | 15/1/45 | W | Luton | Wealdstone |
| Whymark Trevor | 85–86 | 2 | 0 | 2 | 0 | 0 | 4/5/50 | F | Diss T. | Diss T. |
| Wignall Steve | 77–84 | 289 | 47 | 336 | 17 | 10 | 17/9/54 | D | Doncaster R | Aldershot |
| Wilkins Richard | 86–90 | 152 | 22 | 174 | 22 | 0 | 28/5/65 | F\M | Haverhill R | Cambridge U |
| Wilkinson Harry | 52–53 | 1 | 0 | 1 | 0 | 0 | 20/3/26 | WH | Exeter | Folkestone |
| Williams John | 75–78 | 108 | 19 | 127 | 1 | 0 | 26/3/47 | D | Watford | Retired |
| Williams Keith | 87–88 | 10 | 0 | 10 | 0 | 0 | 12/4/57 | M | Bath City | Retired |
| Williams Tommy | 56–61 | 150 | 7 | 157 | 28 | 4 | 10/2/35 | W | Carshalton | Watford |
| Willis Ron | 68–70 | 9 | 1 | 10 | 0 | 0 | 27/12/47 | G | Brentford | South Africa |
| Wingate Tony | 71–72 | 1 | 0 | 1 | 0 | 0 | N.Known | M | Apprentice | Retired Injured |
| Wood Brian | 68–70 | 71 | 6 | 77 | 2 | 0 | 8/12/40 | CH | Orient | Workington |
| Woods Charlie | 1971 | 3 | 0 | 3 | 0 | 0 | 18/3/41 | F | Watford | Blackburn |
| Woods Pat | 63–64 | 36 | 5 | 41 | 0 | 0 | 29/4/33 | FB | Q.P.R. | Australia |
| Wooldridge Steve | 72–73 | 3 | 1 | 4 | 0 | 0 | 18/7/50 | RB | Crystal P | Non League |
| Wright George | 48–55 | 151 | 14 | 165 | 0 | 0 | 10/10/19 | G | Plymouth | Retired |
| Wright John | 53–55 | 4 | 0 | 4 | 0 | 0 | 13/8/33 | G | Local | Gt Bentley |
| Wright Peter | 52–64 | 427 | 21 | 448 | 92 | 6 | 26/1/34 | W | Local | Haverhill R |
| Wright Steve | 77–82 | 121 | 22 | 143 | 2 | 0 | 16/6/59 | CH | Local | Finland |
| Young Scott | 86–88 | 0 | 1 | 1 | 0 | 0 | 22/7/69 | F | Apprentice | Wycombe Wand |
| Youngman Stuart | 84–86 | 6 | 0 | 6 | 1 | 0 | 5/10/65 | M | Apprentice | Non League |

# The Football League Players 1950/51 to 1989/90

| Players | Years | Appearances Lge. | Cup | Tota | Goals Lge. | Cup | Date of Birth | Pos. | Former Club | Succeeding Club |
|---|---|---|---|---|---|---|---|---|---|---|
| Abrahams Paul | 1992 | 23 | 0 | 23 | 6 | 0 | 31/10/73 | F | Apprentice | |
| Ball Steven | 1989 | 28 | 2 | 30 | 4 | 3 | 2/9/69 | M | Norwich City | |
| Barber Fred | 92-93 | 10 | 0 | 10 | 0 | 0 | 2/8/63 | G | Peterbor. Loan | Peterborough |
| Barrett Scott | 89-90 | 13 | 0 | 13 | 0 | 0 | 2/4/63 | G | Stoke C. Loan | Stoke City |
| Betts Simon | 1992 | 23 | 1 | 24 | 0 | 0 | 3/3/73 | M | Scarborough | |
| Blake Mark | 89-90 | 4 | 0 | 4 | 1 | 0 | 19/12/67 | D | Southamp.Loan | Shrewsbury |
| Bruce Marcelle | 89-90 | 29 | 2 | 31 | 1 | 0 | 18/3/71 | D | Apprentice | Baldock |
| Cawley Peter | 92-93 | 24 | 0 | 24 | 3 | 0 | 15/9/65 | D | Barnet | |
| Collins Eammon | 89-90 | 39 | 6 | 35 | 2 | 1 | 22/10/65 | M | Portsmouth | Exeter City |
| Cook Jason | 92-93 | 34 | 2 | 36 | 1 | 0 | 29/12/65 | M | Southend | |
| Devereux Robbie | 89-92 | 8 | 2 | 10 | 0 | 0 | 13/1/71 | M | Ipswich | Sudbury |
| Donald Warren | 92-93 | 10 | 4 | 14 | 0 | 0 | 7/10/64 | M | Northampton | Kettering |
| Emberson Carl | 92-93 | 13 | 0 | 13 | 0 | 0 | 13/7/73 | G | Millwall Loan | Millwall |
| Flowers Paul | 92-93 | 3 | 0 | 3 | 0 | 0 | 7/9/74 | D | Apprentice | |
| Gilbert Billy | 89-90 | 27 | 3 | 30 | 0 | 0 | 10/11/59 | D | Portsmouth | Non League |
| Grace John | 89-90 | 19 | 6 | 25 | 0 | 0 | 12/2/64 | G | Tolka Rovers | Returned to Eire |
| Grainger Martin | 89- | 38 | 3 | 41 | 5 | 0 | 23/8/72 | D | Apprentice | |
| Goddard Karl | 89-90 | 16 | 0 | 16 | 1 | 0 | 29/12/67 | D | Bradford C.Loan | Bradford City |
| Green Ron | 92-93 | 4 | 1 | 5 | 0 | 0 | 3/10/56 | G | Non League | Non League |
| Hagan Jim | 89-90 | 2 | 1 | 3 | 0 | 0 | 10/8/56 | D | Spain | Larne |
| Hansbury Roger | 89-90 | 4 | 0 | 4 | 0 | 0 | 26/1/55 | G | Bir'ham Loan | Cardiff City |
| Hazel Julian | 92- | 2 | 2 | 4 | 0 | 0 | 25/9/73 | F | Apprentice | |
| Hopkins Robert | 92-93 | 14 | 1 | 15 | 1 | 0 | 25/10/61 | M | Shrewsbury | |
| Kelly Tony | 89-90 | 13 | 7 | 20 | 2 | 0 | 1/10/64 | M | West.Brom Loan | Shrewsbury |
| Kinsella Mark | 89- | 44 | 6 | 50 | 6 | 0 | 12/8/72 | M | Home Farm | |
| McGavin Steve | 92- | 37 | 2 | 39 | 9 | 1 | 24/1/69 | F | Sudbury Town | |
| Marrott Andrew | 89-90 | 10 | 0 | 10 | 0 | 0 | 11/10/70 | G | Nott. F. Loan | Nottingham F. |
| Martin Dean | 92-93 | 8 | 0 | 8 | 2 | 0 | 31/8/72 | F | West Ham Loan | West Ham |
| Monk Alistair | 92-93 | 0 | 1 | 1 | 0 | 0 | 8/11/72 | G | Norwich City | Non League |
| Morgan Trevor | 89-90 | 32 | 4 | 36 | 12 | 0 | 30/9/56 | F | Bolton Wands. | |
| Munson Nathan | 92-93 | 1 | 0 | 1 | 0 | 0 | 10/11/74 | G | Apprentice | |
| Newell Paul | 92-93 | 14 | 2 | 16 | 0 | 0 | 23/2/69 | G | Leyton O. Loan | Leyton Orient |
| Oxbrow Darren | 92-93 | 16 | 4 | 20 | 4 | 0 | 1/9/69 | D | Ipswich | Barnet |
| Partner Andy | 92-93 | 1 | 0 | 1 | 0 | 0 | 21/10/74 | D | Apprentice | |
| Pollard John | 89-90 | 9 | 1 | 10 | 1 | 0 | 17/11/71 | D | Apprentice | Halstead |
| Restarick Steve | 89-92 | 1 | 0 | 1 | 0 | 0 | 28/11/71 | F | Apprentice | Chelmsford C. |
| Roberts Paul | 92- | 42 | 4 | 46 | 1 | 0 | 27/4/62 | D | Fisher Ath. | |
| Smith Nicky | 92- | 42 | 4 | 46 | 4 | 0 | 28/1/69 | M | Southend | |
| Sorrell Tony | 92-93 | 5 | 1 | 6 | 1 | 1 | 17/10/66 | M | Peterborough | Barnet |

## GM Vauxhall Conference Players 1990/91 and 1991/92

| Players | Years | Appearances Lge. | Appearances Cup | Appearances Total | Goals Lge. | Goals Cup | Date of Birth | Pos. | Former Club | Succeeding Club |
|---|---|---|---|---|---|---|---|---|---|---|
| Abrahams Paul | 91–92 | 3 | 3 | 6 | 6 | 0 | | F | Apprentice | – |
| Atkins Ian | 90–91 | 41 | 3 | 44 | 7 | 1 | 16/1/57 | D | Birmingham C. | Birmingham C. |
| Barrett Scott * | 90–92 | 84 | 23 | 107 | 1 | 0 | 2/4/63 | G | Stoke City | Gillingham |
| Bennett Gary * | 90–92 | 72 | 17 | 89 | 25 | 10 | 13/11/70 | F | Tottenham H. | Braintree |
| Brooke Gary | 90–91 | 0 | 1 | 1 | 0 | 0 | 24/11/60 | MF | Norwich | non–League |
| Bruce Marcelle | 90–91 | 34 | 2 | 36 | 0 | 0 | 15/3/71 | D | Tottenham H. | Baldock Town |
| Collins Eamonn * | 89–92 | 69 | 17 | 86 | 4 | 1 | 22/10/65 | MF | Portsmouth | Exeter City |
| Cook Jason | 91–92 | 32 | 13 | 45 | 2 | 1 | 29/12/69 | MF | Southend | – |
| Daniels Scott * | 90–91 | 42 | 7 | 49 | 1 | 0 | 22/11/69 | CH | Youth team | Exeter City |
| Dart Julian (later Hazel) | 91–92 | 1 | 2 | 3 | 0 | 0 | 25/9/73 | D | Apprentice | Chelmsford C. |
| Donald Warren | 90–92 | 73 | 19 | 92 | 0 | 0 | 7/10/64 | D | Northampton T. | Kettering T. |
| Duffett Sean | 1991 | 1 | 1 | 2 | 0 | 0 | | F | Eastern Gas Rec. | Wivenhoe T. |
| Elliott Shaun | 90–92 | 54 | 7 | 61 | 0 | 0 | 26/1/58 | D | Blackpool | Gateshead |
| English Tony * | 84–92 | 78 | 21 | 99 | 13 | 2 | 10/10/66 | D/M | Coventry City | – |
| Goodwin James | 90–91 | 3 | 2 | 5 | 0 | 0 | 20/7/74 | D | Apprentice | Halstead Town |
| Grainger Martin | 90–91 | 16 | 11 | 27 | 0 | 0 | 23/8/72 | D/M | Apprentice | – |
| Gray Simon | 91–92 | 2 | 1 | 3 | 0 | 0 | | D | Ipswich Town | Wivenhoe T |
| Hannigan Wayne | 91–92 | 0 | 1 | 1 | 0 | 0 | | MF | Home Farm | |
| Hedman Rudi * | 91–92 | 7 | 0 | 7 | 0 | 0 | 16/11/64 | MF | Junior | Crystal Palace |
| Kinsella Mark * | 89–93 | 49 | 14 | 63 | 3 | 4 | 12/8/72 | MF | Home Farm | – |
| Leworthy David | 90–91 | 9 | 0 | 9 | 0 | 0 | 22/10/62 | F | Reading | Farnborough |
| McDonough Roy | 90–92 | 64 | 16 | 80 | 34 | 4 | 16/10/58 | F | Southend U. | – |
| McGavin Steve | 90–92 | 7 | 14 | 21 | 8 | 8 | 24/1/69 | F | Sudbury Town | – |
| Marmon Neale * | 90–91 | 36 | 8 | 44 | 2 | 3 | 21/4/61 | D | Hanover | Homberg |
| Martin David | 91–92 | 8 | 2 | 10 | 0 | 0 | 25/4/63 | D | Southend U. | Southend U. |
| Masters Mike | 90–92 | 21 | 8 | 29 | 6 | 2 | | F | Albany Capitals | Newbury T. |
| Osbourne Garry | 90–91 | 6 | 0 | 6 | 0 | 0 | | M | Telford United | non–League |
| Partner Andy | 91–92 | 0 | 1 | 1 | 0 | 0 | | D | Apprentice | – |
| Phillips Ian * | 90–91 | 3 | 1 | 4 | 0 | 0 | 23/4/59 | D | Kettering | Harwich |
| Radford Mark * | 90–91 | 3 | 2 | 5 | 0 | 0 | 20/12/68 | M | Apprentice | Bury Town |
| Rees Mark | 90–91 | 1 | 0 | 1 | 0 | 0 | 13/10/61 | F | Walsall | Luxembourg |
| Restarick Steve | 91–92 | 5 | 7 | 12 | 5 | 5 | 28/7/71 | F | Apprentice | Chelmsford C. |
| Roberts Paul | 91–92 | 35 | 11 | 46 | 1 | 0 | 27/4/62 | D | Fisher Athletic | – |
| Ryan Laurie | 90–91 | 10 | 3 | 13 | 2 | 0 | 15/10/63 | F | Cambridge U. | |
| Scott Morrys | 90–91 | 3 | 0 | 3 | 0 | 0 | | F | | |
| Smith Nick | 90–92 | 86 | 20 | 106 | 8 | 3 | 28/1/69 | M | Southend United | – |
| Stewart Ian | 91–92 | 10 | 4 | 14 | 2 | 3 | 10/9/61 | F | Aldershot | |
| Walsh Mario * | 90–91 | 32 | 6 | 38 | 17 | 1 | 19.1.66 | F | Southend United | Redbridge |
| Yates Mark | 90–91 | 25 | 3 | 28 | 6 | 0 | 24.1.70 | F | Birmingham C. | Burnley |

* = Player with Club in pre–Conference days (Appearances and goals are total, unless appeared in a separate pre–Conference period).

**Note: (Pages 120–127) All player records include substitute appearances**

# CHAPTER 12

## THE MANAGERS

Eighteen men have occupied the manager's chair at Layer Road during United's history. The longest serving being Benny Fenton from 1954 to 1963, and the shortest that of Ron Meades – for four days in the early fifties.

In chronological order they were:– Ted David, Syd Fieldus, Ted Fenton (these three were Secretary/Managers in Southern League Days). Jimmy Allen was manager when the club were admitted to the Football League. Then came Ron Meades, Jack Butler, Benny Fenton, Neil Franklin, Dick Graham, Jim Smith, Bobby Roberts, Allan Hunter, Cyril Lea, Mike Walker, Roger Brown, Jock Wallace, Mick Mills, Ian Atkins and the present incumbent Roy McDonough. There have also been a number of Caretaker/Managers – between permanent appointments – notably Alf Miller, Denis Mochan and Steve Foley, three times.

There are various opinions on which one was the best, an argument that of course can never be satisfactorily resolved.

**Ted Davis** – starting from scratch – did a marvellous job in the two full seasons he had at the helm before the Second World War brought his stewardship to a close.

**Ted Fenton** was the architect of that remarkable F.A. Cup run of the late forties and his brother Benny came within a whisker of getting the club in the Second Division in 1957.

**Dick Graham**, took the team into the last eight of the F.A. Cup – remember that astonishing win over Leeds United – and also saw his boys win the Watney Cup.

Others feel that the vintage years were when **Jim Smith** held sway with Bobby Roberts as his coach. Who can say? But it does from time to time provide the chance, for friendly argument and nostalgia, especially among the old–timers.

### EDWIN "TED" DAVIS
### June 1937 to September 1939

Ted, or to give him his full name Edwin Davis took over as the Secretary/Manager of the newly formed Colchester United F.C. on the 21st of June 1937. His brief to sign a team of professionals as cheaply as possible, but also good enough to hold their own in the Southern League. No easy task!

Davis in his time had played for Huddersfield Town and Blackburn Rovers at First Division level in the 1920's and later spent ten years as Secretary/Manager of Bath City, themselves a Southern League club of substance.

So from the start he knew his way around and had an extensive network of contacts as evidenced by the players he signed. Perhaps his shrewdest acquisition was experienced half–back James Baker from Bristol Rovers who continued playing and organising the training – he was in effect the U's first Coach.

Davis also brought with him from Bath groundsman Jock Duncan who was to give the club 25 years of invaluable service in that capacity. Quite apart from his signings however, Davis was a very careful man.

Fred Draycott had legions of stories on his personal tightness and how getting him to buy a drink was an occasion to remember! Nevertheless the Secretary/Manager's canny approach to money matters was to prove of great value in the Club's formative years.

One legend regarding Davis however, must be corrected. In the newspapers of the day he is credited as having won an F.A. Cup Winners medal with Huddersfield Town in 1922. Certainly he was on the Yorkshire club's books at the time and was their regular goalkeeper in the Football League. But Mutch was their 'keeper in that Cup Winning side and according to Huddersfield records only eleven medals were issued to their players.

Davis was busily planning for his third season at Layer Road when the Second World War broke out. He ended his service by assisting acting Chairman W.H. Clark to pack and make an inventory of all the club's loose property which was put into storage. The trophies in their possession were deposited at the National Provincial Bank. He died at his home in Bath, at the age of 60.

### SYD FIELDUS
### June 1945 to April 1946

Syd Fieldus, who was exempt from Military service – but who won the O.B.E. for his work with the Home Guard – first arrived at Layer Road from Brentford. In the two pre–war seasons he was a part–time pro. while also pursuing his career as a commercial traveller.

During the war years he kept in close touch with the Directors and when Layer Road became available again for football, Fieldus was Secretary/Manager in an honorary capacity from June 1945 until Ted Fenton was appointed in 1946. He also continued as a player mainly in the reserves until the late forties.

It was largely due to the efforts of Fieldus and the then honourary treasurer, Claude Orrin, that football in the Southern League restarted in 1945. The Board of Directors were evenly divided on the subject and it was only the persistence of these two men that swayed the issue in the end.

It was Fieldus too, with Major Dai Rees – the Army Liaison Officer – who arranged for a steady flow of footballers serving in the Colchester area to be available for games with United. He continued to act as assistant Secretary in an honorary capacity until May 1948, when Claude Orrin became a full time employee of the club.

## TED FENTON
**April 1946 to June 1948**

Ted Fenton joined the club from Charlton as Manager on the 15th of April 1946. Though that 45/46 season had yielded a small profit of £182, money was still short. Because of National Service commitments it was impossible to field a settled team. Nevertheless the first twelve months with Ted at the helm found the balance sheets showing a profit of £448.

He was not exactly new to Layer Road for back in the 1930/31, season while an amateur on West Ham's books, he had played a few games for Colchester Town in their Spartan League days.

Despite every financial stringency money was still in short supply. Fenton made full use of his many contacts in the game and soon the team that was to shock the football world was taking shape. It could be fairly said that the fantastic cup run of 47/48 was instrumental in the U's finally gaining Football League status two years later. Details of that giant killing run are dealt with elsewhere. But it must not be overlooked that the team also did well in the Southern League and that the crowds were flocking to Layer Road. Gates regularly topped the 8,000 mark and in the 48/49 season more than 225,000 people passed through the turnstiles.

Not surprisingly Fenton's managerial abilities were noted in higher spheres, and at the end of June 1948 he left Layer Road to join West Ham United where he later became manager. His last appointment as a Manager was with Southend United. Ted was killed in a car accident in Leicestershire, aged 77, in July 1992.

## JIMMY ALLEN
**July 1948 to April 28th 1953**

The new man appointed in his place was Jimmy Allen who took up his duties on the 22nd of July 1948. Finances had improved somewhat and Allen's appointment – he had been a well known goalkeeper with Portsmouth in his day – sparked off a new wave of interest. By mid–August more than 500 season tickets had been sold (only 252 were taken up the previous season). The newcomer soon demonstrated he was not a man to take lightly. He cancelled the U's first trial match, and at the next Board Meeting reported that he had taken the action off his own bat because the pitch was carrying excessive weed growth and needed a lot of attention before it was fit for play.

Indeed throughout his stay, of almost five years, he was frequently at loggerheads with the Directors and according to the local scribes of the day the Directors were a bit afraid of him, and his temper. Soon after his appointment, he brought in Alf Miller, a 31 year–old from Plymouth, a centre forward who had also seen service with Portsmouth, Southampton and Southport, and made him coach in place of Jock Kearton, who left the club.

A good Southern League season under his guidance in 1949/50 ended with the U's being elected to the Third Division South when the section was expanded to 24 clubs. Gillingham, exiled from the Football League since Ipswich Town replaced them in 1938, were the other successful applicant.

The initial three seasons in the Football League were fairly successful, but despite several attempts Allen failed to convince the Directors that floodlights for Layer Road should be a number one priority. He also disagreed with the Directors when they decided to sell Vic Keeble to Newcastle United for £15,000. On the other side of the coin, when Rotherham United moved in with an offer of £6,000 for Kevin McCurley, Allen wanted to take the money. But the Board asked a £10,000 fee and the chance was lost, though later on McCurley himself turned down the chance to join the Yorkshire side.

The long drawn out divergences of opinion finally came to a head on the 28th of April 1953. The Supporters' Club reported that they did not consider the club could afford a full time manager, and suggested instead a Player/Manager. They felt there was a lack of discipline in the club with players strolling about the town at all hours, and that the trainer and the groundsman were inefficient. Mr. Allen said he felt very strongly about the matter and thought the Supporters' Club were being allowed by the Board to interfere in affairs that did not concern them. Accordingly he tendered his resignation to take effect from the 2nd of May 1953, and for three weeks or so Miller, the coach, and secretary Claude Orrin carried out the manager's duties from that date until the 11th June.

## RON MEADES
**June 11th to June 15th 1953.**

On June the lst, Les Henley (Reading), George Hepplewhite (Preston North End), Harry Medhurst (late of Chelsea) and Ron Meades (who claimed he had played for Cardiff City and was now managing Wadebridge Town) were interviewed for the job; Peter Carey of Manchester United was also considered. Ten days later it was announced that Ron Meades had been appointed. Arthur Wood of the Essex County Standard seeking more details on Meades, for his piece in the paper, from Cardiff and Wadebridge, unearthed some rather disturbing news.

The result was that after just four days the offer to Meades was withdrawn, the Colchester Board finding his credentials unsatisfactory. Meades, however, was definitely given the manager's job and he in fact signed a contract. He actually took the chair at a players meeting the day after his appointment.

## JACK BUTLER
### June 16th 1953 to January 14th 1955.

On June the 16th, on the recommendation of Tom Whittaker – Secretary/Manager of Arsenal – Jack Butler took over the reins. Butler had spent 16 years with Arsenal as a player and then gone on to coach the Belgium National Team, coached at Leicester, had spells as manager of Torquay and Crystal Palace, and at the time of his appointment was in charge of Royal Daring F.C. in Belgium.

His wages were set at £12 a week with £5 a week expenses, and a house provided at £1–10p. a week. He appointed Bill Light as trainer in place of Alf Miller, who left the club, and Andy Brown as Reserve Team Coach.

The team, however, had a poor season and ended up having to apply for re–election. But with 45 votes the U's comfortably retained their place, as did Walsall with 32. However, there was again a poor start to the next season and of the first 13 home games only two were won; they were also knocked out of the F.A. Cup by Reading in the First Round.

By Christmas the Manager had suffered what was later diagnosed as a nervous breakdown. The club sent him away on vacation for two weeks at their expense, and then gave him indefinite leave until his contract expired in June. In the event Butler tendered his resignation on the 14th of January 1955, and was paid off in an amicable settlement.

## BENNY FENTON
### February 1955 to November 1963

After the Meades fiasco, and the unhappy reign of Butler, the Board approached the question of a new manager with great caution. There were 42 applicants for the job but early in February a decision was made to offer it on a one year contract to Benny Fenton, then with Charlton Athletic. Fenton however declined the offer, but a week later accepted a revised deal, as did Charlton who were asking a fee. In the end the club just managed to keep clear of the foot of the table that season and Fenton set about the task of strengthening the side. His first signing was goalkeeper Percy Ames.

Benny continued as Player/Manager until the summer of 1958, when he finally hung up his boots. But he was to remain in the Boss's seat until the 16th of November 1963, when he departed to join the staff at West Ham, thus following in his older brother Ted's footsteps.

During his long spell at Layer Road he had come close to taking the team into the Second Division in the 56/57 season when Ipswich pipped the U's in a nailbiting finish to the season. A year later he was successful in keeping Colchester in Division Three when the old North and South sections were scrapped and Division Four formed.

In the F.A. Cup, however, in his first three seasons at the club the U's went out in the First Round on each occasion. In fact in only one season under his management was there a decent Cup run, that was in 1958/59, when they were beaten by Arsenal at Highbury in a Fourth Round replay.

Nevertheless, the second Fenton era at Layer Road was marked by pretty good results in the League and gates holding steady when elsewhere, in the main, they were on the decline. It was also a period when frequent north of the border raids were made and a number of good Scottish players moved to Colchester. Milligan, Forbes, Fowler, Bobby Hill and McLeod to mention but a few. Once more, when he left, there was no shortage of applicants for the Manager's post. This time around 50 were received and Chairman William Allen and Secretary Claude Orrin were entrusted with the task of preparing a short list.

## NEIL FRANKLIN
### December 5th 1963 to May 13th 1965

Those interviewed were Frank O'Farrell, Neil Franklin, Bob Dennison and Arthur Cox, all well known names. One of the applicants – name not dis–closed – was offered the post but declined the terms offered. Franklin was than appointed at a salary of £1,650 a year, with a rent free house, and a car. He took over the reins on the 5th of December 1963, and held the job until he was sacked at a Board meeting on May the 13th 1968.

Franklin was a very popular choice with the fans. He had been England's No. 1 centre–half and was then one of the players who sought their fortunes in Columbia i.e., one of the Bogota boys. That sortie to South America cost him a suspension on his return to this country. After leaving Stoke City he had a spell with Hull City before ending his playing days.

During his first season at the club the Bobby Hunt/Martyn King strike force, which had been so successful, was broken up when Hunt, who had scored 23 goals that season, was sold to Northampton Town in March 1964. In the summer of that year Franklin signed a number of players – mainly it should be said on free transfers – but none of them enjoyed any great success at Layer Road. Price, Salisbury, Connelly and Aitchison's arrivals hardly compensated for the departure of Woods – to Australia – Ramage, Rutter and McCrohan. When King also left for Wrexham in part exchange for another player who flopped (Tecwyn Jones), the natives began to get restless.

There were calls for the Manager's head when the team were held to a home draw by Bideford in the F.A. Cup. Though the U's won the replay there was a lot of undercurrent in that 64/65 season. More departures and signings followed but of the new men only Bobbie Blackwood and Reg Stratton matched up to requirements.

During this period Bill Light retired as trainer and John Anderson arrived in his place. By the end of the 1965/66 season, the average gate had dwindled to just over 5,159. On a happier note the advance of Brian Hall and Derek Trevis in particular, and the arrival of Sandy Kennon in goal, had added some stability to the side.

When the team went seven home games unbeaten in September and October of the following campaign it looked as if better times were round the corner. The progress, however, proved transient and the 67/68 season produced only two wins in the last 24 games, and this inevitably led to Franklin's departure at the end of the season.

**DICK GRAHAM**
**June 1st 1968 to October 1972**

On the 31st of May 1968, three men - A. McShane, J. Quigley and R. Graham - were interviewed, and on June the 1st "Dick" Graham took over as the new manager, the salary having by now risen to £2,500 plus a club car. The new man courted controversy right from the start. His first edict was to ban the Press from travelling on the team coach, a ban that was to have repercussions in subsequent years. Yet apart from that Graham proved to be an outstanding Manager from a press point of view. Always good for a gimmick or a quote he was a great motivator, and a master of the unexpected.

He could also be rather tetchy and had "principles" - and that proved to be a flaw in his managerial duties that he would not compromise. It was this question of principals that led to his unfortunate exit from the club some years later, after what he considered was unwarranted criticism at a shareholders' meeting.

From the outset Dick had a policy of signing proven players to do an immediate job of team rebuilding while at the same time bringing in youngsters - Micky Cook, Steve Foley, Steve Leslie, John McLaughlin etc. - with an eye to the future.

Among his early signings were Roy Massey, who's career was to be cut short through injury, Tony Macedo, Ken Jones, Bobbie Cram, Brian Owen, John Kurila, Brian Gibbs and Micky Mahon. In fact in the early days of Graham's reign it was a job to keep tabs on all the comings and goings. He also persuaded the Directors to enter a team in the South East Counties League, and then had to bow reluctantly to a Board decision to sell Duncan Forbes to Norwich for £10,000 and Derek Trevis for £11,000 to Walsall.

Another significant milestone during his reign was the purchase of the Layer Road Ground from the Council for £12,000, and of course the advent of Bill Graver as Chairman on the Board.

The F.A. Cup defeat of Leeds United and winning the Watney Cup are dealt with elsewhere, and it was sad - but perhaps inevitable - that Graham left in some acrimony after a shareholders meeting in October 1972.

**JIM SMITH**
**October 1972 to June 1975**

When his successor was announced the question on everyone's lips was *"Jim who?"*. The new man, Jim Smith, had been an average Fourth Division player before drifting into non-League football at Boston where he became Player/Manager. He moved in at Layer Road as a virtual unknown in early November and soon created a good impression with his wholehearted and no nonsense approach to the job in hand. For a short time he had Joe Hooley as his trainer and right hand man, but this arrangement only lasted to the end of the year, and on the 3rd of January 1973, Bobby Roberts arrived from Coventry City to take over as coach. The Smith-Roberts partnership soon had things buzzing, and from then until Smith's departure to manage Blackburn Rovers in June 1975, Layer Road fans were treated to some of the best football ever seen on the ground.

Smith of course went on to become one of the most respected Managers in the game, with Rovers, Birmingham City, Queens Park Rangers, Newcastle United, and now Portsmouth.

Bobby Svarc and John Foggatt followed their old boss from Boston and proved to be a fine strike force. Ray Harford, later to become Coach, and after that Manager at Fulham and Luton, was another of his early signings. Strict on discipline Smith made a rule that all players must live within 18 miles of the ground.

The summer of 1973 saw him make more shrewd singings, Micky Packer and Barry Dyson came on free transfers, and Mike Walker joined from Watford for a £4,000 fee to start his 14 year stint with the club as goalkeeper, then coach, and finally - briefly - as Manager. Midfielder Jimmy Lindsay and John Williams, both ex-Watford men, were his last signings before moving on up the management ladder.

In addition to a strong first team, Smith left behind a number of up and coming youngsters who were to make their mark in the seasons ahead, notably Lindsay Smith, Ian Allinson and Stewart Bright.

**BOBBY ROBERTS**
**June 19th 1975 to April 1982**

The Board had no hesitation in appointing Bobby Roberts - who was and still is, regarded as one of the best coaches in the business - as the new man in charge. Blackburn paid the U's around £9,000 compensation for spiriting away their Manager, and Roberts took over on the 19th of June 1975.

He was to be in charge for almost seven years, a period of dwindling gates and increasing financial problems for the club.

In retrospect with little money available to buy players he did a thoroughly sound job. Almost as soon as he took over Svarc – who had cost £6,000 from Boston – was sold to Blackburn for £20,000 to ease the financial situation. He was given a little money to spend, and Bobby Gough for £7,000 and Colin Garwood for £4,000 from Huddersfield, proved he had an eye for a player. Both were to score a fair quota of goals.

Very much his own man, and not the best communicator, he was the opposite to the outgoing Jim Smith. But he could be firm when the occasion demanded, as six players – Paul Dyer, Steve Dowman, Lindsay Smith, Steve Foley, Bobbie Gough and Ian Allinson – found when they disobeyed orders while on a training session at Egham, and were promptly fined and sent home.

Another good buy of his was Steve Wignall, at £5,000 from Doncaster, and a brilliant bit of business with the sale of Trevor Lee to Gillingham for £90,000, which is still the club record for a transfer fee received. Apart from Allinson however, other youngsters of whom the club had high hopes, Harvey, Evans, Cotton and Ward for example failed to develop. This, coupled with the departures of some of the old guard – Froggatt, Garwood and Williams – led to a decline in playing fortunes. A rift developed in the Boardroom and in somewhat acrimonious circumstances Bobby Roberts was sacked after refusing the opportunity to resign. The manner of his dismissal also led to changes at Board level and some other departures from the Layer Road scene.

**ALLAN HUNTER**
**May 1982 to January 1983**

After much speculation and many rumours, Allan Hunter, a much capped Northern Ireland international, and a pillar of the Ipswich Town side for many seasons was appointed Player-Coach. A very popular choice who soon found management a task that was not to his liking. He disliked the administrative side of the work and soon came to the conclusion that he had not the temperament for the job. Noted for his honesty, after just a few months in charge, he tendered his resignation, and in spite of a lot of pressure to reconsider his decision, he refused to change his mind. He later came along to Layer Road to see his lad Lee play, who had signed as a full professional, but after returning briefly as coach he now enjoys his football purely as a spectator.

**CYRIL LEA**
**February 1983 – March 1986**

Hunter, during his time as manager, had surprised many people by appointing Cyril Lea as his Coach. In his time at Portman Road as a player, when Lea was coach, the two had not always seen eye to eye. Obviously however, there was a mutual respect. Consequent on Hunter's departure, Lea at first on a caretaker and then on a permanent basis became United's 13th Manager. Brought up in a hard school Cyril had played with distinction for Orient, Ipswich and Wales in his time. Along with his coach, Stewart Houston, the former Manchester United player, it could be fairly said of him that Colchester United never had a fitter side. Some of the players used to moan about the running and training routine, and were a bit afraid of the little man, but they played for him. He also got the best out of what he had got in the line of players. Throughout his time there was no money available to buy or to pay good money to attract better quality performers.

Looking at the season by season record under his leadership, it must be admitted he did wonders working on a shoestring. There can be little doubt that had money been available to buy just one or two quality players, the club would have made it into Division Three. It could also be argued that had not a couple of players been signed against his express wishes the Board would have saved themselves quite a bit of money and a lot of embarrassment.

Cyril's departure towards the end of the 1985/86 season saw Mike Walker, who had been in charge of the Reserve Team, in the role of Caretaker/Manager. The team finished the campaign with a spectacular run of results, and on the basis of this Mike was appointed manager, but without a contract. He persuaded Allan Hunter to rejoin the club in a coaching capacity and also recruited the services of former player Steve Foley to coach the Y.T.S. boys at Layer Road.

**MIKE WALKER**
**April 1986 to November 1987**

Mike had joined the club as a player from Watford in June 1973. He played in 451 League and 71 Cup games in goal for the senior side, and then had a spell in charge of the Reserve Team in the Eastern Counties League.

The team took time to settle at the start of the 1987/88 season, but then had a run of seven League games without defeat. Walker won the October Fourth Division Manager of the Month award. On Sunday the 1st of November 1987, he took a team to Burnham Ramblers to play a Friendly match, and that evening had a meeting with the recently appointed Chairman, Jonathan Crisp. In view of the good start to the campaign Walker was undoubtedly expecting to discuss a raise in salary.

What happened at that meeting has never been officially disclosed! Suffice to say the Chairman said Walker resigned, whilst Walker maintained he was sacked. Whatever the truth of the matter, supporters of the club were not happy, and the Chairman lost a lot of face over the Walker affair. Walker soon found another job with Norwich City, and in the 1992/93 season piloted The Canaries into Europe, after they finished third in the Premier League.

## ROGER BROWN
**November 4th 1987 to October 16th 1988**

Steve Foley took over in a temporary capacity for the game against Rochdale – a game that was won 4–1. The Chairman pulled off his second big surprise – some say with hindsight he made his second big mistake. Roger Brown, who had very limited experience as a Manager – with Poole Town and a season as player–coach at Bournemouth – moved in almost overnight to take over the Manager's chair. After being Fourth Division Manager of the Month in December 1987, the rest of his reign at Layer Road was inconspicuous to say the least. From being top of the table on the 1st of January 1988, the U's slumped, losing 12, drawing 6 and winning just 4 of the last 22 League games.

Just two wins in the opening ten League games of the 88/89 season put severe pressure on the Chairman and the Manager. Home gates slumped to just over 1,000. Matters came to a head with a shattering 8–0 defeat by Leyton Orient, and the Manager, with his pride severely injured, resigned.

## STEVE FOLEY Temporary Manager
**October 16th 1988 to January 21st 1989**

Having burnt his fingers twice in a year Mr. Crisp was not, unexpectedly, very chary when considering his next move. Steve Foley for the second time in 12 months found himself in temporary charge. He faced an awesome task with team morale low. Points continued to be few and far between, but a good F.A. Cup run was an unexpected bonus.

Some felt that Foley should have been given the opportunity as Manager, although Foley himself said he did not consider he was ready for the post, and the Chairman came in for much flack for not solving the problem.

## JOCK WALLACE
**January 89 to December 20th 1989**

Belatedly, at the end of January 1989, Jock Wallace was persuaded out of retirement in Spain. This proved, both resultwise and attendance wise a major coup. How the U's came from behind to preserve their League status is now a matter of history. Jock finally had to give up the seat for health reasons and became a Director of the club.

With Wallace in charge, Alan Ball as Coach, Brian Owen as Physiotherapist and Steve Foley reverting to Youth Team Coach, the club had on paper a management team equal, if not better than many First and Second Division clubs. In fact Jock brought about a remarkable transformation with gates rising from under 2,000 before his advent, to top the 4,000 mark on many occasions. When he arrived on the scene the team had not won a Football League game since October the 4th, and were at the bottom of the table with just three wins to their name. They looked certain relegation candidates. Between February the 5th and the end of the season they won nine and drew eight matches, until finally a 2–1 victory at Darlington on the 29th of April 1989 – before a crowd of 7,126 – condemned The Quakers to Conference football.

The reprieve, however, was only temporary. In 1989/90 only one game was won between the end of September and the New Year. Alan Ball left the club in October, and with Jock Wallace himself a very sick man, the team (31 players were used during the season) never picked itself up off of the bottom. Jock himself had to retire through ill health, and Steve Foley once again took over the hot seat on a caretaker basis.

## MICK MILLS
**January 1990 – May 1991**

Mick Mills the former Ipswich Town skipper and England International, who had left Stoke City the previous October when Alan Ball left Colchester to take over as Manager at the Victoria Ground, was Mr. Crisp's choice as the new man in charge. To be fair to Mills the U's were in almost terminal decline at the time. When the club were relegated at the end of the season, Mills, and Sammy Chung – who he had brought to Layer Road as coach – both left when Colchester's bid to win The Conference at the first time of asking was not achieved.

## ROY McDONOUGH
**June 1991 to Date**

With changes on the Board many fans were surprised when Roy McDonough was appointed Player/Coach. He was in his second spell at Layer Road as a player, and it was certainly no fault of his that the U's just failed – they finished second – to win the Conference in the 1990/91 season. He duly delivered the goods in his first season in charge both on and off the field, and fully deserved his chance as Manager when the U's returned to the Football League in May 1992.

# Giant Killers

(The following is an extract from the book *'Giant Killers'* published in 1972. With the permission of the Author, Frank Rowland)

When Colchester United happen to do something sensational in the Cup, the National Press play it up so much that the rest of Britain must think that life, for Colchester fans, is one long Cup run. This alas, is far from the truth. It is a case of "Bad news is no news" and fortunately, our bad seasons get little publicity.

Take the 1948-49 season for instance. As soon as it became known that we were at home to Reading in the first round, all of the enthusiasm of the previous season spilled over once more and people began to make arrangements for Wembley! It really only became a question of who we were going to defeat in the second round, and in order to make sure they were in at the start of another Giant killing act. 19,072 crammed into Layer Road (this was before the days of all ticket matches) and this still remains the official ground record. How many of these would actually have seen the match must remain doubtful, but as it happens, nobody did.

When we got in, the fog was so thick that we could only just see the far touchline. As time went on, first the corner flag was swallowed up in the fog, then the far edge of the penalty area, then the furthermost goal post (that is at "our" end) disappeared. When, finally, even the near side post could not be seen, the referee took the courageous and correct decision that, as he couldn't see anything, he would abandon the game. The score was 0-0 and nobody could see anything anyway. The 19,072 people squeezed themselves out of the ground and groped their way home, all (well, almost all) convinced that the weather had saved Reading from a terrible hiding.

So the match had to be replayed in midweek, in the afternoon of course, as we had no floodlights then. In spite of this, there was a crowd of 13,371 to see the expected slaughter.

They saw it! Reading won 4-2, with one of the previous season's heroes, "Spud" Cater getting both Colchester goals. Here again, it shows how times have changed, as I have a clear memory of "Spud", all five feet and a few inches of him, charging the keeper over the line, ball and all, and the goal was allowed. Today, a forward has only to get close enough to a goalkeeper so as to offend him with 'BO' and the referee immediately gives a free kick.

As well as the 'ups', there were also the 'downs'. The following seasons were not only down, they were positively subterranean. We were beaten 1-0, away, by amateur side Wealdstone in the fourth qualifying round the following season, and 1-0 at Bournemouth the season after that.

1951-52 saw a little progress, but hardly of the "Giant Killing" variety. We beat Port Vale 3-1 and Bristol City 2-1 (they had a young lad called John Atyeo playing for them!), but were then drawn away to Barnsley, where we lost 3-0. My two sons, David and Bob, and I, have memories of this match also. We couldn't go as we were attending an R.A.F.A. Children's party, but we took a radio set along and left it in the passage outside. As the time for the football results approached, we crept from the room and when we returned, the entertainer had a job to raise a smile from three of his audience I can tell you. By now, Ted Fenton, having put the name of Colchester firmly on the football map, had departed to manage West Ham.

Fenton's successor, Jimmy Allen, must always be remembered as the man who put the U's into the Football League Division Three. Unfortunately however, neither he nor the next manager Jack Butler, could generate a cup run and we had begun to realise that 1948 was probably one of those "once in a lifetime" occasions.

There was a little bit of excitement for some of us in the 1952-53 cup, as after a couple of easy home draws against Weymouth (4-0) and Llanelly (3-2), we were drawn away in the third round to Rotherham.

Bob and I set out by car on a day that once looked distinctly misty. By the time we got to Rotherham, it was downright foggy and the gates had not been opened as they were waiting for the referee to inspect things. Great! Drive all that way and then have a match fogged off. But we were lucky and extremely happy, as not only was the match played, but we drew 2-2, and right at the end our goalkeeper George Wright saved a penalty. Once again, may I point out, how times have changed. Not only were we able to park in a street right by the ground, but the local crowd, seeing our blue and white bedecked car, came over to shake hands with us and wish us luck in the replay. Can you see that happening nowadays? All we should get in all probability, would be a brick through the windscreen.

Never mind, even if it's a bit late; thank you Rotherham.

# APPENDIX STATISTICS 1937 - 1993

The statistics pages that follow have been designed for easy reference and are generally self explanatory, however the following notes explain various specific details.

The first page for each season includes the general details of each Football League (or Southern League or GM Vauxhall Conference) match played that season. Fixture dates, Results, Attendances and (Colchester) Goalscorers are self-explanatory. Under 'Goalscorers', 'pen' refers to a goal scored from a penalty and 'O.G.' an own goal. Opposition teams shown in upper case refer to Colchester United home matches (lower case an 'away' match).

All players that have appeared for the Club in League and/or major Cup matches are entered at right angles to the general details, and their appearance(s) are shown by a number (their position) for the appropriate match. For pre-war matches (numbered shirts were not used), the number shown refers to the normally accepted position for the period; e.g. '1' = goalkeeper, '2' = right back, '11' = left winger, etc. Substitutes, where they made an appearance during the appropriate game, are included, as '12' and/or '14'. Substitute number 12 replaced the player suffixed * (e.g. 8*), and number 14 replaced the player suffixed + (e.g. 10+)

The second seasonal page provides details of major Cup matches, which follow a similar pattern to the League games on the upper page. The left hand column indicates the round of that Cup match, e.g. 4Q = 4th qualify-ing, 1st = 1st round, S/F = semi-final, 1/2L = 1st round second leg, etc.

# SEASON 1937/38 Southern League

| No. | Date | Opposition | Res | Goalscorers | Wood | Williams | Wallis | Thacker | Smith R. | Smith G. | Simnet | Ritchie | Pritchard | Pendergast | Ormesher | Mayes | Leslie | Hodge | Haley | Fieldus | Fairchild | Day | Crisp | Collins | Cheyne | Bennett | Barraclough | Baker | Youngs | Dunn |
|---|---|---|---|---|---|---|---|---|---|---|---|---|---|---|---|---|---|---|---|---|---|---|---|---|---|---|---|---|---|---|
| 1 | 28 Aug | Yeovil & P | 0-3 | | 1 | | | | | 10 | 4 | 11 | | 2 | | | 7 | 5 | | | | 8 | 6 | | | 9 | | | | 3 |
| MW | 2 Sep | BATH | 6-1 | Hodge, Pritchard(2), Smith.R(3) | 1 | | | | | 10 | | 11 | | 2 | | | 7 | 5 | 4 | | | 8 | 6 | | | 9 | | | | 3 |
| 2 | 4 | IPSWICH | 3-3 | Cheyne, Crisp, Wood | 1 | | | | | 10 | | 11 | | 2 | | | 7 | 5 | 4 | | | 8 | 6 | | | 9 | | | | 3 |
| 3 | 11 | YEOVIL & P | 0-0 | | 1 | | | 11 | | 10 | | | | 2 | | | 7 | 5 | 4 | | | 8 | 6 | | | 9 | | | | 3 |
| 4 | 18 | GUILDFORD C | 5-0 | Crisp, Pritchard(3), Smith.R | 1 | | | | | 10 | | 11 | | 2 | | | 7 | 5 | 4 | | | 8 | 6 | | | 9 | | | | 3 |
| MW | 23 | FOLKESTONE | 1-0 | Baker | 1 | | 6 | 11 | | 8 | | 10 | | 2 | | | 7 | 5 | 4 | | | | | | | 9 | | | | 3 |
| 5 | 25 | Aldershot Res | 0-0 | | 1 | | 6 | 11 | | 10 | | 8 | | 2 | | | 7 | 5 | 4 | | | | | | | 9 | | | | 3 |
| 6 | 29 | Torquay Res | 2-2 | Baker, Smith.R | 1 | | 10 | 11 | | | 6 | | | 2 | | | 7 | 5 | 4 | | | 8 | | | | 9 | | | | 3 |
| MW | 2 Oct | Bath | 4-3 | Crisp(pen), Hodge(2), Pritchard | 1 | | 6 | | | 10 | | 11 | | 2 | | | 7 | 5 | 4 | | | 8 | | | | 9 | | | | 3 |
| MW | 7 | TUNBRIDGE WELLS | 1-2 | Smith.R | 1 | | | | | 10 | | 11 | | 2 | | | 7 | 5 | 4 | 6 | | 8 | | | | 9 | | | | 3 |
| 7 | 9 | Plymouth Res | 4-5 | Cheyne, Pritchard, Smith.R AN Other | 1 | | 5 | | | 10 | | 11 | | 2 | 6 | | 7 | | 4 | | | 8 | | | | 9 | | | | 3 |
| MW | 20 | Portsmouth 'A' | 4-3 | Cheyne(2), Pritchard, Smith.R | 1 | | | 11 | | 10 | | 7 | | 2 | 6 | | | 8 | 4 | | | 8 | | | | 9 | | | | 3 |
| 8 | 23 | CHELTENHAM | 3-2 | Crisp, Fielding, Richie | 1 | | | | | 10 | | 11 | | | 8 | | 7 | 5 | 4 | 2 | | | 6 | | | 9 | | | | 3 |
| MW | 30 | Dartford | 2-1 | Cheyne, Pritchard | 1 | | | | | 10 | | 11 | | 2 | | | 7 | 5 | 4 | | | 9 | 6 | | 8 | | | | | 3 |
| 9 | 6 Nov | Newport Res | 2-2 | Cheyne, Smith.G | 1 | | | 11 | | 10 | | 7 | | 2 | | | | 5 | 4 | | | 9 | 6 | | 8 | | | | | 3 |
| 10 | 13 | NORWICH RES | 2-2 | Crisp, Smith.G | 1 | | | 11 | | 10 | | 7 | | 2 | | | | 5 | 4 | | | 9 | 6 | | 8 | | | | | 3 |
| MW | 17 | Aldershot Res | 1-3 | Crisp | 1 | | | 11 | | 10 | | 7 | 9 | 2 | | | | 5 | 8 | | | | 6 | | 4 | | | | | 3 |
| 11 | 20 | Folkestone | 4-2 | Cheyne, Fielding, Hodge(2) | 1 | | | 11 | | 10 | | | | 2 | 9 | | 7 | 5 | 4 | | | 8 | 6 | | | | | | | 3 |
| MW | 25 | Norwich Res | 1-2 | Barraclough | 1 | | | 11 | 9 | 10 | | | | 2 | | | 7 | 5 | 4 | | | 8 | 6 | | | | | | | 3 |
| 12 | 27 | ALDERSHOT RES | 2-0 | Fielding, Hodge | 1 | | | 11 | | 10 | | | | 2 | 9 | | 7 | 5 | | | | 8 | 6 | | 4 | | | | | 3 |
| 13 | 4 Dec | Swindon Res | 5-1 | Hodge, Pritchard(4) | 1 | | | | | 10 | | 11 | | 2 | 9 | | 7 | 5 | | | | 8 | 6 | | 4 | | | | | 3 |
| MW | 11 | ALDERSHOT RES | 1-0 | Cheyne | 1 | | | | | 10 | | 11 | | 2 | | | 7 | 5 | | | 8 | 9 | 6 | | 4 | | | | | 3 |
| 14 | 18 | FOLKESTONE | 7-1 | Cheyne, Day(3), Hodge(2), Pritchard | 1 | | | 11 | | 10 | | | 9 | 2 | | | 7 | 5 | | | | 8 | 6 | | 4 | | | | | 3 |
| 15 | 27 | EXETER RES | 3-1 | Barraclough, Cheyne, Day | 1 | | | 11 | | 10 | | | 9 | 2 | | | 7 | 5 | | | 8 | | 6 | | 4 | | | | | 3 |
| 16 | 1 Jan | BARRY | 6-1 | Cheyne, Day, Hodge, Prendegast(3) | 1 | | | 11 | | 10 | | | 9 | | | 2 | 7 | 5 | | | 8 | | 6 | | 4 | | | | | 3 |
| 17 | 8 | Cheltenham | 2-2 | Cheyne, Prendergast | 1 | | | | | 10 | | 11 | | 2 | | | 7 | 5 | | | 8 | 9 | 6 | | 4 | | | | | 3 |
| 18 | 15 | DARTFORD | 2-0 | Prendergast, Pritchard | 1 | | | 11 | | 10 | | | | | | 2 | 7 | 5 | | | 8 | 9 | 6 | | 4 | | | | | 3 |
| MW | 29 | PORTSMOUTH 'A' | 2-1 | Cheyne, Prendergast | 1 | | | 11 | | 10 | | | | 2 | | | 7 | 5 | | | 8 | 9 | 6 | | 4 | | | | | 3 |
| MW | 31 | Millwall Res | 0-2 | | 1 | | 10 | | | | | 11 | 9 | 2 | 6 | | | 5 | | | 7 | | | | 4 | | | | 8 | 3 |
| 19 | 5 Feb | Ipswich | 2-3 | Cheyne, Pritchard | 1 | | 4 | 11 | | 10 | | | | 2 | 9 | | 7 | 5 | | | | 8 | 6 | | | | | | | 3 |
| 20 | 12 | Barry | 1-2 | Cheyne | 1 | | 6 | 11 | | 10 | | | | 2 | | | 7 | 5 | | | | 8 | | | 4 | | | | 9 | 3 |
| 21 | 19 | Dartford | 0-3 | | 1 | | | 11 | | 10 | | | 9 | 2 | | | 7 | 5 | | | 8 | | 6 | | 4 | | | | | 3 |
| 22 | 24 | TUNBRIDGE WELLS | 3-1 | Barraclough, Cheyne, Hodge | | 1 | 4 | 11 | | 10 | | | | 2 | | | 7 | 5 | | | 8 | 9 | 6 | | | | | | | 3 |
| 23 | 26 | BRISTOL R RES | 1-0 | Pritchard | | 1 | 4 | 11 | | 10 | | | | 2 | | | 7 | 5 | | | 8 | 9 | 6 | | | | | | | 3 |
| MW | 3 Mar | DARTFORD | 1-0 | Barraclough | 1 | | 4 | 11 | | | | | | 2 | | 3 | 7 | 5 | | | | 8 | 6 | | | | 9 | 10 | | |
| 24 | 5 | Bristol R Res | 1-2 | Wallis | 1 | | 6 | 11 | | 10 | | | | 2 | | 3 | 7 | 5 | | | 8 | | | | 4 | | | 9 | | |
| MW | 10 | GUILDFORD C | 5-0 | Cheyne, Day(2), Hodge, Wallis | | 1 | 6 | | | 8 | | 11 | 9 | 2 | | 3 | 7 | 5 | | | | | | | 4 | | | 10 | | |
| MW | 12 | Folkestone | 2-2 | Cheyne, Crisp | | 1 | 6 | | | 8 | | 11 | 9 | 2 | | | 7 | 5 | | | | | | | 4 | | | 10 | | 3 |
| MW | 19 | NORWICH RES | 3-0 | Cheyne, Hodge, Thacker | | 1 | 6 | | | 10 | | 11 | | 2 | | | 7 | 5 | 8 | | | | | | 4 | | 9 | | | 3 |
| MW | 23 | Tunbridge Wells | 1-0 | Hodge | 1 | | 6 | | | 10 | | 11 | | 2 | | | 7 | 5 | 8 | | | | | | 4 | | | 9 | | 3 |
| 25 | 26 | TORQUAY RES | 4-0 | Cheyne, Wallis(3) | 1 | | 6 | 11 | | 10 | | 7 | | 2 | | | | 5 | 8 | | | | | | 4 | | | 9 | | 3 |
| 26 | 2 Apr | Guildford C | 2-3 | Cheyne, Hodge | 1 | | 5 | | | 10 | | 11 | | 2 | | | 7 | | 6 | | | 8 | | | 4 | | | 9 | | 3 |
| 27 | 9 | Exeter Res | 1-2 | Hodge | 1 | | 5 | | | 10 | | 11 | | 2 | 6 | | 7 | | 8 | | | | | | 4 | | 9 | | | 3 |
| 28 | 15 | Bath | 3-2 | Day(3) | 1 | | 5 | | | 10 | | 11 | 9 | 2 | | | 7 | | 4 | | | | | | | | | 6 | 8 | 3 |
| 29 | 16 | SWINDON RES | 7-1 | Cheyne(2), Crisp(3)(2pens), Day, Hodge | 1 | | 5 | | | 10 | | 11 | 9 | 2 | 4 | | 7 | | 8 | | | | | | | | | 6 | | 3 |
| 30 | 18 | BATH | 1-1 | Cheyne | 1 | | 5 | | | 10 | | 11 | 9 | 2 | 4 | | 7 | | 8 | | | | | | | | | 6 | | 3 |

## (Southern League continued)

| No. | Date | Opposition | Res | Goalscorers | | | | | | | | | | | | | | | | | | | | | | | | | | |
|---|---|---|---|---|---|---|---|---|---|---|---|---|---|---|---|---|---|---|---|---|---|---|---|---|---|---|---|---|---|---|
| 31 | 21 Apr | Norwich Res | 2–5 | Crisp, Pritchard | | 1 | 5 | | | 10 | | 11 | | 2 | 4 | | 7 | | 8 | | | 9 | | | | | | 6 | | 3 |
| 32 | 23 | Tunbridge Wells | 0–3 | | 1 | | | 11 | | | 5 | | | 2 | 4 | 3 | | | | | | | 6 | 7 | | | 9 | 10 | 8 | |
| 33 | 30 | NEWPORT RES | 8–0 | Cheyne, Crisp, Hodge, Prichard(4), Wallis | 1 | | 5 | | | 10 | | 11 | | 2 | 4 | | 7 | | 8 | | | 9 | | | | | | 6 | | 3 |
| 34 | 2 May | Guildford C | 4–1 | Crisp, Hodge, Pritchard(2) | 1 | | 5 | | | 10 | | 11 | | | 4 | 2 | 7 | | 8 | | | 9 | | | | | | 6 | | 3 |
| 35 | 5 | MILLWALL RES | 3–2 | Cheyne, Pritchard, Wallis | 1 | | 5 | | | 10 | | 11 | | | 4 | 2 | 7 | | 8 | | | 9 | | | | | | 6 | | 3 |
| 36 | 7 | PLYMOUTH | 2–3 | Cheyne(2)(1pen) | 1 | | 5 | | | 10 | | 11 | | | 4 | 2 | 7 | | 8 | | | 9 | | | | | | 6 | | 3 |

N.B. Numbered games refer to Southern League matches, 'MW' games refer to Mid–week Southern League games

## Southern League Cup

| Rd | Date | Opposition | Res | Goalscorers | | | | | | | | | | | | | | | | | | | | | | | | | | |
|---|---|---|---|---|---|---|---|---|---|---|---|---|---|---|---|---|---|---|---|---|---|---|---|---|---|---|---|---|---|---|
| 1st | 16 Sep | NORWICH RES | 7–3 | Cheyne(2), Hodge, Pritchard(2), A.Smith(2) | 1 | | | | | 10 | | 11 | | 2 | | | 7 | 5 | 4 | | | 8 | 6 | | | 9 | | | | 3 |
| 2nd | 16 Dec | GUILDFORD C | 2–0 | Cheyne, Day | 1 | | | 11 | | 10 | | | 9 | 2 | | | 7 | 5 | 4 | | | 8 | 6 | | | | | | | 3 |
| SF/1 | 30 May | Dartford | 2–0 | Day, Hodge | 1 | | 6 | | | 10 | | 11 | 9 | 2 | 4 | | 7 | 5 | 8 | | | | | | | | | | | 3 |
| SF/2 | 7 Apr | DARTFORD | 8–1 | Cheyne(2), Crisp, Day(3), Hodge(2) | 1 | | 5 | | | 10 | | 11 | 9 | 2 | 4 | | 7 | | 8 | | | | 6 | | | | | | | 3 |
| F/1 | 19 | Yeovil & P | 1–2 | Cheyne | | 1 | 5 | | | 10 | | 11 | 9 | 2 | 6 | | 7 | | 4 | | | 8 | | | | | | | | 3 |
| F/2 | 27 | YEOVIL & P | 3–1 | Cheyne, Pritchard(2) | 1 | | 5 | | | 10 | | 11 | | 2 | 4 | | 7 | | 8 | | | 9 | 6 | | | | | | | 3 |

[Copyright Photograph by West End Studio.

*Back Row :* **Mr. C. H. S. Le Ball, Mr. L. W. Daniell, Mr. E. Davis** (Secretary-Manager), **Mr. G. M. Morris, Mr. L. A. Boult.**

*Middle Row :* **Mr. W. Allen** (Vice-Chairman), **Mr. W. K. Howard, Mr. P. C. Cook, J. E. Evans, G. W. Leslie, R. Dunn, J. W. Baker, J. Collins, G. T. Ritchie, Mr. W. H. Clark, Mr. B. Myers, Mr. A. E. Warner** (Accountant).

*Front Row :* **Councillor R. Wright, A. Wood, K. Mayes, G. Crisp, A. Pritchard, Councillor M. Pye** (Chairman), **R. Smith, J. Hodge, A. Cheyne, W. Barraclough, Councillor Wm. C. Harper.**

# SEASON 1938/39 Southern League

| No. | Date | Opposition | Res | Goalscorers | Dunn | Light | Youngs | Allen | Astill | Baker | Birch | Cheyne | Crisp | Fieldus | Haley | Hodge | Leslie | Matthews | Mayes | Merritt | Morris | Murray | Pritchard | Ritchie | Smith | Thacker | Wallis | Worton | Burditt | Law | Main |
|---|---|---|---|---|---|---|---|---|---|---|---|---|---|---|---|---|---|---|---|---|---|---|---|---|---|---|---|---|---|---|---|
| 1 | 27 Aug | GILLINGHAM | 2-0 | Matthews, Wallis | | 1 | | | 11 | | 2 | 10 | | | | 7 | 5 | 9 | | | 6 | | | | 4 | | 8 | 3 | | | |
| 2 | 3 Sep | ARSENAL 'A' | 2-0 | Cheyne, Morris | | 1 | | | | | 2 | 10 | 11 | | | 7 | 5 | 9 | | | 6 | | | | 4 | | 8 | 3 | | | |
| 3 | 7 | Dartford | 1-0 | Cheyne | | 1 | | | | | 2 | 10 | 11 | | | 7 | 5 | 9 | | | 6 | | | | 4 | | 8 | 3 | | | |
| 4 | 10 | YEOVIL & P. | 8-1 | Astill, Cheyne, Morris, Pritchard(3), Wallis(2) | | 1 | | | 11 | | 2 | 10 | | | | 7 | 5 | | | | 6 | | 9 | | 4 | | 8 | 3 | | | |
| 5 | 15 | DARTFORD | 4-0 | Astill(2), Pritchard(2) | | 1 | | | 11 | 10 | 2 | | | | | 7 | 5 | | | | 6 | | 9 | | 4 | | 8 | 3 | | | |
| MW | 22 | Norwich Res. | 2-0 | Astill, O.G. | | 1 | | 2 | 11 | 10 | | | | | | 7 | 5 | | | | 6 | | 9 | | 4 | | 8 | 3 | | | |
| 6 | 24 | Exeter Res. | 1-2 | Pritchard | | 1 | | | 11 | | 2 | 10 | | | | 7 | 5 | | | | 6 | | 9 | | 4 | | 8 | 3 | | | |
| MW | 28 | Folkestone | 2-1 | Hodge, Pritchard | | 1 | | 2 | 11 | 10 | | | | | | 7 | 5 | | | | 6 | | 9 | | 4 | | 8 | 3 | | | |
| 7 | 1 Oct | CARDIFF RES. | 3-2 | Pritchard, Wallis(2) | | 1 | | | 11 | | 2 | 10 | | | | 7 | 5 | | | | 6 | | 9 | | 4 | | 8 | 3 | | | |
| MW | 6 | TUNBRIDGE WELLS | 2-2 | Astill, Wallis | | 1 | | | 11 | | 2 | 10 | | | | 7 | 5 | | | | 6 | | 9 | | 4 | | 8 | 3 | | | |
| 8 | 8 | Aldershot Res. | 1-0 | Crisp | | 1 | | | | | 2 | | 11 | | | 7 | 5 | | | 10 | 6 | | 9 | | 4 | | 8 | 3 | | | |
| 9 | 13 | FOLKESTONE | 1-0 | Pritchard | | 1 | | | | 5 | 2 | | 11 | | | 7 | | | | 10 | 6 | | 9 | | 4 | | 8 | 3 | | | |
| MW | 20 | PORTSMOUTH 'A' | 4-1 | Cheyne(3), Thacker | | 1 | | | 11 | | 2 | 10 | | | | 7 | | | 8 | | 5 | | | | 4 | 9 | 6 | 3 | | | |
| 10 | 22 | Cheltenham | 1-2 | Pritchard | | 1 | | | 11 | 8 | 2 | 10 | | | | 7 | | | | | 5 | | 9 | | 4 | | 6 | 3 | | | |
| MW | 27 | ALDERSHOT RES. | 1-3 | Smith | | 1 | | | 11 | 5 | 2 | 10 | | | | 7 | | | | | 6 | | 9 | | 4 | | 8 | 3 | | | |
| 11 | 29 | BRISTOL R. RES. | 3-1 | Cheyne(3) | | 1 | | | 11 | 5 | 2 | 10 | | | | 7 | | | | | 6 | | 9 | | 4 | | 8 | 3 | | | |
| 12 | 5 Nov | Norwich Res. | 5-1 | Crisp(2), Pritchard(3) | | 1 | | | | 5 | 2 | 10 | 11 | | | 7 | | | 8 | | 6 | | 9 | | | | 4 | 3 | | | |
| 13 | 19 | Yeovil & P. | 1-2 | Pritchard | | 1 | | | | 4 | 2 | 10 | 11 | | | 7 | 5 | | | | 6 | | 9 | | | | 8 | 3 | | | |
| 14 | 3 Dec | CHELTENHAM | 3-1 | Cheyne(2), Hodge | | 1 | | | 11 | | 2 | 10 | | | | 7 | 5 | 8 | | | 6 | | 9 | | | | 4 | 3 | | | |
| 15 | 10 | BATH | 4-0 | Cheyne, Hodge(2), Matthews | | 1 | | | 11 | | 2 | 10 | | | | 7 | 5 | 9 | | | 6 | | 8 | | | | 4 | 3 | | | |
| MW | 14 | Aldershot Res. | 2-1 | Hodge, Matthews | | 1 | | | | | 2 | | 11 | | | 7 | 5 | 9 | | | 6 | | 8 | | 4 | | 10 | 3 | | | |
| 16 | 17 | Bristol R. Res. | 1-0 | Wallis | | 1 | | | 11 | | 2 | 10 | | | | 7 | 5 | | | | 6 | | 9 | | 4 | | 8 | 3 | | | |
| 17 | 31 | BARRY | 5-1 | Hodge, Pritchard, Wallis(3) | | 1 | | | 11 | 4 | 2 | | | | | 7 | 5 | | 8 | | 6 | | 9 | | | | 10 | 3 | | | |
| 18 | 7 Jan | Tunbridge W. | 2-0 | Pritchard(2) | | 1 | | | 11 | 8 | 2 | | | | | 7 | 5 | | | | 6 | | 9 | | 4 | | 10 | 3 | | | |
| MW | 9 | Millwall Res. | 2-1 | Crisp, Pritchard | | 1 | | | 11 | 8 | 2 | | 10 | | | 7 | 5 | | | | 6 | | 9 | | 4 | | | 3 | | | |
| 19 | 14 | Gillingham | 3-1 | Crisp, Hodge, Pritchard | | 1 | | | 11 | 8 | 2 | | 10 | | | 7 | 5 | | | | 6 | | 9 | | 4 | | | 3 | | | |
| 20 | 21 | NEWPORT RES. | 7-0 | Astill(2), Hodge(2), Pritchard, Wallis(2) | | 1 | | | 11 | 8 | 2 | | | | | 7 | 5 | | | | 6 | | 9 | | 4 | | 10 | 3 | | | |
| MW | 2 Feb | FOLKESTONE | 3-1 | Astill, Wallis(2) | | 1 | | | 11 | | 2 | | | | | 7 | 5 | | | | 6 | 8 | 9 | | 4 | | 10 | 3 | | | |
| 21 | 4 | SWINDON RES. | 3-1 | Astill(2), Morris | | 1 | | | 11 | | 2 | 8 | | | | 7 | 5 | | | | 6 | | 9 | | 4 | | 10 | 3 | | | |
| MW | 8 | Guildford | 0-1 | | | 1 | | | 11 | | 2 | | | | | 7 | 5 | | | | 6 | 8 | 9 | | 4 | | 10 | 3 | | | |
| 22 | 11 | Torquay Res. | 2-0 | Baker, Pritchard | | 1 | | | 11 | 8 | 2 | | | | | 7 | 5 | | | | 6 | | 9 | | 4 | | 10 | 3 | | | |
| MW | 15 | Tunbridge W. | 1-2 | Pritchard | | 1 | | | 11 | 8 | 2 | | 7 | | | 7 | 5 | | | | 6 | | 9 | | 4 | | 10 | 3 | | | |
| 23 | 18 | ALDERSHOT RES. | 2-0 | Hodge, Murray | | 1 | | | 11 | | 2 | 10 | | | | | 5 | | | | 4 | 8 | 9 | | | | 6 | 3 | | | |
| MW | 23 | GUILDFORD | 3-0 | Astill, Cheyne, Morris | | 1 | | | 11 | | 2 | 10 | | | | 7 | 5 | | | | 4 | 8 | 9 | | | | 6 | 3 | | | |
| 24 | 25 | Folkestone | 4-1 | Astill, Pritchard(2), Wallis | | 1 | | | 11 | 8 | 2 | | | | | 7 | 5 | | | | 6 | | 9 | | 4 | | 10 | 3 | | | |
| 25 | 2 Mar | EXETER RES. | 6-1 | Astill(2), Murray, Pritchard(3) | | | 1 | | 11 | | 2 | | | | | 7 | 5 | | | 10 | 4 | 8 | 9 | | | | 6 | 3 | | | |
| 26 | 4 | Plymouth Res. | 3-0 | Hodge, Murray, Pritchard | | | 1 | | | 10 | 2 | | 11 | | | 7 | 5 | | | | 4 | 8 | 9 | | | | 6 | 3 | | | |
| 27 | 11 | Swindon Res. | 1-2 | Pritchard | | | 1 | | 11 | 10 | 2 | | | | | 7 | 5 | | | | 4 | 8 | 9 | | | | 6 | 3 | | | |
| MW | 16 | DARTFORD | 8-0 | Cheyne, Crisp(2), Hodge, Murray, Pritchard(2), Wallis | | | 1 | | | | 2 | 10 | 11 | | | 7 | 5 | | | | 4 | 8 | 9 | | | | 6 | 3 | | | |
| 28 | 18 | Cardiff Res. | 0-3 | | | 1 | | | | | 2 | 10 | 11 | | | 7 | 5 | | | | 4 | 8 | 9 | | | | 6 | 3 | | | |
| MW | 22 | Portsmouth 'A' | 0-1 | | 1 | | | | 7 | | 2 | | 11 | | | | 5 | | | | 6 | 8 | 9 | | 4 | | 10 | 3 | | | |
| MW | 23 | MILLWALL RES. | 2-1 | Astill(2) | 1 | | | | 11 | | 2 | 10 | 7 | | | | 5 | | | | 6 | 8 | 9 | | | | 4 | 3 | | | |
| 29 | 25 | Newport Res. | 1-0 | Cheyne | 1 | | | | 11 | | 2 | 10 | | | | 7 | 5 | | | | 6 | 8 | 9 | | | | 4 | 3 | | | |
| 30 | 29 | Arsenal 'A' | 0-0 | | | | 1 | | | | 2 | 10 | 11 | | | 7 | 5 | | | | 6 | 8 | 9 | | | | 4 | 3 | | | |
| 31 | 30 | TUNBRIDGE W. | 1-1 | Murray | | | 1 | | | | 2 | 10 | 11 | | | 7 | 5 | | | | 6 | 8 | 9 | | | | 4 | 3 | | | |

| | | | | | | | | | | | | | | | | | | | | | | | | | | | | | | | |
|---|---|---|---|---|---|---|---|---|---|---|---|---|---|---|---|---|---|---|---|---|---|---|---|---|---|---|---|---|---|---|---|
| 32 | 1 Apr | TORQUAY RES. | 5-1 | Cheyne, Crisp, Pritchard(3) | | | 1 | | | | 2 | 10 | 11 | | | 7 | 5 | | | | 6 | 8 | 9 | | | | 4 | 3 | | | |
| 33 | 7 | GUILDFORD | 1-0 | Pritchard | | | 1 | | 11 | | 2 | 10 | | | | 7 | 5 | | | | 4 | 8 | 9 | | | | 6 | 3 | | | |
| 34 | 8 | WORCESTER | 1-1 | Pritchard | | | 1 | | 11 | | 2 | 10 | | | | 7 | 5 | | | | 4 | 8 | 9 | | | | 6 | 3 | | | |
| 35 | 10 | Guildford | 1-3 | Crisp | | | 1 | | 11 | | 2 | 10 | 7 | | | | 5 | | | | 4 | 8 | 9 | | | | 6 | 3 | | | |
| 36 | 11 | NORWICH RES. | 5-1 | Cheyne, Hodge(2), Wallis(2) | | | 1 | | | | 2 | 10 | 11 | | | 7 | 5 | | | | 4 | 8 | 9 | | | | 6 | 3 | | | |
| 37 | 15 | Barry | 2-0 | Crisp, Matthews | | | 1 | | | | 2 | 10 | 11 | | | | 5 | 7 | | | 4 | 8 | 9 | | | | 6 | 3 | | | |
| 38 | 20 | Bath | 3-0 | Hodge(2), Pritchard | | 1 | | | | | 2 | 10 | 11 | | | 7 | 5 | | | | 4 | 8 | 9 | | | | 6 | 3 | | | |
| 39 | 22 | PLYMOUTH RES. | 2-3 | Cheyne, Pritchard | | | 1 | | | | 2 | 10 | 11 | | | 7 | 5 | | | | 4 | 8 | 9 | | | | 6 | 3 | | | |
| 40 | 24 | Chelmsford | 0-0 | | | | 1 | | | | 2 | 10 | 11 | | | 7 | 5 | | | | 4 | 8 | 9 | | | | 6 | 3 | | | |
| 41 | 27 | Worcester | 0-1 | | | | 1 | | | | 2 | | 11 | | | 7 | 5 | | | | 4 | 8 | 9 | | 6 | | 10 | 3 | | | |
| 42 | 29 | IPSWICH RES. | 4-0 | Birch, Hodge, Wallis(2) | | | 1 | | 11 | | 2 | | 10 | | | 7 | 5 | | | | 6 | 8 | | | 4 | | 9 | 3 | | | |
| 43 | 1 May | CHELMSFORD | 2-2 | Astill, Morris | | | 1 | | 11 | | 2 | | | | | 7 | 5 | | | | 6 | 8 | 9 | | 4 | | 10 | 3 | | | |
| MW | 2 | Dartford | 2-2 | Pritchard, Wallis | | 1 | | | | | 2 | | 11 | | | 7 | 5 | | | | 6 | 8 | 9 | | 4 | | 10 | 3 | | | |
| MW | 4 | NORWICH RES. | 2-4 | Morris, Wallis | | | 1 | 3 | | | | | 11 | 4 | 2 | 7 | | | | 10 | 6 | 8 | | | 5 | | 9 | | | | |
| 44 | 6 | Ipswich Res. | 3-2 | Astill, Cheyne, Pritchard | | | 1 | | 11 | | 2 | 10 | | | | 7 | 5 | | | | 4 | 8 | 9 | | | | 6 | 3 | | | |

## Southern League Cup

| | | | | | | | | | | | | | | | | | | | | | | | | | | | | | | | |
|---|---|---|---|---|---|---|---|---|---|---|---|---|---|---|---|---|---|---|---|---|---|---|---|---|---|---|---|---|---|---|---|
| 1st | 17 Sep | IPSWICH RES. | 5-0 | Astill(2), Cheyne, Hodge, Pritchard | | 1 | | | 11 | | 2 | 10 | | | | 7 | 5 | | | | 6 | | 9 | | 4 | | 8 | 3 | | | |
| 2nd | 28 Jan | ARSENAL 'A' | 3-1 | Astill, Pritchard, Wallis | | 1 | | | 11 | | 2 | 8 | | | | 7 | 5 | | | | 6 | | 9 | | 4 | | 10 | 3 | | | |
| 3rd | 13 Apr | FOLKESTONE | 2-0 | Cheyne, Pritchard | | | 1 | | | | 2 | 10 | 11 | | | 7 | 5 | | | | 4 | | 9 | 6 | | | 8 | 3 | | | |

## F.A.Cup

| | | | | | | | | | | | | | | | | | | | | | | | | | | | | | | | |
|---|---|---|---|---|---|---|---|---|---|---|---|---|---|---|---|---|---|---|---|---|---|---|---|---|---|---|---|---|---|---|---|
| 4Q | 12 Nov | ILFORD | 4-1 | Crisp, Hodge, Pritchard, Wallis | | 1 | | | | 4 | 2 | 10 | 11 | | | 7 | 5 | | | | 6 | | 9 | | | | 8 | 3 | | | |
| 1st | 26 | Folkestone | 1-2 | Leslie | | 1 | | | | 4 | 2 | 10 | 11 | | | 7 | 5 | | | | 6 | | 9 | | | | 8 | 3 | | | |

## Season 1939/40 Southern League (Abandoned)

| | | | | | | | | | | | | | | | | | | | | | | | | | | | | | | | |
|---|---|---|---|---|---|---|---|---|---|---|---|---|---|---|---|---|---|---|---|---|---|---|---|---|---|---|---|---|---|---|---|
| 1 | 26 Aug | PLYMOUTH RES. | 3-1 | Birch, Cheyne, Law | | 1 | | | 11 | | 2 | 10 | | | | | | | | | 5 | 7 | | | | | 6 | 3 | 8 | 9 | 4 |
| 2 | 31 | CHELMSFORD | 1-2 | Cheyne | | 1 | | | 11 | | 2 | 10 | | | | | | | | | 5 | 8 | 9 | | | | 6 | 3 | | 7 | 4 |
| 3 | 2 Sep | IPSWICH RES. | 0-0 | | | 1 | | | 11 | | 2 | 10 | | 7 | | | 5 | | | | 4 | | | | | | 6 | 3 | 8 | 9 | |

## Southern League Cup (1938/39 Season)

| | | | | | | | | | | | | | | | | | | | | | | | | | | | | | | | |
|---|---|---|---|---|---|---|---|---|---|---|---|---|---|---|---|---|---|---|---|---|---|---|---|---|---|---|---|---|---|---|---|
| S/F/1 | 28 Aug | Norwich Res. | 5-1 | Astill(2), Birch, Law, Pritchard | | 1 | | | 11 | | 2 | | | | | | | | | | 5 | 8 | 9 | | | | 6 | 3 | 10 | 7 | 4 |

15 Friendly matches were played following the abandonment of the 1939/40 season Southern League.

The following players took part (with number of appearances in brackets):

Allan (12), Birch (15), Bidewell (2), Brooks (5), Burns (1), Cárter (2), Cheyne (7), Dunn (6), Edwards (1), H.Fieldus (1), S.Fieldus (9), Jenkins (1), Law (4), Leach (2), Leslie (15), Little (12), Morris (15), Mullane (1), Pettett (8), Prendergast (6), Potts (1), Rees (9), Simpson (3), Storey (2), Smith (12), Thompson (2), Woodcock(1).

C. Allan. W. Light.

Some of the players signed for the abortive 1939/40 season.
Only Allan, Light and Fieldus remained at the club after the war.

S. Fieldus. A. Pritchard.

# SEASON 1945/46 Southern League

| Match | Brown.H | Dawson / Dring | Jeffries / Kingston | Light / Wilkie | Allan / Andrews | Bamford / Barnard | Beach / Beveridge | Bidewell / Bower | Bramhall / Browne | Buckley / Cameron | Canham / Collins | Coulson / Day | Bickmore / Dudley | Duquemin / Ferguson | Fieldus / Fletcher | Fox / Godfrey | Gotts / Gray | Gregg / Harmon | Hawksworth / Heal | Hodgson / Hogg | Holnes / Holmes | Hornby / Hubbard | Hutchings / Inskip | James / Jenkins | Jones L. / Jones S. | Kernohan / Leighton | Milne / Munro | Muttitt / Nelson | O'Sullivan / Rawcliffe | Reeves / Rightun | Robinson / Robson | Shiels / Smale | Smirke / Southam | Stanyon / Steele | Sutton / Thacker | Thompson / Titcombe | Tobin / Townsend | West / Westwood | Williams / Willmott | Brown.R / Jones.C | Green.A / Green J. |
|---|---|---|---|---|---|---|---|---|---|---|---|---|---|---|---|---|---|---|---|---|---|---|---|---|---|---|---|---|---|---|---|---|---|---|---|---|---|---|---|---|---|
| 1 | | | | 1 | | | | 2 | | | | | | | | 8 | | 10 | | | | 11 | | 5 | | | 3 | | | 9 | 6 | | 4 | | | 7 | | | | | |
| 2 | | | | 1 | | | 4 | 2 | | | | | | | | 8 | | 9 | | | | 11 | | 5 | | | 3 | | | 7 | 10 6 | | | | | | | | | | |
| 3 | | 1 | | | | | 4 | 2 | 8 | | | 9 | | | | | | 10 | | | | 11 | | 5 | | | 3 | | | | 6 | | | | | 7 | | | | | |
| 4 | | 1 | | | | | | 2 | 6 | | | | | | | 10 | 4 | | | | 3 | | | 5 | | 9 | | | | 7 | | | 8 | 11 | | | | | | | |
| 5 | | 1 | | | 3 | | | 2 | | 11 10 | | | | | | | | | | | | | 7 | 5 | | 9 | | | 4 | 4 | | | 6 | | | 8 | | | | | |
| 6 | 1 | | | | 10 | | | 2 | | | | | | | | | | | 6 | | | 11 | | 5 | | | | 10 | | | | | 3 | | | 7 | | | 9 8 | | |
| 7 | 1 | | | | | | | 2 | 4 | | | | | | | | | | 6 | | | 11 | | 5 | | | | | | | | | 3 | | 8 | 7 | | | 9 | | |
| 8 | 1 | | | | | | | 2 | | | | | | | | | | 10 9 | 6 | | | 11 | | 5 | | | | | | 4 | | | 8 3 | | | | | | 7 | | |
| 9 | | | | 1 | | 9 | | 2 | | | | | | | | | | 10 8 | 6 | | | | | 5 4 | | | | | | | | | 3 | | 11 | | | | 7 | | |
| 10 | 1 | | | | | | | 2 | | | | | | 10 | | | | 9 | 6 | | | 11 | | 5 4 | | | | | | | 8 | | 3 | | 7 | | | | | | |
| 11 | 1 | | | | | 9 | | 2 | | | | | 11 | 10 | | | | | 8 | | | | | 5 | 6 | | | | | | | 3 | | | | | | 4 | 7 | | |
| 12 | 1 | | | | | 9 | | 2 | | | | | | 10 | | | | | 11 | | | | | 5 4 | 8 3 | | | | | | | | 6 | | | | | | 7 | | |
| 13 | 1 | | | | | | | 2 | | | 9 | | | | | | | | 11 | | | | | 5 4 | | 6 | | | | | | | 10 | | | 7 | | | | 3 | 8 |
| 14 | 1 | | | | | | | 2 | | | | | | 10 | | | | | 11 | | 8 | | | 5 4 | 3 | 6 | | | | | | | 9 | | | | | | 7 | | |
| 15 | 1 | | | | | | 9 7 | 2 | | | | | | | 3 | | | 10 | | 11 | 8 | | | 5 4 | | 6 | | | | | | | | | | | | | | | |
| 16 | 1 | | | | | | | 2 | | | | | | 10 | | | | 9 | | | 8 | 11 | | 5 4 | 6 | | | | | | | 3 | | 7 | | | | | | | |
| 17 | | | 1 | | | | | 2 | | | 11 | | 9 | | | | | 10 | | | | | 6 | 5 | 4 | | | | | 7 | | 3 | 8 | | | | | | | | |
| 18 | | | 1 | | | | | 2 | | | 11 | | | | | | | 10 | | 9 | 8 | | 6 | 5 | 4 | | | | | 7 | | 3 | | | | | | | | | |
| 19 | | | | | | | | 2 | | | | | | | 9 | | | | | 8 | | | 6 | 5 | 4 | | | | 10 | | | 3 7 | | | | | | 11 | | 1 | |
| 20 | | | | | | | | 9 2 | | | | | | | | | | 11 | | 8 | | | 6 | 5 | 4 | | | | 10 | | | 3 7 | | | | | | | | 1 | |

N.B. Numbers in left–hand column of Southern League & Cup tables correspond to match numbers in tables below.

## Southern League Cup

| Match | Brown.H | Dawson / Dring | Jeffries / Kingston | Light / Wilkie | Allan / Andrews | Bamford / Barnard | Beach / Beveridge | Bidewell / Bower | Bramhall / Browne | Buckley / Cameron | Canham / Collins | Coulson / Day | Bickmore / Dudley | Duquemin / Ferguson | Fieldus / Fletcher | Fox / Godfrey | Gotts / Gray | Gregg / Harmon | Hawksworth / Heal | Hodgson / Hogg | Holnes / Holmes | Hornby / Hubbard | Hutchings / Inskip | James / Jenkins | Jones L. / Jones S. | Kernohan / Leighton | Milne / Munro | Muttitt / Nelson | O'Sullivan / Rawcliffe | Reeves / Rightun | Robinson / Robson | Shiels / Smale | Smirke / Southam | Stanyon / Steele | Sutton / Thacker | Thompson / Titcombe | Tobin / Townsend | West / Westwood | Williams / Willmott | Brown.R / Jones.C | Green.A / Green J. |
|---|---|---|---|---|---|---|---|---|---|---|---|---|---|---|---|---|---|---|---|---|---|---|---|---|---|---|---|---|---|---|---|---|---|---|---|---|---|---|---|---|---|
| 1 | | | 1 | | | 9 | | 2 | | | | | | 11 | | | | 10 | | | | | | 5 4 | | 6 | | | | | | | | | | | 8 | | 7 | 3 | |
| 2 | | | | | | | | 2 | | | 11 | | | | | | | | | 9 | | | 6 | 5 | 4 | | | | 10 | | | 3 7 | | | | | | | | 1 | 8 |
| 3 | | | | | | | | 9 2 | | | | | | | | | | 8 | | 7 | | | 6 | 5 | 4 | | | | 10 | | | 3 11 | | | | | | | | 1 | |
| 4 | | | | | | | | 9 2 | | | 7 | | | | | | | | | | | | 6 | 5 | 4 | | | 8 | 10 | | | 3 11 | | | | | | | | 1 | |
| 5 | | | | | | | | 9 2 | | | 11 | | | | | | | 10 | | | | | 6 | 5 | 4 | | | | 8 | | | 3 7 | | | | | | | | 1 | |
| 6 | | | | | | | | 7 2 | | | | | | 9 | 8 | 4 | | | | | | | 6 | | | | | | 10 | | | 3 11 | 5 | | | | | | | 1 | |
| 7 | | | 1 | | | | | 9 2 | | | 11 | | | | | | | | | 8 | | | 6 | 5 | 4 | | | | 10 | | | 3 7 | | | | | | | | | |
| 8 | 1 | | | | | | | 2 | | | 11 | 9 | | | | | | | | 7 | | | 6 | | 5 | | | 8 | 10 | | | 3 | 4 | | | | | | | | |
| 9 | | | 1 | | | 6 | | 8 2 | | | | 5 | | | | | 7 | | | 11 | | | | | | | 3 | 4 | 10 | | | | | | 9 | | | | | | |
| 10 | 1 | | | | | | 9 | 2 | | | 11 | | | | | | | | | 7 | | | 6 | 5 | 4 | | | | 10 | | | 3 | | | | | 8 | | | | |

## F.A.Cup

| Match | Brown.H | Dawson / Dring | Jeffries / Kingston | Light / Wilkie | Allan / Andrews | Bamford / Barnard | Beach / Beveridge | Bidewell / Bower | Bramhall / Browne | Buckley / Cameron | Canham / Collins | Coulson / Day | Bickmore / Dudley | Duquemin / Ferguson | Fieldus / Fletcher | Fox / Godfrey | Gotts / Gray | Gregg / Harmon | Hawksworth / Heal | Hodgson / Hogg | Holnes / Holmes | Hornby / Hubbard | Hutchings / Inskip | James / Jenkins | Jones L. / Jones S. | Kernohan / Leighton | Milne / Munro | Muttitt / Nelson | O'Sullivan / Rawcliffe | Reeves / Rightun | Robinson / Robson | Shiels / Smale | Smirke / Southam | Stanyon / Steele | Sutton / Thacker | Thompson / Titcombe | Tobin / Townsend | West / Westwood | Williams / Willmott | Brown.R / Jones.C | Green.A / Green J. |
|---|---|---|---|---|---|---|---|---|---|---|---|---|---|---|---|---|---|---|---|---|---|---|---|---|---|---|---|---|---|---|---|---|---|---|---|---|---|---|---|---|---|
| 4Q | | 1 | | | | | | | | | | | | | | | | 10 9 | 6 | | | 11 | | 5 | | | 2 | | | | 4 | 3 | | | | 7 | | | 8 | | |

| No. | Date | Opposition | Res | Attend | Goalscorers |
|---|---|---|---|---|---|
| 1 | 25 Aug | Chelmsford | 2-1 | | Hornby, Titcombe |
| 2 | 1 Sep | CHELMSFORD | 3-4 | | Harmon, Reeves, Robinson |
| 3 | 15 | Bedford | 0-2 | | |
| 4 | 22 | Yeovil | 0-8 | | |
| 5 | 29 | BEDFORD | 1-4 | | Southam |
| 6 | 6 Oct | CHELTENHAM | 1-0 | | Hornby |
| 7 | 13 | CARDIFF RES. | 1-0 | | Hornby |
| 8 | 10 Nov | BATH | 3-1 | | Gregg, Harmon, Smale |
| 9 | 17 | Hereford | 1-3 | | Harmon |
| 10 | 24 | WORCESTER | 2-1 | | Rightun(2) |
| 11 | 8 Dec | Barry | 0-0 | | |
| 12 | 15 | YEOVIL | 3-3 | | Barnard, Hawksworth, Willmott |
| 13 | 29 | Cheltenham | 0-1 | | |
| 14 | 12 Jan | HEREFORD | 0-3 | | |
| 15 | 26 | Worcester | 2-6 | | Beach(2) |
| 16 | 2 Feb | Bath | 0-8 | | |
| 17 | 9 | BARRY | 5-0 | | Collins, Dudley(2), Harmon, Rightun |
| 18 | 16 | Swindon Res. | 0-1 | | |
| 19 | 23 | SWINDON RES. | 5-1 | | Hodgson(2), S.Jones, Smale, Westwood |
| 20 | 16 Mar | CARDIFF RES. | 0-0 | | |

## Southern League Cup

| No. | Date | Opposition | Res | Attend | Goalscorers |
|---|---|---|---|---|---|
| 1 | 19 Jan | GUILDFORD | 3-1 | | Townsend(3) |
| 2 | 9 Mar | Cheltenham | 1-0 | | Hodgson |
| 3 | 23 | SWINDON RES. | 2-0 | | Bidewell, Smale |
| 4 | 28 | Bedford | 2-2 | | Bidewell, Rawcliffe |
| 5 | 30 | CHELTENHAM | 3-3 | | Bidewell(2), Shiels |
| 6 | 3 Apr | Chelmsford | 0-2 | | |
| 7 | 6 | Swindon Res. | 2-4 | | Hodgson, Rawcliffe |
| 8 | 11 | CHELMSFORD | 1-1 | | Collins |
| 9 | 13 | Guildford | 5-2 | | Bamford, Rawcliffe, Sutton(3) |
| 10 | 18 | BEDFORD | 3-3 | | Bower, Hodgson, S.Jones |

## F.A.Cup

| No. | Date | Opposition | Res | Attend | Goalscorers |
|---|---|---|---|---|---|
| 4 Q | 3 Nov | Wisbech | 0-5 | | |

OFFICIAL PROGRAMME PRICE TWOPENCE

Colchester Garrison XI
VERSUS
A Combined Services XI

COLCHESTER GARRISON XI
Colours: PURPLE SHIRTS

RIGHT] Brown [LEFT
(17th I.T.C.)

Bower (Detention Barracks) Jones (No. 1 Infantry Holdg. Battn.)

Jenkins (15th I.T.C.) Fenton (No. 1 Infantry Holdg. Battn.) Captain Southam (15th I.T.C.)

Townsend (16th I.T.C.) Robinson (16th I.T.C.) Barnard (No. 1 Infantry Holdg. Battn.) Nelson (15th I.T.C.) Ferguson (No. 1 Infantry Holdg. Battn.)

Referee: Lieut. PEMBROKE (The Suffolk Regt.)

Linesmen: Mr. Harris (Colchester) Mr. Earle (Prittlewell)

Smith, L. (Aston Villa and England) Edelston (Reading and England) Lawton (Chelsea and England) Captain Jones, L. (Arsenal and Wales) Woodgate (West Ham)

Burgess (Spurs and Wales) Smith, G. (Brentford and England) Soo (Leicester and England)

Kinsell (W.B.A. and England) Winter (Chelsea and Wales)

LEFT] Swift [RIGHT
(Manchester City and England)

A COMBINED SERVICES XI
Colours:

At LAYER ROAD GROUND
THURSDAY, DECEMBER 13th, 1945. Kick-off 2.30 p.m.

PROCEEDS IN AID OF SERVICES CHARITY FUNDS

BAND OF THE 17th I.T.C.
(By kind permission of the Commanding Officer, Lt.-Col. R. H. A. Lucas)

# SEASON 1946–47 Southern League

| No. | Date | Opposition | Res | Goalscorers | Walker | Chiswick | Jelly | Wright | Biggs | Bott | Bower | Cant | Cater | Collins | Curry | Fenton | Fieldus | Finch | Gibbs | Gillespie | Harding | Hillman | Hodgson | Hutchings | Jeffries | Kettle | Leah | Neville | Page | Ross | Shiels | Smith S. | Stamper | Stewart | Swift | Tobin | Turner |
|---|---|---|---|---|---|---|---|---|---|---|---|---|---|---|---|---|---|---|---|---|---|---|---|---|---|---|---|---|---|---|---|---|---|---|---|---|---|
| 1 | 31 Aug | GLOUCESTER | 2–3 | Curry, Stewart | | | | 1 | | | 2 | | 8 | | 10 | 5 | | 7 | | | | | | 6 | | | | | | 4 | 3 | 11 | | 9 | | | |
| 2 | 4 Sep | Chelmsford | 0–3 | | | | 1 | | | 11 | 2 | 9 | 10 | | 8 | 5 | | 7 | | | | | | 6 | | | | | | | 3 | | | | | 4 | |
| 3 | 7 | Exeter Res | 1–3 | Cater | | | | 1 | | | 2 | 9 | 10 | | 8 | 5 | | 11 | | | | | 7 | 6 | | | | | | 4 | 3 | | | | | | |
| 4 | 14 | HEREFORD | 2–1 | Cater, Hodgson | 3 | | | 1 | | | 2 | 9 | 10 | 11 | 8 | 4 | | | | | 5 | | 7 | 6 | | | | | | | | | | | | | |
| 5 | 19 | MILLWALL RES | 3–2 | Cater, Curry, O.G. | 3 | | | 1 | | | 2 | 11 | 10 | | 8 | 4 | | | | | 5 | | 7 | 6 | | | | | | | | | | | | | 9 |
| 6 | 28 | WORCESTER | 3–2 | Curry, Turner(2,1pen) | 3 | 1 | | | | 11 | 2 | | 10 | | 8 | 4 | | | | | | 7 | | 6 | | | | | | | 5 | | | | | | 9 |
| 7 | 5 Oct | YEOVIL | 4–3 | Cant(2), Cater(2) | 3 | 1 | | | | | 2 | 9 | 10 | 11 | 8 | 4 | | | | | 5 | 7 | | 6 | | | | | | | | | | | | | |
| 8 | 12 | Hereford | 0–0 | | 3 | 1 | | | | | 2 | | 10 | 11 | 4 | | | | | | 5 | 7 | 8 | 6 | | | | | | | | | | | | | 9 |
| 9 | 19 | EXETER RES | 6–1 | Cater, Curry, Turner(4) | 3 | 1 | | | | | 2 | | 10 | 11 | 8 | 4 | | | | | 5 | 7 | | 6 | | | | | | | | | | | | | 9 |
| 10 | 2 Nov | Bath | 3–3 | Curry, Fenton, Hillman | 3 | 1 | | | | | 2 | | 10 | 11 | 8 | 4 | | | | | 5 | 7 | | 6 | | | | | | | | | | | | | 9 |
| 11 | 9 | Worcester | 5–3 | Collins(2), Turner(3) | 3 | 1 | | | | | 2 | | 10 | 11 | 8 | 4 | | | | | 5 | 7 | | 6 | | | | | | | | | | | | | 9 |
| 12 | 23 | GRAVESEND & N | 1–3 | Collins | 3 | 1 | | | | | 2 | | 10 | 11 | 8 | 4 | | | | | 5 | 7 | | 6 | | | | | | | | | | | | | 9 |
| 13 | 7 Dec | CHELMSFORD | 3–2 | Cater(2), Turner | 3 | 1 | | | | | 2 | | 10 | | 8 | 4 | | | | | | 7 | | 6 | | | | 11 | | | | | | | 5 | | 9 |
| 14 | 25 | GILLINGHAM | 0–1 | | 3 | 1 | | | | | 2 | | 10 | | 8 | 4 | | | | | | 7 | | 6 | | | | 11 | | | | | | | 5 | | 9 |
| 15 | 26 | Gillingham | 2–4 | Curry(2) | 3 | 1 | | | | | 2 | | 10 | | 8 | 5 | | | | | | 7 | | 6 | | 4 | | 11 | | | | | | | | | 9 |
| 16 | 4 Jan | CHELTENHAM | 2–2 | Curry, Turner(pen) | 3 | | | 1 | | | | | 10 | | 8 | 5 | | | | | | 7 | | 6 | | 4 | | 11 | | | | | | | | | 9 |
| 17 | 18 | Barry | 1–2 | Curry | 3 | | | 1 | | | 2 | | 11 | | 8 | 5 | | | | | | 7 | 10 | 6 | | 4 | | | | | | | | | | | 9 |
| 18 | 8 Feb | BARRY | 2–0 | Neville, Turner | 3 | | | 1 | | | 2 | | 10 | | | 5 | | | | | | 7 | 8 | 6 | | 4 | | 11 | | | | | | | | | 9 |
| 19 | 17 | Millwall Res | 1–1 | Curry | 3 | | | 1 | | | 2 | | 10 | | 8 | 5 | | | | | | 7 | 9 | 6 | | 4 | | 11 | | | | | | | | | |
| 20 | 1 Mar | Gravesend & N | 0–3 | | 3 | | | 1 | | | 2 | | 11 | | 10 | 5 | | | 8 | | | 7 | 9 | 6 | | | | | | 4 | | | | | | | |
| 21 | 23 | Yeovil | 1–1 | Curry | 5 | | | 1 | | | 2 | | 11 | | 8 | 6 | | | | | | 7 | | 4 | | 3 | | | | | | 10 | | | | | 9 |
| 22 | 29 | Cheltenham | 4–1 | Smith, Turner(3) | 3 | | | 1 | | | 2 | | 11 | | 8 | 6 | | | | | | 7 | | 4 | | | | | 5 | | | 10 | | | | | 9 |
| 23 | 5 Apr | Guildford | 1–2 | Turner | 3 | | | 1 | | | 2 | | 11 | | 8 | 6 | | | | | | 7 | | 4 | | | | | 5 | | | 10 | | | | | 9 |
| 24 | 12 | GUILDFORD | 2–0 | Cater, Hillman | 3 | | | 1 | | | 2 | | 11 | | 8 | 6 | | | | | | 7 | | | | 4 | | | 5 | | | 10 | | | | | 9 |
| 25 | 19 | Merthyr Tydfil | 0–4 | | 3 | | | 1 | | | 2 | | | | 8 | | 11 | | | | | 7 | | | | 4 | | | 5 | | | 10 | 6 | | | | 9 |
| 26 | 26 | BATH | 3–2 | Curry, Fenton, Turner | 3 | | | 1 | | | 2 | | 11 | | 8 | 6 | | | | | | 7 | | | | 4 | | | 5 | | | 10 | | | | | 9 |
| 27 | 3 May | METHYR TYDFIL | 2–1 | Hillman, Smith | 3 | | | 1 | | | 2 | | 11 | | 8 | 6 | | | | | | 7 | | | | 4 | | | 5 | | | 10 | | | | | 9 |
| 28 | 10 | Dartford | 1–3 | Curry | 3 | | | 1 | | | 2 | | 11 | | 8 | | | | | | | 7 | | | | 4 | | | 5 | | | 10 | 6 | | | | 9 |
| 29 | 17 | Bedford | 0–2 | | 3 | | | 1 | 10 | | | | 11 | | 8 | 6 | | | | 4 | | 7 | | | | 2 | | | 5 | | | | | | | | 9 |
| 30 | 24 | BEDFORD | 4–0 | Cater, Gillespie, Turner(2) | 3 | | | 1 | 10 | | 2 | | 11 | | 8 | 6 | | | | 4 | | 7 | | | | | | | 5 | | | | | | | | 9 |
| 31 | 26 | DARTFORD | 2–1 | Biggs, Curry | | 1 | | | 10 | | 2 | | 11 | | 8 | 6 | | | | 4 | | 7 | | | | 3 | | | 5 | | | | | | | | 9 |
| 32 | 31 | Gloucester | 5–2 | Biggs(2), Curry, Turner(2) | 3 | | | 1 | 10 | | 2 | | 11 | | 8 | | | | | 4 | | 7 | | | | 6 | | | 5 | | | | | | | | 9 |

## Southern League Cup

| | | | | | | | | | | | | | | | | | | | | | | | | | | | | | | | | | | | | | |
|---|---|---|---|---|---|---|---|---|---|---|---|---|---|---|---|---|---|---|---|---|---|---|---|---|---|---|---|---|---|---|---|---|---|---|---|---|---|
| 1 | 26 Sep | CHELMSFORD | 2–4 | Turner(2) | 3 | | | 1 | | | 2 | | 10 | | 8 | 5 | | | | | | 7 | 11 | 6 | | | 4 | | | | | | | | | | 9 |
| 2 | 26 Oct | Bedford | 5–0 | Cater, Collins(2), Curry, Hutchings | 3 | 1 | | | | | 2 | | 10 | 11 | 8 | 4 | | | | | 5 | 7 | | 6 | | | | | | | | | | | | | 9 |
| 3 | 12 Dec | MILLWALL RES. | 3–2 | Cater, Neville, Turner | 3 | 1 | | | | | 2 | | 10 | | 8 | 4 | | | | | | 7 | | 6 | | | | 11 | | | | | | 5 | | 9 |
| 4 | 11 Jan | Chelmsford | 4–1 | Hillman(2), Hodgson(2) | 3 | | | 1 | | | 2 | | 11 | | 8 | 5 | | | | | | 7 | 10 | 6 | | 4 | | | | | | | | | | | 9 |
| 5 | 25 | BEDFORD | 2–1 | Curry, Hillman | 3 | | | 1 | | | 2 | | 11 | | 8 | 5 | | | | | | 7 | 10 | 6 | | 4 | | | | | | | | | | | 9 |
| S/F | 7 Jun | Gillingham | 2–3 | Cater, Curry | 3 | | 1 | | | | 2 | | 11 | | 8 | 6 | | | | 4 | | 7 | | | 10 | | | | 5 | | | | | | | | 9 |

## F.A.Cup

| | | | | | | | | | | | | | | | | | | | | | | | | | | | | | | | | | | | | | |
|---|---|---|---|---|---|---|---|---|---|---|---|---|---|---|---|---|---|---|---|---|---|---|---|---|---|---|---|---|---|---|---|---|---|---|---|---|---|
| 4Q | 16 Nov | GOTHIC | 5–1 | Cant(2), Cater, Curry, Hillman, | 3 | 1 | | | | | 2 | 9 | 10 | 11 | 8 | 4 | | | | | 5 | 7 | | 6 | | | | | | | | | | | | | |
| 1st | 30 | Reading | 0–5 | | 3 | 1 | | | | | 2 | | 10 | 11 | 8 | 4 | | | | | 5 | 7 | | 6 | | | | | | | | | | | | | 9 |

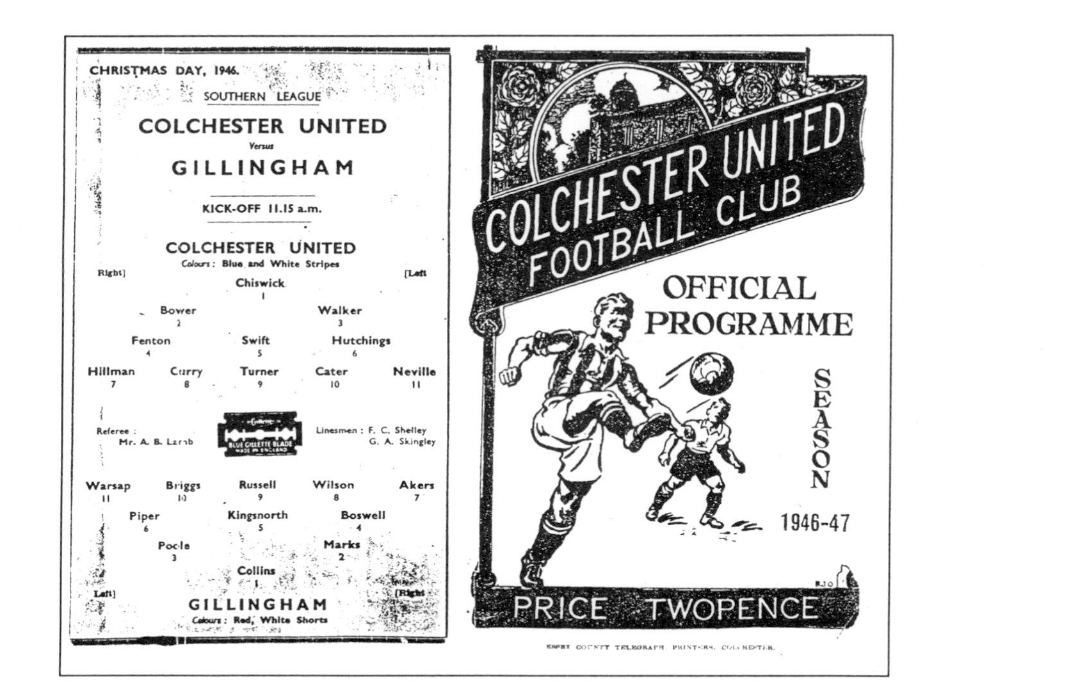

# SEASON 1947–48

## Southern League

| No. | Date | Opposition | Res | Goalscorers | Lamare | Setchell | Wright | Allen | Bearryman | Biggs | Bower | Brown | Cater | Curry | Cutting | Darmody | Fenton | Gillespie | Hillman | Keeble | Kettle | Leah | Page | Rist | Stamper | Townrow | Turner | Walker | Williams |
|---|---|---|---|---|---|---|---|---|---|---|---|---|---|---|---|---|---|---|---|---|---|---|---|---|---|---|---|---|---|
| 1 | 30 Aug | Bedford | 5–1 | Cater(2), Keeble(3) | | | 1 | 3 | 4 | 10 | | 6 | 11 | 8 | | | | | 7 | 9 | 2 | | | 5 | | | | | |
| 2 | 6 Sep | GLOUCESTER | 8–0 | Biggs, Cater, Curry, Hillman(3), Turner(2) | | | 1 | 3 | 4 | 10 | | 6 | 11 | 8 | | | | | 7 | | 2 | | 5 | | | | 9 | | |
| 3 | 13 | Hereford | 0–0 | | | | 1 | 3 | 4 | 10 | | 6 | 11 | 8 | | | | | 7 | | 2 | | 5 | | | | 9 | | |
| 4 | 27 | Yeovil | 0–2 | | | | 1 | 3 | 4 | 10 | | 6 | 11 | 8 | | | | | | | 2 | | 5 | | | | 9 | | 7 |
| 5 | 11 Oct | BATH | 4–2 | Hillman, Turner(2), O.G. | | | 1 | 3 | 4 | | | 6 | 11 | 8 | | | | | 7 | 10 | 2 | | | 5 | | | 9 | | |
| 6 | 18 | WORCESTER | 1–3 | Turner | | | 1 | 3 | 4 | 10 | | 6 | 11 | 8 | | | | | 7 | | 2 | | | 5 | | | 9 | | |
| 7 | 1 Nov | TORQUAY RES | 5–0 | Curry, Fenton, Turner(3) | | | 1 | 3 | | 10 | | 6 | 11 | 8 | | | 4 | | 7 | | 2 | | 5 | | | | 9 | | |
| 8 | 8 | Gravesend & N | 2–1 | Cater, Fenton | | | 1 | 3 | | 10 | | 6 | 11 | 8 | | | 4 | | 7 | | 2 | | 5 | | | | 9 | | |
| 9 | 22 | MERTHYR TYDFIL | 1–1 | Turner(pen) | | | 1 | 3 | 4 | 10 | | 6 | 11 | 8 | | | 5 | | 7 | | 2 | | | | | | 9 | | |
| 10 | 6 Dec | Barry | 5–2 | Curry(3), Cutting, Keeble | 1 | | | 3 | 4 | | | 6 | 11 | 8 | 10 | | | | 7 | 9 | 2 | | | 5 | | | | | |
| 11 | 20 | BEDFORD | 3–0 | Curry(2), Turner | | | 1 | 3 | 4 | | | 6 | 11 | 8 | 10 | | 5 | | 7 | | 2 | | | | | | 9 | | |
| 12 | 25 | GILLINGHAM | 3–0 | Curry, Turner(2) | 1 | | | 3 | 4 | | | 6 | 11 | 8 | 10 | | 5 | | 7 | | 2 | | | | | | 9 | | |
| 13 | 26 | Gillingham | 2–2 | Curry, Turner | | | 1 | 3 | 4 | | | 6 | 11 | 8 | 10 | | | | 7 | | 2 | | | 5 | | | 9 | | |
| 14 | 27 | Cheltenham | 2–5 | Curry, Keeble | 1 | | | | 4 | | | | | 8 | 10 | | | | | 9 | 2 | 11 | 5 | 6 | | | | 3 | 7 |
| 15 | 3 Jan | CHELTENHAM | 1–2 | Fenton | | | 1 | 3 | 4 | | | 6 | | 8 | 10 | | 5 | | 7 | 11 | 2 | | | | | | 9 | | |
| 16 | 31 | Torquay Res | 1–1 | Cutting | 1 | | | 3 | 6 | | | 4 | 11 | | 10 | | | | | | 2 | | | 5 | | 8 | 9 | | 7 |
| 17 | 14 Feb | EXETER RES | 6–0 | Curry(2), Cutting(2), Turner, O.G. | | | 1 | 3 | 6 | | | | 11 | 8 | 10 | | 5 | | 7 | | 2 | | | 4 | | | 9 | | |
| 18 | 21 | Merthyr Tydfil | 1–1 | Cutting | | | 1 | 3 | 6 | | | 4 | 11 | 8 | 10 | | 5 | | 7 | | 2 | | | | | | 9 | | |
| 19 | 28 | Lovell's | 2–2 | Townrow(2) | | | 1 | 3 | 4 | | 2 | 6 | 11 | 8 | 10 | | 5 | | | | | | | | | 7 | 9 | | |
| 20 | 6 Mar | Worcester | 4–2 | Cater, Cutting, Hillman, O.G. | | | 1 | 3 | 4 | | 2 | 6 | 11 | 8 | 10 | | 5 | | 7 | | | | | | | | 9 | | |
| 21 | 13 | Bath | 1–1 | Brown | | | 1 | 3 | 4 | | | 6 | 11 | 8 | 10 | | 5 | | 7 | | 2 | | | | | | 9 | | |
| 22 | 17 | Dartford | 1–1 | Bearryman | | | 1 | 3 | 4 | | | 6 | 11 | 8 | | | | | | | 2 | | | 5 | | 10 | 9 | | 7 |
| 23 | 20 | CHELMSFORD | 2–0 | Cutting(2) | | | 1 | 3 | 4 | | | 6 | 11 | 8 | 10 | | 5 | | 7 | | 2 | | | | | | 9 | | |
| 24 | 26 | GUILDFORD | 1–1 | Bearryman | | | 1 | 3 | 4 | | | 6 | 11 | 8 | 10 | | 5 | | 7 | | 2 | | | | | | 9 | | |
| 25 | 27 | GRAVESEND & N | 6–1 | Cuury(2), Cutting(2), Keeble, Turner | | | 1 | 3 | 4 | | | 6 | | 8 | 10 | | 5 | | 7 | 11 | 2 | | | | | | 9 | | |
| 26 | 29 | Guildford | 2–1 | Cutting, Turner | | | 1 | 3 | 4 | | | 6 | | 7 | 10 | 5 | | | | 11 | 2 | | | | | 8 | 9 | | |
| 27 | 1 Apr | DARTFORD | 6–1 | Keeble(2), Turner(4,1pen) | | | 1 | 3 | 4 | | | 6 | | 7 | 10 | 5 | | | | 11 | 2 | | | | | 8 | 9 | | |
| 28 | 3 | BARRY | 4–0 | Curry, Turner(3) | | | 1 | 3 | 4 | | | | | 8 | 10 | | 5 | | 7 | 11 | 2 | | | | 6 | | 9 | | |
| 29 | 10 | HEREFORD | 1–1 | Fenton | | | 1 | 3 | 4 | | | | | 8 | 10 | | 5 | | 7 | 11 | 2 | | | | 6 | | 9 | | |
| 30 | 14 | Exeter Res | 1–2 | Townrow | | | 1 | 3 | 6 | | | | | | 10 | 5 | 4 | | 7 | 11 | 2 | | | | | 8 | 9 | | |
| 31 | 17 | Gloucester | 3–1 | Cater, Cutting, Turner | | | 1 | 3 | 4 | | | | 11 | | 10 | | 5 | | 7 | | 2 | | | | 6 | 8 | 9 | | |
| 32 | 21 | Chelmsford | 1–2 | Curry | | | 1 | 3 | 4 | | | 6 | 11 | 8 | 10 | | | | 7 | | 2 | | | 5 | | | 9 | | |
| 33 | 24 | YEOVIL | 3–0 | Brown, Curry, Turner | | 1 | | | 4 | | | 6 | 11 | 8 | 10 | | 5 | | 7 | | 2 | | | | | | 9 | 3 | |
| 34 | 1 May | LOVELL'S | 0–2 | | | 1 | | | 4 | | 2 | 3 | 11 | 8 | | | 5 | | 7 | 9 | | | | | 6 | 10 | | | |

# Southern League Cup

| | | | | | | | | | | | | | | | | | | | | | | | | | | | | | |
|---|---|---|---|---|---|---|---|---|---|---|---|---|---|---|---|---|---|---|---|---|---|---|---|---|---|---|---|---|---|
| 1st | 11 Sep | CHELMSFORD | 3-0 | Cater, Gillespie, Hillman | | | 1 | 3 | 4 | | | 6 | 11 | 8 | | | | 10 | 7 | | 2 | | 5 | | | | 9 | | |
| 1st\2 | 24 | Chelmsford | 2-1 | Biggs, Cater | | | 1 | 3 | 4 | 10 | | 6 | 11 | 8 | | | | | 7 | | 2 | | 5 | | | | 9 | | |
| 2nd | 16 Oct | Bedford | 3-3 | Curry, Fenton, Rist(pen) | | | 1 | 3 | 4 | | | 6 | | 8 | 11 | | 10 | | 9 | | 2 | | | 5 | | | 9 | | |
| 2nd\2 | 17 Jan | BEDFORD | 4-0 | Bearryman | 1 | | | 3 | 4 | | | 6 | 11 | | 10 | | | | 7 | 9 | 2 | | | 5 | | 8 | | | |
| 3rd | 4 Feb | CHELTENHAM | 7-1 | Bearryman, Cater(2), Curry(3), Cutting | | | 1 | 3 | 4 | | 2 | 6 | 11 | 8 | 10 | | 5 | | 7 | | | | | | | | 9 | | |
| 3rd\2 | 10 | Cheltenham | 4-0 | Cater(2), Townrow, Turner | | | 1 | 3 | 4 | | | 6 | 11 | 10 | | | | | | | 2 | | | 5 | | 8 | 9 | | 7 |
| S\F | 19 Apr | Gravesend & N | 1-1 | Bearryman | | | 1 | 3 | 6 | | | 10 | | 8 | | | 5 | | | 11 | 7 | | | | 4 | | 9 | 2 | |
| S\F\R | 26 | GRAVESEND & N | 3-1 | Curry(2), Townrow | | | 1 | | 4 | | | 3 | | 8 | | | 5 | | 7 | 11 | 2 | | | | 6 | 10 | 9 | | |

# F A Cup

| | | | | | | | | | | | | | | | | | | | | | | | | | | | | | |
|---|---|---|---|---|---|---|---|---|---|---|---|---|---|---|---|---|---|---|---|---|---|---|---|---|---|---|---|---|---|
| 4th\Q | 15 Nov | CHELMSFORD | 3-1 | Curry(2), Turner | | | 1 | 3 | 4 | 10 | | 6 | 11 | 8 | | | 5 | | 7 | | 2 | | | | | | 9 | | |
| 1st | 29 | BANBURY SPEN | 2-1 | Brown, Curry | | | 1 | 3 | 4 | | | 6 | 11 | 8 | 10 | | 5 | | | | 2 | | | | | | 9 | | |
| 2nd | 13 Dec | WREXHAM | 1-0 | Curry | | | 1 | 3 | 4 | | | 6 | 11 | 8 | 10 | | 5 | | 7 | | 2 | | | | | | 9 | | |
| 3rd | 10 Jan | HUDDERSFIELD | 1-0 | Curry | | | 1 | 3 | 4 | | | 6 | 11 | 8 | 10 | | 5 | | 7 | | 2 | | | | | | 9 | | |
| 4th | 24 | BRADFORD | 3-2 | Curry(2), Cutting | | | 1 | 3 | 4 | | | 6 | 11 | 8 | 10 | | 5 | | 7 | | 2 | | | | | | 9 | | |
| 5th | 7 Feb | Blackpool | 0-5 | | | | 1 | 3 | 6 | | | 4 | 11 | 8 | 10 | | 5 | | 7 | | 2 | | | | | | 9 | | |

Line-ups for F.A.Cup match versus Bradford P.A.
Colchester Team (Left side). (Middle) Turner, Fenton, Wright, Brown, Bearryman, Allen.
(Front) Hillman, Cutting, Kettle, Curry, Cater.

# SEASON 48–49 Southern League

| No. | Date | Opposition | Res | Attend | Goalscorers | Davies | Keeble | Whitehead | Wright.G | Wright.H | Allen | Bearryman | Brown | Cater | Cranfield | Curry | Cutting | Foxall | George | Hildyard | Hillman | Kettle | Maffey | Miller | Nunn | Stamper | Townrow | Turner |
|---|---|---|---|---|---|---|---|---|---|---|---|---|---|---|---|---|---|---|---|---|---|---|---|---|---|---|---|---|
| 1 | 21 Aug | Cheltenham | 1-1 | 3400 | Cutting | | | | | 1 | 3 | 4 | 6 | | 11 | 8 | 10 | 7 | | | | 2 | | | 5 | | | 9 |
| 2 | 28 | BEDFORD | 2-2 | 8945 | Curry, Foxall | | | | | 1 | 3 | 4 | 6 | | 11 | 8 | 10 | 7 | | | | 2 | | | 5 | | | 9 |
| 3 | 1 Sep | Chelmsford | 1-2 | 12550 | Turner(pen) | | | | | 1 | 3 | 4 | | | 11 | 8 | 10 | 7 | | | | 2 | | 6 | | 5 | | 9 |
| 4 | 4 | Barry | 1-3 | | Turner | | | 1 | | | 3 | | 6 | | 11 | 8· | 10 | 7 | | | | 2 | | 4 | | 5 | | 9 |
| 5 | 11 | KIDDERMINSTER | 4-0 | 8271 | Allen, Foxall, Turner(2) | | | 1 | | | 3 | 4 | 6 | 11 | | 8 | 10 | 7 | | | | 2 | | | | 5 | | 9 |
| 6 | 18 | Bath | 3-1 | | Curry, Turner(2) | | | 1 | | | 3 | 4 | 6 | 11 | | 8 | 10 | 7 | | | | 2 | | | | 5 | | 9 |
| 7 | 23 | Lovell's | 1-1 | | Curry | | | 1 | | | 3 | 4 | 6 | 11 | 7 | 8 | 10 | | | | | 2 | | | | 5 | | 9 |
| 8 | 25 | CHELMSFORD | 3-2 | 14048 | Keeble(2), Cutting | | 9 | 1 | | | 3 | 4 | 6 | 11 | | 8 | 10 | 7 | | | | 2 | | | | 5 | | |
| 9 | 16 Oct | Chingford | 5-1 | | Curry, Cutting, Foxall, Turner(2) | | | 1 | | | 3 | 4 | 6 | 11 | | 8 | 10 | 7 | | | | 2 | | | | 5 | | 9 |
| 10 | 6 Nov | Torquay Res | 3-1 | | Cutting, Turner(2) | | | 1 | | | 3 | 4 | 6 | 11 | | 8 | 10 | 7 | | | | 2 | | | | 5 | | 9 |
| 11 | 13 | TORQUAY RES | 3-2 | 8775 | Cutting, Foxall, Turner(pen) | | | 1 | | | 3 | 4 | 6 | 11 | | 8 | 10 | 7 | | | | 2 | | | | 5 | | 9 |
| 12 | 20 | Yeovil | 1-0 | | Cutting | | | 1 | | | 3 | 4 | 6 | 11 | | 8 | 10 | 7 | | | | 2 | | | | 5 | | 9 |
| 13 | 18 Dec | Hereford | 3-2 | | Curry(2), O.G. | | | 1 | | | | 4 | 6 | 11 | | 8 | 10 | 7 | | | | 2 | 3 | | | 5 | | 9 |
| 14 | 25 | GLOUCESTER | 1-1 | 7706 | Turner | | | 1 | | | | 4 | 6 | 11 | | 8 | 10 | 7 | | | | 2 | 3 | | | 5 | | 9 |
| 15 | 27 | HASTINGS | 5-1 | 7736 | Cater, Cutting(2), Hillman, Turner | | | 1 | | | | 4 | 6 | 11 | | 8 | 10 | | | | 7 | 2 | 3 | | | 5 | | 9 |
| 16 | 1 Jan | Gillingham | 1-1 | | Turner(pen) | | | 1 | | | | 4 | 6 | 11 | | 8 | 10 | | | | 7 | 2 | 3 | | | 5 | | 9 |
| 17 | 8 | Hastings | 0-2 | | | | | 1 | | | | 4 | 6 | 11 | | 8 | 10 | 7 | | | | 2 | 3 | | | 5 | | 9 |
| 18 | 15 | Dartford | 1-5 | | Cutting | | | 1 | | | | 4 | 6 | 11 | | 8 | 10 | 7 | | | | 2 | 3 | | | 5 | | 9 |
| 19 | 22 | CHELTENHAM | 2-2 | 7722 | Curry, Foxall | | | 1 | | | | 4 | 6 | 11 | | 8 | 10 | 7 | | | | 2 | 3 | | | 5 | | 9 |
| 20 | 29 | Bedford | 2-0 | 2400 | Turner(pen) | | | 1 | | | | 4 | 6 | 10 | | 8 | | 11 | | | 7 | 2 | 3 | | | 5 | | 9 |
| 21 | 5 Feb | BARRY | 3-0 | 7522 | Curry, Hillman, Turner | | | 1 | | | | 4 | 6 | 10 | | 8 | | 11 | | | 7 | 2 | 3 | | 5 | | | 9 |
| 22 | 12 | Kidderminster | 3-1 | | Cater, Turner, O.G. | | | 1 | | | | 4 | 6 | 10 | | 8 | | 11 | | | 7 | 2 | 3 | | | 5 | | 9 |
| 23 | 19 | BATH | 4-0 | 8264 | Curry(2), Foxall, Hillman | | | 1 | | | | 4 | 6 | 10 | | 8 | | 11 | | | 7 | 2 | 3 | | | 5 | | 9 |
| 24 | 26 | MERTHYR TYDFIL | 5-2 | 9328 | Curry, Turner(4,1pen) | | | 1 | | | | 4 | 6 | 10 | | 8 | | 11 | | | 7 | 2 | 3 | | | 5 | | 9 |
| 25 | 5 Mar | CHINGFORD | 4-0 | 7990 | Cutting(2), Hillman, Turner | | | 1 | | | | 4 | 6 | 10 | | | 8 | 11 | | | 7 | 2 | 3 | | | 5 | | 9 |
| 26 | 10 | TONBRIDGE | 4-0 | 4525 | Cater, Turner(3,1pen) | | | 1 | | | | 4 | 6 | 10 | | 8 | | 11 | | | 7 | 2 | 3 | | | 5 | | 9 |
| 27 | 12 | EXETER RES | 4-2 | 8066 | Keeble, Curry, Cutting | | 9 | 1 | | | | 4 | | | | 8 | 10 | 11 | | | 7 | 2 | 3 | | 6 | 5 | | |
| 28 | 16 | Exeter Res | 1-1 | 2314 | Hillman | | 9 | 1 | | | 3 | 4 | | 10 | | 8 | | 11 | | | 7 | | 2 | | 6 | 5 | | |
| 29 | 19 | Gravesend & N | 2-0 | | Curry, Cutting | | 9 | 1 | | | 3 | 4 | 6 | | | 8 | 10 | 11 | | | 7 | | 2 | | | 5 | | |
| 30 | 24 | DARTFORD | 1-2 | 7156 | Turner | | | 1 | | | 3 | 4 | 6 | | | 8 | 10 | 11 | | | 7 | | 2 | | | 5 | | 9 |
| 31 | 26 | YEOVIL | 1-1 | 10247 | Foxall | | 9 | 1 | | | 3 | 4 | 6 | | | | 10 | 11 | | | 7 | 2 | | | | 5 | 8 | |
| 32 | 2 Apr | LOVELL'S | 4-2 | | Curry, Cutting, Turner, O.G. | | | 1 | | | 3 | 4 | | | 11 | 8 | 10 | | | | 7 | 2 | 6 | | 5 | | | 9 |
| 33 | 11 | GRAVESEND & N | 0-0 | | | | | 1 | | | | 4 | | | | 8 | 10 | 11 | | | 7 | 2 | 3 | | 6 | 5 | | 9 |
| 34 | 15 | GUILDFORD | 0-1 | 10799 | | | | 1 | | | | 4 | | 11 | | 8 | 10 | | 7 | | | 2 | 3 | | 6 | 5 | | 9 |
| 35 | 16 | Tonbridge | 3-3 | | Curry, George, Turner | | 11 | 1 | | | | 4 | | | | 8 | 10 | | 7 | | | 2 | 3 | | 6 | 5 | | 9 |
| 36 | 18 | Guildford | 0-1 | | | | 9 | 1 | | | 3 | 4 | | 11 | | 8 | 10 | | 7 | | | 2 | | | 6 | 5 | | |
| 37 | 21 | Worcester | 2-4 | | Cater, Curry | | | 1 | | | 3 | 4 | | 11 | | 8 | 10 | | 7 | | | 2 | 6 | | | 5 | | 9 |
| 38 | 23 | Merthyr Tydfil | 0-2 | | | | 1 | | | | | 4 | 6 | 11 | | 8 | 10 | 7 | 9 | | | 2 | 3 | | | 5 | | |
| 39 | 28 | WORCESTER | 3-0 | 5445 | Keeble(2), Maffey | 1 | 9 | | | | 3 | 4 | | 11 | | 8 | 10 | | | | 7 | 2 | 6 | | | 5 | | |
| 40 | 30 | Gloucester | 1-6 | | Allen(pen) | 1 | 9 | | | | 3 | 4 | | 11 | | 8 | 10 | | | | 7 | 2 | 6 | | | 5 | | |
| 41 | 5 May | HEREFORD | 4-0 | | Keeble, Cater, Curry, Hillman | | 9 | | 1 | | 3 | 4 | | 11 | | 8 | 10 | | | 5 | 7 | 2 | 6 | | | | | |
| 42 | 7 | GILLINGHAM | 2-3 | 9340 | Keeble, Allen(pen) | | 9 | | 1 | | 3 | 4 | | 11 | | 8 | 10 | | | | 7 | 2 | 6 | | | 5 | | |

## F.A.Cup

| Rd | Date | Opponent | Score | Att | Scorers | | | | | | | | | | | | | | | | | | | | | | | |
|---|---|---|---|---|---|---|---|---|---|---|---|---|---|---|---|---|---|---|---|---|---|---|---|---|---|---|---|---|
| 1st | 27 Nov | READING * | 1-1 | 19072 | Curry * Abandoned | | | 1 | | | 3 | 4 | 6 | 11 | | 8 | 10 | 7 | | | | 2 | | | | 5 | | 9 |
| 1st | 4 Dec | READING | 2-4 | 13371 | Cater(2) | | | 1 | | | 3 | 4 | 6 | 11 | | 8 | 10 | 7 | | | | 2 | | | | 5 | | 9 |

## Southern League Cup

| Rd | Date | Opponent | Score | Att | Scorers | | | | | | | | | | | | | | | | | | | | | | | |
|---|---|---|---|---|---|---|---|---|---|---|---|---|---|---|---|---|---|---|---|---|---|---|---|---|---|---|---|---|
| P | 26 Aug | EXETER RES | 3-1 | 8606 | Cutting, Hillman, Turner | | | | | 1 | 3 | 4 | 6 | 11 | | 8 | 10 | | | | 7 | 2 | | | 5 | | | 9 |
| 1st | 21 Oct | BEDFORD | 6-0 | 4131 | Cater, Curry, Foxall(2), Turner | | | 1 | | | 3 | 4 | 6 | 11 | | 8 | 10 | 7 | | | | 2 | | | | 5 | | 9 |
| 2nd | 11 Dec | Chelmsford | 3-2 | 11102 | Curry, Cutting(2) | | | 1 | | | | 4 | 6 | 11 | | 8 | 10 | 7 | | | | 2 | 3 | | | 5 | | 9 |
| SF | 6 Apr | Gillingham | 4-2 | 11042 | Foxall(2), Hillman | | 9 | 1 | | | | 4 | | | | 8 | 10 | 11 | | | 7 | 2 | 3 | | 6 | 5 | | |
| 47/48F | 22 Apr | Merthyr Tydfill | 0-5 | 8521 | | | 7 | | | 1 | 3 | 4 | 6 | 11 | | 8 | 10 | | | | | 2 | | | | 5 | | 9 |
| F | 2 May | Yeovil | 0-3 | | | 1 | 9 | | | | 3 | 4 | | | | 8 | 10 | 11 | | | 7 | 2 | 6 | | | 5 | | |

*Bob Curry trying to get out of a muddle against Cheltenham. Arthur Turner looks on sympathetically.*

# SEASON 49-50 Southern League

| No. | Date | Opposition | Res | Attend | Goalscorers | Wright | Allen | Beach | Bearryman | Bowler | Cater | Curry | Cutting | Foxall | Gallego | Hillman | Keeble | Kettle | Layton | Maffey | Moore | Sales | Sharpe | Stewart | Turner |
|---|---|---|---|---|---|---|---|---|---|---|---|---|---|---|---|---|---|---|---|---|---|---|---|---|---|
| 1 | 20 Aug | WEYMOUTH | 3-0 | 9897 | Curry(2), Layton | 1 | 3 | | 4 | | | 8 | 10 | 7 | 11 | | 9 | 2 | 6 | | | | | 5 | |
| 2 | 27 | HEADINGTON | 4-1 | 9203 | Curry, Keeble(2) O.G. | 1 | 3 | | 4 | | | 8 | 10 | 7 | 11 | | 9 | 2 | 6 | | | | | 5 | |
| 3 | 1 Sep | Gloucester | 3-2 | | Cutting, Keeble(2) | 1 | 3 | | 4 | | 11 | 8 | 10 | 7 | | | 9 | 2 | 6 | | | | | 5 | |
| 4 | 3 | Bath | 1-1 | | Bearryman | 1 | 3 | | 4 | | 11 | 8 | 10 | 7 | | | 9 | 2 | 6 | | | | | 5 | |
| 5 | 8 | Chingford | 1-3 | | Curry | 1 | 3 | | 4 | | 11 | 8 | 10 | 7 | | | 9 | 2 | | | 6 | | | 5 | |
| 6 | 10 | Chelmsford | 2-2 | | Allen(pen), Keeble | 1 | 3 | | 4 | | 11 | 8 | 10 | 7 | | | 9 | 2 | | | 6 | | | 5 | |
| 7 | 14 | Cheltenham | 3-1 | | Curry, Foxall, Gallego | 1 | 3 | | 4 | | | 8 | 10 | 7 | 11 | | 9 | 2 | | | 6 | | | 5 | |
| 8 | 17 | CHELMSFORD | 4-1 | 14718 | Allen(pen), Cutting(2), Keeble | 1 | 3 | | 4 | | | 8 | 10 | 11 | | 7 | 9 | 2 | | | 6 | | | 5 | |
| 9 | 22 | WORCESTER | 4-1 | 8542 | Bearryman, Curry, Keeble(2) | 1 | 3 | | 4 | | | 8 | 10 | 11 | | 7 | 9 | 2 | | | 6 | | | 5 | |
| 10 | 24 | GILLINGHAM | 2-1 | 10942 | Curry, Keeble | 1 | 3 | | 4 | | | 8 | 10 | | 11 | 7 | 9 | 2 | | | 6 | | | 5 | |
| 11 | 29 | HEREFORD | 3-2 | 6998 | Allen(pen), Cutting, Keeble | 1 | 3 | | 4 | 2 | | 8 | 10 | 11 | | 7 | 9 | | 6 | | | | | 5 | |
| 12 | 1 Oct | Dartford | 0-2 | | | 1 | 3 | | 4 | 2 | | 8 | 10 | 11 | | 7 | 9 | | 6 | | | | | 5 | |
| 13 | 8 | BATH | 5-0 | 9003 | Curry, Cuuting, Foxall, Keeble(2) | 1 | | 3 | 4 | | | 8 | 10 | 11 | | 7 | 9 | | 6 | 2 | | | | 5 | |
| 14 | 15 | Tonbridge | 2-0 | | Kettle(2) | 1 | | 3 | 4 | | | 8 | 10 | 11 | | 7 | 9 | | 6 | 2 | | | | 5 | |
| 15 | 20 | Lovell's | 2-1 | | Curry, Keeble | 1 | | 3 | 4 | | | 8 | 10 | 11 | | 7 | 9 | | | 2 | 6 | 5 | | | |
| 16 | 22 | YEOVIL | 2-1 | 10632 | Cutting(2) | 1 | | 3 | 4 | | | 8 | 10 | 11 | | 7 | | | 6 | 2 | | | 9 | 5 | |
| 17 | 29 | Torquay Res | 5-3 | | Curry(3), Hillman, Keeble | 1 | | 3 | 4 | | | 8 | 10 | 11 | | 7 | 9 | | 6 | 2 | | | | 5 | |
| 18 | 5 Nov | LOVELL'S | 4-0 | 6231 | Curry(2), Keeble, Layton(pen) | 1 | | 3 | 4 | | | 8 | 10 | 11 | | 7 | 9 | 2 | 6 | | | | | 5 | |
| 19 | 19 | KIDDERMINSTER | 8-0 | 7320 | Bearryman, Curry, Cutting, Foxall, Keeble(4) | 1 | | 3 | 4 | | | 8 | 10 | 11 | | 7 | 9 | 2 | 6 | | | | | 5 | |
| 20 | 26 | Exeter Res | 3-2 | | Curry, Keeble(2) | 1 | | 3 | 4 | | | 8 | 10 | 11 | | 7 | 9 | 2 | 6 | | | | | 5 | |
| 21 | 3 Dec | Weymouth | 0-0 | | | 1 | | 3 | 4 | | | 8 | 10 | 11 | | 7 | 9 | 2 | 6 | | | | | 5 | |
| 22 | 10 | HASTINGS | 1-0 | 6536 | Layton(pen) | 1 | | 3 | 4 | | | 8 | 10 | 11 | | 7 | 9 | 2 | 6 | | | | | 5 | |
| 23 | 24 | Bedford | 4-2 | | Curry, Cutting, Keeble(2) | 1 | | 3 | 4 | | | 8 | 10 | 11 | | 7 | 9 | 2 | 6 | | | | | 5 | |
| 24 | 26 | BEDFORD | 1-0 | 9083 | Cutting | 1 | | 3 | 4 | | | 8 | 10 | 11 | | 7 | 9 | 2 | 6 | | | | | 5 | |
| 25 | 27 | Hastings | 5-0 | | Cuury(2), Foxall, Keeble(2) | 1 | | 3 | 4 | | | 8 | 10 | 11 | | 7 | 9 | 2 | 6 | | | | | 5 | |
| 26 | 31 | MERTHYR TYDFIL | 3-0 | 9957 | Cutting, Keeble(2) | 1 | | 3 | 4 | | | 8 | 10 | 11 | | 7 | 9 | 2 | 6 | | | | | 5 | |
| 27 | 7 Jan | GLOUCESTER | 6-1 | 8329 | Cutting, Foxall, Keeble(2), Layton, O.G. | 1 | | 3 | 4 | | | 8 | 10 | 11 | | 7 | 9 | 2 | 6 | | | | | 5 | |
| 28 | 14 | BARRY | 2-0 | 9131 | Keeble, Layton | 1 | | 3 | 4 | | | | 10 | 11 | | 7 | 9 | 2 | 6 | | | | | 5 | 8 |
| 29 | 28 | Gravesend & N | 1-2 | | Keeble | 1 | | 3 | 4 | | | | 10 | 11 | 7 | | 9 | 2 | 6 | | | | | 5 | 8 |
| 30 | 4 Feb | Headington | 3-2 | | Curry, Cutting, Keeble | 1 | | 3 | 4 | | | 8 | 10 | 11 | 7 | | 9 | 2 | 6 | | | | | 5 | |
| 31 | 11 | CHINGFORD | 3-0 | 7797 | Curry, Cutting(2) | 1 | | 3 | 4 | | | 8 | 10 | 11 | 7 | | 9 | 2 | 6 | | | | | 5 | |
| 32 | 4 Mar | Hereford | 1-0 | | Curry | 1 | | 3 | 4 | | | 8 | 10 | 11 | 7 | | 9 | 2 | 6 | | | | | 5 | |
| 33 | 18 | Worcester | 3-1 | | Hillman, Keeble, Layton(pen) | 1 | | 3 | 4 | | | 8 | 10 | 11 | | 7 | 9 | 2 | 6 | | | | | 5 | |
| 34 | 23 | CHELTENHAM | 2-2 | 5352 | Cutting, Hillman | 1 | 3 | | 4 | | | | 10 | 11 | | 7 | 9 | 2 | | | 6 | | | 5 | 8 |
| 35 | 25 | Kidderminster | 1-1 | | Keeble | 1 | | 3 | 4 | | | | 10 | 11 | | 7 | 9 | 2 | | | 6 | | | 5 | 8 |
| 36 | 1 Apr | Yeovil | 0-1 | | | 1 | | 3 | 4 | | | 8 | 10 | 11 | | 7 | 9 | 2 | 6 | | | | | 5 | |
| 37 | 7 | GUILDFORD | 2-1 | 10841 | Cutting(2) | 1 | | 3 | 4 | | | 8 | 10 | 11 | | 7 | 9 | 2 | 6 | | | | | 5 | |
| 38 | 8 | DARTFORD | 1-0 | 8443 | Keeble | 1 | | 3 | 4 | | | | 8 | 11 | | 7 | 9 | 2 | 10 | | 6 | | | 5 | |
| 39 | 10 | Guildford | 1-1 | | Keeble | 1 | | 3 | 4 | | | | 8 | 11 | | 7 | 9 | 2 | 10 | | 6 | | | 5 | |
| 40 | 13 | TONBRIDGE | 2-0 | 6003 | Keeble, Layton | 1 | | 3 | 4 | | | | 8 | 11 | | 7 | 9 | 2 | 10 | | 6 | | | 5 | |
| 41 | 15 | TORQUAY RES | 0-0 | 7617 | | 1 | | 3 | 4 | | | | 10 | 11 | | 7 | 9 | 2 | 6 | | 8 | | | 5 | |
| 42 | 20 | GRAVESEND & N | 2-2 | 7549 | Cutting, Keeble | 1 | | 3 | 4 | | | | 10 | 11 | | 7 | 9 | 2 | 6 | | | | | 5 | 8 |
| 43 | 22 | EXETER RES | 3-0 | 8111 | Keeble(2), O.G. | 1 | 3 | | 4 | | | 8 | 10 | 11 | | 7 | 9 | 2 | 6 | | | | | 5 | |
| 44 | 26 | Merthyr Tydfil | 0-5 | | | 1 | 3 | | 4 | | | 8 | 10 | 11 | | 7 | 9 | 2 | 6 | | | | | 5 | |
| 45 | 29 | Gillingham | 1-6 | | Keeble | 1 | 3 | | 4 | | | 8 | 10 | 11 | | 7 | 9 | 2 | 6 | | | | | 5 | |
| 46 | 6 May | BARRY | 0-0 | | | 1 | | 3 | 4 | | | 8 | 10 | 11 | | 7 | 9 | 2 | 6 | | | | | 5 | |

## S.L.Cup

| | | | | | | | | | | | | | | | | | | | | | | | | | |
|---|---|---|---|---|---|---|---|---|---|---|---|---|---|---|---|---|---|---|---|---|---|---|---|---|---|
| 2nd | 12 Oct | Gillingham | 1-0 | 6639 | Curry | 1 | | 3 | 4 | | | 8 | 10 | 11 | | 7 | 9 | | 6 | 2 | | | | 5 | |
| 3rd | 21 Jan | Chelmsford | 2-1 | | Bearryman, Cutting | 1 | | 3 | 4 | | | | 10 | 11 | | 7 | 9 | 2 | 6 | | | | | 5 | 8 |
| S/F | 11 Mar | TONBRIDGE | 3-2 | 10130 | Curry, Keeble(2) | 1 | | 3 | 4 | | | 8 | 10 | 11 | | 7 | 9 | 2 | 6 | | | | | 5 | |
| F/1st | 27 Apr | Bath | 3-0 | | Cutting(2), Hillman | 1 | 3 | | 4 | | | 8 | 10 | 11 | | 7 | 9 | 2 | 6 | | | | | 5 | |
| F/2nd | 3 May | BATH | 3-4 | | Hillman, Keeble(2) | 1 | | 3 | 4 | | | 8 | 10 | 11 | | 7 | 9 | 2 | 6 | | | | | 5 | |

## F.A.Cup

| | | | | | | | | | | | | | | | | | | | | | | | | | |
|---|---|---|---|---|---|---|---|---|---|---|---|---|---|---|---|---|---|---|---|---|---|---|---|---|---|
| 4th/Q | 12 Nov | Wealdstone | 0-1 | | | 1 | | 3 | 4 | | | 8 | 10 | 11 | | 7 | 9 | 2 | 6 | | | | | 5 | |

*Enthusiasm for the team; from the supporters (below), and the secretary Mr.C.H.Orrin and his wife (right).*

# SEASON 1950–51 Division Three (South)

| No. | Date | Opposition | Res | Attend | Goalscorers | Bircham | Wright.G | Allen | Bearryman | Church | Cullum | Curry | Cutting | Elder | Gallego | Harrison | Hillman | Jones | Keeble | Kettle | Layton | Locherty | McKim | Rochford | Rowlands | Stewart | Turner |
|---|---|---|---|---|---|---|---|---|---|---|---|---|---|---|---|---|---|---|---|---|---|---|---|---|---|---|---|
| 1 | 19 Aug | Gillingham | 0–0 | 19542 | | | 1 | 3 | 4 | 11 | | 8 | | 6 | | | | 7 | | 2 | | | 10 | | | 5 | 9 |
| 2 | 23 | Swindon | 1–1 | 15690 | Curry | | 1 | 3 | 4 | 11 | | 8 | | 6 | | | | 7 | | 2 | | | 10 | | | 5 | 9 |
| 3 | 26 | BRISTOL R | 0–0 | 13687 | | | 1 | 3 | 4 | 11 | | 8 | | 6 | | | | 7 | | 2 | | | 10 | | | 5 | 9 |
| 4 | 31 | SWINDON | 4–1 | 12579 | Church, Curry, Turner(2) | | 1 | 3 | 4 | 11 | | 8 | | 6 | | | | 7 | | 2 | | | 10 | | | 5 | 9 |
| 5 | 2 Sep | Crystal P | 3–1 | 22373 | Curry, McKim, Turner | | 1 | 3 | 4 | 11 | | 8 | | 6 | | | | 7 | | 2 | | | 10 | | | 5 | 9 |
| 6 | 7 | BOURNEMOUTH | 4–1 | 14100 | Curry(2), Turner(2) | | 1 | 3 | 4 | 11 | | 8 | | 6 | | | | 7 | | 2 | | | 10 | | | 5 | 9 |
| 7 | 9 | BRIGHTON | 4–1 | 13792 | Jones, McKim(2), Turner | | 1 | 3 | 4 | 11 | | 8 | | 6 | | | | 7 | | 2 | | | 10 | | | 5 | 9 |
| 8 | 13 | Bournemouth | 0–2 | 18686 | | | 1 | 3 | 4 | | | 8 | | 6 | 11 | | | 7 | | 2 | | | 10 | | | 5 | 9 |
| 9 | 16 | Newport | 0–2 | 16021 | | | 1 | 3 | 4 | 11 | | 8 | | 6 | | | | 7 | | 2 | | | 10 | | | 5 | 9 |
| 10 | 23 | NORWICH | 2–3 | 13843 | Curry, Cutting | | 1 | 3 | 4 | | | 8 | 10 | 6 | | | | 7 | 11 | 2 | | | | | | 5 | 9 |
| 11 | 30 | Northampton | 1–2 | 10160 | Locherty | | 1 | 3 | 4 | 11 | | 8 | | 6 | | 2 | | 7 | | | | 10 | | | | 5 | 9 |
| 12 | 7 Oct | EXETER | 0–1 | 10860 | | | 1 | 3 | 4 | 11 | | 8 | | 6 | | | | 7 | 9 | 2 | | | 10 | | | 5 | |
| 13 | 14 | Southend | 2–4 | 21000 | Curry, Turner | | 1 | 3 | 4 | | | 8 | 10 | 6 | | | | 7 | 11 | 2 | | | | | | 5 | 9 |
| 14 | 21 | READING | 1–1 | 11469 | Cutting | | 1 | 3 | 4 | 11 | | 8 | 10 | 6 | | | | 7 | | 2 | | | | | | 5 | 9 |
| 15 | 28 | Plymouth | 1–7 | 20727 | Curry | | 1 | 3 | 4 | 11 | | 8 | 10 | 6 | | | | 7 | | 2 | | | | | | 5 | 9 |
| 16 | 4 Nov | IPSWICH | 2–3 | 14037 | Church, Turner | | 1 | 3 | 4 | 11 | | 8 | 10 | 6 | | 2 | | 7 | | | | | | | | 5 | 9 |
| 17 | 18 | WALSALL | 0–1 | 9548 | | | 1 | 3 | 4 | 11 | | 8 | 10 | | | 2 | | 7 | | | 6 | | | | | 5 | 9 |
| 18 | 2 Dec | MILLWALL | 3–0 | 9695 | Church(2), Curry | | 1 | 3 | 4 | 11 | | 8 | | 6 | | 2 | | 7 | | | | 10 | | | | 5 | 9 |
| 19 | 9 | Leyton O | 1–1 | 8760 | Curry | | 1 | 3 | 4 | 11 | | 8 | | 6 | | 2 | | 7 | | | | 10 | | | | 5 | 9 |
| 20 | 16 | GILLINGHAM | 4–2 | 6941 | Church, Curry(2), Elder | | 1 | 3 | 4 | 11 | | 8 | | 6 | | 2 | | 7 | | | | 10 | | | | 5 | 9 |
| 21 | 23 | Bristol R | 1–1 | 14475 | Jones | | 1 | 3 | 4 | 11 | | 8 | | 6 | | 2 | | 7 | | | | 10 | | | | 5 | 9 |
| 22 | 25 | Nottingham F | 0–0 | 17033 | | | 1 | 3 | 4 | 11 | | 8 | | 6 | | 2 | | 7 | | | | 10 | | | | 5 | 9 |
| 23 | 26 | NOTTINGHAM F | 0–2 | 12874 | | | 1 | 3 | 4 | | | | 8 | 6 | 11 | 2 | | 7 | | | | 10 | | | | 5 | 9 |
| 24 | 30 | CRYSTAL P | 1–0 | 8587 | Cutting | | 1 | 3 | 4 | 11 | | | 8 | 6 | | 2 | | 7 | | | | 10 | | | | 5 | 9 |
| 25 | 13 Jan | Brighton | 1–3 | 11360 | Allen(pen) | | 1 | 3 | 4 | 11 | | | 8 | 6 | | | | 7 | | 2 | | 10 | | | | 5 | 9 |
| 26 | 20 | NEWPORT | 1–1 | 8230 | Turner | | 1 | 3 | 4 | 11 | | | 8 | 6 | | 2 | | 7 | | | | 10 | | | | 5 | 9 |
| 27 | 27 | ALDERSHOT | 1–0 | 9285 | Elder | | 1 | 3 | 4 | 11 | | | 10 | 6 | | 2 | | 7 | 9 | | | | 8 | | | 5 | |
| 28 | 3 Feb | Norwich | 1–1 | 25669 | Keeble | | 1 | 3 | 4 | 11 | | | | 6 | | 2 | | 7 | 9 | | | | 8 | | | 5 | 10 |
| 29 | 10 | Watford | 0–2 | 8798 | | | 1 | 3 | 4 | 11 | | | | 6 | | 2 | | 7 | 9 | | | | 10 | | | 5 | 8 |
| 30 | 17 | NORTHAMPTON | 2–1 | 7048 | Curry, McKim | 1 | | | 4 | 11 | | 8 | | 6 | | 2 | | 7 | 9 | | | | 10 | 3 | | 5 | |
| 31 | 24 | Exeter | 0–5 | 7334 | | 1 | | | 4 | 11 | | 8 | | 6 | | 2 | | 7 | | | | | 10 | 3 | | 5 | 9 |
| 32 | 3 Mar | SOUTHEND | 1–3 | 12360 | Turner | 1 | | | 4 | 11 | | 8 | | 6 | | 2 | | 7 | | | | | 10 | | 3 | 5 | 9 |
| 33 | 10 | Reading | 2–3 | 15896 | Church, Turner | 1 | | | 4 | 11 | | 8 | | 6 | | 2 | 7 | | 9 | | | | | | 3 | 5 | 10 |
| 34 | 17 | PLYMOUTH | 3–0 | 8746 | Keeble(3) | 1 | | | 4 | 11 | | 8 | | 6 | | 2 | 7 | | 9 | | | | | | 3 | 5 | 10 |
| 35 | 23 | TORQUAY | 3–1 | 12443 | Elder(pen), Keeble, Turner | 1 | | | 4 | 11 | | 8 | | 6 | | 2 | 7 | | 9 | | | | | | 3 | 5 | 10 |
| 36 | 23 | Ipswich | 0–3 | 19093 | | 1 | | | 4 | | | 8 | | 6 | 11 | 2 | 7 | | 9 | | | | | | 3 | 5 | 10 |
| 37 | 26 | Torquay | 1–4 | 8000 | Cullum | | 1 | | 4 | | 7 | 8 | | 6 | 11 | 2 | | | 9 | | | | | | 3 | 5 | 10 |
| 38 | 31 | LEYTON O | 1–0 | 9291 | Church | | 1 | | 4 | 11 | | 8 | | 6 | | 2 | | 7 | 9 | | | | | | 3 | 5 | 10 |
| 39 | 7 Apr | Walsall | 2–4 | 7097 | McKim(2) | | 1 | | 4 | 11 | | | | 6 | | 2 | | 7 | 9 | | | | 8 | | 3 | 5 | 10 |
| 40 | 11 | Aldershot | 0–2 | 5821 | | | 1 | | 4 | 11 | | | | 10 | | 2 | | 7 | 9 | | 6 | | 8 | | 3 | 5 | |
| 41 | 14 | WATFORD | 4–1 | 8073 | Church(2), Keeble, McKim | | 1 | | 4 | 11 | | | | 10 | | 2 | | 7 | 9 | | 6 | | 8 | | 3 | 5 | |
| 42 | 16 | Port Vale | 1–1 | 8600 | Elder | | 1 | | 4 | 11 | | | | 10 | | 2 | | 7 | 9 | | 6 | | 8 | | 3 | 5 | |
| 43 | 21 | Milwall | 0–2 | 17728 | | | 1 | | 4 | 11 | | | | 10 | | 2 | | 7 | 9 | | 6 | | 8 | | 3 | 5 | |
| 44 | 25 | Bristol C | 2–0 | 10000 | Keeble, Rowlands | | 1 | | 4 | 11 | | | | 10 | | 2 | | 7 | 9 | | 6 | | 8 | | 3 | 5 | |
| 45 | 28 | BRISTOL C | 1–1 | 7202 | Church | | 1 | | 4 | 11 | | | | 10 | | 2 | | 7 | 9 | | 6 | | 8 | | 3 | 5 | |
| 46 | 5 May | PORT VALE | 1–1 | 8414 | McKim | | 1 | | 4 | 11 | | 8 | | 6 | | 2 | | 7 | 9 | | | | 10 | | 3 | 5 | |

## F.A.Cup

| | | | | | | | | | | | | | | | | | | | | | | | | | | | | |
|---|---|---|---|---|---|---|---|---|---|---|---|---|---|---|---|---|---|---|---|---|---|---|---|---|---|---|---|---|
| 4th/Q | 11 Nov | Woodford | 7–1 | 7000 | Curry(2), Cutting, Jones, Layton, Turner(2) | | 1 | 3 | 4 | 11 | | 8 | 10 | | | 2 | | 7 | | | 6 | | | | | 5 | 9 |
| 1st | 25 | Bournemouth | 0–1 | 15359 | | | 1 | 3 | 4 | 11 | | 8 | | 6 | | 2 | | 7 | | | | 10 | | | | 5 | 9 |

(Back) J.Allen (Man.), Turner, Bearryman, Wright, Stewart, Layton, R.Allen, ? , Miller
(Front) Hillman, Curry, Keeble, Foxhall.

DIVISION III (SOUTH)

| | P | W | D | L | F | A | Pts. |
|---|---|---|---|---|---|---|---|
| Nottm. Forest | 46 | 30 | 10 | 6 | 110 | 40 | 70 |
| Norwich C. | 46 | 25 | 14 | 7 | 82 | 45 | 64 |
| Reading | 46 | 21 | 15 | 10 | 88 | 53 | 57 |
| Plymouth Arg. | 46 | 24 | 9 | 13 | 85 | 55 | 57 |
| Millwall | 46 | 23 | 10 | 13 | 80 | 57 | 56 |
| Bristol R. | 46 | 20 | 15 | 11 | 64 | 42 | 55 |
| Southend U. | 46 | 21 | 10 | 15 | 92 | 69 | 52 |
| Ipswich T. | 46 | 23 | 6 | 17 | 69 | 58 | 52 |
| Bournemouth | 46 | 22 | 7 | 17 | 65 | 57 | 51 |
| Bristol C. | 46 | 20 | 11 | 15 | 64 | 59 | 51 |
| Newport Co. | 46 | 19 | 9 | 18 | 77 | 70 | 47 |
| Port Vale | 46 | 16 | 13 | 17 | 60 | 65 | 45 |
| Brighton | 46 | 13 | 17 | 16 | 71 | 79 | 43 |
| Exeter C. | 46 | 18 | 6 | 22 | 62 | 85 | 42 |
| Walsall | 46 | 15 | 10 | 21 | 52 | 62 | 40 |
| Colchester U. | 46 | 14 | 12 | 20 | 63 | 76 | 40 |
| Swindon T. | 46 | 18 | 4 | 24 | 55 | 67 | 40 |
| Aldershot | 46 | 15 | 10 | 21 | 56 | 88 | 40 |
| Leyton O. | 46 | 15 | 8 | 23 | 53 | 75 | 38 |
| Torquay U. | 46 | 14 | 9 | 23 | 64 | 81 | 37 |
| Northampton | 46 | 10 | 16 | 20 | 55 | 67 | 36 |
| Gillingham | 46 | 13 | 9 | 24 | 69 | 101 | 35 |
| Watford | 46 | 9 | 11 | 26 | 54 | 88 | 29 |
| C. Palace | 46 | 8 | 11 | 27 | 33 | 84 | 27 |

# SEASON 1951–52 Division Three (South)

| No. | Date | Opposition | Res | Attend | Goalscorers | Coombes | Wright.G | Aitchison | Bearryman | Church | Cutting | Davidson | Elder | Harrison | Hunt.R.M | Jones | Keeble | Kettle | McCurley | McKim | Moore | Rookes | Rowlands | Scott | Stewart | Turner | Wright.P |
|---|---|---|---|---|---|---|---|---|---|---|---|---|---|---|---|---|---|---|---|---|---|---|---|---|---|---|---|
| 1 | 18 Aug | Brighton | 1–5 | 15000 | Jones | | 1 | | 4 | 11 | | | 6 | 2 | | 7 | 9 | | | 10 | | 3 | | 8 | 5 | | |
| 2 | 23 | NORWICH | 1–1 | 14085 | Keeble | | 1 | | 4 | 11 | | | 6 | 2 | | 7 | 9 | | | | | 3 | | 8 | 5 | 10 | |
| 3 | 25 | CRYSTAL P | 1–2 | 10135 | Turner | | 1 | | 4 | 11 | | | 6 | 2 | | 7 | 9 | | | | | 3 | | 8 | 5 | 10 | |
| 4 | 29 | Norwich | 2–5 | 24705 | Cutting(2) | | 1 | | 4 | 11 | 10 | | 6 | 2 | | 7 | 9 | | | | | | 3 | 8 | 5 | | |
| 5 | 1 Sep | Swindon | 1–2 | 10667 | Keeble | | 1 | | 4 | 11 | 10 | | 6 | 2 | | 7 | 9 | | | | | | 3 | 8 | 5 | | |
| 6 | 5 | Plymouth | 1–3 | 17892 | Elder(pen) | | 1 | | 4 | 11 | 10 | | 6 | 2 | | 7 | | | | | | | 3 | 8 | 5 | 9 | |
| 7 | 8 | LEYTON O | 0–1 | 10266 | | | 1 | | 4 | 11 | 10 | | 6 | 2 | | 7 | 9 | | | | | | 3 | 8 | 5 | | |
| 8 | 13 | PLYMOUTH | 1–0 | 8992 | Keeble | | 1 | | 4 | | 10 | 11 | 6 | 2 | | 7 | 9 | | | | | | 3 | 8 | 5 | | |
| 9 | 15 | Walsall | 3–1 | 7327 | Cutting(2), Keeble | | 1 | | 4 | | 10 | 11 | 6 | 2 | | 7 | 9 | | | | | | 3 | 8 | 5 | | |
| 10 | 22 | SHREWSBURY | 2–2 | 10314 | Cutting, Keeble | | 1 | | 4 | | 10 | 11 | 6 | 2 | | 7 | 9 | | | | | | 3 | 8 | 5 | | |
| 11 | 29 | Aldershot | 1–1 | 9013 | Keeble | | 1 | | 4 | | 10 | 11 | 6 | 2 | | 7 | 9 | | | | | 3 | | 8 | 5 | | |
| 12 | 6 Oct | TORQUAY | 0–0 | 9614 | | | 1 | | 4 | | 10 | 11 | 6 | 2 | | 7 | 9 | | | | | | 3 | 8 | 5 | | |
| 13 | 13 | Ipswich | 2–0 | 19275 | Cutting, Keeble | | 1 | | 4 | 11 | 10 | | 6 | 2 | | 7 | 9 | | | | | | 3 | 8 | 5 | | |
| 14 | 20 | BRISTOL C | 4–1 | 9552 | Cutting, Keeble(3) | | 1 | | 4 | 11 | 10 | | 6 | 2 | | 7 | 9 | | | | | | 3 | 8 | 5 | | |
| 15 | 27 | Port Vale | 1–1 | 9600 | Cutting | | 1 | | 4 | 11 | 10 | 7 | 6 | 2 | | | 9 | | | | | | 3 | 8 | 5 | | |
| 16 | 3 Nov | NORTHAMPTON | 2–5 | 10325 | Church, Keeble | | 1 | | 4 | 11 | 10 | | 6 | 2 | | 7 | 9 | | | | | | 3 | 8 | 5 | | |
| 17 | 10 | Reading | 2–4 | 14230 | Scott | | 1 | | 4 | 11 | 10 | | 6 | 2 | | 7 | 9 | | | | | | 3 | 8 | 5 | | |
| 18 | 17 | NEWPORT | 2–1 | 7229 | Cutting, Keeble | | 1 | | 4 | 11 | 10 | | 6 | 2 | | 7 | 9 | | | | | 3 | | 8 | 5 | | |
| 19 | 1 Dec | BOURNEMOUTH | 1–1 | 8902 | Church | | 1 | | 4 | 11 | 10 | 7 | 6 | 2 | | | 9 | | | | | 3 | | 8 | 5 | | |
| 20 | 8 | Millwall | 1–1 | 15285 | Turner | | 1 | | 4 | 11 | 10 | 7 | 6 | 2 | | | | | | | | 3 | | 8 | 5 | | |
| 21 | 22 | Crystal P | 2–2 | 11547 | McKim(2) | | 1 | | 4 | 11 | | 7 | 6 | 2 | | | 9 | | | 10 | | | 3 | 8 | 5 | | |
| 22 | 25 | Gillingham | 2–1 | 8000 | Aitchison, Keeble | | 1 | 7 | 4 | 11 | | | 6 | | | | 9 | | | 10 | | 2 | 3 | 8 | 5 | | |
| 23 | 26 | GILLINGHAM | 1–0 | 11127 | Aitchison | | 1 | 7 | 4 | 11 | | | 6 | | | | 9 | | | 10 | | 2 | 3 | 8 | 5 | | |
| 24 | 29 | SWINDON | 2–0 | 7407 | Keeble, McKim | | 1 | 7 | 5 | 11 | | | 6 | | | | 9 | 2 | | 10 | 4 | | 3 | 8 | | | |
| 25 | 5 Jan | Leyton O | 0–7 | 12000 | | | 1 | 7 | 5 | 11 | | | 6 | | | | 9 | 2 | | 10 | 4 | | 3 | 8 | | | |
| 26 | 16 | Watford | 1–0 | 3245 | McKim | | 1 | | 4 | 11 | | 7 | 6 | 2 | | | | | | 10 | | 3 | | 8 | 5 | 9 | |
| 27 | 19 | WALSALL | 3–2 | 7240 | Keeble(2), McKim | | 1 | | 4 | 11 | | 7 | 6 | 2 | | | 9 | | | 10 | | 3 | | 8 | 5 | | |
| 28 | 26 | Shrewsbury | 0–1 | 7981 | | | 1 | 7 | 4 | 11 | | | 6 | 2 | | | 9 | | | 10 | | 3 | | 8 | 5 | | |
| 29 | 2 Feb | EXETER | 1–0 | 7692 | McKim | | 1 | 7 | 4 | 11 | | | 6 | 2 | | | | | | 10 | | 3 | | 8 | 5 | 9 | |
| 30 | 9 | ALDERSHOT | 0–2 | 7663 | | | 1 | | 4 | 11 | | 7 | 6 | 2 | | | | | | 10 | | 3 | | 8 | 5 | 9 | |
| 31 | 16 | Torquay | 1–3 | 6603 | McKim | | 1 | | 4 | 11 | | 7 | 6 | 2 | | | | | | 10 | | 3 | | 8 | 5 | 9 | |
| 32 | 23 | Exeter | 0–0 | 7500 | | | 1 | 7 | 4 | 11 | 10 | | 6 | 2 | | | | | | | | 3 | 9 | 8 | 5 | | |
| 33 | 1 Mar | IPSWICH | 1–0 | 15175 | Rowlands | | 1 | 7 | 4 | 11 | | | 6 | 2 | | | | | | 10 | | 3 | 9 | 8 | 5 | | |
| 34 | 8 | Bristol C | 0–2 | 12657 | | 1 | | 7 | 4 | 11 | | | 6 | 2 | | | | | | 10 | | 3 | 9 | 8 | 5 | | |
| 35 | 15 | PORT VALE | 0–0 | 7559 | | 1 | | | 4 | 11 | | 7 | 10 | 2 | 6 | | | | | 8 | | 3 | | | 5 | 9 | |
| 36 | 22 | Northampton | 0–2 | 10260 | | 1 | | | 4 | 7 | | | 6 | 2 | | | | | 9 | 10 | | 3 | | 8 | 5 | | 11 |
| 37 | 3 Apr | READING | 4–1 | 7340 | McCurley(2), McKim(2) | 1 | | | 4 | 7 | | | 6 | 2 | | | | | 9 | 10 | | 3 | | 8 | 5 | | 11 |
| 38 | 5 | Newport | 1–0 | 7000 | McCurley | 1 | | | 4 | | | 7 | 6 | 2 | | | | | 9 | 10 | | 3 | | 8 | 5 | | 11 |
| 39 | 11 | BRISTOL R | 2–1 | 12440 | Elder(pen), Scott | 1 | | | 4 | | | 7 | 6 | 2 | | | | | 9 | 10 | | | 3 | 8 | 5 | | 11 |
| 40 | 12 | SOUTHEND | 1–0 | 11967 | McCurley | 1 | | | 4 | | | 7 | 6 | 2 | | | | | 9 | 10 | | | 3 | 8 | 5 | | 11 |
| 41 | 14 | Bristol R | 0–6 | 10630 | | 1 | | | 4 | 7 | | | 6 | 2 | | | | | 9 | 10 | | | 3 | 8 | 5 | | 11 |
| 42 | 19 | Bournemouth | 0–5 | 8666 | | 1 | | | 4 | 7 | | | 6 | 2 | | | | | 9 | 10 | | | 3 | 8 | 5 | | 11 |
| 43 | 22 | Southend | 2–3 | 7500 | Church, McCurley | 1 | | | 4 | 11 | | 7 | | 2 | 6 | | | | 9 | 10 | | | 3 | 8 | 5 | | |
| 44 | 26 | MILLWALL | 2–2 | 8259 | McCurley, Scott | 1 | | | 4 | 7 | | | 6 | | | | | 2 | 9 | 10 | | 3 | | 8 | 5 | | 11 |
| 45 | 1 Apr | BRIGHTON | 0–0 | 7075 | | 1 | | | 4 | 7 | | | 6 | 2 | | | | | 9 | 10 | | 3 | | 8 | 5 | | 11 |
| 46 | 3 | WATFORD | 1–0 | 6128 | McKim | 1 | | | 4 | 11 | | 7 | | 2 | 6 | | | | 9 | 10 | | 3 | | 8 | 5 | | |

# F.A.Cup

| 1st | 24 Nov | PORT VALE | 3-1 | 10119 | Elder(pen), Keeble, Scott | | 1 | | 4 | 11 | 10 | | 6 | 2 | | 7 | 9 | | | | | 3 | | 8 | 5 | | |
|---|---|---|---|---|---|---|---|---|---|---|---|---|---|---|---|---|---|---|---|---|---|---|---|---|---|---|---|
| 2nd | 15 Dec | BRISTOL C | 2-1 | 9988 | Davidson, Scott | | 1 | | 4 | 11 | 10 | | 6 | 2 | | | 9 | | | | | 3 | | 8 | 5 | | |
| 3rd | 12 Jan | Barnsley | 0-3 | 24429 | | | 1 | | 4 | 11 | | 7 | 6 | 2 | | | 9 | | | 10 | | 3 | | 8 | 5 | | |

(Back) Miller, Rowlands, Moore, ? , Stewart, Harrison, Rochford.
(Front) Bearryman, Church, Jones, Curry, Layton.

DIVISION III (SOUTH)

| | P | W | D | L | F | A | Pts. |
|---|---|---|---|---|---|---|---|
| Plymouth Arg. | 46 | 29 | 8 | 9 | 107 | 53 | 66 |
| Reading | 46 | 29 | 3 | 14 | 112 | 60 | 61 |
| Norwich C. | 46 | 26 | 9 | 11 | 89 | 50 | 61 |
| Millwall | 46 | 23 | 12 | 11 | 74 | 53 | 58 |
| Brighton | 46 | 24 | 10 | 12 | 87 | 63 | 58 |
| Newport Co. | 42 | 21 | 12 | 13 | 77 | 76 | 54 |
| Bristol R. | 46 | 20 | 12 | 14 | 89 | 53 | 52 |
| Northampton | 46 | 22 | 5 | 19 | 93 | 74 | 49 |
| Southend U. | 46 | 19 | 10 | 17 | 75 | 66 | 48 |
| Colchester U. | 46 | 17 | 12 | 17 | 56 | 77 | 46 |
| Torquay U. | 46 | 17 | 10 | 19 | 86 | 98 | 44 |
| Aldershot | 46 | 18 | 8 | 20 | 78 | 89 | 44 |
| Port Vale | 46 | 14 | 15 | 17 | 50 | 66 | 43 |
| Bournemouth | 46 | 16 | 10 | 20 | 69 | 75 | 42 |
| Bristol C. | 46 | 15 | 12 | 19 | 58 | 69 | 42 |
| Swindon T. | 46 | 14 | 14 | 18 | 51 | 68 | 42 |
| Ipswich T. | 46 | 16 | 9 | 21 | 63 | 74 | 41 |
| Leyton O. | 46 | 16 | 9 | 21 | 55 | 68 | 41 |
| C. Palace | 46 | 15 | 9 | 22 | 61 | 80 | 39 |
| Shrewsbury T. | 46 | 13 | 10 | 23 | 62 | 86 | 36 |
| Watford | 46 | 13 | 10 | 23 | 57 | 81 | 36 |
| Gillingham | 46 | 11 | 13 | 22 | 71 | 81 | 35 |
| Exeter C. | 46 | 13 | 9 | 24 | 65 | 86 | 35 |
| Walsall | 46 | 13 | 5 | 28 | 55 | 94 | 31 |

# SEASON 1952-53 Division Three (South)

| No. | Date | Opposition | Res | Attend | Goalscorers | Coombs | Wright.G | Aitchison | Barlow | Bearryman | Bicknell | Church | Edwards | Elder | French | Grice | Harrison | Hill.Bert | Jones | McCurley | McKim | Rookes | Rowlands | Scott | Stewart | Wilkinson | Wright.P |
|---|---|---|---|---|---|---|---|---|---|---|---|---|---|---|---|---|---|---|---|---|---|---|---|---|---|---|---|
| 1 | 23 Aug | IPSWICH | 0-0 | 14674 | | 1 | | | | 4 | | 11 | | 6 | | | 2 | | 7 | 9 | 10 | 3 | | 8 | 5 | | |
| 2 | 28 | READING | 2-1 | 9190 | McKim(2) | 1 | | | | 4 | | 11 | | 6 | | | 2 | | 7 | 9 | 10 | 3 | | 8 | 5 | | |
| 3 | 30 | Aldershot | 0-0 | 8278 | | 1 | | | | 4 | | 11 | | 6 | | | 2 | | 7 | 9 | 10 | 3 | | 8 | 5 | | |
| 4 | 3 Sep | Reading | 0-2 | 13908 | | 1 | | | | 4 | | 11 | | 6 | | | 2 | | 7 | 9 | 10 | 3 | | 8 | 5 | | |
| 5 | 6 | SWINDON | 3-1 | 9062 | Church, Edwards, McKim | 1 | | | | 4 | | 11 | 9 | 6 | | | 2 | | 7 | | 10 | 3 | | 8 | 5 | | |
| 6 | 11 | BRISTOL R | 0-3 | 8909 | | 1 | | | | 4 | | 11 | | 6 | | 7 | 2 | | | 9 | 10 | 3 | | 8 | 5 | | |
| 7 | 13 | Q.p.r. | 0-1 | 13837 | | 1 | | | 10 | 4 | | 11 | | 6 | | 7 | 2 | | | 9 | | 3 | 5 | 8 | | | |
| 8 | 15 | Bristol R | 1-3 | 17336 | Elder(pen) | 1 | | | | 4 | | 7 | | 6 | | | 2 | | | 9 | 10 | 3 | 5 | 8 | | | 11 |
| 9 | 20 | SHREWSBURY | 1-0 | 7779 | Scott | 1 | | | 10 | 4 | | 11 | | 6 | | 7 | 2 | | | 9 | | 3 | | 8 | 5 | | |
| 10 | 23 | Bristol C | 2-3 | 12615 | Barlow, Rowlands | 1 | | | 10 | 4 | | 7 | | 6 | | | 2 | | | 9 | | 3 | | 8 | 5 | | 11 |
| 11 | 27 | Walsall | 3-0 | 7736 | Church, Grice, McCurley | 1 | | | 10 | 4 | | 11 | | 6 | | 7 | 2 | | | 9 | | 3 | | 8 | 5 | | |
| 12 | 4 Oct | GILLINGHAM | 1-1 | 8529 | Church, | 1 | | | 10 | 4 | 5 | 11 | | 6 | 3 | 7 | 2 | | | 9 | | | | 8 | | | |
| 13 | 11 | Bournemouth | 0-1 | 11679 | | 1 | | | | 4 | 5 | 11 | | 6 | | 7 | 2 | | | 9 | 10 | 3 | | 8 | | | |
| 14 | 18 | SOUTHEND | 3-3 | 10589 | Church, McKim, McCurley | 1 | | | | 4 | 5 | 11 | 9 | 6 | | | 2 | | | 7 | 10 | 3 | | 8 | | | |
| 15 | 25 | Watford | 0-2 | 16100 | | 1 | | | | 4 | 5 | 11 | 9 | 6 | | | 2 | | | 7 | 10 | 3 | | 8 | | | |
| 16 | 1 Nov | BRIGHTON | 0-0 | 8139 | | | 1 | | 8 | 4 | 3 | 11 | 9 | 6 | | | 2 | | | 7 | 10 | | | | 5 | | |
| 17 | 8 | Newport | 1-0 | 9000 | McKim | | 1 | | 8 | 4 | 3 | 11 | 9 | 6 | | | 2 | | | 7 | 10 | | | | 5 | | |
| 18 | 29 | TORQUAY | 4-1 | 6846 | Barlow, Church(2), McKim | | 1 | | 8 | 4 | | 11 | 9 | 6 | | | 2 | | | 7 | 10 | 3 | | | 5 | | |
| 19 | 13 Dec | LEYTON O | 3-1 | 6622 | McCurley(2), McKim | | 1 | | 8 | 4 | | 11 | | 6 | | | 2 | | | 9 | 10 | 3 | | 7 | 5 | | |
| 20 | 20 | Ipswich | 2-2 | 12572 | McCurley, McKim | | 1 | | 8 | 4 | | 11 | | 6 | | | 2 | | | 9 | 10 | 3 | | 7 | 5 | | |
| 21 | 26 | Norwich | 0-3 | 19859 | | | 1 | | 8 | 4 | | 11 | | 6 | | | 2 | | | 9 | 10 | 3 | | 7 | 5 | | |
| 22 | 3 Jan | ALDERSHOT | 1-2 | 7438 | McCurley | | 1 | | 8 | 4 | | 11 | | 6 | | | 2 | | | 9 | 10 | 3 | | 7 | 5 | | |
| 23 | 17 | Swindon | 1-0 | 8545 | McKim | | 1 | | 8 | 4 | | | | 6 | | | 2 | | 7 | 9 | 10 | 3 | | | 5 | | 11 |
| 24 | 21 | Exeter | 0-2 | 3951 | | | 1 | | 8 | 4 | | | | 6 | | | 2 | | 7 | 9 | 10 | 3 | | | 5 | | 11 |
| 25 | 24 | Q.P.R. | 1-1 | 9150 | Rowlands | | 1 | 11 | | 4 | | | 8 | 6 | | | 2 | | 7 | 9 | | 3 | 10 | | 5 | | |
| 26 | 31 | EXETER | 3-1 | 5643 | Barlow, Elder(pen), Rowlands | | 1 | 7 | 8 | 4 | | | | 6 | | | 2 | | | 9 | | 3 | 10 | | 5 | | 11 |
| 27 | 7 Feb | Shrewsbury | 0-3 | 7624 | | | 1 | | 8 | 4 | | 11 | | 6 | | | 2 | | | 9 | | 3 | 10 | 7 | 5 | | |
| 28 | 14 | WALSALL | 6-1 | 5102 | McCurley(3), McKim(3) | | 1 | | 8 | 4 | | 11 | | 6 | | | 2 | | | 9 | 10 | 3 | | 7 | 5 | | |
| 29 | 21 | Gillingham | 1-1 | 1000 | McCurley | | 1 | | 8 | 4 | | | | 6 | | | 2 | | | 9 | 10 | 3 | | 7 | 5 | | 11 |
| 30 | 28 | BOURNEMOUTH | 1-1 | 7858 | McCurley | | 1 | | | 4 | | 7 | | 6 | | | 2 | | | 9 | 10 | 3 | | 8 | 5 | | 11 |
| 31 | 7 Mar | Southend | 0-4 | 10250 | | | 1 | | | 4 | | 7 | 8 | 6 | | | 2 | | | 9 | 10 | 3 | | | 5 | | 11 |
| 32 | 14 | WATFORD | 1-1 | 6667 | McCurley | | 1 | | | 4 | | 11 | | | | 7 | 2 | | | 9 | 10 | 3 | | 8 | 5 | 6 | |
| 33 | 19 | CRYSTAL P | 3-0 | 3382 | McCurley(2), McKim | | 1 | | | 4 | | 11 | | 6 | | | 2 | | 7 | 9 | 10 | 3 | | 8 | 5 | | |
| 34 | 21 | Brighton | 0-0 | 12366 | | | 1 | | | 4 | | 11 | | 6 | | | 2 | | 7 | 9 | 10 | 3 | | 8 | 5 | | |
| 35 | 28 | NEWPORT | 3-3 | 6200 | Church, Elder(pen), McCurley | | 1 | | | 4 | | 11 | | 6 | | | 2 | | 7 | 9 | 10 | 3 | | 8 | 5 | | |
| 36 | 3 Apr | COVENTRY | 0-1 | 10618 | | | 1 | | 10 | 4 | | 11 | | 6 | | | 2 | | 7 | 9 | | 3 | | 8 | 5 | | |
| 37 | 4 | Crystal P | 1-3 | 12099 | Church | | 1 | | 10 | 4 | | 11 | | 6 | | | 2 | | 7 | 9 | | 3 | | 8 | 5 | | |
| 38 | 6 | Coventry | 2-2 | 11284 | Bearryman, Edwards | | 1 | | 10 | 4 | | | 9 | 6 | | | 2 | | | 7 | | 3 | | 8 | 5 | | 11 |
| 39 | 11 | BRISTOL C | 3-1 | 7519 | Barlow, Edwards(2) | | 1 | | 10 | | | | 9 | 6 | | | 2 | 4 | | 7 | | 3 | | 8 | 5 | | 11 |
| 40 | 16 | Northampton | 0-2 | 7982 | | | 1 | | 10 | | | 11 | 9 | 6 | | | 2 | 4 | | 7 | | 3 | | 8 | 5 | | |
| 41 | 18 | Torquay | 1-5 | 7269 | Barlow | | 1 | | 10 | 4 | | | 9 | 6 | | 11 | 2 | | | 7 | | 3 | | 8 | 5 | | |
| 42 | 23 | MILLWALL | 0-0 | 8127 | | | 1 | | 10 | 4 | | | 9 | 6 | | 11 | 2 | | | 7 | | 3 | | 8 | 5 | | |
| 43 | 25 | NORTHAMPTON | 1-2 | 8122 | Barlow | | 1 | 7 | 10 | 4 | | | 9 | 6 | | 11 | 2 | | | | | 3 | | 8 | 5 | | |
| 44 | 27 | Millwall | 1-3 | 7970 | P.Wright | 1 | | | 10 | 4 | | | 9 | 6 | | 7 | 2 | | | | | 3 | | 8 | 5 | | 11 |
| 45 | 30 | Leyton O | 3-5 | 2553 | Edwards, Scott, P.Wright | 1 | | | 10 | 4 | | | 9 | 6 | | 7 | 2 | | | | | 3 | | 8 | 5 | | 11 |
| 46 | 2 May | NORWICH | 0-4 | 10029 | | 1 | | | | 4 | | 11 | | 6 | | 7 | 2 | | | 9 | 10 | 3 | | 8 | 5 | | |

# F.A.Cup

| | | | | | | | | | | | | | | | | | | | | | | | | | | | |
|---|---|---|---|---|---|---|---|---|---|---|---|---|---|---|---|---|---|---|---|---|---|---|---|---|---|---|---|
| 1st | 22 Nov | Weymouth | 1-1 | 8000 | | | 1 | | 8 | 4 | 3 | 11 | 9 | 6 | | | 2 | | | 7 | 10 | | | | 5 | | |
| 1st/R | 27 | WEYMOUTH | 4-0 | 4314 | Edwards(2), McKim | | 1 | | 8 | 4 | 3 | 11 | 9 | 6 | | | 2 | | | 7 | 10 | | | | 5 | | |
| 2nd | 6 Dec | LLANELLY | 3-2 | 9693 | Barlow, Church, McCurley | | 1 | | 8 | 4 | | 11 | 9 | 6 | | | 2 | | | 7 | 10 | 3 | | | 5 | | |
| 3rd | 10 Jan | Rotherham | 2-2 | 16547 | McCurley(2) | | 1 | | 8 | 4 | | 11 | | 6 | | | 2 | | | 9 | 10 | 3 | | 7 | 5 | | |
| 3rd/R | 15 | ROTHERHAM | 0-2 | 8991 | | | 1 | | 8 | 4 | | 11 | | 6 | | | 2 | | | 9 | 10 | 3 | | 7 | 5 | | |

## Colchester United Football Club Ltd.

# TRIAL MATCH

### *Saturday, 16th August, 1952*

LAYER ROAD GROUND, COLCHESTER

KICK-OFF 3.15 p.m.

**WHITES**

*RIGHT* | *LEFT*

Coombs 1

Harrison 2 — Rookes 3

Bearryman 4 — Stewart 5 — Elder 6

Grice 7 — Cullum 8 — Edwards 9 — Barlow 10 — Wright (P.) 11

*Referee :* Mr. A. S. Thomas

*Linesmen :* Mr L. Lawrence, Mr. R. H. Wopling

Church 11 — McKim 10 — McCurley 9 — Scott 8 — Jones 7

Hunt 6 — Rowlands 5 — Hill 4

Bicknell 3 — Kettle 2

Wright (G.) 1

*LEFT* | *RIGHT*

**STRIPES**

| DIVISION III (SOUTH) | P | W | D | L | F | A | Pts. |
|---|---|---|---|---|---|---|---|
| Bristol R. | 46 | 26 | 12 | 8 | 92 | 46 | 64 |
| Millwall | 46 | 24 | 14 | 8 | 82 | 44 | 62 |
| Northampton | 46 | 26 | 10 | 10 | 109 | 70 | 62 |
| Norwich C. | 46 | 25 | 10 | 11 | 99 | 55 | 60 |
| Bristol C. | 46 | 22 | 15 | 9 | 95 | 61 | 59 |
| Coventry C. | 46 | 19 | 12 | 15 | 77 | 62 | 50 |
| Brighton | 46 | 19 | 12 | 15 | 81 | 75 | 50 |
| Southend U. | 46 | 18 | 13 | 15 | 69 | 74 | 49 |
| Bournemouth | 46 | 19 | 9 | 18 | 74 | 69 | 47 |
| Watford | 46 | 15 | 17 | 14 | 62 | 63 | 47 |
| Reading | 46 | 19 | 8 | 19 | 69 | 64 | 46 |
| Torquay U. | 46 | 18 | 9 | 19 | 87 | 88 | 45 |
| C. Palace | 46 | 15 | 13 | 18 | 66 | 82 | 43 |
| Leyton O. | 46 | 16 | 10 | 20 | 68 | 73 | 42 |
| Newport Co. | 46 | 16 | 10 | 20 | 70 | 82 | 42 |
| Ipswich T. | 46 | 13 | 15 | 18 | 60 | 69 | 41 |
| Exeter C. | 46 | 13 | 14 | 19 | 61 | 71 | 40 |
| Swindon T. | 46 | 14 | 12 | 20 | 64 | 79 | 40 |
| Aldershot | 46 | 12 | 15 | 19 | 61 | 77 | 39 |
| Gillingham | 46 | 12 | 15 | 19 | 55 | 74 | 39 |
| Q.P.R. | 46 | 12 | 15 | 19 | 61 | 82 | 39 |
| Colchester U. | 46 | 12 | 14 | 20 | 59 | 76 | 38 |
| Shrewsbury T. | 46 | 12 | 12 | 22 | 68 | 91 | 36 |
| Walsall | 46 | 7 | 10 | 29 | 56 | 118 | 24 |

# SEASON 1953–54 Division Three (South)

| No. | Date | Opposition | Res | Attend | Goalscorers | Coombs | Wright.G | Barlow | Bearryman | Bicknell | Church | Cullum | Dale | Elder | French | Grice | Harris.Tom | Harrison | Hill.Bert | Hunt.R.M | Keene | Kettle | Lewis | McCurley | McKim | Plant | Scott | Stewart | Wright.P |
|---|---|---|---|---|---|---|---|---|---|---|---|---|---|---|---|---|---|---|---|---|---|---|---|---|---|---|---|---|---|
| 1 | 20 Aug | TORQUAY | 3-1 | 8841 | Barlow, Elder, McCurley | | 1 | 10 | | | 11 | | | 6 | | | | | | | 7 | | 3 | 9 | | | 8 | | |
| 2 | 22 | Ipswich | 0-3 | 18130 | | | 1 | 10 | 4 | | 11 | | | 6 | | | | 2 | | | 7 | | 3 | 9 | | | 8 | 5 | |
| 3 | 26 | Exeter | 2-1 | 10589 | Barlow, McCurley | | 1 | 10 | 4 | | | | | 6 | | 7 | | 2 | | | 11 | | 3 | 9 | | | 8 | 5 | |
| 4 | 29 | CRYSTAL P | 4-1 | 6811 | Barlow, McCurley(2), Scott | | 1 | 10 | 4 | | | | | 6 | | 7 | | 2 | | | 11 | | 3 | 9 | | | 8 | 5 | |
| 5 | 3 Sep | EXETER | 0-1 | 8791 | | | 1 | 10 | 4 | | | | | 6 | | 7 | | 2 | | | 11 | | 3 | 9 | | | 8 | 5 | |
| 6 | 5 | Bristol C | 0-3 | 17219 | | | 1 | 10 | 4 | | | | | 6 | | 7 | | 2 | | | 11 | | 3 | 9 | | | 8 | 5 | |
| 7 | 9 | Norwich | 1-2 | 22228 | Scott | | 1 | 10 | 4 | | | | | | | | | | 6 | | 7 | 2 | 3 | 9 | | | 8 | 5 | 11 |
| 8 | 12 | ALDERSHOT | 3-0 | 8170 | Barlow, Bearryman, McCurley | | 1 | 10 | 4 | | | | | | | | | | 6 | | 7 | 2 | 3 | 9 | | | 8 | 5 | 11 |
| 9 | 17 | NORWICH | 0-1 | 10218 | | | 1 | | 4 | | | | | | 2 | | | | 6 | | 7 | | 3 | 9 | 10 | | 8 | 5 | 11 |
| 10 | 19 | Swindon | 0-3 | 12284 | | | 1 | | 4 | | | | | | 2 | 7 | | | 6 | | 11 | | 3 | 9 | 10 | | 8 | 5 | |
| 11 | 23 | Southampton | 1-2 | 14842 | McKim | | 1 | | 4 | | | | | 6 | | 7 | | 2 | | | | | 3 | 9 | 10 | | 8 | 5 | 11 |
| 12 | 26 | WALSALL | 1-1 | 7643 | Grice | | 1 | 10 | 4 | | | | | 6 | | 7 | | 2 | | | | | 3 | 9 | | | 8 | 5 | 11 |
| 13 | 1 Oct | SOUTHAMPTON | 0-1 | 6705 | | | 1 | 10 | 4 | | | | | 6 | | | | 2 | | | 7 | | 3 | 9 | | | 8 | 5 | 11 |
| 14 | 3 | Shrewsbury | 1-3 | 9915 | Barlow | | 1 | 10 | 4 | | | | | 6 | | | | 2 | | | 7 | | 3 | 9 | | | 8 | 5 | 11 |
| 15 | 10 | COVENTRY | 0-3 | 8174 | | | 1 | 10 | 4 | | | | | 6 | | | 9 | 2 | | | | 2 | 3 | 7 | | | 8 | 5 | 11 |
| 16 | 17 | Gillingham | 0-2 | 8296 | | | 1 | 10 | 4 | | 9 | | | 6 | | | | 2 | | | | | 3 | 7 | | | 8 | 5 | 11 |
| 17 | 24 | NORTHAMPTON | 1-1 | 7599 | Elder(pen) | | 1 | 8 | 4 | | 11 | | | 6 | | 7 | | 2 | | | | | 3 | 9 | 10 | | | 5 | |
| 18 | 31 | Torquay | 1-3 | 6251 | McCurley | | 1 | 8 | 4 | | 11 | | | 6 | | 7 | | 2 | | | | | 3 | 9 | 10 | | | 5 | |
| 19 | 7 Nov | WATFORD | 2-2 | 6505 | Barlow, McCurley | | 1 | 8 | 4 | 5 | | | | 6 | | | | 2 | | | 7 | | 3 | 9 | | | 10 | | 11 |
| 20 | 14 | Brighton | 0-1 | 6000 | | | 1 | 10 | 4 | 5 | | | | 6 | | | | 2 | | | 7 | | 3 | 9 | | | 8 | | 11 |
| 21 | 28 | Reading | 0-2 | 12036 | | | 1 | 8 | 4 | 5 | | | | 6 | | 7 | 11 | | | | | | 3 | 9 | | | 10 | | |
| 22 | 5 Dec | L.ORIENT | 1-0 | 6819 | Grice | | 1 | 8 | 4 | 5 | | | | 6 | | 11 | 7 | 2 | | | | | 3 | 9 | | | 10 | | |
| 23 | 19 | IPSWICH | 1-2 | 10316 | Scott | | 1 | 8 | 4 | 5 | | | | 6 | | 11 | | 2 | | | | | 3 | 9 | 10 | | 7 | | |
| 24 | 25 | Q.P.R. | 5-0 | 6155 | Barlow(2), McKim(2), Scott | | 1 | 8 | 4 | 5 | | | | 6 | | | | 2 | | | 11 | | 3 | 9 | 10 | | 7 | | |
| 25 | 26 | Q.p.r. | 0-0 | 10674 | | | 1 | 8 | 4 | 5 | | | | 6 | | | | 2 | | | 11 | | 3 | 9 | 10 | | 7 | | |
| 26 | 2 Jan | Crystal P | 1-0 | 6971 | McCurley | | 1 | 8 | 4 | 5 | | | 10 | 6 | | | | 2 | | | 11 | | 3 | 9 | | | 7 | | |
| 27 | 9 | NEWPORT | 2-2 | 6434 | Barlow, Dale | | 1 | 8 | 4 | 5 | | | 10 | 6 | | | | 2 | | | | | 3 | 9 | | | 7 | | 11 |
| 28 | 16 | BRISTOL C | 0-2 | 7931 | | | 1 | 8 | 4 | 5 | 9 | | 10 | 6 | | | | 2 | | | | | 3 | | | | 7 | | 11 |
| 29 | 23 | Aldershot | 0-3 | 4502 | | | 1 | 8 | 4 | 5 | | 9 | 10 | 6 | | | | 2 | | | | | 3 | | | | 7 | | 11 |
| 30 | 6 Feb | SWINDON | 2-2 | 6824 | Dale, Plant | | 1 | 8 | | 5 | | | 10 | 6 | | | | 2 | 4 | | | | 3 | | | 9 | 7 | | 11 |
| 31 | 13 | Walsall | 3-2 | 9819 | Plant(2), P.Wright | 1 | | 8 | | 5 | | | 10 | 6 | | | | 2 | 4 | | | | 3 | | | 9 | 7 | | 11 |
| 32 | 20 | SHREWSBURY | 3-1 | 7852 | Barlow, Keene, Plant | 1 | | 8 | | 5 | | | 10 | 6 | | | | 2 | 4 | | 11 | | 3 | | | 9 | 7 | | |
| 33 | 27 | Coventry | 1-2 | 11852 | Plant | 1 | | 8 | | 5 | | | 10 | 6 | | | | 2 | 4 | | 11 | | 3 | | | 9 | 7 | | |
| 34 | 6 Mar | GILLINGHAM | 0-1 | 8651 | | 1 | | 8 | | 5 | | | 10 | 6 | | | | 2 | 4 | | | | 3 | 7 | | 9 | | | 11 |
| 35 | 13 | Southend | 0-3 | 8100 | | 1 | | 8 | 4 | | | | 10 | 6 | | | | 2 | | | | | 3 | 7 | | 9 | | 5 | 11 |
| 36 | 20 | READING | 2-4 | 6726 | Elder(2)(both pen) | 1 | | | 4 | | | | 8 | 6 | | | | 2 | | | | | 3 | 11 | 10 | 9 | 7 | 5 | |
| 37 | 27 | Watford | 0-3 | 10466 | | 1 | | | | | | | 8 | 6 | | | | 2 | 4 | | | | 3 | 11 | 10 | 9 | 7 | 5 | |
| 38 | 3 Apr | BRIGHTON | 1-1 | 8282 | Bert Hill | | 1 | | | | | | 8 | 6 | | | | 2 | 4 | | 11 | | 3 | | 10 | 9 | 7 | 5 | |
| 39 | 10 | L.Orient | 1-3 | 9309 | McKim | | 1 | | | | | | 8 | 6 | | | | 2 | 4 | | 11 | | 3 | | 10 | 9 | 7 | 5 | |
| 40 | 16 | BOURNEMOUTH | 1-1 | 8223 | Dale | | 1 | | 4 | | | | 8 | 6 | | | | 2 | | | 11 | | 3 | | 10 | 9 | 7 | 5 | |
| 41 | 17 | MILLWALL | 3-0 | 7450 | Bearryman, McKim(2) | | 1 | | 4 | | | | 8 | 6 | | 11 | | 2 | | | | | 3 | | 10 | 9 | 7 | 5 | |
| 42 | 19 | Bournemouth | 2-4 | 7778 | Dale, P.Wright | | 1 | | 4 | 5 | | | 8 | | | 7 | | 2 | 6 | | | | 3 | | 10 | 9 | | | 11 |
| 43 | 22 | Newport | 1-1 | 7396 | Plant | | 1 | | 4 | 5 | | | 8 | | | 7 | | 2 | 6 | | | | 3 | | 10 | 9 | | | 11 |
| 44 | 24 | Northampton | 0-3 | 7344 | | | 1 | | 4 | | | | 8 | | | 7 | | 2 | 6 | | | | 3 | | 10 | 9 | | 5 | 11 |
| 45 | 26 | Millwall | 0-0 | 5572 | | | 1 | | | 5 | | | 8 | | | 7 | | 2 | 4 | 6 | | | 3 | | 10 | 9 | | | 11 |
| 46 | 29 | SOUTHEND | 0-1 | 6035 | | | 1 | | 4 | | | | 8 | | | 11 | | 2 | | 6 | | | 3 | 9 | 10 | 7 | | 5 | |

# F.A.Cup

| | | | | | | | | | | | | | | | | | | | | | | | | | | | | | |
|---|---|---|---|---|---|---|---|---|---|---|---|---|---|---|---|---|---|---|---|---|---|---|---|---|---|---|---|---|---|
| 1st | 21 Nov | MILLWALL | 1-1 | 9765 | McCurley | | 1 | 8 | 4 | 5 | 11 | | | 6 | | | | 2 | | | 7 | | 3 | 9 | | | 10 | | |
| 1st/R | 23 | Millwall | 0-4 | 8898 | | | 1 | 8 | 4 | 5 | | | | 6 | | | | | | | 7 | 2 | 3 | 9 | | | 10 | | 11 |

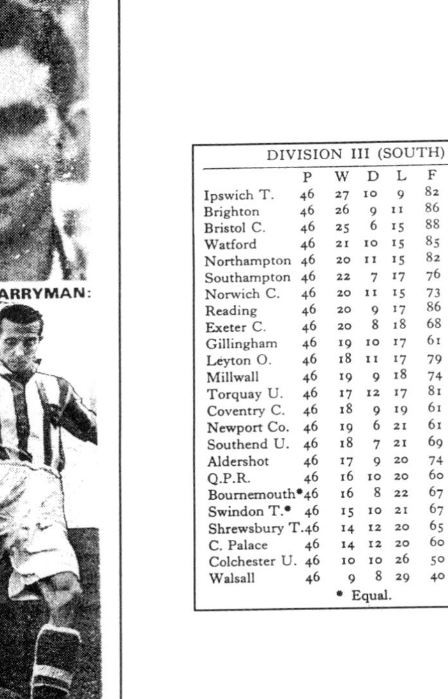

HARRY BEARRYMAN:

JOHNNY McKIM:

McKim suffered a bad injury during the season; Bearryman retired and joined the Police in 1954. (Centre) Bert Barlow and son Peter have a unique niche in the annals of the club. At 38 years 204 days Bart was the oldest League player (in March 1954), Peter made his debut on the 9th of January 1950 aged 14 days short of 17 - the youngest League player for the U's.

DIVISION III (SOUTH)

| | P | W | D | L | F | A | Pts. |
|---|---|---|---|---|---|---|---|
| Ipswich T. | 46 | 27 | 10 | 9 | 82 | 51 | 64 |
| Brighton | 46 | 26 | 9 | 11 | 86 | 61 | 61 |
| Bristol C. | 46 | 25 | 6 | 15 | 88 | 66 | 56 |
| Watford | 46 | 21 | 10 | 15 | 85 | 69 | 52 |
| Northampton | 46 | 20 | 11 | 15 | 82 | 55 | 51 |
| Southampton | 46 | 22 | 7 | 17 | 76 | 63 | 51 |
| Norwich C. | 46 | 20 | 11 | 15 | 73 | 66 | 51 |
| Reading | 46 | 20 | 9 | 17 | 86 | 73 | 49 |
| Exeter C. | 46 | 20 | 8 | 18 | 68 | 58 | 48 |
| Gillingham | 46 | 19 | 10 | 17 | 61 | 66 | 48 |
| Leyton O. | 46 | 18 | 11 | 17 | 79 | 73 | 47 |
| Millwall | 46 | 19 | 9 | 18 | 74 | 77 | 47 |
| Torquay U. | 46 | 17 | 12 | 17 | 81 | 88 | 46 |
| Coventry C. | 46 | 18 | 9 | 19 | 61 | 56 | 45 |
| Newport Co. | 46 | 19 | 6 | 21 | 61 | 81 | 44 |
| Southend U. | 46 | 18 | 7 | 21 | 69 | 71 | 43 |
| Aldershot | 46 | 17 | 9 | 20 | 74 | 86 | 43 |
| Q.P.R. | 46 | 16 | 10 | 20 | 60 | 68 | 42 |
| Bournemouth• | 46 | 16 | 8 | 22 | 67 | 70 | 40 |
| Swindon T.• | 46 | 15 | 10 | 21 | 67 | 70 | 40 |
| Shrewsbury T. | 46 | 14 | 12 | 20 | 65 | 76 | 40 |
| C. Palace | 46 | 14 | 12 | 20 | 60 | 86 | 40 |
| Colchester U. | 46 | 10 | 10 | 26 | 50 | 78 | 30 |
| Walsall | 46 | 9 | 8 | 29 | 40 | 87 | 26 |

• Equal.

# SEASON 1954–55 Division Three (South)

| No. | Date | Opposition | Res | Attend | Goalscorers | Kirk | Wright.G | Wright.J | Aitchison | Birch | Dale | Dunne | Elder | Fenton | George | Grice | Harris.Trevor | Harrison | Hill.Bert | Hunt.R.M | Kettle | Leonard | Lewis | McCourt | McCurley | McKim | Plant | Stewart | Wright.P |
|---|---|---|---|---|---|---|---|---|---|---|---|---|---|---|---|---|---|---|---|---|---|---|---|---|---|---|---|---|---|
| 1 | 21 Aug | SWINDON | 0-0 | 9767 | | 1 | | | | 7 | 8 | | 6 | | | | | 2 | | | | 10 | 3 | 4 | 9 | | | 5 | 11 |
| 2 | 25 | Exeter | 2-2 | 11500 | Grice, Leonard | 1 | | | | 7 | 8 | | 6 | | | 11 | | 2 | | | | 10 | 3 | 4 | | | 9 | 5 | |
| 3 | 28 | Crystal P | 0-0 | 14348 | | 1 | | | | 7 | 8 | | | | | 11 | | 2 | | 6 | | 10 | 3 | 4 | | | 9 | 5 | |
| 4 | 2 Sep | EXETER | 1-2 | 7963 | Plant | 1 | | | | 7 | 8 | | | | | 11 | | 2 | 6 | | | 10 | 3 | 4 | | | 9 | 5 | |
| 5 | 4 | NORTHAMPTON | 4-1 | 7467 | Birch, Plant(3) | 1 | | | | 7 | 8 | | | | | 11 | | 2 | | 6 | | | 3 | 4 | | 10 | 9 | 5 | |
| 6 | 9 | BRISTOL C | 0-2 | 8522 | | 1 | | | | 7 | 8 | | | | | 11 | | 2 | | 6 | | | 3 | 4 | | 10 | 9 | 5 | |
| 7 | 11 | Watford | 0-2 | 13794 | | 1 | | | | | 8 | | | | | 11 | | 2 | | 6 | | | 3 | 4 | 7 | 10 | 9 | 5 | |
| 8 | 14 | Bristol C | 0-4 | 18455 | | 1 | | | | | 8 | | 4 | | | | | 2 | | 6 | | 11 | 3 | | 7 | 10 | 9 | 5 | |
| 9 | 18 | BOURNEMOUTH | 3-3 | 7801 | Dale, Grice, Plant | 1 | | | | 7 | 8 | | 4 | | | 11 | | 2 | | 6 | | | 3 | | | 10 | 9 | 5 | |
| 10 | 23 | NORWICH | 1-0 | 8506 | Dale | 1 | | | | 7 | 8 | | 4 | | | | | 2 | | 6 | | 11 | 3 | | | 10 | 9 | 5 | |
| 11 | 25 | Q.p.r. | 1-4 | 11738 | Birch | 1 | | | | 7 | 8 | | 4 | | | 11 | | 2 | | 6 | | | 3 | | | 10 | 9 | 5 | |
| 12 | 29 | Norwich | 2-0 | 15672 | Dale, Plant | | 1 | | 7 | | 8 | | | | | 11 | | 2 | 4 | 6 | | | 3 | | | 10 | 9 | 5 | |
| 13 | 2 Oct | NEWPORT | 1-0 | 8691 | McKim | 1 | | | 7 | | | | | | | 11 | | 2 | 4 | 6 | | 8 | 3 | | | 10 | 9 | 5 | |
| 14 | 9 | BRIGHTON | 2-4 | 9334 | McKim, Plant(pen) | 1 | | | 7 | | 8 | | | | | 11 | | 2 | 4 | 6 | | | 3 | | | 10 | 9 | 5 | |
| 15 | 16 | Brentford | 2-3 | 10200 | Grice, McKim | 1 | | | 7 | | 8 | | 6 | | 2 | 11 | | | | | | | 3 | 4 | | 10 | 9 | 5 | |
| 16 | 23 | COVENTRY | 0-1 | 8124 | | 1 | | | 7 | | 8 | | 6 | | | 11 | | 2 | 4 | | | | 3 | | | 10 | 9 | 5 | |
| 17 | 30 | Walsall | 1-3 | 11117 | McKim | 1 | | | | | | | | | | 7 | | 2 | 4 | 6 | | 8 | 3 | 9 | | 10 | | 5 | 11 |
| 18 | 6 Nov | MILLWALL | 0-2 | 7551 | | 1 | | | 7 | | | | | | | 11 | | 2 | 4 | 6 | | 8 | 3 | | | 10 | 9 | 5 | |
| 19 | 13 | Leyton O | 0-2 | 16782 | | 1 | | | | 7 | 8 | | 6 | | 2 | | | | 4 | | | | 3 | | | 10 | 9 | 5 | 11 |
| 20 | 27 | Reading | 0-4 | 6512 | | 1 | | | | | 10 | | 6 | | 2 | | | | 4 | | | 8 | 3 | | 7 | | 9 | 5 | 11 |
| 21 | 4 Dec | SHREWSBURY | 2-4 | 5168 | Plant, P. Wright | 1 | | | | | | | 6 | | | | | 2 | | | | 8 | 3 | 4 | 7 | 10 | 9 | 5 | 11 |
| 22 | 18 | Swindon | 1-1 | 5254 | Plant | 1 | | | | 7 | | | | | 6 | 11 | | 2 | 4 | | | 8 | 3 | | | 10 | 9 | 5 | |
| 23 | 25 | Aldershot | 2-2 | 5123 | McKim, P. Wright | 1 | | | | | | | | | 6 | 7 | | 2 | 4 | | | 8 | 3 | | | 10 | 9 | 5 | 11 |
| 24 | 27 | ALDERSHOT | 1-1 | 7967 | P. Wright | 1 | | | | | | | 6 | | | 7 | | 2 | 4 | | | 8 | 3 | | | 10 | 9 | 5 | 11 |
| 25 | 1 Jan | CRYSTAL P | 2-0 | 5806 | Plant, P. Wright | 1 | | | | | | | 6 | | | 7 | | 2 | 4 | | | 8 | 3 | | | 10 | 9 | 5 | 11 |
| 26 | 8 | Southampton | 1-0 | 12449 | Grice | 1 | | | | | 11 | | 6 | | | 7 | | 2 | 4 | | | 8 | 3 | | | 10 | 9 | 5 | |
| 27 | 22 | WATFORD | 1-3 | 6700 | Grice | 1 | | | | | 11 | | 6 | | | 7 | | 2 | 4 | | | 8 | 3 | | | 10 | 9 | 5 | |
| 28 | 5 Feb | Bournemouth | 0-2 | 7417 | | | 1 | | | | | | | | 2 | 7 | | | 4 | 6 | | 8 | 3 | | | 10 | 9 | 5 | 11 |
| 29 | 12 | Q.P.R. | 1-0 | 4903 | Leonard | | 1 | | | | | | 3 | | | 7 | | | 4 | | 2 | 8 | | 6 | | 10 | 9 | 5 | 11 |
| 30 | 19 | Newport | 0-0 | 5000 | | 1 | | | | | 10 | | 3 | | | 7 | | 2 | | | 4 | 8 | | 6 | | | 9 | 5 | 11 |
| 31 | 26 | Brighton | 1-1 | 11074 | Dale | | 1 | | | | 10 | | 3 | | | 7 | | 2 | 4 | 6 | | 8 | | | | | 9 | 5 | 11 |
| 32 | 5 Mar | BRENTFORD | 3-2 | 8251 | Elder(pen), Leonard, Plant | | 1 | | | | 10 | | 3 | 4 | | 7 | | 2 | | 6 | | 8 | | | | | 9 | 5 | 11 |
| 33 | 12 | Coventry | 0-0 | 10058 | | | 1 | | | | | | 3 | 4 | | 7 | | 2 | | 6 | | 8 | | | | 10 | 9 | 5 | 11 |
| 34 | 19 | WALSALL | 2-2 | 7361 | Grice, P. Wright | | 1 | | | | 10 | | 3 | 4 | | 7 | | 2 | | 6 | | 8 | | | | | 9 | 5 | 11 |
| 35 | 26 | Millwall | 2-5 | 8349 | Leonard, P. Wright | 1 | | | | | 10 | | | 4 | | 7 | | 2 | | 6 | | 8 | 3 | | | | 9 | 5 | 11 |
| 36 | 31 | TORQUAY | 0-2 | 3517 | | | 1 | | | | 10 | | 3 | 4 | | | | 2 | | 6 | | 8 | | | 9 | | 7 | 5 | 11 |
| 37 | 2 Apr | LEYTON O | 2-2 | 9448 | Fenton, Plant | | 1 | | | | | | 3 | 10 | | 11 | | | 4 | 6 | | | 2 | | 9 | 8 | 7 | 5 | |
| 38 | 8 | SOUTHEND | 2-0 | 10809 | Fenton, Stewart | | 1 | | | | 4 | | 3 | 10 | | 11 | | | | 6 | | | 2 | | 9 | 8 | 7 | 5 | |
| 39 | 9 | Gillingham | 1-2 | 11002 | Elder(pen) | | 1 | | | | 4 | 6 | 3 | | | 8 | | | | | | 10 | 2 | | 9 | | 7 | 5 | 11 |
| 40 | 11 | Southend | 2-4 | 14000 | Leonard, McKim | | 1 | | | | 4 | | 3 | | | 11 | | | | 6 | | 8 | 2 | | 9 | 10 | 7 | 5 | |
| 41 | 16 | READING | 0-2 | 8000 | | 1 | | | | | 4 | | 3 | 10 | | 11 | | | | 6 | | 8 | 2 | | 9 | | 7 | 5 | |
| 42 | 18 | Northampton | 1-6 | 3198 | McKim | 1 | | | | | 6 | | | 4 | | 7 | 5 | 2 | | | | 8 | 3 | | 9 | 10 | | | 11 |
| 43 | 23 | Shrewsbury | 0-2 | 6735 | | 1 | | | | | 6 | | | 4 | | 7 | | 2 | | | | 8 | 3 | | 9 | 10 | | 5 | 11 |
| 44 | 28 | GILLINGHAM | 2-2 | 5300 | P. Wright(2) | 1 | | | | | 6 | | | 4 | | 7 | | 2 | | | | 8 | 3 | | 9 | 10 | | 5 | 11 |
| 45 | 30 | SOUTHAMPTON | 3-5 | 6386 | McCurley, Plant, P. Wright | | | 1 | | | 4 | | | | | 7 | | 2 | | 6 | | 8 | 3 | | 9 | | 10 | 5 | 11 |
| 46 | 4 May | Torquay | 1-2 | 2907 | Birch | | | 1 | | 7 | 4 | | 3 | | | | | | | 6 | | 8 | 2 | | 9 | 10 | | 5 | 11 |

## F.A.Cup

| | | | | | | | | | | | | | | | | | | | | | | | | | | | | | |
|---|---|---|---|---|---|---|---|---|---|---|---|---|---|---|---|---|---|---|---|---|---|---|---|---|---|---|---|---|---|
| 1st | 20 Nov | Reading | 3–3 | 12800 | Birch, Grice, McKim | | 1 | | | 7 | | | 6 | | 2 | 11 | | | 4 | | | | 3 | | 9 | 10 | 8 | 5 | |
| 1st/R | 25 | READING | 1–2 | 4636 | Elder(pen) | | 1 | | | 7 | | | 6 | | 2 | 11 | | | 4 | | | | 3 | | 9 | 10 | 8 | 5 | |

Elder, made 212 first team appearances for the U's between 1950 and 1955, credited with never missing a penalty. Peter Wright (right) at aged 20 established himself in the first team during the season.

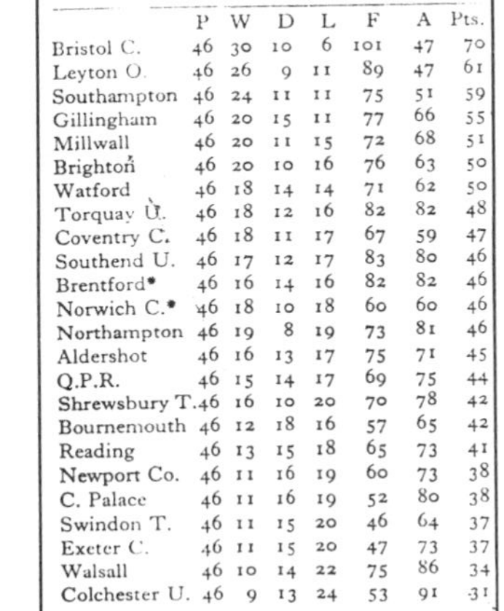

| | P | W | D | L | F | A | Pts. |
|---|---|---|---|---|---|---|---|
| Bristol C. | 46 | 30 | 10 | 6 | 101 | 47 | 70 |
| Leyton O. | 46 | 26 | 9 | 11 | 89 | 47 | 61 |
| Southampton | 46 | 24 | 11 | 11 | 75 | 51 | 59 |
| Gillingham | 46 | 20 | 15 | 11 | 77 | 66 | 55 |
| Millwall | 46 | 20 | 11 | 15 | 72 | 68 | 51 |
| Brighton | 46 | 20 | 10 | 16 | 76 | 63 | 50 |
| Watford | 46 | 18 | 14 | 14 | 71 | 62 | 50 |
| Torquay U. | 46 | 18 | 12 | 16 | 82 | 82 | 48 |
| Coventry C. | 46 | 18 | 11 | 17 | 67 | 59 | 47 |
| Southend U. | 46 | 17 | 12 | 17 | 83 | 80 | 46 |
| Brentford* | 46 | 16 | 14 | 16 | 82 | 82 | 46 |
| Norwich C.* | 46 | 18 | 10 | 18 | 60 | 60 | 46 |
| Northampton | 46 | 19 | 8 | 19 | 73 | 81 | 46 |
| Aldershot | 46 | 16 | 13 | 17 | 75 | 71 | 45 |
| Q.P.R. | 46 | 15 | 14 | 17 | 69 | 75 | 44 |
| Shrewsbury T. | 46 | 16 | 10 | 20 | 70 | 78 | 42 |
| Bournemouth | 46 | 12 | 18 | 16 | 57 | 65 | 42 |
| Reading | 46 | 13 | 15 | 18 | 65 | 73 | 41 |
| Newport Co. | 46 | 11 | 16 | 19 | 60 | 73 | 38 |
| C. Palace | 46 | 11 | 16 | 19 | 52 | 80 | 38 |
| Swindon T. | 46 | 11 | 15 | 20 | 46 | 64 | 37 |
| Exeter C. | 46 | 11 | 15 | 20 | 47 | 73 | 37 |
| Walsall | 46 | 10 | 14 | 22 | 75 | 86 | 34 |
| Colchester U. | 46 | 9 | 13 | 24 | 53 | 91 | 31 |

# SEASON 1955-56 Division Three (South)

| No. | Date | Opposition | Res | Attend | Goalscorers | Ames | Wright.J | Blake.R | Dale | Dobson | Fenton | Fisher | Fowler | Grice | Harris | Harrison | Hill.B | Hill.R | Hunt.R.M | Hunt.W | McCurley | McLeod | Noble.A | Plant | Stewart | Wright.P |
|---|---|---|---|---|---|---|---|---|---|---|---|---|---|---|---|---|---|---|---|---|---|---|---|---|---|---|
| 1 | 20 Aug | Exeter | 0-0 | 13000 | | 1 | | | 6 | | 3 | | 10 | 7 | | 2 | 4 | | | | 9 | 8 | | | 5 | 11 |
| 2 | 24 | Bournemouth | 1-3 | 8066 | McCurley | 1 | | | 6 | | 3 | | 10 | 7 | | 2 | 4 | | | | 9 | 8 | | | 5 | 11 |
| 3 | 27 | SOUTHEND | 3-6 | 8915 | Fowler, McCurley(2,1pen) | 1 | | | 6 | | 3 | | 10 | 7 | | 2 | 4 | | | 5 | 9 | 8 | | | | 11 |
| 4 | 1 Sep | BOURNEMOUTH | 1-0 | 6964 | Fowler | 1 | | | 6 | | 4 | 3 | 10 | 7 | | 2 | | | | | 9 | 8 | | | 5 | 11 |
| 5 | 3 | Coventry | 0-2 | 23171 | | 1 | | | 6 | | | 3 | 10 | 7 | | 2 | 4 | | | | 9 | 8 | | | 5 | 11 |
| 6 | 8 | Leyton O | 0-6 | 13483 | | 1 | | 11 | 6 | | 4 | 3 | 10 | 7 | | 2 | | | | | 9 | 8 | | | 5 | |
| 7 | 10 | BRENTFORD | 0-3 | 7843 | | 1 | | | | | 4 | 3 | 10 | 7 | | 2 | 6 | | | | 9 | 8 | | | 5 | 11 |
| 8 | 15 | LEYTON O | 2-1 | 7191 | Harrison, McCurley | 1 | | | | | 4 | 3 | | 7 | | 2 | 6 | | | | 9 | 8 | | 10 | 5 | 11 |
| 9 | 17 | Watford | 1-1 | 9326 | McCurley | 1 | | | | | 4 | | | 7 | 3 | 2 | 6 | | | | 9 | 8 | | 10 | 5 | 11 |
| 10 | 21 | Norwich | 1-1 | 13555 | Plant | 1 | | | | | 4 | 3 | | 7 | | 2 | 6 | | | | 9 | 8 | | 10 | 5 | 11 |
| 11 | 24 | READING | 0-3 | 8125 | | 1 | | | | | | 3 | | 7 | | 2 | 4 | | 6 | | 9 | 8 | | 10 | 5 | 11 |
| 12 | 29 | GILLINGHAM | 1-1 | 5208 | Stewart | 1 | | | 6 | | 4 | 3 | | 7 | | 2 | | | | | 9 | 8 | | 10 | 5 | 11 |
| 13 | 1 Oct | Millwall | 1-0 | 11807 | Grice | 1 | | | 6 | | | 3 | | 7 | | 2 | 4 | | | | 9 | 8 | | 10 | 5 | 11 |
| 14 | 8 | Torquay | 2-1 | 7419 | McCurley, P.Wright | 1 | | | 6 | | | 3 | | 7 | | 2 | 4 | | | | 9 | 8 | | 10 | 5 | 11 |
| 15 | 15 | NEWPORT | 2-1 | 8225 | Plant(2) | 1 | | | 6 | | | 3 | | 7 | | 2 | 4 | | | | 9 | 8 | | 10 | 5 | 11 |
| 16 | 22 | Swindon | 1-3 | 6373 | Plant | 1 | | | 6 | | | 3 | | 7 | | 2 | 4 | | | | 9 | 8 | | 10 | 5 | 11 |
| 17 | 29 | Q.p.r. | 4-1 | 7339 | Grice, McCurley(3) | 1 | | | 6 | | 4 | 3 | | 7 | | 2 | | | | | 9 | 8 | | 10 | 5 | 11 |
| 18 | 5 Nov | Northampton | 2-0 | 13000 | Grice, McCurley | 1 | | | 6 | | 4 | 3 | | 7 | | 2 | | | | | 9 | 8 | | 10 | 5 | 11 |
| 19 | 12 | ALDERSHOT | 4-0 | 8695 | McCurley(2), McLeod, P.Wright | 1 | | | 6 | | 4 | 3 | | 7 | | 2 | | | | | 9 | 8 | | 10 | 5 | 11 |
| 20 | 26 | BRIGHTON | 3-3 | 9010 | McCurley(3) | 1 | | | 6 | | 4 | 3 | | 7 | | 2 | | | | | 9 | 8 | | 10 | 5 | 11 |
| 21 | 3 Dec | Southampton | 0-3 | 11072 | | 1 | | | 6 | | 4 | 3 | | 7 | 2 | | | | | | 9 | 8 | | 10 | 5 | 11 |
| 22 | 17 | EXETER | 5-1 | 6179 | Fenton(pen), Grice, Plant, P.Wright(2) | 1 | | | 6 | | 4 | 3 | | 7 | | 2 | | | | | 9 | 8 | | 10 | 5 | 11 |
| 23 | 24 | Southend | 0-4 | 7500 | | 1 | | | | | | 3 | | 7 | | 2 | 4 | | 6 | | 9 | 8 | | 10 | 5 | 11 |
| 24 | 26 | IPSWICH | 3-3 | 13176 | McCurley, Plant, O.G. | 1 | | | 6 | | 4 | 3 | | 7 | | 2 | | | | | 9 | 8 | | 10 | 5 | 11 |
| 25 | 27 | Ipswich | 1-3 | 22644 | McCurley | 1 | | | | | | 3 | | 7 | | 2 | 4 | | 6 | | 9 | 8 | 10 | | 5 | 11 |
| 26 | 31 | COVENTRY | 2-0 | 8618 | McCurley, Plant | 1 | | | 6 | | 4 | 3 | | 7 | | 2 | | | | | 9 | 8 | | 10 | 5 | 11 |
| 27 | 7 Jan | Crystal P | 1-1 | 6438 | Plant | 1 | | | 6 | | 4 | 3 | | 7 | | 2 | | | | | 9 | 8 | | 10 | 5 | 11 |
| 28 | 14 | Brentford | 2-2 | 8500 | McCurley, P.Wright | 1 | | | 6 | | 4 | 3 | | 7 | | 2 | | | | | 9 | 8 | | 10 | 5 | 11 |
| 29 | 21 | WATFORD | 4-1 | 7699 | Grice, McCurley, Plant, P.Wright | 1 | | | 6 | | 4 | 3 | 5 | 7 | | 2 | | | | | 9 | 8 | | 10 | | 11 |
| 30 | 28 | SHREWSBURY | 2-0 | 5679 | Grice, McCurley | | 1 | | 6 | | 4 | 3 | 5 | 7 | | 2 | | | | | 9 | 8 | | 10 | | 11 |
| 31 | 11 Feb | MILLWALL | 1-2 | 4811 | McLeod | | 1 | | 6 | | 4 | 3 | 5 | 7 | | 2 | | | | | 9 | 8 | | 10 | | 11 |
| 32 | 18 | TORQUAY | 3-2 | 6906 | Plant(3) | 1 | | | 6 | | 4 | 3 | | 7 | | 2 | | | | | 9 | 8 | | 10 | 5 | 11 |
| 33 | 25 | Newport | 0-0 | 5588 | | 1 | | | 6 | | | 3 | | 7 | | 2 | 4 | | | | 9 | 8 | | 10 | 5 | 11 |
| 34 | 27 | Reading | 3-1 | 4667 | Dale, McCurley, P.Wright | 1 | | | 6 | | 4 | 3 | | 7 | | 2 | | | | | 9 | 8 | | 10 | 5 | 11 |
| 35 | 3 Mar | SWINDON | 5-0 | 6836 | Dale, Fisher, Plant(3) | 1 | | | 6 | | 4 | 3 | | 7 | | 2 | | | | | 9 | 8 | | 10 | 5 | 11 |
| 36 | 10 | Q.P.R. | 2-6 | 7905 | McCurley, P.Wright | 1 | | | 6 | | 4 | 3 | | 7 | | 2 | | | | | 9 | 8 | | 10 | 5 | 11 |
| 37 | 17 | NORTHAMPTON | 2-0 | 8333 | McCurley, Plant | 1 | | | 6 | | 4 | 3 | | 7 | | 2 | | | | | 9 | 8 | | 10 | 5 | 11 |
| 38 | 24 | Aldershot | 0-1 | 3874 | | 1 | | | 6 | 7 | 4 | 3 | | | | 2 | | | | | 9 | 8 | | 10 | 5 | 11 |
| 39 | 30 | WALSALL | 1-1 | 9130 | McCurley | 1 | | | 6 | 7 | 4 | 3 | | | | 2 | | | | | 9 | 8 | | 10 | 5 | 11 |
| 40 | 31 | CRYSTAL P | 2-4 | 7397 | Fenton, Hill.B | 1 | | | 6 | | 4 | 3 | 5 | | | 2 | 7 | | | | 9 | 8 | | 10 | | 11 |
| 41 | 2 Apr | Walsall | 0-0 | 15179 | | 1 | | 7 | 6 | 8 | 4 | 2 | 3 | | | | | 10 | | | 9 | | | | 5 | 11 |
| 42 | 7 | Brighton | 0-2 | 17364 | | 1 | | 7 | 6 | 8 | | 2 | 3 | | | | 4 | 10 | | | 9 | | | | 5 | 11 |
| 43 | 14 | SOUTHAMPTON | 3-2 | 5560 | Hill.R, McCurley(2) | 1 | | 7 | 6 | | | 2 | 3 | | | | 4 | 10 | | | 9 | | | 8 | 5 | 11 |
| 44 | 21 | Shrewsbury | 1-2 | 6976 | O.G. | 1 | | | 6 | 7 | | 2 | 3 | | | | 4 | | | | 9 | 8 | | 10 | 5 | 11 |
| 45 | 25 | Gillingham | 1-2 | 5622 | Plant | 1 | | | 6 | 8 | | 2 | 3 | | | | 4 | 10 | | | 9 | | | 7 | 5 | 11 |
| 46 | 28 | NORWICH | 3-2 | 8004 | McCurley(2), P.Wright | 1 | | 7 | 6 | | | 3 | | | | 2 | 4 | | | | 9 | 8 | | 10 | 5 | 11 |

# F.A.Cup

| | | | | | | | | | | | | | | | | | | | | | | | | | | |
|---|---|---|---|---|---|---|---|---|---|---|---|---|---|---|---|---|---|---|---|---|---|---|---|---|---|---|
| 1st | 19 Nov | Torquay | 0-2 | 8823 | | 1 | | | 6 | | 4 | 3 | | 7 | | 2 | | | | | 9 | 8 | | 10 | 5 | 11 |

COLCHESTER UNITED F.C.

**BACK ROW** (*l. to r.*) **Fisher : Harrison : Fenton : Ames : Dale : Stewart.**
**FRONT ROW** (*l. to r.*) **Grice : MacLeod : McCurley : Plant : Wright.**

DIVISION III (SOUTH)

| | P | W | D | L | F | A | Pts. |
|---|---|---|---|---|---|---|---|
| Leyton O. | 46 | 29 | 8 | 9 | 106 | 49 | 66 |
| Brighton | 46 | 29 | 7 | 10 | 112 | 50 | 65 |
| Ipswich T. | 46 | 25 | 14 | 7 | 106 | 60 | 64 |
| Southend U. | 46 | 21 | 11 | 14 | 88 | 80 | 53 |
| Torquay U. | 46 | 20 | 12 | 14 | 86 | 63 | 52 |
| Brentford | 46 | 19 | 14 | 13 | 69 | 66 | 52 |
| Norwich C. | 46 | 19 | 13 | 14 | 86 | 82 | 51 |
| Coventry C. | 46 | 20 | 9 | 17 | 73 | 60 | 49 |
| Bournemouth | 46 | 19 | 10 | 17 | 63 | 51 | 48 |
| Gillingham | 46 | 19 | 10 | 17 | 69 | 71 | 48 |
| Northampton | 46 | 20 | 7 | 19 | 67 | 71 | 47 |
| Colchester U. | 46 | 18 | 11 | 17 | 76 | 81 | 47 |
| Shrewsbury T. | 46 | 17 | 12 | 17 | 69 | 66 | 46 |
| Southampton | 46 | 18 | 8 | 20 | 91 | 81 | 44 |
| Aldershot | 46 | 12 | 16 | 18 | 70 | 90 | 40 |
| Exeter City | 46 | 15 | 10 | 21 | 58 | 77 | 40 |
| Reading | 46 | 15 | 9 | 22 | 70 | 79 | 39 |
| Q.P.R. | 46 | 14 | 11 | 21 | 64 | 86 | 39 |
| Newport Co. | 46 | 15 | 9 | 22 | 58 | 79 | 39 |
| Walsall | 46 | 15 | 8 | 23 | 68 | 84 | 38 |
| Watford | 46 | 13 | 11 | 22 | 52 | 85 | 37 |
| Millwall | 46 | 15 | 6 | 25 | 83 | 100 | 36 |
| C. Palace | 46 | 12 | 10 | 24 | 54 | 83 | 34 |
| Swindon T. | 46 | 8 | 14 | 24 | 34 | 78 | 30 |

# SEASON 1956–57

## Division Three (South)

| No. | Date | Opposition | Res | Attend | Goalscorers | Ames | Barrell | Blake | Dale | Fenton | Fisher | Fowler | Harrison | Hill, Bert | Hill, Bobby | King | McCurley | McLeod | Milligan | Parker | Plant | Smith | Stewart | Williams | Wright P. |
|---|---|---|---|---|---|---|---|---|---|---|---|---|---|---|---|---|---|---|---|---|---|---|---|---|---|
| 1 | 18 Aug | SOUTHEND | 3-2 | 11454 | Barrell, McCurley, P.Wright | 1 | 7 | | 6 | 4 | 3 | | 2 | | | | 9 | | 5 | | 10 | 8 | | | 11 |
| 2 | 22 | Crystal P | 4-2 | 9400 | Plant, Smith(3) | 1 | 7 | | 6 | 4 | 3 | | 2 | | 10 | | | | 5 | | 9 | 8 | | | 11 |
| 3 | 25 | Northampton | 0-1 | 9869 | | 1 | | | 6 | | 2 | 3 | | 4 | 7 | | 9 | | 5 | | 10 | 8 | | | 11 |
| 4 | 27 | CRYSTAL P | 3-3 | 6979 | Fenton(pen), Fowler, Bobby Hill | 1 | | | 6 | 4 | 2 | 3 | | | 7 | 9 | | | 5 | | 10 | 8 | | | 11 |
| 5 | 1 Sep | Q.P.R. | 1-1 | 8179 | Plant | 1 | | | 6 | 4 | 2 | 3 | | | | 9 | | 7 | 5 | | 10 | 8 | | | 11 |
| 6 | 5 | Southampton | 1-2 | 11000 | Plant | 1 | | | 6 | 4 | 3 | | 2 | | 7 | | 9 | | 5 | | 8 | 10 | | | 11 |
| 7 | 8 | Plymouth | 3-2 | 10000 | Smith, P.Wright | 1 | | | 6 | | 5 | 3 | | 4 | 7 | | 9 | | 2 | | 8 | 10 | | | 11 |
| 8 | 10 | SOUTHAMPTON | 3-1 | 7208 | McCurley, Plant, Smith | 1 | | | 6 | 4 | 5 | 3 | | | 7 | | 9 | | 2 | | 8 | 10 | | | 11 |
| 9 | 15 | READING | 3-2 | 8908 | Dale, Fenton(pen), Plant | 1 | | | 6 | 4 | 2 | 3 | | | 7 | | 9 | | 5 | | 8 | 10 | | | 11 |
| 10 | 19 | Eseter | 2-0 | 8360 | Plant, Smith | 1 | | | 6 | 4 | 2 | 3 | | | 7 | | 9 | | 5 | | 8 | 10 | | | 11 |
| 11 | 22 | Newport | 0-1 | 12426 | | 1 | | | 6 | | 2 | 3 | | 4 | 7 | | 9 | | 5 | | 8 | 10 | | | 11 |
| 12 | 24 | EXETER | 4-0 | 6754 | Fenton, McCurley, Plant(2) | 1 | | | 6 | 4 | 2 | 3 | | | 7 | | 9 | | 5 | | 8 | 10 | | | 11 |
| 13 | 29 | SHREWSBURY | 6-0 | 9784 | Fisher, McCurley(3), Plant(2) | 1 | | | 6 | 4 | 2 | 3 | | | 7 | | 9 | | 5 | | 8 | 10 | | | 11 |
| 14 | 6 Oct | Ipswich | 1-3 | 20431 | Plant | 1 | | | 6 | 4 | 2 | 3 | | | 7 | | 9 | | 5 | | 8 | 10 | | | 11 |
| 15 | 13 | BOURNEMOUTH | 3-0 | 9363 | McCurley, Plant, Smith | 1 | | | 6 | 4 | 2 | 3 | | | 7 | | 9 | | 5 | | 8 | 10 | | | 11 |
| 16 | 20 | Torquay | 2-4 | 8753 | Dale, Bobby Hill | 1 | | | 6 | 4 | 2 | 3 | | | 7 | | 9 | | 5 | | 8 | 10 | | | 11 |
| 17 | 27 | MILLWALL | 2-1 | 9548 | McCurley, P.Wright | 1 | | | 6 | 4 | 2 | 3 | | | 7 | | 9 | | 5 | | 8 | 10 | | | 11 |
| 18 | 3 Nov | Brighton | 0-0 | 13601 | | 1 | 11 | | 6 | 4 | | 3 | | | 7 | | 9 | | 2 | | 8 | 10 | 5 | | |
| 19 | 10 | GILLINGHAM | 0-0 | 8891 | | 1 | | | 6 | 4 | 2 | 3 | | | 7 | | 9 | | 5 | | 8 | 10 | | | 11 |
| 20 | 24 | BRENTFORD | 1-0 | 7290 | Bobby Hill | 1 | | | 6 | 4 | 2 | 3 | | | 10 | | 9 | | 5 | | 8 | | | 7 | 11 |
| 21 | 1 Dec | Aldershot | 1-2 | 4416 | Bobby Hill | 1 | | | 6 | 4 | 2 | 3 | | | 10 | | 9 | | 5 | | 8 | | | 7 | 11 |
| 22 | 15 | Southend | 2-3 | 7500 | Milligan, Plant | 1 | | | 6 | 4 | 2 | 3 | | | | | 9 | | 5 | | 8 | 10 | | 7 | 11 |
| 23 | 22 | NORTHAMPTON | 5-1 | 5899 | McLeod(2), Smith, P.Wright(2) | 1 | | | 6 | 4 | 2 | 3 | | | | | | 8 | 5 | | 10 | 9 | | 7 | 11 |
| 24 | 25 | NORWICH | 1-1 | 6376 | Plant | 1 | | | 6 | 4 | | | | | | | | 8 | | | 10 | | | 7 | 11 |
| 25 | 26 | Norwich | 2-1 | 8462 | King, Williams | 1 | | | 6 | | | | | 4 | 8 | 9 | | | | | | 9 | 5 | 7 | |
| 26 | 29 | Q.p.r. | 1-1 | 8760 | Fisher(pen) | 1 | 11 | | 6 | | 2 | 3 | | 4 | 8 | | | | 5 | | 10 | 9 | | 7 | |
| 27 | 5 Jan | COVENTRY | 3-2 | 7302 | Bobby Hill, Plant, P.Wright | 1 | | | 6 | | 2 | 3 | | 4 | 8 | | | | 5 | | 10 | 9 | | 7 | 11 |
| 28 | 12 | PLYMOUTH | 2-1 | 7732 | Plant, Williams | 1 | | | 6 | 4 | 2 | 3 | | | 8 | | | | 5 | | 10 | 9 | | 7 | 11 |
| 29 | 19 | Reading | 3-0 | 9502 | Smith(3) | 1 | | | 6 | 4 | 2 | 3 | | | 8 | | | | 5 | | 10 | 9 | | 7 | 11 |
| 30 | 26 | Coventry | 4-2 | 14834 | Fenton, Plant, Smith, P.Wright | 1 | | | 6 | 4 | 2 | 3 | | | 8 | | | | 5 | | 10 | | | 7 | 11 |
| 31 | 2 Feb | NEWPORT | 1-0 | 9700 | Bobby Hill | 1 | | | 6 | | 2 | 3 | | 4 | 8 | | | | 5 | | 10 | | | 7 | 11 |
| 32 | 9 | Shrewsbury | 3-1 | 11151 | Plant(2), Williams | 1 | | | 6 | 4 | 2 | 3 | | | 8 | | 9 | | 5 | | 10 | | | 7 | 11 |
| 33 | 16 | IPSWICH | 0-0 | 18559 | | 1 | | | 6 | 4 | 2 | 3 | | | 8 | | 9 | | 5 | | 10 | 9 | | 7 | 11 |
| 34 | 23 | Bournemouth | 1-1 | 21239 | Fenton | 1 | | | | 4 | 2 | 3 | | 6 | 8 | | 9 | | 5 | | 10 | 9 | | 7 | 11 |
| 35 | 2 Mar | TORQUAY | 2-1 | 12555 | Plant(2) | 1 | | | | 4 | 2 | 3 | | 6 | 8 | | | | 5 | | 10 | 10 | | 7 | 11 |
| 36 | 9 | Watford | 0-0 | 10434 | | 1 | | | | 4 | 2 | 3 | | 6 | 8 | | | | | | 10 | 10 | 5 | 7 | 11 |
| 37 | 16 | BRIGHTON | 0-0 | 10459 | | 1 | | | | 4 | 2 | 3 | | 6 | | | 9 | | | | 8 | 10 | 5 | 7 | 11 |
| 38 | 23 | Gillingham | 2-1 | 9981 | Plant, O.G. | 1 | | | | 4 | 2 | 3 | | 6 | | | 9 | | | | 8 | | 5 | 7 | 11 |
| 39 | 30 | SWINDON | 1-1 | 9275 | P.Wright | 1 | | | | 4 | 2 | 3 | | 6 | | | 9 | | | | 8 | | 5 | 7 | 11 |
| 40 | 6 Apr | Brentford | 1-1 | 12869 | Fenton | 1 | | | | 4 | 2 | 3 | | 6 | 10 | | 9 | | | | 8 | | 5 | 7 | 11 |
| 41 | 13 | ALDERSHOT | 1-1 | 8975 | Fenton(pen) | 1 | | | | 4 | 2 | 3 | | | 7 | | 9 | 8 | | 6 | 10 | 10 | 5 | | 11 |
| 42 | 19 | WALSALL | 2-1 | 12770 | Fenton(pen), Bobby Hill | 1 | | 7 | | 4 | 2 | 3 | | | 10 | | 9 | | | 6 | 8 | 8 | 5 | | 11 |
| 43 | 20 | Millwall | 1-3 | 14273 | Plant | 1 | | | | 4 | 2 | 3 | | | 7 | | 9 | | | 6 | 8 | | 5 | | 11 |
| 44 | 22 | Walsall | 1-2 | 9400 | Smith | 1 | | 7 | | 4 | 2 | 3 | | | 10 | | | | | 6 | 9 | | 5 | | 11 |
| 45 | 27 | Swindon | 1-4 | 9600 | Plant | 1 | | | | 4 | 2 | 3 | | | 10 | | 9 | | | 6 | 8 | | 5 | 7 | 11 |
| 46 | 29 | WATFORD | 2-0 | 9226 | Bert Hill, McCurley | 1 | | | | | 2 | 3 | | 4 | 10 | | 9 | | | 6 | 8 | | 5 | 7 | 11 |

# F.A.Cup

| 1st | 17 Nov | SOUTHEND | 1-4 | 11280 | McCurley | 1 | | | 6 | 4 | 2 | 3 | | | 7 | | 9 | | 5 | | 8 | 10 | | | 11 |
|---|---|---|---|---|---|---|---|---|---|---|---|---|---|---|---|---|---|---|---|---|---|---|---|---|---|

COLCHESTER UNITED
Football Supporters' Club
Annual

An Incident during the Match between Colchester United and Coventry last December

Official Handbook, 1956-57

PRICE - SIXPENCE

| | P | W | D | L | F | A | Pts. |
|---|---|---|---|---|---|---|---|
| Ipswich T. | 46 | 25 | 9 | 12 | 101 | 54 | 59 |
| Torquay U. | 46 | 24 | 11 | 11 | 89 | 64 | 59 |
| Colchester U. | 46 | 22 | 14 | 10 | 84 | 56 | 58 |
| Southampton | 46 | 22 | 10 | 14 | 76 | 52 | 54 |
| Bournemouth | 46 | 19 | 14 | 13 | 88 | 62 | 52 |
| Brighton | 46 | 19 | 14 | 13 | 86 | 65 | 52 |
| Southend U. | 46 | 18 | 12 | 16 | 73 | 65 | 48 |
| Brentford | 46 | 16 | 16 | 14 | 78 | 76 | 48 |
| Shrewsbury T. | 46 | 15 | 18 | 13 | 72 | 79 | 48 |
| Q.P.R. | 46 | 18 | 11 | 17 | 61 | 60 | 47 |
| Watford | 46 | 18 | 10 | 18 | 72 | 75 | 46 |
| Newport Co. | 46 | 16 | 13 | 17 | 65 | 62 | 45 |
| Reading | 46 | 18 | 9 | 19 | 80 | 81 | 45 |
| Northampton | 46 | 18 | 9 | 19 | 66 | 73 | 45 |
| Walsall | 46 | 16 | 12 | 18 | 80 | 74 | 44 |
| Coventry C. | 46 | 16 | 12 | 18 | 74 | 84 | 44 |
| Millwall | 46 | 16 | 12 | 18 | 64 | 84 | 44 |
| Plymouth Arg. | 46 | 16 | 11 | 19 | 68 | 73 | 43 |
| Aldershot | 46 | 15 | 12 | 19 | 79 | 92 | 42 |
| C. Palace | 46 | 11 | 18 | 17 | 62 | 75 | 40 |
| Exeter C. | 46 | 12 | 13 | 21 | 61 | 79 | 37 |
| Gillingham | 46 | 12 | 13 | 21 | 54 | 85 | 37 |
| Swindon T. | 46 | 15 | 6 | 25 | 66 | 96 | 36 |
| Norwich C. | 46 | 8 | 15 | 23 | 61 | 94 | 31 |

# SEASON 1957–58 Division Three (South)

| No. | Date | Opposition | Res | Attend | Goalscorers | Ames | Blake | Dobson | Evans | Fenton | Fisher | Fowler | Harris | Hill.Bert | Hill.Bob | Hunt.R.M | Langman | McCurley | McLeod | McNeill | Milligan | Parker | Plant | Rumney | Williams | Wright.P |
|---|---|---|---|---|---|---|---|---|---|---|---|---|---|---|---|---|---|---|---|---|---|---|---|---|---|---|
| 1 | 24 Aug | TORQUAY | 3-0 | 9760 | McCurley(pen), P.Wright(2) | 1 | | | | | 2 | 3 | 6 | | | | | 9 | 8 | | 5 | 4 | 10 | | 7 | 11 |
| 2 | 26 | Q.p.r. | 0-1 | 12135 | | 1 | | | | | 2 | 3 | 6 | | | | | 9 | 8 | | 5 | 4 | 10 | | 7 | 11 |
| 3 | 31 | Brentford | 3-3 | 12730 | Parker, P.Wright(2) | 1 | | | | | 2 | 3 | 6 | | | | | 9 | 8 | | 5 | 4 | 10 | | 7 | 11 |
| 4 | 2 Sep | Q.P.R. | 2-1 | 8992 | McCurley, P.Wright | 1 | 7 | | | | 5 | 3 | 6 | | 8 | | | 9 | | | | 4 | 10 | 2 | | 11 |
| 5 | 7 | Southend | 3-2 | 19000 | McCurley(pen), Plant, P.Wright | 1 | | | | | 5 | 3 | 6 | | | | | 9 | 8 | | | 4 | 10 | 2 | 7 | 11 |
| 6 | 9 | READING | 1-3 | 8774 | McCurley | 1 | | | | | 5 | 3 | 6 | | | | | 9 | 8 | | | 4 | 10 | 2 | 7 | 11 |
| 7 | 14 | NORWICH | 1-2 | 11077 | McCurley | 1 | | | | | 2 | 3 | | 6 | 8 | | | 9 | | | 5 | 4 | 10 | | 7 | 11 |
| 8 | 18 | Reading | 0-7 | 13811 | | 1 | | | | | 2 | 3 | | 6 | 8 | | | 9 | | | 5 | 4 | 10 | | 7 | 11 |
| 9 | 21 | Bournemouth | 1-1 | 16057 | McNeill | 1 | 7 | | | 6 | 2 | 3 | | | | | | 9 | 8 | 10 | 5 | 4 | | | | 11 |
| 10 | 26 | Northampton | 1-4 | 4000 | Plant | 1 | 7 | | | 6 | 2 | 3 | | | | | | 9 | | 10 | 5 | 4 | 8 | | | 11 |
| 11 | 28 | WALSALL | 1-1 | 7366 | P.Wright | 1 | | | | | 2 | 3 | | 4 | | | | 9 | 10 | | 5 | 6 | 8 | | 7 | 11 |
| 12 | 30 | NORTHAMPTON | 1-0 | 4391 | P.Wright | 1 | | 5 | | 6 | 2 | 3 | | 4 | 10 | | | 9 | | | | | 8 | | 7 | 11 |
| 13 | 5 Oct | Coventry | 0-1 | 14423 | | 1 | | | | | 2 | 11 | 5 | 4 | 10 | | | 9 | | | | 6 | 8 | 3 | 7 | |
| 14 | 9 | Plymouth | 1-1 | 22250 | McLeod | 1 | | | | 6 | 2 | 3 | | 4 | | | | 9 | 10 | | 5 | | 8 | | 7 | 11 |
| 15 | 12 | EXETER | 3-0 | 7930 | McCurley, Plant(2) | 1 | | | | | 2 | 3 | | 4 | 7 | | | 9 | 10 | | 5 | 6 | 8 | | | 11 |
| 16 | 15 | Watford | 1-1 | 6580 | P.Wright | 1 | 7 | | | | 2 | 3 | | 4 | | | | 9 | 10 | | 5 | 6 | 8 | | | 11 |
| 17 | 19 | Gillingham | 3-2 | 8000 | McCurley(2), Williams | 1 | | | | 10 | 2 | 3 | | 4 | | | | 9 | | | 5 | 6 | 8 | | 7 | 11 |
| 18 | 26 | MILLWALL | 2-1 | 9260 | Plant, P.Wright | 1 | | | | 6 | 2 | 3 | | 4 | | | | 9 | 10 | | 5 | | 8 | | 7 | 11 |
| 19 | 2 Nov | Swindon | 0-4 | 14198 | | 1 | | | | | 2 | 3 | | 4 | | | | 9 | 10 | | 5 | 6 | 8 | | 7 | 11 |
| 20 | 9 | ALDERSHOT | 1-1 | 7569 | Fenton | 1 | | | | 6 | 2 | 3 | | | | | | 9 | 10 | | 5 | 4 | 8 | | 7 | 11 |
| 21 | 23 | PORT VALE | 2-1 | 9106 | Plant, Williams | 1 | | | 10 | 6 | 2 | 3 | | 4 | | | 9 | | | | 5 | | 8 | | 7 | 11 |
| 22 | 30 | Newport | 2-2 | 9000 | Langman, Plant | 1 | | | 10 | 6 | 2 | 3 | | 4 | | | 9 | | | | 5 | | 8 | | 7 | 11 |
| 23 | 14 Dec | Brighton | 2-5 | 9716 | Fisher(pen), Williams | 1 | | | 10 | | 2 | 3 | | 4 | | | 9 | | | | 5 | 6 | 8 | | 7 | 11 |
| 24 | 21 | Torquay | 3-1 | 5749 | Evans, P.Wright(2) | 1 | | | 10 | | 2 | 3 | | 4 | | | 9 | | | | 5 | 6 | 8 | | 7 | 11 |
| 25 | 26 | WATFORD | 4-0 | 9379 | Langman, Plant(3) | 1 | | | 10 | | 2 | 3 | | 4 | 7 | | 9 | | | | 5 | 6 | 8 | | | 11 |
| 26 | 28 | BRENTFORD | 1-1 | 9548 | Langman | 1 | | | 10 | | 2 | 3 | | 4 | 7 | | 9 | | | | 5 | 6 | 8 | | | 11 |
| 27 | 4 Jan | Shrewsbury | 0-0 | 5600 | | 1 | | 5 | 10 | 6 | 2 | 3 | | 4 | 7 | | 9 | | | | | | 8 | | | 11 |
| 28 | 11 | SOUTHEND | 1-0 | 9357 | Williams | 1 | | | 10 | 6 | | 3 | | 4 | | | 9 | | | | 5 | | 8 | | 7 | 11 |
| 29 | 18 | Norwich | 1-1 | 17523 | Plant | 1 | | | 10 | 6 | 2 | 3 | | 4 | | | 9 | | | | 5 | | 8 | | 7 | 11 |
| 30 | 1 Feb | BOURNEMOUTH | 3-2 | 8091 | Evans(2), Williams | 1 | | | 10 | 6 | 2 | 3 | | | | | 9 | | | | 5 | 4 | 8 | | 7 | 11 |
| 31 | 8 | Walsall | 0-3 | 7639 | | 1 | | | 10 | 6 | 2 | 3 | | 4 | | | 9 | | | | 5 | | 8 | | 7 | 11 |
| 32 | 15 | COVENTRY | 4-1 | 8613 | Fenton(2 both pen), Plant(2) | 1 | | 5 | 10 | 6 | 2 | 3 | | 4 | | | 9 | | | | | | 8 | | 7 | 11 |
| 33 | 22 | Exeter | 3-4 | 7636 | Evans, Langman, Plant | 1 | | 5 | 10 | 6 | 2 | 3 | | 4 | | | 9 | | | | | | 8 | | 7 | 11 |
| 34 | 1 Mar | GILLINGHAM | 3-2 | 8158 | Langman, Plant(2) | 1 | | 5 | 10 | 6 | 2 | 3 | | 4 | | | 9 | | | | | | 8 | | 7 | 11 |
| 35 | 8 | Millwall | 4-1 | 7307 | Langman, Plant, P.Wright(2) | 1 | | 5 | 10 | | 2 | 3 | | 4 | | | 9 | | | | | 6 | 8 | | 7 | 11 |
| 36 | 15 | SWINDON | 1-3 | 9241 | Langman | 1 | | | 10 | 6 | 2 | 3 | | 4 | | | 9 | | | | 5 | | 8 | | 7 | 11 |
| 37 | 22 | Port Vale | 0-2 | 7161 | | 1 | | 5 | 10 | | | 3 | | 4 | 7 | | 9 | | | | | 6 | 8 | | | 11 |
| 38 | 29 | BRIGHTON | 1-2 | 8751 | Evans | 1 | | 5 | 10 | 4 | 2 | 3 | | | 7 | | 9 | | | | | 6 | 8 | | | 11 |
| 39 | 4 Apr | Crystal P | 1-1 | 17787 | Plant | 1 | | 5 | 10 | | 2 | 3 | | 4 | | | 8 | 9 | | | | | 7 | | | 11 |
| 40 | 7 | CRYSTAL P | 1-1 | 9528 | Evans | 1 | | 5 | 10 | 4 | 2 | 3 | | | | | 8 | 9 | | | | 6 | 7 | | | 11 |
| 41 | 12 | NEWPORT | 1-1 | 7472 | Langman | 1 | | 5 | 10 | 4 | 2 | 3 | | | | | 9 | 7 | | | | 6 | 8 | | | 11 |
| 42 | 16 | Aldershot | 1-2 | 2630 | Plant | 1 | | 5 | 10 | 4 | 2 | 3 | | | | | 9 | 7 | | | | 6 | 8 | | | 11 |
| 43 | 19 | Southampton | 2-3 | 13842 | McCurley(2) | 1 | 7 | 5 | | | 2 | 3 | | 4 | | 6 | | 9 | 8 | | | | 10 | | | 11 |
| 44 | 21 | SHREWSBURY | 3-0 | 7092 | Evans, McCurley, P.Wright | 1 | 7 | 5 | 8 | | 2 | 3 | | 4 | | 6 | | 9 | | | | | 10 | | | 11 |
| 45 | 26 | PLYMOUTH | 1-2 | 8599 | Blake | 1 | 7 | 5 | 8 | | 2 | 3 | | 4 | | 6 | | 9 | | | | | 10 | | | 11 |
| 46 | 1 May | SOUTHAMPTON | 4-2 | 8914 | Blake, McCurley, McLeod, P.Wright | 1 | 7 | 5 | | 4 | 2 | 3 | | | | 6 | 10 | 9 | 8 | | | | | | | 11 |

# F.A.Cup

| 1st | 16 Nov | Wisbech | 0-1 | 9552 | | 1 | | 5 | | | 3 | | | 4 | | | | 9 | 10 | | 2 | 6 | 8 | | 7 | 11 |
|---|---|---|---|---|---|---|---|---|---|---|---|---|---|---|---|---|---|---|---|---|---|---|---|---|---|---|

Ken Plant (left) and Kevin McCurley (right) out training with manager Benny Fenton.

DIVISION III (SOUTH)

| | P | W | D | L | F | A | Pts. |
|---|---|---|---|---|---|---|---|
| Brighton | 46 | 24 | 12 | 10 | 88 | 64 | 60 |
| Brentford | 46 | 24 | 10 | 12 | 82 | 56 | 58 |
| Plymouth Arg. | 46 | 25 | 8 | 13 | 67 | 48 | 58 |
| Swindon T. | 46 | 21 | 15 | 10 | 79 | 50 | 57 |
| Reading | 46 | 21 | 13 | 12 | 79 | 51 | 55 |
| Southampton | 46 | 22 | 10 | 14 | 112 | 72 | 54 |
| Southend U. | 46 | 21 | 12 | 13 | 90 | 58 | 54 |
| Norwich C. | 46 | 19 | 15 | 12 | 75 | 70 | 53 |
| Bournemouth | 46 | 21 | 9 | 16 | 81 | 74 | 51 |
| Q.P.R. | 46 | 18 | 14 | 14 | 64 | 65 | 50 |
| Newport Co. | 46 | 17 | 14 | 15 | 73 | 67 | 48 |
| Colchester U. | 46 | 17 | 13 | 16 | 77 | 79 | 47 |
| Northampton | 46 | 19 | 6 | 21 | 87 | 79 | 44 |
| C. Palace | 46 | 15 | 13 | 18 | 70 | 72 | 43 |
| Port Vale | 46 | 16 | 10 | 20 | 67 | 58 | 42 |
| Watford | 46 | 13 | 16 | 17 | 59 | 77 | 42 |
| Shrewsbury T. | 46 | 15 | 10 | 21 | 49 | 71 | 40 |
| Aldershot | 46 | 12 | 16 | 18 | 59 | 89 | 40 |
| Coventry C. | 46 | 13 | 13 | 20 | 61 | 81 | 39 |
| Walsall | 46 | 14 | 9 | 23 | 61 | 75 | 37 |
| Torquay U. | 46 | 11 | 13 | 22 | 49 | 74 | 35 |
| Gillingham | 46 | 13 | 9 | 24 | 52 | 81 | 35 |
| Millwall | 46 | 11 | 9 | 26 | 63 | 91 | 31 |
| Exeter C. | 46 | 11 | 9 | 26 | 57 | 99 | 31 |

# SEASON 1958-59 Division Three

| No. | Date | Opposition | Res | Attend | Goalscorers | Ames | Blake | Evans | Fisher | Fowler | Hammond | Harris | Hill.R | Hunt.R.H | Johnstone | King | Langman | McLeod | Marshall | McCurley | Milligan | Parker | Plant | Williams | Wright.P |
|---|---|---|---|---|---|---|---|---|---|---|---|---|---|---|---|---|---|---|---|---|---|---|---|---|---|
| 1 | 23 Aug | BURY | 1-3 | 9394 | Langman | 1 | | | 2 | 3 | 6 | | | | | 9 | 10 | | | | 5 | 4 | 8 | 7 | 11 |
| 2 | 25 | NORWICH | 2-1 | 9379 | Blake(2) | 1 | 7 | | 2 | 3 | | | | 6 | | 9 | 10 | 8 | | | 5 | 4 | | | 11 |
| 3 | 30 | Q.p.r. | 2-4 | 9733 | Langman(2) | 1 | 7 | | 2 | 3 | | | | 6 | | 9 | 10 | 8 | | | 5 | 4 | | | 11 |
| 4 | 3 Sep | Norwich | 2-1 | 25132 | Evans, Langman | 1 | | 10 | 2 | 3 | | | | 6 | | | 9 | 8 | | | 5 | 4 | | 7 | 11 |
| 5 | 6 | ROCHDALE | 2-1 | 8141 | Langman,McLeod | 1 | | 10 | 2 | 3 | | | | 6 | | | 9 | 8 | | | 5 | 4 | | 7 | 11 |
| 6 | 8 | ACCRINGTON | 1-0 | 7380 | Langman | 1 | | 10 | 2 | 3 | | | | 6 | | | 9 | 8 | | | 5 | 4 | | 7 | 11 |
| 7 | 17 | Accrington | 1-1 | 8350 | O.G. | 1 | | 10 | 2 | 3 | | | | 6 | | | 9 | 8 | | | 5 | 4 | | 7 | 11 |
| 8 | 20 | PLYMOUTH | 2-0 | 10033 | Evans(2)(1pen) | 1 | | 10 | 2 | 3 | | | | 6 | | | 9 | 8 | | | 5 | 4 | | 7 | 11 |
| 9 | 24 | Southend | 1-1 | 12000 | Langman | 1 | | 10 | 2 | 3 | | | | 6 | | | 9 | 8 | | | 5 | 4 | | 7 | 11 |
| 10 | 27 | Tranmere | 3-3 | 14000 | McLeod(2), O.G. | 1 | | 10 | 2 | 3 | | | | 6 | | | 9 | 8 | | | 5 | 4 | | 7 | 11 |
| 11 | 29 | SOUTHEND | 0-1 | 6833 | | 1 | 7 | 10 | 2 | 3 | 6 | | | | | | 9 | 8 | | | 5 | 4 | | | 11 |
| 12 | 4 Oct | STOCKPORT | 8-2 | 8298 | Fisher(3), Langman(2), McLeod(3) | 1 | 7 | 10 | 2 | 3 | 6 | | | | | | 9 | 8 | | | 5 | 4 | | | 11 |
| 13 | 8 | Reading | 0-0 | 17401 | | 1 | 7 | 10 | | 3 | 6 | | | | | | 9 | 8 | 2 | | 5 | 4 | | | 11 |
| 14 | 11 | WREXHAM | 1-1 | 9204 | Evans | 1 | 7 | 10 | | 3 | 6 | | | | | | 9 | 8 | 2 | | 5 | 4 | | | 11 |
| 15 | 16 | Doncaster | 1-2 | 2786 | Blake | 1 | 7 | 10 | | 3 | 6 | | | | | | 9 | 8 | 2 | | 5 | 4 | | | 11 |
| 16 | 18 | Bradford | 3-1 | 12307 | Langman, Plant(2) | 1 | 7 | | | 3 | 4 | | | 6 | | | 9 | 8 | 2 | | 5 | | 10 | | 11 |
| 17 | 25 | HULL | 1-3 | 9277 | McCurley | 1 | 7 | | | 3 | 4 | | | 6 | | | | 8 | 2 | 9 | 5 | | 10 | | 11 |
| 18 | 1 Nov | Brentford | 1-2 | 11930 | Langman | 1 | 7 | | 2 | 3 | 6 | | | | | | 9 | 8 | | | 5 | 4 | 10 | | 11 |
| 19 | 8 | SWINDON | 1-0 | 8001 | Plant | 1 | 7 | | 2 | 3 | 6 | | | | | | 9 | 8 | 5 | | | 4 | 10 | | 11 |
| 20 | 22 | NEWPORT | 3-2 | 7271 | Blake, P.Wright | 1 | 7 | | 2 | 3 | | | | 6 | | | 9 | 8 | | | 5 | 4 | 10 | | 11 |
| 21 | 29 | Chesterfield | 2-2 | 7140 | P.Wright(2) | 1 | 7 | 4 | 2 | 3 | | | | 6 | | | 9 | 8 | | | 5 | | 10 | | 11 |
| 22 | 20 Dec | Bury | 0-0 | 11615 | | 1 | | 10 | 2 | 3 | 6 | | | | | | 9 | 8 | | | 5 | 4 | | 7 | 11 |
| 23 | 26 | BOURNEMOUTH | 3-1 | 9182 | Langman, McLeod, Williams | 1 | | 10 | 2 | 3 | 6 | | | | | | 9 | 8 | | | 5 | 4 | | 7 | 11 |
| 24 | 27 | Bournemouth | 1-1 | 12404 | Williams | 1 | | 10 | 2 | 3 | 6 | | | | | | 9 | 8 | | | 5 | 4 | | 7 | 11 |
| 25 | 3 Jan | Q.P.R. | 3-0 | 8719 | Evans, Fisher, Langman | 1 | 7 | 10 | 2 | 3 | 6 | | | | | | 9 | 8 | | | 5 | 4 | | | 11 |
| 26 | 31 | DONCASTER | 1-0 | 8658 | Langman | 1 | | 10 | 2 | 3 | 6 | | | | | | 9 | 8 | | | 5 | 4 | | 7 | 11 |
| 27 | 2 Feb | Mansfield | 2-3 | 5155 | R.Hill, McCurley | 1 | | | 2 | 3 | | | 8 | 6 | | | 9 | | | 10 | 5 | 4 | | 7 | 11 |
| 28 | 7 | Plymouth | 1-1 | 22686 | Evans | 1 | | 10 | | 3 | 6 | | 8 | | | | 9 | | 2 | | 5 | 4 | | 7 | 11 |
| 29 | 14 | TRANMERE | 1-1 | 7160 | O.G. | 1 | | 10 | | 3 | 6 | | | | | | 9 | 8 | 2 | | 5 | 4 | | 7 | 11 |
| 30 | 21 | Stockport | 1-0 | 5734 | Williams | 1 | | 10 | | 3 | 6 | | | | | | 9 | 8 | 2 | | 5 | 4 | | 7 | 11 |
| 31 | 23 | NOTTS COUNTY | 4-1 | 4406 | Langman(2), McCurley, P.Wright | 1 | | 10 | | 3 | 6 | | | | | | 8 | | 2 | 9 | 5 | 4 | | 7 | 11 |
| 32 | 28 | Wrexham | 0-2 | 8635 | | 1 | | | | 3 | 6 | | 8 | | | | 9 | 10 | 2 | | 5 | 4 | | 7 | 11 |
| 33 | 7 Mar | BRADFORD | 3-2 | 7139 | Langman, McCurley, Williams | 1 | | | | 3 | 6 | | | | | | 10 | 8 | 2 | 9 | 5 | 4 | | 7 | 11 |
| 34 | 14 | Hull | 0-3 | 16668 | | 1 | | | | 3 | 6 | | | | | | 10 | 8 | 2 | 9 | 5 | 4 | | 7 | 11 |
| 35 | 16 | Rochdale | 1-0 | 3510 | Langman | 1 | 11 | | | 3 | 4 | | | 6 | | | 9 | 8 | 2 | | 5 | | | 7 | 10 |
| 36 | 21 | BRENTFORD | 0-4 | 8775 | | 1 | 11 | | | 3 | 6 | | | | | | 9 | 8 | 2 | | 5 | 4 | | 7 | 10 |
| 37 | 27 | SOUTHAMPTON | 1-3 | 8943 | McCurley | 1 | | | | 3 | 4 | | | 6 | | | 10 | 8 | 2 | 9 | 5 | | | 7 | 11 |
| 38 | 28 | Swindon | 0-2 | 8976 | | 1 | 7 | | | 3 | 4 | | 8 | 6 | | | 9 | | 2 | | 5 | | | 10 | 11 |
| 39 | 30 | Southampton | 0-3 | 8502 | | 1 | 7 | | | 3 | 4 | | 8 | 6 | | | 9 | | 2 | | 5 | | | 10 | 11 |
| 40 | 4 Apr | MANSFIELD | 1-3 | 5901 | Milligan(pen) | 1 | | | | 3 | 4 | | 8 | 6 | | | 9 | 10 | 2 | | 5 | | | 7 | 11 |
| 41 | 18 | CHESTERFIELD | 1-0 | 5433 | Langman | 1 | 7 | | 2 | 3 | 6 | | 8 | | 10 | | 9 | | 5 | | | 4 | | | 11 |
| 42 | 20 | READING | 3-1 | 5590 | Evans(2)(1pen), McLeod | 1 | 7 | 10 | 2 | 3 | 6 | | | | | | 9 | 8 | | | 5 | 4 | | | 11 |
| 43 | 25 | Notts County | 1-0 | 4733 | Evans | 1 | 11 | 10 | 3 | | 6 | | 8 | | | | 9 | | 2 | | 5 | 4 | | 7 | |
| 44 | 27 | HALIFAX | 3-1 | 5769 | Blake, Evans(pen), Williams | 1 | 11 | 10 | 3 | | 6 | | | | | | 9 | 8 | 2 | | 5 | 4 | | 7 | |
| 45 | 30 | Halifax | 1-4 | 5458 | Evans | 1 | 11 | 10 | 3 | | | 6 | | | | | 9 | 8 | 2 | | 5 | 4 | | 7 | |
| 46 | 4 May | Newport | 1-0 | 4702 | P.Wright | 1 | 7 | 10 | 3 | | 6 | | | | | | | 8 | 2 | 9 | 5 | 4 | | | 11 |

# F.A.Cup

| | | | | | | | | | | | | | | | | | | | | | | | | | |
|---|---|---|---|---|---|---|---|---|---|---|---|---|---|---|---|---|---|---|---|---|---|---|---|---|---|
| 1st | 15 Nov | BATH | 2-0 | 10636 | Langman, Plant | 1 | 7 | | 2 | 3 | | | | 6 | | | 9 | 8 | | | 5 | 4 | 10 | | 11 |
| 2nd | 6 Dec | YEOVIL | 1-1 | 10890 | Plant | 1 | 7 | | 2 | 3 | | | | 6 | | | 9 | 8 | | | 5 | 4 | 10 | | 11 |
| 2ndR | 11 | Yeovil | 7-1 | 10000 | Langman(4), McLeod(2), Williams | 1 | | 10 | 2 | 3 | 6 | | | | | | 9 | 8 | | | 5 | 4 | | 7 | 11 |
| 3rd | 10 Jan | CHESTERFIELD | 2-0 | 9723 | Evans, Langman | 1 | 7 | 10 | 2 | 3 | 6 | | | | | | 9 | 8 | | | 5 | 4 | | | 11 |
| 4th | 24 | ARSENAL | 2-2 | 16000 | Evans, Langman | 1 | 7 | 10 | 2 | 3 | 6 | | | | | | 9 | 8 | | | 5 | 4 | | | 11 |
| 4th/R | 28 | Arsenal | 0-4 | 62686 | | 1 | 7 | 10 | 2 | 3 | 6 | | | | | | 9 | 8 | | | 5 | 4 | | | 11 |

COLCHESTER UNITED

Back row: N. Langman, R. Hunt, D. Parker, P. Ames, J. Wright, T. Williams, M. King, C. Hammond.
Centre row: Bill Light (Trainer), P. Wright, J. Roe, T. Harris, R. Blake, B. Dobson, A. Marshall, C. Milligan, I. Johnstone, J. Evans, Andy Brown (Asst. Trainer).
Front row: K. Plant, S. McLeod, A. Springett, A. Miller, Ben Fenton (Manager), J. Fowler, G. Fisher (Capt.), R. Hill, H. McNeil

| | P | W | D | L | F | A | Pts. |
|---|---|---|---|---|---|---|---|
| Plymouth Arg. | 46 | 23 | 16 | 7 | 89 | 59 | 62 |
| Hull C. | 46 | 26 | 9 | 11 | 90 | 55 | 61 |
| Brentford | 46 | 21 | 15 | 10 | 76 | 49 | 57 |
| Norwich C. | 46 | 22 | 13 | 11 | 89 | 62 | 57 |
| Colchester U. | 46 | 21 | 10 | 15 | 71 | 67 | 52 |
| Reading | 46 | 21 | 8 | 17 | 78 | 63 | 50 |
| Tranmere R. | 46 | 21 | 8 | 17 | 82 | 67 | 50 |
| Southend U. | 46 | 21 | 8 | 17 | 85 | 80 | 50 |
| Halifax T. | 46 | 21 | 8 | 17 | 80 | 77 | 50 |
| Bury | 46 | 17 | 14 | 15 | 69 | 58 | 48 |
| Bradford C. | 46 | 18 | 11 | 17 | 84 | 76 | 47 |
| Bournemouth | 46 | 17 | 12 | 17 | 69 | 69 | 46 |
| Q.P.R. | 46 | 19 | 8 | 19 | 74 | 77 | 46 |
| Southampton | 46 | 17 | 11 | 18 | 88 | 80 | 45 |
| Swindon T. | 46 | 16 | 13 | 17 | 59 | 57 | 45 |
| Chesterfield | 46 | 17 | 10 | 19 | 67 | 64 | 44 |
| Newport Co. | 46 | 17 | 9 | 20 | 69 | 68 | 43 |
| Wrexham | 46 | 14 | 14 | 18 | 63 | 77 | 42 |
| Accrington S. | 46 | 15 | 12 | 19 | 71 | 87 | 42 |
| Mansfield T. | 46 | 14 | 13 | 19 | 73 | 98 | 41 |
| Stockport Co. | 46 | 13 | 10 | 23 | 65 | 78 | 36 |
| Doncaster R. | 46 | 14 | 5 | 27 | 50 | 90 | 33 |
| Notts Co. | 46 | 8 | 13 | 25 | 55 | 96 | 29 |
| Rochdale | 46 | 8 | 12 | 26 | 37 | 79 | 28 |

# SEASON 1959-60 Division Three

| No. | Date | Opposition | Res | Attend | Goalscorers | Ames | Blake | Dobson | Evans | Fisher | Fowler | Hammond | Hill.R | Hunt.R.R | Hunt.R.M | Johnstone | King | Laidlaw | Langman | McLeod | Marshall | McCurley | Millfir | Milligan | Parker | Roe | Williams | Wright.P |
|---|---|---|---|---|---|---|---|---|---|---|---|---|---|---|---|---|---|---|---|---|---|---|---|---|---|---|---|---|
| 1 | 22 Aug | Bury | 1-3 | 11509 | Langman | 1 | 7 | | 10 | | 3 | 6 | | | | | | | 9 | 8 | 2 | | | 5 | 4 | | | 11 |
| 2 | 24 | GRIMSBY | 2-2 | 9689 | McLeod(2) | 1 | 7 | | | | 3 | 6 | | | | | | | 10 | 8 | 2 | 9 | | 5 | 4 | | | 11 |
| 3 | 29 | BARNSLEY | 2-2 | 8246 | Fisher(pen), Williams | 1 | | | | 2 | 3 | 6 | 8 | | | 10 | 9 | | | | | | | 5 | 4 | | 7 | 11 |
| 4 | 1 Sep | Grimsby | 1-4 | 14000 | P.Wright | 1 | | | | 2 | 3 | 6 | 8 | | | | 9 | | | | | | 10 | 5 | 4 | | 7 | 11 |
| 5 | 5 | Southampton | 2-4 | 14704 | King, Williams | 1 | | | | | 3 | 6 | 8 | | | | 9 | 2 | | | | | 10 | 5 | 4 | | 7 | 11 |
| 6 | 7 | HALIFAX | 1-0 | 8305 | Williams | 1 | | | 10 | | 3 | 6 | 8 | | | | 9 | 2 | | | | | | 5 | 4 | | 7 | 11 |
| 7 | 12 | READING | 4-2 | 7683 | King, Langman(2), P.Wright | 1 | | | | | 3 | 6 | 8 | | | | 10 | 2 | 9 | | | | | 5 | 4 | | 7 | 11 |
| 8 | 14 | Halifax | 2-3 | 5865 | King, McLeod | 1 | 7 | | | | 3 | 6 | | | | | 10 | 2 | 9 | 8 | | | | 5 | 4 | | | 11 |
| 9 | 19 | Shrewsbury | 1-4 | 9068 | Langman | 1 | 7 | | | | 3 | 6 | 8 | | | | 10 | 2 | 9 | | | | | 5 | 4 | | | 11 |
| 10 | 21 | MANSFIELD | 3-0 | 8202 | King(2) | 1 | 7 | | | | 3 | 6 | 8 | | | | 10 | 2 | 9 | | | | | 5 | 4 | | | 11 |
| 11 | 26 | PORT VALE | 3-1 | 7822 | King(3) | 1 | | | | | 3 | 6 | 8 | | | | 10 | 2 | 9 | | | | | 5 | 4 | | 7 | 11 |
| 12 | 28 | Mansfield | 3-1 | 5406 | King(3) | 1 | | | | | 3 | 6 | 8 | | | | 10 | 2 | 9 | | | | | 5 | 4 | | 7 | 11 |
| 13 | 3 Oct | Norwich | 2-3 | 27759 | Langman, Milligan | 1 | | | | | 3 | 6 | 8 | | | | 10 | | 9 | | | | | 5 | 4 | 2 | 7 | 11 |
| 14 | 6 | Brentford | 0-2 | 14750 | | 1 | | | | | 3 | 6 | 8 | | | | 10 | | 9 | | | | | 5 | 4 | 2 | 7 | 11 |
| 15 | 10 | WREXHAM | 3-1 | 7683 | Evans, R.Hill, Langman | 1 | | | 10 | | 3 | | 8 | | 6 | | | 2 | 9 | | | | | 5 | 4 | | 7 | 11 |
| 16 | 12 | BRENTFORD | 2-1 | 7790 | Langman, P.Wright | 1 | | | 10 | | 3 | 6 | 8 | | | | | 2 | 9 | | | | | 5 | 4 | | 7 | 11 |
| 17 | 17 | Tranmere | 1-1 | 8532 | Langman | 1 | | | | | 3 | 6 | 8 | | | | 10 | 2 | 9 | | | | | 5 | 4 | | 7 | 11 |
| 18 | 24 | BOURNEMOUTH | 1-2 | 7938 | Williams | 1 | | | 10 | | 3 | 6 | 8 | | | | | | 9 | | 2 | | | 5 | 4 | | 7 | 11 |
| 19 | 31 | Bradford | 0-0 | 8436 | | 1 | | 9 | | | 3 | 6 | 8 | | | | | 2 | | 10 | | | | 5 | 4 | | 7 | 11 |
| 20 | 7 Nov | NEWPORT | 2-1 | 6620 | Williams, P.Wright | 1 | | 9 | | | 3 | 6 | 8 | | | | | 2 | | 10 | | | | 5 | 4 | | 7 | 11 |
| 21 | 21 | SWINDON | 0-0 | 6537 | | 1 | | | | | 3 | 6 | 8 | | | | 10 | 2 | | | | 9 | | 5 | 4 | | 7 | 11 |
| 22 | 28 | York | 3-2 | 6881 | King, McCurley(2)(1pen) | 1 | | | | | 3 | 6 | 8 | | | | 10 | 2 | | | | 9 | | 5 | 4 | | 7 | 11 |
| 23 | 12 Dec | Accrington | 2-1 | 2116 | McCurley(2) | 1 | | | | | 3 | 6 | 8 | | | | 10 | 2 | | | | 9 | | 5 | 4 | | 7 | 11 |
| 24 | 19 | BURY | 3-0 | 5503 | King, McCurley, Williams | 1 | | | | | 3 | 6 | 8 | | | | 10 | 2 | | | | 9 | | 5 | 4 | | 7 | 11 |
| 25 | 26 | Q.p.r. | 1-3 | 6480 | McCurley | 1 | | | | | 3 | 6 | 8 | | | | 10 | 2 | | | | 9 | | 5 | 4 | | 7 | 11 |
| 26 | 28 | Q.P.R. | 2-0 | 9095 | McCurley, P.Wright | 1 | | | | | 3 | 6 | 8 | | | | 10 | 2 | | | 5 | 9 | | | 4 | | 7 | 11 |
| 27 | 2 Jan | Barnsley | 1-2 | 5526 | King | 1 | | | | | 3 | 6 | 8 | | | | 10 | 2 | | | | 9 | | 5 | 4 | | 7 | 11 |
| 28 | 9 | Chesterfield | 1-1 | 5193 | P.Wright | 1 | | | | | 3 | 6 | 8 | | | | 10 | 2 | | | | 9 | | 5 | 4 | | 7 | 11 |
| 29 | 23 | Reading | 1-2 | 7486 | King | 1 | | | | | 3 | 6 | 8 | | | | 10 | 2 | | | | 9 | | 5 | 4 | | 7 | 11 |
| 30 | 30 | COVENTRY | 0-0 | 7200 | | 1 | | | | | 3 | 6 | 8 | | | | 10 | 2 | | | | 9 | | 5 | 4 | | 7 | 11 |
| 31 | 6 Feb | SHREWSBURY | 3-2 | 7144 | R.Hill(2), Williams | 1 | | | | | 3 | 6 | 8 | | | | 10 | 2 | 9 | | | | | 5 | 4 | | 7 | 11 |
| 32 | 13 | Port Vale | 1-1 | 10248 | King | 1 | | | | | 3 | 6 | 8 | | | | 10 | 2 | 9 | | | | | 5 | 4 | | 7 | 11 |
| 33 | 20 | NORWICH | 3-0 | 13053 | King(3) | 1 | | | | | 3 | 6 | 8 | | | | 10 | 2 | 9 | | | | | 5 | 4 | | 7 | 11 |
| 34 | 27 | Wrexham | 1-1 | 8836 | King | 1 | | | | | 3 | 6 | 8 | | | | 10 | 2 | 9 | | | | | 5 | 4 | | 7 | 11 |
| 35 | 5 Mar | TRANMERE | 4-0 | 6857 | Blake, Hammond, R.Hill, King | 1 | 7 | | | | 3 | 6 | 8 | | | | 10 | 2 | 9 | | | | | 5 | 4 | | | 11 |
| 36 | 12 | Bournemouth | 2-3 | 9256 | King(2) | 1 | 7 | | | | 3 | 6 | 8 | | | | 10 | 2 | 9 | | | | | 5 | 4 | | | 11 |
| 37 | 19 | YORK | 2-2 | 6599 | R.R.Hunt, King | 1 | 7 | | | | 3 | 6 | 8 | 9 | | | 10 | 2 | | | | | | 5 | 4 | | | 11 |
| 38 | 21 | SOUTHAMPTON | 1-1 | 10100 | Laidlaw | 1 | 7 | | | | 3 | 6 | 8 | | | | 9 | 2 | | 10 | | | | 5 | 4 | | | 11 |
| 39 | 26 | Newport | 2-3 | 4332 | King, P.Wright | 1 | 7 | | | | 3 | 6 | 8 | | | | 9 | 2 | | 10 | | | | 5 | 4 | | | 11 |
| 40 | 2 Apr | CHESTERFIELD | 1-0 | 6079 | King | 1 | 7 | | | | 3 | 6 | 8 | | | | 10 | 2 | 9 | | | | | 5 | 4 | | | 11 |
| 41 | 9 | Swindon | 3-4 | 7342 | King, Williams, P.Wright | 1 | | | | | 3 | 6 | | | | | 10 | 2 | 9 | 8 | | | | 5 | 4 | | 7 | 11 |
| 42 | 15 | SOUTHEND | 2-3 | 10317 | King, P.Wright | 1 | | | | | 3 | 6 | | | | | 10 | 2 | 9 | 8 | | | | 5 | 4 | | 7 | 11 |
| 43 | 16 | BRADFORD | 2-1 | 5765 | Langman(2) | 1 | 7 | | | | 3 | | | | 6 | | 10 | 2 | 9 | 8 | 5 | | 4 | | | | | 11 |
| 44 | 18 | Southend | 0-1 | 12533 | | 1 | | | | | 3 | 6 | 8 | | | | 10 | 2 | 9 | | | | | 5 | 4 | | 7 | 11 |
| 45 | 23 | Coventry | 1-3 | 8382 | P.Wright | 1 | | | | | 3 | | | | 6 | | 10 | 2 | 9 | 8 | | | 4 | 5 | | | 7 | 11 |
| 46 | 30 | ACCRINGTON | 5-1 | 5215 | King(2), Langman, Williams, P.Wright | 1 | | | | 2 | 3 | 6 | | | | | 10 | 5 | 9 | 8 | | | 4 | | | | 7 | 11 |

# F.A.Cup

| 1st | 14 Nov | Q.P.R. | 2-3 | 8860 | McCurley, Wright.P | 1 | | | | | 3 | 6 | 8 | | | | 10 | 2 | | | | 9 | | 5 | 4 | | 7 | 11 |
|---|---|---|---|---|---|---|---|---|---|---|---|---|---|---|---|---|---|---|---|---|---|---|---|---|---|---|---|---|

(Back): Milligan, Hammond, Parker, Ames, Fowler, Laidlaw.
(Front): Williams, Hill, Langman, King, Wright.

**THIRD DIVISION**

| | P | W | D | L | F | A | Pts |
|---|---|---|---|---|---|---|---|
| 1 Southampton | 46 | 26 | 9 | 11 | 106 | 75 | 61 |
| 2 Norwich | 46 | 24 | 11 | 11 | 82 | 54 | 59 |
| 3 Shrewsbury | 46 | 18 | 16 | 12 | 97 | 75 | 52 |
| 4 Coventry | 46 | 21 | 10 | 15 | 78 | 63 | 52 |
| 5 Grimsby | 46 | 18 | 16 | 12 | 87 | 70 | 52 |
| 6 Brentford | 46 | 21 | 9 | 16 | 78 | 61 | 51 |
| 7 Bury | 46 | 21 | 9 | 16 | 64 | 51 | 51 |
| 8 QPR | 46 | 18 | 13 | 15 | 73 | 54 | 49 |
| 9 Colchester | 46 | 18 | 11 | 17 | 83 | 74 | 47 |
| 10 Bournemouth | 46 | 17 | 13 | 16 | 72 | 72 | 47 |
| 11 Reading | 46 | 18 | 10 | 18 | 84 | 77 | 46 |
| 12 Southend | 46 | 19 | 8 | 19 | 76 | 74 | 46 |
| 13 Newport | 46 | 20 | 6 | 20 | 80 | 79 | 46 |
| 14 Port Vale | 46 | 19 | 8 | 19 | 80 | 79 | 46 |
| 15 Halifax | 46 | 18 | 10 | 18 | 70 | 72 | 46 |
| 16 Swindon | 46 | 19 | 8 | 19 | 69 | 78 | 46 |
| 17 Barnsley | 46 | 15 | 14 | 17 | 65 | 66 | 44 |
| 18 Chesterfield | 46 | 18 | 7 | 21 | 71 | 84 | 43 |
| 19 Bradford City | 46 | 15 | 12 | 19 | 66 | 74 | 42 |
| 20 Tranmere | 46 | 14 | 13 | 19 | 72 | 75 | 41 |
| 21 York | 46 | 13 | 12 | 21 | 57 | 73 | 38 |
| 22 Mansfield | 46 | 15 | 6 | 25 | 81 | 112 | 36 |
| 23 Wrexham | 46 | 14 | 8 | 24 | 68 | 101 | 36 |
| 24 Accrington | 46 | 11 | 5 | 30 | 57 | 123 | 27 |

# SEASON 1960-61

## Division Three

| No. | Date | Opposition | Res | Attend | Goalscorers | Ames | Baines | Blake | Carey | Eagles | Fowler | Hammond | Harris | Hill | Howe | Hunt.R.M | Hunt.R.R | King | Laidlaw | Langman | McLeod | Marshall | Millar | Milligan | Parker | Rumney | Williams | Wright.J | Wright.P |
|---|---|---|---|---|---|---|---|---|---|---|---|---|---|---|---|---|---|---|---|---|---|---|---|---|---|---|---|---|---|
| 1 | 20 Aug | HULL | 4-0 | 6731 | Hammond(2 both pen), King(2) | 1 | | | | | 3 | 6 | | 8 | 11 | | | 10 | 2 | 9 | | | | 5 | 4 | | 7 | | |
| 2 | 22 | GRIMSBY | 1-1 | 7194 | King | 1 | | | | | 3 | 6 | | 8 | 11 | | | 10 | 2 | 9 | | | | 5 | 4 | | 7 | | |
| 3 | 27 | Reading | 1-2 | 7775 | Howe | 1 | | | | | 3 | 6 | | 8 | 11 | | | 10 | | 9 | | | | 5 | 4 | 2 | 7 | | |
| 4 | 30 | Grimsby | 1-2 | 11000 | King | 1 | | | | | 3 | 6 | | 8 | 11 | | | 10 | | 9 | | | | 5 | 4 | 2 | 7 | | |
| 5 | 3 Sep | COVENTRY | 4-3 | 5431 | Hammond(p),King,Langman,Williams | 1 | | | | | 3 | 6 | | 8 | 11 | | | 10 | | 9 | | | | 5 | 4 | 2 | 7 | | |
| 6 | 5 | BARNSLEY | 4-2 | 6034 | Hammond(p), Howe, King(2) | 1 | | | | | 3 | 6 | | 8 | 11 | | | 10 | | 9 | | | | 5 | 4 | 2 | 7 | | |
| 7 | 10 | Bristol C | 0-5 | 11808 | | 1 | | | | | 3 | 6 | | 8 | 11 | | | 10 | | 9 | | | | 5 | 4 | 2 | 7 | | |
| 8 | 14 | Barnsley | 0-3 | 3000 | | 1 | | 7 | | | 3 | | | 8 | 11 | 6 | | 10 | | 9 | | | 4 | 5 | | 2 | | | |
| 9 | 17 | Q.P.R. | 0-1 | 5750 | | 1 | | 7 | | | 3 | 6 | | 8 | 11 | | | 10 | | 9 | | | | 5 | 4 | 2 | | | |
| 10 | 20 | Bury | 0-4 | 9253 | | 1 | | 7 | | | 3 | 6 | | 8 | 11 | | | 10 | | 9 | | | | 5 | 4 | 2 | | | |
| 11 | 24 | Notts County | 2-4 | 14134 | Langman, Williams | 1 | | | | | 3 | 6 | | 8 | | | | 10 | | 9 | | | | 5 | 4 | 2 | 7 | | 11 |
| 12 | 26 | BURY | 0-2 | 5263 | | 1 | | | | | 3 | 6 | | 8 | | | | 10 | | 9 | | | | 5 | 4 | 2 | 7 | | 11 |
| 13 | 1 Oct | BOURNEMOUTH | 0-1 | 4576 | | 1 | | | | | 3 | 6 | | 8 | | | | 10 | | 9 | | | | 5 | 4 | 2 | 7 | | 11 |
| 14 | 8 | SHREWSBURY | 1-1 | 4191 | Langman | 1 | | | | | 3 | 6 | | 8 | | | | 10 | | 9 | | | 4 | 5 | | 2 | 7 | | 11 |
| 15 | 15 | Halifax | 1-2 | 6210 | King | 1 | | | | | 3 | | 4 | 10 | | 6 | | 9 | | | 8 | | 2 | 5 | | | 7 | | 11 |
| 16 | 22 | TRANMERE | 0-3 | 4569 | | 1 | | | | | 3 | | 4 | 10 | | 6 | | 9 | | | 8 | | 2 | 5 | | | 7 | | 11 |
| 17 | 29 | Watford | 2-2 | 13031 | King, Williams(pen) | 1 | | | | | 3 | | 4 | 8 | | 6 | | 10 | | 9 | | | 2 | 5 | | | 7 | | 11 |
| 18 | 12 Nov | Swindon | 2-0 | 11782 | Langman(2) | 1 | | | | | 3 | | 4 | 8 | | 6 | 11 | | | 9 | 10 | | 2 | 5 | | | 7 | | |
| 19 | 19 | TORQUAY | 3-3 | 5483 | Fowler, R.R.Hunt, Langman | 1 | | | | | 3 | | 4 | 8 | | 6 | 11 | | | 9 | 10 | | 2 | 5 | | | 7 | | |
| 20 | 3 Dec | SOUTHEND | 2-0 | 5007 | Langman, Williams | 1 | | | | | 3 | | 4 | | | 6 | 11 | 10 | | 9 | 8 | | 2 | 5 | | | 7 | | |
| 21 | 10 | Chesterfield | 3-2 | 3342 | Fowler, Harris(pen), King | 1 | | | | | 3 | | 4 | 7 | | 6 | 11 | 10 | | 9 | 8 | | 2 | 5 | | | | | |
| 22 | 17 | Hull | 1-1 | 6047 | King | 1 | | | | | 3 | | 4 | 7 | | 6 | 11 | 10 | | 9 | 8 | | 2 | 5 | | | | | |
| 23 | 22 | Newport | 2-3 | 6182 | King, Langman | 1 | | | | | 3 | | 4 | 8 | | 6 | 11 | 10 | | 9 | | | 2 | 5 | | | 7 | | |
| 24 | 26 | NEWPORT | 1-1 | 6732 | King | 1 | | | | | 3 | | 4 | 8 | | 6 | 11 | 10 | | 9 | | | 2 | 5 | | | 7 | | |
| 25 | 31 | READING | 2-2 | 5252 | Langman, Williams | 1 | | | | | 3 | | 4 | 8 | | 6 | 11 | 10 | | 9 | | | 2 | 5 | | | 7 | | |
| 26 | 14 Jan | Coventry | 0-2 | 10197 | | | | | 5 | 2 | | | 4 | | | 6 | 10 | | | 9 | | | 8 | 3 | | | 7 | 1 | 11 |
| 27 | 21 | BRISTOL C | 0-1 | 5099 | | 1 | | | | 2 | 3 | | 4 | | | 6 | 10 | | | 9 | 8 | | | 5 | | | 7 | | 11 |
| 28 | 28 | BRENTFORD | 2-4 | 4040 | R.R.Hunt, Williams | 1 | | | | 2 | 3 | 4 | | 8 | | 6 | 11 | | | 9 | 10 | | | 5 | | | 7 | | |
| 29 | 4 Feb | Q.p.r. | 2-3 | 10232 | Williams, P.Wright | 1 | | | 4 | 2 | 3 | 6 | | | | | 10 | | | 9 | 8 | | | 5 | | | 7 | | 11 |
| 30 | 6 | Port Vale | 0-3 | 6504 | | 1 | | | | 2 | 3 | | 4 | | | 6 | 9 | 10 | | | 8 | | | 5 | | | 7 | | 11 |
| 31 | 11 | NOTTS COUNTY | 1-2 | 4634 | Williams | 1 | | | 4 | 2 | 3 | 6 | | | | | 11 | 10 | | 9 | 8 | | | 5 | | | 7 | | |
| 32 | 18 | Bournemouth | 4-4 | 6712 | King(2), McLeod, O.G. | 1 | | | 5 | 2 | 3 | | 4 | | | 6 | 11 | 10 | | 9 | 8 | | | | | | 7 | | |
| 33 | 25 | Southend | 1-2 | 6047 | Eagles | 1 | | | 5 | 2 | 3 | | 4 | | | 6 | 10 | 9 | | | 8 | | | | | | 7 | | 11 |
| 34 | 4 Mar | HALIFAX | 3-1 | 4710 | Harris(pen), McLeod(2) | 1 | 9 | 7 | 5 | 2 | 3 | | 4 | | | 6 | 11 | 10 | | | 8 | | | | | | | | |
| 35 | 7 | Bradford | 1-0 | 7590 | King | 1 | 9 | 7 | 5 | 2 | 3 | | 4 | | | 6 | 11 | 10 | | | 8 | | | | | | | | |
| 36 | 11 | Tranmere | 2-7 | 11299 | King, O.G. | 1 | 9 | 7 | 5 | 2 | 3 | | 4 | | | 6 | 11 | 10 | | | 8 | | | | | | | | |
| 37 | 18 | WATFORD | 1-4 | 4648 | Langman | 1 | | | 5 | 2 | 3 | | 4 | | | 6 | 11 | 8 | | 9 | 10 | | | | | | 7 | | |
| 38 | 25 | Brentford | 0-0 | 4600 | | 1 | | | | 2 | 3 | 6 | | 8 | | | | 10 | | 9 | | | | 5 | 4 | | 7 | | 11 |
| 39 | 31 | WALSALL | 0-4 | 5480 | | 1 | | | | 2 | 3 | 6 | | 8 | | | | 10 | | 9 | | | | 5 | 4 | | 7 | | 11 |
| 40 | 1 Apr | SWINDON | 3-1 | 3182 | R.R.Hunt, King, P.Wright | 1 | | | | 2 | 3 | 6 | 4 | 7 | | | 8 | 9 | | | 10 | | | 5 | | | | | 11 |
| 41 | 3 | Walsall | 0-3 | 12985 | | 1 | | 7 | | 2 | 3 | | 4 | 8 | | 6 | 10 | 9 | | | | | | 5 | | | | | 11 |
| 42 | 8 | Torquay | 1-1 | 4047 | Hill | 1 | | | | | 3 | | 4 | 10 | | 6 | 8 | 9 | | | | | | 5 | | 2 | 7 | | 11 |
| 43 | 15 | PORT VALE | 2-0 | 3500 | King(2) | 1 | | | | | 3 | | 4 | 10 | | 6 | 8 | 9 | | | | | | 5 | | 2 | 7 | | 11 |
| 44 | 22 | Shrewsbury | 2-2 | 6891 | R.M.Hunt, R.R.Hunt | 1 | | | | | 3 | | 4 | 10 | | 6 | 8 | | | 9 | | | | 5 | | 2 | 7 | | 11 |
| 45 | 24 | BRADFORD | 2-4 | 3542 | Langman, P.Wright | 1 | | | 5 | | 3 | | 4 | 10 | | 6 | 8 | | | 9 | | | | | | 2 | 7 | | 11 |
| 46 | 29 | CHESTERFIELD | 4-3 | 3141 | King(3), O.G. | 1 | | | | | 3 | | 4 | | | 6 | 8 | 9 | | | 10 | 5 | | | | 2 | 7 | | 11 |

## F.A.Cup

| | | | | | | | | | | | | | | | | | | | | | | | | | | | | | |
|---|---|---|---|---|---|---|---|---|---|---|---|---|---|---|---|---|---|---|---|---|---|---|---|---|---|---|---|---|---|
| 1st | 5 Nov | MAIDENHEAD | 5–0 | 5771 | R.R.Hunt(2), Langman(2), Williams | 1 | | | | | 3 | | 4 | 8 | | 6 | 11 | 10 | | 9 | | | 2 | 5 | | | 7 | | |
| 2nd | 26 | Aldershot | 1–3 | 8425 | Hill | 1 | | | | | 3 | | 4 | 8 | | 6 | 11 | | | 9 | 10 | | 2 | 5 | | | 7 | | |

## Football League Cup

| | | | | | | | | | | | | | | | | | | | | | | | | | | | | | |
|---|---|---|---|---|---|---|---|---|---|---|---|---|---|---|---|---|---|---|---|---|---|---|---|---|---|---|---|---|---|
| 1st | 10 Oct | NEWCASTLE | 4–1 | 9130 | King(2), Williams, P.Wright | 1 | | | | | 3 | | 4 | 10 | | 6 | | 9 | | | 8 | | | 5 | | 2 | 7 | | 11 |
| 2nd | 31 | SOUTHAMPTON | 0–2 | 6264 | | 1 | | | | | 3 | | 4 | 8 | | 6 | | 10 | | 9 | | | 2 | 5 | | | 7 | | 11 |

PETER WRIGHT PERCY AMES JOHN FOWLER

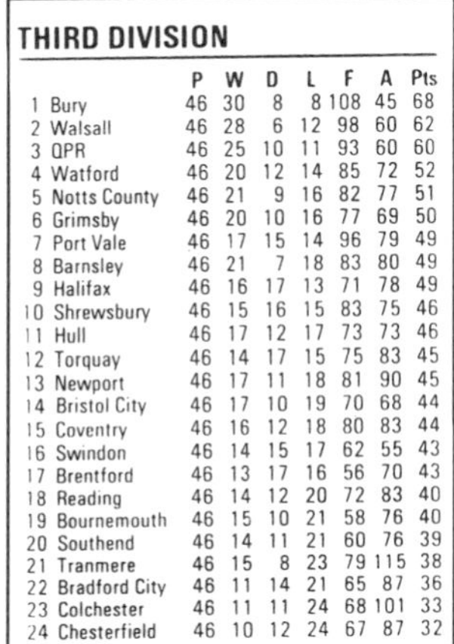

**THIRD DIVISION**

| | | P | W | D | L | F | A | Pts |
|---|---|---|---|---|---|---|---|---|
| 1 | Bury | 46 | 30 | 8 | 8 | 108 | 45 | 68 |
| 2 | Walsall | 46 | 28 | 6 | 12 | 98 | 60 | 62 |
| 3 | QPR | 46 | 25 | 10 | 11 | 93 | 60 | 60 |
| 4 | Watford | 46 | 20 | 12 | 14 | 85 | 72 | 52 |
| 5 | Notts County | 46 | 21 | 9 | 16 | 82 | 77 | 51 |
| 6 | Grimsby | 46 | 20 | 10 | 16 | 77 | 69 | 50 |
| 7 | Port Vale | 46 | 17 | 15 | 14 | 96 | 79 | 49 |
| 8 | Barnsley | 46 | 21 | 7 | 18 | 83 | 80 | 49 |
| 9 | Halifax | 46 | 16 | 17 | 13 | 71 | 78 | 49 |
| 10 | Shrewsbury | 46 | 15 | 16 | 15 | 83 | 75 | 46 |
| 11 | Hull | 46 | 17 | 12 | 17 | 73 | 73 | 46 |
| 12 | Torquay | 46 | 14 | 17 | 15 | 75 | 83 | 45 |
| 13 | Newport | 46 | 17 | 11 | 18 | 81 | 90 | 45 |
| 14 | Bristol City | 46 | 17 | 10 | 19 | 70 | 68 | 44 |
| 15 | Coventry | 46 | 16 | 12 | 18 | 80 | 83 | 44 |
| 16 | Swindon | 46 | 14 | 15 | 17 | 62 | 55 | 43 |
| 17 | Brentford | 46 | 13 | 17 | 16 | 56 | 70 | 43 |
| 18 | Reading | 46 | 14 | 12 | 20 | 72 | 83 | 40 |
| 19 | Bournemouth | 46 | 15 | 10 | 21 | 58 | 76 | 40 |
| 20 | Southend | 46 | 14 | 11 | 21 | 60 | 76 | 39 |
| 21 | Tranmere | 46 | 15 | 8 | 23 | 79 | 115 | 38 |
| 22 | Bradford City | 46 | 11 | 14 | 21 | 65 | 87 | 36 |
| 23 | Colchester | 46 | 11 | 11 | 24 | 68 | 101 | 33 |
| 24 | Chesterfield | 46 | 10 | 12 | 24 | 67 | 87 | 32 |

# SEASON 1961–62 Division Four

| No. | Date | Opposition | Res | Attend | Goalscorers | Abbey | Ames | Coleman | Foster | Forbes | Fowler | Griffiths | Harris | Hill | Hunt.R.R | Hunt.R.M | King | Lundstrum | MacLeod | Millar | Rumney | Wright |
|---|---|---|---|---|---|---|---|---|---|---|---|---|---|---|---|---|---|---|---|---|---|---|
| 1 | 19 Aug | STOCKPORT | 3–0 | 4318 | R.R.Hunt, King, Wright | 5 | 1 | | 7 | | 3 | | 4 | 10 | 8 | 6 | 9 | | | 2 | | 11 |
| 2 | 21 | CARLISLE | 2–0 | 4971 | King, Millar | 5 | 1 | | 7 | | 3 | | 4 | 10 | 8 | 6 | 9 | | | 2 | | 11 |
| 3 | 26 | Oldham | 2–2 | 15746 | Foster, King | 5 | 1 | | 7 | | 3 | | 4 | 10 | 8 | 6 | 9 | | | 2 | | 11 |
| 4 | 29 | Carlisle | 1–1 | 8500 | King | 5 | 1 | | 7 | | 3 | | 4 | 10 | 8 | 6 | 9 | | | 2 | | 11 |
| 5 | 2 Sep | ACCRINGTON | 3–2 | 5129 | King(2), Millar | 5 | 1 | | 7 | | 3 | | 4 | 10 | 8 | 6 | 9 | | | 2 | | 11 |
| 6 | 5 | Doncaster | 4–1 | 3705 | Foster(2), R.R.Hunt, King | 5 | 1 | | 7 | | 3 | | 4 | 10 | 8 | 6 | 9 | | | 2 | | 11 |
| 7 | 9 | Darlington | 2–0 | 8958 | R.R.Hunt, King | 5 | 1 | | 7 | | 3 | | 4 | 10 | 8 | 6 | 9 | | | 2 | | 11 |
| 8 | 16 | HARTLEPOOLS | 6–1 | 5036 | Foster(2), R.R.Hunt(2), Millar(2) | 5 | 1 | | 7 | | 3 | | 4 | 10 | 8 | 6 | 9 | | | 2 | | 11 |
| 9 | 21 | Workington | 2–1 | 5914 | R.R.Hunt, King | 5 | 1 | | 7 | | 3 | | 4 | 10 | 8 | 6 | 9 | | | 2 | | 11 |
| 10 | 23 | Southport | 0–3 | 5258 | | 5 | 1 | | 7 | | 3 | | 4 | 10 | 8 | 6 | 9 | | | 2 | | 11 |
| 11 | 25 | WORKINGTON | 6–1 | 5961 | Harris(pen), R.R.Hunt, King, Wright(3) | 5 | 1 | | | | 3 | | 4 | 7 | 8 | 6 | 9 | | 10 | 2 | | 11 |
| 12 | 30 | TRANMERE | 3–0 | 6446 | R.R.Hunt, King(2) | 5 | 1 | | | | 3 | | 4 | 7 | 8 | 6 | 9 | | 10 | 2 | | 11 |
| 13 | 2 Oct | CHESTER | 5–2 | 7148 | R.R.Hunt(3), McLeod, Millar | 5 | 1 | | | | 3 | | 4 | 7 | 8 | 6 | 9 | | 10 | 2 | | 11 |
| 14 | 7 | York | 0–5 | 5714 | | 5 | 1 | | | | 3 | | 4 | 7 | 8 | 6 | 9 | | 10 | 2 | | 11 |
| 15 | 11 | Chester | 2–2 | 7186 | R.R.Hunt, King | 5 | 1 | | 7 | | 3 | | 4 | | 8 | 6 | 9 | | 10 | | 2 | 11 |
| 16 | 14 | CHESTERFIELD | 3–3 | 6043 | Harris, R.R.Hunt, McLeod | 5 | 1 | | 7 | | 3 | | 4 | | 8 | 6 | 9 | | 10 | 2 | | 11 |
| 17 | 21 | Gillingham | 1–2 | 8962 | R.R.Hunt | 5 | 1 | | 7 | | 3 | | 4 | 10 | 8 | 6 | 9 | | | 2 | | 11 |
| 18 | 28 | MILLWALL | 2–2 | 6868 | Abrey, R.R.Hunt | 5 | 1 | | 7 | | 3 | | 4 | 10 | 8 | 6 | 9 | | | 2 | | 11 |
| 19 | 11 Nov | BARROW | 1–1 | 4553 | R.R.Hunt | 5 | 1 | | 7 | | 3 | | 4 | 10 | 8 | 6 | 9 | | | 2 | | 11 |
| 20 | 18 | Rochdale | 1–0 | 4618 | R.R.Hunt | 5 | 1 | 9 | 7 | | 3 | | 4 | 10 | 8 | 6 | | | | 2 | | 11 |
| 21 | 2 Dec | Exeter | 2–0 | 4530 | R.R.Hunt(2) | 5 | 1 | | 7 | | 3 | | 4 | 10 | 8 | 6 | 9 | | | 2 | | 11 |
| 22 | 9 | WREXHAM | 2–4 | 5587 | R.R.Hunt, King | 5 | 1 | | 7 | | 3 | | 4 | 10 | 8 | 6 | 9 | | | 2 | | 11 |
| 23 | 16 | Stockport | 4–1 | 2803 | R.R.Hunt, King(2), Wright | 5 | 1 | | 7 | | 3 | | 4 | 10 | 8 | 6 | 9 | | | 2 | | 11 |
| 24 | 23 | OLDHAM | 5–1 | 3782 | R.R.Hunt(2), King(2), Wright | 5 | 1 | | 7 | | 3 | | 4 | 10 | 8 | 6 | 9 | | | 2 | | 11 |
| 25 | 26 | Bradford | 1–4 | 5571 | King | 5 | 1 | | 7 | | 3 | | 4 | 10 | 8 | 6 | 9 | | | 2 | | 11 |
| 26 | 30 | BRADFORD | 9–1 | 4415 | Hill, R.R.Hunt(4)(1pen), King(4) | 5 | 1 | | 7 | | 3 | | 4 | 10 | 8 | 6 | 9 | | | 2 | | 11 |
| 27 | 13 Jan | Accrington | 4–0 | 1411 | Foster, R.R.Hunt, Wright(2) | 5 | 1 | | 7 | | 3 | | 4 | 10 | 8 | 6 | 9 | | | 2 | | 11 |
| 28 | 15 | Mansfield | 0–4 | 5880 | | 5 | 1 | | | | 3 | | 4 | 10 | 8 | 6 | 9 | 7 | | 2 | | 11 |
| 29 | 20 | DARLINGTON | 2–0 | 4923 | R.R.Hunt, King | 5 | 1 | | 7 | | 3 | | 4 | 10 | 8 | 6 | 9 | | | 2 | | 11 |
| 30 | 27 | CREWE | 5–3 | 5435 | Harris, R.R.Hunt(2), King, Wright | 5 | 1 | | 7 | | 3 | | 4 | 10 | 8 | 6 | 9 | | | 2 | | 11 |
| 31 | 3 Feb | Hartlepools | 1–1 | 6738 | King | 5 | 1 | | 7 | | 3 | 2 | 4 | 10 | | 6 | 9 | | 8 | | | 11 |
| 32 | 10 | SOUTHPORT | 2–0 | 5379 | Hill, R.R.Hunt | 5 | 1 | | 7 | | 3 | 2 | 4 | 10 | 8 | 6 | 9 | | | | | 11 |
| 33 | 17 | Tranmere | 2–5 | 6481 | King, Wright | 5 | 1 | | 7 | | 3 | 2 | 4 | 10 | 8 | 6 | 9 | | | | | 11 |
| 34 | 24 | YORK | 3–1 | 4633 | R.R.Hunt, King, Wright | 5 | 1 | | 7 | | 3 | 2 | 4 | | 8 | 6 | 9 | | 10 | | | 11 |
| 35 | 3 Mar | Chesterfield | 1–4 | 2906 | King | 5 | 1 | | 7 | | 3 | 2 | 4 | 10 | 8 | 6 | 9 | | | | | 11 |
| 36 | 10 | GILLINGHAM | 6–0 | 4503 | Foster(2), Hill, R.R.Hunt, King, Wright | 5 | 1 | | 7 | | 3 | 2 | 4 | 10 | 8 | 6 | 9 | | | | | 11 |
| 37 | 17 | Millwall | 0–2 | 16585 | | 5 | 1 | | 7 | | 3 | 2 | 4 | 10 | 8 | 6 | 9 | | | | | 11 |
| 38 | 23 | MANSFIELD | 2–0 | 5730 | Foster, King | 5 | 1 | | 7 | | 3 | 2 | 4 | 10 | 8 | 6 | 9 | | | | | 11 |
| 39 | 31 | Barrow | 0–4 | 3672 | | 5 | 1 | | 7 | | 3 | 2 | 4 | 10 | 8 | 6 | 9 | | | | | 11 |
| 40 | 7 Apr | ROCHDALE | 1–1 | 4616 | R.R.Hunt | 5 | 1 | | 7 | | 3 | 2 | 4 | 10 | 8 | 6 | 9 | | | | | 11 |
| 41 | 14 | Crewe | 0–4 | 6456 | | | 1 | | 7 | 5 | 3 | 2 | | | 10 | 6 | 9 | | 8 | | 4 | 11 |
| 42 | 20 | ALDERSHOT | 3–0 | 6399 | Harris(pen), McLeod, Wright | | 1 | | | 5 | 3 | 2 | 4 | 7 | 8 | 6 | 9 | | 10 | | | 11 |
| 43 | 21 | EXETER | 2–1 | 5530 | King, Wright | | 1 | | | 5 | 3 | 2 | 4 | 7 | 8 | 6 | 9 | | 10 | | | 11 |
| 44 | 23 | Aldershot | 0–1 | 6338 | | | 1 | | | 5 | 3 | 2 | 4 | 7 | 8 | 6 | 9 | | 10 | | | 11 |
| 45 | 28 | Wrexham | 0–0 | 16027 | | | 1 | | 7 | 5 | 3 | 2 | 4 | 8 | 10 | 6 | 9 | | | | | 11 |
| 46 | 30 | DONCASTER | 5–3 | 6108 | R.R.Hunt(4), King | | 1 | | 7 | 5 | 3 | 2 | 4 | 8 | 10 | 6 | 9 | | | | | 11 |

## F.A.Cup

| Round | Date | Opponent | Score | Att | Scorers | | | | | | | | | | | | | | | | | |
|---|---|---|---|---|---|---|---|---|---|---|---|---|---|---|---|---|---|---|---|---|---|---|
| 1st | 4 Nov | Peterborough | 3–3 | 16469 | Abrey, Hunt.R.R, Wright | 5 | 1 | | 7 | | 3 | | 4 | 10 | 8 | 6 | 9 | | | 2 | | 11 |
| 1st/R | 6 | PETERBOROUGH | 2–2 | 10653 | Hunt.R.R, King | 5 | 1 | | 7 | | 3 | | 4 | 10 | 8 | 6 | 9 | | | 2 | | 11 |
| 1/2R | 13 | Peterborough | 0–3 | 11857 | | 5 | 1 | | 7 | | 3 | | 4 | 10 | 8 | 6 | | | 9 | 2 | | 11 |

## Football League Cup

| Round | Date | Opponent | Score | Att | Scorers | | | | | | | | | | | | | | | | | |
|---|---|---|---|---|---|---|---|---|---|---|---|---|---|---|---|---|---|---|---|---|---|---|
| 1st | 13 Sep | CREWE | 1–2 | 4806 | King | 5 | 1 | | 7 | | 3 | | 4 | 10 | 8 | 6 | 9 | | | 2 | | 11 |

*Photo by Essex County Standard*

**COLCHESTER UNITED, 1961-62**

Left to right (back row): Lundstrum, Millar, Fowler, Ames, G. Gillingham, Abrey, Rumney, Marshall and Loughton; (centre) Foster, Hunt, R. R. Griffiths, King, Hill, Wright, Hunt (R.M.) and Harris; (front) D. Waylen, Miller, Howe, McLeod, G. Watson, D. Mallett, C. Balls and Baines.

### DIVISION 4

| | P | W | D | L | F | A | W | D | L | F | A | Pts |
|---|---|---|---|---|---|---|---|---|---|---|---|---|
| Millwall | 44 | 16 | 3 | 3 | 47 | 18 | 7 | 7 | 8 | 40 | 44 | 56 |
| Colchester U | 44 | 17 | 4 | 1 | 78 | 24 | 6 | 5 | 11 | 26 | 47 | 55 |
| Wrexham | 44 | 12 | 6 | 4 | 56 | 23 | 10 | 3 | 9 | 40 | 33 | 53 |
| Carlisle U | 44 | 15 | 3 | 4 | 35 | 22 | 7 | 5 | 10 | 29 | 41 | 52 |
| Bradford C | 44 | 14 | 5 | 3 | 58 | 32 | 7 | 4 | 11 | 36 | 54 | 51 |
| York C | 44 | 17 | 2 | 3 | 62 | 19 | 3 | 8 | 11 | 22 | 34 | 50 |
| Aldershot | 44 | 16 | 4 | 2 | 56 | 20 | 6 | 1 | 15 | 25 | 40 | 49 |
| Workington | 44 | 12 | 6 | 4 | 40 | 23 | 7 | 5 | 10 | 29 | 47 | 49 |
| Barrow | 44 | 12 | 7 | 3 | 49 | 20 | 5 | 7 | 10 | 25 | 38 | 48 |
| Crewe A | 44 | 16 | 3 | 3 | 53 | 24 | 4 | 3 | 15 | 26 | 46 | 46 |
| Oldham A | 44 | 12 | 7 | 3 | 47 | 26 | 5 | 5 | 12 | 30 | 44 | 46 |
| Rochdale | 44 | 14 | 3 | 5 | 47 | 28 | 5 | 4 | 13 | 24 | 43 | 45 |
| Darlington | 44 | 13 | 5 | 4 | 37 | 24 | 5 | 4 | 13 | 24 | 49 | 45 |
| Mansfield T | 44 | 14 | 3 | 5 | 51 | 19 | 5 | 3 | 14 | 26 | 47 | 44 |
| Tranmere R | 44 | 15 | 2 | 5 | 53 | 37 | 5 | 2 | 15 | 17 | 44 | 44 |
| Stockport Co | 44 | 13 | 3 | 6 | 42 | 27 | 4 | 6 | 12 | 28 | 42 | 43 |
| Southport | 44 | 13 | 5 | 4 | 36 | 25 | 4 | 4 | 14 | 25 | 46 | 43 |
| Exeter C | 44 | 11 | 5 | 6 | 43 | 32 | 2 | 6 | 14 | 19 | 45 | 37 |
| Chesterfield | 44 | 11 | 3 | 8 | 43 | 38 | 3 | 6 | 13 | 27 | 49 | 37 |
| Gillingham | 44 | 10 | 6 | 6 | 48 | 30 | 3 | 5 | 14 | 25 | 64 | 37 |
| Doncaster R | 44 | 8 | 5 | 9 | 34 | 29 | 3 | 2 | 17 | 26 | 56 | 29 |
| Hartlepools U | 44 | 6 | 5 | 11 | 27 | 35 | 2 | 6 | 14 | 25 | 66 | 27 |
| Chester | 44 | 5 | 9 | 8 | 36 | 37 | 2 | 3 | 17 | 18 | 59 | 26 |

Accrington Stanley resigned from the League

# SEASON 1962–63 Division Four

| No. | Date | Opposition | Res | Attend | Goalscorers | Ames | Ramage | Baines | Brown | Coleman | Forbes | Fowler | Grice | Griffiths | Harris | Hill | Hunt.R.R | Hunt.R.M | King | MacLeod | McCrohan | Rumney | Rutter | Stark | Wright | Abrey |
|---|---|---|---|---|---|---|---|---|---|---|---|---|---|---|---|---|---|---|---|---|---|---|---|---|---|---|
| 1 | 18 Aug | Brentford | 1–1 | 9482 | King | 1 | | | | | 5 | 3 | 7 | 2 | 4 | 8 | 10 | 6 | 9 | | | | | | 11 | |
| 2 | 20 | BRISTOL C | 1–0 | 6824 | R.R.Hunt | 1 | | | | | 5 | 3 | 7 | 2 | 4 | 8 | 10 | 6 | 9 | | | | | | 11 | |
| 3 | 25 | COVENTRY | 0–0 | 5781 | | 1 | | | | | 5 | 3 | 7 | 2 | 4 | 8 | 10 | 6 | 9 | | | | | | 11 | |
| 4 | 28 | Bristol C | 2–1 | 12508 | King(2) | 1 | | | | | 5 | 3 | 7 | 2 | 4 | 10 | 8 | 6 | 9 | | | | | | 11 | |
| 5 | 1 Sep | Bournemouth | 1–1 | 9208 | R.R.Hunt | 1 | | 9 | | | 5 | 3 | 7 | 2 | 4 | 10 | 8 | 6 | | | | | | | 11 | |
| 6 | 3 | Port Vale | 2–4 | 11729 | King(2) | 1 | | | | | 5 | 3 | 7 | 2 | 4 | 10 | 8 | 6 | 9 | | | | | | 11 | |
| 7 | 8 | NOTTS COUNTY | 2–2 | 5524 | Hill, O.G. | 1 | | | | | 5 | 3 | 7 | 2 | 4 | 10 | 8 | 6 | 9 | | | | | | 11 | |
| 8 | 10 | PORT VALE | 0–1 | 6039 | | 1 | | | | | 5 | 3 | 7 | 2 | 4 | 10 | 8 | 6 | 9 | | | | | | 11 | |
| 9 | 15 | NORTHAMPTON | 2–2 | 5512 | R.R.Hunt(pen), Wright | 1 | | | | | 5 | 3 | 7 | 2 | | 10 | 8 | 6 | 9 | | 4 | | | | 11 | |
| 10 | 19 | Reading | 1–4 | 5207 | R.R.Hunt | 1 | | | | | 5 | 3 | 7 | 2 | | 10 | 8 | 6 | 9 | | 4 | | | | 11 | |
| 11 | 22 | Southend | 3–2 | 11487 | R.R.Hunt(2), King | 1 | | | | | 5 | 3 | 11 | 2 | | 7 | 10 | 6 | 9 | 8 | 4 | | | | | |
| 12 | 24 | READING | 4–2 | 5999 | Hill, R.R.Hunt(2), King | 1 | | | | | 5 | 3 | 11 | 2 | | 7 | 10 | 6 | 9 | 8 | 4 | | | | | |
| 13 | 29 | MILLWALL | 2–5 | 7096 | Grice, McLeod | 1 | | | | | 5 | 3 | 11 | 2 | | 7 | 10 | 6 | 9 | 8 | 4 | | | | | |
| 14 | 3 Oct | Shrewsbury | 2–1 | 8261 | Grice, Hill | 1 | | | | | 5 | 3 | 11 | 2 | | 7 | 10 | 6 | 9 | 8 | 4 | | | | | |
| 15 | 6 | Hull | 2–2 | 9360 | King(2) | 1 | | | | | 5 | 3 | 11 | 2 | | 7 | 10 | 6 | 9 | 8 | 4 | | | | | |
| 16 | 8 | SHREWSBURY P | 3–2 | 6472 | Grice, R.R.Hunt, King | 1 | | | | | 5 | 3 | 11 | 2 | 6 | 7 | 10 | | 9 | 8 | 4 | | | | | |
| 17 | 13 | CRYSTAL P | 1–2 | 6371 | McCrohan | 1 | | | | | 5 | 3 | 11 | 2 | 6 | 7 | 10 | | 9 | 8 | 4 | | | | | |
| 18 | 20 | Wrexham | 1–4 | 12750 | Coleman | 1 | | | | 9 | 5 | 3 | 7 | 2 | 6 | 8 | | | | 10 | 4 | | | | 11 | |
| 19 | 27 | HALIFAX | 1–1 | 4697 | R.R.Hunt(pen) | 1 | | | 6 | | 5 | 3 | 11 | 2 | | 7 | 10 | | 9 | 8 | 4 | | | | | |
| 20 | 10 Nov | BRIGHTON | 4–1 | 3835 | Hill, King(3) | 1 | | | | | 5 | 3 | 7 | 2 | 4 | 8 | 10 | 6 | 9 | | | | | | 11 | |
| 21 | 17 | Carlisle | 1–3 | 3518 | King | 1 | | | | | 5 | 3 | 7 | 2 | 4 | 8 | 10 | 6 | 9 | | | | | | 11 | |
| 22 | 1 Dec | Peterborough | 2–6 | 11290 | King, Wright | 1 | | | | | 5 | 3 | | 2 | 4 | 7 | 8 | 6 | 9 | | | | | 10 | 11 | |
| 23 | 8 | BARNSLEY | 1–1 | 3071 | King | 1 | | | | | 5 | 3 | 7 | | | | 8 | 6 | 9 | | 2 | 4 | | 10 | 11 | |
| 24 | 15 | BRADFORD | 1–4 | 3059 | R.R.Hunt | 1 | | | | | 5 | 3 | 7 | 2 | | 10 | 8 | 6 | | | 4 | | | 9 | 11 | |
| | 22 | Coventry* | 0–2 | 11803 | * Abandoned | 1 | | | | | 5 | 3 | 7 | | 4 | 10 | 8 | 6 | | | 2 | | | 9 | 11 | |
| 25 | 16 Feb | Millwall | 1–2 | 9783 | R.M.Hunt | 1 | | | | | 5 | 3 | 7 | | 4 | 8 | 10 | 6 | | | 2 | | | 9 | 11 | |
| 26 | 26 | Coventry | 2–2 | 13062 | R.R.Hunt(2) | 1 | | | | | 2 | 3 | 7 | | | 8 | 10 | 6 | 9 | | 4 | | 5 | | 11 | |
| 27 | 4 Mar | HULL | 2–3 | 4365 | King, Wright | 1 | | | | | 2 | 3 | 7 | | | 8 | 10 | 6 | 9 | | 4 | | 5 | | 11 | |
| 28 | 8 | WREXHAM | 1–1 | 4725 | King | 1 | | | | | 2 | 3 | 7 | | | 8 | 10 | 6 | 9 | | 4 | | 5 | | 11 | |
| 29 | 12 | Northampton | 1–3 | 9981 | King | 1 | | | | | 2 | 3 | 7 | | | 8 | 10 | 6 | 9 | | 4 | | 5 | | 11 | |
| 30 | 15 | Halifax | 2–1 | 5053 | R.R.Hunt(pen), R.M.Hunt | | 1 | | | | 2 | 3 | 7 | | | | 8 | 6 | 9 | | 4 | | 5 | 10 | 11 | |
| 31 | 22 | BRISTOL R | 1–0 | 4560 | King | | 1 | | | | 2 | 3 | 7 | | | | 8 | 6 | 9 | | 4 | | 5 | 10 | 11 | |
| 32 | 27 | Crystal P | 1–0 | 11672 | Wright | 1 | | | | | 2 | 3 | 7 | | | | 8 | 6 | 9 | | 4 | | 5 | 10 | 11 | |
| 33 | 30 | Brighton | 0–3 | 6153 | | 1 | | | | | 2 | 3 | 7 | | | | 8 | 6 | 9 | | 4 | | 5 | 10 | 11 | |
| 34 | 1 Apr | Q.p.r. | 2–1 | 7688 | Grice, Wright | 1 | | | | | 2 | 3 | 7 | | | | 8 | 6 | 9 | | 4 | | 5 | 10 | 11 | |
| 35 | 9 | CARLISLE | 2–1 | 4282 | Grice, King | 1 | | | | | 2 | 3 | 7 | | | | 8 | 6 | 9 | | 4 | | 5 | 10 | 11 | |
| 36 | 13 | Swindon | 1–6 | 12157 | King | 1 | | | | | 2 | 3 | 7 | | 4 | | 8 | 6 | 9 | | | | 5 | 10 | 11 | |
| 37 | 15 | Watford | 1–1 | 6749 | King | | 1 | | | | 2 | 3 | 7 | | 4 | | 8 | 6 | 9 | | | | 5 | 10 | 11 | |
| 38 | 16 | WATFORD | 3–2 | 5315 | King, Wright, O.G. | | 1 | | | | 2 | 3 | 7 | | 4 | | 8 | | 9 | | | 6 | 5 | 10 | 11 | |
| 39 | 20 | PETERBOROUGH | 2–0 | 5143 | Grice, R.R.Hunt | | 1 | | | | 2 | 3 | 7 | | | | 8 | | 9 | | 4 | 6 | 5 | 10 | 11 | |
| 40 | 22 | Q.P.R. | 2–1 | 6556 | Grice, R.R.Hunt | | 1 | | | | 2 | 3 | 7 | | | | 8 | | 9 | | 4 | 6 | 5 | 10 | 11 | |
| 41 | 27 | Barnsley | 3–2 | 5283 | Grice, R.R.Hunt, Stark | | 1 | | | | 2 | 3 | 7 | | | | 8 | | 9 | | 4 | 6 | 5 | 10 | 11 | |
| 42 | 4 May | SOUTHEND | 3–1 | 7244 | R.R.Hunt, Stark | | 1 | | | | 2 | 3 | 7 | | | | 8 | | 9 | | 4 | 6 | 5 | 10 | 11 | |
| 43 | 6 | SWINDON | 0–2 | 6952 | | | 1 | | | | 2 | 3 | 7 | | | | 8 | | 9 | | 4 | 6 | 5 | 10 | 11 | |
| 44 | 11 | BOURNEMOUTH | 3–1 | 4414 | R.R.Hunt, King(2) | | 1 | | | | 2 | 3 | 7 | | | | 8 | | 9 | | 4 | 6 | 5 | 10 | 11 | |
| 45 | 14 | Bristol R | 0–2 | 9004 | | | 1 | | | | 2 | 3 | 7 | | | | 8 | | 9 | | 4 | 6 | 5 | 10 | 11 | |
| 46 | 17 | Notts County | 0–6 | 4103 | | | 1 | | | | 2 | 3 | 7 | | | | 8 | | 9 | | 4 | 6 | 5 | 10 | 11 | |

# F.A.Cup

| Rd | Date | Opponent | Score | Att | Scorers | 1 | 2 | 3 | 4 | 5 | 6 | 7 | 8 | 9 | 10 | 11 | 12 | 13 | 14 | 15 | 16 | 17 | 18 | 19 | 20 | 21 |
|---|---|---|---|---|---|---|---|---|---|---|---|---|---|---|---|---|---|---|---|---|---|---|---|---|---|---|
| 1st | 3 Nov | Wimbledon | 1-2 | 8500 | King | 1 | | | 6 | | 5 | 3 | 7 | 2 | | 10 | 8 | | 9 | | 4 | | | | 11 | |

# Football League Cup

| Rd | Date | Opponent | Score | Att | Scorers | 1 | 2 | 3 | 4 | 5 | 6 | 7 | 8 | 9 | 10 | 11 | 12 | 13 | 14 | 15 | 16 | 17 | 18 | 19 | 20 | 21 |
|---|---|---|---|---|---|---|---|---|---|---|---|---|---|---|---|---|---|---|---|---|---|---|---|---|---|---|
| 1st | 6 Sep | Watford | 2-1 | 4726 | Hunt.R, King | 1 | | | | | 5 | 3 | 7 | 2 | 4 | 10 | 8 | 6 | 9 | | | | | | 11 | |
| 2nd | 26 | Northampton | 0-2 | 7771 | | 1 | | | 6 | 10 | | 3 | | 2 | 4 | 7 | | | | 8 | | 9 | | | 11 | 5 |

A wintry scene at Layer Road in the 1962/63 winter.
Sever conditions ensured that no matches were played
between December the 22nd and February the 16th.

## THIRD DIVISION

| | | P | W | D | L | F | A | Pts |
|---|---|---|---|---|---|---|---|---|
| 1 | Northampton | 46 | 26 | 10 | 10 | 109 | 60 | 62 |
| 2 | Swindon | 46 | 22 | 14 | 10 | 87 | 56 | 58 |
| 3 | Port Vale | 46 | 23 | 8 | 15 | 72 | 58 | 54 |
| 4 | Coventry | 46 | 18 | 17 | 11 | 83 | 69 | 53 |
| 5 | Bournemouth | 46 | 18 | 16 | 12 | 63 | 46 | 52 |
| 6 | Peterborough | 46 | 20 | 11 | 15 | 93 | 75 | 51 |
| 7 | Notts County | 46 | 19 | 13 | 14 | 73 | 74 | 51 |
| 8 | Southend | 46 | 19 | 12 | 15 | 75 | 77 | 50 |
| 9 | Wrexham | 46 | 20 | 9 | 17 | 84 | 83 | 49 |
| 10 | Hull | 46 | 19 | 10 | 17 | 74 | 69 | 48 |
| 11 | Crystal Palace | 46 | 17 | 13 | 16 | 68 | 58 | 47 |
| 12 | Colchester | 46 | 18 | 11 | 17 | 73 | 93 | 47 |
| 13 | QPR | 46 | 17 | 11 | 18 | 85 | 76 | 45 |
| 14 | Bristol City | 46 | 16 | 13 | 17 | 100 | 92 | 45 |
| 15 | Shrewsbury | 46 | 16 | 12 | 18 | 83 | 81 | 44 |
| 16 | Millwall | 46 | 15 | 13 | 18 | 82 | 87 | 43 |
| 17 | Watford | 46 | 17 | 8 | 21 | 82 | 85 | 42 |
| 18 | Barnsley | 46 | 15 | 11 | 20 | 63 | 74 | 41 |
| 19 | Bristol Rovers | 46 | 15 | 11 | 20 | 70 | 88 | 41 |
| 20 | Reading | 46 | 16 | 8 | 22 | 74 | 78 | 40 |
| 21 | Bradford PA | 46 | 14 | 12 | 20 | 79 | 97 | 40 |
| 22 | Brighton | 46 | 12 | 12 | 22 | 58 | 84 | 36 |
| 23 | Carlisle | 46 | 13 | 9 | 24 | 61 | 89 | 35 |
| 24 | Halifax | 46 | 9 | 12 | 25 | 64 | 106 | 30 |

# SEASON 1963-64 — Division Three

| No. | Date | Opposition | Res | Attend | Goalscorers | Ames | Docherty | Forbes | Fowler | Grice | Hill | Hunt.R.R | Hunt.R.M | King | McColl | McCrohan | Miller | Ramage | Rumney | Rutter | Stark | Trevis | Woods | Wright |
|---|---|---|---|---|---|---|---|---|---|---|---|---|---|---|---|---|---|---|---|---|---|---|---|---|
| 1 | 24 Aug | BARNSLEY | 4-1 | 3507 | R.R.Hunt(3), Wright | | | 2 | | | 7 | 8 | 6 | | 10 | 4 | | 1 | | 5 | 9 | | 3 | 11 |
| 2 | 27 | Walsall | 1-1 | 9489 | McColl | | | 2 | | | 7 | 8 | 6 | | 10 | 4 | | 1 | | 5 | 9 | | 3 | 11 |
| 3 | 31 | Hull City | 0-0 | 11844 | | | | 2 | | 7 | 10 | | 6 | | 8 | 4 | | 1 | | 5 | 9 | | 3 | 11 |
| 4 | 7 Sep | BOURNEMOUTH | 1-2 | 4348 | Wright | | | 2 | | 7 | 10 | 8 | 6 | | | 4 | | 1 | | 5 | 9 | | 3 | 11 |
| 5 | 9 | WALSALL | 0-0 | 5419 | | | | 2 | | 7 | 10 | 8 | 6 | | | 4 | | 1 | | 5 | 9 | | 3 | 11 |
| 6 | 14 | Wrexham | 4-5 | 6310 | King(2), Stark, Wright | | 4 | 2 | | 7 | | 8 | 6 | 9 | | | | 1 | | 5 | 10 | | 3 | 11 |
| 7 | 16 | Millwall | 1-0 | 9321 | R.R.Hunt | | 4 | 2 | | | 7 | 8 | 6 | 9 | | | | 1 | | 5 | 10 | | 3 | 11 |
| 8 | 21 | Q.P.R. | 2-0 | 5418 | R.R.Hunt(pen), Stark | | | 2 | | 7 | | 8 | 6 | 9 | | 4 | | 1 | | 5 | 10 | | 3 | 11 |
| 9 | 28 | Bristol R | 1-3 | 10724 | Stark | | | 2 | | 7 | | 8 | 6 | 9 | | 4 | | 1 | | 5 | 10 | | 3 | 11 |
| 10 | 30 | MILLWALL | 2-0 | 5482 | Wright | | | 2 | | 7 | | 8 | 6 | 9 | | 4 | | 1 | | 5 | 10 | | 3 | 11 |
| 11 | 5 Oct | OLDHAM | 2-3 | 5190 | R.R.Hunt(2) | | | 2 | | 7 | | 8 | 6 | 9 | | 4 | | 1 | | 5 | 10 | | 3 | 11 |
| 12 | 7 | Southend | 0-0 | 8875 | | | | 2 | | 7 | | 8 | 6 | 9 | | 4 | | 1 | | 5 | 10 | | 3 | 11 |
| 13 | 12 | CREWE | 1-1 | 5232 | King | | 6 | 2 | | 7 | | 8 | | 9 | | 4 | | 1 | | 5 | 10 | | 3 | 11 |
| 14 | 14 | SOUTHEND | 3-3 | 6610 | King, Stark(2) | | 6 | 2 | | 7 | | 8 | | 9 | | 4 | | 1 | | 5 | 10 | | 3 | 11 |
| 15 | 19 | COVENTRY | 2-1 | 7189 | Grice, R.R.Hunt | | 6 | 2 | | 7 | | 8 | | 9 | | 4 | | 1 | | 5 | 10 | | 3 | 11 |
| 16 | 21 | Peterborough | 0-4 | 11505 | | | 6 | 2 | | 7 | | 8 | | 9 | | 4 | | 1 | | 5 | 10 | | 3 | 11 |
| 17 | 26 | Mansfield | 1-1 | 10278 | King | | 6 | 2 | | 7 | | 8 | | 9 | | 4 | | 1 | | 5 | 10 | | 3 | 11 |
| 18 | 28 | PETERBOROUGH | 4-1 | 6966 | R.R.Hunt, King, Stark, Wright | | 6 | 2 | | 7 | | 8 | | 9 | | 4 | | 1 | | 5 | 10 | | 3 | 11 |
| 19 | 2 Nov | BRENTFORD | 1-2 | 7117 | King | | 6 | 2 | | 7 | | 8 | | 9 | | 4 | | 1 | | 5 | 10 | | 3 | 11 |
| 20 | 9 | Shrewsbury | 1-1 | 6427 | Stark | | 6 | 2 | | 7 | 8 | | | 9 | | 4 | | 1 | | 5 | 10 | | 3 | 11 |
| 21 | 23 | Port Vale | 2-0 | 11158 | R.R.Hunt(2) | | 6 | 2 | | 7 | | 8 | | 9 | | 4 | | 1 | | 5 | 10 | | 3 | 11 |
| 22 | 30 | NOTTS COUNTY | 4-0 | 4377 | R.R.Hunt, King(2), Stark | | 6 | | 3 | 7 | | 8 | | 9 | | 4 | | 1 | | 5 | 10 | | 2 | 11 |
| 23 | 14 Dec | Barnsley | 1-1 | 4984 | Stark | | 6 | | 3 | 7 | | 8 | | 9 | | 4 | | 1 | | 5 | 10 | | 2 | 11 |
| 24 | 21 | HULL | 1-1 | 3609 | R.R.Hunt | | 6 | | 3 | 7 | | 8 | | 9 | | 4 | | 1 | | 5 | 10 | | 2 | 11 |
| 25 | 26 | READING | 2-1 | 5607 | R.R.Hunt, King | | 6 | | 3 | 7 | | 8 | | 9 | | 4 | | 1 | | 5 | 10 | | 2 | 11 |
| 26 | 28 | Reading | 3-5 | 7878 | R.R.Hunt, Stark, Wright | | 6 | | 3 | 7 | | 8 | | 9 | | 4 | | 1 | | 5 | 10 | | 2 | 11 |
| 27 | 11 Jan | Bournemouth | 2-2 | 8090 | King, Wright | 1 | 6 | | 3 | 7 | | 8 | | 9 | | 4 | | | | 5 | 10 | | 2 | 11 |
| 28 | 18 | WREXHAM | 4-1 | 4460 | R.R.Hunt(2)(1pen), Stark(2) | 1 | 6 | | 3 | 7 | | 8 | | 9 | | 4 | | | | 5 | 10 | | 2 | 11 |
| 29 | 25 | Luton | 1-3 | 4725 | R.R.Hunt | 1 | 6 | | 3 | 7 | | 8 | | 9 | | 4 | | | | 5 | 10 | | 2 | 11 |
| 30 | 1 Feb | Q.p.r. | 0-0 | 5225 | | 1 | 6 | | 3 | 7 | 10 | 8 | | 9 | | 4 | 11 | | | 5 | | | 2 | |
| 31 | 8 | BRISTOL R | 2-3 | 4747 | King(2) | 1 | 6 | | 3 | 7 | 10 | 8 | | 9 | | 4 | | | | 5 | | | 2 | 11 |
| 32 | 15 | Oldham | 2-2 | 11525 | R.R.Hunt(2)(1pen) | 1 | 6 | | 3 | 7 | 10 | 8 | | 9 | | 4 | | | | 5 | | | 2 | 11 |
| 33 | 22 | Crewe | 4-0 | 3886 | R.R.Hunt, King, Stark | 1 | 6 | | 3 | | 7 | 8 | | 9 | | 4 | | | | 5 | 10 | | 2 | 11 |
| 34 | 24 | BRISTOL C | 1-1 | 4803 | Docherty | 1 | 6 | | 3 | 11 | 7 | 9 | | | 8 | 4 | | | | 5 | 10 | | 2 | |
| 35 | 29 | Crystal P | 0-0 | 15421 | | 1 | 6 | 2 | | 11 | 7 | 8 | | 9 | | 4 | | | | 5 | 10 | | 3 | |
| 36 | 7 Mar | MANSFIELD | 1-1 | 3666 | Grice | 1 | 6 | 2 | 3 | 11 | 7 | | | | 10 | 4 | | | | 5 | 9 | 8 | | |
| 37 | 14 | Brentford | 1-3 | 7050 | Stark | 1 | 6 | 2 | 3 | 11 | 7 | | | | 10 | 4 | | | | 5 | 8 | 9 | | |
| | 21 | CRYSTAL P* | 1-1 | 5333 | King (* Abandoned) | 1 | 6 | 2 | 3 | 11 | 7 | | | 9 | | 4 | | | | 5 | 10 | 8 | | |
| 38 | 27 | Watford | 1-3 | 18393 | Grice | 1 | 6 | 2 | 3 | 11 | 7 | | | 9 | | 4 | | | | 5 | 10 | 8 | | |
| 39 | 28 | Bristol C | 1-3 | 7780 | Stark | 1 | | | 3 | 11 | 7 | | | 9 | 8 | 4 | | | | 5 | 10 | 6 | 2 | |
| 40 | 31 | WATFORD | 1-1 | 6477 | McCrohan(pen) | 1 | 10 | 5 | 3 | 11 | 7 | | | 9 | | 2 | | | 6 | | 8 | 4 | | |
| 41 | 4 Apr | PORT VALE | 1-2 | 3263 | Stark | 1 | 10 | 5 | 3 | 11 | 7 | | | 9 | | 2 | | | 6 | | 8 | 4 | | |
| 42 | 11 | Notts County | 1-3 | 3912 | McCrohan(pen) | 1 | 10 | 5 | 3 | | 7 | | | 9 | | 2 | | | 6 | | 8 | 4 | | 11 |
| 43 | 15 | CRYSTAL P | 1-1 | 5633 | Grice | 1 | 10 | 5 | 3 | 11 | 7 | | | 9 | | 2 | | | 6 | | 8 | 4 | | |
| 44 | 18 | LUTON | 1-1 | 3913 | King | 1 | 10 | 2 | 3 | 11 | 7 | | | 9 | | | | | 6 | 5 | 8 | 4 | | |
| 45 | 20 | SHREWSBURY | 1-0 | 3647 | King | 1 | 6 | 2 | 3 | 7 | 8 | | | 9 | | 4 | | | | 5 | 10 | | | 11 |
| 46 | 23 | Coventry | 0-1 | 36901 | | 1 | 6 | 2 | 3 | 7 | 8 | | | 9 | | 4 | | | | 5 | 10 | | | 11 |

# F.A.Cup

| | | | | | | | | | | | | | | | | | | | | | | | | |
|---|---|---|---|---|---|---|---|---|---|---|---|---|---|---|---|---|---|---|---|---|---|---|---|---|
| 1st | 9 Nov | Brighton | 1–0 | 14400 | R.R.Hunt | | 6 | 2 | | 7 | | 8 | | 9 | | 4 | | 1 | | 5 | 10 | | 3 | 11 |
| 2nd | 7 Dec | Q.P.R. | 0–1 | 6481 | | | 6 | | 3 | 7 | | 8 | | 9 | | 4 | | 1 | | 5 | 10 | | 2 | 11 |

# Football League Cup

| | | | | | | | | | | | | | | | | | | | | | | | | |
|---|---|---|---|---|---|---|---|---|---|---|---|---|---|---|---|---|---|---|---|---|---|---|---|---|
| 2nd | 25 Sep | FULHAM | 5–3 | 7772 | Grice, R.R.Hunt(pen), King, Stark(2) | | | 2 | | 7 | | 8 | 6 | 9 | | 4 | | 1 | | 5 | 10 | | 3 | 11 |
| 3rd | 4 Nov | NORTHAMPTON | 4–1 | 6237 | King, Wright(3) | | 6 | 2 | | 7 | 10 | 8 | | 9 | | 4 | | 1 | | 5 | | | 3 | 11 |
| 4th | 26 | Workington | 1–2 | 8237 | R.R.Hunt | | 6 | 2 | | 7 | | 8 | | 9 | | 4 | | 1 | | 5 | 10 | | 3 | 11 |

(Rear): Loughton, Rumney, Rutter, Ramage, Ames, Forbes, McCrohan, Fowler, Mildenhall.
(Middle): Mansfield, Docherty, Miller, McCall, Waylen, Griffiths, R.Hunt, Woods.
(Front): Grice, R.Hunt, Stark, Hill, Wright.

## THIRD DIVISION

| | | P | W | D | L | F | A | Pts |
|---|---|---|---|---|---|---|---|---|
| 1 | Coventry | 46 | 22 | 16 | 8 | 98 | 61 | 60 |
| 2 | Crystal Palace | 46 | 23 | 14 | 9 | 73 | 51 | 60 |
| 3 | Watford | 46 | 23 | 12 | 11 | 79 | 59 | 58 |
| 4 | Bournemouth | 46 | 24 | 8 | 14 | 79 | 58 | 56 |
| 5 | Bristol City | 46 | 20 | 15 | 11 | 84 | 64 | 55 |
| 6 | Reading | 46 | 21 | 10 | 15 | 79 | 62 | 52 |
| 7 | Mansfield | 46 | 20 | 11 | 15 | 76 | 62 | 51 |
| 8 | Hull | 46 | 16 | 17 | 13 | 73 | 68 | 49 |
| 9 | Oldham | 46 | 20 | 8 | 18 | 73 | 70 | 48 |
| 10 | Peterborough | 46 | 18 | 11 | 17 | 75 | 70 | 47 |
| 11 | Shrewsbury | 46 | 18 | 11 | 17 | 73 | 80 | 47 |
| 12 | Bristol Rovers | 46 | 19 | 8 | 19 | 91 | 79 | 46 |
| 13 | Port Vale | 46 | 16 | 14 | 16 | 53 | 49 | 46 |
| 14 | Southend | 46 | 15 | 15 | 16 | 77 | 78 | 45 |
| 15 | QPR | 46 | 18 | 9 | 19 | 76 | 78 | 45 |
| 16 | Brentford | 46 | 15 | 14 | 17 | 87 | 80 | 44 |
| 17 | Colchester | 46 | 12 | 19 | 15 | 70 | 68 | 43 |
| 18 | Luton | 46 | 16 | 10 | 20 | 64 | 80 | 42 |
| 19 | Walsall | 46 | 13 | 14 | 19 | 59 | 76 | 40 |
| 20 | Barnsley | 46 | 12 | 15 | 19 | 68 | 94 | 39 |
| 21 | Millwall | 46 | 14 | 10 | 22 | 53 | 67 | 38 |
| 22 | Crewe | 46 | 11 | 12 | 23 | 50 | 77 | 34 |
| 23 | Wrexham | 46 | 13 | 6 | 27 | 75 | 107 | 32 |
| 24 | Notts County | 46 | 9 | 9 | 28 | 45 | 92 | 27 |

# SEASON 1964-65 Division Three

| No. | Date | Opposition | Res | Attend | Goalscorers | Ames | Buck.A | Kennon | Aitchison | Connolly | Docherty | Forbes | Fowler | Grice | Griffiths | Hall | Hill | Jones | Kearney | King | Langley | Loughton | Mansfield | McColl | Price | Rumney | Salisbury | Stark | Trevis |
|---|---|---|---|---|---|---|---|---|---|---|---|---|---|---|---|---|---|---|---|---|---|---|---|---|---|---|---|---|---|
| 1 | 22 Aug | CARLISLE | 0-1 | 4420 | | 1 | | | 11 | 9 | 6 | 5 | 3 | 7 | 2 | | | | | 8 | | | | | | | 10 | | 4 |
| 2 | 26 | Luton | 1-3 | 9797 | Stark | 1 | | | 11 | 9 | 6 | 5 | 3 | 7 | 2 | | | | | | | | | | | | 8 | 10 | 4 |
| 3 | 29 | Port Vale | 2-1 | 8190 | Salisbury, Stark | 1 | | | 11 | 9 | 6 | 5 | 3 | 7 | 2 | | | | | | | | | | | | 8 | 10 | 4 |
| 4 | 31 | LUTON | 0-1 | 5115 | | 1 | | | 11 | 9 | 6 | 5 | 3 | 7 | 2 | | | | | | | | | | | | 8 | 10 | 4 |
| 5 | 5 Sept | HULL | 1-2 | 3310 | Trevis | 1 | | | 11 | | 6 | 5 | 3 | 7 | 2 | | 10 | | | 9 | | | | 8 | | | | | 4 |
| 6 | 7 | Mansfield | 1-0 | 11573 | McColl | 1 | | | 11 | 9 | 6 | 5 | 3 | 7 | 2 | | 10 | | | | | | | 8 | | | | | 4 |
| 7 | 12 | BRENTFORD | 0-3 | 3977 | | 1 | | | | 9 | 6 | 5 | 3 | | | | 7 | | 11 | | | | 10 | 8 | | 2 | | | 4 |
| 8 | 14 | MANSFIELD | 0-1 | 3544 | | 1 | | | | | 6 | 5 | 3 | 11 | | | 10 | | 7 | 9 | | | | 8 | | 2 | | | 4 |
| 9 | 19 | Bristol R | 2-2 | 13211 | King, Stark | 1 | | | 11 | | 6 | 5 | 3 | 7 | | | 10 | | | 9 | | | | | | 2 | | 8 | 4 |
| 10 | 26 | OLDHAM | 2-2 | 3642 | King, Trevis | 1 | | | 11 | | 6 | 5 | 3 | 7 | | | 10 | | | 9 | | | | | | 2 | | 8 | 4 |
| 11 | 30 | Grimsby | 0-2 | 8455 | | 1 | | | 11 | | 6 | 5 | 3 | 7 | 2 | | 10 | | | 9 | | | | | | | | 8 | 4 |
| 12 | 3 Oct | EXETER | 0-2 | 5800 | | | 1 | | 11 | 9 | 6 | 5 | 3 | 7 | 2 | | 10 | | | | | | | | | | | 8 | 4 |
| 13 | 5 | GRIMSBY | 0-1 | 3837 | | | 1 | | 11 | | 6 | 5 | 3 | 7 | 2 | | 10 | | 8 | | | | | | | | | 9 | 4 |
| 14 | 10 | Bristol C | 1-1 | 9983 | Langley | | 1 | | 11 | | | 5 | 3 | 7 | | | | 6 | | | 8 | | | | | 2 | 10 | 9 | 4 |
| 15 | 14 | Bournemouth | 1-3 | 7526 | Stark | | 1 | | 11 | | | 5 | 3 | | | | 7 | 6 | | | 8 | | | | | 2 | 10 | 9 | 4 |
| 16 | 17 | Q.P.R. | 1-2 | 3529 | Langley | | 1 | | 11 | | | 5 | 3 | | | | 7 | 6 | | | 8 | | | | | 2 | 7 | 9 | 4 |
| 17 | 19 | BOURNEMOUTH | 4-3 | 3454 | Aitchison, Langley(2), Stark | | 1 | | 11 | 9 | | 5 | 3 | | | | | 6 | | | 8 | | | | | 2 | 7 | 10 | 4 |
| 18 | 24 | Shrewsbury | 0-3 | 4770 | | | 1 | | 11 | 9 | 6 | 5 | 3 | | | | | | | | 8 | | | | | 2 | | 10 | 4 |
| 19 | 26 | WORKINGTON | 1-1 | 3700 | Connolly | | 1 | | 7 | 9 | 6 | 5 | 3 | 11 | | | | | | | 8 | | | | | 2 | 7 | 10 | 4 |
| 20 | 31 | READING | 2-2 | 3350 | Langley, Stark | | 1 | | | 9 | 6 | 5 | 3 | 11 | | | | | | | 8 | | | | | 2 | 10 | 10 | 4 |
| 21 | 7 Nov | Southend | 3-6 | 6941 | Connolly(2), Langley | | 1 | | 7 | 9 | 6 | 2 | 3 | 11 | | | | | | | 8 | 5 | | | | | | | 4 |
| 22 | 20 | Scunthorpe | 0-0 | 7454 | | 1 | | | 11 | 9 | 6 | 2 | 3 | 7 | | | | | | | 8 | 5 | | | | | | 10 | 4 |
| 23 | 28 | WALSALL | 2-1 | 3394 | Connolly, Stark | 1 | | | 11 | 9 | 6 | 2 | 3 | 7 | | | | | | | 8 | 5 | | | | | | 10 | 4 |
| 24 | 12 Dec | Carlisle | 1-4 | 5747 | Aitchison | 1 | | | 11 | 9 | 6 | 2 | 3 | 7 | | | | | | | 8 | 5 | | | | | | 10 | 4 |
| 25 | 19 | PORT VALE | 2-0 | 2528 | Langley, Trevis | 1 | | | 11 | | 6 | 2 | 3 | 7 | | | | 4 | | | 8 | 5 | | | | | | 10 | 9 |
| 26 | 26 | Gillingham | 1-2 | 10692 | Stark | 1 | | | 11 | | 6 | 2 | 3 | 7 | | | | 4 | | | 8 | 5 | | | | | | 10 | 9 |
| 27 | 28 | GILLINGHAM | 2-1 | 3966 | Trevis(2) | 1 | | | 11 | | 6 | 2 | 3 | 7 | | | | 4 | | | 8 | 5 | | | | | | 10 | 9 |
| 28 | 2 Jan | Hull | 1-5 | 16928 | Stark | 1 | | | 11 | | 6 | 2 | 3 | 7 | | | | 4 | | | 8 | 5 | | | | | | 10 | 9 |
| 29 | 9 | Barnsley | 4-1 | 2824 | Docherty, Langley(2), Stark | 1 | | | 11 | | 6 | 2 | 3 | 7 | | | | 4 | | | 8 | 5 | | | | | | 10 | 9 |
| 30 | 16 | Brentford | 0-1 | 9000 | | 1 | | | 11 | | 6 | 2 | 3 | 7 | | | | 4 | | | 8 | 5 | | | | | | 10 | 9 |
| 31 | 23 | BRISTOL R | 1-1 | 4851 | Stark | 1 | | | 11 | | 6 | 2 | 3 | 7 | | | | 4 | | | 8 | 5 | | | | | | 10 | 9 |
| 32 | 30 | Watford | 0-3 | 5720 | | 1 | | | 11 | | 6 | 2 | 3 | 7 | | | | 4 | | | 8 | 5 | | | | | | 10 | 9 |
| 33 | 6 Feb | Oldham | 1-3 | 6926 | Salisbury | 1 | | | 11 | | 6 | 2 | | 7 | | | | 4 | | | 8 | 5 | | | 3 | | 10 | | 9 |
| 34 | 13 | EXETER | 1-1 | 3073 | Langley | 1 | | | 11 | | 6 | 2 | 3 | 7 | | | | 4 | | | 8 | 5 | | | | | 10 | | 9 |
| 35 | 20 | BRISTOL C | 2-3 | 2905 | Stark(2) | 1 | | | 11 | | 6 | 2 | 3 | 7 | | | | 4 | | | 8 | 5 | | | | | | 8 | 10 |
| 36 | 26 | Q.p.r. | 0-5 | 4462 | | 1 | | | 11 | 9 | 6 | 2 | 3 | 7 | | | | 4 | | | 8 | 5 | | | | | | | 10 |
| 37 | 6 Mar | WATFORD | 0-0 | 3385 | | | | 1 | | | 6 | 2 | | 7 | | 11 | | 4 | | | 8 | 5 | | | 3 | | | 9 | 10 |
| 38 | 13 | Reading | 1-1 | 5502 | Connolly | | | 1 | | 9 | 6 | 2 | | 7 | | 11 | | 4 | | | 8 | 5 | | | 3 | | | | 10 |
| 39 | 20 | SOUTHEND | 3-1 | 2929 | Connolly, Langley, O.G. | | | 1 | | 9 | 6 | 2 | | 7 | | 11 | | 4 | | | 8 | 5 | | | 3 | | | | 10 |
| 40 | 26 | Barnsley | 2-1 | 3070 | Hall, Loughton | | | 1 | 11 | | 6 | 2 | | 7 | | 9 | | 4 | | | 8 | 5 | | | 3 | | | | 10 |
| 41 | 3 Apr | SCUNTHORPE | 2-1 | 3212 | Grice, Trevis | | | 1 | | 9 | 6 | 2 | | 7 | | 11 | | 4 | | | 8 | 5 | | | 3 | | | | 10 |
| 42 | 10 | Walsall | 1-2 | 2766 | Langley | | | 1 | | 9 | 6 | 2 | | 7 | | 11 | | 4 | | | 8 | 5 | | | 3 | | | | 10 |
| 43 | 16 | PETERBOROUGH | 0-1 | 6074 | | | | 1 | | 9 | 6 | 2 | | 7 | | 11 | | 4 | | | 8 | 5 | | | 3 | | | | 10 |
| 44 | 17 | SHREWSBURY | 0-4 | 3058 | | | | 1 | | | 6 | 2 | | 7 | | 11 | 10 | 4 | | | 8 | 5 | | | 3 | | | | 9 |
| 45 | 19 | Peterborough | 1-4 | 6262 | Aitchison | | | 1 | 7 | | | 2 | | | | 11 | 10 | 4 | | | 9 | 5 | | | 3 | | 8 | | 6 |
| 46 | 23 | Workington | 0-1 | 3001 | | | | 1 | 4 | | 6 | 2 | | 7 | | 11 | 10 | | | | 9 | | | | 3 | | 8 | | 5 |

# F.A.Cup

| | | | | | | 1 | 2 | 3 | 4 | 5 | 6 | 7 | 8 | 9 | 10 | 11 | 12 | 13 | 14 | 15 | 16 | 17 | 18 | 19 | 20 | 21 | 22 | 23 | 24 |
|---|---|---|---|---|---|---|---|---|---|---|---|---|---|---|---|---|---|---|---|---|---|---|---|---|---|---|---|---|---|
| 1st | 14 Nov | BIDEFORD | 3-3 | 4566 | King, Salisbury, Trevis | | 1 | | 7 | 9 | 6 | 2 | 3 | 11 | | | | | | | 8 | 5 | | | | | 10 | | 4 |
| 1st/R | 18 | Bideford | 2-1 | 4513 | Connolly, Stark | 1 | | | 11 | 9 | 6 | 2 | 3 | 7 | | | | | | | 8 | 5 | | | | | | 10 | 4 |
| 2nd | 5 Dec | Torquay | 0-2 | 4724 | | 1 | | | 11 | 9 | 6 | 2 | 3 | 7 | | | | | | | 8 | 5 | | | | | | 10 | 4 |

# Football League Cup

| | | | | | | 1 | 2 | 3 | 4 | 5 | 6 | 7 | 8 | 9 | 10 | 11 | 12 | 13 | 14 | 15 | 16 | 17 | 18 | 19 | 20 | 21 | 22 | 23 | 24 |
|---|---|---|---|---|---|---|---|---|---|---|---|---|---|---|---|---|---|---|---|---|---|---|---|---|---|---|---|---|---|
| 1st | 2 Sep | TORQUAY | 1-1 | 2218 | Aitchison | 1 | | | 11 | | 6 | 5 | 3 | 7 | 2 | | | | | 9 | | | | 8 | | | 10 | | 4 |
| 1st/R | 10 | Torquay | 0-3 | 4683 | | 1 | | | | ? | | ? | ? | ? | ? | | ? | | | | | | | ? | | | | | |

Printed Reserve team programmes were issued at this time, and consisted of a single page, double sided sheet priced 2d. (1p)

PRICE TWOPENCE

**Colchester United Football Club**

Monday, 22nd March, 1965 Kick-off 7.30 p.m.

LAYER ROAD GROUND, COLCHESTER

ESSEX PROFESSIONAL CUP : SEMI-FINAL

**COLCHESTER UNITED**

*Versus*

**CLACTON TOWN**

COLCHESTER UNITED

*Colours:* BLUE AND WHITE

RIGHT] Neil Kennon 1 [LEFT

Duncan Forbes 2 Ray Price 3

John Docherty 4 Mick Loughton 5 Derek Trevis 6

Billy Stark 8 Garry Salisbury 10

Bobby Hill 7 Pat Connolly 9 John Hornsby 11

Referee: R. A. L. WILLIAMS (Thorpe Bay)

Linesmen: D. M. GROUNDS (Billericay) *Yellow Flag*

H. R. J. HILL (Laindon) *Red Flag*

Kavanagh 11 Constant 10 Meacher 9 Coleman 8 Smith 7

Dellar 6 Phelan 5 Drinkwater 4

Hayward 3 Johnstone 2

LEFT] Wright 1 [RIGHT

CLACTON TOWN

*Colours:* WHITE

**THIRD DIVISION**

| | | P | W | D | L | F | A | Pts |
|---|---|---|---|---|---|---|---|---|
| 1 | Carlisle | 46 | 25 | 10 | 11 | 76 | 53 | 60 |
| 2 | Bristol City | 46 | 24 | 11 | 11 | 92 | 55 | 59 |
| 3 | Mansfield | 46 | 24 | 11 | 11 | 95 | 61 | 59 |
| 4 | Hull | 46 | 23 | 12 | 11 | 91 | 57 | 58 |
| 5 | Brentford | 46 | 24 | 9 | 13 | 83 | 55 | 57 |
| 6 | Bristol Rovers | 46 | 20 | 15 | 11 | 82 | 58 | 55 |
| 7 | Gillingham | 46 | 23 | 9 | 14 | 70 | 50 | 55 |
| 8 | Peterborough | 46 | 22 | 7 | 17 | 85 | 74 | 51 |
| 9 | Watford | 46 | 17 | 16 | 13 | 71 | 64 | 50 |
| 10 | Grimsby | 46 | 16 | 17 | 13 | 68 | 67 | 49 |
| 11 | Bournemouth | 46 | 18 | 11 | 17 | 72 | 63 | 47 |
| 12 | Southend | 46 | 19 | 8 | 19 | 78 | 71 | 46 |
| 13 | Reading | 46 | 16 | 14 | 16 | 70 | 70 | 46 |
| 14 | QPR | 46 | 17 | 12 | 17 | 72 | 80 | 46 |
| 15 | Workington | 46 | 17 | 12 | 17 | 58 | 69 | 46 |
| 16 | Shrewsbury | 46 | 15 | 12 | 19 | 76 | 84 | 42 |
| 17 | Exeter | 46 | 12 | 17 | 17 | 51 | 52 | 41 |
| 18 | Scunthorpe | 46 | 14 | 12 | 20 | 65 | 72 | 40 |
| 19 | Walsall | 46 | 15 | 7 | 24 | 55 | 80 | 37 |
| 20 | Oldham | 46 | 13 | 10 | 23 | 61 | 83 | 36 |
| 21 | Luton | 46 | 11 | 11 | 24 | 51 | 94 | 33 |
| 22 | Port Vale | 46 | 9 | 14 | 23 | 41 | 76 | 32 |
| 23 | Colchester | 46 | 10 | 10 | 26 | 50 | 89 | 30 |
| 24 | Barnsley | 46 | 9 | 11 | 26 | 54 | 90 | 29 |

# SEASON 1965-66 Division Four

| No. | Date | Opposition | Res | Attend | Goalscorers | Buck.A | Kennon | Aitchison | Bell | Blackwood | Buck.D | Bullock | Forbes | Fowler | Grice | Hall | Hornsby | Jones | Kaye | Laitt | Loughton | Mansfield | Phillips | Price | Raine | Stark | Stratton | Trevis |
|---|---|---|---|---|---|---|---|---|---|---|---|---|---|---|---|---|---|---|---|---|---|---|---|---|---|---|---|---|
| 1 | 21 Aug | Port Vale | 0-1 | 11212 | | | 1 | 8 | 6 | | | | 2 | | | 3 | 11 | | 7 | | 5 | | | | | 10 | 9 | 4 |
| 2 | 23 | HALIFAX | 1-0 | 4473 | Kaye | | 1 | 8 | 6 | | | | 2 | | | 3 | 11 | | 7 | | 5 | | | | | 10 | 9 | 4 |
| 3 | 28 | CREWE | 1-1 | 4040 | Stark | | 1 | 10 | 6 | | | | 2 | | 11 | 3 | | | 7 | | 5 | | | | | 8 | 9 | 4 |
| 4 | 4 Sep | Bradford | 2-1 | 2692 | Aitchison, Stratton | | 1 | 8 | | 10 | | | 2 | | 11 | 3 | | 6 | 7 | | 5 | | | | | | 9 | 4 |
| 5 | 11 | BARNSLEY | 4-0 | 5082 | Aitchison, Phillips(3) | | 1 | 8 | | 6 | | | 2 | | 11 | 3 | | | 7 | | 5 | | 10 | | | | 9 | 4 |
| 6 | 14 | Halifax | 1-1 | 2773 | Stratton | | 1 | 8 | | 6 | | | 2 | | 11 | 3 | | | 7 | | 5 | | 10 | | | | 9 | 4 |
| 7 | 18 | ROCHDALE | 2-0 | 4968 | Stratton(2) | | 1 | 8 | | 6 | | | 2 | | 11 | 3 | | | 7 | | 5 | | 10* | 12 | | | 9 | 4 |
| 8 | 24 | Tranmere | 0-2 | 8821 | | | 1 | | | 6 | | | 2 | | 7 | 3* | 11 | | 8 | | 5 | | 10 | | 12 | | 9 | 4 |
| 9 | 2 Oct | STOCKPORT | 3-2 | 4968 | Phillips, Stratton(2) | | 1 | | | 6 | | | 2 | 11 | 7 | 3 | | 8 | | | 5 | | 10 | | | | 9 | 4 |
| 10 | 7 | Notts County | 0-1 | 5681 | | | 1 | 8* | | 6 | | | 2 | 11 | 12 | 3 | | | 7 | | 5 | | 10 | | | | 9 | 4 |
| 11 | 9 | Barrow | 0-3 | 5378 | | | 1 | | | 6 | | | 2 | | 11 | 3 | | 8 | 7 | | 5 | | 10 | | | | 9 | 4 |
| 12 | 16 | HARTLEPOOLS | 2-0 | 4421 | Stratton, Trevis | | 1 | | 6 | 8 | 12 | | 2 | | 11 | 3 | | | 7 | | 5 | | 10 | | | | 9* | 4 |
| | 22 | Doncaster* | 1-0 | 4263 | * Abandoned Blackwood | | 1 | | | 8 | | | 2 | | | 3 | 11 | | 7 | | 5 | | 10 | | 4 | | 9 | 6 |
| 13 | 30 | SOUTHPORT | 0-0 | 4169 | | 1 | | | | 6 | | 8 | 2 | | 11 | 3 | | | 7 | 12 | 5 | | 10 | | | | 9* | 4 |
| 14 | 6 Nov | Wrexham | 3-2 | 3743 | Hall, Loughton, Phillips | | 1 | | | 9 | | 8 | 2 | 3 | | 11 | | | 7 | | 5 | | 10 | | 6 | | | 4 |
| 15 | 20 | Aldershot | 3-1 | 3097 | Blackwood, Phillips, Trevis | | 1 | | | 9 | | 8 | 2 | 3 | | 11 | | | 7 | | 5 | | 10 | | 6 | | | 4 |
| 16 | 22 | NOTTS COUNTY | 4-1 | 2768 | Bullock, Forbes, Hall, O.G. | | 1 | | | 9 | | 8 | 2 | 3 | | 11 | | | 7 | | 5 | | 10 | | 6 | | | 4 |
| 17 | 27 | NEWPORT | 3-2 | 3593 | Hall(3) | | 1 | | | 9 | | 8 | 2 | 3 | | 11 | | | 7 | | 5 | | 10 | | 4 | | | 6 |
| 18 | 4 Dec | Doncaster | 0-2 | 6035 | | | 1 | | | 9 | | 8 | 2 | 3 | | 11 | | | 7 | | 5 | | 10 | | 4 | | | 6 |
| 19 | 11 | CHESTERFIELD | 3-0 | 3867 | Blackwood, Bullock, Hall | | 1 | | | 9 | | 8 | 2 | 3 | | 11 | | | 7 | | 5 | | 10 | | 4 | | | 6 |
| 20 | 18 | Harlepools | 1-0 | 3967 | Phillips | | 1 | | | 9 | | 8 | 2 | 3 | | 11 | | | 7 | | 5 | | 10 | | 4 | | | 6 |
| 21 | 27 | CHESTER | 1-1 | 7840 | Phillips | | 1 | | | 9 | | 8 | 2 | 3 | | 11 | | | 7 | | 5 | | 10 | | 4 | | | 6 |
| 22 | 28 | Chester | 1-2 | 8361 | Bullock | | 1 | | | 4 | | 8 | | | | 3 | 11 | | 7 | | 5 | | 10 | 2 | | | 9 | 6 |
| 23 | 1 Jan | BARROW | 2-2 | 4676 | Blackwood | | 1 | | | 10 | | 8 | | 3 | | 11 | | | 7 | | 5 | | | 2 | 4 | | 9 | 6 |
| 24 | 8 | Bradford p.a. | 0-1 | 5867 | | | 1 | | | 4 | | 8 | | 3 | | 11 | | | 7 | | 5 | | 10 | 2 | | | 9 | 6 |
| 25 | 15 | DONCASTER | 2-1 | 3778 | Bullock(2) | | 1 | | 6 | 10 | | 8 | | | | 3 | | | 7 | | 5 | 9 | | 2 | | | 11 | 4 |
| 26 | 29 | PORT VALE | 3-0 | 4481 | Hornsby, Phillips, O.G. | | 1 | | | 9 | | 8 | 2 | | | 3 | 11 | | 7 | | 5 | 12 | 10 | | 4 | | | 6* |
| 27 | 5 Feb | Crewe | 2-0 | 5470 | Phillips(2) | | 1 | | 6 | | | 8 | 2 | | | 3 | 11 | | 7 | | 5 | | 10 | | 4 | | 9 | |
| 28 | 12 | Lincoln | 2-0 | 2294 | Phillips, Stratton | | 1 | | 6 | | | 8 | 2* | | | 3 | 11 | | 7 | | 5 | 12 | 10 | | 4 | | 9 | |
| 29 | 19 | BRADFORD | 0-1 | 4936 | | | 1 | | | 6 | | 8 | 2 | | | 3 | 11 | | 7 | | 5 | | 10 | | 4 | | 9 | |
| 30 | 26 | Barnsley | 1-1 | 3166 | Hall | | 1 | | | 6 | | 8 | 2 | 3 | | 11 | | | 7 | | 5 | | 10 | | | | 9 | 4 |
| 31 | 28 | BRADFORD P.A. | 6-3 | 4921 | Bullock(3), Kaye, Stratton, Trevis | | 1 | | | 6 | | 8 | 2 | 3 | | 11 | | | 7 | | 5 | | 10 | | | | 9 | 4 |
| 32 | 5 Mar | LINCOLN | 3-0 | 5055 | Bullock, Hall, Phillips | | 1 | | | 6 | | 8 | 2 | 3 | | 11 | | | 7 | | 5 | | 10 | | | | 9 | 4 |
| 33 | 11 | Rochdale | 1-0 | 1780 | Stratton | | 1 | | | 6 | | 8 | 2 | 3 | | 11 | | | 7 | | 5* | | 10 | | 12 | | 9 | 4 |
| 34 | 19 | TRANMERE | 2-1 | 6611 | Stratton(2) | | 1 | | | 6 | | 8 | 2 | 3 | | 11 | | | 7 | | 5 | | 10 | | | | 9 | 4 |
| 35 | 25 | Stockport | 0-1 | 6500 | | | 1 | 12 | | 6 | | 8 | 2 | 3 | | 11 | | | 7* | | 5 | | 10 | | | | 9 | 4 |
| 36 | 2 Apr | WREXHAM | 1-1 | 5012 | Stratton | | 1 | | | 4 | | 8 | 2 | 3 | 7 | 11 | | | | | 5 | | 10 | | | | 9 | 6 |
| 37 | 8 | LUTON | 2-2 | 10200 | Stratton(2) | | 1 | | | 4 | | 8 | 2 | 3 | 7 | 11 | | | | | 5* | | 10 | | 12 | | 9 | 6 |
| 38 | 9 | Torquay | 1-0 | 7678 | Aitchison | | 1 | 7 | | 10 | | 8 | 2 | | | 3 | 11 | | | | 5 | | | | 4 | | 9 | 6 |
| 39 | 11 | Luton | 1-1 | 15245 | Stratton | | 1 | 7 | | 10 | | 8 | 2 | | | 3 | 11 | | | | 5 | | | | 4 | | 9 | 6 |
| 40 | 16 | ALDERSHOT | 0-0 | 5356 | | | 1 | | | 10 | | 8 | 2 | | | 3 | 11 | | 7 | | 5 | | | | 4 | | 9 | 6 |
| 41 | 25 | DARLINGTON | 0-1 | 7353 | | | 1 | 7 | | 11 | | 8 | 2 | | | 3 | | | | | 5 | | 10 | | 4 | | 9 | 6 |
| 42 | 30 | TORQUAY | 0-2 | 5922 | | | 1 | 7 | | 10 | | 8 | 2 | 3 | | 11 | | | | | 5 | | | | 4 | | 9 | 6 |
| 43 | 7 May | Chesterfield | 4-2 | 3943 | Bullock(2), Hall, Stratton | | 1 | | | 4 | | 8 | 2 | 3 | | 11 | | | 7 | | | 10 | | | 5 | | 9 | 6 |
| 44 | 10 | Southport | 1-0 | 4983 | Mansfield | | 1 | | | 4 | | 8 | 2 | 3 | | 11 | | | 7 | | 5 | 10 | | | | | 9 | 6 |
| 45 | 16 | Darlington | 0-2 | 12474 | | | 1 | | | 4 | | 8 | 2 | 3 | | 11 | | | 7 | | 5 | 10 | | | | | 9 | 6 |
| 46 | 28 | Newport | 1-2 | 2905 | Trevis | | 1 | 7 | | 4 | | 8 | 2 | 3 | | 11 | | | | | 5 | 10 | | | | | 9 | 6 |

# F.A.Cup

| 1st | 13 Nov | Q.P.R. | 3–3 | 6693 | Blackwood, Hall | | 1 | | | 9 | | 8 | 2 | 3 | | 11 | 12 | | 7 | | 5 | | 10 | | 6 | | | 4 |
|---|---|---|---|---|---|---|---|---|---|---|---|---|---|---|---|---|---|---|---|---|---|---|---|---|---|---|---|---|
| 1st/R | 17 | Q.p.r. | 0–4 | 6166 | | | 1 | | 12 | 9 | | 8 | 2 | 3 | | 11 | | | 7 | | 5 | | 10 | | 4 | | | 6 |

# Football League Cup

| 1st | 1 Sept | EXETER | 2–1 | 2988 | Stratton(2) | | 1 | 8 | | 10 | | | 2 | | 11 | 3 | | 4 | 7 | | 5 | | | | | | 9 | 6 |
|---|---|---|---|---|---|---|---|---|---|---|---|---|---|---|---|---|---|---|---|---|---|---|---|---|---|---|---|---|
| 2nd | 22 | MIDDLESBROUGH | 2–4 | 7777 | Hall, Stratton | | 1 | | | 10 | | | 2 | | 7 | 3 | 11 | | 8 | | 5 | | | | 4 | | 9 | 6 |

THIS SEASON'S PLAYING STAFF.

**Back Row.** Barratt, Loughton, Freeman, Stark, Trevis, Forbes, Stratton, Manager Neil Franklin. **Middle Row.** Trainer John Anderson, Jones, Raine, Price, Buck, Kennon, **Front Row.** Lamont, Mansfield, Kaye, Hornsby, Bell, Blackwood, Aitchison.

*Photo by courtesy of The "Essex County Standard"*

**DIVISION 4**

| | P | W | D | L | F | A | W | D | L | F | A | Pts |
|---|---|---|---|---|---|---|---|---|---|---|---|---|
| Doncaster R | 46 | 15 | 6 | 2 | 49 | 21 | 9 | 5 | 9 | 36 | 33 | 59 |
| Darlington | 46 | 16 | 3 | 4 | 41 | 17 | 9 | 6 | 8 | 31 | 36 | 59 |
| Torquay U | 46 | 17 | 2 | 4 | 43 | 20 | 7 | 8 | 8 | 29 | 29 | 58 |
| Colchester U | 46 | 13 | 7 | 3 | 45 | 21 | 10 | 3 | 10 | 25 | 26 | 56 |
| Tranmere R | 46 | 15 | 1 | 7 | 56 | 32 | 9 | 7 | 7 | 37 | 34 | 56 |
| Luton T | 46 | 19 | 2 | 2 | 65 | 27 | 5 | 6 | 12 | 25 | 43 | 56 |
| Chester | 46 | 15 | 5 | 3 | 52 | 27 | 5 | 7 | 11 | 27 | 43 | 52 |
| Notts Co | 46 | 9 | 8 | 6 | 32 | 25 | 10 | 4 | 9 | 29 | 28 | 50 |
| Newport Co | 46 | 14 | 6 | 3 | 46 | 24 | 4 | 6 | 13 | 29 | 51 | 48 |
| Southport | 46 | 15 | 6 | 2 | 47 | 20 | 3 | 6 | 14 | 21 | 49 | 48 |
| Bradford | 46 | 14 | 2 | 7 | 59 | 31 | 7 | 3 | 13 | 43 | 61 | 47 |
| Barrow | 46 | 12 | 8 | 3 | 48 | 31 | 4 | 7 | 12 | 24 | 45 | 47 |
| Stockport Co | 46 | 12 | 4 | 7 | 42 | 29 | 6 | 2 | 15 | 29 | 41 | 42 |
| Crewe A | 46 | 12 | 4 | 7 | 42 | 23 | 4 | 5 | 14 | 19 | 40 | 41 |
| Halifax T | 46 | 11 | 6 | 6 | 46 | 31 | 4 | 5 | 14 | 21 | 44 | 41 |
| Barnsley | 46 | 11 | 6 | 6 | 43 | 24 | 4 | 4 | 15 | 31 | 54 | 40 |
| Aldershot | 46 | 12 | 6 | 5 | 47 | 27 | 3 | 4 | 16 | 28 | 57 | 40 |
| Hartlepools U | 46 | 13 | 4 | 6 | 44 | 22 | 3 | 4 | 16 | 19 | 53 | 40 |
| Port Vale | 46 | 12 | 7 | 4 | 38 | 18 | 3 | 2 | 18 | 10 | 41 | 39 |
| Chesterfield | 46 | 8 | 9 | 6 | 37 | 35 | 5 | 4 | 14 | 25 | 43 | 39 |
| Rochdale | 46 | 12 | 1 | 10 | 46 | 27 | 4 | 4 | 15 | 25 | 60 | 37 |
| Lincoln C | 46 | 9 | 7 | 7 | 37 | 29 | 4 | 4 | 15 | 20 | 53 | 37 |
| Bradford C | 46 | 10 | 5 | 8 | 37 | 34 | 2 | 8 | 13 | 26 | 60 | 37 |
| Wrexham | 46 | 10 | 4 | 9 | 43 | 43 | 3 | 5 | 15 | 29 | 61 | 35 |

# SEASON 1966-67

## Division Three

| No. | Date | Opposition | Res | Attend | Goalscorers | Buck.A | Kennon | Barlow | Blackwood | Bullock | Forbes | Hall | Hodgson | Kaye | Loughton | Mansfield | Martin | Mochan | Price.R | Raine | Shires | Stratton | Trevis | Westlake |
|---|---|---|---|---|---|---|---|---|---|---|---|---|---|---|---|---|---|---|---|---|---|---|---|---|
| 1 | 20 Aug | MIDDLESBROUGH | 2-3 | 4382 | Bullock, Stratton | 1 | | | 4 | 8 | 2 | 3 | 9 | 7 | 5 | | 11 | | | | | 10 | 6 | |
| 2 | 27 | Shrewsbury | 1-2 | 4819 | Stratton | 1 | | | | 8 | 2 | 3 | 9 | | 5 | | 11 | | | 4 | 7 | 10 | 6 | |
| 3 | 3 Sep | WATFORD | 2-1 | 4232 | Hodgson, Stratton(pen) | 1 | | | | 8 | 2 | 3 | 9 | | 5 | | 11 | | | 4 | 7 | 10 | 6 | |
| 4 | 6 | Swindon | 1-1 | 11600 | Hodgson | 1 | | | | 8 | 2 | 3 | 9 | 12 | 5 | | 11 | | | 4* | 7 | 10 | 6 | |
| 5 | 10 | BRISTOL R | 3-1 | 4736 | Hodgson, Stratton, O.G. | 1 | | | | 8 | 2 | 3 | 9 | | 5 | | 11 | | | 4 | 7 | 10 | 6 | |
| 6 | 17 | Oxford | 1-1 | 6503 | Hodgson | 1 | | | | 8 | 2 | 3 | 9 | | 5 | | 11 | | | 4 | 7 | 10 | 6 | |
| 7 | 24 | OLDHAM | 3-2 | 5921 | Hodgson(2), O.G. | 1 | | | | 8 | 2 | 7 | 9 | | 5 | | 11 | 3 | | 4 | | 10 | 6 | |
| 8 | 26 | SWINDON | 2-1 | 7874 | Forbes, Hodgson | 1 | | | | 8 | 2 | 7 | 9 | | 5 | | 11 | 3 | | 4 | | 10 | 6 | |
| 9 | 30 | Scunthorpe | 1-3 | 5222 | Stratton | 1 | | | | 8 | 2 | 7 | 9 | | 5 | | 11 | 3 | | 4 | | 10 | 6 | |
| 10 | 8 Oct | Reading | 3-2 | 7213 | Martin, Shires(2) | 1 | | | | 8 | 2 | 3 | 9 | | 5 | | 11 | 12 | | 4* | 7 | 10 | 6 | |
| 11 | 15 | DONCASTER | 5-0 | 6461 | Bullock(2), Hodgson, Stratton(2) | 1 | | | | 8 | 2 | 3 | 9 | | 5 | | 11 | | | 4 | 7 | 10 | 6 | |
| 12 | 17 | LEYTON ORIENT | 2-2 | 8969 | Stratton(2) | 1 | | | | 8 | 2 | 3* | 9 | | | 12 | 11 | 6 | | 5 | 7 | 10 | 4 | |
| 13 | 22 | Mansfield | 0-2 | 6028 | | 1 | | | | 8 | 2 | 3 | 9 | | | | 11 | 6 | | 5 | 7 | 10 | 4 | |
| 14 | 29 | GRIMSBY | 4-0 | 6330 | Bullock, Hodgson, Stratton(2) | 1 | | | | 8 | 2 | 3 | 9 | | 5 | | 11 | | | 4 | 7 | 10 | 6 | |
| 15 | 4 Nov | Walsall | 0-1 | 8192 | | 1 | | | | 8 | 2 | 11 | 9 | | 5 | | 11 | 3 | | 4 | | 10 | 6 | |
| 16 | 12 | PETERBOROUGH | 1-4 | 6353 | Hodgson | 1 | | | | 8 | 2 | 3 | 9 | | 5 | | 11 | | | 4 | 7 | 10 | 6 | |
| 17 | 14 | Leyton Orient | 3-3 | 5714 | Hodgson, Stratton(2) | 1 | | | 6 | 8 | 2 | 3 | 9 | | 5 | | 11 | | | | 7 | 10 | 4 | |
| 18 | 19 | Torquay | 0-5 | 5056 | | 1 | | | 6 | 8 | 2 | 3 | 9 | | 5 | | 11 | | | | 7 | 10 | 4 | |
| 19 | 3 Dec | Darlington | 4-0 | 5706 | Mansfield(2), Martin, Stratton | | 1 | | 6 | | 2 | 3 | 9 | 7 | | 8 | 11 | | | 5 | | 10 | 4 | |
| 20 | 10 | Q.P.R. | 1-3 | 8195 | Stratton | | 1 | | 6 | | 2 | 3 | 9 | 7 | | 8 | 11 | 12 | | 5* | | 10 | 4 | |
| 21 | 17 | Middlesbrough | 0-4 | 8891 | | | 1 | | | | 2 | 3 | 9 | 7 | 5* | 8 | 11 | 12 | | 6 | | 10 | 4 | |
| 22 | 26 | Bournemouth | 1-1 | 5478 | Martin | | 1 | | | 12 | 5 | 3 | 9 | 8 | | | 11 | 2 | | 6 | 7* | 10 | 4 | |
| 23 | 27 | BOURNEMOUTH | 2-0 | 6140 | Bullock, Hodgson | | 1 | 7 | | 8 | 5 | 3 | 9 | | | | 11 | 2 | | 6 | | 10 | 4 | |
| 24 | 31 | SHREWSBURY | 3-1 | 4980 | Bullock, Hodgson, Stratton | | 1 | | | 8 | 5 | 3 | 9 | 7 | | | 11 | 2 | | 6 | | 10 | 4 | |
| 25 | 14 Jan | Bristol R | 1-4 | 15415 | Stratton | | 1 | | | 8 | 5 | 3 | 9 | 7 | 4 | | 11 | 2 | | | | 10 | 6 | |
| 26 | 21 | OXFORD | 1-2 | 4755 | Stratton | 1 | | | | 8 | 5 | 3 | 9 | 7 | 4 | | 11 | 2 | | | | 10 | 6 | |
| 27 | 28 | Workington | 0-1 | 2589 | | 1 | | | | | 2 | 9 | 8 | 7 | 5 | | 11 | 3 | | 4 | | 10 | 6 | |
| 28 | 4 Feb | Oldham | 0-4 | 8961 | | 1 | | | 6 | | 2 | | 9 | | 5 | 8 | 11 | 3 | | | 7 | 10 | 4 | |
| 29 | 11 | SCUNTHORPE | 0-1 | 3965 | | | 1 | | 6 | 8 | 5 | 3 | 9 | 7 | | | 11 | 2 | | | | 10 | 4 | |
| 30 | 18 | Gillingham | 1-2 | 6147 | Stratton | | 1 | | 6 | 8 | 5 | 3 | | | | 7 | 11 | 2 | | 4 | | 10 | | 9 |
| 31 | 25 | READING | 2-0 | 4331 | Stratton, Westlake | | 1 | | 6 | 8 | 5 | 3 | 7 | | | | 11 | 2 | | | | 10 | 4 | 9 |
| 32 | 3 Mar | Doncaster | 4-1 | 8481 | Martin(2)(1pen), Stratton, Westlake | | 1 | | 6 | 8 | 5 | 3 | 7 | | | | 11 | 2 | | | | 10 | 4 | 9 |
| 33 | 11 | GILLINGHAM | 0-0 | 4915 | | | 1 | | 6 | 8* | 5 | 3 | 7 | | | | 11 | 2 | 12 | | | 10 | 4 | 9 |
| 34 | 18 | MANSFIELD | 3-0 | 4175 | Bullock, Martin, Westlake | | 1 | | 6 | 8 | 5 | 3 | 7 | | | | 11 | 2 | | | | 10 | 4 | 9 |
| 35 | 24 | SWANSEA | 3-1 | 7277 | Bullock(2), Hodgson | | 1 | | | 8 | 5 | 3 | 7 | | | | 11 | 2 | | 4 | | 10 | 6 | 9 |
| 36 | 25 | Grimsby | 0-0 | 4487 | | | 1 | | | 8 | 5 | 3 | 7 | | 6 | | 11 | 2 | | | | 10 | 4 | 9 |
| 37 | 27 | Swansea | 0-1 | 5748 | | | 1 | | | 8 | 5 | 3 | 7 | | 6 | | 11 | 2 | | | | 10 | 4 | 9 |
| 38 | 1 Apr | WALSALL | 5-1 | 4809 | Bullock(2), Martin, Westlake(2) | | 1 | | 6 | 8 | 5 | 3 | 7 | | | | 11 | 2 | | | | 10 | 4 | 9 |
| 39 | 8 | Peterborough | 1-2 | 5362 | Hodgson | | 1 | | 6 | 8 | 5 | 3 | 7 | | | | 11 | 2 | | | | 10 | 4 | 9 |
| 40 | 10 | WORKINGTON | 2-2 | 4767 | Bullock, Hodgson | | 1 | | | 8 | 5 | 3 | 7 | | | | 11 | 2 | | 6 | | 10 | 4 | 9 |
| 41 | 15 | TORQUAY | 1-0 | 5672 | Stratton | | 1 | | 6 | 8 | 5 | 3 | 7 | | | | 11 | 2 | | | | 10 | 4 | 9 |
| 42 | 22 | Brighton | 1-1 | 10567 | Stratton | | 1* | 7 | 6 | 8 | 5 | 3 | 9 | | | | 11 | 2 | | 12 | | 10 | 4 | |
| 43 | 29 | DARLINGTON | 2-3 | 4578 | Martin, Stratton | 1 | | 7 | 6 | 8 | 5 | 3 | 9* | | | | 11 | 2 | | | | 10 | 4 | 12 |
| 44 | 6 May | Q.p.r. | 1-2 | 10935 | Hall | 1 | | | 6 | 8 | 5 | 3 | | | | 7 | 11 | 2 | | | | 10 | 4 | 9 |
| 45 | 9 | Watford | 0-0 | 20169 | | 1 | | 12 | 6 | 8 | 5 | 3 | 9 | | | 7 | 11* | 2 | | | | 10 | 4 | |
| 46 | 13 | BRIGHTON | 3-2 | 4238 | Bullock(3) | 1 | | | 6 | 8 | 5 | 3 | 9 | | | | 11 | 2 | | | | 10 | 4 | 7 |

# F.A.Cup

| | | | | | | | | | | | | | | | | | | | | | | | | |
|---|---|---|---|---|---|---|---|---|---|---|---|---|---|---|---|---|---|---|---|---|---|---|---|---|
| 1st | 26 Nov | Gainsborough | 1–0 | 3968 | Hall | | 1 | | 6 | | 2 | 3 | 9 | 8 | | | 11 | 12 | | 5 | 7 | 10 | 4 | |
| 2nd | 7 Jan | PETERBOROUGH | 0–3 | 9081 | | | 1 | | | 8 | 5 | 3 | 9 | 7 | 4 | | 11 | 2 | | 12 | | 10 | 6 | |

# Football League Cup

| | | | | | | | | | | | | | | | | | | | | | | | | |
|---|---|---|---|---|---|---|---|---|---|---|---|---|---|---|---|---|---|---|---|---|---|---|---|---|
| 1st | 23 Aug | Q.p.r. | 0–5 | 5497 | | 1 | | | 4* | 8 | 2 | 3 | 9 | 7 | 5 | | 11 | | | | 12 | 10 | 6 | |

Back Row: B. Hall, D. Trevis, D. Charlesworth, R. Price, A. Buck, S. Kennon, M Loughton,. D. Forbes. A. Redrobe.
Centre: J. Anderson (Trainer), A. Shires, A. Kaye, K. Hodgson, P. Bullock, R. Stratton, J. Martin, J. Mansfield, B. Blackwood D. Raine N. Franklin (Manager).
Front: R. Freeman. P. Barlow, D. Lamont.

*Photo by courtesy of the Essex County Standard*

**THIRD DIVISION**

| | | P | W | D | L | F | A | Pts |
|---|---|---|---|---|---|---|---|---|
| 1 | QPR | 46 | 26 | 15 | 5 | 103 | 38 | 67 |
| 2 | Middlesbrough | 46 | 23 | 9 | 14 | 87 | 64 | 55 |
| 3 | Watford | 46 | 20 | 14 | 12 | 61 | 46 | 54 |
| 4 | Reading | 46 | 22 | 9 | 15 | 76 | 57 | 53 |
| 5 | Bristol Rovers | 46 | 20 | 13 | 13 | 76 | 67 | 53 |
| 6 | Shrewsbury | 46 | 20 | 12 | 14 | 77 | 62 | 52 |
| 7 | Torquay | 46 | 21 | 9 | 16 | 73 | 54 | 51 |
| 8 | Swindon | 46 | 20, | 10 | 16 | 81 | 59 | 50 |
| 9 | Mansfield | 46 | 20 | 9 | 17 | 84 | 79 | 49 |
| 10 | Oldham | 46 | 19 | 10 | 17 | 80 | 63 | 48 |
| 11 | Gillingham | 46 | 15 | 16 | 15 | 58 | 62 | 46 |
| 12 | Walsall | 46 | 18 | 10 | 18 | 65 | 72 | 46 |
| 13 | Colchester | 46 | 17 | 10 | 19 | 76 | 73 | 44 |
| 14 | Leyton Orient | 46 | 13 | 18 | 15 | 58 | 68 | 44 |
| 15 | Peterborough | 46 | 14 | 15 | 17 | 66 | 71 | 43 |
| 16 | Oxford | 46 | 15 | 13 | 18 | 61 | 66 | 43 |
| 17 | Grimsby | 46 | 17 | 9 | 20 | 61 | 68 | 43 |
| 18 | Scunthorpe | 46 | 17 | 8 | 21 | 58 | 73 | 42 |
| 19 | Brighton | 46 | 13 | 15 | 18 | 61 | 71 | 41 |
| 20 | Bournemouth | 46 | 12 | 17 | 17 | 39 | 57 | 41 |
| 21 | Swansea | 46 | 12 | 15 | 19 | 85 | 89 | 39 |
| 22 | Darlington | 46 | 13 | 11 | 22 | 47 | 81 | 37 |
| 23 | Doncaster | 46 | 12 | 8 | 26 | 58 | 117 | 32 |
| 24 | Workington | 46 | 12 | 7 | 27 | 55 | 89 | 31 |

# SEASON 1967-68 Division Three

| No. | Date | Opposition | Res | Attend | Goalscorers | Adams | Buck.A | Barlow | Blackwood | Bullock | Forbes | Fowler | Hall | Hodgson | Joslyn | Lamont | Loughton | Mansfield | Martin | McKechnie | Mochan | Oliver | Price.T | Shires | Stratton | Trevis | Walker |
|---|---|---|---|---|---|---|---|---|---|---|---|---|---|---|---|---|---|---|---|---|---|---|---|---|---|---|---|
| 1 | 19 Aug | OLDHAM | 0-0 | 3989 | | 1 | | | 6 | 8 | 2 | | | 9 | | | 5 | 7 | 11 | | 3 | | | | 10 | 4 | |
| 2 | 26 | Bristol R | 1-1 | 8260 | Hall | 1 | | | 6 | 8 | 2 | | 9 | 10 | | | 5 | 7 | 11 | | 3 | | | | | 4 | |
| 3 | 5 Sep | BARROW | 3-2 | 3609 | Bullock, Mochan, Stratton | 1 | | | 6 | 8 | 2 | | | 9 | | | 5 | 7 | 11 | | 3 | | | | 10 | 4 | |
| 4 | 4 | Southport | 3-2 | 7008 | Bullock, Hodgson(2) | 1 | | | 6 | 8 | 5 | | 3 | 9 | | | | 7 | 11 | | 2 | | | | 10 | 4 | |
| 5 | 9 | Oxford | 1-3 | 5873 | Hall | 1 | | | 6 | 8 | 5 | 11 | 3 | 9 | | | | 7 | | | 2 | | | | 10 | 4 | |
| 6 | 16 | BURY | 0-0 | 4331 | | 1 | | | 6 | 8 | 2 | | 11 | 9 | | | 5 | | | 10 | 3 | | 7 | | | 4 | |
| 7 | 23 | Bournemouth | 2-1 | 5766 | McKechnie(2) | 1 | | | 6 | 8 | 2 | | 11 | 9 | | | 5 | | | 10 | 3 | | 7 | | | 4 | |
| 8 | 25 | SOUTHPORT | 1-1 | 5873 | Bullock | 1 | | | 6 | 8 | 2 | | 11 | 9 | | | 5 | | | 10 | 3 | | 7 | | | 4 | |
| 9 | 29 | Tranmere R | 2-4 | 7133 | Bullock, McKechnie | 1 | | | 6 | 8 | 2 | | 11 | | | | 5 | | | 10 | 3 | | 7 | | 9 | 4 | |
| 10 | 2 Oct | WATFORD | 2-1 | 6420 | McKechnie(2) | 1 | | | 6 | 8 | 2 | | 11 | | | | 5 | | | 10 | 3 | | 7 | | 9 | 4 | |
| 11 | 7 | BRIGHTON | 0-0 | 5075 | | 1 | | | 6 | 8 | 2 | | 11 | | | | 5* | | | 10 | 3 | | 7 | | 9 | 4 | 12 |
| 12 | 14 | Shrewsbury | 0-4 | 4162 | | 1 | | | 6 | 8 | 5 | | 11 | | | | | | | 10 | 3 | | 7 | | 9 | 4 | 2 |
| 13 | 21 | SWINDON | 2-1 | 4907 | Blackwood, T.Price | 1 | | | 10 | 8 | 5 | | 3 | | | | | | 11 | 9 | 2 | | 7 | | | 4 | 6 |
| 14 | 24 | Watford | 1-1 | 10669 | Bullock | 1 | | | 10 | 8 | 5 | | 3 | | | | | | 11 | 9 | 2 | | 7 | | | 4 | 6 |
| 15 | 28 | Reading | 0-1 | 5741 | | 1 | | | 10 | 8* | 5 | | 3 | 12 | | | 6 | | 11 | 9 | | | 7 | | | 4 | 2 |
| 16 | 4 Nov | TORQUAY | 3-5 | 3249 | Hodgson, Shires, Stratton | 1 | | 9 | 6 | | 2 | | | 9 | | 12 | 5 | | 11 | 8* | | | | 7 | 10 | 4 | 3 |
| 17 | 11 | Grimsby | 2-1 | 3667 | Barlow, Blackwood | 1 | | 9 | 11 | | 5 | 3 | | | | | 6 | | | | | | 8 | 7 | 10 | 4 | 2 |
| 18 | 13 | Barrow | 0-5 | 5685 | | 1 | | | 6 | | 5 | 3 | | 8 | | | | | 11 | | | | 7 | | 10 | 4 | 2 |
| 19 | 18 | GILLINGHAM | 2-2 | 4190 | Stratton(2) | 1 | | | 6 | | 5 | | 3 | 9 | | | | | 11 | 8 | 2 | | 7 | | 10 | 4 | |
| 20 | 25 | Walsall | 1-1 | 10001 | Forbes | 1 | | | 11 | | 5 | | 3 | | | | | | | 10 | 2 | | 8 | 7 | 9 | 4 | 6 |
| 21 | 2 Dec | NORTHAMPTON | 2-1 | 3505 | T.Price, Trevis | 1 | | | 11 | | 5 | | 3 | | | | | | | 10 | 2 | | 8 | 7 | 9 | 4 | 6 |
| 22 | 16 | Oldham | 1-2 | 4177 | Barlow | 1 | | 9 | 8 | | 5 | | 3 | | | | 6* | | | 10 | 2 | | 7 | | 11 | 4 | 12 |
| 23 | 23 | BRISTOL R | 2-0 | 4324 | Barlow, Stratton | 1 | | 9 | 8 | | 5 | | 11 | | 2 | | | | | | 3 | | 7 | | 10 | 4 | 6 |
| 24 | 26 | Mansfield | 1-2 | 6679 | Stratton | 1 | | 9 | 8 | | 5 | | 11 | | 2 | | | | | | 3 | | 7 | | 10 | 4 | 6 |
| 25 | 30 | MANSFIELD | 1-2 | 4180 | Stratton | 1 | | 9 | 10 | | 5 | | 3 | | 2 | | 6 | 8 | | | | | 7 | | 11 | 4 | |
| 26 | 20 Jan | Bury | 0-2 | 7000 | | 1 | | | 11 | | 5 | | 3 | | | | | 8 | | 10 | 2 | | | 7 | 9 | 4 | 6 |
| 27 | 3 Feb | BOURNEMOUTH | 0-1 | 4075 | | 1 | | | 6 | 10 | 5 | | 3 | | | | 12 | 8 | 11 | | 2 | | 7 | | 9* | 4 | |
| 28 | 10 | TRANMERE | 1-2 | 3739 | Martin | 1 | | 12 | 9 | | 5 | | 3 | | | | | 8 | 11* | | 2 | | | 7 | 10 | 4 | 6 |
| 29 | 17 | Peterborough | 1-3 | 5066 | Loughton | 1 | | 9 | 6 | | 5 | | 11 | | 2 | | 4 | 8 | | 10 | 3 | | 7 | | | | |
| 30 | 24 | Brighton | 0-0 | 6512 | | 1 | | | 6 | | 5 | | 3 | | | | | 8* | | 10 | 2 | 9 | 7 | 11 | | 4 | 12 |
| 31 | 26 | SCUNTHORPE | 1-0 | 3979 | Barlow | 1 | | 8 | 6 | | 5 | | 3 | | | | | | 11 | | 2 | 9 | 7 | | 10 | 4 | |
| 32 | 2 Mar | SHREWSBURY | 0-3 | 3877 | | 1 | | 8 | 6 | | 5 | | 3 | | 2 | | | | 11 | | | 9 | 7 | | 10 | 4 | |
| 33 | 9 | Scunthorpe | 1-5 | 3003 | Mochan | 1 | | | 6 | | 5 | | 3 | | 2 | | | 8 | 10* | | 7 | 9 | | | 11 | 4 | 12 |
| 34 | 16 | Swindon | 1-1 | 13515 | Martin | 1 | | | 11 | 8 | 5 | | 3 | | | | 6 | | 10 | | 2 | 9 | 7 | | | 4 | |
| 35 | 23 | READING | 2-5 | 3136 | Bullock(2) | | 1 | | 10 | 8 | 5 | | 3 | | | | 6* | | 11 | | 2 | 12 | 7 | | 9 | 4 | |
| 36 | 25 | OXFORD | 1-2 | 3516 | Stratton | | 1 | | 10 | | 5 | | 3 | | | | 6 | 12 | 11 | | 2 | 8* | 7 | | 9 | 4 | |
| 37 | 30 | Torquay | 0-3 | 9801 | | 1 | | 8* | 10 | | 5 | | 3 | | | | 6 | 12 | 11 | | 2 | | 7 | | 9 | 4 | |
| 38 | 6 Apr | GRIMSBY | 1-3 | 3231 | Blackwood | 1 | | | 10 | 8 | 5 | | 3 | | | | 6 | | 11 | | 2 | | 7 | | 9 | 4 | |
| 39 | 12 | STOCKPORT | 1-1 | 4059 | Loughton | 1 | | 12 | 6 | | 5 | | 3 | | | | 8 | | 11 | 10 | 2 | 9 | 7* | | | 4 | |
| 40 | 13 | Gillingham | 0-1 | 5734 | | 1 | | | 12 | | 5 | | 3 | | 7 | | 6 | | 10* | 8 | 2 | 9 | | 11 | | 4 | |
| 41 | 15 | Stockport | 0-1 | 7149 | | 1 | | 7 | 11 | | 5 | | 3 | | 12 | | 6 | 8* | | 10 | 2 | 9 | | | | 4 | |
| 42 | 20 | WALSALL | 2-2 | 2764 | Loughton(2) | 1 | | 9 | 6 | | 2 | | 11 | | 12 | | 5 | | | 8 | 3 | 10 | 7 | | | 4* | |
| 43 | 22 | Orient | 1-1 | 6125 | Stratton | 1 | | | 6 | 8 | 2 | | 11 | | | | 5 | | | 12 | 3* | 10 | 7 | | 9 | 4 | |
| 44 | 27 | Northampton | 2-2 | 6859 | Loughton, T.Price | 1 | | 9 | | | 5 | | 3 | | 10 | | 6 | | 11 | | 2 | 8 | 7 | | | 4 | |
| 45 | 4 May | ORIENT | 1-1 | 3124 | Martin | 1 | | 9 | | | 5 | | 3 | | 6 | | 10 | | 11 | | 2 | 8 | 7 | | | 4 | |
| 46 | 11 | PETERBOROUGH | 1-5 | 2483 | Trevis | 1 | | | 10 | | 9 | | 3 | | 6 | | 5 | | 11 | | 2 | 8 | 7 | | | 4 | |

## F.A.Cup

| | | | | | | | | | | | | | | | | | | | | | | | | | | | |
|---|---|---|---|---|---|---|---|---|---|---|---|---|---|---|---|---|---|---|---|---|---|---|---|---|---|---|---|
| 1st | 12 Dec | Torquay | 1–1 | 6655 | Barlow | 1 | | 9 | 11 | | 5 | | 3 | | | | 6 | 8 | 7 | 10 | 2 | | | | 12 | 4 | |
| 1st/R | 18 | TORQUAY | 2–1 | 7079 | Trevis(2) | 1 | | 9 | 6 | | 5 | | 3 | | | | | 8 | 11 | 10* | 2 | | 7 | | | 4 | 12 |
| 2nd | 6 Jan | Chelmsford | 2–0 | 16400 | McKechnie, Stratton | 1 | | | 6 | | 5 | | 3* | | | | | 8 | 11 | 10 | 2 | | 7 | | 9 | 4 | 12 |
| 3rd | 27 | W.B.A. | 1–1 | 15981 | Stratton | 1 | | | 6 | 12 | 5 | | 3 | | | | | 8 | 11 | 10* | 2 | | 7 | | 9 | 4 | |
| 3rd/R | 31 | W.b.a. | 0–4 | 40008 | | 1 | | | 6 | 10 | 5 | | 3 | | | | 12 | 8 | 11 | | 2 | | 7 | | 9 | 4 | |

## Football League Cup

| | | | | | | | | | | | | | | | | | | | | | | | | | | | |
|---|---|---|---|---|---|---|---|---|---|---|---|---|---|---|---|---|---|---|---|---|---|---|---|---|---|---|---|
| 1st | 23 Aug | Brighton | 0–4 | 10745 | | 1 | | | 6 | 8 | 2 | | | 9 | | | 5 | 7 | 11 | | 3 | | | | 10 | 4 | |

(Back): Forbes, Adams, Trevis, Joslyn, Loughton, Hall. (Front): Price, Mansfield, Barlow, Blackwood, Stratton.

**THIRD DIVISION**

| | P | W | D | L | F | A | Pts |
|---|---|---|---|---|---|---|---|
| 1 Oxford | 46 | 22 | 13 | 11 | 69 | 47 | 57 |
| 2 Bury | 46 | 24 | 8 | 14 | 91 | 66 | 56 |
| 3 Shrewsbury | 46 | 20 | 15 | 11 | 61 | 49 | 55 |
| 4 Torquay | 46 | 21 | 11 | 14 | 60 | 56 | 53 |
| 5 Reading | 46 | 21 | 9 | 16 | 70 | 60 | 51 |
| 6 Watford | 46 | 21 | 8 | 17 | 74 | 50 | 50 |
| 7 Walsall | 46 | 19 | 12 | 15 | 74 | 61 | 50 |
| 8 Barrow | 46 | 21 | 8 | 17 | 65 | 54 | 50 |
| 9 Peterborough | 46 | 20 | 10 | 16 | 79 | 67 | 50 |
| 10 Swindon | 46 | 16 | 17 | 13 | 74 | 51 | 49 |
| 11 Brighton | 46 | 16 | 16 | 14 | 57 | 55 | 48 |
| 12 Gillingham | 46 | 18 | 12 | 16 | 59 | 63 | 48 |
| 13 Bournemouth | 46 | 16 | 15 | 15 | 56 | 51 | 47 |
| 14 Stockport | 46 | 19 | 9 | 18 | 70 | 75 | 47 |
| 15 Southport | 46 | 17 | 12 | 17 | 65 | 65 | 46 |
| 16 Bristol Rovers | 46 | 17 | 9 | 20 | 72 | 78 | 43 |
| 17 Oldham | 46 | 18 | 7 | 21 | 60 | 65 | 43 |
| 18 Northampton | 46 | 14 | 13 | 19 | 58 | 72 | 41 |
| 19 Leyton Orient | 46 | 12 | 17 | 17 | 46 | 62 | 41 |
| 20 Tranmere | 46 | 14 | 12 | 20 | 62 | 74 | 40 |
| 21 Mansfield | 46 | 12 | 13 | 21 | 51 | 67 | 37 |
| 22 Grimsby | 46 | 14 | 9 | 23 | 52 | 69 | 37 |
| 23 Colchester | 46 | 9 | 15 | 22 | 50 | 87 | 33 |
| 24 Scunthorpe | 46 | 10 | 12 | 24 | 56 | 87 | 32 |

# SEASON 1968-69 Division Four

| No. | Date | Opposition | Res | Attend | Goalscorers | Adams | Buck.A | Macedo | Willis | Barlow | Bickles | Brown | Dyson | Forbes | Gibbs | Hall | Hodgson | Honeywood | Joslyn | Light | Mansfield | Martin | Mochan | Moughton | Oliver | O'Rourke | Perryman | Price | Rowan | Simpson | Trevis | Wood |
|---|---|---|---|---|---|---|---|---|---|---|---|---|---|---|---|---|---|---|---|---|---|---|---|---|---|---|---|---|---|---|---|---|
| 1 | 10 Aug | Brentford | 0-4 | 7580 | | 1 | | | | | | | | 4 | | 5 | | 2 | 9 | | 12 | 10* | | 3 | 8 | | | 11 | | 6 | 7 | |
| 2 | 17 | ROCHDALE | 0-0 | 3969 | | 1 | | | | | | | | 5 | | 3 | | 6 | 4 | | 10* | 11 | | 9 | 9 | | | 7 | | 12 | 8 | |
| 3 | 24 | Chester | 1-5 | 5813 | Simpson | 1 | | | | | | | 11 | 5 | | 3 | | 6 | 4 | 7 | | | 2* | 8 | 9 | | 12 | | | 10 | | |
| 4 | 26 | SCUNTHORPE | 0-4 | 3771 | | | 1 | | | 11 | | | 12 | 5 | | 3 | | | | 8 | 9 | | | 4* | | | 2 | 7 | | 10 | 6 | |
| 5 | 31 | DONCASTER | 1-2 | 3199 | Simpson | 1 | | | | | | | 11 | 2 | | 8 | | 6* | 4 | 10 | | 7 | | | 12 | | | | | 8 | 9 | 5 |
| 6 | 7 Sept | YORK | 1-0 | 3756 | Light | | | 1 | | | | | | 8 | | 3 | | | 5 | 9 | | | 2 | | 7 | | | 11 | | 10 | 4 | 6 |
| 7 | 14 | Bradford | 1-1 | 6879 | Light | | | 1 | | | | | 11 | | 10 | 3* | | 12 | 5 | 9 | | | 2 | | 8 | | | | | 7 | 4 | 6 |
| 8 | 16 | Chesterfield | 2-0 | 4693 | Gibbs, Trevis | | | 1 | | | | | 11* | | 10 | 3 | | 12 | 5 | 9 | | | 2 | | 8 | | | | | 7 | 4 | 6 |
| 9 | 20 | PORT VALE | 1-0 | 6441 | Joslyn | | | 1 | | | | | 11 | | 10 | 3 | | | 5 | 9 | | | 2 | | 8 | | | | | 7 | 4 | 6 |
| 10 | 28 | Exeter | 1-1 | 5146 | Simpson | | | 1 | | | 5 | | 11 | | 8 | 3 | | | 4 | 9 | | | 2 | | 10 | | | | | 7 | | 6 |
| 11 | 4 Oct | GRIMSBY | 2-1 | 7543 | Gibbs(2) | | | 1 | | | 5 | | 11 | | 10 | 3 | | | 4 | 9 | | | 2 | | 8 | | | | | 7 | | 6 |
| 12 | 8 | Scunthorpe | 3-2 | 2748 | Bickles, Gibbs(2) | | | 1 | | | 5 | | 11 | | 10 | 3 | | | 4 | 9 | | | 2 | | 8 | | | | | 7 | | 6 |
| 13 | 12 | Newport | 0-1 | 3262 | | | | 1 | | | 5 | | 11 | | 8 | 3 | | | 4 | 9 | | | 2 | | 10 | | | | | 7 | | 6 |
| 14 | 19 | DARLINGTON | 0-0 | 6323 | | | | 1 | | | 5 | | 11 | | 10 | 3 | | | 4 | 9 | | | 2 | | 8 | | | | | 7 | | 6 |
| 15 | 26 | Lincoln | 3-0 | 6833 | Hall, Oliver, O.G. | | | 1 | | | 5 | 10 | 11 | | 9 | 3 | | | | 8 | | | 2 | | 7 | | | | | 4 | | 6 |
| 16 | 2 Nov | WREXHAM | 2-1 | 5806 | Oliver, Price | | | 1 | | | 5 | 7 | 11 | | 10* | 3 | | 12 | | 9 | | | 2 | | 8 | | | 4 | | | | 6 |
| 17 | 4 | WORKINGTON | 3-0 | 6702 | Light, Oliver, Price | | | 1 | | | 5 | 7 | 11 | | | 3 | | 6 | | 9 | | | 2 | | 8 | | | 4 | | 10 | | |
| 18 | 9 | Bradford | 1-2 | 2011 | Oliver | | | 1 | | | 5 | 7* | 11 | | | 3 | | 12 | | 9 | | | 2 | | 8 | | | 4 | | 10 | | 6 |
| 19 | 23 | Swansea | 0-2 | 5080 | | | | | 1 | | | 7 | 11 | | | 3 | | | 6 | 9 | | | 2 | | | 8* | | | 10 | 12 | | 5 |
| 20 | 29 | SOUTHEND | 4-0 | 10604 | Dyson(pen), Gibbs, Oliver, Simpson | | | | 1 | | 5 | | 11 | | 10 | 3 | | | | 9 | | | 2 | | 8 | | | | 7 | 4 | | 6 |
| 21 | 14 Dec | NEWPORT | 2-1 | 3532 | Light, Wood | | | | 1 | | 5 | | 11 | | 10 | 3 | | | | 9 | | | 2 | | 8 | | | 4 | | 7 | | 6 |
| 22 | 26 | Grimsby | 4-2 | 5559 | Bickles, Light(2), Oliver | | | 1 | | | 5 | | 11 | | 10 | 3 | | | 4 | 9 | | | 2 | | 8 | | | | | 7 | | 6 |
| 23 | 11 Jan | Wrexham | 3-0 | 7471 | Gibbs, Light(2) | | | 1 | | | 5 | | 11 | | 8 | 3 | | | 4 | 10 | | | 2 | | 7 | | | | | 9 | | 6 |
| 24 | 18 | BRADFORD | 3-0 | 5914 | Dyson, Hall, Oliver | | | 1 | | | 5 | 12 | 11 | | 10 | 3 | | | 4 | 9 | | | 2 | | 8* | | | | | 7 | | 6 |
| 25 | 24 | Workington | 1-0 | 2584 | Oliver | | | 1 | | | 5 | | 11 | | 10 | 3 | | | 4 | 9 | | | 2 | | 8 | | | | | 7 | | 6 |
| 26 | 1 Feb | Aldershot | 2-1 | 8383 | Dyson, Gibbs | | | 1 | | | 5 | | 11 | | 10 | 3 | | | 4 | 9 | | | 2 | | 8 | | | | | 7 | | 6 |
| 27 | 14 | Southend | 1-3 | 12681 | Light | | | 1 | | | 5 | 12 | 11* | | 10 | 3 | | | 4 | 9 | | | 2 | | 8 | | | | | 7 | | 6 |
| 28 | 22 | NOTTS COUNTY | 1-1 | 6612 | Gibbs | | | 1 | | | 5 | | 11 | | 10 | 3 | | | 4 | 9 | | | 2 | | 8 | | | | | 7 | | 6 |
| 29 | 28 | BRENTFORD | 2-1 | 7268 | Joslyn, Light | | | 1 | | | 5 | | 11 | | 10 | 3 | 7* | 4 | 6 | 9 | | | 2 | | 8 | | | 12 | | | | |
| 30 | 4 Mar | Halifax | 1-2 | 3400 | O.G. | | | 1 | | | 5 | 4* | 11 | | 10 | 3 | | | 6 | 9 | | | 2 | | 8 | | | 12 | | 7 | | |
| 31 | 8 | Rochdale | 0-4 | 4988 | | | | 1 | | | 5 | | 11 | | 10 | 3 | | 6 | 2 | 9 | | 12 | | | 8* | | | | | 7 | | 4 |
| 32 | 10 | ALDERSHOT | 2-0 | 6577 | Hall, Light | | | 1 | | | | | 11 | | 9 | 3 | | 12 | 4 | 8 | | 10 | 2 | | | | | 7 | | 6 | | 5* |
| 33 | 14 | CHESTERFIELD | 1-1 | 7312 | Oliver | | | 1 | | | 5 | | 11 | | 9 | 3 | | | 4 | 10 | | 8 | 2 | | 12 | | | 7* | | 6 | | |
| 34 | 22 | Doncaster | 0-1 | 10799 | | | | 1 | | | 5 | 12 | 11* | | 9 | 3 | | | 4 | 10 | | 8 | 2 | | 7 | | | | | 6 | | |
| 35 | 24 | LINCOLN | 1-1 | 6787 | Joslyn | | | 1 | | | 5* | 7 | | | 9 | 3 | | 12 | 4 | 10 | | | 2 | | 8 | | | 11 | | 6 | | |
| 36 | 29 | York | 0-2 | 3140 | | | | 1 | | | | 9 | 11 | | 10 | 3* | | 5 | 4 | 8 | | | 2 | | 12 | | | 7 | | 6 | | |
| 37 | 4 Apr | CHESTERFIELD | 1-0 | 7180 | Brown | | | 1 | | | 5 | 10 | 11 | | 8 | 3 | | | 4 | 9* | | | 2 | | 12 | | | 6 | | 7 | | |
| 38 | 5 | EXETER | 1-0 | 5650 | Light | | | 1 | | | 5 | | 11 | | 9 | 3 | | | 4 | 8 | | | 2 | | 10 | | | 7 | | 6 | | |
| 39 | 8 | Peterborough | 1-0 | 6548 | Brown | | | 1 | | | 5 | 8 | 11 | | 10 | 3 | | | 4 | 9 | | | 2 | | | | | 7 | | 6 | | |
| 40 | 12 | Port Vale | 0-0 | 3774 | | | | 1 | | | 5 | 6 | 11 | | 10 | 3 | | | 4 | 9 | | | 2 | | | | | 8 | | 7 | | |
| 41 | 14 | PETERBOROUGH | 2-2 | 6564 | Bickles, Brown | | | 1 | | | 5 | 8 | 11 | | 10 | 3 | | | 4 | | | | 2 | | 12 | | | 9 | | 7 | | 6* |
| 42 | 18 | BRADFORD | 1-1 | 8196 | Gibbs | | | 1 | | | 5 | 9 | 11 | | 10 | 3 | | | 6 | 12 | | | 2 | | 8 | | | 4 | | 7* | | |
| 43 | 21 | HALIFAX | 0-0 | 7429 | | | | 1 | | | 5 | 7 | | | 10 | 3 | | 4 | | 9 | | | 2 | | 8 | | | 11 | | | | 6 |
| 44 | 25 | SWANSEA | 0-1 | 7136 | | | | 1 | | | 5 | 10 | 11 | | 8 | 3 | | | 4 | 9 | | | 2 | | 12 | | | | | 7 | | 6* |
| 45 | 28 | Darlington | 1-1 | 7505 | Gibbs | | | 1 | | | 5 | 9 | 11 | | 8 | 3 | | 6 | 12 | 10 | | | 2 | | 7* | | | | | 4 | | |
| 46 | 2 May | Notts County | 0-2 | 3576 | | | | 1 | | | 5* | 9 | 11 | | 8 | 3 | | 6 | 4 | 10 | | | 2 | | 12 | | | | | 7 | | |

## F.A.Cup

| | | | | | | | | | | | | | | | | | | | | | | | | | | | | | | | | | |
|---|---|---|---|---|---|---|---|---|---|---|---|---|---|---|---|---|---|---|---|---|---|---|---|---|---|---|---|---|---|---|---|---|---|
| 1st | 16 Nov | CHESHAM H | 5–0 | 5497 | Hall(2), Light(2), Price | | | 1 | | | | 7 | 11 | | | 3 | | 4 | 6 | 9 | | 12 | 2 | | | 8 | | 10 | | | | 5 |
| 2nd | 7 Dec | EXETER | 0–1 | 6180 | | | | 1 | | | 5 | 12 | 11 | | 10 | 3 | | | | 9* | | | 2 | | 8 | | | | 7 | 4 | | 6 |

## Football League Cup

| | | | | | | | | | | | | | | | | | | | | | | | | | | | | | | | | | |
|---|---|---|---|---|---|---|---|---|---|---|---|---|---|---|---|---|---|---|---|---|---|---|---|---|---|---|---|---|---|---|---|---|---|
| 1st | 14 Aug | READING | 2–0 | 3824 | Hall, Oliver(pen) | 1 | | | | | | | | 5 | | 3 | | 6 | 4 | | 10 | 11 | | 2 | 9 | | | 7 | | | 8 | |
| 2nd | 4 Sep | WORKINGTON | 0–1 | 3523 | | 1 | | | | | | | | 5 | | 9 | | 6 | 4 | | 10 | 11 | | | | | 2 | 7 | | 3 | 8 | |

COLCHESTER UNITED 1968-69. Back: Roger Joslyn, Ernie Adams, Alan Buck, Colin Moughton. Centre: John Anderson (trainer); Jim Oliver, Peter Barlow, Duncan Forbes (now Norwich), Derek Trevis (now Walsall), John Mansfield (now Brentwood), Brian Hall, Dick Graham (manager). Front: Gerry Perryman, Terry Price, Adrian Webster, Ken Hodgson, Brian Honeywood, Denis Mochan, John Martin.

**FOURTH DIVISION**

| | P | W | D | L | F | A | Pts |
|---|---|---|---|---|---|---|---|
| 1 Doncaster | 46 | 21 | 17 | 8 | 65 | 38 | 59 |
| 2 Halifax | 46 | 20 | 17 | 9 | 53 | 37 | 57 |
| 3 Rochdale | 46 | 18 | 20 | 8 | 68 | 35 | 56 |
| 4 Bradford City | 46 | 18 | 20 | 8 | 65 | 46 | 56 |
| 5 Darlington | 46 | 17 | 18 | 11 | 62 | 45 | 52 |
| 6 Colchester | 46 | 20 | 12 | 14 | 57 | 53 | 52 |
| 7 Southend | 46 | 19 | 13 | 14 | 78 | 61 | 51 |
| 8 Lincoln | 45 | 17 | 17 | 12 | 54 | 52 | 51 |
| 9 Wrexham | 46 | 18 | 14 | 14 | 61 | 52 | 50 |
| 10 Swansea | 46 | 19 | 11 | 16 | 58 | 54 | 49 |
| 11 Brentford | 46 | 18 | 12 | 16 | 64 | 65 | 48 |
| 12 Workington | 46 | 15 | 17 | 14 | 40 | 43 | 47 |
| 13 Port Vale | 46 | 16 | 14 | 16 | 46 | 46 | 46 |
| 14 Chester | 46 | 16 | 13 | 17 | 76 | 66 | 45 |
| 15 Aldershot | 46 | 19 | 7 | 20 | 66 | 66 | 45 |
| 16 Scunthorpe | 46 | 18 | 8 | 20 | 61 | 60 | 44 |
| 17 Exeter | 46 | 16 | 11 | 19 | 66 | 65 | 43 |
| 18 Peterborough | 46 | 13 | 16 | 17 | 60 | 57 | 42 |
| 19 Notts County | 46 | 12 | 18 | 16 | 48 | 57 | 42 |
| 20 Chesterfield | 46 | 13 | 15 | 18 | 43 | 50 | 41 |
| 21 York | 46 | 14 | 11 | 21 | 53 | 75 | 39 |
| 22 Newport | 46 | 11 | 14 | 21 | 49 | 74 | 36 |
| 23 Grimsby | 46 | 9 | 15 | 22 | 47 | 69 | 33 |
| 24 Bradford PA | 46 | 5 | 10 | 31 | 32 | 106 | 20 |

# SEASON 1969–70 Division Four

| No. | Date | Opposition | Res | Attend | Goalscorers | Smith.G | Willis | Bickles | Brown | Cook | Cram | Dennis | Dyson | Gibbs | Hall | Howe | Howlett | Jones | Joslyn | Light | Massey | Mochan | Oliver | Pitt | Presland | Slater | Whittaker | Wood |
|---|---|---|---|---|---|---|---|---|---|---|---|---|---|---|---|---|---|---|---|---|---|---|---|---|---|---|---|---|
| 1 | 9 Aug | Lincoln | 3-3 | 6761 | Gibbs(2), Massey | 1 | | | 6 | | | | | 10 | 3 | 2 | 5 | | 4 | 9 | 8 | | 12 | 7* | | | 11 | |
| 2 | 16 | WREXHAM | 2-0 | 5292 | Gibbs, Whittaker | 1 | | 5 | 10 | | | | | 4 | 3 | 2 | | | | 7 | 8 | | 9 | | | | 11 | 6 |
| 3 | 23 | Notts County | 1-1 | 4901 | Massey | 1 | | 5 | 10 | | | | | 4 | 3 | 2 | | | | 7 | 8 | | 9 | | | | 11 | 6 |
| 4 | 25 | PETERBOROUGH | 2-1 | 7133 | Gibbs, Hall | 1 | | 5 | 10 | | | | | 4 | 3 | 2 | 12 | | 7 | | 8 | | 9 | | | | 11 | 6 |
| 5 | 30 | PORTVALE | 0-0 | 6323 | | 1 | | 5 | 10 | | | | | 4 | 3 | 2 | | | 12 | 7* | 8 | | 9 | | | | 11 | 6 |
| 6 | 6 Sep | Darlington | 2-3 | 3767 | Massey(2) | 1 | | | 4 | | | | | 10 | | 2 | 5 | | 3 | 9 | 8 | | 12 | 7* | | | 11 | 6 |
| 7 | 13 | CREWE | 1-0 | 5084 | Massey | 1 | | | 12 | | | | | 8 | 3 | 2 | 6 | | 4 | 10* | 9 | | 7 | | | | 11 | 5 |
| 8 | 16 | Oldham | 2-1 | 3993 | Brown, Massey | 1 | | 6 | 7 | | | | | 8 | 3 | 2 | | | 4 | | 9 | | 10 | | | | 11 | 5 |
| 9 | 20 | Hartlepool | 0-0 | 3667 | | 1 | | 5 | 7 | | | | | 8 | 3 | 2 | | | 4 | | 9 | | 10 | | | | 11 | 6 |
| 10 | 27 | SWANSEA | 1-1 | 5748 | Massey | 1 | | 5 | 10 | | | | | 8 | 3 | 2 | | | 4 | | 9 | | 7 | | | | 11 | 6 |
| 11 | 29 | SCUNTHORPE | 0-2 | 6328 | | 1 | | 5 | | | | | | 8 | 3 | 2 | 12 | | 4 | 7 | 9 | | 10* | | | | 11 | 6 |
| 12 | 4 Oct | Newport | 1-4 | 2996 | Whittaker | 1 | | 5 | 7 | | | | | | 3 | 2 | 8 | | 4 | 10 | 9 | | | 12 | | | 11 | 6* |
| 13 | 6 | Wrexham | 2-4 | 11967 | Brown, Hall | 1 | | 5 | 8 | 12 | | | | | 3 | 2 | 9* | | 4 | 10 | | | | 7 | | | 11 | 6 |
| 14 | 11 | BRADFORD | 2-1 | 4440 | Brown, Whittaker | | 1 | 5 | 10 | | | | 12 | | 3 | 2 | | | 4 | 9 | 8* | | | 7 | 6 | | 11 | |
| 15 | 18 | York | 2-4 | 3981 | Brown, Hall | | 1 | 5* | 8 | | | | 7 | | 9 | 2 | 12 | | 4 | 10 | | | | | 6 | | 11 | 3 |
| 16 | 25 | CHESTER | 0-1 | 3754 | | 1 | | | 10 | | | | | 7 | 9 | | 6 | | 4 | 8* | | 3 | | 12 | 2 | | 11 | 5 |
| 17 | 1 Nov | Aldershot | 1-1 | 5966 | Brown | 1 | | | 9 | 2 | | | 10 | | 3 | | | | 4 | 8 | | | | | 6 | 7 | 11 | 5 |
| 18 | 8 | SOUTHEND | 0-2 | 6021 | | 1 | | 4 | 8 | | | | 12 | 9 | 3 | | | | 2 | | | | 11* | | 6 | 7 | 10 | 5 |
| 19 | 22 | GRIMSBY | 3-2 | 3474 | Brown(2), Gibbs | 1 | | 5 | 9 | 2 | | | 11 | 10 | 3 | | | 6 | 8 | | | | | | | 7 | | 4 |
| 20 | 25 | Northampton | 1-1 | 3256 | Brown | 1 | | 5 | 9 | 2 | | | 11 | 10 | 3 | | | 6 | 8 | 12 | | | | | | 7 | | 4* |
| 21 | 13 Dec | Crewe | 1-0 | 2670 | Jones | 1 | | 6 | 9 | 2 | | | 11 | 8 | 3 | | | 10 | 4 | | | | | | | | 7 | 5 |
| 22 | 20 | DARLINGTON | 2-1 | 2571 | Gibbs, Jones | 1 | | 6 | 10 | 2 | | | 7 | 9 | 3 | | | 8 | 4 | | | | | | | | 11 | 5 |
| 23 | 26 | NOTTS COUNTY | 2-1 | 4759 | Gibbs(2) | 1 | | 5 | 9 | 2 | | | 11 | 8 | 3 | | | 10 | 4 | | | | | | | | 7 | 6 |
| 24 | 10 Jan | HARTLEPOOL | 1-1 | 3200 | Jones | 1 | | 5 | 9 | 2 | | | 11 | 8 | 3 | | | 10 | 4 | | | | | | | | 7 | 6 |
| 25 | 17 | Swansea | 0-1 | 8008 | | 1 | | 6 | 12 | 11 | 8 | | | 10 | 3 | 2 | | 7 | 4 | | 9* | | | | | | | 5 |
| 26 | 24 | WORKINGTON | 3-0 | 4265 | Gibbs, Jones, Whittaker | 1 | | 6 | 9 | 2 | 4 | | | 8 | 3 | | | 10 | | | | | 7 | | | | 11 | 5 |
| 27 | 27 | Scunthorpe | 1-1 | 6276 | Jones | 1 | | | 7 | 2 | 4 | | | 8 | 3 | | | 10 | 5 | | | | 9 | | | | 11 | 6 |
| 28 | 31 | NEWPORT | 1-1 | 4679 | Gibbs | 1 | | | 7 | 2 | 4 | | | 8 | 3 | | | 10 | 5 | | | | 9 | | | | 11 | 6 |
| 29 | 7 Feb | Bradford | 1-0 | 2972 | Brown | 1 | | 5 | 7 | 2 | 4 | | | 8 | 3 | | | 10 | | | | | 9 | | | | 11 | 6 |
| 30 | 21 | Southend | 1-2 | 6778 | Oliver | 1 | | 5 | 7* | 2 | 4 | | | 8 | 3 | | | 10 | 12 | | | | 9 | | | | 11 | 6 |
| 31 | 28 | YORK | 3-0 | 3803 | Gibbs, Jones(2) | 1 | | 5 | | 2 | 7 | | | 8 | 3 | | | 10 | 4 | | | | 9 | | | | 11 | 6 |
| 32 | 2 Mar | CHESTERFIELD | 4-1 | 5665 | Gibbs, Jones(2), Wood | 1 | | 5* | | 2 | 7 | | | 8 | 11 | 3 | 12 | 10 | 4 | | | | 9 | | | | | 6 |
| 33 | 11 | Exeter | 1-2 | 4010 | Jones | 1 | | | | 2 | 7 | | | 9 | 11 | 3* | 5 | 10 | 4 | | 12 | | | | | | 8 | 6 |
| 34 | 14 | BRENTFORD | 1-1 | 4878 | Jones | 1 | | 5 | | 2 | 7 | | | 8 | 11 | 3 | | 10 | 4 | | 9 | | | | | | | 6 |
| 35 | 18 | Workington | 1-1 | 2368 | Jones | 1 | | | | 2 | 7 | | | 9 | 10 | 3 | 5 | 11 | 4 | | 8 | | | | | | | 6 |
| 36 | 21 | Chesterfield | 0-2 | 9257 | | 1 | | | | 2* | 7 | | | 8 | 11 | 3 | 5 | 10 | 4 | | 9 | | | | | | 12 | 6 |
| 37 | 27 | ALDERSHOT | 3-1 | 6163 | Howe, Jones(2) | 1 | | 5 | | | 4 | | 10 | 11 | 3 | 2 | | 8 | 12 | 7 | 9* | | | | | | | 6 |
| 38 | 28 | EXETER | 2-1 | 3842 | Gibbs, Jones | 1 | | 5 | 7* | | 4 | | 11 | 8 | 3 | 2 | | 9 | 12 | 10 | | | | | | | | 6 |
| 39 | 1 Apr | Chester | 0-1 | 2580 | | 1 | | 5 | | | 11 | | 7 | 9 | 3 | 2 | | 10 | 4 | 8 | | | | | | | | 6 |
| 40 | 4 | Peterborough | 1-1 | 4168 | Jones | 1 | | 5* | 7 | | | | | 8 | 3 | 2 | 12 | 9 | 4 | 10 | | | | | | | 11 | 6 |
| 41 | 6 | NORTHAMPTON | 0-3 | 3776 | | 1 | | | | | 7 | | | 8 | 3 | 2 | 5 | 10 | 4 | 9 | | | | | | | 11 | 6 |
| 42 | 13 | OLDHAM | 3-1 | 2921 | Hall, Joslyn, Whittaker | | 1 | 5 | | | 3 | | | 8 | 11 | 2 | | 10 | 4 | 9 | | | | | | | 7 | 6 |
| 43 | 18 | Brentford | 0-2 | 4720 | | 1 | | 5 | | | 3 | | | 8 | 11 | 2 | 12 | 10 | 4 | 9 | | | | | | | 7* | 6 |
| 44 | 22 | LINCOLN | 2-0 | 2611 | Whittaker(2) | 1 | | 5 | 11* | | 6 | 12 | | 8 | 3 | 2 | | 10 | 4 | 9 | | | | | | | 7 | |
| 45 | 25 | Port Vale | 1-1 | 5626 | Dyson | 1 | | | | | 6 | 5 | 7 | 9 | 3 | | | 10 | 4 | 8 | | | | | | | 11 | 2 |
| 46 | 28 | Grimsby | 3-5 | 2074 | Gibbs, Light(2) | 1 | | | | | 2 | 5 | 11 | 8 | 3 | | | 10 | 4 | 7 | | | | | | | 9 | 6 |

## F.A.Cup

| | | | | | | | | | | | | | | | | | | | | | | | | | | | | |
|---|---|---|---|---|---|---|---|---|---|---|---|---|---|---|---|---|---|---|---|---|---|---|---|---|---|---|---|---|
| 1st | 15 Nov | Newport | 1–2 | 4224 | O.G. | 1 | | 5 | 7 | 2 | | | | 8 | 3 | | | | | 10 | 9* | | 12 | | 8 | | 11 | 4 |

## Football League Cup

| | | | | | | | | | | | | | | | | | | | | | | | | | | | | |
|---|---|---|---|---|---|---|---|---|---|---|---|---|---|---|---|---|---|---|---|---|---|---|---|---|---|---|---|---|
| 1st | 13 Aug | READING | 1–1 | 5165 | Massey | | 1* | 5 | 10 | | | | | 4 | 3 | | 2 | | 12 | 7 | 8 | | 9 | | | | 11 | 6 |
| 1st/R | 20 | Reading | 3–0 | 11065 | Massey(3) | 1 | | 5 | 10 | | | | | 4 | 3 | | | | 2 | 7 | 8 | | 9 | | | | 11 | 6 |
| 2nd | 3 Sep | Ipswich | 0–4 | 19012 | | 1 | | 5 | 10 | | | | | 4 | 3 | 2 | 12 | | | 7* | 8 | | | 9 | | | 11 | 6 |

# U's new directors

● United's two new directors, Mr. Derek Lamberth and Mr. Robert Jackson, with manager Dick Graham, and chairman of directors Mr. Bill Graver.

**FOURTH DIVISION**

| | | P | W | D | L | F | A | Pts |
|---|---|---|---|---|---|---|---|---|
| 1 | Chesterfield | 46 | 27 | 10 | 9 | 77 | 32 | 64 |
| 2 | Wrexham | 46 | 26 | 9 | 11 | 84 | 49 | 61 |
| 3 | Swansea | 46 | 21 | 18 | 7 | 66 | 45 | 60 |
| 4 | Port Vale | 46 | 20 | 19 | 7 | 61 | 33 | 59 |
| 5 | Brentford | 46 | 20 | 16 | 10 | 58 | 39 | 56 |
| 6 | Aldershot | 46 | 20 | 13 | 13 | 78 | 65 | 53 |
| 7 | Notts County | 46 | 22 | 8 | 16 | 73 | 62 | 52 |
| 8 | Lincoln | 46 | 17 | 16 | 13 | 66 | 52 | 50 |
| 9 | Peterborough | 46 | 17 | 14 | 15 | 77 | 69 | 48 |
| 10 | Colchester | 46 | 17 | 14 | 15 | 64 | 63 | 48 |
| 11 | Chester | 46 | 21 | 6 | 19 | 58 | 66 | 48 |
| 12 | Scunthorpe | 46 | 18 | 10 | 18 | 67 | 65 | 46 |
| 13 | York | 46 | 16 | 14 | 16 | 55 | 62 | 46 |
| 14 | Northampton | 46 | 16 | 12 | 18 | 64 | 55 | 44 |
| 15 | Crewe | 46 | 16 | 12 | 18 | 51 | 51 | 44 |
| 16 | Grimsby | 46 | 14 | 15 | 17 | 54 | 58 | 43 |
| 17 | Southend | 46 | 15 | 10 | 21 | 59 | 85 | 40 |
| 18 | Exeter | 46 | 14 | 11 | 21 | 57 | 59 | 39 |
| 19 | Oldham | 46 | 13 | 13 | 20 | 60 | 65 | 39 |
| 20 | Workington | 46 | 12 | 14 | 20 | 46 | 64 | 38 |
| 21 | Newport | 46 | 13 | 11 | 22 | 53 | 74 | 37 |
| 22 | Darlington | 46 | 13 | 10 | 23 | 53 | 73 | 36 |
| 23 | Hartlepool | 46 | 10 | 10 | 26 | 42 | 82 | 30 |
| 24 | Bradford P A | 46 | 6 | 11 | 29 | 41 | 96 | 23 |

# SEASON 1970–71 Division Four

| No. | Date | Opposition | Res | Attend | Goalscorers | Sherratt | Smith.G | Bloss | Burgess | Cook | Cram | Crawford | Dennis | Garvey | Gibbs | Gilchrist | Hall | Jones | Joslyn | Kurila | Leslie | Lewis | Mahon | Massey | Owen | Painter | Simmons | Smith.L | Whitaker |
|---|---|---|---|---|---|---|---|---|---|---|---|---|---|---|---|---|---|---|---|---|---|---|---|---|---|---|---|---|---|
| 1 | 15 Aug | HARTLEPOOL | 1–0 | 4866 | Gibbs | | 1 | | | 2 | 6 | 10 | | 5 | 8 | 3 | 11 | 9 | 4 | | | | 7 | | | | | | |
| 2 | 22 | Chester | 1–2 | 5447 | Owen | | 1 | | | | 2 | 10 | | 5 | 8 | 3 | 7 | 11 | | 4 | | | 9 | | 6 | | | | |
| 3 | 29 | NORTHAMPTON | 1–1 | 5220 | Owen | | 1 | | | | 2 | 10 | | 5 | 8 | 3 | 11 | 9 | | 6 | | | 7 | 12 | 4* | | | | |
| 4 | 31 | Barrow | 2–0 | 2422 | Crawford | | 1 | | | | 6 | 10 | | 5 | 8 | 2 | 3 | 7 | | 4 | | | 9 | 11 | | | | | |
| 5 | 4 Sep | Southport | 1–2 | 3792 | Gibbs | | 1 | | | | 6 | 10 | | 5 | 8 | 2 | 3 | 7 | | 4 | | | 9* | 11 | | | | | 12 |
| 6 | 12 | NOTTS COUNTY | 2–3 | 4285 | Crawford, Gibbs | | 1 | | | | 7 | 10 | | 5 | 8 | 3 | 2 | 9 | | 6 | | | 11 | | 4 | | | | |
| 7 | 18 | Bournemouth | 1–4 | 7769 | Crawford | | 1 | | | 2 | 11 | 8* | | 5 | 9 | | 3 | 7 | 4 | 6 | | | 10 | | 12 | | | | |
| 8 | 21 | Darlington | 0–0 | 4042 | | 1 | | | | 2 | 3 | 9 | | 5 | 8 | | | 7 | 4 | 6 | | | | 10 | | | | | 11 |
| 9 | 25 | CREWE | 3–0 | 5012 | Crawford(3) | 1 | | | | 2 | 3 | 10 | | 5 | 8 | 9 | | 7 | 4 | 6 | | | | | | | | | 11 |
| 10 | 30 | Workington | 1–1 | 2350 | Gibbs | 1 | | | | 2 | 3 | 10 | | 5 | 8 | 9 | | 7 | 4 | 6 | | | | 12 | | | | | 11 |
| 11 | 3 Oct | Peterborough | 2–1 | 5935 | Gibbs, Massey | 1 | | | | 2 | 3 | 10 | | 5 | 8 | 11 | | 7 | 4 | 6 | | | | 9 | | | | | |
| 12 | 9 | OLDHAM | 1–2 | 5423 | Crawford | 1 | | | | 2 | 3 | 10 | | 5 | 8 | 11 | 12 | 7 | 4 | 6 | | | | 9* | | | | | |
| 13 | 17 | Hartlepool | 2–1 | 2193 | Gibbs, Massey | | 1 | | | | 2 | 8 | | 5 | 9 | 3 | 11 | 10 | | 4 | | | 7 | 12 | 6* | | | | |
| 14 | 19 | YORK | 1–0 | 4457 | Crawford | | 1 | | | | 2 | 8 | | 5 | 9 | 6* | 3 | 10 | | 4 | | | 7 | 11 | 12 | | | | |
| 15 | 23 | Stockport | 0–0 | 5113 | | | 1 | | | 4 | 2 | 11 | | 5 | 8 | | 3 | 10 | | 6 | | | 9 | 7 | | | | | |
| 16 | 30 | ALDERSHOT | 5–2 | 5848 | Crawford, Hall, Jones(2), O.G. | | 1 | | | 2 | 10 | 9 | | 5 | 8 | 4 | 3 | 7 | | 6 | | | 11 | | | | | | |
| 17 | 7 Nov | Exeter | 2–2 | 4420 | Jones, Owen | | 1 | | | 2 | 4 | 10 | | 5 | 8 | | 3 | 7 | | 6 | | | 11 | 9 | | | | | |
| 18 | 10 | Newport | 3–1 | 1973 | Jones, Owen(2) | | 1 | | | 2 | 4 | 10 | | 5 | 8 | | 3 | 7 | | 6 | | | 11 | 9 | | | | | |
| 19 | 13 | SOUTHEND | 1–1 | 7777 | Crawford | | 1 | | | 2 | 4 | 10 | | 5 | 8 | | 3 | 7 | | 6 | | | 11 | 9 | | | | | |
| 20 | 28 | BRENTFORD | 4–0 | 4673 | Cram, Crawford(2), Gibbs | | 1 | | | 2 | 4* | 10 | | 5 | 8 | 11 | 3 | 7 | | 6 | | | 12 | 9 | | | | | |
| 21 | 5 Dec | Cambridge | 1–2 | 5183 | Crawford | | 1 | | | 2 | | 10 | | 5 | 8 | 11 | 3 | 7 | | 6 | | | 4 | 9 | | | | | |
| 22 | 18 | CHESTER | 0–1 | 4342 | | | 1 | | | 2 | 4 | 10 | 12 | 5* | 8 | 11 | 3 | | | 6 | | | 9 | | | 7 | | | |
| 23 | 26 | Lincoln | 2–1 | 5919 | Lewis, Simmons | | 1 | | | 2 | 4 | 10 | | | 11 | 5 | 3 | | | 6 | | 7 | 9 | | | | 8 | | |
| 24 | 8 Jan | WORKINGTON | 2–1 | 5239 | Cram, Crawford | | 1 | | | 2 | 4 | 10 | | 12 | 5 | 11 | 3 | | | 6 | | 8* | 9 | | | | 7 | | |
| 25 | 16 | York | 1–1 | 3804 | Kurila | | 1 | | | 2 | 4 | 9 | | 5 | 11 | | 3 | | | 6 | | 8 | 10 | | | | 7 | | |
| 26 | 5 Feb | CAMBRIDGE | 2–1 | 6469 | Crawford(2) | | 1 | | | | 4 | 10 | | 5 | 7 | 2 | 3 | | | 6 | | 9 | 11 | | | | 8 | | |
| 27 | 20 | NEWPORT | 4–2 | 6444 | Crawford, Lewis(2)(1pen), Mahon | | 1 | | 12 | 4 | 3 | 10 | | 5 | 11 | | 2* | | | 6 | | 7 | 9 | | | | 8 | | |
| 28 | 22 | GRIMSBY | 1–0 | 7253 | Mahon | | 1 | | | 4 | 3 | 10 | | 5 | 7 | | 2 | | | 6 | | 11 | 9 | | | | 8 | | |
| 29 | 26 | Aldershot | 1–0 | 7609 | Cram | | 1 | | | 4 | 3 | 10 | | 5 | 7 | | 2 | | | 6 | | 8 | 11 | | | | 9 | | |
| 30 | 8 Mar | DARLINGTON | 2–0 | 7110 | Crawford, Simmons | 1 | | | | 4 | 3 | 10 | | 5 | 7 | | 2 | | | 6 | | 9 | 11 | | | | 8 | | |
| 31 | 12 | Southend | 1–1 | 9406 | O.G. | 1 | | | | 4 | 3 | 10 | | 5 | 7 | | 2 | | | 6 | | 9 | 11 | | | | 8 | | |
| 32 | 16 | Scunthorpe | 0–2 | 3715 | | 1 | | | | 4 | 3 | 10 | | 5 | 7 | | 2 | 11 | | 6 | | 9* | | | | | 8 | | 12 |
| 33 | 20 | EXETER | 1–1 | 5630 | Crawford | | 1 | | | 2 | 6 | 8 | | 5 | 7 | | 3 | 10 | | 4 | | 11 | | | | | | | 9 |
| 34 | 22 | SCUNTHROPE | 2–0 | 5592 | Crawford(2) | | 1 | | | 2 | 4 | 8 | | 5 | 7 | | 3 | 10 | | 6 | | 11 | 9 | | | | | | |
| 35 | 27 | SOUTHPORT | 1–0 | 5909 | Crawford | | 1 | | | 2 | 4 | 8 | | 5 | 7 | | 3 | 10 | | 6 | | 11 | 9 | | | | | | |
| 36 | 29 | Brentford | 0–1 | 9190 | | | 1 | | 11 | 2 | 4 | 8 | | 5 | 7 | | 3 | 10 | | 6 | | 9 | | | | | | | |
| 37 | 3 Apr | Northampton | 1–2 | 7909 | Kurila | | 1 | | 2* | 12 | 4 | 10 | | 5 | 7 | | 3 | 8 | | 6 | | 11 | 9 | | | | | | |
| 38 | 9 | PETERBOROUGH | 3–0 | 7650 | Gibbs, Gilchrist, Hall | | 1 | | | | 2 | 8 | | 5 | 10 | 4 | 3 | 7 | | 6 | | 9 | 11 | | | | | | |
| 39 | 10 | LINCOLN | 1–1 | 6430 | Gibbs | | 1 | | | 2 | | 8 | | 5 | 10 | 4 | 3 | 7 | | 6 | | 9* | 11 | | | | | | 12 |
| 40 | 12 | Notts County | 0–4 | 14084 | | 1* | | | 12 | 2 | | 8 | | 5 | 9 | 4 | 3 | 10 | | 6 | | | 11 | | | | | | 7 |
| 41 | 17 | Oldham | 0–4 | 10405 | | | 1 | | 10 | 2 | 4 | 9* | 12 | 5 | 8 | 7 | 3 | | | 6 | | | 11 | | | | | | |
| 42 | 20 | Grimsby | 1–3 | 4166 | Burgess | | 1 | | 6 | 2 | 4 | | | 5 | 11* | 7 | 3 | | | 8 | 9 | | 10 | | | | | 12 | |
| 43 | 23 | BOURNEMOUTH | 1–1 | 4168 | Crawford | | 1 | | 4 | 2 | 7 | 9 | | 5 | 10 | 8 | 3 | | | 6 | | | 11 | | | | | | |
| 44 | 26 | BARROW | 4–1 | 3502 | Bloss, Cram(pen), Hall, Mahon | | 1 | 6 | 4 | 2 | 7 | 10 | | 5 | 12 | 8* | 3 | | | | 9 | | 11 | | | | | | |
| 45 | 1 Mar | Crewe | 3–0 | 2796 | Crawford, Hall, Mahon | | 1 | | 4 | | 7 | 10 | | 5 | 6 | 8 | 3 | 9 | | 2 | | | 11 | | | | | | |
| 46 | 7 | Stockport | 1–1 | 5477 | Gibbs | | 1 | | 4 | | 2 | 8 | | 5 | 9 | 7 | 3 | 10 | | 6 | | | 11 | | | | | | |

## F.A.Cup

| | | | | | | | | | | | | | | | | | | | | | | | | | | | | | |
|---|---|---|---|---|---|---|---|---|---|---|---|---|---|---|---|---|---|---|---|---|---|---|---|---|---|---|---|---|---|
| 1st | 21 Nov | RINGMER | 3–0 | 6139 | Crawford(3) | | 1 | | | 2 | 4 | 10 | | 5 | 8 | 12 | 3 | 9 | | 6 | | | 11* | 7 | | | | | |
| 2nd | 12 Dec | CAMBRIDGE | 3–0 | 7348 | Garvey, Gilchrist, Jones | | 1 | | | 2 | 4 | 10 | | 5 | | 11 | 3 | 7* | | 6 | | | 9 | | 12 | | | | 8 |
| 3rd | 5 Jan | Barnet | 1–0 | 4909 | Mahon | | 1 | | | 2 | 4 | 10 | | 12 | 5 | 11 | 3 | | | 6 | | 8 | 9 | | | | 7 | | |
| 4th | 23 | Rochdale | 3–3 | 12321 | Crawford, Lewis, Simmons | | 1 | | | 3 | 4 | 11 | | 5 | 9* | 12 | 2 | | | 6 | | 8 | 10 | | | | 7 | | |
| 4th/R | 25 | ROCHDALE | 5–0 | 11205 | Crawford, Lewis, Mahon, Simmons, O.G. | | 1 | | | 12 | 2 | 11 | | 5 | 4 | 10 | 3 | | | 6 | | 7 | 9 | | | | 8 | | |
| 5th | 13 Feb | LEEDS | 3–2 | 16000 | Crawford(2), Simmons | | 1 | | | 12 | 3 | 10 | | 5 | 11 | 4 | 2 | | | 6 | | 7 | 9 | | | | 8 | | |
| 6th | 6 Mar | Everton | 0–5 | 53028 | | | 1 | | | | 4 | 11 | | 5 | 9 | 2 | 3 | 12 | | 6 | | 7 | 10 | | | | 8 | | |

## Football League Cup

| | | | | | | | | | | | | | | | | | | | | | | | | | | | | | |
|---|---|---|---|---|---|---|---|---|---|---|---|---|---|---|---|---|---|---|---|---|---|---|---|---|---|---|---|---|---|
| 1st | 19 Aug | CAMBRIDGE | 5–0 | 6952 | Hall, Jones(2)(1pen), Owen(2) | | 1 | | | | 2 | 10 | | 5 | 8 | 3 | 7 | 11 | | 6 | | | 9 | | 4 | | | | |
| 2nd | 9 Sep | BRIMINGHAM | 1–1 | 8085 | Jones | | 1 | | | | 7 | 10 | | 5 | 8 | 2 | 3 | 9 | | 6 | | | 11 | | 4 | | | | |
| 2/R | 15 | Birmingham | 1–2 | 17606 | Jones | | 1 | | | 4 | 7 | 10 | | 5 | 8 | 2 | 3 | 9 | 11 | 6 | | | | | | | | | |

Everton
official matchday magazine 5p

Chairman
G A Watts

Vice Chairman
J P Hacking

Directors
J C Sharp
N W Coffey
John Moores
T H W Scott
A W Waterworth JP

Manager
Harry Catterick

Secretary
W Dickinson

Promotions Manager
David Exall

Colchester United

F.A. Cup Sixth Round

Kick-off 3.0 p.m.
Saturday, 6th March 1971

teamcheck

EVERTON
(Royal Blue Shirts, White Shorts)
1 ~~Gordon WEST~~ ANDY RANKIN
2 Tommy WRIGHT
3 Henry NEWTON
4 Howard KENDALL
5 Roger KENYON
6 Colin HARVEY
7 Jimmy HUSBAND
8 Alan BALL
9 Joe ROYLE
10 John HURST
11 Johnny MORRISSEY
12 DEREK JOHNSON

JACK SHARP SPORTS LIVERPOOL

COLCHESTER UNITED
(Red Shirts and Shorts)
1 Graham SMITH
2 Bobby CRAM
3 Brian HALL
4 John GILCHRIST
5 Brian GARVEY
6 John KURILA
7 Brian LEWIS
8 Dave SIMMONS
9 Ray CRAWFORD
10 Mick MAHON
11 Brian GIBBS
12 MICK COOK

Referee:
Jack Taylor (Wolverhampton)

Linesmen:
F. E. Bassett, Swindon (Red Flag)
T. Farley, Co. Durham (Orange Flag)

| FOURTH DIVISION | P | W | D | L | F | A | Pts |
|---|---|---|---|---|---|---|---|
| 1 Notts County | 46 | 30 | 9 | 7 | 89 | 36 | 69 |
| 2 Bournemouth | 46 | 24 | 12 | 10 | 81 | 46 | 60 |
| 3 Oldham | 46 | 24 | 11 | 11 | 88 | 63 | 59 |
| 4 York | 46 | 23 | 10 | 13 | 78 | 54 | 56 |
| 5 Chester | 46 | 24 | 7 | 15 | 69 | 55 | 55 |
| 6 Colchester | 46 | 21 | 12 | 13 | 70 | 54 | 54 |
| 7 Northampton | 46 | 19 | 13 | 14 | 63 | 59 | 51 |
| 8 Southport | 46 | 21 | 6 | 19 | 63 | 57 | 48 |
| 9 Exeter | 46 | 17 | 14 | 15 | 67 | 68 | 48 |
| 10 Workington | 46 | 18 | 12 | 16 | 48 | 49 | 48 |
| 11 Stockport | 46 | 16 | 14 | 16 | 49 | 65 | 46 |
| 12 Darlington | 46 | 17 | 11 | 18 | 58 | 57 | 45 |
| 13 Aldershot | 46 | 14 | 17 | 15 | 66 | 71 | 45 |
| 14 Brentford | 46 | 18 | 8 | 20 | 66 | 62 | 44 |
| 15 Crewe | 46 | 18 | 8 | 20 | 75 | 76 | 44 |
| 16 Peterborough | 46 | 18 | 7 | 21 | 70 | 71 | 43 |
| 17 Scunthorpe | 46 | 15 | 13 | 18 | 56 | 61 | 43 |
| 18 Southend | 46 | 14 | 15 | 17 | 53 | 66 | 43 |
| 19 Grimsby | 46 | 18 | 7 | 21 | 57 | 71 | 43 |
| 20 Cambridge | 46 | 15 | 13 | 18 | 51 | 66 | 43 |
| 21 Lincoln | 46 | 13 | 13 | 20 | 70 | 71 | 39 |
| 22 Newport | 46 | 10 | 8 | 28 | 55 | 85 | 28 |
| 23 Hartlepool | 46 | 8 | 12 | 26 | 34 | 74 | 28 |
| 24 Barrow | 46 | 7 | 8 | 31 | 51 | 90 | 22 |

The end of the road in the incredible F.A.Cup run.

# SEASON 1971–72 Division Four

| No. | Date | Opposition | Res | Attend | Goalscorers | Bloss | Bourne | Burgess | Burnside | Cook | Cram | Foley | Garvey | Gibbs | Gilchrist | Hall | Jones | Kurila | Leslie | Lewis | Mahon | McLaughlin | Mills | Owen | Simmons | Smith.B | Smith.G | Smith.L | Woods | Wingate |
|---|---|---|---|---|---|---|---|---|---|---|---|---|---|---|---|---|---|---|---|---|---|---|---|---|---|---|---|---|---|---|
| 1 | 14 Aug | Lincoln | 0-2 | 6607 | | 10* | | 3 | | | 2 | | 5 | 9 | 6 | | 12 | | | 7 | 11 | | | 4 | 8 | | 1 | | | |
| 2 | 20 | HARTLEPOOL | 1-0 | 5614 | O.G. | | | 2 | | | 12 | | 5 | 8 | 3 | 12 | 4* | 6 | | 11 | 7 | | | 10 | | | 1 | | | |
| 3 | 28 | Bury | 0-3 | 2557 | | | | 6 | | | 2 | | 5 | 8 | 3 | 9 | 12 | 4* | | 10 | 7 | | | 10 | | 1 | | | | |
| 4 | 31 | Newport | 1-2 | 4168 | Lewis | | | 6 | | 12 | 2 | | 5 | 8 | 3* | 11 | 4 | | 9 | 11 | 7 | | | 9 | | 1 | | | | |
| 5 | 3 Sep | SOUTHPORT | 1-0 | 5439 | Mahon | 6 | | 4 | | 2 | 5 | | | 9 | | | | | 10 | 8 | 11 | | | 10 | | | 1 | | | |
| 6 | 11 | Darlington | 0-2 | 2683 | | 6 | | 4 | | | 5 | | 2 | 9 | | 3 | 12 | | 10* | 7 | 11 | | | 7 | | | 1 | | | |
| 7 | 17 | CREWE | 4-2 | 6133 | Burgess, Leslie, Lewis, Mahon | 8 | | 4 | | | 3 | | | 7 | 2 | 5 | 12 | | 10 | 9* | 11 | | | 8 | | | 1 | | | |
| 8 | 25 | Northampton | 1-1 | 5800 | Hall | 6 | | 4 | | 7 | 5 | | 3 | 9 | 2 | 12 | 8* | | 10 | | 11 | | | 6 | | | 1 | | | |
| 9 | 28 | Scunthorpe | 0-2 | 5111 | | 6 | | | | 12 | 3 | | 5 | 9* | 2 | 7 | 4 | | 10 | | 11 | | | | 8 | | 1 | | | |
| 10 | 1 Oct | CHESTER | 1-0 | 6048 | Leslie | 7 | | | | 6 | 2 | | 3 | 12 | 4 | 5 | | 6 | 8 | 9 | 11 | | | | 10 | | 1 | | | |
| 11 | 9 | Aldershot | 2-0 | 5285 | Leslie, Lewis | 8 | | 4 | | 2 | 5 | | | 12 | | 3 | 9 | 6 | 10 | 7 | 11 | | | | | | 1 | | | |
| 12 | 15 | LINCOLN | 5-2 | 5834 | Bloss, Hall, Lewis(3) | 10 | | 4 | | 2 | 5 | | | 12 | | 3 | 9 | 6 | 8 | 7 | 11 | | | | | | 1 | | | |
| 13 | 18 | SOUTHEND | 1-0 | 9867 | Leslie | 10 | | 5 | | 2 | 4 | | | 12 | | 3 | 9 | 6 | 8 | 7 | 11 | | | | | | 1 | | | |
| 14 | 23 | Cambridge | 2-4 | 7238 | Jones(2) | 10 | | 5 | | 2 | 4 | | | 12 | | 3 | 9 | 6 | 8 | 7 | 11* | | | | | | 1 | | | |
| 15 | 29 | GILLINGHAM | 2-2 | 6622 | Kurila, Lewis | | | 5 | | | 4 | | | 2 | 3 | 12 | 9 | 6 | 8 | 7 | 11 | | | | 10* | | 1 | | | |
| 16 | 6 Nov | Barrow | 2-2 | 1954 | Gibbs, Kurila | | | | | 2 | 4 | | 5 | 11 | 10 | 3 | 9 | 6 | 8 | 7 | | | | | | | 1 | | | |
| 17 | 13 | BRENTFORD | 1-1 | 6898 | Jones | | | | | 2 | 4 | | 5 | 8 | 11 | 3 | 10* | | 9 | 7 | 12 | | | | | | 1 | | | |
| 18 | 26 | EXETER | 3-0 | 5116 | Foley(2), Lewis | 10 | | 5 | | | 6 | 4 | 2 | 12 | | 3 | | | 9 | 7* | 11 | | | | | 1 | | | 8 | |
| 19 | 3 Dec | Stockport | 2-2 | 2043 | Mahon(2) | 10 | | 5 | | | 2 | 4* | 6 | 7 | | 3 | | | 9 | | 11 | | | | 12 | 1 | | | 8 | |
| 20 | 18 | Southport | 0-3 | 2657 | | 10 | | 5 | | 4 | 3 | | 6 | | | 2 | | | 12 | 9 | 11 | | | | 7* | 1 | | | 8 | |
| 21 | 27 | PETERBOROUGH | 1-1 | 7750 | Leslie | 8 | | 5 | | 10 | 2 | 4 | 6 | | | 3 | | | 9 | 7 | 11* | | | | 12 | 1 | | | | |
| 22 | 1 Jan | Crewe | 4-2 | 1992 | Cook, Hall, Leslie, Lewis(pen) | 8 | | 5 | | 5 | 2 | 4 | | | | 3 | | | 9 | 7 | | 12 | | | 10 | 1 | | 11 | | |
| 23 | 8 | BURY | 0-0 | 4924 | | 8 | | 55 | | 2 | 6 | 4 | | | | 3 | | | 9 | 7 | | | | | 10 | 1 | | 11 | | |
| 24 | 15 | Doncaster | 0-2 | 3247 | | 8 | | 5 | | 2 | 6 | 4 | 12 | 7 | | 3 | | | 9 | 7* | | | | | 10 | 1 | | 11 | | |
| 25 | 21 | SCUNTHORPE | 1-1 | 4867 | Gibbs | | | 5 | | 2 | 4 | 9 | 12 | 6 | | 3 | | | 8 | | 10 | | | | 7 | 1 | | 11 | | |
| 26 | 28 | Southend | 4-1 | 8871 | Foley, Leslie(2), Mahon | | | 5 | | 2 | 4 | 9 | 6 | 11 | | 3 | | | 8 | | 10 | | | | 12 | 1 | | | | |
| 27 | 5 Feb | Workington | 0-1 | 2170 | | | | 5 | | 2 | 4 | 9 | 6 | 11* | 7 | 3 | | | 8 | | 10 | | | | 12 | 1 | | | | |
| 28 | 12 | CAMBRIDGE | 1-1 | 5663 | Lewis | 9 | | 5 | | 2 | 4 | | 6 | 11 | 7 | 3 | | | 8 | 7 | 10 | | | | 12 | 1 | | | | |
| 29 | 19 | Gillingham | 2-0 | 5313 | Leslie(2) | | | 5 | | 2 | 4 | | 6 | 9 | | 3 | 10* | | 8 | 7 | 11 | | | | | 1 | | 12 | | |
| 30 | 26 | BARROW | 0-1 | 4618 | | | | 5 | | 2 | 4 | | 6 | 11 | | 3 | 9 | | 8 | 7 | 10 | | | | | 1 | | 12 | | |
| 31 | 4 Mar | Brentford | 2-0 | 9210 | Lewis, Mahon | | | 5 | | 2 | 4 | | 6 | | | 3 | | | 8 | 7 | 9 | | 10 | | | 1 | | 11 | | |
| 32 | 11 | ALDERSHOT | 1-0 | 3776 | Lewis | | | 5 | 9 | 2 | 4 | | 6 | | | 3 | | | 8 | 7 | 10 | | 12 | | | 1 | | 11 | | |
| 33 | 13 | DONCASTER | 1-2 | 5004 | L.Smith | | | 5 | 7 | 2 | 4 | | 6 | | | 3 | | | 8 | 10 | 9 | | | | | 1 | | 11 | | |
| 34 | 18 | Hartlepool | 2-3 | 2621 | Garvey, Mahon | | | 5 | | 2 | | | 6* | 11 | | 9 | | | 8 | | 7 | 3 | 4 | | | 1 | | 10 | | 12 |
| 35 | 21 | Grimsby | 0-3 | 13288 | | | | 5 | 7 | 2 | 4 | | | 6 | | 3 | | | 8 | | 9 | | | | 10 | 1 | | 11 | | |
| 36 | 24 | DARLINGTON | 4-3 | 3865 | Burgess, Leslie, Lewis, Simmons | | | 5 | 10 | 2 | 4 | | 6 | | | 3 | | | 9 | 7 | 11 | | | | 8 | 1 | | | | |
| 37 | 31 | NORTHAMPTON | 2-0 | 5375 | Lewis(pen), Simmons | | | 5 | 10 | 2 | 4 | | 6 | | | 3 | | | 9 | 7 | 11 | | | | 8 | 1 | | | | |
| 38 | 1 Apr | Peterborough | 0-4 | 4367 | | | | 5 | 10 | 2 | | 3 | 6 | 9 | | | | | | 4 | 11 | 12 | | | 8* | 1 | | 7 | | |
| 39 | 3 | Chester | 1-2 | 3315 | Lewis(pen) | | 12 | | 9 | 2 | | 4 | 5 | 6 | | | | | | 11 | 7 | 3 | 10* | | | 1 | | 8 | | |
| 40 | 7 | WORKINGTON | 1-0 | 3930 | Foley | | | 6 | 10 | 2 | | 4 | 5 | 7 | | | | | 8 | | 11 | 3 | | | 9 | 1 | | | | |
| 41 | 10 | READING | 2-1 | 4110 | Gibbs, Leslie | | 5* | 6 | 10 | 2 | | 4 | | 7 | | | | | 8 | | 11 | 3 | | | 9 | 1 | | 12 | | |
| 42 | 15 | Exeter | 3-3 | 4052 | Burgess, Gibbs(pen) | | | 6 | 10 | 2 | | 4* | 5 | 7 | | | | | 8 | | 11 | 3 | | | 9 | 1 | | 12 | | |
| 43 | 17 | GRIMSBY | 0-1 | 5086 | | | | 6 | 11 | 2 | | | 5 | 7 | | | | | 8 | | 10 | 3 | 12 | | 9 | 1 | | 4 | | |
| 44 | 21 | STOCKPORT | 3-2 | 4010 | Burgess(2), Simmons | | | 6 | 10* | 2 | | 4 | | 5 | | 7 | | | 8 | | 11 | 3 | | | 9 | 1 | | 12 | | |
| 45 | 24 | NEWPORT | 2-3 | 4311 | Burgess(2), | | | 6 | | 10 | | 4* | 5 | 12 | | 2 | | | 9 | | 11 | 3 | | | 8 | 1 | | 7 | | |
| 46 | 29 | Reading | 4-2 | 3202 | Burgess, Leslie, L.Smith(2) | | | 5 | 10 | 2 | | 4 | | 6 | | 3 | | | 7 | | 11 | 12 | | | 8 | 1 | | 9 | | |

## F.A.Cup

| | | | | | | | | | | | | | | | | | | | | | | | | | | | | | | |
|---|---|---|---|---|---|---|---|---|---|---|---|---|---|---|---|---|---|---|---|---|---|---|---|---|---|---|---|---|---|---|
| 1st | 20 Nov | SHREWSBURY | 1–4 | 5773 | Hall | | | | | 2 | 8 | | 5 | 9 | 4* | 3 | 10 | 6 | 12 | 7 | 11 | | | | | | 1 | | | |

## Football League Cup

| | | | | | | | | | | | | | | | | | | | | | | | | | | | | | | |
|---|---|---|---|---|---|---|---|---|---|---|---|---|---|---|---|---|---|---|---|---|---|---|---|---|---|---|---|---|---|---|
| 1st | 18 Aug | BRENTFORD | 3–1 | 6125 | Lewis(2), Mahon | | | 2 | | | | | 5 | 8 | 3 | 12 | 4 | 6 | | 11 | 7 | | | 10 | 9* | | 1 | | | |
| 2nd | 8 Sep | SWINDON | 4–1 | 7437 | Lewis(3), Mahon | 6 | | 4 | | 6 | 5 | | 12 | 9 | | 3 | | | 10 | 7* | 11 | | | 8 | | | 1 | | | |
| 3rd | 5 Oct | Blackpool | 0–4 | 11042 | | 7 | | 4 | | | 5 | | 6 | 10 | 2 | | | | 12 | 8 | 11 | | | 3 | 9* | | 1 | | | |

### FOURTH DIVISION

| | | P | W | D | L | F | A | Pts |
|---|---|---|---|---|---|---|---|---|
| 1 | Grimsby | 46 | 28 | 7 | 11 | 88 | 56 | 63 |
| 2 | Southend | 46 | 24 | 12 | 10 | 81 | 55 | 60 |
| 3 | Brentford | 46 | 24 | 11 | 11 | 76 | 44 | 59 |
| 4 | Scunthorpe | 46 | 22 | 13 | 11 | 56 | 37 | 57 |
| 5 | Lincoln | 46 | 21 | 14 | 11 | 77 | 59 | 56 |
| 6 | Workington | 46 | 16 | 19 | 11 | 50 | 34 | 51 |
| 7 | Southport | 46 | 18 | 14 | 14 | 66 | 46 | 50 |
| 8 | Peterborough | 46 | 17 | 16 | 13 | 82 | 64 | 50 |
| 9 | Bury | 46 | 19 | 12 | 15 | 73 | 59 | 50 |
| 10 | Cambridge | 46 | 17 | 14 | 15 | 62 | 60 | 48 |
| 11 | Colchester | 46 | 19 | 10 | 17 | 70 | 69 | 48 |
| 12 | Doncaster | 46 | 16 | 14 | 16 | 56 | 63 | 46 |
| 13 | Gillingham | 46 | 16 | 13 | 17 | 61 | 67 | 45 |
| 14 | Newport | 46 | 18 | 8 | 20 | 60 | 72 | 44 |
| 15 | Exeter | 46 | 16 | 11 | 19 | 61 | 68 | 43 |
| 16 | Reading | 46 | 17 | 8 | 21 | 56 | 76 | 42 |
| 17 | Aldershot | 46 | 9 | 22 | 15 | 48 | 54 | 40 |
| 18 | Hartlepool | 46 | 17 | 6 | 23 | 58 | 69 | 40 |
| 19 | Darlington | 46 | 14 | 11 | 21 | 64 | 82 | 39 |
| 20 | Chester | 46 | 10 | 18 | 18 | 47 | 56 | 38 |
| 21 | Northampton | 46 | 12 | 13 | 21 | 66 | 79 | 37 |
| 22 | Barrow | 46 | 13 | 11 | 22 | 40 | 71 | 37 |
| 23 | Stockport | 46 | 9 | 14 | 23 | 55 | 87 | 32 |
| 24 | Crewe | 46 | 10 | 9 | 27 | 43 | 69 | 29 |

# SEASON 1972-73 Division Four

| No. | Date | Opposition | Res | Attend | Goalscorers | Kelly | McInally | Smith.B | Binks | Bloss | Bourne | Brown | Cook | Foley | Hall | Harford | Leslie | Mahon | McLaughlin | Mills | Morgan | Moss | Noble | Simmons | Smith.J | Smith.L | South | Svarc | Thomas | Wooldridge | Roberts |
|---|---|---|---|---|---|---|---|---|---|---|---|---|---|---|---|---|---|---|---|---|---|---|---|---|---|---|---|---|---|---|---|
| 1 | 12 Aug | HEREFORD | 1–0 | 6093 | Foley | | | 1 | | 10 | | | | 4 | | | 7 | 11 | 3 | | 5 | 8 | 6 | 12 | | 9 | | | | 2 | |
| 2 | 19 | Hartlepool | 1–2 | 5472 | O.G. | | | 1 | 6 | 10 | | | 2 | | 3 | | 9 | 11 | | | 5 | 8* | 4 | 12 | | | | | 7 | | |
| 3 | 26 | NEWPORT | 1–3 | 3639 | Mahon | | | 1 | | | | | 2 | 7 | 12 | | 9* | 10 | 3 | 11 | 6 | 4 | | 8 | | | 5 | | | | |
| 4 | 30 | Chester | 0–4 | 4304 | | | | 1 | | 6 | | | 12 | 10 | | | | 9 | 3 | | 5 | 7 | 4 | 8 | | 11 | | | | 2 | |
| 5 | 2 Sep | Darlington | 1–2 | 1251 | Moss | | | 1 | | 10 | | | 2 | 6 | | | | 9 | 3 | | 4 | 8 | 5 | 7 | | 11 | | | 12 | | |
| 6 | 8 | CREWE | 5–1 | 2767 | Mahon, McLaughlin, Simmons(3) | | | 1 | 6 | 10 | | | 2 | 4 | | | | 11 | 3 | | | 8 | 5 | 9 | | 12 | | | 7 | | |
| 7 | 16 | Barnsley | 0–4 | 2297 | | | | 1 | 5 | 11 | | | 2 | 4 | | | 12 | 10 | 3* | | | 9 | 6 | 8 | | | | | 7 | | |
| 8 | 20 | Southport | 0–1 | 2527 | | | | 1 | 6 | 10* | | | 2 | 4 | | | | 11 | | | 12 | 8 | 5 | | | 9 | | | 7 | 3 | |
| 9 | 22 | NORTHAMPTON | 2–2 | 3543 | Mahon, McLaughlin | | | 1 | 6 | 11 | | | 2 | 4 | | | | 10 | 3 | | | 8 | 5 | 9 | | 12 | | | 7 | | |
| 10 | 25 | BRADFORD | 0–0 | 3474 | | | | 1 | 6* | 10 | | | 2 | 4 | | | | 11 | 3 | | 5 | 8 | | 9 | | 12 | | | 7 | | |
| 11 | 30 | Exeter | 0–1 | 5005 | | | | 1 | | | | | 2 | 4 | 11 | | | 10 | 3 | | | | 5 | 9 | | 8 | 6 | | 7 | 12 | |
| 12 | 7 Oct | Lincoln | 2–3 | 6268 | Moss, Simmons | | | 1 | | | | | 2 | 4 | 11 | | | 10 | 3 | | | 8 | 5 | 9 | | 12 | 6 | | 7 | | |
| 13 | 9 | ALDERSHOT | 2–3 | 3445 | Mahon, Moss | | | 1 | | | | | 2* | 4 | 11 | | | 7 | 3 | | | 8 | 5 | 9 | | 12 | 6 | | 10 | | |
| 14 | 13 | WORKINGTON | 1–1 | 2997 | Simmons | | | 1 | | | | | 2 | 4 | 7 | | | 11 | 3 | | 5 | 9 | 6 | 8 | | 12 | | | 10 | | |
| 15 | 20 | Cambridge | 0–3 | 4465 | | | | 1 | | | | | 2 | 4 | 7 | | | 11 | 3 | 5 | 12 | 9 | 6 | 8* | | | | | 10 | | |
| 16 | 23 | Peterborough | 2–2 | 5648 | Mahon(2) | | | 1 | 5* | | | | 2 | 4 | 11 | | 10 | 7 | 3 | 6 | | 8 | 12 | | | 9 | | | | | |
| 17 | 28 | MANSFIELD | 1–1 | 3789 | Mahon(pen) | | | 1 | 4 | | | | 8 | 11 | 3 | | | 7 | 2 | | 6 | | 5 | 9 | | 10 | | | | 12 | |
| 18 | 4 Nov | Bradford | 0–3 | 3047 | | 1 | | | 4 | 7 | | | 2* | | 11 | | | 10 | 3 | | 6 | 8 | 5 | 9 | | | | | 12 | | |
| 19 | 10 | SOUTHPORT | 3–1 | 3306 | Foley, Mahon, Thomas | | 1 | | | 7* | | | | 10 | 3 | | | 11 | 2 | | 6 | | 5 | 8 | 12 | 9 | | | 4 | | |
| 20 | 25 | Reading | 1–0 | 4955 | Foley, | | 1 | | | | | | 4 | 7 | 3 | | 10 | 11 | 2 | 12 | 6 | | 5 | 8 | | 9 | | | | | |
| 21 | 16 Dec | Doncaster | 0–1 | 1888 | | | 1 | | | 12 | | | 4 | 7* | 3 | | 10 | 11 | 2 | | 6 | | 5 | 8 | | 9 | | | | | |
| 22 | 23 | BURY | 2–1 | 2739 | Foley, Morgan | | 1 | | | 12 | | | 4 | 7 | 3 | | 10 | 11 | 2 | | 6 | | 5 | | | 9 | | | 8 | | |
| 23 | 26 | Northampton | 0–4 | 3298 | | | 1 | | | 8* | | | 4 | 7 | 3 | | | 11 | 2 | 12 | 6 | | 5 | | | 9 | | | 10 | | |
| 24 | 29 | HARTLEPOOL | 1–1 | 3172 | Mahon | | 1 | | 6 | | | 4 | 2 | | | | 8 | 11 | 3 | | 5 | 12 | | | | 9 | | 10 | 7* | | |
| 25 | 6 Jan | Newport | 0–1 | 3465 | | | 1 | | | | | 4 | 2 | | | 6 | 8 | 11* | 3 | | 5 | 12 | | | | 9 | | 10 | 7 | | |
| 26 | 19 | DARLINGTON | 1–0 | 3360 | Mahon | | 1 | | | 12 | | 4 | 2 | 9 | | 6 | 10 | 11 | 3 | | 5 | | | 8 | | | | | 7 | | |
| 27 | 27 | Crewe | 2–1 | 1825 | Simmons, Thomas | | 1 | | | | | 4 | 2 | 12 | | 6 | 10 | 11 | 3 | | 5 | | | 8 | | 9 | | | 7 | | |
| 28 | 3 Feb | Aldershot | 0–2 | 3574 | | | 1 | | | | | 4 | 2 | 12 | | 5 | 10 | 11 | 3 | | | | 6 | 8 | | 9 | | | 7 | | |
| 29 | 10 | BARNSLEY | 1–2 | 3148 | Svarc | | 1 | | | | | 4 | 2 | | | 5 | 12 | 11 | 3 | | | | 6 | 8 | | 9* | | 10 | 7 | | |
| 30 | 17 | Hareford | 1–4 | 7624 | Svarc | | | 1 | | | | 6 | 3 | 4 | | 5 | 7 | 11 | 2* | | | | 12 | 9 | | 10 | | 8 | | | |
| 31 | 24 | DONCASTER | 1–1 | 2550 | Foley | | 1 | | | | | 4 | 2 | 8 | | 6 | 7 | 11 | | | 5 | | 3 | | | 10 | | 9 | 12 | | |
| 32 | 3 Mar | LINCOLN | 0–2 | 2649 | | | 1 | | | | | 4 | 3 | 11 | | 6 | 7* | 8 | | | 5 | | 2 | 12 | | 10 | | 9 | | | |
| 33 | 5 | TORQUAY | 1–1 | 2636 | Leslie(pen) | | 1 | | | | | 3 | 8 | 11 | | 6 | 7 | 10 | | | 5 | | 2 | | 4 | 12 | | 9 | | | |
| 34 | 10 | Workington | 0–1 | 1297 | | | 1 | | | 12 | | 3 | 2 | | | 6 | 7 | 11 | | | 5 | | | | 4 | 10* | | 9 | 8 | | |
| 35 | 16 | CAMBRIDGE | 0–1 | 3888 | | | 1 | | | | | 3 | 8 | | | 6 | 7 | | 2 | | 5 | | | | 4 | 10 | | 9 | 11* | | 12 |
| 36 | 19 | Stockport | 0–2 | 3056 | | | 1 | | | | | 3 | 8 | | | 6* | 7 | | 2 | | 5 | | | | 4 | 10 | | 9 | 11 | | 12 |
| 37 | 24 | Mansfield | 1–1 | 4664 | Foley | | 1 | | | | | 10* | 9 | 7 | | 6 | | 11 | 3 | | 5 | | | | 4 | 12 | | 8 | 2 | | |
| 38 | 30 | READING | 2–2 | 3092 | Leslie(pen), Svarc | | 1 | | | | | 5 | 10 | 7 | | | 9* | 11 | 3 | | 6 | | | | 4 | 12 | | 8 | 2 | | |
| 39 | 6 Apr | Gillingham | 1–2 | 3072 | Svarc(pen) | | 1 | | | | | 9 | 7 | 10 | | 5 | 12 | 11* | 3 | | 6 | | | | 4 | | | 8 | 2 | | |
| 40 | 9 | PETERBOROUGH | 1–0 | 2437 | Foley | | 1 | | | | | 4 | 7 | 9 | | 6 | 10 | 11 | 3 | | 5 | | | | | 12 | | 8 | 2 | | |
| 41 | 13 | STOCKPORT | 3–0 | 2772 | Mahon(2), Svarc | | 1 | | | | | 4 | 7 | 9 | | 6 | 10 | 11 | 3 | | 5 | | | | | 12 | | 8 | 2 | | |
| 42 | 16 | EXETER | 1–2 | 3489 | Svarc | | 1 | | | | | 4 | 7 | 9 | | 6 | 10 | 11 | 3 | | 5 | | | | | 12 | | 8 | 2 | | |
| 43 | 20 | Torquay | 0–0 | 4081 | | | 1 | | | | | 4 | 7 | 9 | | 5 | 10 | 11 | 3 | 12 | | | | | | 6 | | 8 | 2 | | |
| 44 | 23 | Bury | 0–4 | 3079 | | | 1 | | | | | 4 | 7 | 9 | | 5 | 10 | 11 | 3 | 12 | | | | | | 6 | | 8 | 2 | | |
| 45 | 27 | CHESTER | 2–3 | 2680 | Harford, Svarc | | 1 | | | | 5 | 4 | 7 | 9 | | 6 | 10 | 11 | 3 | | | | | | | 12 | | 8 | 2 | | |
| 46 | 30 | GILLINGHAM | 4–0 | 2590 | Foley, Leslie, L.Smith, Svarc | | 1 | | | | 5 | 3 | 4 | 9 | | 6 | 7* | 11 | 2 | 12 | | | | | | 10 | | 8 | | | |

## F.A.Cup

| | | | | | | | | | | | | | | | | | | | | | | | | | | | | | | | |
|---|---|---|---|---|---|---|---|---|---|---|---|---|---|---|---|---|---|---|---|---|---|---|---|---|---|---|---|---|---|---|---|
| 1st | 18 Nov | BOGNOR REGIS | 6-0 | 4321 | Foley, Hall, Morgan, Simmons(3) | 1 | | | | 12 | | | 7 | 3 | | | 11 | 2* | | 6 | | 5 | 8 | 4 | 9 | | | 10 | | |
| 2nd | 9 Dec | Bournemouth | 0-0 | 11164 | | | 1 | | 12 | | | | 4 | 7 | 3 | | 10 | 11 | 2 | | 6 | | 5 | 8 | | 9 | | | | | |
| 2R/R | 11 | BOURNEMOUTH | 0-2 | 7419 | | | 1 | | | 12 | | | 4 | 7* | 3 | | 10 | 11 | 2 | | 6 | | 5 | 8 | | 9 | | | | | |

## Football League Cup

| | | | | | | | | | | | | | | | | | | | | | | | | | | | | | | | |
|---|---|---|---|---|---|---|---|---|---|---|---|---|---|---|---|---|---|---|---|---|---|---|---|---|---|---|---|---|---|---|---|
| 1st | 16 Aug | Gillingham | 0-1 | 3966 | | | | 1 | | | | | | 4 | | | 7 | 11 | 3 | | 5 | 8 | 6 | 12 | | 9 | | | 10 | 2 | |

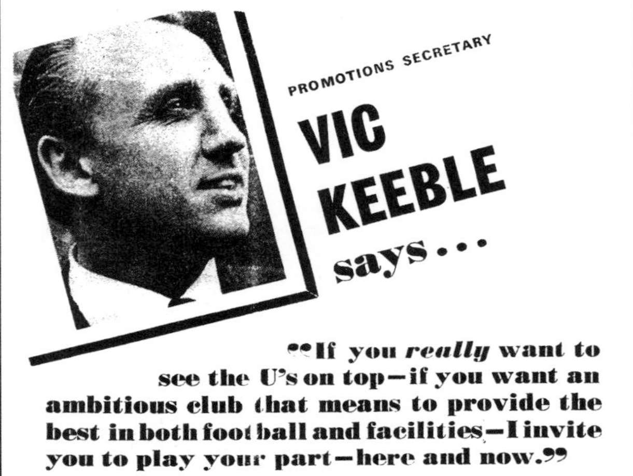


### FOURTH DIVISION

| | P | W | D | L | F | A | Pts |
|---|---|---|---|---|---|---|---|
| 1 Southport | 46 | 36 | 10 | 10 | 71 | 48 | 62 |
| 2 Hereford | 46 | 23 | 12 | 11 | 56 | 38 | 58 |
| 3 Cambridge | 48 | 20 | 17 | 9 | 67 | 57 | 57 |
| 4 Aldershot | 46 | 22 | 12 | 12 | 60 | 38 | 56 |
| 5 Newport | 46 | 22 | 12 | 12 | 64 | 44 | 56 |
| 6 Mansfield | 46 | 20 | 14 | 12 | 78 | 51 | 54 |
| 7 Reading | 46 | 17 | 18 | 11 | 51 | 38 | 52 |
| 8 Exeter | 46 | 18 | 14 | 14 | 57 | 51 | 50 |
| 9 Gillingham | 46 | 19 | 11 | 16 | 63 | 58 | 49 |
| 10 Lincoln | 46 | 16 | 16 | 14 | 64 | 57 | 48 |
| 11 Stockport | 46 | 18 | 12 | 16 | 53 | 53 | 48 |
| 12 Bury | 46 | 14 | 18 | 14 | 58 | 51 | 46 |
| 13 Workington | 46 | 17 | 12 | 17 | 59 | 61 | 46 |
| 14 Barnsley | 46 | 14 | 16 | 16 | 58 | 60 | 44 |
| 15 Chester | 46 | 14 | 15 | 17 | 61 | 52 | 43 |
| 16 Bradford | 46 | 16 | 11 | 19 | 61 | 65 | 43 |
| 17 Doncaster | 46 | 15 | 12 | 19 | 49 | 58 | 42 |
| 18 Torquay | 46 | 12 | 17 | 17 | 44 | 47 | 41 |
| 19 Peterborough | 46 | 14 | 13 | 19 | 71 | 76 | 41 |
| 20 Hartlepool | 46 | 12 | 17 | 17 | 34 | 49 | 41 |
| 21 Crewe | 46 | 9 | 18 | 19 | 38 | 61 | 36 |
| 22 Colchester | 46 | 10 | 11 | 25 | 48 | 76 | 31 |
| 23 Northampton | 46 | 10 | 11 | 25 | 40 | 73 | 31 |
| 24 Darlington | 46 | 7 | 15 | 24 | 42 | 85 | 29 |

Vic Keeble, a player from the pre-League and early Football League days returned to Colchester as Promotions Secretary.

# SEASON 1973-74 Division Four

| No. | Date | Opposition | Res | Attend | Goalscorers | Walker | Aimson | Anderson | Slinkell | Cook | Dominey | Dyson | Foley | Harford | Leslie | Mahon | McLaughlin | Mills | Moore | Morgan | Packer | Rowe | Silvester | Smith.A | Smith.L | Svarc | Taylor | Thomas |
|---|---|---|---|---|---|---|---|---|---|---|---|---|---|---|---|---|---|---|---|---|---|---|---|---|---|---|---|---|
| 1 | 25 Aug | Barnsley | 1-0 | 2560 | Svarc | 1 | 9* | | | 7 | | 4 | 10 | 6 | | 11 | 2 | | | 5 | 3 | | | | | 8 | | 12 |
| 2 | 1 Sep | CREWE | 3-2 | 4078 | Aimson, Morgan, Svarc | 1 | 9 | | | 7 | | 4 | 10 | 5 | | 11 | 2 | | | 6 | 3 | | | | | 8* | | 12 |
| 3 | 7 | Northampton | 0-0 | 4916 | | 1 | | | | 7 | | 4 | 10 | 5 | 12 | 11 | 2 | | | 6 | 3 | | | | | 8 | | 9 |
| 4 | 11 | READING | 0-0 | 4565 | | 1 | | | | 7 | | 4 | 10 | 6 | 12 | 11 | 2 | | | 6 | 3 | | | | | 8 | | 9 |
| 5 | 15 | NEWPORT | 4-1 | 3523 | Leslie, Morgan, Svarc, Thomas | 1 | | | | 7 | | 4 | 10 | 6 | 11* | | 2 | | | 5 | 3 | | | | 12 | 8 | | 9 |
| 6 | 19 | Torquay | 4-0 | 3488 | Dyson, Leslie, Svarc, Thomas | 1 | | | | 7 | | 4 | 10 | 6 | 11 | 12 | 2 | | | 5 | 3 | | | | | 8* | | 9 |
| 7 | 22 | Swansea | 0-2 | 1981 | | 1 | | | | 7 | | 4 | 10 | 6 | 11* | 12 | 2 | | | 5 | 3 | | | | | 8 | | 9 |
| 8 | 28 | EXETER | 1-0 | 5466 | Leslie | 1 | | | | 7 | | 4 | 9 | 6 | 11 | 12 | 2 | | | 5* | 3 | | | | | 8 | | 10 |
| 9 | 2 Oct | TORQUAY | 2-2 | 5291 | Svarc(2) | 1 | | | | 4 | | 6 | 10* | 5 | 7 | 11 | 2 | | | | 3 | | | | 12 | 8 | | 9 |
| 10 | 6 | Hartlepool | 0-0 | 1919 | | 1 | | | | 2 | | 4 | | 5 | | 11 | 3 | 12 | | | 6 | | 9 | | 10 | 8 | | 7 |
| 11 | 12 | DARLINGTON | 3-0 | 5089 | Foley(2), Svarc | 1 | | | | 7 | | 4 | 10 | 6 | | | 2 | | | 5 | 3* | | 9 | | 12 | 8 | | 11 |
| 12 | 19 | SCUNTHORPE | 2-0 | 4862 | Morgan, Svarc | 1 | | | | 2 | | 4 | 10 | 6 | 12 | | 3 | | | 5 | | | 9* | | 11 | 8 | | 7 |
| 13 | 24 | Reading | 1-1 | 12310 | Svarc | 1 | | | | 3 | | 4 | 10 | 6 | 9* | | 2 | 12 | | 5 | | | | | | 8 | | 11 |
| 14 | 27 | Rotherham | 0-0 | 4594 | | 1 | | | | 7 | | 4 | 10 | 6 | | 12 | 2 | 9 | | 5 | | | | | 3 | 8 | | 11 |
| 15 | 2 Nov | WORKINGTON | 3-0 | 5342 | Cook, Harford, Morgan | 1 | | | | 11 | | 4 | 10 | 6 | | 12 | 2 | | | 5 | | | 9 | | 3 | 8 | | 7 |
| 16 | 10 | Mansfield | 2-2 | 3033 | Foley(2) | 1 | | | | 10 | | 4 | 9 | 6 | | 11 | 2 | 12 | | | | | | 5 | 3 | 8 | | 7 |
| 17 | 14 | Chester | 4-0 | 1973 | Svarc(4) | 1 | | | | 11 | | 4 | 9 | 6* | | 10 | 2 | | | | 3 | | | 5 | 12 | 8 | | 7 |
| 18 | 17 | STOCKPORT | 3-1 | 4966 | Dyson(2)(both pen), Foley | 1 | | | | 10 | | 4 | 9 | 6 | | 11 | 2* | | | | 3 | | | 5 | 12 | 8 | | 7 |
| 19 | 1 Dec | BRADFORD | 4-0 | 3468 | Dyson, Morgan, Svarc(2) | 1 | | | | 10 | | 4 | 9 | 6 | | 12 | | 7 | | 5 | 3 | | | 2 | 11 | 8 | | |
| 20 | 8 | Gillingham | 1-4 | 8411 | L.Smith | 1 | | | 12 | 10 | | 4 | 9 | 6 | | | | | | 5* | 3 | | | 2 | 11 | 8 | | 7 |
| 21 | 15 | Stockport | 3-0 | 1472 | Foley(2), Svarc | 1 | | | 11 | 10 | | 4 | 9 | 6 | | | | 12 | | 5 | 3 | | | 2 | | 8 | | 7 |
| 22 | 22 | Exeter | 0-1 | 3638 | | 1 | | | 10 | 2 | | 4 | 9 | 6 | | | | 11* | | | 3 | | | 5 | 12 | 8 | | 7 |
| 23 | 26 | PETERBOROUGH | 1-1 | 7960 | Svarc | 1 | | | 11 | 2 | | 4 | 9 | 6 | | | | 12 | | | 3 | | | 5 | 10 | 8 | | 7 |
| 24 | 29 | NORTHAMPTON | 1-0 | 5042 | Dyson(pen) | 1 | | | 11* | 10 | | 4 | 9 | 6 | | | | | | 5 | 3 | | | 2 | 12 | 8 | | 7 |
| 25 | 1 Jan | Crewe | 2-1 | 2383 | Dyson, Svarc | 1 | | | 10* | 11 | | 4 | 9 | 6 | | | | 12 | | 5 | 3 | | | 2 | | 8 | | 7 |
| 26 | 5 | LINCOLN | 4-1 | 4398 | Leslie, Morgan, Svarc(2) | 1 | | | | 11 | | 4 | | 6 | 9 | | | 12 | | 5 | 3 | | | | 10 | 8 | | 7 |
| 27 | 12 | Newport | 3-1 | 3304 | Cook, Leslie, Thomas | 1 | | | | 11 | | 4 | | 6 | 9 | | | 2 | | 5 | 3 | | | | 10 | 8 | | 7 |
| 28 | 19 | BARNSLEY | 2-0 | 5793 | Dyson(pen), Svarc | 1 | | | | 11 | | 4 | 10 | 6 | 9 | | | 2* | | 5 | 3 | | | 2 | 12 | 8 | | 7 |
| 29 | 27 | Doncaster | 0-2 | 4285 | | 1 | | | | 11 | | 4 | 9 | 6 | 10* | | | | | 5 | 3 | | | 2 | 12 | 8 | | 7 |
| 30 | 3 Feb | Bury | 0-2 | 7796 | | 1 | 10* | | | | | | 9 | 6 | 11 | | | 4 | | 5 | 3 | 12 | | 2 | | 8 | | 7 |
| 31 | 8 | SWANSEA | 2-0 | 5040 | Morgan, Svarc | 1 | | 11 | | | | | 10 | 6 | 9 | | | 4 | | 5 | 3 | | | 2 | 12 | 8 | | 7 |
| 32 | 16 | Darlington | 0-1 | 2275 | | 1 | | 11 | | 3 | | | 10 | 6 | 8 | | | 4* | | 5 | | | | 2 | 12 | 9 | | 7 |
| 33 | 22 | HARTLEPOOL | 3-0 | 5608 | Aimson, A.Smith, Svarc | 1 | 12 | 9 | | 11 | | | 7* | 6 | 10 | | | 4 | | 5 | | | | 2 | 3 | 8 | | |
| 34 | 2 Mar | Peterborough | 0-2 | 10714 | | 1 | | 9 | | 11 | | | 7 | 6 | 10 | | | 4* | | 5 | 12 | | | 2 | 3 | 8 | | |
| 35 | 8 | ROTHERHAM | 0-1 | 5180 | | 1 | | | | 11 | | 4 | 10 | 6 | 9* | | | | | 5 | 3 | | | 2 | 12 | 8 | | 7 |
| 36 | 16 | Scunthorpe | 0-1 | 2139 | | 1 | | | | 11 | | 4 | | 6 | 9 | | | | 10* | 5 | 3 | | | 2 | | 8 | 12 | 7 |
| 37 | 19 | BURY | 1-1 | 4748 | Moore | 1 | | | | 11 | | 4 | | 6 | 12 | | | | 10 | 5 | | | | 2 | 3 | 8 | 9* | 7 |
| 38 | 22 | MANSFIELD | 1-0 | 4695 | Morgan | 1 | | | | 11 | | 4 | | 6 | | | | | 10 | 5 | 12 | | | 2 | 3 | 8 | 9 | 7 |
| 39 | 27 | Lincoln | 1-0 | 2638 | Svarc | 1 | | | | 9 | | | | 6 | | | | 12 | 10 | 5 | 11 | | | 2 | 3 | 8 | 4* | 7 |
| 40 | 30 | Workington | 4-1 | 1103 | Moore, Svarc, Thomas, O.G. | 1 | | | | 9 | | 4 | | 6 | | | | 12 | 10 | 5 | 11* | | | 2 | 3 | 8 | | 7 |
| 41 | 2 Apr | DONCASTER | 3-0 | 5124 | Cook(2), Moore | 1 | | | | 9 | | 4 | | 6 | 12 | | | | 10 | 5 | 11 | | | 2 | 3 | 8 | | 7* |
| 42 | 5 | CHESTER | 1-1 | 6371 | Moore | 1 | | | | 9 | | 4* | | 6 | 11 | | | | 10 | 5 | | | | 2 | 3 | 8 | 12 | 7 |
| 43 | 12 | BRENTFORD | 2-1 | 8154 | Moore(2) | 1 | | | | 9 | | | | 6 | 11 | | | 4 | 10 | 5 | | | | 2 | 3 | 8 | 12 | 7* |
| 44 | 16 | Brentford | 0-0 | 7480 | | 1 | | | | 9 | 12 | | | 6 | 11 | | | 4 | 10 | 5 | | | | 2 | 3 | 8 | 7* | |
| 45 | 20 | GILLINGHAM | 0-2 | 10007 | | 1 | | | | 9 | 12 | | | 6 | 11* | | | 4 | 10 | 5 | | | | 2 | 3 | 8 | 7 | |
| 46 | 27 | Bradford | 1-1 | 3702 | Moore | 1 | | | | 9 | 5 | | | 6 | 12 | | | 4 | 10 | | 11 | | | 2 | 3 | 8 | 7 | |

## F.A.Cup

| | | | | | | | | | | | | | | | | | | | | | | | | | | | | |
|---|---|---|---|---|---|---|---|---|---|---|---|---|---|---|---|---|---|---|---|---|---|---|---|---|---|---|---|---|
| 1st | 24 Nov | PETERBOROUGH | 2-3 | 9664 | Harford, Mahon | 1 | | | | 10 | | 4 | 9 | 6 | | 11 | 2 | | | 5* | 8 | | | | 12 | 8 | | 7 |

## Football League Cup

| | | | | | | | | | | | | | | | | | | | | | | | | | | | | |
|---|---|---|---|---|---|---|---|---|---|---|---|---|---|---|---|---|---|---|---|---|---|---|---|---|---|---|---|---|
| 1st | 29 Aug | Gillingham | 2-4 | 3991 | Cook, Svarc | 1 | 9 | | | 7 | | 4* | 10 | 6 | | 11 | 2 | | | 5 | 3 | | | | | 8 | | 12 |

Barry Smith in a training session with the Colchester United ladies' soccer team.

**FOURTH DIVISION**

| | | P | W | D | L | F | A | Pts |
|---|---|---|---|---|---|---|---|---|
| 1 | Peterborough* | 46 | 27 | 11 | 8 | 75 | 38 | 65 |
| 2 | Gillingham* | 46 | 25 | 12 | 9 | 90 | 49 | 62 |
| 3 | Colchester* | 46 | 24 | 12 | 10 | 73 | 36 | 60 |
| 4 | Bury* | 46 | 24 | 11 | 11 | 81 | 49 | 59 |
| 5 | Northampton | 46 | 20 | 13 | 13 | 63 | 48 | 53 |
| 6 | Reading | 46 | 16 | 19 | 11 | 58 | 37 | 51 |
| 7 | Chester | 46 | 17 | 15 | 14 | 54 | 55 | 49 |
| 8 | Bradford | 46 | 17 | 14 | 15 | 58 | 52 | 48 |
| 9 | Newport† | 46 | 16 | 14 | 16 | 56 | 65 | 45 |
| 10 | Exeter† | 45 | 18 | 8 | 19 | 58 | 55 | 44 |
| 11 | Hartlepool | 46 | 16 | 12 | 18 | 48 | 47 | 44 |
| 12 | Lincoln | 46 | 16 | 12 | 18 | 63 | 67 | 44 |
| 13 | Barnsley | 46 | 17 | 10 | 19 | 58 | 64 | 44 |
| 14 | Swansea | 46 | 16 | 11 | 19 | 45 | 46 | 43 |
| 15 | Rotherham | 46 | 15 | 13 | 18 | 56 | 58 | 43 |
| 16 | Torquay | 46 | 13 | 17 | 16 | 52 | 57 | 43 |
| 17 | Mansfield | 46 | 13 | 17 | 16 | 62 | 69 | 43 |
| 18 | Scunthorpe† | 45 | 14 | 12 | 19 | 47 | 64 | 42 |
| 19 | Brentford | 46 | 12 | 16 | 18 | 48 | 50 | 40 |
| 20 | Darlington | 46 | 13 | 13 | 20 | 40 | 62 | 39 |
| 21 | Crewe | 46 | 14 | 10 | 22 | 43 | 71 | 38 |
| 22 | Doncaster | 46 | 12 | 11 | 23 | 47 | 80 | 35 |
| 23 | Workington | 46 | 11 | 13 | 22 | 43 | 74 | 35 |
| 24 | Stockport | 46 | 7 | 20 | 19 | 44 | 69 | 34 |

# SEASON 1974–75 Division Three

| No. | Date | Opposition | Res | Attend | Goalscorers | Walker | Allinson | Bunkell | Cameron | Cook | Dominey | Dyson | Foley | Froggatt | Harford | Leslie | Lindsay | McDonald | Morgan | Packer | Rowe | Sims | Smith.A | Smith.L | Svarc | Thomas |
|---|---|---|---|---|---|---|---|---|---|---|---|---|---|---|---|---|---|---|---|---|---|---|---|---|---|---|
| 1 | 17 Aug | WATFORD | 1–1 | 5715 | Leslie | 1 | | | | 11 | | 12 | | 9 | 5 | 4 | 10 | | | 6 | | | 2 | 3 | 8 | 7 |
| 2 | 24 | Blackburn | 2–3 | 8390 | Cook, Froggatt | 1 | | | | 11 | 12 | | | 9 | 5 | 4 | 10 | | | 6 | | | 2 | 3* | 8 | 7 |
| 3 | 31 | BOURNEMOUTH | 1–0 | 4930 | Cook | 1 | | | | 11 | | | | 9 | 6 | 4 | 10 | | 5 | 12 | | | 2 | 3 | 8 | 7 |
| 4 | 7 Sep | Chesterfield | 1–1 | 3477 | Svarc | 1 | | | | 11 | | | | 9 | 6 | 4 | 10 | | 5 | 12 | | | 2 | 3 | 8 | 7 |
| 5 | 14 | CHARLTON | 3–0 | 5527 | Leslie(pen), Svarc, Thomas | 1 | | 12 | | 11 | | | | 9 | 6 | 4 | | | 5 | 3 | | | 2 | 10 | 8 | 7 |
| 6 | 17 | PLYMOUTH | 1–0 | 5389 | Packer | 1 | | | | 11 | 12 | | | 9 | | 4 | 10 | | 5 | 6 | | | 2 | 3 | 8 | 7 |
| 7 | 21 | Aldershot | 1–0 | 3539 | Svarc | 1 | | | | 11 | | | | 9 | 6 | 4 | 10 | | 5 | 3 | | | 2 | 12 | 8 | 7* |
| 8 | 24 | Bury | 0–0 | 5223 | | 1 | | | | 11 | | | | 9 | 6 | 4 | 10 | | 5 | 3 | | | 2 | 12 | 8 | 7 |
| 9 | 28 | WALSALL | 1–2 | 4877 | Svarc | 1 | | | | 11 | | | | 9 | 6 | 4* | 10 | | 5 | 3 | | | 2 | 12 | 8 | 7 |
| 10 | 30 | Port Vale | 2–2 | 3700 | Froggatt, Lindsay | 1 | | | | 11 | 12 | | | 9 | 5 | | 10 | | | 6 | 7 | | 2 | 3 | 8 | 4 |
| 11 | 5 Oct | GILLINGHAM | 4–2 | 4684 | Froggatt(2), Svarc(2) | 1 | | 12 | | 11 | | | | 9 | 5 | 4 | 10 | | | 6 | | | 2 | 3 | 8 | 7 |
| 12 | 12 | Preston | 2–0 | 10259 | Harford(2) | 1 | | 12 | | 11* | | | | 9 | 5 | 4 | 10 | | | 6 | | | 2 | 3 | 8 | 7 |
| 13 | 15 | PORT VALE | 2–0 | 5184 | Svarc(2) | 1 | | 12 | | 11 | | | | 9 | 5 | 4 | 10 | | | 6 | | | 2 | 3 | 8 | 7 |
| 14 | 23 | Hereford | 1–3 | 6390 | Thomas | 1 | | 2 | | 1 | 6 | 12 | | 9 | | 4 | 10 | | | | | | 5 | 3 | 8 | 7 |
| 15 | 26 | Halifax | 1–1 | 1935 | Svarc | 1 | | 12 | | 11* | 5 | 6 | | 9 | | 4 | 10 | | | | | | 2 | 3 | 8 | 7 |
| 16 | 29 | SOUTHEND | 1–1 | 6547 | Lindsay(pen) | 1 | | 12 | | 11 | | 6 | | 9 | 5 | | 10 | | | 3 | | | 2 | 4 | 8 | 7 |
| 17 | 2 Nov | WREXHAM | 1–1 | 4432 | Svarc | 1 | | 4 | | 11 | | | | 9 | 5 | | 10 | | | 6 | 12 | | 2 | 3 | 8 | 7 |
| 18 | 6 | HEREFORD | 1–2 | 5131 | Svarc | 1 | | 12 | | 11 | | | | 9 | 5 | 4 | 10 | | | 6* | | | 2 | 3 | 8 | 7 |
| 19 | 9 | Huddersfield | 2–3 | 5233 | Froggatt, Svarc | 1 | | 3 | | 1 | 6 | | | 9 | 5 | 4 | 10 | | | | | | 2 | 12 | 8 | 7 |
| 20 | 15 | GRIMSBY | 5–0 | 4489 | Froggatt(3), Svarc(2) | 1 | | 11* | | 3 | 2 | | | 9 | 5 | 4 | 10 | | | 6 | 12 | | | 7 | 8 | |
| 21 | 30 | Swindon | 1–4 | 10072 | Svarc | 1 | | 11* | | 2 | 6 | | | 9 | 5 | 4 | 10 | | | 3 | | | | 12 | 8 | 7 |
| 22 | 6 Dec | TRANMERE | 2–1 | 4555 | Froggatt, L.Smith | 1 | | 12 | | 7 | 2 | | | 9 | 6 | 4 | 10 | | 5 | 3 | | | | 11 | 8 | |
| 23 | 20 | CRYSTAL P | 1–1 | 6814 | Leslie | 1 | | 7 | | 11 | 6 | | | 9 | 5 | 4 | 10 | | | 2 | | | | 3 | 8 | 2 |
| 24 | 28 | PETERBOROUGH | 4–1 | 7790 | Cook, Dominey, Froggatt, O.G. | 1 | | 7 | | 11 | 6 | 12 | | 9 | 5 | | 10 | | | 3 | | | | 4 | 8 | 2* |
| 25 | 1 Jan | Charlton | 1–4 | 5246 | Dyson, | 1 | | 7 | | 11 | 6 | 8 | | 9 | 5 | | 10* | | 2 | 4 | 12 | | | 3 | | |
| 26 | 4 | ALDERSHOT | 0–0 | 5096 | | 1 | | | | 11 | 2 | 4* | | 9 | 5 | | 10 | | 6 | 3 | 7 | 8 | | 12 | | |
| 27 | 10 | Tranmere | 0–2 | 2819 | | 1 | | 12 | | 11 | 6 | 4 | 7* | 9 | 5 | | 10 | | | 3 | | 8 | 2 | | | |
| | 18 | SWINDON | 3–0 | 4441 | Cook, Lindsay, Morgan.(abandoned) | 1 | | 4 | | 10 | 6 | | 7 | 9 | | | 11 | | 5 | 3 | 12 | | 2 | | 8 | |
| 28 | 25 | Brighton | 0–2 | 9937 | | 1 | | 4 | | 10 | 6 | | 7 | 9 | | | 11 | | 5 | 3 | | | 2 | 12 | 8* | |
| 29 | 1 Feb | HUDDERSFIELD | 3–2 | 3921 | Dominey, Froggatt(2) | 1 | | 4 | | 10 | 6 | | 7* | 9 | 5 | | 11 | | | | 12 | | 2 | 3 | 8 | |
| 30 | 8 | Wrexham | 1–2 | 3435 | Lindsay | 1 | | 4 | 2 | 10 | 6 | | 12 | 9 | 5 | | 11 | 7 | | | | | | 3 | 8* | |
| 31 | 15 | BRIGHTON | 2–2 | 4161 | McDonald, Svarc | 1 | | 4 | 2 | 11 | 6 | | 12 | 9 | 5 | | 10* | 7 | | | | | | 3 | 8 | |
| 32 | 22 | Grimsby | 1–1 | 5608 | McDonald | 1 | | 4 | 2 | 3 | | | 11 | 9 | 5 | 12 | 10 | 7* | | | | | | 6 | 8 | |
| 33 | 1 Mar | Bournemouth | 2–0 | 4578 | Foley, Froggatt | 1 | | 4 | 2 | 3 | | | 11 | 9 | 5 | 12 | 10 | 7 | | | | | | 6 | 8 | |
| 34 | 4 | SWINDON | 2–0 | 4041 | Svarc(2) | 1 | | 4 | 2 | 3 | | | 11 | 9 | 5 | 12 | 10 | 7 | | | | | | 6 | 8 | |
| 35 | 15 | Walsall | 2–5 | 4914 | Foley, Lindsay | 1 | | 4 | | 3 | 2* | | 11 | 9 | 5 | 7 | 10 | | | | | | | 6 | 8 | 12 |
| 36 | 19 | Watford | 2–1 | 3914 | Froggatt, Svarc | 1 | | 4 | | 3 | 12 | | 11 | 9 | 5 | 7 | 10* | | | | | | | 6 | 8 | 2 |
| 37 | 22 | CHESTERFIELD | 1–2 | 4152 | Lindsay | 1 | | 4 | | 3 | | | 11 | 9 | 5 | 7* | 10 | | | | 12 | | | 6 | 8 | 2 |
| 38 | 25 | Crystal P | 1–2 | 6851 | Froggatt | 1 | | 4* | | 3 | 12 | | 11 | 9 | 5 | 7 | 10 | | | | | | | 6 | 8 | 2 |
| 39 | 28 | Peterborough | 0–1 | 7559 | | 1 | | 1 | | 3 | 5 | | 11 | 9 | | 7 | 10 | | | 8 | 12 | | | 6 | | 2* |
| 40 | 4 Apr | HALIFAX | 2–0 | 3541 | Rowe, Svarc | 1 | | 4 | | 3 | 5 | | | 9 | 12 | 7 | 10 | | | 2 | 11 | | | 6* | 8 | |
| 41 | 12 | Gillingham | 1–2 | 6504 | Rowe | 1 | | 4 | | 2 | 12 | | | 9 | 5 | 11 | 10 | | | 3 | 7* | | | 6 | 8 | |
| 42 | 15 | Plymouth | 0–1 | 23551 | | 1 | | 12 | | 3 | 2* | | 10 | 9 | 5 | 7 | 11 | | | 4 | | | | 6 | 8 | |
| 43 | 19 | PRESTON | 2–2 | 5228 | Bunkell, Svarc | 1 | 12 | 11 | | 2 | | | 7 | 9 | 5 | 4 | 10* | | | 6 | | | | 3 | 8 | |
| 44 | 22 | BLACKBURN | 2–0 | 4183 | Lindsay, Svarc | 1 | | 12 | | 11 | 2 | | 7 | 9 | 5 | 4 | 10 | | | 6 | | | | 3 | 8 | |
| 45 | 25 | Southend | 1–1 | 5924 | Foley | 1 | | | | 11 | 2 | | 7 | 9 | 5* | 4 | 10 | | | 3 | 12 | | | 6 | 8 | |
| 46 | 2 May | BURY | 3–2 | 3202 | Froggatt, Svarc(2) | 1 | | | | 11 | 2 | | 7 | 9 | 5* | 4 | 10 | | | 3 | 12 | | | 6 | 8 | |

# F.A.Cup

| | | | | | | | | | | | | | | | | | | | | | | | | | | |
|---|---|---|---|---|---|---|---|---|---|---|---|---|---|---|---|---|---|---|---|---|---|---|---|---|---|---|
| 1st | 23 Nov | Watford | 1–0 | 8228 | Froggatt | 1 | | 3 | | 11 | 6 | | | 9 | 5 | 4 | 10 | | | | | | 2 | | 8 | 7 |
| 2nd | 14 Dec | Leatherhead | 0–1 | 3500 | | 1 | | 12 | | 7 | 6 | | | 9 | 5 | 4 | 10 | | | 3 | | | | 11 | 8 | 2 |

# Football League Cup

| | | | | | | | | | | | | | | | | | | | | | | | | | | |
|---|---|---|---|---|---|---|---|---|---|---|---|---|---|---|---|---|---|---|---|---|---|---|---|---|---|---|
| 1st | 20 Aug | OXFORD | 1–0 | 4609 | Lindsay(pen) | 1 | | | | 11 | | 12 | | 9 | 5 | 4 | 10 | | | 6 | | | 2 | 3 | 8 | 7 |
| 2nd | 11 Sep | Southend | 2–0 | 7856 | Leslie(2) | 1 | | | | 11 | 2 | | | 9 | 6 | 4 | | | 5 | 10 | | | 2 | 3 | 8 | 7 |
| 3rd | 9 Oct | CARLISLE | 2–0 | 7842 | Leslie, Svarc | 1 | | | | 11 | | | | 9 | 6 | 4 | 10 | | 5 | 3 | | | 2 | 12 | 8 | 7 |
| 4th | 13 Nov | SOUTHAMPTON | 0–0 | 9515 | | 1 | | 3 | | 11 | 6 | | | 9 | 5 | 4 | 10 | | | | | | 2 | 12 | 8 | 7 |
| 4th\R | 25 | Southampton | 1–0 | 11492 | Dominey | 1 | | 6 | | 11 | 2 | | | 9 | 5 | 4 | 10 | | | 3 | | | | 12 | 8 | 7 |
| 5th | 3 Dec | ASTON VILLA | 1–2 | 11871 | Froggatt | 1 | | 11 | | 2 | 6 | | | 9 | 5 | 4 | 10 | | | 3 | | | | 12 | 8 | 7 |

(Back) Roberts (Trainer), Packer, Thomas, Foley, Dominey, L.Smith, Harford, Morgan, Froggatt, A.Smith, Dyson, Lindsay, J.Smith (Manager). (Front) Cook, Svarc, Walker, Rowe, McInally, Bunckell, Leslie

**THIRD DIVISION**

| | P | W | D | L | F | A | Pts |
|---|---|---|---|---|---|---|---|
| 1 Blackburn | 46 | 22 | 16 | 8 | 68 | 45 | 60 |
| 2 Plymouth | 46 | 24 | 11 | 11 | 79 | 58 | 59 |
| 3 Charlton Ath | 46 | 22 | 11 | 13 | 76 | 61 | 55 |
| 4 Swindon | 46 | 21 | 11 | 14 | 64 | 58 | 53 |
| 5 Crystal Palace | 46 | 18 | 15 | 13 | 66 | 57 | 51 |
| 6 Port Vale | 46 | 18 | 15 | 13 | 61 | 54 | 51 |
| 7 Peterborough | 46 | 19 | 12 | 15 | 47 | 53 | 50 |
| 8 Walsall | 46 | 18 | 13 | 15 | 67 | 52 | 49 |
| 9 Preston NE | 46 | 19 | 11 | 16 | 63 | 56 | 49 |
| 10 Gillingham | 46 | 17 | 14 | 15 | 65 | 60 | 48 |
| 11 Colchester | 46 | 17 | 13 | 16 | 70 | 63 | 47 |
| 12 Hereford | 46 | 16 | 14 | 16 | 64 | 66 | 46 |
| 13 Wrexham | 46 | 15 | 15 | 16 | 65 | 55 | 45 |
| 14 Bury | 46 | 16 | 12 | 18 | 53 | 50 | 44 |
| 15 Chesterfield | 46 | 16 | 12 | 18 | 62 | 66 | 44 |
| 16 Grimsby | 46 | 15 | 13 | 18 | 55 | 64 | 43 |
| 17 Halifax | 46 | 13 | 17 | 16 | 49 | 65 | 43 |
| 18 Southend | 46 | 13 | 16 | 17 | 46 | 51 | 42 |
| 19 Brighton | 46 | 16 | 10 | 20 | 56 | 64 | 42 |
| 20 Aldershot | 46 | 14 | 11 | 21 | 53 | 63 | 38* |
| 21 Bournemouth | 46 | 13 | 12 | 21 | 44 | 58 | 38 |
| 22 Tranmere | 46 | 14 | 9 | 23 | 55 | 57 | 37 |
| 23 Watford | 46 | 10 | 17 | 19 | 52 | 75 | 37 |
| 24 Huddersfield | 46 | 11 | 10 | 25 | 47 | 76 | 32 |

*One point deducted for playing unregistered player.

# SEASON 1975-76 Division Three

| No. | Date | Opposition | Res | Attend | Goalscorers | Bond | Walker | Allinson | Anderson | Bright | Bunkell | Cook | Dominey | Dyer | Foley | Froggatt | Garwood | Gough | Harrison | Leslie | O'Donnell | Packer | Smith.L | Svarc | Telford | Thomas | Williams | Roberts |
|---|---|---|---|---|---|---|---|---|---|---|---|---|---|---|---|---|---|---|---|---|---|---|---|---|---|---|---|---|
| 1 | 16 Aug | Preston | 1-2 | 6324 | Svarc |  | 1 |  |  |  | 4 | 3 | 12 | 11 |  | 9 |  |  | 5 |  | 2 | 6 | 10 | 8 |  | 7 |  |  |
| 2 | 23 | MANSFIELD | 0-2 | 3333 |  |  | 1 |  | 10 |  | 4 | 7 | 5 | 12 |  | 9 |  |  |  |  |  | 6 | 11 | 8 |  | 2 | 3 |  |
| 3 | 30 | Crystal P | 2-3 | 13713 | Bunkell, Svarc |  | 1 |  |  |  | 4 | 7 | 6 |  |  | 9 |  |  | 5 | 12 |  | 10 | 11 | 8 |  | 2 | 3 |  |
| 4 | 6 Sep | HALIFAX | 0-1 | 2819 |  |  | 1 |  | 11 |  | 4 | 7 | 6 | 12 |  | 9 |  |  | 5 | 10 |  |  |  | 8 |  | 2 | 3 |  |
| 5 | 13 | Hereford | 0-0 | 5577 |  |  | 1 |  | 11 |  |  | 7 | 6 | 4 | 12 | 9 |  |  |  | 10 |  | 5 |  | 8 |  | 2 | 3 |  |
| 6 | 20 | BRIGHTON | 2-0 | 3176 | Froggatt, Svarc |  | 1 |  | 11 |  |  | 7 | 5 | 2 | 12 | 9 |  |  |  | 4 |  | 6 |  | 8 |  | 10 | 3 |  |
| 7 | 24 | Chester | 0-1 | 3954 |  |  | 1 |  | 11 |  |  | 7 | 5 | 2 | 12 | 9 |  |  |  | 4 |  | 6 |  | 8 |  | 10 | 3 |  |
| 8 | 27 | Swindon | 1-0 | 5750 | Packer |  | 1 |  | 11 |  | 12 | 7 | 5 | 2 | 10 | 9 |  |  |  | 4 |  | 6 |  | 8 |  |  | 3 |  |
| 9 | 4 Oct | BURY | 0-0 | 3035 |  |  | 1 |  | 12 |  | 4 | 7 | 5 | 2 | 10 | 9 |  |  |  | 8 |  | 6 | 11 |  |  |  | 3 |  |
| 10 | 11 | WALSALL | 2-0 | 2980 | Dominey, Froggatt |  | 1 |  | 12 |  | 4 | 7 | 5 | 2 | 10 | 9 |  |  |  | 8 |  | 6 | 11 |  |  |  | 3 |  |
| 11 | 18 | Aldershot | 2-2 | 3586 | Foley(2) |  | 1 |  | 12 |  | 4 | 7 | 5 | 2 | 10 | 9 |  |  |  | 8 |  | 6 | 11 |  |  |  | 3 |  |
| 12 | 21 | ROTHERHAM | 0-0 | 3468 |  |  | 1 |  | 12 |  | 4 | 7 | 5 | 2 | 10 | 9 |  |  |  | 8 |  | 6 | 11 |  |  |  | 3 |  |
| 13 | 25 | PORT VALE | 1-0 | 3053 | Foley |  | 1 |  | 12 |  | 4 | 7 | 5 | 2 | 10 | 9 |  |  |  | 8 |  | 6 | 11 |  |  |  | 3 |  |
| 14 | 1 Nov | Millwall | 1-1 | 7492 | L.Smith |  | 1 |  | 12 |  | 4 | 7 | 5 | 2 | 10 | 9 |  |  |  | 8 |  | 6 | 11 |  |  |  | 3 |  |
| 15 | 5 | Chesterfield | 1-3 | 2906 | L.Smith |  | 1 |  | 10 | 12 | 4 | 7 | 5 | 2 |  | 9 |  |  |  | 8 |  | 6 | 11 |  |  |  | 3 |  |
| 16 | 8 | SHREWSBURY | 1-1 | 3088 | L.Smith |  | 1 |  | 10 | 12 | 4 | 7 | 5 | 2 |  | 9 |  |  |  | 8 |  | 6 | 11 |  |  |  | 3 |  |
| 17 | 15 | Cardiff | 0-2 | 6781 |  |  | 1 |  | 10 | 9 | 4 | 7 | 5 | 2 |  |  |  |  | 12 | 8 |  | 6 | 11 |  |  |  | 3 |  |
| 18 | 29 | Gillingham | 1-0 | 5402 | Foley |  | 1 |  |  | 12 | 4 | 7 | 5 | 2 | 10 | 9 |  |  |  | 8 |  | 6 | 11 |  |  |  | 3 |  |
| 19 | 6 Dec | SHEFF WED | 2-1 | 3534 | Cook, L.Smith |  | 1 |  |  |  | 4 | 7 | 5 | 2 | 10 | 9 |  |  | 12 | 8 |  | 6 | 11 |  |  |  | 3 |  |
| 20 | 13 | Wrexham | 1-1 | 2143 | Froggatt |  | 1 |  |  |  | 4 | 7 | 5 | 2 | 10 | 9 |  |  |  | 8 |  | 6 | 11 |  |  | 12 | 3 |  |
| 21 | 20 | WREXHAM | 0-2 | 2603 |  |  | 1 |  |  | 12 | 4 | 7 | 5 | 2 | 10 | 9 |  |  |  | 8 |  | 6 | 11 |  |  |  | 3 |  |
| 22 | 26 | Southend | 0-2 | 6127 |  |  | 1 | 12 | 9 | 4 |  | 7 | 5 | 2 | 10 |  |  |  |  | 8 |  | 6 | 11 |  |  |  | 3 |  |
| 23 | 27 | GRIMSBY | 1-0 | 3136 | Foley |  | 1 | 12 | 9 | 2 | 4 | 7 | 5 |  | 10 |  |  |  |  | 8 |  | 6 | 11 |  |  |  | 3 |  |
| 24 | 10 Jan | CRYSTAL P | 0-3 | 6240 |  |  | 1 |  |  |  | 4 | 7 | 5 | 2 | 10 | 11 |  | 8 |  | 12 |  | 6 | 9 |  |  |  | 3 |  |
| 25 | 14 | Peterborough | 1-3 | 7453 | Packer |  | 1 |  | 9 |  | 4 | 7 | 5 | 2 | 10 | 11 |  | 8 |  |  |  | 6 | 12 |  |  |  | 3 |  |
| 26 | 17 | Brighton | 0-6 | 16302 |  |  | 1 |  | 9 |  | 12 | 7 | 5 | 2 | 10 | 11 |  | 8 |  | 4 |  | 6 | 3 |  |  |  |  |  |
| 27 | 24 | HEREFORD | 1-4 | 2626 | Telford | 1 |  |  |  | 2 | 4 | 7 | 5 |  | 10 | 11 |  | 8 |  |  |  | 6 | 12 |  | 9 |  | 3 |  |
| 28 | 31 | Rotherham | 0-2 | 3943 |  | 1 |  |  |  | 2 | 4 |  | 12 | 10 |  | 9 |  | 8 | 5 | 7 |  | 6 | 11 |  |  |  | 3 |  |
| 29 | 7 Feb | CHESTERFIELD | 2-3 | 2245 | Bunkell(pen), Leslie |  | 1 |  |  | 2 | 4 | 10 | 6 |  |  | 9 |  | 8 | 5 | 7 |  |  | 11 |  | 12 |  | 3 |  |
| 30 | 14 | Shrewsbury | 0-1 | 4485 |  | 1 |  | 12 |  | 2 | 4 | 3 | 6 | 10 |  | 9 | 7 | 8 |  |  |  | 5 | 11 |  |  |  |  |  |
| 31 | 21 | CARDIFF | 3-2 | 3248 | Froggatt, Garwood(2) |  | 1 |  |  | 2 | 4 | 3 | 12 | 11 | 10 | 9 | 7 | 8 |  |  |  | 6 | 5 |  |  |  |  |  |
| 32 | 24 | CHESTER | 1-0 | 3534 | Gough |  | 1 |  |  | 2 | 4 | 3 | 12 | 11 |  | 9 | 7 | 8 |  |  |  | 6 | 5 |  |  |  | 10 |  |
| 33 | 28 | Port Vale | 2-3 | 3803 | Dyer(2) |  | 1 |  |  | 2 | 4 | 3 | 10 | 11 |  | 9 | 7 | 8 |  | 12 |  | 6 | 5 |  |  |  |  |  |
| 34 | 13 Mar | Walsall | 1-1 | 5371 | Leslie |  | 1 |  |  | 2 | 4 | 3 | 10 |  |  | 9 | 7 | 8 |  | 11 |  | 6 | 5 |  |  |  | 12 |  |
| 35 | 16 | ALDERSHOT | 2-0 | 3040 | Gough, Leslie |  | 1 |  |  | 2 | 4 | 3 | 12 |  | 10 | 9 | 7 | 8 |  | 11 |  | 6 | 5 |  |  |  |  |  |
| 36 | 20 | GILLINGHAM | 2-2 | 3981 | Bunkell(pen), Leslie |  | 1 |  |  | 2 | 4 | 3 | 5 |  | 12 | 9 | 7 | 8 |  | 11 |  | 6 | 10 |  |  |  |  |  |
| 37 | 23 | MILLWALL | 0-1 | 4573 |  |  | 1 |  |  | 2 | 4 | 3 | 12 |  | 10 | 9 | 7 | 8 |  | 11 |  | 6 | 5 |  |  |  |  |  |
| 38 | 27 | Sheff Wed | 0-1 | 6905 |  |  | 1 |  |  | 2 | 4 | 3 | 12 |  | 10 | 9 | 7 | 8 |  | 11 |  | 6 | 5 |  |  |  |  |  |
| 39 | 3 Apr | PRESTON | 1-1 | 2657 | Leslie |  | 1 | 12 |  | 2 | 4 | 10 | 8 |  |  | 9 | 7 |  |  | 11 |  | 6 | 5 |  |  |  | 3 |  |
| 40 | 6 | SWINDON | 1-2 | 2694 | Leslie |  | 1 |  |  | 2 | 4 |  | 12 | 10 |  | 9 | 7 | 8 |  | 11 |  | 6 | 5 |  |  |  | 3 |  |
| 41 | 12 | Bury | 0-0 | 4505 |  |  | 1 |  |  |  | 4 |  | 12 | 2 | 10 | 9 | 7 | 8 |  | 11 |  | 6 | 5 |  |  |  | 3 |  |
| 42 | 16 | PETERBOROUGH | 1-1 | 3687 | Bunkell(pen) |  | 1 | 9 |  |  | 4 |  | 12 | 2 | 10 |  | 7 | 8 |  | 11 |  | 6 | 5 |  |  |  | 3 |  |
| 43 | 17 | SOUTHEND | 2-1 | 4260 | Froggatt, Gough |  | 1 | 7 |  | 12 | 4 | 10 |  | 2 |  | 9 |  | 8 |  | 11 |  | 6 | 5 |  |  |  | 3 |  |
| 44 | 19 | Grimsby | 1-0 | 4862 | Gough |  | 1 |  |  | 12 | 4 |  |  | 2 | 10 | 9 | 7 | 8 |  | 11 |  | 6 | 5 |  |  |  | 3 |  |
| 45 | 24 | Mansfield | 0-0 | 7407 |  |  | 1 |  |  | 12 | 4 |  |  | 2 | 10 | 9 | 7 | 8 |  | 11 |  | 6 | 5 |  |  |  | 3 |  |
| 46 | 26 | Halifax | 1-1 | 856 | Gough |  | 1 | 7 |  | 2 | 4 |  |  | 10 | 9 |  |  | 8 |  | 11 |  | 6 | 5 |  |  |  | 3 |  |

# F.A.Cup

| | | | | | | | | | | | | | | | | | | | | | | | | | | | | |
|---|---|---|---|---|---|---|---|---|---|---|---|---|---|---|---|---|---|---|---|---|---|---|---|---|---|---|---|---|
| 1st | 22 Nov | DOVER | 3-3 | 3765 | Dominey, Leslie, L.Smith | | 1 | | 9 | 12 | 4 | 7 | 5 | 2 | 10 | | | | | 8 | | 6 | 11 | | | | 3 | |
| 2nd | 26 | Dover | 1-4 | 3779 | Packer(pen) | | 1 | | 12 | | 4 | 7 | 5 | 2 | | 9 | | | 10 | 8 | | 6 | 11 | | | | 3 | |

# Football League Cup

| | | | | | | | | | | | | | | | | | | | | | | | | | | | | |
|---|---|---|---|---|---|---|---|---|---|---|---|---|---|---|---|---|---|---|---|---|---|---|---|---|---|---|---|---|
| 1st | 19 Aug | Crystal P | 0-3 | 10006 | | | 1 | 12 | | | 4 | 3 | 5 | 10 | | 9 | | | | | | 6 | 11 | 8 | | 2 | | 7 |
| 1st\2l | 25 | CRYSTAL P | 3-1 | 3912 | L.Smith, Svarc(2) | | 1 | | | | 4 | 7 | 5 | 10 | | 9 | | | | | | 6 | 11 | 8 | | 2 | 3 | |

COLCHESTER UNITED 1975

*Front row (left to right)*: REEVE, JARVIS, DOWMAN, ALINSON, BARNET, BRIGHT.
*Seated*: JOHN HILLIER, VIC KEEBLE, TREVOR DODWELL, STANLEY FIRTH, JACK RIPPINGALE, ANTONY BUCK, M.P., GORDON PARKER, NIGEL FITCH and BOBBY ROBERTS.
*Standing*: RAY COLE, SVARC, DYER, BUNKELL, WALTER, SMELT, LESLIE, PACKER, COOK, TOM CHENEY.
*Back row*: DOMINEY, WILLIAMS, HARRISON, FROGGATT, THOMAS, SMITH and FOLEY.

## THIRD DIVISION

| | P | W | D | L | F | A | Pts |
|---|---|---|---|---|---|---|---|
| 1 Hereford | 46 | 26 | 11 | 9 | 86 | 55 | 63 |
| 2 Cardiff | 46 | 22 | 13 | 11 | 69 | 48 | 57 |
| 3 Millwall | 46 | 20 | 16 | 10 | 54 | 43 | 56 |
| 4 Brighton | 46 | 22 | 9 | 15 | 78 | 53 | 53 |
| 5 Crystal Palace | 46 | 18 | 17 | 11 | 61 | 46 | 53 |
| 6 Wrexham | 46 | 20 | 12 | 14 | 66 | 55 | 52 |
| 7 Walsall | 46 | 18 | 14 | 14 | 74 | 61 | 50 |
| 8 Preston | 46 | 19 | 10 | 17 | 62 | 57 | 48 |
| 9 Shrewsbury | 46 | 19 | 10 | 17 | 61 | 59 | 48 |
| 10 Peterborough | 46 | 15 | 18 | 13 | 63 | 63 | 48 |
| 11 Mansfield | 46 | 16 | 15 | 15 | 58 | 52 | 47 |
| 12 Port Vale | 46 | 15 | 16 | 15 | 55 | 54 | 46 |
| 13 Bury | 46 | 14 | 16 | 16 | 51 | 46 | 44 |
| 14 Chesterfield | 46 | 17 | 9 | 20 | 69 | 69 | 43 |
| 15 Gillingham | 46 | 12 | 19 | 15 | 58 | 68 | 43 |
| 16 Rotherham | 46 | 15 | 12 | 19 | 54 | 65 | 42 |
| 17 Chester | 46 | 15 | 12 | 19 | 53 | 62 | 42 |
| 18 Grimsby | 46 | 15 | 10 | 21 | 62 | 74 | 40 |
| 19 Swindon | 46 | 16 | 8 | 22 | 62 | 75 | 40 |
| 20 Sheff Wed | 46 | 12 | 16 | 18 | 48 | 59 | 40 |
| 21 Aldershot | 46 | 13 | 13 | 20 | 59 | 75 | 39 |
| 22 Colchester | 46 | 12 | 14 | 20 | 41 | 65 | 38 |
| 23 Southend | 46 | 12 | 13 | 21 | 65 | 75 | 37 |
| 24 Halifax | 46 | 11 | 13 | 22 | 41 | 61 | 35 |

# SEASON 1976–77 Division Four

| No. | Date | Opposition | Res | Attend | Goalscorers | Ellis | Walker | Allinson | Bright | Bunkell | Cook | Dominey | Dowman | Dyer | Foley | Froggatt | Garwood | Gough | Leslie | Packer | Smith.L | Williams |
|---|---|---|---|---|---|---|---|---|---|---|---|---|---|---|---|---|---|---|---|---|---|---|
| 1 | 21 Aug | Cambridge | 0–2 | 3056 | | | 1 | 9 | | 4 | 11 | | | 2 | | | 7 | 8 | 10 | 6 | 5 | 3 |
| 2 | 24 | HALIFAX | 3–0 | 2489 | Allinson(2), Gough | | 1 | 9 | | 4 | 11 | | 12 | 2 | | | 7 | 8 | 10 | 6 | 5 | 3 |
| 3 | 28 | Rochdale | 0–1 | 1440 | | | 1 | 12 | | 4 | 11 | | | 2 | | 9 | 7 | 8 | 10 | 6 | 5 | 3 |
| 4 | 4 Sep | EXETER | 3–1 | 2516 | Cook, Froggatt, Garwood | | 1 | 10 | | 4 | 11 | | | 2 | | 9 | 7 | 8 | | 6 | 5 | 3 |
| 5 | 11 | Watford | 1–2 | 5386 | Dowman | | 1 | 10 | | | 11 | | 12 | 2 | | 9 | 7 | 8 | 4 | 6 | 5 | 3 |
| 6 | 18 | CREWE | 3–2 | 2519 | Allinson, Froggatt, Garwood | | 1 | 10 | | 4 | 11 | | | 2 | | 9 | 7 | 8 | 2 | 6 | 5 | 3 |
| 7 | 25 | Bournemouth | 0–0 | 3881 | | | 1 | 10 | 2 | 4 | 11 | | | | 7 | 9 | | 8 | 12 | 6 | 5 | 3 |
| 8 | 1 Oct | WORKINGTON | 3–1 | 2957 | Garwood(2), Gough | | 1 | 10 | 2 | 12 | 11 | | | | 4 | 9 | 7 | 8 | | 6 | 5 | 3 |
| 9 | 8 | Southend | 0–0 | 6690 | | | 1 | 10 | 2 | | 11 | | | | 4 | 9 | 12 | 8 | 7 | 6 | 5 | 3 |
| 10 | 16 | HARTLEPOOL | 6–2 | 3180 | Allinson, Garwood(3), Gough(2) | | 1 | 10 | 2 | | 11 | | | | 4 | 9 | 7 | 8 | 12 | 6 | 5 | 3 |
| 11 | 23 | Scunthorpe | 0–2 | 3157 | | | 1 | 10 | 2 | | 11 | | | 12 | 4 | 9 | 7 | | 8 | 6 | 5 | 3 |
| 12 | 25 | Doncaster | 2–3 | 3856 | Cook, Packer(pen) | | 1 | 10 | | | 2 | 4 | | 12 | 8 | 9 | 7 | | 11 | 6 | 5 | 3 |
| 13 | 30 | BRENTFORD | 2–1 | 3607 | Cook, Garwood | | 1 | 10 | | | 4 | | 12 | 2 | 9 | | 7 | 8 | 11 | 6 | 5 | 3 |
| 14 | 1 Nov | TORQUAY | 4–0 | 3102 | Dowman, Garwood(2), Gough | | 1 | 10 | | | 4 | | 6 | 2 | | 9 | 7 | 8 | 11 | | 5 | 3 |
| 15 | 12 | STOCKPORT | 1–0 | 3948 | Dowman | | 1 | 11 | | 12 | 4 | | 6 | 2 | | 9 | 7 | 8 | 10 | | 5 | 3 |
| 16 | 27 | Barnsley | 1–0 | 5662 | Garwood | | 1 | 12 | | | 4 | | 6 | 2 | | 9 | 7 | 8 | 11 | 10 | 5 | 3 |
| 17 | 4 Dec | DARLINGTON | 4–0 | 2951 | Dowman(2), Gough, L.Smith | | 1 | 11 | | | 2 | | 6 | | | 9 | 7 | 8 | 4 | 10 | 5 | 3 |
| 18 | 18 | Bradford | 0–1 | 4173 | | | 1 | 12 | | | 2 | | 6 | 11 | | 9 | 7 | 8 | 4 | 10 | 5 | 3 |
| 19 | 27 | ALDERSHOT | 1–0 | 6007 | L.Smith | | 1 | 11 | | | 2 | | 6 | 12 | | 9 | 7 | 8 | 4 | 10 | 5 | 3 |
| 20 | 29 | Swansea | 1–2 | 5666 | Bunkell | | 1 | 11 | | 7 | 2 | | 6 | 3 | | 9 | 12 | 8 | 4 | 10 | 5 | |
| 21 | 1 Jan | NEWPORT | 5–0 | 4614 | Dowman, Garwood, Gough(2),Smith | | 1 | 11 | | 10 | 2 | | 6 | 3 | | 9 | 7 | 8 | 4 | | 5 | |
| 22 | 3 | Brentford | 4–1 | 4610 | Dowman, Garwood, Gough(2) | | 1 | 11 | | 10 | 2 | 12 | 6 | 3 | | 9 | 7 | 8 | 4 | | 5 | |
| 23 | 18 | SOUTHPORT | 4–1 | 5634 | Allinson, Bunkell, Garwood, Packer(pen) | | 1 | 11 | | 10 | 2 | | 6 | | | 9 | 7 | 8 | 4 | 12 | 5 | 3 |
| 24 | 21 | CAMBRIDGE | 0–1 | 7639 | | | 1 | 10 | | | 2 | 12 | 6 | 11 | | 9 | 7 | 8 | | 4 | 5 | 3 |
| 25 | 5 Feb | ROCHDALE | 1–0 | 4943 | Dowman | | 1 | | | 10 | 2 | | 6 | | | 9 | 7 | 8 | 4 | 11 | 5 | 3 |
| 26 | 12 | Exeter | 0–1 | 6132 | | | 1 | | | 10 | 2 | | 6 | 12 | | 9 | 7 | 8 | 4 | 11 | 5 | 3 |
| 27 | 19 | WATFORD | 1–0 | 5678 | Packer(pen) | 1 | | 12 | | 10 | 2 | | 6 | | | 9 | 7 | 8 | 4 | 11 | 5 | 3 |
| 28 | 22 | Newport | 2–1 | 1575 | Gough(2) | 1 | | 10 | | | 2 | | 6 | 12 | | 9 | 7 | 8 | 4 | 11 | 5 | 3 |
| 29 | 26 | Crewe | 0–1 | 2410 | | | 1 | 10 | | | 2 | | 6 | 12 | | 9 | 7 | 8 | 4 | 11 | 5 | 3 |
| 30 | 4 Mar | BOURNEMOUTH | 1–0 | 4948 | Froggatt | | 1 | 10 | | | 2 | | 6 | | 12 | 9 | 7 | 8 | 4 | 11 | 5 | 3 |
| 31 | 8 | Halifax | 2–1 | 2097 | Leslie, Packer | | 1 | | | | 2 | | 6 | 11 | 7 | 9 | | 8 | 4 | 10 | 5 | 3 |
| 32 | 12 | Workington | 4–2 | 1223 | Dowman, Froggatt, Gough, Packer | | 1 | | | | 2 | | 6 | 11 | 7 | 9 | | 8 | 4 | 10 | 5 | 3 |
| 33 | 19 | SOUTHEND | 0–1 | 6637 | | | 1 | | | 10 | 2 | | 6 | 11 | 7 | 9 | 12 | 8 | 4 | 5 | | 3 |
| 34 | 21 | Huddersfield | 0–0 | 7508 | | | 1 | | | 12 | 2 | | 6 | 11 | | 9 | 7 | 8 | 4 | 10 | 5 | 3 |
| 35 | 26 | Hartlepool | 2–2 | 1822 | Allinson, Dowman | | 1 | 8 | | 10 | 2 | 12 | 6 | 11 | | 9 | 7 | | 4 | | 5 | 3 |
| 36 | 2 Apr | SCUNTHORPE | 1–1 | 3799 | Leslie | | 1 | 10 | | | 2 | | 6 | 12 | | 9 | 7 | 8 | 4 | 11 | 5 | 3 |
| 37 | 5 | Aldershot | 1–1 | 2586 | Gough | | 1 | 12 | | | 2 | | 6 | 10 | | 9 | 7 | 8 | 4 | 11 | 5 | 3 |
| 38 | 8 | SWANSEA | 1–1 | 5184 | Dowman | | 1 | 12 | | | 2 | | 6 | 10 | | 9 | 7 | 8 | 4 | 11 | 5 | 3 |
| 39 | 11 | Torquay | 2–2 | 3189 | Dowman, Gough | | 1 | 12 | | 10 | 2 | | 6 | 11 | | 9 | 7 | 8 | 4 | | 5 | 3 |
| 40 | 15 | DONCASTER | 1–0 | 4668 | Gough | | 1 | 10 | | | 2 | | 6 | 11 | | 9 | 7 | 8 | 4 | 12 | 5 | 3 |
| 41 | 19 | HUDDERSFIELD | 3–1 | 5051 | Garwood, L.Smith(2) | | 1 | 10 | | | 2 | | 6 | 11 | | 9 | 7 | 8 | 4 | | 5 | 3 |
| 42 | 22 | Stockport | 1–1 | 2826 | Garwood | | 1 | 12 | | | 4 | | 6 | 2 | | 9 | 7 | 8 | 11 | 10 | 5 | 3 |
| 43 | 29 | BARNSLEY | 1–0 | 5802 | L.Smith | | 1 | 10 | | | 4 | | 6 | 2 | | 9 | 7 | 8 | 11 | 12 | 5 | 3 |
| 44 | 3 May | Southport | 3–1 | 867 | Froggatt(2), Gough | | 1 | 10 | | | 4 | | 6 | 2 | | 9 | 7 | 8 | 11 | 12 | 5 | 3 |
| 45 | 7 | Darlington | 0–2 | 1964 | | | 1 | 12 | | | 4 | | 6 | 2 | | 9 | 7 | 8 | 11 | 10 | 5 | 3 |
| 46 | 14 | BRADFORD | 2–1 | 8912 | Allinson, O.G. | | 1 | 11 | | | 2 | | 6 | 12 | | 9 | 7 | 8 | 4 | 10 | 5 | 3 |

# F.A.Cup

| | | | | | | | | | | | | | | | | | | | | | | |
|---|---|---|---|---|---|---|---|---|---|---|---|---|---|---|---|---|---|---|---|---|---|---|
| 1st | 20 Nov | Cambridge | 1–1 | 5090 | Packer(pen) | | 1 | 12 | | | 4 | | 6 | 2 | | 9 | 7 | 8 | 11 | 10 | 5 | 3 |
| 1st\R | 24 | CAMBRIDGE | 2–0 | 6041 | Garwood, Leslie | | 1 | 12 | | | 4 | | 6 | 2 | | 9 | 7 | 8 | 11 | 10 | 5 | 3 |
| 2nd | 11 Dec | BRENTFORD | 0–0 | 5286 | (Abandoned) | | 1 | 11 | | | 2 | | 6 | 12 | | 9 | 7 | 8 | 4 | 10 | 5 | 3 |
| 2nd | 20 | BRENTFORD | 3–2 | 4730 | Froggatt, Gough, Packer(pen) | | 1 | 11 | | | 2 | | 6 | 12 | | 9 | 7 | 8 | 4 | 10 | 5 | 3 |
| 3rd | 8 Jan | Kettering | 3–2 | 7176 | Froggatt, Garwood(2) | | 1 | 12 | | 10 | 2 | | 6 | 11 | | 9 | 7 | 8 | 4 | | 5 | 3 |
| 4th | 29 | DERBY | 1–1 | 14030 | Garwood | | 1 | | | 10 | 2 | | 6 | 11 | | 9 | 7 | 8 | 4 | 12 | 5 | 3 |
| 4th\R | 2 Feb | Derby | 0–1 | 22155 | | | 1 | | | 10 | 2 | | 6 | 12 | | 9 | 7 | 8 | 4 | 11 | 5 | 3 |

# Football League Cup

| | | | | | | | | | | | | | | | | | | | | | | |
|---|---|---|---|---|---|---|---|---|---|---|---|---|---|---|---|---|---|---|---|---|---|---|
| 1st | 14 Aug | Millwall | 1–2 | 4599 | L.Smith | | 1 | 12 | | 4 | 11 | | | 2 | | 9 | 7 | 8 | 10 | 6 | 5 | 3 |
| 1st\2l | 17 | MILLWALL | 2–1 | 3155 | Garwood, Gough | | 1 | 12 | | 4 | 11 | | | 2 | | 9 | 7 | 8 | 10 | 6 | 5 | 3 |
| 1st\R | 30 | MILLWALL | 4–4 | 3695 | Bunkell(pen), Garwood(3) | | 1 | 12 | | 4 | 11 | | | 2 | | 9 | 7 | 8 | 10 | 6 | 5 | 3 |

Back Row (L to R) Andy Loveless Glenn Reeve, Ray Cole (Physio), Bobby Roberts (Manager), Ray Harford (Coach), Tony Evans, Russell Cotton.
Centre Row (L to R.) Barry Dominey, Mick Packer (Captain), John Froggatt, Mike Walker, Ian Cranstone, Colin Garwood, Ray Bunkell, Lindsay Smith
Front Row (L to R) Ian Allinson Micky Cook, Stewart Bright, Steve Dowman, Steve Leslie, John Williams, Paul Dyer, Bobby Gough, Steve Foley.

## FOURTH DIVISION

| | P | W | D | L | F | A | W | D | L | F | A | Pts |
|---|---|---|---|---|---|---|---|---|---|---|---|---|
| Cambridge U | 46 | 16 | 5 | 2 | 57 | 18 | 10 | 8 | 5 | 30 | 22 | 65 |
| Exeter C | 46 | 17 | 5 | 1 | 40 | 13 | 8 | 7 | 8 | 30 | 33 | 62 |
| Colchester U | 46 | 19 | 2 | 2 | 51 | 14 | 6 | 7 | 10 | 26 | 29 | 59 |
| Bradford C | 46 | 16 | 7 | 0 | 51 | 18 | 7 | 6 | 10 | 27 | 33 | 59 |
| Swansea C | 46 | 18 | 3 | 2 | 60 | 30 | 7 | 5 | 11 | 32 | 38 | 58 |
| Barnsley | 46 | 16 | 5 | 2 | 45 | 18 | 7 | 4 | 12 | 17 | 21 | 55 |
| Watford | 46 | 15 | 7 | 1 | 46 | 13 | 3 | 8 | 12 | 21 | 37 | 51 |
| Doncaster R | 46 | 16 | 2 | 5 | 47 | 25 | 5 | 7 | 11 | 24 | 40 | 51 |
| Huddersfield T | 46 | 15 | 5 | 3 | 36 | 15 | 4 | 7 | 12 | 24 | 34 | 50 |
| Southend U | 46 | 11 | 9 | 3 | 35 | 19 | 4 | 10 | 9 | 17 | 26 | 49 |
| Darlington | 46 | 13 | 5 | 5 | 37 | 25 | 5 | 8 | 10 | 22 | 39 | 49 |
| Crewe A | 46 | 16 | 6 | 1 | 36 | 15 | 3 | 5 | 15 | 11 | 45 | 49 |
| Bournemouth | 46 | 13 | 8 | 2 | 39 | 13 | 2 | 10 | 11 | 15 | 31 | 48 |
| Stockport Co | 46 | 10 | 10 | 3 | 29 | 19 | 3 | 9 | 11 | 24 | 38 | 45 |
| Brentford | 46 | 14 | 3 | 6 | 48 | 27 | 4 | 4 | 15 | 29 | 49 | 43 |
| Torquay U | 46 | 12 | 5 | 6 | 33 | 22 | 5 | 4 | 14 | 26 | 45 | 43 |
| Aldershot | 46 | 10 | 8 | 5 | 29 | 19 | 6 | 3 | 14 | 20 | 40 | 43 |
| Rochdale | 46 | 8 | 7 | 8 | 32 | 25 | 5 | 5 | 13 | 18 | 34 | 38 |
| Newport Co | 46 | 11 | 6 | 6 | 33 | 21 | 3 | 4 | 16 | 9 | 37 | 38 |
| Scunthorpe U | 46 | 11 | 6 | 6 | 32 | 24 | 2 | 5 | 16 | 17 | 49 | 37 |
| Halifax T | 46 | 11 | 6 | 6 | 36 | 18 | 0 | 8 | 15 | 11 | 40 | 36 |
| Hartlepool | 46 | 8 | 9 | 6 | 30 | 20 | 2 | 3 | 18 | 17 | 53 | 32 |
| Southport | 46 | 3 | 12 | 8 | 17 | 28 | 0 | 7 | 16 | 16 | 49 | 25 |
| Workington | 46 | 3 | 7 | 13 | 23 | 42 | 1 | 4 | 18 | 18 | 60 | 19 |

# SEASON 1977-78 Division Three

| No. | Date | Opposition | Res | Attend | Goalscorers | Walker | Allinson | Bunkell | Cook | Cotton | Dowman | Dyer | Evans | Foley | Froggatt | Garwood | Gough | Leslie | Packer | Rowles | Wignall | Williams | Wright |
|---|---|---|---|---|---|---|---|---|---|---|---|---|---|---|---|---|---|---|---|---|---|---|---|
| 1 | 20 Aug | Gillingham | 3-1 | 3450 | Foley, Gough, Packer | 1 | 11 | | 2 | | 6 | 12 | | 10 | 9 | 7 | 8 | 4 | 5 | | | 3 | |
| 2 | 23 | BRADFORD | 3-0 | 4371 | Froggatt, Gough, Leslie | 1 | 11 | 10 | 2 | | 6 | 12 | | | 9 | 7 | 8 | 4 | 5 | | | 3 | |
| 3 | 27 | CHESTER | 2-0 | 4169 | Gough(2) | 1 | 11 | 10 | 2 | | 6 | 12 | | | 9 | 7 | 8 | 4 | 5 | | | 3 | |
| 4 | 2 Sep | Tranmere | 0-1 | 3263 | | 1 | 11 | 10 | 2 | | 6 | 12 | | | 9 | 7 | 8 | 4 | 5 | | | 3 | |
| 5 | 9 | PLYMOUTH | 3-1 | 5719 | Dowman, Gough, Williams | 1 | 11 | 10 | 2 | | 6 | 12 | | | 9 | 7 | 8 | 4 | 5 | | | 3 | |
| 6 | 13 | Portsmouth | 0-0 | 11757 | | 1 | 11 | 10 | 2 | | 6 | 5 | | 4 | 9 | 7 | 8 | | | | 12 | 3 | |
| 7 | 17 | Rotherham | 0-1 | 4906 | | 1 | 11 | 10 | | | 6 | 2 | | 4 | 9 | 7 | 8 | | 5 | | 12 | 3 | |
| 8 | 24 | PRESTON | 0-0 | 4978 | | 1 | 11 | | 2 | | 6 | 12 | | 10 | 9 | 7 | 8 | 4 | 5 | | | 3 | |
| 9 | 27 | PORT VALE | 2-3 | 4820 | Garwood, Gough | 1 | 11 | 10 | 2 | | 6 | 4 | | | 9 | 7 | 8 | | 5 | | 12 | 3 | |
| 10 | 1 Oct | Carlisle | 3-1 | 4611 | Garwood(2), Gough | 1 | 11 | 10 | 2 | | 6 | 4 | | | 9 | 7 | 8 | | 5 | | 3 | | 12 |
| 11 | 5 | Chesterfield | 0-0 | 4575 | | 1 | 11 | 10 | 2 | | 6 | 4 | | | 9 | 7 | 8 | 12 | 5 | | 3 | | |
| 12 | 8 | HEREFORD | 0-0 | 4586 | | 1 | 11 | 10 | 2 | | 6 | 12 | | | 9 | 7 | 8 | 4 | 5 | | | 3 | |
| 13 | 14 | OXFORD | 1-1 | 4893 | Foley | 1 | 11 | | 2 | | 6 | 10 | | 7 | 9 | 7 | 8 | 4 | 5 | | | 3 | |
| 14 | 22 | Cambridge | 0-2 | 5423 | | 1 | 11 | | 2 | | 6 | 12 | | 10 | 9 | 12 | 8 | 4 | 5 | | | 3 | |
| 15 | 28 | PETERBOROUGH | 3-0 | 4827 | Allinson, Gough, Packer | 1 | 11 | 10 | 2 | | 6 | 12 | | | 9 | 7 | 8 | 4 | 5 | | 3 | | |
| 16 | 5 Nov | Walsall | 2-4 | 4231 | Allinson, Garwood | 1 | 11 | 10 | 2 | | 6 | 12 | | | 9 | 7 | 8 | 4 | 5 | | 3 | | |
| 17 | 11 | SWINDON | 2-0 | 4788 | Bunkell, Garwood | 1 | 11 | 10 | 2 | | 6 | | | | 9 | 7 | 8 | 4 | 5 | | 3 | 12 | |
| 18 | 19 | Wrexham | 1-2 | 9198 | Wignall | 1 | 11 | 10 | 2 | | 6 | | | 12 | 9 | 7 | 8 | 4 | 5 | | 3 | | |
| 19 | 3 Dec | Sheff Wed | 2-1 | 9000 | Cook, Garwood | 1 | 11 | | 2 | | 6 | | | | 9 | 7 | 8 | 4 | 5 | | 3 | 10 | |
| 20 | 9 | EXETER | 3-1 | 4267 | Dowman, Garwood, Gough | 1 | 11 | 12 | 2 | | 6 | | | 12 | 9 | 7 | 8 | 4 | 5 | | 3 | 10 | |
| 21 | 26 | LINCOLN | 1-1 | 5840 | Froggatt | 1 | 11 | | 2 | | 6 | | | | 9 | 7 | 8 | 4 | 5 | 12 | 3 | 10 | |
| 22 | 27 | Bury | 1-1 | 5409 | Foley | 1 | 11 | | 2 | | 6 | 5 | | 12 | | 7 | 8 | 4 | | 9 | 3 | 10 | |
| 23 | 31 | Shrewsbury | 0-1 | 4336 | | 1 | 11 | | 2 | | 6 | | | | 9 | 7 | 8 | 4 | 5 | 12 | 3 | 10 | |
| 24 | 2 Jan | WALSALL | 1-1 | 6039 | Gough | 1 | 11 | | 2 | | 6 | | | 7 | | 12 | 8 | 4 | 5 | 9 | 3 | 10 | |
| 25 | 7 | Bradford | 2-1 | 3266 | Dowman, Gough | 1 | | | 2 | | 6 | 10 | | 7 | 9 | 11 | 8 | 4 | 5 | 12 | 3 | | |
| 26 | 13 | GILLINGHAM | 1-1 | 6447 | Gough | 1 | 10 | | 2 | | 6 | 12 | | 7 | 9 | 11 | 8 | 4 | 5 | | 3 | | |
| 27 | 21 | Chester | 1-2 | 2355 | Rowles | 1 | 10 | | 2 | | 6 | 11 | | 7 | 9 | | | 4 | 5 | 8 | 3 | 12 | |
| 28 | 27 | TRANMERE | 0-0 | 4465 | | 1 | 10 | | 2 | | 6 | 12 | | 7 | | 11 | 8 | 4 | 5 | 9 | 3 | | |
| 29 | 4 Feb | Plymouth | 1-1 | 4639 | Rowles | 1 | 10 | 12 | 2 | | 6 | 11 | | 7 | | | 8 | 4 | 5 | 9 | 3 | | |
| 30 | 25 | CARLISLE | 2-2 | 3867 | Dowman, Garwood | 1 | 10 | | 2 | | 6 | 11 | | 7 | | 8 | | 4 | 5 | 9 | 3 | | |
| 31 | 28 | Preston | 0-4 | 9225 | | 1 | 10 | 11 | 2 | | 6 | 12 | | 7 | | 8 | | 4 | 5 | 9 | 3 | | |
| 32 | 4 Mar | Hereford | 0-1 | 3831 | | 1 | 10 | 6 | 2 | | | 11 | 12 | 7 | | 8 | | 4 | 5 | 9 | 3 | | |
| 33 | 7 | PORTSMOUTH | 4-0 | 3570 | Allinson, Foley, Rowles, O.G. | 1 | 10 | 11 | 2 | | 6 | 12 | | 7 | | | 8 | 4 | 5 | 9 | 3 | | |
| 34 | 11 | Oxford | 0-3 | 4060 | | 1 | 10 | | 2 | | 6 | 11 | 12 | 7 | | | 8 | 4 | 5 | | 3 | 9 | |
| 35 | 14 | Peterborough | 0-1 | 4468 | | 1 | 11 | 10 | 2 | | 6 | 12 | 9 | 7 | | | 8 | 4 | 3 | | 5 | | |
| 36 | 17 | CAMBRIDGE | 2-1 | 5260 | Allinson, Wignall | 1 | 11 | 10 | 2 | | 6 | 12 | 9 | 7 | | | 8 | 4 | 3 | | 5 | | |
| 37 | 25 | BURY | 1-0 | 3661 | Allinson | 1 | 11 | 10 | 2 | | | 12 | 9 | 7 | | | 8 | 4 | 5 | | 3 | 6 | |
| 38 | 27 | Lincoln | 0-0 | 4709 | | 1 | 10 | 9 | 2 | | 6 | 11 | 12 | 7 | | | 8 | 4 | 5 | | 3 | | |
| 39 | 1 Apr | SHREWSBURY | 1-2 | 2910 | Leslie | 1 | 10 | 9 | 2 | | | 12 | 11 | 7 | | | 8 | 4 | 5 | | 3 | 6 | |
| 40 | 4 | CHESTERFIELD | 2-0 | 3300 | Gough, Leslie | 1 | 10 | | 2 | | 6 | 9 | 11 | 7 | | | 8 | 4 | 5 | | | 3 | 12 |
| 41 | 8 | Swindon | 0-0 | 4596 | | 1 | 10 | | 2 | 12 | 6 | 9 | | 7 | | | 8 | 4 | 5 | | | 3 | 11 |
| 42 | 15 | WREXHAM | 1-1 | 5385 | Foley | 1 | 10 | | 2 | | 6 | 9 | | 7 | | | 8 | 4 | 5 | | 11 | 3 | 12 |
| 43 | 22 | Exeter | 0-0 | 3853 | | 1 | 10 | | 2 | 12 | 6 | 9 | | 7 | | | 8 | 4 | 5 | | 11 | 3 | |
| 44 | 24 | Port Vale | 3-0 | 3684 | Allinson, Foley(2) | 1 | 11 | | 2 | 12 | 6 | 7 | | 9 | | | 10 | 4 | 8 | | 5 | 3 | |
| 45 | 29 | SHEFF WED | 1-1 | 4337 | Dowman | 1 | 11 | | | 2 | 6 | 7 | 12 | 9 | | | 10 | 4 | 8 | | 5 | 3 | |
| 46 | 3 May | ROTHERHAM | 0-0 | 2554 | | 1 | 10 | | 2 | | 6 | 11 | | 7 | | | 8 | 4 | 5 | | 3 | 9 | |

## F.A.Cup

| | | | | | | | | | | | | | | | | | | | | | | | | |
|---|---|---|---|---|---|---|---|---|---|---|---|---|---|---|---|---|---|---|---|---|---|---|---|---|
| 1st | 26 Nov | BOURNEMOUTH | 1-1 | 4465 | Gough | 1 | 11 | 10 | 2 | | 6 | 12 | | | 9 | 7 | 8 | 4 | 5 | | 3 | | |
| 1st/R | 28 | Bournemouth | 0-0 | 3838 | | 1 | 11 | 12 | 2 | | 6 | 12 | | | 9 | 7 | 8 | 4 | 5 | | 3 | 10 | |
| 1st/2r | 5 Dec | Bournemouth | 4-1 | 2230 | Dowman, Garwood(3) | 1 | 11 | | 2 | | 6 | | | 12 | 9 | 7 | 8 | 4 | 5 | | 3 | 10 | |
| 2nd | 17 | Watford | 0-2 | 11907 | | 1 | 11 | | 2 | | 6 | 12 | | 5 | 9 | 7 | 8 | 4 | | | 3 | 10 | |

## Football League Cup

| | | | | | | | | | | | | | | | | | | | | | | | |
|---|---|---|---|---|---|---|---|---|---|---|---|---|---|---|---|---|---|---|---|---|---|---|---|
| 1st/1l | 13 Aug | Aldershot | 1-1 | 2574 | Gough | 1 | 11 | 12 | 2 | | 6 | | | 10 | 9 | 7 | 8 | 4 | 5 | | | 3 | |
| 1st/2l | 16 | ALDERSHOT | 4-1 | 3360 | Dowman, Froggatt(2), O.G. | 1 | 11 | 12 | 2 | | 6 | | | 10 | 9 | 7 | 8 | 4 | 5 | | | 3 | |
| 2nd | 31 | Blackburn | 1-1 | 6193 | Garwood | 1 | 11 | 10 | 2 | | 6 | 12 | | | 9 | 7 | 8 | 4 | 5 | | | 3 | |
| 2nd/r | 7 Sep | BLACKBURN | 4-0 | 5843 | Allinson, Garwood, Gough(2) | 1 | 11 | 10 | 2 | | 6 | 12 | | | 9 | 7 | 8 | 4 | 5 | | | 3 | |
| 3rd | 26 Oct | Leeds | 0-4 | 17713 | | 1 | 11 | 4 | 2 | 12 | 6 | 10 | | | 9 | 7 | 8 | | 5 | | | 3 | |

John Gilchrist (on the left) –
one of the 1970/71 F.A.Cup Heroes.

### THIRD DIVISION

| | | P | W | D | L | F | A | Pts |
|---|---|---|---|---|---|---|---|---|
| 1 | Wrexham | 46 | 23 | 15 | 8 | 78 | 45 | 61 |
| 2 | Cambridge | 46 | 23 | 12 | 11 | 72 | 51 | 58 |
| 3 | Preston | 46 | 20 | 16 | 10 | 63 | 38 | 56 |
| 4 | Peterborough | 46 | 20 | 16 | 10 | 47 | 33 | 56 |
| 5 | Chester | 46 | 16 | 22 | 8 | 59 | 56 | 54 |
| 6 | Walsall | 46 | 18 | 17 | 11 | 61 | 50 | 53 |
| 7 | Gillingham | 46 | 15 | 20 | 11 | 67 | 60 | 50 |
| 8 | Colchester | 46 | 15 | 18 | 13 | 55 | 44 | 48 |
| 9 | Chesterfield | 46 | 17 | 14 | 15 | 58 | 49 | 48 |
| 10 | Swindon | 46 | 16 | 16 | 14 | 67 | 60 | 48 |
| 11 | Shrewsbury | 46 | 16 | 15 | 15 | 63 | 57 | 47 |
| 12 | Tranmere | 46 | 16 | 15 | 15 | 57 | 52 | 47 |
| 13 | Carlisle | 46 | 14 | 19 | 13 | 59 | 59 | 47 |
| 14 | Sheff Wed | 46 | 15 | 16 | 15 | 50 | 52 | 46 |
| 15 | Bury | 46 | 13 | 19 | 14 | 62 | 56 | 45 |
| 16 | Lincoln | 46 | 15 | 15 | 16 | 53 | 61 | 45 |
| 17 | Exeter | 46 | 15 | 14 | 17 | 49 | 59 | 44 |
| 18 | Oxford | 46 | 13 | 14 | 19 | 64 | 67 | 40 |
| 19 | Plymouth | 46 | 11 | 17 | 18 | 61 | 68 | 39 |
| 20 | Rotherham | 46 | 13 | 13 | 20 | 51 | 68 | 39 |
| 21 | Port Vale | 46 | 8 | 20 | 18 | 46 | 67 | 36 |
| 22 | Bradford | 46 | 12 | 10 | 24 | 56 | 86 | 34 |
| 23 | Hereford | 46 | 9 | 14 | 23 | 34 | 60 | 32 |
| 24 | Portsmouth | 46 | 7 | 17 | 22 | 31 | 75 | 31 |

# SEASON 1978–79 Division Three

| No. | Date | Opposition | Res | Attend | Goalscorers | Walker | Allinson | Bunkell | Cook | Cotton | Dowman | Dyer | Evans | Foley | Gough | Hodge | Lee | Leslie | Packer | Rowles | Sharkey | Wignall | Wright |
|---|---|---|---|---|---|---|---|---|---|---|---|---|---|---|---|---|---|---|---|---|---|---|---|
| 1 | 19 Aug | SWANSEA | 2–2 | 2918 | Foley, Rowles | 1 | 11 | | 2 | | 6 | | | 7 | 8 | | | 4 | 3 | 10 | 9 | 5 | 2 |
| 2 | 21 | Brentford | 0–1 | 6800 | | 1 | 11 | | 2 | | 6 | 12 | | 7 | 8 | | | 4 | 3 | 10 | 9* | 5 | |
| 3 | 26 | Sheff Wed | 0–0 | 10685 | | 1 | 11 | | 2 | | 6 | 9 | | 7 | 8 | | | 4* | 3 | 10 | | 5 | 12 |
| 4 | 2 Sep | ROTHERHAM | 0–0 | 2448 | | 1 | 11 | | 2 | | 6 | 9 | | 7 | 8 | | | | 3 | 10 | | 5 | 4 |
| 5 | 8 | Carlisle | 0–4 | 4430 | | 1 | 11 | | 2 | | 6 | | 9 | 7 | 8 | | | | 3 | 10 | | 5 | 4 |
| 6 | 12 | CHESTER | 2–1 | 2311 | Cook, Gough | 1 | 11 | | 2 | | 6 | 9 | | 7 | 8 | | | | 3 | 10 | 12 | 5 | 4* |
| 7 | 15 | SHREWSBURY | 1–0 | 2788 | Foley | 1 | 11 | 12 | 2 | | 6 | 9 | | 7 | 8 | | | | 3 | 10 | 4 | 5 | |
| 8 | 23 | Walsall | 2–2 | 4052 | Foley, Gough | 1 | 11 | | 2 | | 6 | 9 | | 7 | 8 | 12 | | | 3 | 10 | 4 | 5 | |
| 9 | 27 | Exeter | 1–2 | 3421 | Gough | 1 | 11 | | 2 | | 6 | 9 | | 7* | 8 | 10 | | | 3 | 12 | 4 | 5 | |
| 10 | 30 | BLACKPOOL | 3–1 | 3007 | Gough(2), Rowles | 1 | 11 | | 2 | | 6 | 9 | 7 | | 8 | 4 | | | 3 | 10 | | 5 | |
| 11 | 6 Oct | SWINDON | 3–2 | 3324 | Evans, Gough, Rowles | 1 | 11 | 6 | 2 | | | 9 | 7 | | 8 | 4 | | | 3 | 10 | | 5 | |
| 12 | 13 | Lincoln | 0–0 | 3541 | | 1 | 11 | | 2 | | 6 | 9 | 7 | | 8 | 4 | | | 3 | | | 5 | 10 |
| 13 | 18 | Chesterfield | 1–2 | 4394 | Dyer | 1 | 11 | 10 | 2 | | | 9 | 7 | | 8 | 4 | | | 3 | | | 5 | 6 |
| 14 | 20 | SOUTHEND | 1–1 | 5881 | Evans | 1 | 11 | 12 | 2 | | | 9* | 7 | | 8 | 4 | | | 3 | 6 | | 5 | 10 |
| 15 | 28 | Mansfield | 1–1 | 4515 | Wignall | 1 | 11 | 10 | 2 | | 6 | 9 | 7 | | 8 | 4 | | | 3 | | | 5 | |
| 16 | 3 Nov | PLYMOUTH | 2–1 | 4564 | Bunkell, Gough | 1 | 11 | 9 | 2 | | 6 | 12 | | 7 | 8 | 4 | 10 | | 3* | | | 5 | |
| 17 | 11 | Rotherham | 0–1 | 3777 | | 1 | 11 | | 2 | | 6 | 9* | | 7 | 8 | 4 | 10 | | 3 | | | 5 | 12 |
| 18 | 18 | SHEFF WED | 1–0 | 4346 | Wignall | 1 | 11 | 9 | 2 | | 6 | | | 7 | 8 | 4 | 10 | | 3 | | | 5 | |
| 19 | 9 Dec | BURY | 0–0 | 2732 | | 1 | 11 | 9* | 2 | | 6 | 12 | | 7 | 8 | 4 | | | 3 | | | 5 | |
| 20 | 23 | WATFORD | 0–1 | 5424 | | 1 | 11 | | 2 | | 6 | 9 | | | 8 | 4 | 10 | | 3 | 7 | | | 5 |
| 21 | 26 | Oxford | 0–2 | 4892 | | 1 | 12 | | 2 | | 6 | 9* | | 7 | 8 | 4 | | | 3 | 11 | | 5 | 10 |
| 22 | 17 Jan | Chester | 2–2 | 2339 | Foley(2) | 1 | 11 | 10 | 2 | | 6 | 9 | | 7 | 8 | 4 | | | | | | 5 | 3 |
| 23 | 19 | Shrewsbury | 0–2 | 2119 | | 1 | 11 | 12 | 2 | | 6 | 9 | | 7 | 8 | 4 | | | 10* | | | 5 | 3 |
| 24 | 2 Feb | EXETER | 2–2 | 2767 | Allinson(pen), O.G. | 1 | 11 | | 2 | | 6 | 9 | | 7 | 8 | 4 | 10* | | 12 | | | 5 | 3 |
| 25 | 10 | Blackpool | 1–2 | 3446 | Allinson | 1 | 11 | 8 | 2 | | 6 | 9 | | | | 4 | 10 | | 7 | | | 5 | 3 |
| 26 | 23 | LINCOLN | 2–0 | 2861 | Hodge, Lee | 1 | 11 | | 2 | | 6 | 9 | | 8 | | 4 | 10 | | 7 | | | 5 | 3 |
| 27 | 27 | WALSALL | 2–0 | 3135 | Hodge, Wignall | 1 | 11 | | 2 | | 6 | 9 | | 8 | | 4 | 10 | | 7 | | | 5 | 3 |
| 28 | 2 Mar | Southend | 1–1 | 6957 | Lee | 1 | 11 | | 2 | | 6 | 9 | | 8 | | 4 | 10 | | 7 | | | 5 | 3 |
| 29 | 9 | MANSFIELD | 1–0 | 2866 | Gough | 1 | 11 | | 2 | | | 9 | | 8 | 6 | 4 | 10 | | 7 | | | 5 | 3 |
| 30 | 13 | Hull | 0–1 | 4201 | | 1 | 11 | | 2 | | 12 | 9* | | 8 | 6 | 4 | 10 | | 7 | | | 5 | 3 |
| 31 | 17 | Plymouth | 1–1 | 5342 | Dyer | 1 | 11 | | 2 | | | 9 | | 8 | 6 | 4 | 10 | | 7 | | | 5 | 3 |
| 32 | 20 | Swindon | 2–1 | 6678 | Lee(2) | 1 | 11 | | 2 | | 5 | 9 | | 8 | 6 | 4 | 10 | | 7 | | | | 3 |
| 33 | 24 | BRENTFORD | 1–1 | 3528 | Hodge(pen) | 1 | 11 | | 2 | | 5 | 9 | | 8 | 6 | 4 | 10 | | 7 | | | | 3 |
| 34 | 27 | Swansea | 1–4 | 11645 | Lee | 1 | 8 | | 2 | | 5 | 7 | | 6 | 9 | 11 | 10 | | 3 | | | | 4 |
| 35 | 31 | Peterborough | 2–1 | 3559 | Allinson, Gough | 1 | 11 | | 2 | | | 9 | | 7 | 8 | 4 | 10 | | 6 | | | 5 | 3 |
| 36 | 2 Apr | CARLISLE | 2–1 | 2608 | Lee, Wignall | 1 | 11 | | 2 | | | 9 | | 7 | 8 | 4 | 10 | | 6 | | | 5 | 3 |
| 37 | 6 | TRANMERE | 1–0 | 2578 | Lee | 1 | 11 | | 2 | | | 9 | | 7 | 8* | 4 | 10 | | 6 | 12 | | 5 | 3 |
| 38 | 13 | Watford | 3–0 | 17903 | Gough, Lee(2) | 1 | 11 | | 2 | | 9 | | | 7 | 8 | 4 | 10 | | 6 | | | 5 | 3 |
| 39 | 14 | OXFORD | 1–1 | 3897 | Gough | 1 | 11 | | 2 | | 7 | 9 | 12 | | 8 | 4* | 10 | | 6 | | | 5 | 3 |
| 40 | 16 | Gillingham | 0–3 | 12030 | | 1 | 11 | | 2 | 7 | 4 | 9 | | | 8 | | 10 | | 6 | | | 5 | 3 |
| 41 | 21 | HULL | 2–1 | 2762 | Gough, Rowles | 1 | 11 | 6 | 2 | | 4 | 9 | | | 8 | | 10 | | | 7 | | 5 | 3 |
| 42 | 24 | CHESTERFIELD | 0–0 | 6273 | | 1 | 11 | 6 | 2 | | 4 | 9 | | | 8 | | 10 | | | 7 | | 5 | 3 |
| 43 | 28 | Bury | 2–2 | 2905 | Gough, Wright | 1 | 11 | | 2 | | 4 | 9 | | 6 | 8 | | 10 | | | 7 | | 5 | 3 |
| 44 | 4 May | PETERBOROUGH | 4–2 | 2692 | Allinson, Dowman(2), Foley | 1 | 11 | | 2 | | 4 | 9* | | 6 | 8 | | 10 | | 12 | 7 | | 5 | 3 |
| 45 | 7 | GILLINGHAM | 2–2 | 6317 | Allinson, Gough | 1 | 11 | | 2 | | 4 | | | 6 | 8 | | 10 | | 9 | 7 | | 5 | 3 |
| 46 | 9 | Tranmere | 5–1 | 1016 | Gough(2), Lee(2), Packer | 1 | 11 | | 2 | | 4 | | | 6 | 8 | | 10 | | 9 | 7 | | 5 | 3 |

# F.A.Cup

| | | | | | | | | | | | | | | | | | | | | | | | | |
|---|---|---|---|---|---|---|---|---|---|---|---|---|---|---|---|---|---|---|---|---|---|---|---|---|
| 1st | 25 Nov | OXFORD | 4–2 | 4170 | Foley, Gough(3) | 1 | 11 | 9 | 2 | | 6 | | | 7 | 8 | 4 | 10 | | 3 | | | 5 | 12 |
| 2nd | 16 Dec | Leatherhead | 1–1 | 2550 | Gough | 1 | 11 | | 2 | | 6 | 9 | | 7 | 8 | 4 | | | 3 | | | 5 | 10 |
| 2nd/r | 19 | LEATHERHEAD | 4–0 | 3920 | Dowman(2), Gough, Lee | 1 | 11 | | 2 | | 6 | 9 | | | 8 | 4 | 10 | | 3 | | | 5 | 7 |
| 3rd | 9 Jan | Darlington | 1–0 | 3465 | Hodge | 1 | 11 | 10 | 2 | | 6 | 9 | | 7 | 8 | 4 | | | | | | 5 | 3 |
| 4th | 30 | Newport | 0–0 | 10329 | | 1 | 11 | | 2 | | 6 | 9 | | 7 | 8 | 4 | 10 | | | | | 5 | 3 |
| 4th/R | 6 Feb | NEWPORT | 1–0 | 7029 | Gough | 1 | 11 | | 2 | | 6 | | | 7 | 8 | 4 | 10 | | 9 | | | 5 | 3 |
| 5th | 20 | MANCHESTER U | 0–1 | 13171 | | 1 | 11 | | 2 | | 6 | 9 | | 8 | | 4 | 10 | | 7 | | | 5 | 3 |

# Football League Cup

| | | | | | | | | | | | | | | | | | | | | | | | |
|---|---|---|---|---|---|---|---|---|---|---|---|---|---|---|---|---|---|---|---|---|---|---|---|
| 1st/1 | 12 Aug | CHARLTON | 2–3 | 3016 | Dowman, Rowles | 1 | 11 | 4 | 2* | | 6 | 9 | | 7 | 8 | | | | 3 | 10 | 12 | 5 | |
| 1/2L | 15 | Charlton | 0–0 | 7205 | | 1 | 11 | | | | 6 | 9 | | 7 | 8 | | | 4 | 3 | 10 | 2 | 5 | 12 |

JA

" Ah, well, who wants a silly old cup, anyway."

COLCHESTER UNITED

Fairy Tales
The Giant Killers

"ONCE UPON A TIME THERE LIVED A FOOTBALL TEAM..."

**THIRD DIVISION**

| | | P | W | D | L | F | A | Pts |
|---|---|---|---|---|---|---|---|---|
| 1 | Shrewsbury | 46 | 21 | 19 | 6 | 61 | 41 | 61 |
| 2 | Watford | 46 | 24 | 12 | 10 | 83 | 52 | 60 |
| 3 | Swansea | 46 | 24 | 12 | 10 | 83 | 61 | 60 |
| 4 | Gillingham | 46 | 21 | 17 | 8 | 65 | 42 | 59 |
| 5 | Swindon | 46 | 25 | 7 | 14 | 74 | 52 | 57 |
| 6 | Carlisle | 46 | 15 | 22 | 9 | 53 | 42 | 52 |
| 7 | Colchester | 46 | 17 | 17 | 12 | 60 | 55 | 51 |
| 8 | Hull | 46 | 19 | 11 | 16 | 66 | 61 | 49 |
| 9 | Exeter | 46 | 17 | 15 | 14 | 61 | 56 | 49 |
| 10 | Brentford | 46 | 19 | 9 | 18 | 53 | 49 | 47 |
| 11 | Oxford | 46 | 14 | 18 | 14 | 44 | 50 | 46 |
| 12 | Blackpool | 46 | 18 | 9 | 19 | 61 | 59 | 45 |
| 13 | Southend | 46 | 15 | 15 | 16 | 51 | 49 | 45 |
| 14 | Sheff Wed | 46 | 13 | 19 | 14 | 53 | 53 | 45 |
| 15 | Plymouth | 46 | 15 | 14 | 17 | 67 | 68 | 44 |
| 16 | Chester | 46 | 14 | 16 | 16 | 57 | 61 | 44 |
| 17 | Rotherham | 46 | 17 | 10 | 19 | 49 | 55 | 44 |
| 18 | Mansfield | 46 | 12 | 19 | 15 | 51 | 52 | 43 |
| 19 | Bury | 46 | 11 | 20 | 15 | 59 | 65 | 42 |
| 20 | Chesterfield | 46 | 13 | 14 | 19 | 51 | 65 | 40 |
| 21 | Peterborough | 46 | 11 | 14 | 21 | 44 | 63 | 36 |
| 22 | Walsall | 46 | 10 | 12 | 24 | 56 | 71 | 32 |
| 23 | Tranmere | 46 | 6 | 16 | 24 | 45 | 78 | 28 |
| 24 | Lincoln | 46 | 7 | 11 | 28 | 41 | 88 | 25 |

# SEASON 1979/80 Division Three

| No. | Date | Opposition | Res | Attend | Goalscorers | Walker | Allinson | Bunkell | Cook | Cotton | Dowman | Dyer | Evans | Foley | Gough | Harvey | Hodge | Lee | Leslie | Packer | Rowles | Wignall | Wright |
|---|---|---|---|---|---|---|---|---|---|---|---|---|---|---|---|---|---|---|---|---|---|---|---|
| 1 | 18 Aug | Hull | 2-0 | 4453 | Allinson, Hodge | 1 | 11 | | 2 | | | | | 9 | 8 | | 7 | 10 | 4 | 6 | | 5 | 3 |
| 2 | 21 | SHEFF UTD | 1-0 | 4191 | Lee | 1 | 11 | | 2 | | 6 | | | 9 | 8 | | 7 | 10 | 4 | | | 5 | 3 |
| 3 | 25 | Rotherham | 0-3 | 3728 | | 1 | 11 | | 2 | | 6 | | | 9 | 8 | | 7 | 10 | 4 | 5 | 12 | | 3 |
| 4 | 31 | SWINDON | 2-3 | 2794 | Gough, Hodge | 1 | 11 | 6 | | | | | | 9 | 8 | | 7 | 10 | 4 | 2 | 3 | 5 | |
| 5 | 8 Sep | Chesterfield | 0-3 | 4206 | | 1 | 11 | | | | 2 | | | 9 | 8 | | 7 | 10 | 4 | | 3 | 5 | 6 |
| 6 | 15 | SHEFF WED | 0-0 | 3473 | | 1 | 11 | | 2 | | 6 | | | 9 | | | 7 | 10 | 4 | 3 | 5 | | |
| 7 | 18 | MANSFIELD | 2-1 | 2346 | Gough, Lee | 1 | 11 | | 2 | | 6 | | | | 8 | | 7 | 10 | 4 | 9 | | 5 | 3 |
| 8 | 22 | Grimsby | 2-1 | 6962 | Dowman(2) | 1 | 11 | | 2 | | 6 | 9 | | | 8 | | 7 | 10 | 4 | 6 | 12 | 5 | 3 |
| 9 | 29 | BARNSLEY | 0-0 | 3376 | | 1 | 11 | | 2 | | | | | 9 | 8 | | 7 | 10 | 4 | 6 | | 5 | 3 |
| 10 | 1 Oct | Mansfield | 1-0 | 3500 | Lee | 1 | 11 | | 2 | | 6 | | | 9 | 8 | | 7 | 10 | 4 | 3 | | 5 | |
| 11 | 5 | READING | 1-1 | 3330 | Rowles | 1 | 11 | | 2 | | 6 | | | 9 | 8 | | 7 | | 4 | 3 | 10 | 5 | |
| 12 | 9 | Sheff Utd | 2-1 | 18712 | Foley, Gough | 1 | 11 | | 2 | | 6 | 12 | | 9 | 8 | | 7 | | 4 | 3 | 10 | 5 | |
| 13 | 12 | Southend | 1-0 | 5944 | O.G. | 1 | 11 | | 2 | | 6 | | | 9 | 8 | | 7 | | 4 | 3 | 10 | 5 | |
| 14 | 19 | BLACKPOOL | 3-1 | 4383 | Gough, Hodge, Lee | 1 | 11 | | 2 | | 6 | | | 9 | 8 | | 7 | 10 | 4 | 3 | | 5 | |
| 15 | 23 | WIMBLEDON | 4-0 | 4396 | Gough, Hodge(pen), Lee, Wignall | 1 | 11 | | 2 | | 6 | | | 9 | 8 | | 7 | 10 | 4 | 3 | | 5 | |
| 16 | 27 | Blackburn | 0-3 | 6436 | | 1 | 11 | | 2 | | 6 | | | 9 | 8 | | 7 | 10 | 4 | 3 | | 5 | 12 |
| 17 | 2 Nov | HULL | 1-1 | 4510 | Gough | 1 | 11 | | 2 | | 6 | | | 9 | 8 | | 7 | 10 | 4 | 3 | 12 | 5 | |
| 18 | 6 | Wimbledon | 3-3 | 2465 | Gough, Lee, Wignall | 1 | | | 2 | | 6 | | | 9 | 8 | | 7 | 10 | 4 | 11 | 12 | 5 | 3 |
| 19 | 10 | Brentford | 0-1 | 9060 | | 1 | 11 | | 2 | | 6 | | | 9 | 8 | | 7 | 10 | 4 | 3 | 12 | 5 | |
| 20 | 16 | PLYMOUTH | 5-2 | 3520 | Gough, Hodge, Lee, Packer(2) | 1 | | | 2 | | 6 | | | 9 | 8 | | 7 | 10 | 4 | 3 | 11 | 5 | |
| 21 | 1 Dec | Millwall | 2-1 | 7563 | Foley, Lee | 1 | 11 | | 2 | | 6 | | | 9 | 8 | | 7 | 10 | 4 | 3 | 12 | | 5 |
| 22 | 7 | CARLISLE | 1-1 | 4104 | Lee | 1 | 11 | | 2 | | 6 | | | 9 | 8 | | 7 | 10 | 4 | 3 | | 5 | |
| 23 | 21 | Exeter | 1-3 | 2648 | Wright | 1 | | | 2 | | 6 | 9 | 12 | | | | 7 | 10 | 4 | 3 | 11 | 5 | 8 |
| 24 | 26 | GILLINGHAM | 2-2 | 5145 | Allinson, Packer | 1 | 11 | | 2 | | 6 | 7 | | 9 | | | | 10 | 4 | 3 | | 5 | 8 |
| 25 | 29 | ROTHERHAM | 1-1 | 3375 | Lee | 1 | 11 | | 2 | | 6 | | | 9 | | | 7 | 10 | 4 | 3 | 8 | 5 | 12 |
| 26 | 8 Jan | CHESTER | 1-1 | 3251 | Wright | 1 | 11 | | 2 | | 6 | | | 9 | 8 | | 7 | 10 | 4 | 3 | 12 | 8 | |
| 27 | 12 | Oxford | 2-0 | 3857 | Foley, Lee | 1 | 11 | | 2 | | 6 | | | 9 | 8 | | 7 | 10 | 4 | 3 | | 5 | |
| 28 | 18 | CHESTERFIELD | 0-1 | 3763 | | 1 | 11 | | 2 | | 6 | | | 9 | 8 | | 7 | 10 | 4 | 3 | | 5 | 12 |
| 29 | 29 | Bury | 1-0 | 3551 | Rowles | 1 | 11 | | 2 | | 6 | | | 9 | | | 7 | 10 | 4 | 3 | 8 | 5 | |
| 30 | 2 Feb | Sheff Wed | 0-3 | 11958 | | 1 | 11 | | 2 | | 6 | | 12 | 9 | | | 7 | 10 | 4 | 3 | 8 | 5 | |
| 31 | 8 | GRIMSBY | 2-1 | 5149 | Foley, Gough | 1 | | | 2 | | 6 | | | 9 | 8 | | | 10 | 4 | 3 | 7 | 5 | 11 |
| 32 | 16 | Barnsley | 2-1 | 11309 | Dowman, Rowles | 1 | 11 | | 2 | | 6 | | | 9 | | | 7 | 10 | 4 | 3 | 8 | 5 | |
| 33 | 22 | SOUTHEND | 2-1 | 6135 | Leslie, Rowles | 1 | 12 | | 2 | | 6 | | | 9 | 8 | | | 10 | 4 | 3 | 7 | 5 | 11 |
| 34 | 29 | Blackpool | 0-1 | 5594 | | 1 | 8 | | 2 | | 6 | | | 9 | 12 | | 5 | 10 | 4 | 3 | 7 | | 11 |
| 35 | 8 Mar | BLACKBURN | 0-1 | 4957 | | 1 | 11 | | 2 | | 6 | | | 9 | 8 | | | 10 | 4 | 3 | 7 | | 5 |
| 36 | 16 | Reading | 0-2 | 5444 | | 1 | 11 | | 2 | | 6 | | | 9 | 8 | | | 10 | 4 | 3 | 7 | | 5 |
| 37 | 22 | BRENTFORD | 6-1 | 3818 | Dowman, Foley(2), Lee(2), Rowles | 1 | 11 | | 2 | | 6 | | | 9 | | | 7 | 10 | 4 | 3 | 8 | 5 | |
| 38 | 29 | Plymouth | 0-2 | 6330 | | 1 | 11 | | 2 | | 6 | | | | | | 7 | 10 | 4 | 3 | 8 | 5 | 9 |
| 39 | 2 Apr | EXETER | 0-0 | 2780 | | 1 | 11 | | 2 | | 6 | | | 9 | | | 7 | 10 | 4 | 3 | 8 | 5 | |
| 40 | 5 | Gillingham | 2-2 | 6561 | Foley, Lee | 1 | 11 | | 2 | | | | | 9 | 8 | | | 10 | 4 | 3 | 7 | 5 | 6 |
| 41 | 7 | BURY | 2-1 | 3190 | Gough, Lee | 1 | 11 | | 2 | | 6 | | | 9 | 8 | | 12 | 10 | 4 | 3 | 7 | 5 | |
| 42 | 12 | Chester | 1-2 | 2282 | Foley | 1 | 11 | | 2 | | 6 | | 12 | 9 | 8 | | | 10 | 4 | 3 | 7 | 5 | |
| 43 | 19 | MILLWALL | 0-0 | 3296 | | 1 | | | 2 | 11 | | | 7 | 9 | | 8 | | 10 | 4 | 3 | 12 | 5 | 6 |
| 44 | 22 | Swindon | 3-2 | 2985 | Harvey(2), Rowles | 1 | | | 2 | 11 | | | 12 | 9 | | 8 | | 10 | 4 | 3 | 7 | 5 | 6 |
| 45 | 26 | Carlisle | 0-2 | 3702 | | 1 | | | 2 | 11 | | | 7 | 9 | | 8 | 12 | 10 | 4 | 6 | 3 | | 5 |
| 46 | 2 May | OXFORD | 3-0 | 2535 | Packer, Rowles(2) | 1 | | | 2 | 11 | | | | 9 | | 7 | 12 | 10 | 4 | 3 | 8 | 6 | 5 |

## F.A.Cup

| | | | | | | | | | | | | | | | | | | | | | | | |
|---|---|---|---|---|---|---|---|---|---|---|---|---|---|---|---|---|---|---|---|---|---|---|---|
| 1st | 24 Nov | PLYMOUTH | 1–1 | 4064 | Rowles | 1 | 12 | | 2 | | 6 | | | 9 | 8 | | 7 | 10 | 4 | 3 | 11 | | 5 |
| 1st\r | 27 | Plymouth | 1–0 | 6926 | Allinson | 1 | 11 | | 2 | | 6 | | | 9 | 8 | | 7 | 10 | 4 | 3 | | | 5 |
| 2nd | 15 Dec | BOURNEMOUTH | 1–0 | 3693 | Rowles | 1 | 11 | | 2 | | 6 | | | 9 | | | 7 | 10 | 4 | 3 | 8 | 5 | 12 |
| 3rd | 5 Jan | Reading | 0–2 | 7780 | | 1 | 11 | | 2 | | 6 | | | 9 | 8 | | | 10 | 4 | 3 | 12 | 5 | 7 |

## Football League Cup

| | | | | | | | | | | | | | | | | | | | | | | | |
|---|---|---|---|---|---|---|---|---|---|---|---|---|---|---|---|---|---|---|---|---|---|---|---|
| 1st | 11 Aug | WATFORD | 2–0 | 4638 | Gough, Hodge(pen) | 1 | 11 | | 2 | | 6 | | | 9 | 8 | | 7 | 10 | 4 | | | 5 | 3 |
| 1R\2l | 14 | Watford | 1–2 | 10045 | Allinson | 1 | 11 | | 2 | | 6 | | | 9 | 8 | | 7 | 10 | 4 | | | 5 | 3 |
| 2r\1l | 28 | ASTON VILLA | 0–2 | 6221 | | 1 | 11 | | | | 6 | | | 9 | 8 | | 7 | 10 | 4 | 2 | 3 | 5 | |
| 2R\2l | 5 Sep | Aston Villa | 2–0 | 19473 | Gough, Lee | 1 | 11 | | | | 12 | | | 9 | 8 | | 7 | 10 | 4 | 2 | 3 | 5 | 6 |

Steve Foley · Steve Leslie · Eddie Rowles · Mick Packer · Paul Dyer · Trevor Lee · Bobby Hodge

Steve Wignall · Bobby Gough · Micky Cook · Ian Allinson · Mike Walker · Steve Dowman

### THIRD DIVISION

| | | P | W | D | L | F | A | Pts |
|---|---|---|---|---|---|---|---|---|
| 1 | Grimsby | 46 | 26 | 10 | 10 | 73 | 42 | 62 |
| 2 | Blackburn | 46 | 25 | 9 | 12 | 58 | 36 | 59 |
| 3 | Sheff Wed | 46 | 21 | 16 | 9 | 81 | 47 | 58 |
| 4 | Chesterfield | 46 | 23 | 11 | 12 | 71 | 46 | 57 |
| 5 | Colchester | 46 | 20 | 12 | 14 | 64 | 56 | 52 |
| 6 | Carlisle | 46 | 18 | 12 | 16 | 66 | 56 | 48 |
| 7 | Reading | 46 | 16 | 16 | 14 | 66 | 65 | 48 |
| 8 | Exeter | 46 | 19 | 10 | 17 | 60 | 68 | 48 |
| 9 | Chester | 46 | 17 | 13 | 16 | 49 | 57 | 47 |
| 10 | Swindon | 46 | 19 | 8 | 19 | 71 | 63 | 46 |
| 11 | Barnsley | 46 | 16 | 14 | 16 | 53 | 56 | 46 |
| 12 | Sheff United | 46 | 18 | 10 | 18 | 60 | 66 | 46 |
| 13 | Rotherham | 46 | 18 | 10 | 18 | 58 | 66 | 46 |
| 14 | Millwall | 46 | 16 | 13 | 17 | 65 | 59 | 45 |
| 15 | Plymouth | 46 | 16 | 12 | 18 | 59 | 55 | 44 |
| 16 | Gillingham | 46 | 14 | 14 | 18 | 49 | 51 | 42 |
| 17 | Oxford | 46 | 14 | 13 | 19 | 57 | 62 | 41 |
| 18 | Blackpool | 46 | 15 | 11 | 20 | 62 | 74 | 41 |
| 19 | Brentford | 46 | 15 | 11 | 20 | 59 | 73 | 41 |
| 20 | Hull | 46 | 12 | 16 | 18 | 51 | 69 | 40 |
| 21 | Bury | 46 | 16 | 7 | 23 | 45 | 59 | 39 |
| 22 | Southend | 46 | 14 | 10 | 22 | 47 | 58 | 38 |
| 23 | Mansfield | 46 | 10 | 16 | 20 | 47 | 58 | 36 |
| 24 | Wimbledon | 46 | 10 | 14 | 22 | 52 | 81 | 34 |

# SEASON 1980–81 Division Three

| No. | Date | Opposition | Res | Attend | Goalscorers | Walker | Adcock | Allinson | Bremner | Coleman | Cook | Cotton | Crouch | Evans | Foley | Gough | Harvey | Hodge | Lee | Leslie | Longhorn | McDonough | Osborne | Packer | Rowles | Wignall | Wright | Cusenza |
|---|---|---|---|---|---|---|---|---|---|---|---|---|---|---|---|---|---|---|---|---|---|---|---|---|---|---|---|---|
| 1 | 16 Aug | PLYMOUTH | 2-2 | 2061 | Gough, Hodge | 1 | | 3 | | | 2 | 11 | | | 9 | 4 | | 7 | 10 | 12 | | | | 6 | 8* | 5 | | |
| 2 | 20 | Fulham | 0-1 | 4155 | | 1 | | 3 | | | 2 | 11 | | 10 | 9 | 8 | 7* | | 12 | 4 | | | | 6 | | 5 | | |
| 3 | 23 | WALSALL | 1-1 | 1979 | Rowles | 1 | | 11 | | | 2 | | | 12 | 9 | 4* | | 7 | 10 | 3 | | | | 6 | 8 | 5 | | |
| 4 | 30 | Exeter | 0-4 | 3918 | | 1 | | 3 | | | | 11 | | 2 | 9 | | 8 | 7 | 10 | 4 | | | | 6 | | 5 | | |
| 5 | 6 Sep | Burnley | 0-1 | 4391 | | 1 | | 3 | | | 2 | | 12 | 8* | 9 | | | 7 | 10 | 4 | | | | 6 | 11 | 5 | | |
| 6 | 13 | MILLWALL | 3-0 | 2724 | Foley, Lee, Rowles | 1 | | 8 | | | 2 | 7 | 3 | | 9 | | | | 10 | 4 | | | | 6 | 11 | 5 | | |
| 7 | 16 | CHESTERFIELD | 1-1 | 2171 | Lee | 1 | | 3 | | | 2 | | 11 | | 9 | | | 7 | 10 | 4 | | | | 6 | 8 | 5 | | |
| 8 | 20 | Charlton | 2-1 | 4323 | Foley, Hodge | 1 | | 11 | | | 2 | | 3 | | 9 | | | 7 | 10 | 4 | | | | 6 | 8 | 5 | | |
| 9 | 27 | CHESTER | 1-1 | 2147 | Lee | 1 | | 11 | | | 2 | | 3 | | 9 | | | 7 | 10 | 4 | | | | 6 | 8 | 5 | | |
| 10 | 30 | Chesterfield | 0-3 | 6674 | | 1 | | 3 | | | 2 | | 11 | | 9 | | | 7 | 10 | 4 | | | | 6 | 8 | 5 | | |
| 11 | 4 Oct | Huddersfield | 0-2 | 8400 | | 1 | | 11 | | | 2 | 9 | 3 | 12 | | | | 7 | 10 | 4 | 8* | | | 6 | | 5 | | |
| 12 | 7 | PORTSMOUTH | 1-0 | 2702 | Lee | 1 | | 11 | | | 2 | | 3 | | | 8 | | 7 | 10 | 4 | | | | 6 | 9 | 5 | | |
| 13 | 11 | BARNSLEY | 2-2 | 2749 | Gough, Hodge | 1 | | 11 | 12 | | 2 | | 3* | | | 8 | | 7 | 10 | 4 | | | | 6 | 9 | 5 | | |
| 14 | 18 | Blackpool | 1-1 | 6997 | Allinson | 1 | | 11 | 10 | | 2 | | | 3 | | 8 | | 7 | | 4 | | | | 6 | 9 | 5 | | |
| 15 | 22 | Reading | 0-1 | 3955 | | 1 | | 11 | 9 | | 2 | 7 | | | | 8 | | | 10 | 4 | | | | 6 | 3 | 5 | | |
| 16 | 25 | ROTHERHAM | 0-0 | 2623 | | 1 | | 11 | 10 | | 2 | 7 | | | | 8 | | | 9 | 4 | 5 | | | 6 | 3 | | | |
| 17 | 28 | HULL | 2-0 | 2239 | Allinson, Lee | 1 | | 11 | 10 | | 2 | | | | | 8 | | 7 | 9 | 4 | | | | 6 | 3 | 5 | | |
| 18 | 1 Nov | Sheff Utd | 0-3 | 18810 | | 1 | | 11 | 9 | | 2 | 8 | | 7 | | | | | 10 | 4 | 3 | | | 6 | | 5 | | |
| 19 | 4 | Portsmouth | 1-2 | 10895 | Lee | 1 | | 11 | 9 | | 2 | 8 | | 7 | | | | | 10 | 4 | 3 | | | 6 | | 5 | | |
| 20 | 8 | SWINDON | 1-0 | 2153 | Hodge(pen) | 1 | | 11 | 9 | | 2 | | | | | 8* | | 7 | 10 | 4 | 12 | | | 6 | 3 | 5 | | |
| 21 | 11 | FULHAM | 3-2 | 2543 | Allinson(2), Wignall | 1 | | 11 | 9 | | 2 | | | | 12 | | | 7 | 10 | 4 | 8* | | | 6 | 3 | 5 | | |
| 22 | 15 | Plymouth | 1-1 | 4905 | Bremner | 1 | | 11 | 9 | | 2 | | | | 8 | | | 7 | 10 | 4 | | | | 6 | 3 | 5 | | |
| 23 | 29 | OXFORD | 3-0 | 2114 | Bremner(2), Hodge(pen) | 1 | | 11 | 9 | | 2 | | | | 8 | | | 7 | 10 | 4 | | | | 6 | 3 | 5 | | |
| 24 | 6 Dec | Carlisle | 0-4 | 3196 | | 1 | | 11 | 9 | | 2 | | | | 8 | | | 7 | 10 | 4 | | | | 6 | 3 | 5 | | |
| 25 | 20 | NEWPORT | 1-0 | 2160 | Hodge(pen) | 1 | | 11 | 9 | | 2 | | | | | 8 | | 7 | 10 | 4 | 6 | | | | 3 | 5 | | |
| 26 | 26 | Brentford | 1-2 | 6340 | Bremner | 1 | | 11 | 9 | | 2 | 12 | | | | | | 7* | 10 | 4 | 8 | | | 6 | 3 | 5 | | |
| 27 | 27 | GILLINGHAM | 2-1 | 3897 | Lee, Packer(pen) | 1 | | 11 | 9 | | 2 | | | | | 8 | | 12 | 10 | 4 | 7 | | | 6 | | 5 | 3* | |
| 28 | 10 Jan | BLACKPOOL | 3-2 | 2378 | Foley, Gough(2) | 1 | | 11 | 9 | | 2 | | | | 8 | 10 | | | | 4 | 3 | | | 6 | | 5 | 7 | |
| 29 | 17 | Oxford | 1-2 | 3498 | Foley | 1 | | 11 | 9 | | 2 | | | | 8 | 10 | | 12 | | 4 | 3 | | | 6 | | 5 | 7* | |
| 30 | 31 | Walsall | 1-3 | 3195 | Allinson | 1 | | 11 | 9 | | 2 | 8 | | | 10 | | | | | 4 | 7 | | | 3 | | 5 | 6 | |
| 31 | 3 Feb | EXETER | 1-2 | 2359 | Bremner | 1 | | 11 | 9 | | 2 | | | | 8 | 10 | | 7 | | 4 | 3 | | | | | 5 | 6 | |
| 32 | 7 | Millwall | 1-3 | 4565 | Bremner | 1 | | 11 | 9 | | 2 | 7 | | | 10 | | | 8 | | 4 | 3 | | | | | 5 | 6 | |
| 33 | 14 | BURNLEY | 2-1 | 3082 | Bremner, McDonough | 1 | | 11 | 9 | | 2 | 4 | | | 8 | | | | | | 3 | 10 | 7 | 6 | | | 5 | |
| 34 | 21 | Chester | 0-0 | 1778 | | 1 | | 11 | 9 | 3 | 2 | 4 | | | 10 | | | | | | | 8 | 7 | 6 | | | 5 | |
| 35 | 28 | CHARLTON | 2-0 | 4864 | Foley, Packer(pen) | 1 | | 11 | 9 | 3 | 2 | | | | 8 | | | | | 4 | | 10 | 7 | 6 | | | 5 | |
| 36 | 7 Mar | HUDDERSFIELD | 1-2 | 3644 | Packer | 1 | | 11 | 9 | 3 | 2 | | | | 8 | | | | | 4 | | 10 | 7 | 6 | | 5 | | |
| 37 | 17 | Hull | 1-0 | 3584 | Cotton | 1 | | 12 | 9 | | 2 | 11* | | | 8 | | | | | 4 | | 10 | 7 | 6 | | 3 | 5 | |
| 38 | 22 | READING | 1-2 | 3705 | Bremner | 1 | | 12 | 9 | | 2 | 11 | | | 8* | | | | | 4 | | 10 | 7 | 6 | | 3 | 5 | |
| 39 | 28 | Rotherham | 0-2 | 7956 | | 1 | | 12 | 9 | | 2 | 11* | | | 8 | | | | | 4 | | 10 | 7 | 6 | | 5 | 3 | |
| 40 | 4 Apr | SHEFF UTD | 1-1 | 2439 | Allinson | 1 | | 11 | 9 | | 2 | | | | | | | | | 4 | 8 | 10 | 7 | 6 | | 5 | 3 | |
| 41 | 7 | Barnsley | 0-3 | 13283 | | 1 | | 11 | 9 | | 2 | 7 | | | 10 | | | | | 4 | 8 | 12 | | 6 | | 5 | 3* | |
| 42 | 11 | Swindon | 0-3 | 6180 | | 1 | | 11 | 9 | | 2 | | | | 3 | | | | | 4 | 8 | 10 | 7 | 6 | | 5 | | |
| 43 | 18 | Gillingham | 0-0 | 4408 | | 1 | | 11 | 9 | | 2 | | 3 | | 10 | | | | | 4 | 8 | | | 6 | | 5 | 7 | |
| 44 | 20 | BRENTFORD | 0-2 | 2409 | | 1 | | 11 | 9 | 3 | 2 | | | | 7 | | | | | 4 | 8 | 10 | 12 | 6* | | 5 | | |
| 45 | 25 | Newport | 0-1 | 4619 | | 1 | | 11 | 9 | | 2 | 4 | | | 7 | | | | | | 8 | | 10 | 6 | | 5 | 3 | |
| 46 | 2 May | CARLISLE | 1-0 | 1430 | McDonough | 1 | 7 | 11 | 9 | | 2 | | | | | | | | | 12 | 8* | 10 | 4 | 6 | | 5 | 3 | |

## F.A.Cup

| | | | | | | | | | | | | | | | | | | | | | | | | | | | | | |
|---|---|---|---|---|---|---|---|---|---|---|---|---|---|---|---|---|---|---|---|---|---|---|---|---|---|---|---|---|---|
| 1st | 22 Nov | PORTSMOUTH | 3–0 | 5837 | Allinson, Bremner, Lee | 1 | | 11 | 9 | | 2 | | | | 8 | | | 7 | 10 | 4 | | | | 6 | 3 | 5 | | |
| 2nd | 13 Dec | YEOVIL | 1–1 | 3394 | Wignall | 1 | | 11 | 9 | | 2 | | | | | 8 | | 7* | 10 | 4 | 12 | | | 6 | 3 | 8 | | |
| 2/R | 17 | Yeovil | 2–0 | 5803 | Bremner, Lee | 1 | | 11 | 9 | | 2 | | | 8 | | | | | 10 | 4 | 7 | | | 6 | 3 | 5 | | |
| 3rd | 3 Jan | WATFORD | 0–1 | 7769 | | 1 | | 11 | 9 | | 2 | | | | 8 | 12 | | 7* | 10 | 4 | 3 | | | 6 | | 5 | | |

## Football League Cup

| | | | | | | | | | | | | | | | | | | | | | | | | | | | | |
|---|---|---|---|---|---|---|---|---|---|---|---|---|---|---|---|---|---|---|---|---|---|---|---|---|---|---|---|---|
| 1st/1 | 9 Aug | GILLINGHAM | 0–2 | 2514 | | 1 | | 11 | | | | | 2 | 12 | 9 | | | 7 | 10 | | 4* | | | 6 | 8 | 5 | | 3 |
| 1/2l | 12 | Gillingham | 1–2 | 5220 | Gough | 1 | | 11 | | | 2* | 3 | | 12 | 9 | 4 | | 7 | 10 | | | | | 6 | 8 | 5 | | |

Antony Buck, Q.C., M.P.

J.W. Rippingale

R.G.R. Chapman, F.R.I.C.S

M.J. Cadman

N.F. Fitch

H.R. Piper

R.T. Jackson

M. Bennet

### THIRD DIVISION

| | P | W | D | L | F | A | Pts |
|---|---|---|---|---|---|---|---|
| 1 Rotherham | 46 | 24 | 13 | 9 | 62 | 32 | 61 |
| 2 Barnsley | 46 | 21 | 17 | 8 | 72 | 45 | 59 |
| 3 Charlton | 46 | 25 | 9 | 12 | 63 | 44 | 59 |
| 4 Huddersfield | 46 | 21 | 14 | 11 | 71 | 40 | 56 |
| 5 Chesterfield | 46 | 23 | 10 | 13 | 72 | 48 | 56 |
| 6 Portsmouth | 46 | 22 | 9 | 15 | 55 | 47 | 53 |
| 7 Plymouth | 46 | 19 | 14 | 13 | 56 | 44 | 52 |
| 8 Burnley | 46 | 18 | 14 | 14 | 60 | 48 | 50 |
| 9 Brentford | 46 | 14 | 19 | 13 | 52 | 49 | 47 |
| 10 Reading | 46 | 18 | 10 | 18 | 62 | 62 | 46 |
| 11 Exeter | 46 | 16 | 13 | 17 | 62 | 66 | 45 |
| 12 Newport | 46 | 15 | 13 | 18 | 64 | 61 | 43 |
| 13 Fulham | 46 | 15 | 13 | 18 | 57 | 64 | 43 |
| 14 Oxford | 46 | 13 | 17 | 16 | 39 | 47 | 43 |
| 15 Gillingham | 46 | 12 | 18 | 16 | 48 | 58 | 42 |
| 16 Millwall | 46 | 14 | 14 | 18 | 43 | 60 | 42 |
| 17 Swindon | 46 | 13 | 15 | 18 | 51 | 56 | 41 |
| 18 Chester | 46 | 15 | 11 | 20 | 41 | 48 | 41 |
| 19 Carlisle | 46 | 14 | 13 | 19 | 57 | 70 | 41 |
| 20 Walsall | 46 | 13 | 15 | 18 | 59 | 74 | 41 |
| 21 Sheff United | 46 | 14 | 13 | 19 | 65 | 62 | 40 |
| 22 Colchester | 46 | 14 | 11 | 21 | 45 | 65 | 39 |
| 23 Blackpool | 46 | 9 | 14 | 23 | 45 | 75 | 32 |
| 24 Hull | 46 | 8 | 16 | 22 | 40 | 71 | 32 |

# SEASON 1981–82 Division Four

| No. | Date | Opposition | Res | Attend | Goalscorers | Walker | Adcock | Allinson | Bremner | Coleman | Cook | Cotton | Foley | Groves | Hunter | Leslie | Longhorn | Lyons | McDonough | Osborne | Packer | Rowles | Ward | Wignall | Wright |
|---|---|---|---|---|---|---|---|---|---|---|---|---|---|---|---|---|---|---|---|---|---|---|---|---|---|
| 1 | 29 Aug | Hartlepool | 3-1 | 2007 | Bremner(2), Packer(pen) | 1 | 12 | 11 | 8 |  | 2 |  |  |  |  | 4 | 9 |  | 10 | 7* | 3 |  |  | 5 | 6 |
| 2 | 4 Sep | TRANMERE | 4-0 | 2474 | Allinson(2,1pen), Bremner, Cook | 1 | 7 | 11 | 8 | 3 | 2 |  | 12 |  |  | 4 | 9 |  | 10 |  |  |  |  | 5 | 6 |
| 3 | 12 | Sheff Utd | 0-1 | 11293 |  | 1 | 12 | 11 | 8 | 3 | 2 |  | 9* |  |  | 4 |  |  | 10 | 7 |  |  |  | 5 | 6 |
| 4 | 18 | TORQUAY | 3-0 | 2820 | Adcock(2), Cook | 1 | 9 | 11 | 8 | 3 | 2 |  |  |  |  | 4 |  |  | 10 | 7 |  |  |  | 5 | 6 |
| 5 | 22 | ALDERSHOT | 1-1 | 2719 | Coleman | 1 | 7 | 11 | 8 | 3 | 2 |  |  |  |  | 4 |  |  | 10 | 9 |  |  |  | 5 | 6 |
| 6 | 26 | Bradford | 1-2 | 4772 | Leslie | 1 | 7 | 11 | 8 | 3 | 2 |  |  |  |  | 4 |  |  | 10 | 9 |  |  |  | 5 | 6 |
| 7 | 28 | Port Vale | 1-2 | 3351 | MccDonough | 1 | 7 | 11 | 8 | 3 | 2 |  |  |  |  | 4 |  |  | 10 | 9 |  |  |  | 5 | 6 |
| 8 | 2 Oct | NORTHAMPTON | 5-1 | 2760 | Allinson(pen), Bremner(2), Coleman Cook | 1 | 7 | 11 | 8 | 3 | 2 |  |  |  |  | 4* | 12 |  | 10 | 9 |  |  |  | 5 | 6 |
| 9 | 11 | Rochdale | 2-1 | 1366 | Allinson, McDonough | 1 | 7 | 11 | 8 | 3 | 2 |  |  |  |  | 4 |  |  | 10 | 9 |  |  |  | 5 | 6 |
| 10 | 16 | YORK | 4-0 | 3139 | Allinson, Bremner, Leslie, McDonough | 1 | 7* | 11 | 8 | 3 | 2 |  |  |  |  | 4 | 12 |  | 10 | 9 |  |  |  | 5 | 6 |
| 11 | 20 | HEREFORD | 4-0 | 3064 | Allinson, Bremner, Osborne(2) | 1 | 7 | 11 | 8 | 3 | 2 |  |  |  |  | 4 |  |  | 10 | 9 |  |  |  | 5 | 6 |
| 12 | 24 | Halifax | 2-0 | 1374 | Allinson(pen), McDonough | 1 | 7* | 11 | 8 | 3 | 2 |  |  |  |  | 4 | 12 |  | 10 | 9 |  |  |  | 5 | 6 |
| 13 | 30 | WIGAN | 1-2 | 3884 | Coleman | 1 | 7 | 11 | 8 | 3 | 2 |  |  |  |  | 4 | 6* |  | 10 | 9 |  | 12 |  | 5 |  |
| 14 | 2 Nov | Mansfield | 3-1 | 2294 | Allinson(3,1pen), | 1 | 12 | 11 | 8 | 3 | 2 | 7* |  |  |  | 4 |  |  | 10 | 9 |  | 6 |  | 5 |  |
| 15 | 7 | Hull | 3-2 | 3040 | Bremner, McDonough(2) | 1 | 7 | 11 | 8 | 3 | 2 |  |  |  |  | 4 |  |  | 10 | 9 |  |  |  | 5 | 6 |
| 16 | 13 | SCUNTHORPE | 2-1 | 3838 | Allinson, Cook | 1 | 7 | 11 | 8 | 3 | 2 |  |  |  |  | 4* | 12 |  | 10 | 9 |  |  |  | 5 | 6 |
| 17 | 28 | Darlington | 2-1 | 1456 | Bremner, Osborne | 1 | 7 | 11 | 8 | 3 | 2 |  |  |  |  | 4 |  |  |  | 9 |  | 10 |  | 5 | 6 |
| 18 | 4 Dec | BLACKPOOL | 2-1 | 3875 | Allinson, O.G. | 1 | 7* | 11 | 8 | 3 | 2 |  |  |  |  | 4 |  |  | 10 | 9 |  | 12 |  | 5 | 6 |
| 19 | 26 | Bournemouth | 1-1 | 8829 | McDonough | 1 | 12 | 11 | 8 | 3* | 2 |  |  |  |  | 4 |  |  | 10 | 9 |  | 7 |  | 5 | 6 |
| 20 | 16 Jan | BURY | 1-1 | 3504 | Adcock | 1 | 7 | 11 | 8 | 3* | 2 |  |  |  |  | 4 | 12 |  | 10 | 9 |  |  |  | 5 | 6 |
| 21 | 23 | HARTLEPOOL | 3-3 | 2862 | Allinson(pen), McDonough, O.G. | 1 | 7 | 11 | 8 | 3 | 2* |  |  |  |  |  | 12 |  | 10 | 9 | 6 | 4 |  | 5 |  |
| 22 | 30 | Torquay | 0-1 | 2037 |  | 1 | 12 | 11 | 8 | 3 | 2 | 7 |  |  |  |  |  |  | 10 | 9 | 4* |  |  | 5 | 6 |
| 23 | 6 Feb | SHEFF UTD | 5-2 | 5194 | Allinson(2), Bremner, Lyons, McDonough | 1 | 7 | 11 | 8 | 12 | 2 |  |  |  |  |  | 3* | 4 | 10 | 9 |  |  |  | 5 | 6 |
| 24 | 9 | Aldershot | 1-1 | 2324 | Lyons | 1 | 7 | 11 | 8 |  | 2 |  |  |  |  | 12 | 3 | 4 | 10 | 9* |  |  |  | 5 | 6 |
| 25 | 14 | Northampton | 2-1 | 3102 | Allinson, Bremner | 1 | 12 | 11 | 8 |  | 2 |  |  |  |  | 7* | 3 | 4 | 10 | 9 |  |  |  | 5 | 6 |
| 26 | 19 | BRADFORD | 1-2 | 3975 | Cook | 1 | 7 | 11 | 8 |  | 2 |  |  |  |  |  | 3 | 4 | 10 | 9 |  |  |  | 5 | 6 |
| 27 | 26 | ROCHDALE | 3-2 | 2760 | Adcock(2), Bremner | 1 | 7 | 11* | 8 | 5 | 2 | 12 |  |  |  |  | 3 | 4 | 10 | 9 |  |  |  |  | 6 |
| 28 | 2 Mar | Tranmere | 1-2 | 1252 | Bremner | 1 | 7* | 11 | 8 | 5 | 2 | 12 |  |  |  |  | 3 | 4 | 10 | 9 |  |  |  |  | 6 |
| 29 | 5 | York | 0-3 | 1854 |  | 1 |  | 11 | 8 | 5 | 2 | 7 |  |  |  |  | 3 | 12 | 10 | 9 | 4* |  |  |  | 6 |
| 30 | 10 | Hereford | 2-2 | 2060 | Allinson(pen), Osborne | 1 | 12 | 11 | 8* | 3 | 2 | 4 |  |  |  |  |  | 7 | 10 | 9 |  |  |  | 5 | 6 |
| 31 | 12 | HALIFAX | 1-1 | 2464 | Bremner | 1 | 12 | 11 | 8 | 3 | 2 | 7* |  |  |  |  |  | 4 | 10 | 9 |  |  |  | 5 | 6 |
| 32 | 16 | MANSFIELD | 0-1 | 2000 |  | 1 | 7 | 11 | 8 | 3 | 2 |  |  |  |  | 4 |  |  | 10 | 9 |  |  |  | 5 | 6 |
| 33 | 20 | Wigan | 2-3 | 6747 | Bremner, Osborne | 1 |  | 11 | 8 | 3 | 2 | 7 |  |  |  | 4 | 12 |  |  | 9 | 10* |  |  | 5 | 6 |
| 34 | 22 | Stockport | 0-0 | 1740 |  | 1 |  | 11 | 8 | 3 | 2 | 7 |  |  |  | 4 | 10 |  |  | 9 |  |  |  | 5 | 6 |
| 35 | 26 | HULL | 2-0 | 2193 | Bremner, Coleman | 1 | 7* | 12 | 8 | 3 | 2 | 10 |  |  |  | 4 | 11 |  |  | 9 |  |  |  | 5 | 6 |
| 36 | 30 | CREWE | 1-1 | 1904 | Allinson | 1 |  | 11 | 8 | 3 | 2 | 7 |  |  |  | 4 | 10 |  |  | 9 |  |  |  | 5 | 6 |
| 37 | 2 Apr | Scunthorpe | 1-2 | 1762 | Bremner | 1 | 7 | 11 | 8 | 3 | 2 |  |  |  |  | 4 |  |  | 10 | 9 |  |  |  | 5 | 6 |
| 38 | 10 | BOURNEMOUTH | 1-2 | 2662 | Allinson | 1 | 7 | 11 | 8 |  | 2 |  |  | 10 |  | 4 | 3* | 12 |  | 9 | 6 |  |  | 5 |  |
| 39 | 13 | Peterborough | 2-2 | 5402 | Allinson, McDonough | 1 |  | 11 | 8 | 3 | 2 |  |  | 7* |  | 12 |  | 4 | 10 | 9 | 6 |  |  | 5 |  |
| 40 | 17 | Blaackpool | 0-0 | 2298 |  | 1 |  | 11 | 8 | 3 | 2 |  |  | 7 |  | 12 |  | 4 | 10 | 9* | 6 |  |  | 5 |  |
| 41 | 24 | DARLINGTON | 1-0 | 1764 | Bremner | 1 | 12 | 11* | 8 |  | 2 |  |  | 9 |  | 4 |  | 7 | 10 |  | 6 |  | 3 | 5 |  |
| 42 | 27 | PETERBOROUGH | 1-1 | 2212 | Bremner | 1 | 11 |  | 8 |  | 2 |  |  | 9 |  | 4 |  | 7* | 10 |  | 6 |  | 12 | 5 | 3 |
| 43 | 1 May | Bury | 3-4 | 1720 | Bremner, Lyons, McDonough | 1 | 11 |  | 8 | 12 | 2 |  |  | 9 |  | 4 |  | 7* | 10 |  | 6 |  |  | 5 | 3 |
| 44 | 3 | PORT VALE | 1-0 | 1470 | McDonough | 1 | 11 |  | 8 |  | 2 |  |  | 9 |  |  |  | 7 | 10 |  | 6 |  | 3 | 5 | 4 |
| 45 | 7 | STOCKPORT | 0-1 | 2132 |  | 1 | 11 |  | 8 | 12 | 2 |  |  | 9 |  |  |  | 7 | 10 |  | 6 |  | 3 | 5* | 4 |
| 46 | 15 | Crewe | 3-1 | 1226 | Allinson, Bremner, McDonough | 1 | 11 | 4 | 8 |  | 2 |  |  | 9 | 3 |  |  | 7 | 10 |  | 6 |  | 12 | 5 |  |

## F.A.Cup

| | | | | | | | | | | | | | | | | | | | | | | | | | |
|---|---|---|---|---|---|---|---|---|---|---|---|---|---|---|---|---|---|---|---|---|---|---|---|---|---|
| 1st | 21 Nov | NEWPORT | 2-0 | 3535 | Adcock, Leslie | 1 | 7 | 11 | 8 | 3 | 2 | | | | | 12 | | | 10* | 9 | | 4 | | 5 | 6 |
| 2nd | 16 Dec | Brentford | 1-1 | 5550 | Allinson | 1 | | 11 | 8 | 3 | 2 | | | | | 4 | | | 10 | 9 | | 7 | | 5 | 6 |
| 2nd\r | 30 | BRENTFORD | 1-0 | 5532 | No Scorer listed | 1 | | 11 | 8 | 3 | 2 | | | | | 4 | | | 10 | 9 | | 7 | | 5 | 6 |
| 3rd | 4 Jan | Newcastle | 1-1 | 16977 | Wignall | 1 | 12 | 11 | 8 | 3* | 2 | | | | | 4 | | | 10 | 9 | | 7 | | 5 | 6 |
| 3rd\r | 18 | NEWCASTLE | 3-4 | 7505 | Allinson(2,1pen), Cook | 1 | 7 | 11 | 8 | 12 | 2 | | | | | 4* | | | 10 | 9 | | 3 | | 5 | 6 |

## Football League Cup

| | | | | | | | | | | | | | | | | | | | | | | | | | |
|---|---|---|---|---|---|---|---|---|---|---|---|---|---|---|---|---|---|---|---|---|---|---|---|---|---|
| 1st\1l | 1 Sep | GILLINGHAM | 2-0 | 2431 | Allinson(pen), Bremner | 1 | 7 | 11 | 8 | 12 | 2 | | | | | 4 | 9 | | 10 | | 3* | | | 5 | 6 |
| 1st\2l | 15 Sep | Gillingham | 1-1 | 3260 | Bremner | 1 | 7 | 11 | 8 | 3 | 2 | | | | | 4 | | | 10 | 9 | | | | 5 | 6 |
| 2nd\1 | 6 Oct | CAMBRIDGE | 3-1 | 3844 | Cook, McDonough(2) | 1 | 7 | 11 | 8 | 3 | 2 | | | | | 4 | | | 10 | 9 | | | | 5 | 6 |
| 2nd\2 | 27 | Cambridge | 2-3 | 4672 | Allinson, Bremner | 1 | 7* | 11 | 8 | 3 | 2 | | | | | 4 | 12 | | 10 | 9 | | | | 5 | 6 |
| 3rd | 10 Nov | Tranmere | 0-1 | 2505 | | 1 | 12 | 11 | 8 | 3 | 2 | | | | | 4* | | | 10 | 9 | | 7 | | 5 | 6 |

(Players Left to Right)
(Top) Wignall, Longhorn
(Btm.) Leslie, Bremner

### FOURTH DIVISION

| | | P | W | D | L | F | A | Pts |
|---|---|---|---|---|---|---|---|---|
| 1 | Sheff United | 46 | 27 | 15 | 4 | 94 | 41 | 96 |
| 2 | Bradford | 46 | 26 | 13 | 7 | 88 | 45 | 91 |
| 3 | Wigan | 46 | 26 | 13 | 7 | 80 | 46 | 91 |
| 4 | Bournemouth | 46 | 23 | 19 | 4 | 62 | 30 | 88 |
| 5 | Peterborough | 46 | 24 | 10 | 12 | 71 | 57 | 82 |
| 6 | Colchester | 46 | 20 | 12 | 14 | 82 | 57 | 72 |
| 7 | Port Vale | 46 | 18 | 16 | 12 | 56 | 49 | 70 |
| 8 | Hull | 46 | 19 | 12 | 15 | 70 | 61 | 69 |
| 9 | Bury | 46 | 17 | 17 | 12 | 80 | 59 | 68 |
| 10 | Hereford | 46 | 16 | 19 | 11 | 64 | 58 | 67 |
| 11 | Tranmere | 46 | 14 | 18 | 14 | 51 | 56 | 60 |
| 12 | Blackpool | 46 | 15 | 13 | 18 | 66 | 60 | 58 |
| 13 | Darlington | 46 | 15 | 13 | 18 | 61 | 62 | 58 |
| 14 | Hartlepool | 46 | 13 | 16 | 17 | 73 | 84 | 55 |
| 15 | Torquay | 46 | 14 | 13 | 19 | 47 | 59 | 55 |
| 16 | Aldershot | 46 | 13 | 15 | 18 | 57 | 68 | 54 |
| 17 | York | 46 | 14 | 8 | 24 | 69 | 91 | 50 |
| 18 | Stockport | 46 | 12 | 13 | 21 | 48 | 67 | 49 |
| 19 | Halifax | 46 | 9 | 22 | 15 | 51 | 72 | 49 |
| 20 | Mansfield* | 46 | 13 | 10 | 23 | 63 | 81 | 47 |
| 21 | Rochdale | 46 | 10 | 16 | 20 | 50 | 62 | 46 |
| 22 | Northampton | 46 | 11 | 9 | 26 | 57 | 84 | 42 |
| 23 | Scunthorpe | 46 | 9 | 15 | 22 | 43 | 79 | 42 |
| 24 | Crewe | 46 | 6 | 9 | 31 | 29 | 84 | 27 |

* Two points deducted by League.

# SEASON 1982-83 Division Four

| No. | Date | Opposition | Res | Attend | Goalscorers | Chamberlain | Walker | Adcock | Allinson | Beattie | Bowman | Bremner | Coleman | Cook | Groves | Hull | Munter | Keith | Leslie | Linford | Longhorn | Lyons | McDonough | Osborne | Packer | Ward | Wignall |
|---|---|---|---|---|---|---|---|---|---|---|---|---|---|---|---|---|---|---|---|---|---|---|---|---|---|---|---|
| 1 | 28 Aug | HALIFAX | 1-0 | 2610 | McDonough | | 1 | | 7 | | | 12 | 3 | 2 | 4 | | 6 | | 11 | | | 9 | 10* | 8 | | | 5 |
| 2 | 4 Sep | Hereford | 0-0 | 2465 | | | 1 | | 7 | | | | 3 | 2 | 4 | | 6 | | 11 | | | 9 | 10 | 8 | | | 5 |
| 3 | 6 | Port Vale | 0-0 | 2877 | | | 1 | | 7 | | | | 3 | 2 | 4 | | 6 | | 11 | | | 9 | 10 | 8 | | | 5 |
| 4 | 10 | ROCHDALE | 4-1 | 2638 | Allinson(pen), Lyons(2), Wignall | | 1 | | 7 | | | 12 | 3 | 2 | 4 | | 6 | | 11 | | | 9 | 10* | 8 | | | 5 |
| 5 | 17 | Crewe | 1-0 | 2539 | Lyons | | 1 | | 7 | | | 12 | 3 | 2 | 4 | | 6 | | 11 | | | 9 | 10* | 8 | | | 5 |
| 6 | 25 | BLACKPOOL | 4-1 | 2918 | Allinson, Groves, Leslie, Lyons | | 1 | | 7 | 12 | | 10 | 3 | 2 | 4 | | 6* | | 11 | | | 9 | | 8 | | | 5 |
| 7 | 28 | HULL | 0-0 | 2071 | | | 1 | | 7 | | | 10 | 3 | 2 | 4* | | 6 | | 11 | | | 9 | 12 | 8 | | | 5 |
| 8 | 2 Oct | Scunthorpe | 1-2 | 2616 | | | 1 | | 7 | | | 10 | 3 | 2 | 4 | | 6 | | 11* | | | 9 | 12 | 8 | | | 5 |
| 9 | 10 | Swindon | 0-3 | 4473 | Osborne | | 1 | 4 | 7* | 6 | | | 3 | 2 | | | 12 | | 11 | | | 9 | 10 | 8 | | | 5 |
| 10 | 15 | DARLINGTON | 2-2 | 2547 | Allinson, McDonough | | 1 | 4 | 7 | 6* | | | 3 | 2 | | | | | 11 | | 12 | 9 | 10 | 8 | | | 5 |
| 11 | 19 | Northampton | 1-2 | 1955 | Allinson | | 1 | | 7 | 6 | | | 3 | 2 | | | 4 | | 11 | | | 9 | 10 | 8 | | | 5 |
| 12 | 30 | Bury | 0-1 | 2653 | | | 1 | | 7 | | | | 3 | 2 | | | 6 | | 11 | | 4 | 9 | 10 | 8 | | | 5 |
| 13 | 2 Nov | WIMBLEDON | 3-0 | 2219 | Allinson, McDonough(2) | | 1 | | 7 | | | | 3 | 2 | | | 6 | | 11 | | 4 | 9 | 10 | 8 | | | 5 |
| 14 | 5 | MANSFIELD | 2-0 | 2009 | Lyons | | 1 | | 7 | | | 12 | 3 | 2 | | | 6 | | 11 | | 4 | 9 | 10* | 8 | | | 5 |
| 15 | 9 | CHESTER | 1-0 | 2362 | Wignall | | 1 | | 7 | | | 12 | 3 | 2 | | | 6 | | 11* | | 4 | 9 | 10 | 8 | | | 5 |
| 16 | 13 | Tranmere | 4-2 | 1410 | Adcock, Allinson(2), McDonough | | 1 | 12 | 7 | | | 10 | 3 | 2 | | | 6 | | 11 | | 4 | | 9* | 8 | | | 5 |
| 17 | 27 | Bristol C. | 2-0 | 4310 | Allinson, Bremner | | 1 | 12 | 7 | | | 10 | 3* | | | | 6 | | 11 | | 4 | | 9 | 8 | | 2 | 5 |
| 18 | 3 Dec | YORK | 0-0 | 2204 | | | 1 | | 7 | | | 10 | | 2 | | | 6 | | 11 | | 4 | | 9 | 8 | | 3 | 5 |
| 19 | 11 | Hull | 0-3 | 4323 | | | 1 | 12 | 7 | | | 10 | | 2 | | | 6 | | 11* | | 4 | | 9 | 8 | | 3 | 5 |
| 20 | 17 | STOCKPORT | 3-0 | 1625 | Allinson(2), McDonough | | 1 | | 7 | | | 10 | | 2 | | 6 | | | 11 | | 4 | | 9 | 8 | 5 | 3 | |
| 21 | 27 | Peterborough | 1-2 | 4335 | Bremner | | 1 | | 7 | | | 10 | | 2 | | 6 | | | 11 | | 4 | | 9 | 8 | 5 | 3 | |
| 22 | 28 | ALDERSHOT | 0-0 | 2463 | | | 1 | 12 | 7 | | | 10 | | 2 | | 11* | | | | | 4 | | 9 | 8 | 6 | 3 | 5 |
| 23 | 1 Jan | Torquay | 0-2 | 2758 | | | 1 | 10 | 7 | | | | | 2 | | 11 | | 6 | | | | | 9 | 8 | 4 | 3 | 5 |
| 24 | 3 | HARTLEPOOL | 4-1 | 2249 | Adcock(2), Allinson, Wignall | 1 | | 10 | 7* | | | | | 2 | 12 | 11 | | 6 | | | 4 | | 9 | 8 | | 3 | 5 |
| 25 | 7 | HEREFORD | 3-2 | 2236 | Adcock, Allinson(2)(1 pen) | 1 | | 10 | 7 | | | | | 2 | | 11 | | 6 | | | 4 | | 9 | 8 | | 3 | 5 |
| 26 | 14 | Halifax | 0-4 | 1862 | | 1 | | 10 | 7 | | | | 6 | 2 | | 11 | | | | 9 | 4 | | | 8 | | 3 | 5 |
| 27 | 21 | CREWE | 4-3 | 2221 | Adcock(3), Allinson(pen) | | 1 | 10 | 7 | | | | 6 | | | 11 | | 3 | | 9 | 4 | | | 8 | | 2 | 5 |
| 28 | 5 Feb | Blackpool | 2-1 | 1747 | Adcock, Hull | | 1 | 10 | 7 | | | | 6 | | | 11 | | | | 9 | | | 4 | 8 | 2 | 3 | 5 |
| 29 | 15 | Wimbledon | 1-2 | 1753 | Adcock | | 1 | 10 | 7 | | | | 6 | 2 | | 11 | | | | 9 | | | 4 | 8 | 3 | | 5 |
| 30 | 18 | SWINDON | 1-0 | 2386 | Cook | | 1 | 10 | 7 | | | | 6 | 2 | | 11 | | | | 9 | 3 | | 4 | 8 | | | 5 |
| 31 | 26 | Darlington | 3-1 | 1089 | Adcock(2), McDonough | | 1 | 10 | 7 | | | | 6 | 2 | | 11 | | | | 9 | 3 | | 4 | | | | 5 |
| 32 | 1 Mar | NORTHAMPTON | 3-1 | 2501 | Adcock, Allinson(pen), Hull | | 1 | 10 | 7 | | | | 6 | 2 | | 11 | | | 8 | 9 | 3 | | 4 | 8 | | | 5 |
| 33 | 5 | Chester | 1-1 | 1136 | Adcock | | 1 | 10 | 7 | | | | 6 | 2 | | 11 | | | 12 | | 3 | | 4 | 8* | | 9 | 5 |
| 34 | 12 | BURY | 2-1 | 3359 | Allinson, Bowen | | 1 | 10 | 7 | | 9 | | 6 | 2 | | 11 | | | | | 3 | | 4 | 8 | | | 5 |
| 35 | 19 | Mansfield | 1-1 | 2371 | Hull | | 1 | 10 | 7* | | 9 | | 6 | 2 | 12 | 11 | | | | | 3 | | 4 | 8 | | | 5 |
| 36 | 25 | TRANMERE | 3-3 | 2547 | Adcock, Bowen, Osborne | | 1 | 10 | 7 | | 9 | | 6 | 2 | | 11 | | | 12 | | 3 | | 4 | 8* | | | 5 |
| 37 | 1 Apr | PETERBOROUGH | 1-0 | 3759 | Allinson | | 1 | 10* | 7 | | 9 | | 6 | 2 | 12 | 11 | | | | | 3 | | 4 | 8 | | | 5 |
| 38 | 2 | Aldershot | 1-0 | 1670 | Hull | | 1 | 10 | 7* | | 9 | | 6 | 2 | | 11 | | | 12 | | 3 | | 4 | 8 | | | 5 |
| 39 | 9 | York | 0-3 | 2538 | | | 1 | 10 | 7 | | 9 | | 6 | 2 | 12 | 11 | | | | | 3* | | 4 | 8 | | | 5 |
| 40 | 12 | PORT VALE | 1-2 | 3275 | Adcock | | 1 | 10 | 7 | | 9 | | 6 | 2 | 12 | 11 | | | | | 3* | | | 8 | 4 | | 5 |
| 41 | 15 | SCUNTHORPE | 5-1 | 3155 | Adcock(pen), Allinson(2)(1pen), | | 1 | 10 | 7 | | 9 | | 6 | 2 | | 11 | | | 4 | | | | | 8 | 3 | | 5 |
| 42 | 22 | Stockport | 0-3 | 1730 | | | 1 | 10 | 7 | | 9 | | 6 | 2 | 12 | 11 | | | | | 4* | | 3 | 8 | | | 5 |
| 43 | 26 | Rochdale | 1-2 | 1219 | Allinson | | 1 | 10* | 7 | | 9 | | 6 | 2 | 12 | 11 | | | | | | | 4 | 8 | 3 | | 5 |
| 44 | 29 | BRISTOL C. | 3-1 | 2196 | Allinson(pen), Bowen, McDonough | | 1 | 10* | 7 | | 9 | | 6 | 2 | | 11 | | | 4 | | | | 12 | 8 | 3 | | 5 |
| 45 | 2 Mar | Hartlepool | 4-1 | 804 | Allinson, Coleman(2), Groves | | 1 | 10 | 7 | | 9 | | 6 | | 12 | 11* | | | 4 | | | | 2 | 8 | 3 | | 5 |
| 46 | 13 | TORQUAY | 1-0 | 2181 | Wignall | 1 | | 10 | 7 | | 9 | | | | 12 | 11* | | | 4 | | | | 6 | 8 | 3 | 2 | 5 |

## F.A.Cup

| | | | | | | | | | | | | | | | | | | | | | | | | | | | |
|---|---|---|---|---|---|---|---|---|---|---|---|---|---|---|---|---|---|---|---|---|---|---|---|---|---|---|---|
| 1st | 20 Nov | TORQUAY | 0-2 | 2913 | | | 1 | | 7 | | | 10 | 3 | | | | 6 | | 11 | | 4 | | 9 | 8 | | 2 | 5 |

## Milk (Football League) Cup

| | | | | | | | | | | | | | | | | | | | | | | | | | | | |
|---|---|---|---|---|---|---|---|---|---|---|---|---|---|---|---|---|---|---|---|---|---|---|---|---|---|---|---|
| 1st\1l | 31 Aug | ALDERSHOT | 2-0 | 1665 | Groves, Wignall | | 1 | | 7 | | | | 3 | 2 | 4 | | 6 | | 11 | | | 9 | 10 | 8 | | | 5 |
| 1st\2 | 14 Sep | Aldershot | 1-0 | 1680 | Allinson | | 1 | | 7 | | | | 3 | 2 | 4 | | 6 | | 11 | | | 9 | 10 | 8 | | | 5 |
| 2nd\1 | 6 Oct | SOUTHAMPTON | 0-0 | 7967 | | | 1 | 4 | 7 | 6 | | | 3 | 2 | | | | | 11 | | | 9 | 10 | 8 | | | 5 |
| 2nd\2 | 26 | Southampton | 2-4 | 9676 | Allinson(pen), Lyons | | 1 | | 7 | | | | 3 | 2 | | | 4 | | 11 | | | 9 | 10 | 8 | | 6 | 5 |

(Back) Beattie, Coleman, McDonough, Chamberlain, Walker, Longhorn, Wignall, Lyons.
(Middle) Hunter (Coach), Bremner, Allinson, Hadleigh, Adcock, Lea (Manager), Simpson (Physio)
(Front) Packer, Osborne, Cook, Leslie, Ward, Groves

### FOURTH DIVISION

| | | P | W | D | L | F | A | Pts |
|---|---|---|---|---|---|---|---|---|
| 1 | Wimbledon | 46 | 29 | 11 | 6 | 96 | 45 | 98 |
| 2 | Hull | 46 | 25 | 15 | 6 | 75 | 34 | 90 |
| 3 | Port Vale | 46 | 26 | 10 | 10 | 67 | 34 | 88 |
| 4 | Scunthorpe | 46 | 23 | 14 | 9 | 71 | 42 | 83 |
| 5 | Bury | 46 | 24 | 12 | 11 | 76 | 44 | 81 |
| 6 | Colchester | 46 | 24 | 9 | 13 | 75 | 55 | 81 |
| 7 | York | 46 | 22 | 13 | 11 | 88 | 58 | 79 |
| 8 | Swindon | 46 | 19 | 11 | 16 | 61 | 54 | 68 |
| 9 | Peterborough | 46 | 17 | 13 | 16 | 58 | 52 | 64 |
| 10 | Mansfield | 46 | 16 | 13 | 17 | 61 | 70 | 61 |
| 11 | Halifax | 46 | 16 | 12 | 18 | 59 | 66 | 60 |
| 12 | Torquay | 46 | 17 | 7 | 22 | 56 | 65 | 58 |
| 13 | Chester | 46 | 15 | 11 | 20 | 55 | 60 | 56 |
| 14 | Bristol City | 46 | 13 | 17 | 16 | 59 | 70 | 56 |
| 15 | Northampton | 46 | 14 | 12 | 20 | 67 | 75 | 54 |
| 16 | Stockport | 46 | 14 | 12 | 20 | 60 | 79 | 54 |
| 17 | Darlington | 46 | 13 | 13 | 20 | 61 | 71 | 52 |
| 18 | Aldershot | 46 | 12 | 15 | 19 | 61 | 82 | 51 |
| 19 | Tranmere | 46 | 13 | 11 | 22 | 49 | 71 | 50 |
| 20 | Rochdale | 46 | 11 | 16 | 19 | 55 | 73 | 49 |
| 21 | Blackpool | 46 | 13 | 12 | 21 | 55 | 74 | 49 |
| 22 | Hartlepool | 46 | 13 | 9 | 24 | 46 | 76 | 48 |
| 23 | Crewe | 46 | 11 | 8 | 27 | 53 | 71 | 41 |
| 24 | Hereford | 46 | 11 | 8 | 27 | 43 | 79 | 41 |

# SEASON 83–84 Division Four

| No. | Date | Opposition | Res | Attend | Goalscorers | Chamberlain | Adcock | Bowen | Coleman | Cook | Farrell | Groves | Hadley | Hedman | Houston | Hubbick | Hull | Leslie | Mutrie | Nichols | Oldfield | Osborne | Phillips | Taylor | Wignall |
|---|---|---|---|---|---|---|---|---|---|---|---|---|---|---|---|---|---|---|---|---|---|---|---|---|---|
| 1 | 27 Aug | Darlington | 2-0 | 1411 | Adcock, Houston | 1 | 10 | 9 | | 2 | 3 | 7 | 4 | | 6 | | 11 | | | | | 8 | | | 5 |
| 2 | 3 Sep | BLACKPOOL | 2-1 | 2169 | Adcock | 1 | 10 | 9 | | 2 | 3 | 7* | 4 | | 6 | | 11 | | | | 12 | 8 | | | 5 |
| 3 | 6 | BRISTOL C | 0-0 | 2120 | | 1 | 10 | 9 | | 2 | 3 | 7 | 4 | | 6 | | 11 | | | | | 8 | | | 5 |
| 4 | 9 | Stockport | 0-0 | 2077 | | 1 | 10 | 9 | | 2 | | 7 | 4 | | 6 | | 11 | | | | | 8 | 3 | | 5 |
| 5 | 17 | ROCHDALE | 4-0 | 1955 | Adcock(2), Bowen, Wignall | 1 | 10 | 9 | | 2 | | 7 | 4 | | 6 | | 11* | | | | 12 | 8 | 3 | | 5 |
| 6 | 24 | Chesterfield | 1-1 | 4106 | Wignall | 1 | 10 | 9 | | 2 | | 7 | 4 | | 6 | | 11 | | | | | 8 | 3 | | 5 |
| 7 | 26 | Tranmere | 1-2 | 1886 | Adcock(pen) | 1 | 10 | 9 | | 2 | | 7* | 4 | | 6 | | 11 | | | | 12 | 8 | 3 | | 5 |
| 8 | 1 Oct | CHESTER | 1-0 | 1976 | Adcock | 1 | 10 | 9 | | 2 | | 7 | 4 | | 6 | | 11 | 5 | | | | 8 | 3 | | |
| 9 | 7 | York | 0-3 | 6207 | | 1 | 10 | 9 | | 2 | | 7 | 4 | | 6 | | 11 | 5 | | | | 8 | 3 | | |
| 10 | 15 | NORTHAMPTON | 2-2 | 1964 | Cook, Houston | 1 | 10 | 9 | | 2 | | 7* | 4 | | 6 | 12 | 11 | 5 | | | | 8 | 3 | | |
| 11 | 18 | BURY | 1-0 | 1969 | Adcock | 1 | 10 | 9 | | 2 | | 7* | 4 | | | | 11 | 6 | | 12 | | 8 | 3 | | 5 |
| 12 | 22 | Swindon | 1-2 | 2079 | Adcock(pen) | 1 | 10 | 9 | | 2 | | 7 | 4 | | | | 11 | 6 | | 12 | | 8 | 3 | | 5* |
| 13 | 29 | CREWE | 2-0 | 3402 | Adcock(2)(1 pen) | 1 | 10 | 9 | | 2 | | 7 | 4 | | 6 | 12 | 11* | | | 5 | | 8 | 3 | | |
| 14 | 1 Nov | Doncaster | 3-3 | 3491 | Adcock(pen), Bowen, O.G. | 1 | 10 | 9 | | | 2 | 7* | 4 | | 6 | 12 | | 11 | | 5 | | 8 | 3 | | |
| 15 | 5 | READING | 3-0 | 2433 | Adcock, Houston, Hull | 1 | 10 | 9 | | 2 | | 12 | 4 | | 6 | 7 | | 11 | | | | 8* | 3 | | 5 |
| 16 | 12 | Mansfield | 0-0 | 3042 | | 1 | 10 | 9 | | 2 | 8 | | 4 | | 6 | 7 | | 11 | | | | | 3 | | 5 |
| 17 | 26 | Torquay | 1-2 | 1365 | Cook | 1 | 10 | 9 | | 2 | 8 | | 4 | | 6 | 7 | | 11 | | | | | 3 | | 5 |
| 18 | 3 Dec | HARTLEPOOL | 6-0 | 1935 | Groves, Nichols, Osborne(2), Wignall(2) | 1 | 10 | 9 | | 2 | | 7 | | | 6 | | | 11 | | 4 | | 8 | 3 | | 5 |
| 19 | 17 | HALIFAX | 4-1 | 1866 | Adcock, Bowen(2), Houston | 1 | 10* | 9 | | 2 | | 7 | 4 | | 6 | 12 | | 11 | | | | 8 | 3 | | 5 |
| 20 | 26 | Peterborough | 0-2 | 6527 | | 1 | 10 | 9 | | 2 | | 7* | 4 | | 6 | 12 | | 11 | | | | 8 | 3 | | 5 |
| 21 | 27 | ALDERSHOT | 4-1 | 3123 | Adcock(2)(1 pen), Bowen, Wignall | 1 | 10 | 9 | | 2 | | 7 | 4 | | 6 | | | 11 | | | | 8 | 3 | | 5 |
| | 31 | Hereford * | 0-1 | | * (Abandoned) | 1 | 10 | 9 | | | 2 | 7* | 4 | | 6 | 12 | | 11 | | | | 8 | 3 | | 5 |
| 22 | 2 Jan | WREXHAM | 1-1 | 3182 | Adcock | 1 | 10 | 9 | | | 2 | 7 | 4 | | 6 | 12 | | | | 11* | | 8 | 3 | | 5 |
| 23 | 14 | DARLINGTON | 2-1 | 2151 | Adcock(2,1pen) | 1 | 10 | 9 | | 2 | | 7* | 4 | | 6 | 12 | | 11 | | | | 8 | 3 | | 5 |
| 24 | 28 | STOCKPORT | 1-1 | 2213 | Adcock | 1 | 10 | 9 | | 2 | 5 | 12 | 4 | | 6 | | 8 | 11 | 7* | | | | 3 | | |
| 25 | 4 Feb | Chester | 4-1 | 1179 | Bowen(2), Mutrie, Phillips | 1 | 10* | 9 | | 2 | | 12 | 4 | | 6 | | 8 | 11 | 7 | | | | 3 | | 5 |
| 26 | 11 | CHESTERFIELD | 2-0 | 2358 | Adcock, Wignall | 1 | 10 | 9 | | 2 | | 7 | 4 | | 6 | | 8 | 11 | | | | | 3 | | 5 |
| 27 | 14 | DONCASTER | 1-1 | 2821 | Bowen | 1 | 10 | 9 | | 2 | | 7 | 4 | | 6 | | 8 | 11 | | | | | 3 | | 5 |
| 28 | 18 | Crewe | 1-1 | 2532 | Bowen | 1 | 10* | 9 | | 2 | | | 4 | | 6 | | 8 | 11 | 7 | | | 12 | 3 | | 5 |
| 29 | 25 | SWINDON | 0-0 | 2448 | | 1 | 10 | 9 | | 2 | | 12 | 4 | | 6 | | 8 | 11 | 7* | | | | 3 | | 5 |
| 30 | 3 Mar | Bury | 1-1 | 1576 | Adcock(pen) | 1 | 10* | 9 | | 2 | | | 4 | 12 | 6 | | 8 | 11 | 7 | | | | 3 | | 5 |
| 31 | 7 | Reading | 0-1 | 3360 | | 1 | | 9* | | 2 | | 7 | 4 | | 6 | | 8 | 11 | 10 | | | 12 | 3 | | 5 |
| 32 | 10 | MANSFIELD | 1-0 | 2007 | Bowen | 1 | | 9 | | 2 | | 7 | 4 | | 6 | | 8 | | 10 | | | 11 | 3 | | 5 |
| 33 | 17 | YORK | 1-3 | 3032 | Bowen | 1 | 10* | 9 | | 2 | | 7 | 4 | | 6 | | | 11 | 12 | | | 8 | 3 | | 5 |
| 34 | 24 | Northampton | 1-3 | 1494 | Phillips | 1 | 12 | 9 | 5 | 2 | | 7 | 4* | | 6 | | | 11 | 10 | | | 8 | 3 | | |
| 35 | 31 | Bristol C | 1-4 | 6504 | Wignall | 1 | 10 | 9 | | 2 | | 7 | 12 | 4 | 6 | | | 11 | | | | 8 | 3* | | 5 |
| 36 | 4 Apr | Hereford | 1-1 | 2501 | Wignall | 1 | | 9 | | 2 | | 7 | 11 | 4 | 6 | | 8 | | 10 | | | | 3 | | 5 |
| 37 | 7 | TRANMERE | 0-1 | 1679 | | 1 | 12 | 9 | | 2 | | 7* | 11 | 4 | 6 | | 8 | | 10 | | | | 3 | | 5 |
| 38 | 14 | Hartlepool | 0-0 | 1001 | | 1 | 10 | 9 | 5 | 2 | | 7 | 4 | | 6 | | 11 | | | | | 8 | 3 | | |
| 39 | 17 | Rochdale | 0-0 | 1020 | | 1 | 10 | 9 | 2 | | | 7 | 4 | | 6 | | 11 | | | | | 8 | 3 | | 5 |
| 40 | 21 | PETERBOROUGH | 1-1 | 1746 | Adcock | 1 | 10 | 9 | 2 | | 6 | 7 | 4 | | | | 11 | | | | | 8 | 3 | | 5 |
| 41 | 23 | Aldershot | 1-5 | 2446 | Adcock | 1 | 10 | 9 | 2 | | 6 | 7 | 4 | | | | 11 | | 12 | | | 8* | 3 | | 5 |
| 42 | 28 | TORQUAY | 3-0 | 1226 | Adcock, Phillips(pen), O.G. | 1 | 10 | 9 | 2 | | 5 | 7* | 4 | | 6 | | 11 | | 12 | | | 8 | 3 | | |
| 43 | 1 May | Blackpool | 2-3 | 3111 | Adcock, Hull | 1 | 10 | 9 | 2 | | 5 | 7 | 4 | | 6 | | 11 | | | | | 8 | 3 | | |
| 44 | 5 | Wrexham | 2-0 | 1016 | Groves, Osborne | 1 | 10 | 9 | 12 | | 4 | 7* | 2 | | 6 | | 11 | | | | | 8 | 3 | | 5 |
| 45 | 7 | HEREFORD | 3-0 | 1286 | Adcock, Bowen, O.G. | 1 | 10 | 9 | | | 4 | 7 | 2 | | 6 | | 11 | | | | | 8 | 3 | | 5 |
| 46 | 11 | Halifax | 1-4 | 1284 | Mutrie | 1 | 10 | 9 | | | 4 | 7* | 2 | | 6 | | 11 | | 12 | | | 8 | 3 | | 5 |

## F.A.Cup

| | | | | | | | | | | | | | | | | | | | | | | | | | | |
|---|---|---|---|---|---|---|---|---|---|---|---|---|---|---|---|---|---|---|---|---|---|---|---|---|---|---|
| 1 | 19 Nov | Torquay | 2-1 | 2126 | Bowen(2) | 1 | 10 | 9 | | 2 | | | 4 | | 6 | 7 | | 11 | | | | 8 | 3 | | 5 |
| 2 | 10 Dec | WEALDSTONE | 4-0 | 2673 | Bowen(3), Houston | 1 | 10 | 9 | | 2 | | 7 | 4 | | 6 | | | 11 | | | | 8 | 3 | | 5 |
| 3 | 7 Jan | CHARLTON | 0-1 | 6296 | | 1 | 10 | 9 | | | 2* | 7 | 4 | | 6 | 12 | | 11 | | | | 8 | 3 | | 5 |

## Milk (Football League) Cup

| | | | | | | | | | | | | | | | | | | | | | | | | | |
|---|---|---|---|---|---|---|---|---|---|---|---|---|---|---|---|---|---|---|---|---|---|---|---|---|---|
| 1/1 | 30 Aug | READING | 3-2 | 2418 | Adcock(2), Wignall | 1 | 10 | 9 | | 2 | 3 | 7 | 4 | | 6 | | 11 | | | | | 8 | | | 5 |
| 1/2 | 14 Sep | Reading | 3-4 | 3460 | Adcock, Bowen, Wignall | 1 | 10 | 9 | | 2 | 3 | 7* | 4 | | 6 | | 11 | | | | | 8 | | 12 | 5 |
| 2/1 | 4 Oct | Swansea | 1-1 | 3758 | Adcock | 1 | 10 | 9 | | 2 | 3 | 7 | 4 | | 6 | | 11 | 8 | | | | | | | 5 |
| 2/2 | 25 | SWANSEA | 1-0 | 5204 | Adcock | 1 | 10 | | | 2 | 3 | 7 | 4 | | 6 | 9 | 11 | | | 5 | | 8 | | | |
| 3 | 8 Nov | MAN UTD | 0-2 | 13031 | | 1 | 10 | 9 | | 6 | 3 | 12 | 4 | | 6 | 11* | | 7 | | | | 8 | | | 5 |

## Associate Members Cup

| | | | | | | | | | | | | | | | | | | | | | | | | | |
|---|---|---|---|---|---|---|---|---|---|---|---|---|---|---|---|---|---|---|---|---|---|---|---|---|---|
| 1 | 21 Feb | WIMBLEDON | 2-1 | 1888 | Adcock(2)(1 pen) | 1 | 10 | 9 | | 2 | | | 4 | | 6 | | 8 | 11 | 7* | | 12 | | 3 | | 5 |
| 2 | 13 Mar | SOUTHEND | 0-2 | 2841 | | 1 | 10 | 9 | 6* | 2 | | 7 | 4 | | | | 8 | 13 | 12 | | | 11 | 3 | | 5 |

Players (L. to R.)
Top - Bowen, Hull
Btm. - Osborne, Adcock

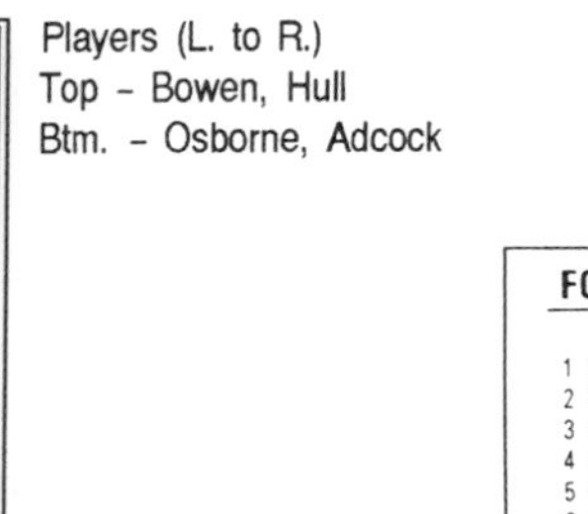

### FOURTH DIVISION

| | | P | W | D | L | F | A | Pts |
|---|---|---|---|---|---|---|---|---|
| 1 | York | 46 | 31 | 8 | 7 | 96 | 39 | 101 |
| 2 | Doncaster | 46 | 24 | 13 | 9 | 82 | 54 | 85 |
| 3 | Reading | 46 | 22 | 16 | 8 | 84 | 56 | 82 |
| 4 | Bristol City | 46 | 24 | 10 | 12 | 70 | 44 | 82 |
| 5 | Aldershot | 46 | 22 | 9 | 15 | 76 | 69 | 75 |
| 6 | Blackpool | 46 | 21 | 9 | 16 | 70 | 52 | 72 |
| 7 | Peterborough | 46 | 18 | 14 | 14 | 72 | 48 | 68 |
| 8 | Colchester | 46 | 17 | 16 | 13 | 69 | 53 | 67 |
| 9 | Torquay | 46 | 18 | 13 | 15 | 59 | 64 | 67 |
| 10 | Tranmere | 46 | 17 | 15 | 14 | 53 | 53 | 66 |
| 11 | Hereford | 46 | 16 | 15 | 15 | 54 | 53 | 63 |
| 12 | Stockport | 46 | 17 | 11 | 18 | 60 | 64 | 62 |
| 13 | Chesterfield | 46 | 15 | 15 | 16 | 59 | 61 | 60 |
| 14 | Darlington | 46 | 17 | 8 | 21 | 49 | 50 | 59 |
| 15 | Bury | 46 | 15 | 14 | 17 | 61 | 64 | 59 |
| 16 | Crewe | 46 | 16 | 11 | 19 | 56 | 57 | 59 |
| 17 | Swindon | 46 | 15 | 13 | 18 | 58 | 56 | 58 |
| 18 | Northampton | 46 | 13 | 14 | 19 | 53 | 78 | 53 |
| 19 | Mansfield | 46 | 13 | 13 | 20 | 66 | 70 | 52 |
| 20 | Wrexham | 46 | 11 | 15 | 20 | 59 | 74 | 48 |
| 21 | Halifax | 46 | 12 | 12 | 22 | 55 | 89 | 45 |
| 22 | Rochdale | 46 | 11 | 13 | 22 | 52 | 80 | 46 |
| 23 | Hartlepool | 46 | 10 | 10 | 26 | 47 | 85 | 40 |
| 24 | Chester | 46 | 7 | 13 | 26 | 45 | 82 | 34 |

# SEASON 84-85 Division Four

| No. | Date | Opposition | Res | Attend | Goalscorers | Chamberlain | Adcock | Bowman | Burman | Day | English A. | English T. | Farrell | Godbold | Groves | Hedman | Houston | Hubbick | Hull | Irving | Osborne | Parkinson | Phillips | Shinners | Youngman |
|---|---|---|---|---|---|---|---|---|---|---|---|---|---|---|---|---|---|---|---|---|---|---|---|---|---|
| 1 | 25 Aug | SOUTHEND | 3-3 | 2378 | Adcock(3) | 1 | 10* | 9 | | 5 | | | 4 | 2 | 7 | | 6 | | 1 | 12 | 8 | | 3 | | |
| 2 | 31 | Scunthorpe | 2-2 | 1818 | Adcock, Bowen | 1 | 10 | 9 | | 5 | | | 4 | 2 | 7 | | 6 | | 11 | | 8 | 12 | 3 | | |
| 3 | 8 Sep | BLACKPOOL | 1-1 | 1772 | Adcock | 1 | 10 | 9 | | | | | 4 | 2* | 7 | | 6 | | 11 | 8 | 12 | 5 | 3 | | |
| 4 | 15 | Bury | 3-4 | 2145 | Adcock, Houston, Hull | 1 | 10 | 9 | | 5 | | | 2 | | 7 | | 6 | | 11 | 12 | 8 | 4 | 3 | | |
| 5 | 19 | Mansfield | 1-0 | 2084 | Bowen | 1 | 10 | 9 | | 5 | | | 2 | | 7* | | 6 | | 11 | 12 | 8 | 4 | 3 | | |
| 6 | 22 | ALDERSHOT | 2-0 | 1641 | Adcock(2) | 1 | 10 | 9 | | 5 | | | 2 | | 7 | | 6 | | 11 | 12 | 8 | 4 | 3 | | |
| 7 | 29 | Northampton | 3-1 | 1595 | Adcock, Bowen, Parkinson | 1 | 10 | 9 | | 5 | | | 2 | 12 | 7 | | 6 | | 11 | | 8 | 4 | 3 | | |
| 8 | 2 Oct | TORQUAY | 2-1 | 1813 | Bowen, Hull | 1 | 10 | 9 | | 5 | | | 2 | | 7 | | 6 | | 11 | 12 | 8 | 4 | 3 | | |
| 9 | 13 | Darlington | 0-4 | 2021 | | 1 | 10* | 9 | | 5 | | | 2 | | 7 | | 6 | | 11 | 12 | 8 | 4 | 3 | | |
| 10 | 16 | EXETER | 3-4 | 1846 | Adcock, Groves, Hull | 1 | 10 | 9 | | 5 | | | 2* | | 7 | | 6 | | 11 | 12 | 8 | 4 | 3 | | |
| 11 | 20 | Chester | 2-1 | 1400 | Adcock(2) | 1 | 10* | 9 | | 5 | | | 2 | | 7 | | 6 | | 11 | 12 | 8 | 4 | 3 | | |
| 12 | 23 | STOCKPORT | 3-0 | 2153 | Groves, Hull(2) | 1 | 10 | 9 | | 5* | | | 2 | | 7 | | 6 | | 11 | 12 | 8 | 4 | 3 | | |
| 13 | 26 | HALIFAX | 1-3 | 2295 | Adcock | 1 | 10 | 9 | | 5 | | | 2 | | 7 | | 6 | | 11 | 12 | 8* | 4 | 3 | | |
| 14 | 3 Nov | Chesterfield | 1-1 | 3614 | Adcock | 1 | 10 | 9* | | 5 | | | 2 | 12 | | | 6 | | 11 | 7 | 8 | 4 | 3 | | |
| 15 | 6 | Tranmere | 1-3 | 1587 | Godbold | 1 | 10 | | | 5 | | | 2 | 12 | | 9 | 6 | | 11 | 7* | 8 | 4 | 3 | | |
| 16 | 9 | HARTLEPOOL | 1-0 | 2136 | Adcock | 1 | 10 | | | 5 | | | 2 | | 7 | 12 | 6 | | 11 | 9* | 8 | 4 | 3 | | |
| 17 | 24 | Rochdale | 1-1 | 1012 | Groves | 1 | 10 | | | 5 | | | 2 | 8 | 7 | 12 | 6 | | 11 | 9 | | 4 | 3 | | |
| 18 | 1 Dec | PETERBOROUGH | 3-1 | 2070 | Adcock, Groves, Irving | 1 | 10 | 12 | | 5 | | | 2 | | 7 | | 6 | | 11 | 9* | 8 | 4 | 3 | | |
| 19 | 15 | Swindon | 1-2 | 2263 | Adcock | 1 | 10 | 11 | 12 | 5 | | | 2 | | 7 | 6 | | | | 9 | 8 | 4 | 3 | | |
| 20 | 21 | Crewe | 4-1 | 1529 | Adcock, Bowen(2), Groves | 1 | 10 | 9 | | 5 | | | 2 | 12 | 7 | 6 | | | | 11 | 8 | 4 | 3 | | |
| 21 | 26 | HEREFORD | 2-2 | 2525 | Adcock, Bowen | 1 | 10 | 9 | 12 | 5 | | | 2 | | 7 | 6 | | | | 11 | 8 | 4 | 3 | | |
| 22 | 28 | PORT VALE | 3-2 | 2014 | Bowen(2,1pen), Groves | 1 | 10 | 9 | 12 | 5 | | | 2 | | 7 | 6 | | | | 11 | 8 | 4 | 3 | | |
| 23 | 1 Jan | Wrexham | 2-2 | 1376 | Irving, Phillips | 1 | 10 | 9 | | 5 | 12 | | 2 | | 7 | 6 | | | | 11 | 8 | 4 | 3 | | |
| 24 | 26 | BURY | 1-0 | 2028 | Osborne | 1 | 10 | 9 | | 5 | | | 2* | | 7 | 6 | 12 | | | 11 | 8 | 4 | 3 | | |
| 25 | 29 | Southend | 5-2 | 2401 | Adcock, Bowen(2), Groves(2) | 1 | 10 | 9 | | 5 | 12 | | | | 7 | 2 | 6 | | | 11 | 8 | 4 | 3* | | |
| 26 | 1 Feb | NORTHAMPTON | 4-1 | 2314 | Adcock, Day, Hedman, Parkinson(pen) | 1 | 10 | | | 5 | 11* | | 12 | | 7 | 2 | 6 | | | 9 | 8 | 4 | 3 | | |
| 27 | 22 | CHESTERFIELD | 3-1 | 2303 | Adcock(3) | 1 | 10 | 9 | | 5 | 12 | | | | 7 | 2 | 6 | | | 11 | 8* | 4 | 3 | | |
| 28 | 26 | MANSFIELD | 2-1 | 2267 | Day, Groves | 1 | | 9 | | 5 | 11 | | | | 7 | 2 | 6 | | 12 | 10 | 8 | 4 | 3 | | |
| 29 | 1 Mar | Halifax | 0-0 | 1022 | | 1 | | 9 | 12 | 5 | 11 | | | | 7 | 2 | 6 | | | 10 | 8 | 4 | 3 | | |
| 30 | 4 | Stockport | 0-1 | 1561 | | 1 | | 9 | | 5 | 11 | | 12 | | 7 | 2 | 6 | | | 10 | 8 | 4 | 3 | | |
| 31 | 8 | CHESTER | 1-1 | 2224 | Irving | 1 | | 9 | 12 | 5 | 11 | | 6 | | 7 | 2 | | | | 10 | 8 | 4 | 3 | | |
| 32 | 15 | DARLINGTON | 1-2 | 1739 | Irving | 1 | | 9 | 12 | 5 | 11 | | 6 | | 7 | 2 | | | | 10 | 8 | 4 | 3 | | |
| 33 | 23 | Exeter | 5-1 | 1825 | Bowen(2), Irving(2), Parkinson | 1 | | 9 | | 5 | 11 | | 12 | | 7 | 2 | 6 | | | 10 | 8 | 4 | 3* | | |
| 34 | 26 | Blackpool | 1-1 | 4057 | English | 1 | | 9 | | 5 | 11 | | 12 | | 7 | 2 | 6 | | | 10 | 8 | 4 | 3 | | |
| 35 | 29 | TRANMERE | 2-1 | 2044 | Day, English | 1 | | 9 | 8 | 5 | 11 | | 12 | | 7 | 2 | 6 | | | 10 | | 4 | 3* | | |
| 36 | 2 Apr | SCUNTHORPE | 1-1 | 2409 | Day | 1 | | 9 | 12 | 5 | 11 | | 3 | | 7 | 2 | 6* | | | 10 | 8 | 4 | | | |
| 37 | 6 | Hereford | 1-2 | 3485 | Bowen(pen) | 1 | | 9 | 11* | 5 | 3 | | 2 | | 7 | 6 | | 12 | | 10 | 8 | 4 | | | |
| 38 | 8 | WREXHAM | 4-1 | 2204 | Bowen, Hubbick, Irving(2) | 1 | | 9 | 11* | 5 | 3 | | 2 | | 7 | 6 | | 12 | | 10 | 8 | 4 | | | |
| 39 | 13 | Hartlepool | 1-2 | 1512 | Parkinson | 1 | | 9 | 11 | 5 | 3 | | 2* | | 7 | 6 | | 12 | | 10 | 8 | 4 | | | |
| 40 | 16 | Torquay | 1-1 | 1191 | Bowen | 1 | | 9 | 11 | 5 | 3 | | 2 | | 7 | 6 | | 12 | | 10 | | 4 | | 8 | |
| 41 | 19 | ROCHDALE | 1-1 | 1858 | Parkinson | 1 | | 9 | 11 | 5 | 3 | | 2 | | 7 | 6 | | 12 | | 10 | | 4 | | 8* | |
| 42 | 23 | Aldershot | 0-1 | 1624 | | 1 | | 9 | 11 | 5 | 3 | | 2 | | 7 | 6 | | 8* | | 10 | | 4 | | | 12 |
| 43 | 27 | Peterborough | 1-0 | 1500 | Hedman | 1 | | 9 | 11 | 5 | 3 | | 2 | | 7 | 6 | | | | 10 | 12 | 4 | | 8 | |
| 44 | 3 May | SWINDON | 1-1 | 1867 | English | 1 | | 9 | 12 | 5 | 2 | | | | 7 | 6 | | | | 10 | 8 | 4 | 3 | 11 | |
| 45 | 6 | Port Vale | 2-3 | 2526 | Groves, Shinners | 1 | | 9 | 12 | 5 | 2 | | | | 7 | 6 | | | | 10 | 8 | 4 | 3 | 11 | |
| 46 | 10 | CREWE | 4-1 | 1864 | Bowen, Hull, Osborne, Parkinson | 1 | 12 | 9 | | 5 | 2 | | 3 | | 7 | 6* | | | | 11 | 8 | 4 | | 10 | |

## F.A.Cup

| | | | | | | | | | | | | | | | | | | | | | | | | | |
|---|---|---|---|---|---|---|---|---|---|---|---|---|---|---|---|---|---|---|---|---|---|---|---|---|---|
| 1st | 17 Nov | Southend | 2-2 | 2935 | Houston, Irving | 1 | 10 | | | 5 | | | 2 | | 7 | 12 | 6 | | 11 | 9* | 8 | 4 | 3 | | |
| 1st\r | 21 | SOUTHEND | 3-2 | 3907 | Adcock, Groves, O.G. | 1 | 10 | | | 5 | | | 2 | 8* | 7 | 12 | 6 | | 11 | 9 | | 4 | 3 | | |
| 2nd | 8 Dec | GILLINGHAM | 0-5 | 4487 | | 1 | 10 | 12 | | 5 | | | 2* | | 7 | 6 | | | 11 | 9 | 8 | 4 | 3 | | |

## Milk (Football League) Cup

| | | | | | | | | | | | | | | | | | | | | | | | | | |
|---|---|---|---|---|---|---|---|---|---|---|---|---|---|---|---|---|---|---|---|---|---|---|---|---|---|
| 1st\1 | 28 Aug | Gillingham | 2-3 | 2689 | Bowen, Houston | 1 | 10 | 9 | | 5 | | | 4 | 2 | 7 | | 6 | | 11* | | 8 | 12 | 3 | | |
| 1st\2 | 4 Sep | GILLINGHAM | 0-2 | 2162 | | 1 | 10 | 9 | | 5 | | | 4* | 2 | 7 | | 6 | | 11 | 12 | 8 | | 3 | | |

## Associate Members Cup (Freight Rover Trophy)

| | | | | | | | | | | | | | | | | | | | | | | | | | |
|---|---|---|---|---|---|---|---|---|---|---|---|---|---|---|---|---|---|---|---|---|---|---|---|---|---|
| 1st\1 | 23 Jan | Gillingham | 2-2 | 962 | Adcock, Groves | 1 | 10 | 9 | | 5 | 12 | | 2* | | 7 | 6 | 13 | | | 11 | 8 | 4 | 3 | | |
| 1st\2 | 5 Feb | GILLINGHAM | 2-0 | 1762 | Adcock(2) | 1 | 10* | | | | 11 | 12 | 5 | | 7* | 2 | 6 | | 13 | 9 | 8 | 4 | 3 | | |
| 2nd | 13 Mar | Walsall | 0-1 | 4108 | | 1 | | 9 | | 5 | 11 | | 6 | | 7 | 2 | | | | 10 | 8 | 4 | 3 | | |

Back Row: Steve Allen, Noel Parkinson, Perry Groves, Alec Chamberlain, David Gadsdon, Rudi Hedman, Andy Farrell, Tony Adcock.
2nd Row: C. Watson (Dev. Sec.), Ken Curtis (Dev. Man.), Mike Walker, Roger Osborne, Russell Irving, Stewart Houston, Keith Bowen, Michael Whytock, Simon Burman, Cyril Lea (Manager), Tony Willoughby (Sporting U's Promoter), Dee Elwood (Admin. Ass.).
3rd Row: John Schultz (Director), Ron West (Director), Sir Antony Buck Q.C. M.P. (Club Patron), Maurice Cadman (Chairman), Harry Piper (Vice-Chairman), Nigel Fitch (Director), Martin Bennet (Club Sec.), Tony Coker (Accountant), Eddie Keegan (Commercial Consultant).
Front Row: Ian Phillips, Jeff Hull, Stuart Youngman, Robin Reid, Alex Chappell.

### FOURTH DIVISION

| | | P | W | D | L | F | A | Pts |
|---|---|---|---|---|---|---|---|---|
| 1 | Chesterfield | 46 | 26 | 13 | 7 | 64 | 35 | 91 |
| 2 | Blackpool | 46 | 24 | 14 | 8 | 73 | 39 | 86 |
| 3 | Darlington | 46 | 24 | 13 | 9 | 66 | 49 | 85 |
| 4 | Bury | 46 | 24 | 12 | 10 | 76 | 50 | 84 |
| 5 | Hereford | 46 | 22 | 11 | 13 | 65 | 47 | 77 |
| 6 | Tranmere | 46 | 24 | 3 | 19 | 83 | 66 | 75 |
| 7 | Colchester | 46 | 20 | 14 | 12 | 87 | 65 | 74 |
| 8 | Swindon | 46 | 21 | 9 | 16 | 62 | 58 | 72 |
| 9 | Scunthorpe | 46 | 19 | 14 | 13 | 83 | 62 | 71 |
| 10 | Crewe | 46 | 18 | 12 | 16 | 65 | 69 | 66 |
| 11 | Peterborough | 46 | 16 | 14 | 16 | 54 | 53 | 62 |
| 12 | Port Vale | 46 | 14 | 18 | 14 | 61 | 59 | 60 |
| 13 | Aldershot | 46 | 17 | 8 | 21 | 56 | 63 | 59 |
| 14 | Mansfield | 46 | 13 | 18 | 15 | 41 | 38 | 57 |
| 15 | Wrexham | 46 | 15 | 9 | 22 | 67 | 70 | 54 |
| 16 | Chester | 46 | 15 | 9 | 22 | 60 | 72 | 54 |
| 17 | Rochdale | 46 | 13 | 14 | 19 | 55 | 69 | 53 |
| 18 | Exeter | 46 | 13 | 14 | 19 | 57 | 79 | 53 |
| 19 | Hartlepool | 46 | 14 | 10 | 22 | 54 | 67 | 52 |
| 20 | Southend | 46 | 13 | 11 | 22 | 58 | 83 | 50 |
| 21 | Halifax | 46 | 14 | 5 | 26 | 42 | 69 | 50 |
| 22 | Stockport | 46 | 13 | 9 | 25 | 58 | 79 | 47 |
| 23 | Northampton | 46 | 14 | 5 | 27 | 53 | 74 | 47 |
| 24 | Torquay | 46 | 9 | 14 | 23 | 38 | 63 | 41 |

# SEASON 1985/86 Division Four

| No. | Date | Opposition | Res | Attend | Goalscorers |
|---|---|---|---|---|---|
| 1 | 17 Aug | STOCKPORT | 3–1 | 1719 | Osborne, Day, Adcock |
| 2 | 24 | Wrexham | 1–2 | 2298 | Reeves |
| 3 | 27 | ALDERSHOT | 4–0 | 1928 | A.English, Adcock, Groves, Hedman |
| 4 | 31 | Torquay | 1–2 | 1023 | Adcock |
| 5 | 6 Sep | HALIFAX | 3–1 | 2023 | Adcock(2), Bowen |
| 6 | 14 | Tranmere | 4–3 | 1362 | A.English, Groves, Parkinson, Day |
| 7 | 17 | CAMBRIDGE U. | 4–1 | 2574 | Adock(3), Groves |
| 8 | 21 | Orient | 2–1 | 2577 | Parkinson, Bowen |
| 9 | 27 | PORT VALE | 1–0 | 3110 | Bowen |
| 10 | 1 Oct | Burnley | 2–0 | 3375 | Adcock, Bowen |
| 11 | 4 | EXETER | 1–1 | 3927 | Day |
| 12 | 12 | Mansfield | 1–2 | 3364 | A.English |
| 13 | 18 | SCUNTHORPE | 1–1 | 3462 | Reeves |
| 14 | 22 | Southebd | 4–2 | 8120 | Bowen, Groves(3) |
| 15 | 26 | NORTHAMPTON | 0–2 | 2872 | |
| 16 | 2 Nov | Hereford | 0–2 | 3081 | |
| 17 | 6 | Chester | 0–4 | 2809 | |
| 18 | 8 | ROCHDALE | 0–1 | 2624 | |
| 19 | 23 | Preston | 2–3 | 2793 | Parkinson, Adcock |
| 20 | 14 Dec | Hartlepool | 1–4 | 2507 | Hedman |
| 21 | 20 | WREXHAM | 5–2 | 1683 | Adcock(2), Groves, Hedman, O.G. |
| 22 | 28 | Aldershot | 1–1 | 1757 | Day |
| 23 | 1 Jan | Swindon | 1–2 | 8802 | Parkinson |
| 24 | 3 | HEREFORD | 4–1 | 2214 | Parkinson(2), T.English, Phillips |
| 25 | 11 | TORQUAY | 0–0 | 2063 | |
| 26 | 17 | Stockport | 1–1 | 2366 | Groves |
| 27 | 24 | TRANMERE | 1–2 | 2013 | Parkinson |
| 28 | 31 | Halifax | 2–2 | 989 | Baker, Adcock |
| 29 | 4 Feb | SOUTHEND | 2–0 | 1915 | Adcock, O.G. |
| 30 | 1 Mar | Port Vale | 1–1 | 2726 | Groves |
| 31 | 8 | Exeter | 2–2 | 1520 | Adcock, Burman |
| 32 | 14 | MANSFIELD | 0–0 | 1956 | |
| 33 | 22 | Northampton | 0–1 | 2035 | |
| 34 | 25 | CREWE | 1–2 | 1356 | A.English |
| 35 | 28 | SWINDON | 1–1 | 2997 | A.English |
| 36 | 31 | Peterborough | 2–1 | 2316 | A.English, Baker |
| 37 | 4 Apr | CHESTER | 2–3 | 2281 | A.English(2) |
| 38 | 8 | ORIENT | 4–0 | 1771 | Ferguson, Phillips, Day, A.English |
| 39 | 12 | Rochdale | 3–3 | 1182 | Ferguson, Farrell, T.English |
| 40 | 15 | Scunthorpe | 1–1 | 1238 | Ferguson |
| 41 | 18 | PRESTON | 4–0 | 2046 | T.English(3), Ferguson |
| 42 | 22 | PETERBOROUGH | 5–0 | 1863 | Reeves, T.English, A.English(3) |
| 43 | 26 | Crewe | 2–0 | 1555 | Groves(2) |
| 44 | 29 | Cambridge | 3–1 | 3115 | Reeves, Ferguson(2) |
| 45 | 2 May | HARTLEPOOL | 3–1 | 2410 | Ferguson, T.English, A.English |
| 46 | 6 | BURNLEY | 2–2 | 2726 | Groves, T.English |

| No. | Chamberlain | Hedman | Phillips | Reeves | Day | Houston | Groves | Osborne | Bowen | Adcock | English A. | Irving | Parkinson | Farrell | Hull | Garne | Turner | English T. | Whymark | Burman | Baker | Ferguson |
|---|---|---|---|---|---|---|---|---|---|---|---|---|---|---|---|---|---|---|---|---|---|---|
| 1 | 1 | 2 | 3 | 4 | 5 | 6 | 7* | 8 | 9 | 10 | 11 | 12 | | | | | | | | | | |
| 2 | 1 | 2 | 3 | 4* | 5 | 6 | 7 | | 9 | 10 | 11 | 12 | 8 | | | | | | | | | |
| 3 | 1 | 2 | 3 | 4 | 5 | 6 | 7 | 12 | 9 | 10 | 11* | | 8 | | | | | | | | | |
| 4 | 1 | 2 | 3 | 4 | 5 | 6 | 7 | 12 | 9 | 10 | 11* | | 8 | | | | | | | | | |
| 5 | 1 | 6 | 3 | 4 | 5 | | 7 | | 9 | 10 | 11 | | 8 | 2 | | | | | | | | |
| 6 | 1 | 2 | 3 | 4 | 5 | 6 | 7 | | 9 | 10 | 11 | | 8 | | | | | | | | | |
| 7 | 1 | 2 | 3 | 4* | 5 | 6 | 7 | 12 | 9 | 10 | 11 | | 8 | | | | | | | | | |
| 8 | 1 | 2 | 3 | 4 | 5 | 6 | 7 | | 9 | 10 | 11 | | 8 | | | | | | | | | |
| 9 | 1 | 2 | 3 | 4 | 5 | 6 | 7* | | 9 | 10 | 11 | 12 | 8 | | | | | | | | | |
| 10 | 1 | 2 | 3 | 4 | 5* | 6 | | | 9 | 10 | 11 | 12 | 8 | | 7 | | | | | | | |
| 11 | 1 | 2 | 3 | 4 | 5 | 6 | 7 | | 9 | 10 | 2 | | 8 | | | | | | | | | |
| 12 | 1 | 2 | 3 | 4* | 5 | 6 | 7 | 12 | 9 | 10 | 2 | | 8 | | | | | | | | | |
| 13 | 1 | 2 | 3 | 4 | 5 | 6 | 7 | 12 | 9 | 10 | 2 | | 8* | | | | | | | | | |
| 14 | 1 | 2 | | 4 | 5* | 6 | 7 | | 9 | 10 | 11 | | 8 | 3 | 12 | | | | | | | |
| 15 | 1 | 5 | | 4 | | 6 | 7 | 12 | 9 | 10 | 11 | | 8 | 3 | 11* | | | | | | | |
| 16 | 1 | 5 | | 4 | | 6 | 7 | 9 | | 10 | 11 | 12 | 8 | 3* | 11 | | | | | | | |
| 17 | 1 | 5 | | 4 | | 6 | 7 | | | 10 | 11 | 9 | 8 | 3 | 11 | | | | | | | |
| 18 | 1 | 2 | | 4 | | 6 | 7 | | | 10 | 11 | | 8 | 3 | | 5 | 9* | 12 | | | | |
| 19 | 1 | 2 | | | 5 | 6 | 7 | | | 10 | 11 | | 8 | 3* | | 12 | 4 | | 9 | | | |
| 20 | 1 | 2 | | 4* | 5 | 6 | 7 | | | 10 | 11 | | 8 | | | 3 | | | 9 | 12 | | |
| 21 | 1 | 2 | | | 5 | 6 | 7 | 4 | | 10 | 11 | | 8 | 3 | | | | 12 | | 9* | | |
| 22 | 1 | 2 | 3 | | 5 | 6 | 7* | 4 | | 10 | 11 | | 8 | | | | | 12 | | 9 | | |
| 23 | 1 | 2 | 3 | | 5* | 6 | | 4 | | 10 | 11 | 12 | 8 | | | | | 9 | | 7 | | |
| 24 | 1 | 2 | 3 | | 5* | 6 | | 4 | | 10 | 11 | 12 | 8 | | | | | 9 | | 7 | | |
| 25 | 1 | 2 | 3 | | | 6 | 12 | 4 | | 10 | 11 | | 8 | | | | 7* | 9 | | | 5 | |
| 26 | 1 | 2 | 3 | | | 6 | 9 | 4 | | 10 | 11 | | 8 | | | | 7 | | | | 5 | |
| 27 | 1 | 2 | 3 | | | 6* | 9 | 4 | | 10 | 11 | | 8 | | | | 7 | 12 | | | 5 | |
| 28 | 1 | 2 | | | | | 9 | 4 | | 10 | 3 | 11 | 8 | | | 6 | | | | 7 | 5 | |
| 29 | 1 | 2 | 3 | | | 6 | 9 | 4 | | 10 | 11 | | 8 | | | | | | | 7 | 5 | |
| 30 | 1 | 2 | 3 | | | 6 | 9 | 4 | | 10 | 11 | | 8 | | | | 12 | | | 7* | 5 | |
| 31 | 1 | 2 | 3 | | | 6 | 9 | 4 | | 10 | 11 | | 8 | 11 | | | | 12 | | 7 | 5* | |
| 32 | 1 | 5 | 3 | | | 6 | 9 | 4 | | 10 | 11 | | 8 | 2 | | | | 12 | | 7* | | |
| 33 | 1 | | 3 | | | 6 | 9 | 4 | | 10* | 11 | | 8 | 2 | | | | 12 | | 7 | 5 | |
| 34 | 1 | 2 | 3 | | | 6 | 9 | 4 | | | 11 | | 8 | 7 | | | | 10 | | | 5 | |
| 35 | 1 | 2 | 3 | | | 6 | 9 | 4 | | | 11 | | 8 | 7 | | | | 10 | | | 5 | |
| 36 | 1 | 2 | 3 | | | 6 | 9 | 4 | | | 11 | | 8* | 7 | | | | 10 | | | 5 | 12 |
| 37 | 1 | | 3 | | 2 | 6 | 9 | 4 | | | 11 | | | 7 | | | | 10* | | | 5 | 8 |
| 38 | 1 | | 3 | | 2 | 6 | 7 | 4 | | | 11 | | | 8 | | | 12 | 10 | | | 5 | 9 |
| 39 | 1 | 2 | 3 | | 6 | | 7 | 4 | | | 11 | | | 8 | | | | 10 | | | 5 | 9 |
| 40 | 1 | 2 | 3 | | 6 | | 9 | 4* | | | 11 | | | 7 | | | 12 | 10 | | | 5 | 8 |
| 41 | 1 | 2 | 3 | | 6 | | 9 | 4 | | | 11 | | | 7 | | | 12 | 10 | | | 5 | 8* |
| 42 | 1 | 12 | 3 | 11 | 6 | | 9 | 4 | | | 2 | | | 7* | | | 8 | 10 | | | 5 | |
| 43 | 1 | | 3 | 11 | 6 | | 9 | 4 | | | 2 | | | 7 | | | | 10 | | | 5 | 8 |
| 44 | 1 | | 3 | 11 | 6 | | 9 | 4 | | | 2 | | | 7 | | | | 10 | | | 5 | 8 |
| 45 | 1 | | 3 | 11 | 6 | | 9 | 4 | | | 2 | | | 7 | | | | 10 | | | 5 | 8 |
| 46 | 1 | | 3 | 11* | 6 | | 9 | 4 | | | 2 | | | 7 | | | 12 | 10 | | | 5 | 8 |

# F.A.Cup

| | | | | | | | | | | | | | | | | | | | | | | | | | | | |
|---|---|---|---|---|---|---|---|---|---|---|---|---|---|---|---|---|---|---|---|---|---|---|---|---|---|---|---|
| 1st | 16 Nov | Wycombe W. | 0–2 | 3018 | | 1 | 2 | | 4 | | 6 | 7 | | | | 11 | | 8 | 3 | | 6 | 9 | 10 | | | | |

# Milk (League) Cup

| | | | | | | | | | | | | | | | | | | | | | | | | | | | |
|---|---|---|---|---|---|---|---|---|---|---|---|---|---|---|---|---|---|---|---|---|---|---|---|---|---|---|---|
| 1/1L | 21 Aug | MILLWALL | 2–3 | 1430 | Bowen(2) | 1 | 2 | 3 | 8 | 5 | 6 | 7 | 4 | 9 | 10 | 11 | | 12 | | | | | | | | | |
| 1/2L | 3 Sept | Millwall | 1–4 | 3330 | Bowen(pen) | 1 | 2 | 3 | 4 | 5 | 6 | | 12 | 9 | 10 | 11 | 7 | 8 | | | | | | | | | |

*Back row (left to right):* Paul Keaney, Keith Bowen, Alec Chamberlain, Keith Day, Tony English, Rudi Hedman, Andy Farrell, Tony Polito.
*Third row:* Kirk Game, Tony Adcock, Simon Burman, Perry Groves, Jeff Hull, Sean Norman, Brian Sawyer, John Reeves, Steve Allen (Trainee Physio).
*Second row:* Russell Irving, Roger Osborne, Mike Walker (Coach), Stewart Houston, Cyril Lea (Manager), Ian Phillips, Noel Parkinson, Charlie Simpson (Physiotherapist).
*Front row:* Scott Young, Mark Radford, Steve Turney, Andy Springett.

## FOURTH DIVISION

| | | P | W | D | L | F | A | Pts |
|---|---|---|---|---|---|---|---|---|
| 1 | Swindon | 46 | 32 | 6 | 8 | 82 | 43 | 102 |
| 2 | Chester | 46 | 23 | 15 | 8 | 83 | 50 | 84 |
| 3 | Mansfield | 46 | 23 | 12 | 11 | 74 | 47 | 81 |
| 4 | Port Vale | 46 | 21 | 16 | 9 | 67 | 37 | 79 |
| 5 | Orient | 46 | 20 | 12 | 14 | 79 | 64 | 72 |
| 6 | Colchester | 46 | 19 | 13 | 14 | 88 | 63 | 70 |
| 7 | Hartlepool | 46 | 20 | 10 | 16 | 68 | 67 | 70 |
| 8 | Northampton | 46 | 18 | 10 | 18 | 79 | 58 | 64 |
| 9 | Southend | 46 | 18 | 10 | 18 | 69 | 67 | 64 |
| 10 | Hereford | 46 | 18 | 10 | 18 | 74 | 73 | 64 |
| 11 | Stockport | 46 | 17 | 13 | 16 | 63 | 71 | 64 |
| 12 | Crewe | 46 | 18 | 9 | 19 | 54 | 61 | 63 |
| 13 | Wrexham | 46 | 17 | 9 | 20 | 68 | 80 | 60 |
| 14 | Burnley | 46 | 16 | 11 | 19 | 60 | 65 | 59 |
| 15 | Scunthorpe | 46 | 15 | 14 | 19 | 50 | 55 | 59 |
| 16 | Aldershot | 46 | 17 | 7 | 22 | 66 | 74 | 58 |
| 17 | Peterborough | 46 | 13 | 17 | 16 | 52 | 64 | 56 |
| 18 | Rochdale | 46 | 14 | 13 | 19 | 57 | 77 | 55 |
| 19 | Tranmere | 46 | 15 | 9 | 22 | 74 | 73 | 54 |
| 20 | Halifax | 46 | 14 | 12 | 20 | 60 | 71 | 54 |
| 21 | Exeter | 46 | 13 | 15 | 18 | 47 | 59 | 54 |
| 22 | Cambridge | 46 | 15 | 9 | 22 | 65 | 80 | 54 |
| 23 | Preston | 46 | 11 | 10 | 25 | 54 | 89 | 43 |
| 24 | Torquay | 46 | 9 | 10 | 27 | 43 | 88 | 37 |

# SEASON 1986/87 Division Four

| No. | Date | Opposition | Res | Attend | Goalscorers | Chamberlain | Game | Phillips | Hedman | Baker | Day | Burman | Ferguson | Adcock | Farrell | Reeves | Norman | English A. | Groves | English T. | Hinshelwood | Chatterton | Gorman | Grenfell | Wilkins | Lowe | White |
|---|---|---|---|---|---|---|---|---|---|---|---|---|---|---|---|---|---|---|---|---|---|---|---|---|---|---|---|
| 1 | 23 Aug | Lincoln | 1–3 | 2303 | Adcock | 1 | 2 | 3 | 4 | 5 | 6* | 7 | 8 | 9 | 10 | 11 | 12 | | | | | | | | | | |
| 2 | 29 | EXETER | 1–1 | 1633 | A.English | 1 | | 3 | 2 | 5 | 6 | | 8 | 10* | 7 | 11 | | 4 | 9 | 12 | | | | | | | |
| 3 | 5 Sep | Tranmere | 4–3 | 1281 | Reeves, Adcock, T.English(2) | 1 | 6 | 3 | 2 | 5 | | | 8 | 9 | 4 | 11 | | 7 | | 10 | | | | | | | |
| 4 | 12 | TORQUAY | 3–0 | 2476 | A.English(3) | 1 | 6 | | 3 | 5 | | | 9 | 7 | 12 | 11 | | 8 | | 10* | 2 | 4 | | | | | |
| 5 | 16 | HARTLEPOOL | 2–1 | 2326 | Adcock(2) | 1 | 6 | | 3 | 5 | | | 9 | 7 | 10 | 11 | | 8 | | | 2 | 4 | | | | | |
| 6 | 20 | Rochdale | 0–1 | 1240 | | 1 | 6 | | 3 | 5 | | 12 | 9 | 7 | 10* | 11 | | 8 | | | 2 | 4 | | | | | |
| 7 | 27 | PETERBOROUGH | 1–3 | 2343 | Day | 1 | 6 | | 3 | 5 | 8 | 12 | 9* | | 7 | 11 | | 10 | | | 2 | 4 | | | | | |
| 8 | 1 Oct | Hereford | 3–2 | 2144 | Burman, Hedman, Ferguson | 1 | 5 | 3 | 10 | | 6 | 7 | 9 | | | 11 | | 8 | | | 2 | 4 | | | | | |
| 9 | 3 | WREXHAM | 2–1 | 2633 | Ferguson, O.G. | 1 | 6 | 3 | 10 | | 5 | 7 | 9 | | 11 | | | 8 | | | 2 | 4* | 12 | | | | |
| 10 | 10 | Southend | 1–1 | 4004 | Hedman | 1 | 6 | 3 | 10 | | 5 | 7 | 9 | | 4 | 11 | | 8 | | | 2 | | | | | | |
| 11 | 17 | CARDIFF | 3–1 | 3160 | Reeves, A.English, Burman | 1 | 6 | 3 | 10 | | 5 | 7 | 9 | | 4 | 11 | | 8 | | | 2 | | | | | | |
| 12 | 21 | Crewe | 1–1 | 1812 | T.English | 1 | 6 | 3 | 10 | | 5 | 7 | 9 | | 4 | 11* | | 8 | | 12 | 2 | | | | | | |
| 13 | 24 | Stockport | 1–1 | 1278 | T.English | 1 | 6 | 3 | 11 | | 5 | 7 | 9 | | 4 | | | 8 | | 10 | 2 | | | | | | |
| 14 | 31 | WOLVERHAMPTON | 3–0 | 4741 | Ferguson, A.English O.G. | 1 | 6 | 3 | | | 5 | 7 | 9 | | 4 | | | 8 | | 10 | 2 | | | 11 | | | |
| 15 | 4 Nov | Burnley | 1–2 | 1692 | Ferguson | 1 | 6 | 3 | 12 | | 5 | 7* | 9 | | 4 | | | 8 | | 10 | 2 | | | 11 | | | |
| 16 | 7 | ORIENT | 0–0 | 3924 | | 1 | 6 | 3 | 12 | | 5 | 7* | 9 | | 4 | | | 8 | | 10 | 2 | | | 11 | | | |
| 17 | 21 | Scunthorpe | 2–5 | 1725 | Hedman, Grenfell | 1 | 6 | 3 | 9 | | 5 | | | 7 | | 11 | | 11 | | 10 | 2 | | | 4 | | | |
| 18 | 28 | HALIFAX | 3–1 | 2567 | Farrell, Adcock, Phillips | 1 | 6 | 3 | 9 | | 5 | | | 8 | 7 | | | 11 | | 10 | 2 | | | 4 | | | |
| 19 | 13 Dec | PRESTON N.E. | 0–2 | 2240 | | 1 | | 3 | 9* | 6 | 5 | | | 8 | 7 | | | 11 | | 12 | 2 | | | 4 | 10 | | |
| 20 | 20 | Swansea | 2–1 | 4515 | T.English, Farrell | 1 | | 3 | 12 | 6 | 5 | | | 8 | 7 | | | 11* | | 10 | 2 | | | 4 | | 9* | |
| 21 | 26 | CAMBRIDGE | 1–2 | 3376 | Lowe | 1 | | 3 | 12 | 6 | 5 | | | 8 | 7 | | | | | 10 | 2 | | | 4 | | 9 | |
| 22 | 27 | Aldershot | 0–1 | 2594 | | 1 | | 3 | 11 | 6 | 5 | | | 8 | 7 | | | | | 12 | 2 | | | 4* | 10 | 9 | |
| 23 | 1 Jan | Northampton | 2–3 | 8215 | Adcock (2) | 1 | | 3 | 2 | 6 | 5 | | | 8 | 7 | | 11 | | | 12 | 4 | | | | 10* | 9 | |
| 24 | 3 | SCUNTHORPE | 1–0 | 2100 | Adcock | 1 | 2 | | 3 | 6 | 5 | | | 8 | 7 | | 11 | | | | 4 | | | 10 | | 9 | |
| 25 | 10 | LINCOLN | 2–0 | 1768 | Farrell(2) | 1 | 2 | | 3 | 6 | 5 | | | 8 | 7 | | 11 | | | | 4 | | | 10 | | 9 | |
| 26 | 17 | Exeter | 0–2 | 2553 | | 1 | 2 | | 3 | 6 | 5 | | | 8 | 7 | | 11 | | | | 4 | | | 10 | | 9 | |
| 27 | 23 | TRANMERE | 1–1 | 2167 | Norman | 1 | 6 | 3 | 2 | | 5 | | | 8 | 7* | | 11 | | | | 4 | | | 10 | 12 | 9 | |
| 28 | 31 | Torquay | 1–3 | 1034 | Adcock | 1 | 6 | 3 | 2 | | 5 | | | 10 | 12 | | 11* | | | | 4 | | | 8 | 7 | 9 | |
| 29 | 6 Feb | Hartlepool | 0–1 | 1235 | | 1 | 6 | 3 | | | 5 | | | 8 | | | | 2 | | | 4 | 7 | | 10 | 11 | 9 | |
| 30 | 13 | ROCHDALE | 2–0 | 2020 | T.English, Wilkins | 1 | 6 | 3 | 12 | 5 | | | | 7* | | | | 2 | | 8 | | 4 | | 10 | 11 | 9 | |
| 31 | 21 | Peterborough | 0–2 | 3474 | | 1 | 5 | 3 | 12 | 6 | | | | 7 | | | | 2 | | 8 | | 4 | | 10* | 11 | 9 | |
| 32 | 27 | HEREFORD | 2–0 | 1999 | T.English, Phillips | 1 | | 3 | 5 | 6 | | | | 7 | | | | | | 8 | 2 | 4 | | 10 | 11 | 9 | |
| 33 | 3 Mar | Wolverhampton | 0–2 | 5715 | | 1 | | 3 | 5 | 6 | | | | 12 | | | | | | 8 | 2 | 4 | | 10 | 11 | 9 | 7* |
| 34 | 6 | STOCKPORT | 5–1 | 2001 | Lowe(3), T.English, Day | 1 | | 3 | 6 | | 5 | | | 12 | | | | | | 8* | 2 | 4 | | 10 | 11 | 9 | 7 |
| 35 | 14 | Cardiff | 2–0 | 2222 | Lowe(2) | 1 | | 3* | 6 | | 5 | | | 8 | 12 | | | | | | 2 | 4 | | 10 | 11 | 9 | 7 |
| 36 | 17 | CREWE | 2–1 | 2249 | Day, Lowe | 1 | | 3 | 6 | | 5 | | | 8 | | | | | | 12 | 2 | 4 | | 10 | 11* | 9 | 7 |
| 37 | 20 | SOUTHEND | 1–2 | 3357 | White | 1 | | 3 | 6 | | 5 | | | 8 | | | | | | | 2 | 4 | | 10 | 11 | 9 | 7 |
| 38 | 28 | Wrexham | 1–0 | 1320 | T.English | 1 | | 3 | 6 | | 5 | | | 8 | | | | 2 | | 9 | 10 | 4 | | 10 | 11 | | 7 |
| 39 | 3 Apr | Orient | 0–1 | 3105 | | 1 | | 3 | 6 | | 5 | | | 8 | | | | 2 | | 9* | 10 | 4 | | | 11 | 12 | 7 |
| 40 | 10 | BURNLEY | 1–0 | 2635 | Adcock | 1 | | 3 | 6 | | 5 | | | 8 | | | | 2 | | | 10 | 4 | | | 11 | 9 | 7 |
| 41 | 17 | NORTHAMPTON | 3–1 | 3676 | Wilkins, Chatterton, Hedman | 1 | | | 6 | | 5 | | | 8 | | | 3 | 2 | | | 10 | 4 | | | 11 | 9 | 7 |
| 42 | 21 | Cambridge U. | 1–0 | 2946 | A.English | 1 | | | 6 | | 5 | | | | | 4 | 3 | 2 | | 8 | 10 | | | | 11 | 9 | 7 |
| 43 | 24 | SWANSEA | 2–1 | 3323 | Hinshelwood, Adcock | 1 | | | 6 | | 5 | | | 8 | | 4 | 3 | 2 | | | 10 | | | | 11 | 9 | 7 |
| 44 | 29 | Halifax | 0–0 | 911 | | 1 | | | 6 | | 5 | | | 8 | | 4 | 3 | 2 | | | 10 | 12 | | | 11 | 9 | 7 |
| 45 | 4 May | ALDERSHOT | 0–1 | 4310 | | 1 | | | 6 | | 5 | | | 8 | | 12 | 3 | 2 | | | 10 | 4 | | | 11 | 9* | 7 |
| 46 | 9 | Preston N.E. | 0–1 | 8757 | | 1 | | | 6 | | 5 | | | 8 | 12 | 11* | 3 | 2 | | | 10 | | | | 4 | 9 | 7 |

# F.A.Cup

| | | | | | | | | | | | | | | | | | | | | | | | | | | | |
|---|---|---|---|---|---|---|---|---|---|---|---|---|---|---|---|---|---|---|---|---|---|---|---|---|---|---|---|
| 1st | 15 Nov | Bishop's Stort. | 1–1 | 2413 | T.English | 1 | 6 | 3 | 12 | | 5 | | 9* | 7 | 4 | | | 8 | | 10 | 2 | | | 11 | | | |
| 1/R | 17 | BISHOP'S STORT. | 2–0 | 3516 | T.English, Adcock | 1 | 6 | 3 | 9* | | 5 | | | 7 | 4* | 12 | | 8 | | 10 | 2 | | | 11 | 14 | | |
| 2 | 6 Dec | Aldershot | 2–3 | 2997 | T.English, Grenfell | 1 | 6 | 3 | 9* | | 5 | | 8 | 7 | | | | 11 | | 10 | 2 | | | 4 | 12 | | |

# Littlewoods (League) Cup

| | | | | | | | | | | | | | | | | | | | | | | | | | | | |
|---|---|---|---|---|---|---|---|---|---|---|---|---|---|---|---|---|---|---|---|---|---|---|---|---|---|---|---|
| 1 | 26 Aug | PETERBOROUGH | 0–0 | 1551 | | 1 | 6 | 3 | 2 | 5 | | 4 | 9 | 8 | 7 | 11 | 10 | | | | | | | | | | |
| 1/R | 3 Sept | Peterborough | 0–2 | 2698 | | 1 | 12 | 3 | 2 | 5 | 6* | 14 | 8* | 9 | 7 | 11 | | 4 | | 10 | | | | | | | |

• Nick Chatterton

• John Reeves

• Rudi Hedman

• Richard Wilkins

## FOURTH DIVISION

| | | P | W | D | L | F | A | Pts |
|---|---|---|---|---|---|---|---|---|
| 1 | Northampton | 46 | 30 | 9 | 7 | 103 | 53 | 99 |
| 2 | Preston | 46 | 26 | 12 | 8 | 72 | 47 | 90 |
| 3 | Southend | 46 | 25 | 5 | 16 | 68 | 55 | 80 |
| 4 | Wolves | 46 | 24 | 7 | 15 | 69 | 50 | 79 |
| 5 | Colchester | 46 | 21 | 7 | 18 | 64 | 56 | 70 |
| 6 | Aldershot | 46 | 20 | 10 | 16 | 64 | 57 | 70 |
| 7 | Orient | 46 | 20 | 9 | 17 | 64 | 61 | 69 |
| 8 | Scunthorpe | 46 | 18 | 12 | 16 | 73 | 57 | 66 |
| 9 | Wrexham | 46 | 15 | 20 | 11 | 70 | 51 | 65 |
| 10 | Peterborough | 46 | 17 | 14 | 15 | 57 | 50 | 65 |
| 11 | Cambridge | 46 | 17 | 11 | 18 | 60 | 62 | 62 |
| 12 | Swansea | 46 | 17 | 11 | 18 | 56 | 61 | 62 |
| 13 | Cardiff | 46 | 15 | 16 | 15 | 48 | 50 | 61 |
| 14 | Exeter | 46 | 11 | 23 | 12 | 53 | 49 | 56 |
| 15 | Halifax | 46 | 15 | 10 | 21 | 59 | 74 | 55 |
| 16 | Hereford | 46 | 14 | 11 | 21 | 60 | 61 | 53 |
| 17 | Crewe | 46 | 13 | 14 | 19 | 70 | 72 | 53 |
| 18 | Hartlepool | 46 | 11 | 18 | 17 | 44 | 65 | 51 |
| 19 | Stockport | 46 | 13 | 12 | 21 | 40 | 69 | 51 |
| 20 | Tranmere | 46 | 11 | 17 | 18 | 54 | 72 | 50 |
| 21 | Rochdale | 46 | 11 | 17 | 18 | 54 | 73 | 50 |
| 22 | Burnley | 46 | 12 | 13 | 21 | 53 | 74 | 49 |
| 23 | Torquay | 46 | 10 | 18 | 18 | 56 | 72 | 48 |
| 24 | Lincoln | 46 | 12 | 12 | 22 | 45 | 65 | 48 |

# SEASON 1987/88 Division Four

| No. | Date | Opposition | Res | Attend | Goalscorers |
|---|---|---|---|---|---|
| 1 | 15 Aug | Burnley | 3-0 | 5369 | Walsh, English, Lowe |
| 2 | 21 | TORQUAY | 0-1 | 1372 | |
| 3 | 29 | Scunthorpe | 2-2 | 2003 | Wilkins, White |
| 4 | 31 | SCARBOROUGH | 1-3 | 1525 | Tempest |
| 5 | 4 Sep | Crewe | 0-0 | 1843 | |
| 6 | 12 | PETERBOROUGH | 4-1 | 1164 | White, Tempest, Chatterton, Walsh |
| 7 | 16 | Hereford | 0-1 | 1951 | |
| 8 | 19 | Hartlepool | 1-3 | 1698 | Hinshelwood |
| 9 | 25 | EXETER | 0-2 | 1443 | |
| 10 | 29 | SWANSEA | 2-1 | 1140 | Tempest, Hinshelwood |
| 11 | 3 Oct | Newport | 2-1 | 1200 | Wilkins, Chatterton |
| 12 | 9 | LEYTON ORIENT | 0-0 | 1665 | |
| 13 | 17 | Wrexham | 1-0 | 1493 | Reeves |
| 14 | 20 | CARLISLE | 1-0 | 1328 | Tempest |
| 15 | 24 | Cambridge U. | 1-0 | 2450 | Chatterton |
| 16 | 30 | DARLINGTON | 2-1 | 1659 | Wilkins, Chatterton |
| 17 | 3 Nov | Rochdale | 4-1 | 1399 | Wilkins(2), Chatterton, Hinshelwood |
| 18 | 6 | Halifax | 2-1 | 1432 | Wilkins, Chatterton |
| 19 | 21 | WOLVERHAMPTON | 0-1 | 2413 | |
| 20 | 27 | Stockport | 1-1 | 1703 | Chatterton |
| 21 | 11 Dec | BOLTON | 3-0 | 1725 | Wilkins, White(2) |
| 22 | 18 | Tranmere | 2-0 | 2642 | White(2) |
| 23 | 26 | Exeter | 2-0 | 2675 | Wilkins, Tempest |
| 24 | 28 | CARDIFF | 2-1 | 2599 | Tempest, English |
| 25 | 1 Jan | SCUNTHORPE | 0-3 | 2287 | |
| 26 | 2 | Peterborough | 0-2 | 3665 | |
| 27 | 15 | HARTLEPOOL | 0-0 | 1768 | |
| 28 | 30 | Scarborough | 1-3 | 2155 | Hinshelwood |
| 29 | 5 Feb | CREWE | 1-4 | 1822 | Tempest |
| 30 | 13 | Cardiff | 0-1 | 5458 | |
| 31 | 19 | BURNLEY | 0-1 | 2520 | |
| 32 | 26 | NEWPORT | 0-0 | 1784 | |
| 33 | 1 Mar | Swansea | 2-1 | 4011 | Tempest, White |
| 34 | 4 | WREXHAM | 1-2 | 1797 | Coleman |
| 35 | 12 | Leyton Orient | 0-0 | 3125 | |
| 36 | 19 | Darlington | 0-2 | 2034 | |
| 37 | 25 | CAMBRIDGE U. | 0-0 | 2146 | |
| 38 | 1 Apr | HALIFAX | 2-1 | 1992 | Hinshelwood, Farrell |
| 39 | 4 | Wolverhampton | 0-2 | 13433 | |
| 40 | 8 | ROCHDALE | 1-0 | 1864 | Tempest |
| 41 | 15 | Torquay | 0-0 | 3508 | |
| 42 | 19 | HEREFORD | 1-0 | 1367 | Tempest |
| 43 | 23 | Carlisle | 0-4 | 1496 | |
| 44 | 29 | STOCKPORT | 2-0 | 1607 | Tempest, Wilkins |
| 45 | 2 May | Bolton | 0-4 | 5540 | |
| 46 | 6 | TRANMERE | 0-0 | 1704 | |

| No. | Benstead | Hinshelwood | Norman | Chatterton | Baker | Hedman | White | English | Walsh | Lowe | Wilkins | Reeves | Grenfell | Tempest | Radford | Hill | Smith | Walton | Williams | Angell | Keane | Ray | Keeley | Coleman | Hetzke | Forrest | Farrell | Hicks | Daniel | Hunter |
|---|---|---|---|---|---|---|---|---|---|---|---|---|---|---|---|---|---|---|---|---|---|---|---|---|---|---|---|---|---|---|
| 1 | 1 | 2 | 3 | 4 | 5 | 6 | 7 | 8 | 9 | 10 | 11 | | | | | | | | | | | | | | | | | | | |
| 2 | 1 | 2 | 3 | 4 | 5 | 6 | 7 | 8 | 9* | 10 | 11 | 12 | | | | | | | | | | | | | | | | | | |
| 3 | 1 | 2 | 3* | 4 | 5 | 6 | 7 | 8 | | 10 | 11 | | 12 | 9 | | | | | | | | | | | | | | | | |
| 4 | 1 | 2 | | 4 | 5 | 6 | 7 | 8 | | 10 | 11 | | 3 | 9 | | | | | | | | | | | | | | | | |
| 5 | 1 | 2* | 12 | 4 | | 6 | 7 | 5 | 14 | 10 | 8 | 11 | 3 | 9+ | | | | | | | | | | | | | | | | |
| 6 | 1 | 2 | | 4 | | 6 | 7 | 5 | 12 | 10* | 8 | | 3 | 9 | 11 | | | | | | | | | | | | | | | |
| 7 | 1 | 2 | | 4 | | 6 | 7 | 5 | 10 | | 8 | | 3 | 9 | 11 | | | | | | | | | | | | | | | |
| 8 | 1 | 2 | | 4 | | 6 | 7 | 5 | 10* | 12 | 8 | 11 | 3 | 9 | | | | | | | | | | | | | | | | |
| 9 | 1 | 2 | 14 | 4 | | 6 | 7* | 5 | 12 | 10+ | 8 | 11 | 3 | 9 | | | | | | | | | | | | | | | | |
| 10 | 1 | 2 | 10 | 4 | | 6 | 7 | 5 | | | 8 | 11 | 3 | 9 | | | | | | | | | | | | | | | | |
| 11 | 1 | 2 | 10 | 4 | 5 | 6 | 7 | | 12 | | 8* | 11 | 3 | 9 | | | | | | | | | | | | | | | | |
| 12 | 1 | 2 | 10 | 4 | 5 | 6 | 7 | | | | 8 | 11 | 3 | 9 | | | | | | | | | | | | | | | | |
| 13 | 1 | 2 | | 4 | 5 | 6 | 7 | 10 | | 12 | 8* | 11 | 3 | 9 | | | | | | | | | | | | | | | | |
| 14 | 1 | 2 | | 4 | 5 | 6 | 7 | 10 | | | 8 | 11 | 3 | 9 | | | | | | | | | | | | | | | | |
| 15 | 1 | 2 | | 4 | 5 | 6 | 7* | 10 | | 12 | 8 | 11 | 3 | 9 | | | | | | | | | | | | | | | | |
| 16 | 1 | 2 | | 4 | 5 | 6 | 7* | 10 | 12 | | 8 | 11+ | 3 | 9 | | 14 | | | | | | | | | | | | | | |
| 17 | 1 | 2 | | 4* | 5 | 6 | 7 | 10 | | | 8 | 11 | 3 | 9 | | 12 | | | | | | | | | | | | | | |
| 18 | 1 | 2 | | 4 | 5 | | 7 | 10 | | | 8 | 11 | 3 | 9 | | | 6 | | | | | | | | | | | | | |
| 19 | | 6 | | 4 | 5 | 2 | 7 | 10 | | | 8 | 11 | 3 | 9 | | | | 1 | | | | | | | | | | | | |
| 20 | | 6 | | 4 | 5 | 2 | 7* | 10 | 12 | | 8 | 11 | 3+ | 9 | | 14 | | 1 | | | | | | | | | | | | |
| 21 | | 2 | | 4 | | 3 | 7 | 10 | | | 8 | | 11 | 9 | | 5 | | 1 | 6 | | | | | | | | | | | |
| 22 | | 2 | | 4 | | 3 | 7 | 10 | | | 8 | | 12 | 9 | | 6 | | 1 | 11 | 5* | | | | | | | | | | |
| 23 | | 2 | | 4 | | 3 | 7 | 10 | | | 8 | | 11 | 9 | | 5 | | 1 | 6 | | | | | | | | | | | |
| 24 | | 2 | | 4 | | 3 | 7 | 10 | | | 8 | | 11 | 9 | | 5 | | 1 | 6 | | | | | | | | | | | |
| 25 | | 2 | | 4 | | 3 | 7 | 10 | | | 8 | | 11* | 9 | | 5 | | 1 | 6 | | 12 | | | | | | | | | |
| 26 | | 2 | | 4 | 5 | 3 | 7* | | | | 8 | | 10 | 9 | | 6 | | 1 | 11 | | 12 | | | | | | | | | |
| 27 | | 2 | | | | 3 | 7 | 6 | | | 8 | | 11 | 9 | | 5 | | 1 | 4 | | 10 | | | | | | | | | |
| 28 | | 11 | | | | 2 | 7 | 6* | | | 8 | | 3 | 9 | 4 | 5 | | 1 | | | 10+ | 12 | | | | | | | | |
| 29 | | 2 | | | | 3 | 7 | 10 | | | 8 | | 11 | 9 | 4* | 6 | | 1 | | | 12 | | 5 | | | | | | | |
| 30 | | 2 | | | | 3 | 7 | 10 | | | 4 | | 11 | 9 | | 6 | | 1 | | | 8 | | 5 | | | | | | | |
| 31 | | 4 | | | | 14 | 7 | 10 | | | 8+ | | 11* | 9 | | 6 | 2 | 1 | | | 12 | | 5 | 3 | | | | | | |
| 32 | | 4 | | | | | 7 | 10 | | | 8 | | 11 | 9 | | 6 | 2 | 1 | | | | | 5 | 3 | | | | | | |
| 33 | | 4 | | | | | 7 | 10 | | | 8* | | 11 | 9 | | 6 | 2 | 1 | | | 12 | | | 3 | 5 | | | | | |
| 34 | | 4 | | | | | 7 | 10 | | | 8 | | 11 | 9 | | 6 | 2 | | | | | | | 3 | 5 | 1 | | | | |
| 35 | | 4 | | | | 2 | | 10 | | | 8 | | 11 | 9 | | 6 | | | | | 7 | | | 3 | 5 | 1 | | | | |
| 36 | | 4 | | | | 2 | | 10 | | | 8 | | 11 | 9 | | 6 | | | | | 7 | | | 3 | 5 | 1 | | | | |
| 37 | | 4 | | | | 2 | | 10 | | | 8 | | 11 | 9 | 3 | 6 | | | | | 7* | | | | 5 | 1 | 12 | | | |
| 38 | | 4 | | | | 2 | 7 | 10 | | | 8 | | 11 | 9 | 3 | 6 | | | 5* | | | | | | | 1 | 12 | | | |
| 39 | | 4* | | | | 2 | 7 | 10 | | | 8 | | 11 | 9 | 3 | 6 | | | 5 | | | | | | | 1 | 12 | | | |
| 40 | | | | | | 2* | | 10 | | | 8 | 12 | 11+ | 9 | 3 | 6 | 4 | | 14 | | | | | | | 1 | 7 | 5 | | |
| 41 | | 11+ | | | | 2 | 14 | 10 | | | 8 | | | 9 | 3* | 6 | 4 | | | | 12 | | | | | 1 | 7 | 5 | | |
| 42 | | | | | | 2 | | 10 | | | 8 | 11 | | 9 | 3 | 6 | 4 | | | | 12 | | | | | 1 | 7* | 5 | | |
| 43 | | | | | | 3 | 7 | 6 | | | 8 | 11 | | 9 | 4+ | | 2 | | | | 10* | | | | | 1 | 12 | 5 | 14 | |
| 44 | | | | | | 4 | 7 | 6 | | | 8* | 11 | 3 | 9 | 12 | | 2 | | | | 10 | | | | | 1 | | 5 | | |
| 45 | | | | | | 4 | 7* | 6 | | | 8 | 11+ | 3 | 9 | 12 | | 2 | 1 | | | 10 | | | | | | 14 | 5 | | |
| 46 | | | | | | 2 | 7 | 6 | | | 8 | | 11 | 9 | 3 | | | 1 | | | | | | | | | 10 | 5 | | 4 |

# F.A.Cup

| Round | Date | Opponent | Result | Att | Scorers | | | | | | | | | | | | | | | | | | | | | | | | | | | | | | |
|---|---|---|---|---|---|---|---|---|---|---|---|---|---|---|---|---|---|---|---|---|---|---|---|---|---|---|---|---|---|---|---|---|---|---|---|
| 1st | 14 Nov | TAMWORTH | 3–0 | 3215 | Wilkins, Tempest, Chatterton (pen) | | 6 | | 4 | 5 | 2 | 7 | 10 | | | 8 | 11 | 3 | 9 | | | | 1 | | | | | | | | | | | | |
| 2nd | 5 Dec | HEREFORD | 3–2 | 2216 | Chatterton, Wilkins, Hill | | 2 | | 4 | 5 | 3 | 7 | 10 | 12 | 14 | 8* | | 11 | 9 | | 6 | | 1 | | | | | | | | | | | | |
| 3rd | 11 Jan | Plymouth | 0–2 | 10351 | | | 2 | | 4* | | 3 | 7 | 10 | 12 | | 8 | | 11 | 9 | | 5 | | 1 | | | | | | | | | | | | |

# Littlewoods (League) Cup

| Round | Date | Opponent | Result | Att | Scorers | | | | | | | | | | | | | | | | | | | | | | | | | | | | | | Lake |
|---|---|---|---|---|---|---|---|---|---|---|---|---|---|---|---|---|---|---|---|---|---|---|---|---|---|---|---|---|---|---|---|---|---|---|---|
| 1/1L | 18 Aug | Fulham | 1–3 | 2782 | White | | 2 | 3 | 4 | 5 | 6 | 7 | 8 | 9 | 10 | 11 | 12 | | | | | | | | | | | | | | | | | | 1 |
| 1/2L | 25 | FULHAM | 0–2 | 1554 | | | 2 | 3* | 4 | 5 | 6 | 7 | 8 | 9* | 10 | 11 | 12 | 14 | | | | | 1 | | | 6 | | | | | | | | | |

Back Row — Left to Right: John Chandler (Physiotherapist), Tony English, John Reeves, Mario Walsh, Rhys Jones, Roger Brown (Manager), Colin Hill, Richard Wilkins, Rudi Hedman, Steve Foley (Coach).
Front Row — Left to Right: Stephen Grenfell, Nick Chatterton, Dale Tempest, Paul Hinshelwood (Captain), Gary Smith, Sean Norman, Simon Lowe, Winston White.

**DIVISION 4**

| | P | W | D | L | F | A | W | D | L | F | A | Pts |
|---|---|---|---|---|---|---|---|---|---|---|---|---|
| Wolves | 46 | 15 | 3 | 5 | 47 | 19 | 12 | 6 | 5 | 35 | 24 | 90 |
| Cardiff C | 46 | 15 | 6 | 2 | 39 | 14 | 9 | 7 | 7 | 27 | 27 | 85 |
| Bolton W | 46 | 16 | 5 | 2 | 42 | 12 | 7 | 6 | 10 | 24 | 30 | 78 |
| Scunthorpe U | 46 | 14 | 5 | 4 | 42 | 20 | 6 | 12 | 5 | 34 | 31 | 77 |
| Torquay U | 46 | 10 | 7 | 6 | 34 | 16 | 11 | 7 | 5 | 32 | 25 | 77 |
| Swansea C | 46 | 9 | 7 | 7 | 35 | 28 | 11 | 3 | 9 | 27 | 28 | 70 |
| Peterboro' U | 46 | 10 | 5 | 8 | 28 | 26 | 10 | 5 | 8 | 24 | 27 | 70 |
| Leyton Orient | 46 | 13 | 4 | 6 | 55 | 27 | 6 | 8 | 9 | 30 | 36 | 69 |
| Colchester U | 46 | 10 | 5 | 8 | 23 | 22 | 9 | 5 | 9 | 24 | 29 | 67 |
| Burnley | 46 | 12 | 5 | 6 | 31 | 22 | 8 | 2 | 13 | 26 | 40 | 67 |
| Wrexham | 46 | 13 | 3 | 7 | 46 | 26 | 7 | 3 | 13 | 23 | 32 | 66 |
| Scarborough | 46 | 12 | 8 | 3 | 38 | 19 | 5 | 6 | 12 | 18 | 29 | 65 |
| Darlington | 46 | 13 | 6 | 4 | 39 | 25 | 5 | 5 | 13 | 32 | 44 | 65 |
| Tranmere R* | 46 | 14 | 2 | 7 | 43 | 20 | 5 | 7 | 11 | 18 | 33 | 64 |
| Cambridge U | 46 | 10 | 6 | 7 | 32 | 24 | 6 | 7 | 10 | 18 | 28 | 61 |
| Hartlepool U | 46 | 9 | 7 | 7 | 25 | 25 | 6 | 7 | 10 | 25 | 32 | 59 |
| Crewe A | 46 | 7 | 11 | 5 | 25 | 19 | 6 | 8 | 9 | 32 | 34 | 58 |
| Halifax T† | 46 | 11 | 7 | 5 | 37 | 25 | 3 | 7 | 13 | 17 | 34 | 55 |
| Hereford U | 46 | 8 | 7 | 8 | 25 | 27 | 6 | 5 | 12 | 16 | 32 | 54 |
| Stockport Co | 46 | 7 | 7 | 9 | 26 | 26 | 5 | 8 | 10 | 18 | 32 | 51 |
| Rochdale | 46 | 5 | 9 | 9 | 28 | 34 | 6 | 6 | 11 | 19 | 42 | 48 |
| Exeter C | 46 | 8 | 6 | 9 | 33 | 29 | 3 | 7 | 13 | 20 | 39 | 46 |
| Carlisle U | 46 | 9 | 5 | 9 | 38 | 33 | 3 | 3 | 17 | 19 | 53 | 44 |
| Newport Co | 46 | 4 | 5 | 14 | 19 | 36 | 2 | 2 | 19 | 16 | 69 | 25 |

# SEASON 1988/89 Division Four

| No. | Date | Opposition | Res | Attend | Goalscorers | Walton | Hedman | Cartwright | Barnett | Hetzke | Hill | Wilkins | White | Tempest | Swindlehurst | Grenfell | English | Bedford | Radford | Hicks | Hunter | Daniels | Walsh | Bennett | Kelly | Coombe | Chatterton | Allinson | Taylor | Coleman | McAllister | McGee | Warner | Stafford | Pollard | Scott |
|---|---|---|---|---|---|---|---|---|---|---|---|---|---|---|---|---|---|---|---|---|---|---|---|---|---|---|---|---|---|---|---|---|---|---|---|---|
| 1 | 27 Aug | YORK | 1–0 | 1644 | Tempest | 1 | 2 | 3 | 4 | 5 | 6 | 7 | 8 | 9 | 10 | 11 | | | | | | | | | | | | | | | | | | | | |
| 2 | 2 Sep | Tranmere | 0–0 | 3401 | | 1 | | 3 | 4 | 5 | 6 | 7 | 8 | 9 | 10 | 11* | 2 | 12 | | | | | | | | | | | | | | | | | | |
| 3 | 9 | DONCASTER | 0–1 | 1726 | | 1 | | 3 | | | 6* | 7 | 8 | 9 | 10 | 11+ | 2 | 12 | 4 | 5 | 14 | | | | | | | | | | | | | | | |
| 4 | 16 | Wrexham | 2–2 | 2873 | Swindlehurst(2) | 1 | 2 | 3 | | | 6 | 7 | 8* | 9 | 10 | | | 11 | 4 | 5 | 12 | | | | | | | | | | | | | | | |
| 5 | 20 | SCARBOROUGH | 3–1 | 1420 | Swindlehurst, Tempest, Wilkins | 1 | 2 | 3 | 4* | | 6 | 7 | 8 | 9 | 10 | | | 11 | 12 | 5 | | | | | | | | | | | | | | | | |
| 6 | 24 | Burnley | 0–2 | 7177 | | 1 | 2 | 3 | 4 | | 6 | 7 | 8 | 9 | 10 | | | 11* | 12 | 5 | | | | | | | | | | | | | | | | |
| 7 | 1 Oct | LINCOLN | 1–3 | 1529 | Swindlehurst | 1 | 2 | 3 | 4 | | 6 | 11* | 8 | 9 | 10 | | | | 12 | 5 | 7 | | | | | | | | | | | | | | | |
| 8 | 4 | Carlisle | 2–1 | 2193 | Tempest, Swindlehurst | 1 | 2 | 3 | 4 | | 6 | 11 | 8 | 9 | 10 | | | | | 5 | 7 | | | | | | | | | | | | | | | |
| 9 | 8 | SCUNTHORPE | 1–2 | 1299 | Hedman | 1 | 2 | 3 | 4 | | 6 | 11* | 8 | 9 | 10 | | | | 12 | 5 | 7 | | | | | | | | | | | | | | | |
| 10 | 15 | Leyton Orient | 0–8 | 3421 | | 1 | 2 | 3 | 4* | | 6 | 11 | 8 | 9 | 10 | | | | 12 | 5 | 7 | | | | | | | | | | | | | | | |
| 11 | 21 | CAMBRIDGE U. | 1–2 | 2138 | English | 1 | 2 | | 4* | | 6 | 7 | | 9 | | 11+ | 8 | 3 | 12 | 5 | | | 10 | 14 | | | | | | | | | | | | |
| 12 | 25 | Rotherham | 0–2 | 4066 | | 1 | 2 | | | | 6 | 7 | | 9* | 10 | 11+ | 8 | 3 | 12 | 5 | | | 14 | | 4 | | | | | | | | | | | |
| 13 | 28 | STOCKPORT | 1–1 | 1643 | Tempest | 1 | 2 | | | | 6 | 7 | | 9 | | | 8 | 3 | 11* | 5 | 12 | | 10 | | 4 | | | | | | | | | | | |
| 14 | 4 Nov | Crewe | 1–3 | 2787 | Walsh | 1 | 2 | | | | 6 | 7 | | 9 | | 12 | 8 | 3 | 11* | 5+ | | 14 | 10 | | 4 | | | | | | | | | | | |
| 15 | 8 | Halifax | 2–3 | 2176 | Kelly, Wilkins | 1 | 2 | | 11 | | 6* | 7 | | 9 | | | 8 | 3 | | 5 | | 12 | 10 | | 4 | | | | | | | | | | | |
| 16 | 11 | TORQUAY | 2–2 | 1926 | English, Kelly | | 2 | | 11* | | 6 | 7+ | | 9 | | 12 | 8 | 3 | 12 | 5 | | 14 | 10 | | 4 | 1 | | | | | | | | | | |
| 17 | 25 | DARLINGTON | 1–2 | 1550 | Radford | | 2 | | 11 | | | | | 9 | | | 6+ | 3 | 7 | 5 | | 14 | 10 | 8* | 4 | 1 | 12 | | | | | | | | | |
| 18 | 3 Dec | Exeter | 2–4 | 2132 | Swindlehurst, Tempest | | 7 | | | 14 | 2 | | | 12 | 9 | | | 3 | 11+ | 5 | | 6 | 10 | | 4 | 1 | 8* | | | | | | | | | |
| 19 | 16 | Rochdale | 1–1 | 1258 | Walsh | 1 | 2 | | 8 | 14 | 6 | 9 | | 12 | | | 7 | 3 | | | | 5 | 10* | | 4+ | | | 11 | | | | | | | | |
| 20 | 26 | PETERBOROUGH | 1–2 | 2828 | Walsh | 1 | | | 8 | 6 | 2 | 9 | | 12 | | | 7* | 3 | | 14 | | 5+ | 10 | | 4 | | | 11 | | | | | | | | |
| 21 | 30 | HARTLEPOOL | 1–2 | 2359 | English | 1 | | | 8 | 6 | 2+ | 9 | | 12 | | | 7 | 3 | 14 | | | 5 | 10 | | 4 | | | 11* | | | | | | | | |
| 22 | 2 Jan | Grimsby | 2–2 | 4472 | Walsh, Allinson | 1 | | | 8 | 6 | | 9+ | | 12 | | | 2 | 3 | 14 | 5 | | 7 | 10 | | 4 | | | 11* | | | | | | | | |
| 23 | 13 | TRANMERE | 2–3 | 3458 | Walsh(2) | 1 | | | 8+ | 6 | 12 | | | 9 | | | 2 | 3 | | 5* | | 7 | 10 | | 4 | | | 11 | 14 | | | | | | | |
| 24 | 21 | York | 0–2 | 2219 | | 1 | | | | 6 | 12 | | | 9* | | | 8 | 3 | | 5 | | 7 | 10 | | 4+ | | | 11 | 14 | 2 | | | | | | |
| 25 | 4 Feb | Scarborough | 0–0 | 1913 | | | | | 7 | 5 | 6 | 9 | | | | | 8 | 3 | | 2 | | | 10 | | | | | 11 | 4 | | 1 | | | | | |
| 26 | 10 | BURNLEY | 2–2 | 3809 | Allinson, Walsh | | | | 12 | 5 | 6 | 9 | | | | | 8 | 3 | | 2 | | | 10 | | | | | 7 | 4 | | 1 | 11* | | | | |
| 27 | 18 | Scunthorpe | 3–2 | 4286 | Wilkins, English, Warner | | | | | 5 | 6 | 9 | | | | | 8 | 3 | | 2 | | 12 | 10* | | | | | 7 | 4 | | 1 | 11+ | 14 | | | |
| 28 | 24 | LEYTON ORIENT | 1–0 | 4269 | Allinson | | | | 8 | 5 | 6 | 9* | | | | | | 3 | | 2 | | | | 12 | | | | 7 | 4 | | 1 | 11 | 10 | | | |
| 29 | 28 | ROTHERHAM | 1–1 | 3671 | Allinson | | | | | 5 | 6 | 11 | | 9 | | | 8 | 3 | | 2 | | | | 12 | | | | 7 | 4* | | 1 | | 10 | | | |
| 30 | 5 Mar | Cambridge U. | 1–3 | 4205 | Wilkins | | | | | 5+ | 6 | 11 | | 10 | | | 8 | | 14 | 2 | | 12 | | 7 | | | | | 4 | | 1 | | 9 | 3* | | |
| 31 | 10 | CREWE | 2–1 | 3088 | English(2) | | | | | | 6 | 11 | | 12 | | | 8 | | 4 | 10 | | | | 7 | | | | | | 2 | 1 | | 9* | 3 | | |
| 32 | 13 | Stockport | 0–1 | 2027 | | | | | | | 6 | 10 | | 4 | | | 7 | | 11 | 8 | | | | | | | | | | 2 | 1 | | 9 | 3 | | |
| 33 | 18 | Doncaster | 1–3 | 1237 | Walsh | | | | | | 6 | 8 | | | | | 7 | | 11* | 5 | | | 10 | | | | | 9 | 4 | 2 | 1 | | 12 | 3 | | |
| 34 | 24 | GRIMSBY | 0–0 | 4507 | | | | | | 5 | 6 | | | | | | 2 | 11* | | 8 | | | 10 | | | | | 7* | 4 | | 1 | | 12 | 3 | | 9 |
| 35 | 27 | Peterborough | 0–3 | 3529 | | | | | | 5 | 6 | | | | | | 7 | 11* | | 4 | | | 10 | | | | | 9 | | 2+ | 1 | | 12 | 3 | | 8 |
| 36 | 31 | ROCHDALE | 3–0 | 3631 | Scott, Bennett, Wilkins | | | | | 5 | 6 | 11* | | | | | 8 | | 4 | 14 | | | 10+ | 7 | | | | 12 | | | 1 | | | 3 | | 9 |
| 37 | 4 Apr | HEREFORD | 1–1 | 2862 | English | | | | | 5+ | 6 | 11 | | | | | 8 | | 4 | 14 | | | | 7 | | | | 10 | | | 1 | | 12 | 3 | | 9 |
| 38 | 8 | Hartlepool | 1–2 | 1501 | Scott | | | | | | 6 | 12 | | | | | 7 | | 4 | 2 | | | | 8+ | | | | 11 | | 14 | 1 | | 10* | 3 | | 9 |
| 39 | 12 | Hereford | 1–1 | 2015 | Scott | | | | | | 6 | 7 | | 10 | | | 8 | | 12 | 2 | | | | | | | | 11 | 4* | 14 | 1 | | | 3 | | 9 |
| 40 | 15 | Lincoln | 1–1 | 3519 | Wilkins | | | | | | 6 | 7 | | 10+ | | | 8 | | 12 | 2 | | | | | | | | 11 | 4 | 14 | 1 | | | 3 | | 9 |
| 41 | 21 | CARLISLE | 1–1 | 3906 | Scott | | | | | | 6 | 7 | | 12 | | | 8 | | | 2+ | | | 10 | | | | | 11 | 4 | | 1 | | | 3* | | 9 |
| 42 | 25 | WREXHAM | 2–1 | 2918 | Allinson, Hetzke | | | | | 5 | 6 | 7 | | 10+ | | | 3 | | 8 | | | | 14 | | | | | 11 | 4 | 2* | 1 | | | | | 9 |
| 43 | 29 | Darlington | 2–1 | 7126 | Walsh, Scott | | | | | 5 | 6 | 7+ | | | | | 8 | | 14 | | | | 10 | | | | | 11 | 4 | | 1 | | 12 | 3 | | 9 |
| 44 | 1 May | HALIFAX | 3–2 | 5065 | Wilkins, Warner, Allinson | | | | | 5 | 6 | 7 | | | | | 8 | | 2 | | | | 10 | | | | | 11 | 4* | 14 | 1 | | 12 | 3 | | 9 |
| 45 | 5 | EXETER | 4–0 | 5256 | Walsh, Allinson, Pollard, English | 1 | | | | 5 | 6 | 7 | | | | | 8 | | 4+ | | | | 10 | | | | | 11 | | | | | 12 | 3 | 14 | 9 |
| 46 | 13 | Torquay | 3–1 | 2066 | Warner, Hetzke, Tempest | 1 | | | | 5 | 6 | 7 | | 12 | | | 8 | | 4+ | | | | 10* | | | | | 11 | | | | | 9 | 3 | 14 | |

# F.A.Cup

| Rd | Date | Opponent | Score | Att | Scorers | | | | | | | | | | | | | | | | | | | | | | | | | | | | | | | | |
|---|---|---|---|---|---|---|---|---|---|---|---|---|---|---|---|---|---|---|---|---|---|---|---|---|---|---|---|---|---|---|---|---|---|---|---|---|
| 1st | 19 Nov | Fulham | 1–0 | 4481 | Walsh | | 2 | | 11 | | 6 | | | 9 | | | 8 | 3 | 7 | 5 | | | 10 | | 4 | 1 | | | | | | | | | | |
| 2nd | 10 Dec | SWANSEA | 2–2 | 2715 | Hedman, Wilkins | 1 | 2 | | | | 6 | 11 | | | 9* | | 8 | 3 | 12 | 5 | | 7 | 10 | | 4 | | | | | | | | | | | |
| 2/2R | 13 | Swansea | 3–1 | 4045 | Hedman, Walsh, Wilkins | 1 | 2 | | 8 | | 6 | 9* | | 12 | | | 7 | 3 | 11 | | | 5 | 10 | | 4 | | | | | | | | | | | |
| 3rd | 7 Jan | Shrewsbury | 3–0 | 3982 | Walsh, Allison(pen), O.G. | 1 | | | 8 | 6 | | | | 9 | | | 2 | 3 | | 5 | | 7 | 10 | | 4 | | | 11 | | | | | | | | |
| 4th | 28 | Sheffield United | 3–3 | 14406 | Hicks, Hill, Hetzke | 1 | | | | 6 | 4 | | | 9 | | | 8 | 3 | 12 | 5 | | 7 | 10* | | | | | 11 | | 2 | | | | | | |
| 4/4R | 31 | SHEFFIELD UNITED | 0–2 | 7638 | | 1 | | | 14 | 5 | 4 | 12 | | 10 | 8* | | 7 | 3 | | | | 6 | 9* | | | | | 11 | | 2 | | | | | | |

# Littlewoods (League) Cup

| Rd | Date | Opponent | Score | Att | Scorers | | | | | | | | | | | | | | | | | | | | | | | | | | | | | | | | |
|---|---|---|---|---|---|---|---|---|---|---|---|---|---|---|---|---|---|---|---|---|---|---|---|---|---|---|---|---|---|---|---|---|---|---|---|---|
| 1/1L | 29 Aug | NORTHAMPTON | 0–0 | 1698 | | 1 | 2 | 3 | 4 | 5 | 6 | 7 | 8 | 9 | 10 | 11 | | | | | | | | | | | | | | | | | | | | |
| 1/2L | 6 Sept | Northampton | 0–5 | 3957 | | 1 | | 3 | 4 | 5* | 6 | 7 | 8 | 9 | 10 | 11* | | 2 | 12 | 14 | | | | | | | | | | | | | | | | |

(Back): Chandler (physio), Baker, Grenfell, Hinshelwood, Lowe, Walker (manager), Walsh, Wilkins, English, Headman, Hunter (coach)
(Front): White, Young, Radford, Lake, Chatterton, Norman, Reeves.

**DIVISION 4**

| | P | W | D | L | F | A | W | D | L | F | A | Pts |
|---|---|---|---|---|---|---|---|---|---|---|---|---|
| Rotherham U | 46 | 13 | 6 | 4 | 44 | 18 | 9 | 10 | 4 | 32 | 17 | 82 |
| Tranmere R | 46 | 13 | 6 | 2 | 34 | 13 | 6 | 11 | 6 | 28 | 30 | 80 |
| Crewe A | 46 | 13 | 7 | 3 | 42 | 24 | 8 | 8 | 7 | 25 | 24 | 78 |
| Scunthorpe U | 46 | 11 | 9 | 3 | 40 | 22 | 10 | 5 | 8 | 37 | 35 | 77 |
| Scarborough | 46 | 12 | 7 | 4 | 33 | 23 | 9 | 7 | 7 | 34 | 39 | 77 |
| Leyton Orient | 46 | 16 | 2 | 5 | 61 | 19 | 5 | 10 | 8 | 25 | 31 | 75 |
| Wrexham | 46 | 12 | 7 | 4 | 44 | 28 | 7 | 7 | 9 | 33 | 35 | 71 |
| Cambridge U | 46 | 13 | 7 | 3 | 45 | 25 | 5 | 7 | 11 | 26 | 37 | 68 |
| Grimsby T | 46 | 11 | 9 | 3 | 33 | 18 | 6 | 6 | 11 | 32 | 41 | 66 |
| Lincoln C | 46 | 12 | 6 | 5 | 39 | 26 | 6 | 4 | 13 | 25 | 34 | 64 |
| York C | 46 | 10 | 8 | 5 | 43 | 27 | 7 | 5 | 11 | 19 | 36 | 64 |
| Carlisle U | 46 | 9 | 6 | 8 | 26 | 25 | 6 | 9 | 8 | 27 | 27 | 60 |
| Exeter C | 46 | 14 | 4 | 5 | 46 | 23 | 4 | 2 | 17 | 19 | 45 | 60 |
| Torquay U | 46 | 15 | 2 | 6 | 32 | 23 | 2 | 6 | 15 | 13 | 37 | 59 |
| Hereford U | 46 | 11 | 8 | 4 | 40 | 27 | 3 | 8 | 12 | 26 | 45 | 58 |
| Burnley | 46 | 12 | 6 | 5 | 35 | 20 | 2 | 7 | 14 | 17 | 41 | 55 |
| Peterboro' U | 46 | 10 | 3 | 10 | 29 | 32 | 4 | 9 | 10 | 23 | 42 | 54 |
| Rochdale | 46 | 10 | 10 | 3 | 32 | 26 | 3 | 4 | 16 | 24 | 56 | 53 |
| Hartlepool U | 46 | 10 | 6 | 7 | 33 | 33 | 4 | 4 | 15 | 17 | 45 | 52 |
| Stockport Co | 46 | 8 | 10 | 5 | 31 | 20 | 2 | 11 | 10 | 23 | 32 | 51 |
| Halifax T | 46 | 10 | 7 | 6 | 42 | 27 | 3 | 4 | 16 | 27 | 48 | 50 |
| Colchester U | 46 | 8 | 7 | 8 | 35 | 30 | 4 | 7 | 12 | 25 | 48 | 50 |
| Doncaster R | 46 | 9 | 6 | 8 | 32 | 32 | 4 | 4 | 15 | 17 | 46 | 49 |
| Darlington | 46 | 3 | 12 | 8 | 28 | 38 | 5 | 6 | 12 | 25 | 38 | 42 |

# SEASON 1989/90 Division Four

| No. | Date | Opposition | Res | Attend | Goalscorers | Grace | Hicks | Rooke | English A. | Daniels | Radford | Bennett | Collins | Wilkins | Scott | Allinson | Hansbury | Taylor | Kinsella | Pollard | Stafford | Blake | Devereux | Gilbert | English T. | Morgan | Bruce | Hagan | Grainger | Warner | Ball | Barrett | Marmon | Goddard | Marriott |
|---|---|---|---|---|---|---|---|---|---|---|---|---|---|---|---|---|---|---|---|---|---|---|---|---|---|---|---|---|---|---|---|---|---|---|---|
| 1 | 19 Aug | Chesterfield | 1–1 | 3000 | Radford | 1 | 2 | 3 | 4 | 5 | 6 | 7 | 8 | 9 | 10 | 11 | | | | | | | | | | | | | | | | | | | |
| 2 | 26 | HALIFAX | 2–2 | 2404 | Bennett, Radford | | 2 | 3* | 4 | 5 | 6 | 7 | 8 | 9 | 10 | 11+ | 1 | 12 | 14 | | | | | | | | | | | | | | | | |
| 3 | 2 Sep | Grimsby | 1–4 | 4678 | Allinson | | 2 | 3 | 4 | 5 | 6* | 7 | 8 | 9 | 10+ | 11 | 1 | 12 | | 14 | | | | | | | | | | | | | | | |
| 4 | 8 | HEREFORD | 1–1 | 3269 | Allinson | | 2 | | 4 | 5 | | 7 | 8 | 9 | | 11 | 1 | 10 | | | 3 | 6 | | | | | | | | | | | | | |
| 5 | 16 | Rochdale | 2–2 | 1466 | Collins, Blake | | 2 | | 4 | 5 | 12 | 7* | 8 | 9 | | 11 | 1 | 10 | | | 3 | 6 | | | | | | | | | | | | | |
| 6 | 23 | SCARBOROUGH | 0–0 | 2420 | | 1 | 2 | | 3 | 5 | 4* | 7 | 8 | 9 | | 11 | | 10 | | | 12 | 6 | | | | | | | | | | | | | |
| 7 | 26 | MAIDSTONE | 4–1 | 2946 | Radford, Allinson, Taylor, Bennett | 1 | 2 | | 3 | 5 | 10 | 7* | 8 | 9 | 12 | 11 | | 4 | | | | 6 | | | | | | | | | | | | | |
| 8 | 30 | Carlisle | 0–1 | 3979 | | 1 | 2 | | 6 | 5 | 10* | 7 | 8 | 9 | 12 | 11 | | 4 | | | 3 | | | | | | | | | | | | | | |
| 9 | 7 Oct | Aldershot | 0–4 | 2092 | | 1 | 2 | 3 | 6 | 5 | 11+ | 14 | 8 | 9 | 10 | 7* | | 4 | | 12 | | | | | | | | | | | | | | | |
| 10 | 13 | YORK | 0–2 | 3274 | | 1 | 2 | | 6 | 5 | 3 | 7* | 8 | 9 | 10 | 11 | | 4 | | | | | 12 | | | | | | | | | | | | |
| 11 | 17 | WREXHAM | 1–3 | 2564 | Scott | 1 | 2 | | 6 | 5 | 3 | 7+ | 8 | 9 | 10* | 11 | | 4 | 14 | 12 | | | | | | | | | | | | | | | |
| 12 | 21 | Scunthorpe | 0–4 | 3254 | | 1 | 9 | | 6 | 5 | 11* | | 8+ | | | 12 | | 4 | | 2 | 14 | | 7 | 3 | 10 | | | | | | | | | | |
| 13 | 28 | PETERBOROUGH | 0–1 | 3460 | | 1 | 2 | | 7 | 5 | | 12 | 8 | 11 | | | | 4 | | | 3 | | | 6* | 10 | 9 | | | | | | | | | |
| 14 | 1 Nov | Exeter | 1–2 | 3905 | A.English | 1 | 2 | | 7 | 5 | | 12 | 8 | 11 | | | | 4 | | | 3 | | | 6 | 10 | 9* | | | | | | | | | |
| 15 | 4 | Burnley | 0–0 | 6145 | | 1 | 2 | | | 5 | | 7 | 8 | 11 | | | | 4 | 14 | 12 | 3 | | | 6 | 10+ | 9* | | | | | | | | | |
| 16 | 10 | CAMBRIDGE U. | 1–2 | 3771 | T.English | 1 | | | | 5 | | 7 | 8+ | 11 | | | | 4 | 14 | 12 | 3 | | | 6* | 10 | 9 | 2 | | | | | | | | |
| 17 | 24 | Gillingham | 3–3 | 3816 | T.English, Bennett, Morgan | 1 | | | 4 | 5 | | 7 | 8 | 11 | | | | | | | 3 | | | 6 | 10 | 9 | 2 | | | | | | | | |
| 18 | 2 Dec | LINCOLN | 0–1 | 2517 | | 1 | | | 4 | 5 | | 7 | 8 | 11+ | 12 | | | 14 | | | 3 | | | 6 | 10 | 9* | | 2 | | | | | | | |
| 19 | 16 | TORQUAY | 0–3 | 1720 | | 1 | | | 4 | 5 | | 7 | | 9 | | 11* | | 10 | | | | | | 6 | 12 | | 2 | 8 | 3 | | | | | | |
| 20 | 26 | Southend | 2–0 | 5563 | Grainger, T.English | 1 | | | 4 | 5 | | 7 | | 8 | 11+ | | | 9 | | | 3 | | | 6* | 10 | | 2 | | 12 | 14 | | | | | |
| 21 | 30 | Doncaster | 0–2 | 2942 | | 1 | | | 4 | 5 | 6+ | 7 | | 8* | | | | 9 | | 14 | 3 | | | | 10 | 11 | 2 | | 12 | | | | | | |
| 22 | 1 Jan | HARTLEPOOL | 3–1 | 3826 | Morgan, Grainger, Radford | 1 | | | 4 | 5 | 6 | | | | 12 | | | 8+ | 7 | | 3 | | | | 10* | 9 | 2 | | 11 | | 14 | | | | |
| 23 | 5 | STOCKPORT | 0–1 | 3609 | | 1 | | | 4 | 5 | 6 | 7 | 8 | | | | | | | | 3 | | | | | 9 | 2 | | 11 | 10 | | | | | |
| 24 | 12 | Halifax | 1–1 | 1397 | Scott | | | | 6 | 5 | 11* | 10+ | 7 | 9 | 14 | | | 4 | | | 3 | | | | | 12 | 2 | | | | 8 | 1 | | | |
| 25 | 20 | CHESTERFIELD | 1–0 | 3016 | Wilkins | | | | 3 | 5 | 11 | | 7 | 10 | 12 | | | 4 | | | | | | | | 9 | 2 | | | | 8* | 1 | 6 | | |
| 26 | 27 | York | 1–3 | 2311 | Wilkins | | 14 | | 3 | 5 | 11* | 12 | 7 | 10 | | | | 4 | | | | | | | | 9 | 2 | | | | 8+ | 1 | 6 | | |
| 27 | 3 Feb | Scarborough | 2–2 | 1786 | A.English, Morgan | | | | 8 | 5 | 11* | 12 | 7 | 10 | | | | 4 | | | | | | | | 9 | 2 | | | | | 1 | 6 | 3 | |
| 28 | 10 | ROCHDALE | 1–2 | 2744 | Morgan | | | | 8 | 5 | 11* | 12 | 7 | 10 | | | | 4+ | | | | | | 14 | | 9 | 2 | | | | | 1 | 6 | 3 | |
| 29 | 17 | Lincoln | 1–2 | 3284 | Wilkins | | | | 8 | 5 | | 11* | 7 | 10 | 12 | | | | | | | | | 4 | | 9 | 2 | | | | | 1 | 6 | 3 | |
| 30 | 20 | GRIMSBY | 1–0 | 3026 | Bruce | | | | 8 | 5 | | | 7 | 10 | 11* | | | 12 | | | | | | 4 | | 9 | 2 | | | | | 1 | 6 | 3 | |
| 31 | 23 | GILLINGHAM | 2–0 | 4456 | Morgan, Scott | | | | 8 | 5 | | 12 | 7 | 10 | 11* | | | | | | | | | 4 | | 9 | 2 | | | | | 1 | 6 | 3 | |
| 32 | 2 Mar | Stockport | 1–1 | 3452 | Goddard | | | | 8 | 5 | | | 7 | 10 | 11 | | | | | | | | | 4 | | 9 | 2 | | | | | 1 | 6 | 3 | |
| 33 | 6 | CARLISLE | 4–0 | 3752 | Wilkins, Marmon, Morgan(2) | | | | 8 | 5 | | | 7 | 10* | 11 | | | 12 | | | | | | 4 | | 9 | 2 | | | | | 1 | 6 | 3 | |
| 34 | 10 | Maidstone | 1–4 | 2856 | Morgan | | 12 | | 8 | 5 | | | 7 | 10 | 11* | | | | | | | | | 4 | | 9 | 2 | | | | | 1 | 6 | 3 | |
| 35 | 14 | Hereford | 0–2 | 2253 | | | 12 | | 8 | 5 | | | 7 | 10 | | | | | | | 3* | | | 4 | 11 | 9 | 2 | | | | | 1 | 6 | | |
| 36 | 17 | ALDERSHOT | 1–0 | 2682 | Morgan | | 14 | | 3 | 5 | | 12 | 7* | 10 | 11+ | | | 8 | | | | | | 4 | | 9 | 2 | | | | | 1 | 6 | | |
| 37 | 24 | Wrexham | 2–3 | 4653 | Marmon, O.G. | | | | 8 | 5 | | | 7 | 10 | | | | 11 | | | | | | 4 | | 9 | 2 | | | | | | 6 | 3 | 1 |
| 38 | 31 | SCUNTHORPE | 1–0 | 2920 | Morgan | | | | 8 | 5 | | 7 | | 10* | | | | 11 | | | | | | 4 | | 9 | 2 | | | | | | 6 | 3 | 1 |
| 39 | 7 Apr | Peterborough | 0–1 | 4025 | | | | | 8 | 5 | | 7 | | 10 | | | | 11 | | | | | | 4 | | 9 | 2 | | | | | | 6 | 3 | 1 |
| 40 | 10 | EXETER | 0–1 | 3369 | | | | | 8 | 5 | | | | 10 | 12 | | | 11 | | | | | | 4 | 7* | 9 | 2 | | | | | | 6 | 3 | 1 |
| 41 | 14 | Hartlepool | 2–0 | 3397 | Bennett, Collins | | | | 2 | 5 | | 12 | 7 | 10 | 11* | | | 8 | | | | | | 4 | | 9 | | | | | | | 6 | 3 | 1 |
| 42 | 16 | SOUTHEND | 0–2 | 5283 | | | | | 2 | 5 | | 7* | 8 | 10 | 12 | | | 11 | | | | | | 4+ | | 9 | 14 | | | | | | 6 | 3 | 1 |
| 43 | 21 | Torquay | 1–4 | 1521 | Morgan | | | | 8 | 5* | | 14 | 7 | 10 | 12 | | | | | | | | | 4 | | 9 | 2 | | 11+ | | | | 6 | 3 | 1 |
| 44 | 24 | DONCASTER | 2–0 | 2641 | Marmon(2) | | | | 8 | 5 | | 11 | 7 | 10 | | | | | | | | | | 4 | | 9 | 2 | | | | | | 6 | 3 | 1 |
| 45 | 29 | Cambridge U. | 0–4 | 4558 | | | | | 8 | 5 | 3 | 11* | 7 | 10 | 12 | | | 14 | | | | | | 4+ | | 9 | 2 | | | | | | 6 | | 1 |
| 46 | 5 May | BURNLEY | 1–2 | 2788 | Morgan | | 4 | | 3 | 5 | | 7 | 8+ | 10 | | | | 11 | 14 | | | | | | | 9 | 2 | | 12 | | | | 6 | | 1 |

# F.A.Cup

| | | | | | | | | | | | | | | | | | | | | | | | | | | | | | | | | | | | |
|---|---|---|---|---|---|---|---|---|---|---|---|---|---|---|---|---|---|---|---|---|---|---|---|---|---|---|---|---|---|---|---|---|---|---|---|
| 1st | 18 Nov | Brentford | 1–0 | 4171 | Bennett | 1 | | | 4 | 5 | | 7 | 8 | 11 | | | | 12 | | | 3 | | | 6 | 10* | 9 | 2 | | | | | | | | |
| 2nd | 9 Dec | BIRMINGHAM | 0–2 | 3858 | | 1 | | | 4 | 5 | | 7 | 8* | 11 | | | | 12 | | | | | | 6 | 10 | 9 | 2 | 3 | | | | | | | |

# Littlewoods (League) Cup

| | | | | | | | | | | | | | | | | | | | | | | | | | | | | | | | | | | | |
|---|---|---|---|---|---|---|---|---|---|---|---|---|---|---|---|---|---|---|---|---|---|---|---|---|---|---|---|---|---|---|---|---|---|---|---|
| 1st | 21 Aug | SOUTHEND | 3–4 | 3537 | Scott(2), Bennett | 1 | 2 | 3 | 4 | 5 | 6* | 7 | 8 | 9 | 10 | 11 | | 12 | | | | | | | | | | | | | | | | | |
| 2nd | 28 | Southend | 1–2 | 3763 | Collins | 1 | 2 | 3 | 4 | 5 | 6* | 7 | 8 | 9 | 10* | 11 | | 12 | 14 | | | | | | | | | | | | | | | | |

COLCHESTER UNITED 1989–90 *Back row (left to right):* Steve Ball, Billy Gilbert, John Grace, Scott Daniels, Tom English.
*Centre row:* Brian Owen, Eamonn Collins, Gary Bennett, Clive Stafford, Mark Radford, Trevor Morgan, Stuart Hicks, Richard Wilkins, John Pollard, Sammy Chung (Coach).
*Front row:* Martin Grainger, Robert Devereaux, Mark Kinsella, Mick Mills (Manager), Tony English, Marcel Bruce, Robert Scott, Les Taylor.

**DIVISION 4**

| | P | W | D | L | F | A | W | D | L | F | A | Pts |
|---|---|---|---|---|---|---|---|---|---|---|---|---|
| Exeter C | 46 | 20 | 3 | 0 | 50 | 14 | 8 | 2 | 13 | 33 | 34 | 89 |
| Grimsby T | 46 | 14 | 4 | 5 | 41 | 20 | 8 | 9 | 6 | 29 | 27 | 79 |
| Southend U | 46 | 15 | 3 | 5 | 35 | 14 | 7 | 6 | 10 | 26 | 34 | 75 |
| Stockport Co | 46 | 13 | 6 | 4 | 45 | 27 | 8 | 5 | 10 | 23 | 35 | 74 |
| Maidstone U | 46 | 14 | 4 | 5 | 49 | 21 | 8 | 3 | 12 | 28 | 40 | 73 |
| Cambridge U | 46 | 14 | 3 | 6 | 45 | 30 | 7 | 7 | 9 | 31 | 36 | 73 |
| Chesterfield | 46 | 12 | 9 | 2 | 41 | 19 | 7 | 5 | 11 | 22 | 31 | 71 |
| Carlisle U | 46 | 15 | 4 | 4 | 38 | 20 | 6 | 4 | 13 | 23 | 40 | 71 |
| Peterboro' U | 46 | 10 | 8 | 5 | 35 | 23 | 7 | 9 | 7 | 24 | 23 | 68 |
| Lincoln C | 46 | 11 | 6 | 6 | 30 | 27 | 7 | 8 | 8 | 18 | 21 | 68 |
| Scunthorpe U | 46 | 9 | 9 | 5 | 42 | 25 | 8 | 6 | 9 | 27 | 29 | 66 |
| Rochdale | 46 | 11 | 4 | 8 | 28 | 23 | 9 | 2 | 12 | 24 | 32 | 66 |
| York C | 46 | 10 | 5 | 8 | 29 | 24 | 6 | 11 | 6 | 26 | 29 | 64 |
| Gillingham | 46 | 9 | 8 | 6 | 28 | 21 | 8 | 3 | 12 | 18 | 27 | 62 |
| Torquay U | 46 | 12 | 2 | 9 | 33 | 29 | 3 | 10 | 10 | 20 | 37 | 57 |
| Burnley | 46 | 6 | 10 | 7 | 19 | 18 | 8 | 4 | 11 | 26 | 37 | 56 |
| Hereford U | 46 | 7 | 4 | 12 | 31 | 32 | 8 | 6 | 9 | 25 | 30 | 55 |
| Scarborough | 46 | 10 | 5 | 8 | 35 | 28 | 5 | 5 | 13 | 25 | 45 | 55 |
| Hartlepool U | 46 | 12 | 4 | 7 | 45 | 33 | 3 | 6 | 14 | 21 | 55 | 55 |
| Doncaster R | 46 | 7 | 7 | 9 | 29 | 29 | 7 | 2 | 14 | 24 | 31 | 51 |
| Wrexham | 46 | 8 | 8 | 7 | 28 | 28 | 5 | 4 | 14 | 23 | 39 | 51 |
| Aldershot | 46 | 8 | 7 | 8 | 28 | 26 | 4 | 7 | 12 | 21 | 43 | 50 |
| Halifax T | 46 | 5 | 9 | 9 | 31 | 29 | 7 | 4 | 12 | 26 | 36 | 49 |
| Colchester U | 46 | 9 | 3 | 11 | 26 | 25 | 2 | 7 | 14 | 22 | 50 | 43 |

# SEASON 1990-91

## GM Vauxhall Conference

| No. | Date | Opposition | Res | Attend | Goalscorers | Barrett | English | Atkins | Collins | Daniels | Marmon | Kinsella | Bennett | Scott | Yates | Smith | Radford | Bruce | Donald | Walsh | Grainger | Ryan | Rees | McDonough | Masters | Elliott | Hedman | Leworthy | McGavin | Osbourne | Taylor | Brooke | Pollard | Restarick | Kinsella | Hannigan |
|---|---|---|---|---|---|---|---|---|---|---|---|---|---|---|---|---|---|---|---|---|---|---|---|---|---|---|---|---|---|---|---|---|---|---|---|---|
| 1 | 18 Aug | Yeovil | 0-2 | 4169 | | 1 | 2 | 3 | 4 | 5 | 6 | 7* | 8 | 9 | 10 | 11 | 12 | | | | | | | | | | | | | | | | | | | |
| 2 | 22 | Welling | 1-1 | 1828 | Yates | 1 | 2 | 3 | 4 | 5 | 6 | 10 | 8* | 14 | 9 | 11 | 7+ | 12 | | | | | | | | | | | | | | | | | | |
| 3 | 25 | MERTHYR | 3-1 | 2008 | Collins, Bennett, Yates | 1 | 2 | 3 | 4 | 5 | 6 | 10 | 8 | | 9 | 11 | 12 | 7* | | | | | | | | | | | | | | | | | | |
| 4 | 27 | Fisher | 0-0 | 1395 | | 1 | 2 | 3 | 4 | 5 | 6 | 10 | 8+ | 12 | 9 | 11 | | 7* | 14 | | | | | | | | | | | | | | | | | |
| 5 | 1 Sept | NORTHWICH | 4-0 | 1966 | English, Yates, Walsh(2) | 1 | 2 | 3 | 4 | 5 | 6 | 7 | 8 | | 9 | 11 | | | | 10 | | | | | | | | | | | | | | | | |
| 6 | 8 | Barrow | 2-2 | 1441 | Yates, Walsh | 1 | 2 | 3 | 4 | 5 | 6 | 7* | 8+ | | 9 | 11 | | | 14 | 10 | 12 | | | | | | | | | | | | | | | |
| 7 | 15 | TELFORD | 2-0 | 2164 | Daniels, Walsh | 1 | 2 | 3 | 4 | 5 | 6 | | 8 | | 9 | 11 | | | 7 | 10 | | | | | | | | | | | | | | | | |
| 8 | 19 | Boston | 3-1 | 1620 | Bennett, Walsh(2) | 1 | 2* | 3 | 4 | 5 | 6 | 14 | 8+ | | 9 | 11 | | | 7 | 10 | | 12 | | | | | | | | | | | | | | |
| 9 | 22 | CHELTENHAM | 3-1 | 2527 | Atkins(pen), Bennett, Walsh | 1 | 2 | 3 | 4 | 5 | 6 | | 8* | | 9 | 11 | | | 7 | 10 | | 12 | 14 | | | | | | | | | | | | | |
| 10 | 29 | Runcorn | 0-3 | 861 | Atkins(2)(1pen), Marmon | 1 | 2 | 3 | 4 | 5 | 6 | | 8* | | 9 | 11 | | | 7 | 10 | | 12 | | | | | | | | | | | | | | |
| 11 | 6 Oct | Macclesfield | 0-1 | 1100 | | 1 | 2 | 3 | 4 | 5 | 6 | 12 | 8* | | 9 | 11 | | | 7 | 10 | | | | | | | | | | | | | | | | |
| 12 | 13 | SUTTON | 1-0 | 2716 | | 1 | 2 | 3 | 4 | 5 | 6 | 12 | 8* | | 9 | 11 | | | 7 | 10+ | | | | 14 | | | | | | | | | | | | |
| 13 | 20 | Bath | 2-1 | 1078 | Atkins(pen), Yates | 1 | 2 | 3 | 4 | 5 | 6 | | 8* | | 9 | 11 | | | 7 | 10 | | | | 14 | | | | | | | | | | | | |
| 14 | 27 | BARROW | 1-0 | 2650 | Walsh | 1 | 2 | 3 | 4 | 5 | 6 | | 8 | | 9* | 11 | | | 7 | 10 | | | | 12 | | | | | | | | | | | | |
| 15 | 3 Nov | STAFFORD | 2-0 | 2403 | English, Walsh | 1 | 2 | 3 | 4 | 5 | 6 | | 8 | | 9 | 11 | | | 7 | 10* | | | | 12 | | | | | | | | | | | | |
| 16 | 10 | Kettering | 0-1 | 5020 | | 1 | 2 | 3 | 4 | 5 | 6 | | 8 | | 9* | 11 | | | 7 | 10 | | | | 12 | | | | | | | | | | | | |
| 17 | 24 | Wycombe | 2-2 | 2970 | Yates, Walsh | 1 | 2 | 3 | 4 | 5 | 6 | | 8 | | 9+ | 11 | | | 7 | 10 | | | | 12 | 14 | | | | | | | | | | | |
| 18 | 1 Dec | Stafford | 2-0 | 1304 | Marmon, McDonough | 1 | 2 | 3 | 4 | 5 | 6 | | 12 | | 8 | 11 | | | 7 | 10* | | | | 9 | | | | | | | | | | | | |
| 19 | 15 | Merthyr | 0-3 | 710 | | 1 | 2 | | 4 | 5 | 6 | | | | 9 | 11* | | 12 | 7 | 10+ | | 8 | | | 14 | 3 | | | | | | | | | | |
| 20 | 22 | Cheltenham | 2-0 | 1379 | English, Walsh | 1 | 2 | 3 | 4 | 5 | 6 | | 12 | | 9 | 11 | | | 7+ | 10 | | | | | 8+ | 14 | | | | | | | | | | |
| 21 | 26 | BARNET | 0-0 | 3946 | | 1 | 2 | 3 | 4 | 5 | 6 | | | | 8+ | 11 | | | 7 | 10 | | | | 12 | 9* | 14 | | | | | | | | | | |
| 22 | 29 | BOSTON | 3-1 | 2416 | Collins, English, Walsh | 1 | 2 | 3 | 4 | 5 | 6 | | 8* | | | 11 | | | 7 | 10 | | | | 9+ | 14 | 12 | | | | | | | | | | |
| 23 | 1 Jan | Barnet | 1-3 | 5105 | Walsh | 1 | | 3 | 4 | 5 | 6 | | 8+ | | 12 | 11 | | | 7 | 10 | | | | 9* | 14 | 2 | | | | | | | | | | |
| 24 | 5 | SLOUGH | 2-1 | 2715 | Bennett, Walsh | 1 | | 3 | 4* | 5 | 6 | | 8 | | 12 | 11 | | | 7 | 10 | | | | 9+ | 14 | 2 | | | | | | | | | | |
| 25 | 19 | Altrincham | 2-2 | 1388 | McDonough, English | 1 | 12 | 3 | 4* | 5 | 6+ | | 8 | | 14 | 11 | | | 7 | 10 | | | | 9 | | 2 | | | | | | | | | | |
| 26 | 26 | Sutton | 1-0 | 1496 | McDonough | 1 | 2 | 3 | 4* | 5 | | | 8 | | 10 | 11 | | | 7 | | | | | 9 | 14 | 6 | | | | | | | | | | |
| 27 | 2 Mar | BATH | 2-0 | 2277 | Atkins, Walsh | 1 | 2 | 3 | 4 | 5 | 6 | | 8* | | | 11 | | | 7 | 10+ | | 12 | | 9 | 14 | | | | | | | | | | | |
| 28 | 5 | Slough | 2-0 | 1120 | McDonough(2) | 1 | 2 | 3 | 4* | 5 | 6 | | 8+ | | | 11 | | | 7 | 10 | | 14 | | 9 | | 12 | | | | | | | | | | |
| 29 | 9 | MACCLESFIELD | 1-0 | 2735 | Atkings(pen) | 1 | 2 | 3 | 4 | 5 | 6 | | 8* | | | 11 | | | 7 | 10 | | 12 | | 9 | | | | | | | | | | | | |
| 30 | 12 | RUNCORN | 2-2 | 2969 | Bennett, Ryan | 1 | 2 | 3 | 4 | 5 | 6 | | 8 | | | 11 | | | 7 | 10* | | 12 | | 9 | | | | | | | | | | | | |
| 31 | 23 | FISHER | 2-1 | 2493 | McDonough, Walsh | 1 | 2 | 3 | 4 | 5 | | | 8 | | | 11 | | | 7 | 10 | | | | 9 | | 6 | | | | | | | | | | |
| 32 | 26 | Wycombe | 0-1 | 3200 | | 1 | 2 | 3 | 4 | 5 | 7 | | | | | 11 | | | 14 | 10+ | | 8 | | 9* | 12 | 6 | | | | | | | | | | |
| 33 | 30 | YEOVIL | 0-1 | 3115 | | 1 | 2 | 3 | 4 | 5 | 6 | | 8* | | | 11 | | | 12 | 14 | | | | 9 | | | 7+ | 10 | | | | | | | | |
| 34 | 2 Apr | Gateshead | 2-1 | 753 | Leworthy, McDonough | 1 | 2 | 3 | | 5 | | | | | | 11* | | | 4 | 10+ | | | | 9 | | 6 | 7 | 8 | 12 | 14 | | | | | | |
| 35 | 6 | Northwich | 2-2 | 1094 | McDonough, Walsh | 1 | 2 | 3 | 4 | 5 | | | | | | | | | | 10 | | | | 9 | | 6 | 7 | 8 | | 11 | | | | | | |
| 36 | 9 | WELLING | 2-1 | 2889 | English, Atkings(pen) | 1 | 2 | 3 | 4 | 5 | | | | | | | | | | 10 | | | | 9 | | 6 | 7 | 8* | 12 | 11 | | | | | | |
| 37 | 17 | KETTERING | 3-1 | 5084 | English, Donald, Bennett | 1 | 2 | 3 | | 5 | | | 9 | | | | | | 4 | 10* | | | | | | 6 | 7 | 8 | 12 | 11 | | | | | | |
| 38 | 20 | ALTRINCHAM | 1-1 | 6986 | Leworthy | 1 | 2 | 3 | | 5 | 6 | | 10 | | | | | | 4 | | | | | 9* | | | 7 | 8 | 12 | 11 | | | | | | |
| 39 | 22 | Kidderminster | 0-0 | 1721 | | 1 | 2 | 3 | 10+ | 5 | 6 | | 9 | | | | | | 4 | | | | | | | 14 | 7 | 8 | 12 | 11* | | | | | | |
| 40 | 26 | Telford | 2-0 | 1592 | | 1 | 2 | 10 | | 5+ | 6 | | 9* | | | | | | 4 | | 11 | 12 | | | | 3 | 7 | 8 | 14 | | | | | | | |
| 41 | 30 | GATESHEAD | 3-0 | 2367 | Bennett, Leworthy(2) | 1 | 2 | 3 | | | 6 | 12 | 8+ | | | | | | 4 | | 11 | 14 | | | | 5 | 7 | 10 | 9* | | | | | | | |
| 42 | 4 May | KIDDERMINSTER | 2-0 | 3481 | Ryan, Bennett | 1 | 2 | 3 | | | 5 | 12 | 8* | | | | | | 4 | | 11 | 10 | | | | 6 | 7 | | 9 | | | | | | | |

## F.A.Cup

| | | | | | | | | | | | | | | | | | | | | | | | | | | | | | | | | | | | | |
|---|---|---|---|---|---|---|---|---|---|---|---|---|---|---|---|---|---|---|---|---|---|---|---|---|---|---|---|---|---|---|---|---|---|---|---|---|
| 1st | 17 Nov | READING | 2-1 | 3761 | Atkins(pen), Marmon | 1 | 2 | 3 | 4 | 5 | 6 | | 8 | | 9 | 11 | | | 7 | 10 | | | | | | | | | | | | | | | | |
| 2nd | 12 Dec | LEYTON ORIENT | 0-0 | 6150 | | 1 | 2 | 3 | 4 | 5 | 6 | | 12 | | 8* | 11 | | | 7 | 10 | | | | 9 | | | | | | | | | | | | |
| 2/R | 18 | Leyton Orient | 1-4 | 4165 | Masters | 1 | 2 | 3 | 4 | 5+ | 6 | | 14 | | 9 | | | 12 | 7 | 10 | 11 | | | | 8* | | | | | | | | | | | |

## Bob Lord Trophy

| | | | | | | | | | | | | | | | | | | | | | | | | | | | | | | | | | | | | |
|---|---|---|---|---|---|---|---|---|---|---|---|---|---|---|---|---|---|---|---|---|---|---|---|---|---|---|---|---|---|---|---|---|---|---|---|---|
| 1st | 21 Jan | Fisher | * | 293 | Restarick(2), Marmon | 1 | 8 | 3 | | | 6 | | | | 4 | 11* | 14 | 2 | | | | 10 | | | 9 | | | | | | | 7+ | 5 | 12 | | |
| 2nd | 26 Feb | Sutton | 0-2 | 582 | | 1 | | | | | 6 | | | | | | 8+ | 2 | 7 | | 3 | 9* | | | 10 | | | | | | 4 | | 5 | 12 | 11 | 14 |

* After Extra Time

## F.A. Trophy

| | | | | | | | | | | | | | | | | | | | | | | | | | | | | | | | | | | | | |
|---|---|---|---|---|---|---|---|---|---|---|---|---|---|---|---|---|---|---|---|---|---|---|---|---|---|---|---|---|---|---|---|---|---|---|---|---|
| 1st | 15 Jan | Windsor & Eton | 1-0 | 727 | Bennett | 1 | 12 | 3 | 4 | 5 | 6 | | 8 | | | 11 | | | 7 | 10 | | | | 9 | 14 | 2 | | | | | | | | | | |
| 2nd | 2 Feb | RUNCORN | 2-0 | 2348 | Walsh, Marmon | 1 | 2 | 3 | 4 | 5 | 12 | | 8 | | 14 | 11 | | | 7 | 10 | | | | 9 | | 6 | | | | | | | | | | |
| 3rd | 23 | WIVENHOE | 3-0 | 4923 | Bennett(2), McDonough | 1 | 2 | 3 | 4 | 5 | 6 | | 8 | | | 11 | | | 7 | 10 | 12 | 14 | | 9 | | | | | | | | | | | | |
| 4th | 16 Mar | WITTON | 0-2 | 3079 | | 1 | 2 | 3 | 4 | 5 | | | 8 | | | 11 | | | 7 | | | 10* | | 9 | 12 | 6 | | | | | | | | | | |

(Back): Foley & Phillips (Coaches), Grainger, Daniels, Patten, Barrett, Walsh, English, Bevis (Physio), McDonough (P/Coach). (Front): McGavin, Kinsella. N.Smith, Donald, Restarick, Bennett, Elliot, Collins.

### GM VAUXHALL CONFERENCE

| | | Home | | | | | Away | | | | | |
|---|---|---|---|---|---|---|---|---|---|---|---|---|
| | P | W | D | L | F | A | W | D | L | F | A | Pts |
| BARNET | 42 | 13 | 4 | 4 | 50 | 23 | 13 | 5 | 3 | 53 | 29 | 87 |
| COLCHESTER UNITED | 42 | 16 | 4 | 1 | 41 | 13 | 9 | 6 | 6 | 27 | 22 | 85 |
| ALTRINCHAM | 42 | 12 | 6 | 3 | 48 | 22 | 11 | 7 | 3 | 39 | 24 | 82 |
| KETTERING TOWN | 42 | 12 | 6 | 3 | 38 | 18 | 11 | 5 | 5 | 29 | 28 | 80 |
| WYCOMBE WANDERERS | 42 | 15 | 3 | 3 | 46 | 17 | 6 | 8 | 7 | 29 | 29 | 74 |
| TELFORD UNITED | 42 | 11 | 3 | 7 | 30 | 21 | 9 | 4 | 8 | 32 | 31 | 67 |
| MACCLESFIELD TOWN | 42 | 11 | 4 | 6 | 38 | 22 | 6 | 8 | 7 | 25 | 30 | 63 |
| RUNCORN | 42 | 12 | 4 | 5 | 44 | 23 | 4 | 8 | 11 | 25 | 36 | 58 |
| MERTHYR TYDFIL | 42 | 9 | 5 | 7 | 37 | 24 | 7 | 4 | 10 | 25 | 37 | 57 |
| BARROW | 42 | 10 | 8 | 3 | 34 | 24 | 5 | 4 | 12 | 25 | 41 | 57 |
| WELLING UNITED | 42 | 7 | 10 | 4 | 32 | 27 | 6 | 5 | 10 | 22 | 30 | 54 |
| NORTHWICH VICTORIA | 42 | 8 | 7 | 6 | 33 | 30 | 5 | 6 | 10 | 32 | 45 | 52 |
| KIDDERMINSTER HARRIERS | 42 | 8 | 5 | 8 | 33 | 30 | 6 | 5 | 10 | 23 | 37 | 52 |
| YEOVIL TOWN | 42 | 9 | 5 | 7 | 35 | 29 | 4 | 6 | 11 | 20 | 29 | 50 |
| STAFFORD RANGERS | 42 | 7 | 9 | 5 | 30 | 26 | 5 | 5 | 11 | 18 | 25 | 50 |
| CHELTENHAM TOWN | 42 | 8 | 6 | 7 | 29 | 25 | 4 | 6 | 11 | 25 | 47 | 48 |
| GATESHEAD | 42 | 10 | 3 | 8 | 32 | 38 | 4 | 3 | 14 | 20 | 54 | 48 |
| BOSTON UNITED | 42 | 9 | 4 | 8 | 40 | 31 | 3 | 7 | 11 | 15 | 38 | 47 |
| SLOUGH TOWN | 42 | 9 | 4 | 8 | 31 | 29 | 4 | 2 | 15 | 20 | 51 | 46 |
| BATH CITY | 42 | 9 | 4 | 8 | 33 | 27 | 1 | 8 | 12 | 16 | 34 | 42 |
| SUTTON UNITED | 42 | 6 | 8 | 9 | 29 | 33 | 4 | 3 | 14 | 33 | 49 | 38 |
| FISHER ATHLETIC | 42 | 3 | 9 | 9 | 22 | 30 | 2 | 6 | 13 | 16 | 49 | 30 |

# SEASON 1991–92 GM Conference

| No. | Date | Opposition | Res | Attend | Goalscorers | Barrett | Donald | Grainger | Kinsella | English | Elliott | Collins | Bennett | McDonough | McGavin | Smith | Goodwin | Phillips | Abrahams | Gray | Roberts | Cook | Restarick | Hazel * | Masters | Stewart | Martin | Hannigan | Partner | Duffett |
|---|---|---|---|---|---|---|---|---|---|---|---|---|---|---|---|---|---|---|---|---|---|---|---|---|---|---|---|---|---|---|
| 1 | 17 Aug | MACCLESFIELD | 2–1 | 2293 | Bennett, McGavin | 1 | 2 | 3 | 4 | 5 | 6 | 7 | 8 | 9 | 10 | 11 | | | | | | | | | | | | | | |
| 2 | 24 | BARROW | 1–1 | 1480 | Kinsella | 1 | 2 | 3 | 4 | 5 | 6 | 7 | 8 | 9 | 10 | 11 | | | | | | | | | | | | | | |
| 3 | 26 | Slough | 4–2 | 2226 | McDonough(4) | 1 | 2 | 3 | 4 | 5* | 6 | 7 | 8 | 9 | 10+ | 11 | | 12 | 14 | | | | | | | | | | | |
| 4 | 31 | BATH | 5–0 | 2416 | Bennett(3), McGavin(2) | 1 | 2 | 3 | 4 | 5 | 6 | 7 | 8 | 9+ | 10 | 11 | | | 14 | | | | | | | | | | | |
| 5 | 7 Sept | Witton | 2–2 | 1045 | Collins, McDonough | 1 | 2 | 3 | 4 | 5 | 6 | 7 | 8 | 9 | 10 | 11 | | | | | | | | | | | | | | |
| 6 | 10 | FARNBOROUGH | 2–3 | 2954 | Collins, McGavin | 1 | 2 | 3+ | 4 | 5 | 6 | 7 | 8 | 9 | 10 | 11 | 14 | | | | | | | | | | | | | |
| 7 | 13 | YEOVIL | 4–0 | 2979 | English, Bennett(2), McGavin | 1 | 2 | 3 | 4 | 5 | 6 | 7 | 8 | 9+ | 10 | 11 | | | 14 | | | | | | | | | | | |
| 8 | 21 | Cheltenham | 1–1 | 1157 | McDonough | 1 | 2 | 3 | 4 | 5 | 6 | 7 | 8 | 9 | | 11 | | | | 10 | | | | | | | | | | |
| 9 | 28 | Wycombe | 2–1 | 5186 | Barrett, Smith | 1 | 2 | | 4 | 5 | 6 | 7 | 8 | 9 | 10 | 11 | | | | | 3 | | | | | | | | | |
| 10 | 5 Oct | ALTRINCHAM | 3–3 | 2853 | McDonough, McGavin, O.G. | 1 | 2 | | 4 | 5 | 6 | 7 | 8 | 9 | 10 | 11 | | | | | 3 | | | | | | | | | |
| 11 | 12 | RUNCORN | 2–1 | 2617 | Bennett, McDonough(pen) | 1 | 2 | | 14 | 5 | 6 | 7 | 8+ | 9 | 10 | 11 | | | | | 3 | 4 | | | | | | | | |
| 12 | 19 | Telford | 3–0 | 1109 | McDonough(2)(1pen), Smith | 1 | 2 | | 14 | 5 | 6 | 7 | 8 | 9* | 10 | 11 | | 12 | | | 3 | 4+ | | | | | | | | |
| 13 | 30 | Yeovil | 1–0 | 2385 | Bennett | 1 | 2 | | 4 | 5 | 6 | 7 | 8* | 9 | 10 | 11 | 12 | | | | 3 | | | | | | | | | |
| 14 | 2 Nov | STAFFORD | 2–0 | 2139 | McDonough, Smith | 1 | 2+ | | 4 | 5 | 6 | 7 | 8 | 9* | 10 | 11 | 14 | | | | 3 | 12 | 14 | | | | | | | |
| 15 | 9 | Farnborough | 2–0 | 3069 | Elliott, Bennett | 1 | 2 | | 4 | 5 | 6 | 7 | 8+ | 9* | 10 | 11 | | | | | 3 | 12 | | | | | | | | |
| 16 | 23 | WELLING | 3–1 | 2933 | English, Bennett, Cook | 1 | 2 | | 4 | 5 | 6 | 7 | 8 | 9* | 10 | 11 | | | | | 3 | 12 | | | | | | | | |
| 17 | 30 | Northwich | 1–1 | 1042 | McDonough | 1 | 2 | 5 | 14 | | 6 | 7 | | 9 | 10 | 11* | | 4 | | | 3 | 8 | | | | | | | | |
| 18 | 3 Dec | Stafford | 3–3 | 961 | Bennett(2), McGavin | 1 | 2 | | 4 | | 6 | 7 | 8 | 9 | 10 | 11 | | | | | 3 | 5 | | | | | | | | |
| 19 | 7 | WYCOMBE | 3–0 | 5862 | McGavin(2), Bennett | 1 | 2 | | 4 | | 6 | 7 | 8 | 9 | 10 | 11 | | | | | 3 | 5 | | | | | | | | |
| 20 | 14 | Gateshead | 2–0 | 542 | Bennett, McDonough | 1 | 2 | | 4 | | 6 | 7 | 8 | 9 | | 11 | | | | | 3 | 5 | 10 | | | | | | | |
| 21 | 21 | WITTON | 3–2 | 2842 | Bennett, McGavin, English | 1 | 2 | | 4+ | 12 | 6 | 7 | 8* | 9 | 10 | 11 | | | | 14 | 3 | 5 | | | | | | | | |
| 22 | 26 | Redbridge | 1–2 | 2327 | McDonough | 1 | 2 | | 4 | 5 | 6 | 12 | 8 | 9 | 10* | 11 | | | | | 3 | 7+ | 14 | | | | | | | |
| 23 | 28 | Runcorn | 3–1 | 883 | Cook, McGavin, Bennett | 1 | 2 | | 12 | 5 | 6 | 7 | 8 | 9 | 10 | 11 | | | | | 3 | 4+ | | | | | | | | |
| 24 | 1 Jan | REDBRIDGE | 1–0 | 4773 | McGavin | 1 | 2 | | 12 | 5 | 6 | 7 | 8* | 9 | 10 | 11 | | | | | 3 | 4+ | 14 | | | | | | | |
| 25 | 4 | Merthyr | 0–2 | 1032 | | 1 | | 14 | 4 | 5 | 6 | 7 | 8* | 9 | 10 | 11 | | | | | 3 | 2+ | 12 | | | | | | | |
| 26 | 18 | CHELTENHAM | 4–0 | 2643 | Kinsella, McGavin(2), McDonough | 1 | 2 | 12 | 4 | 5 | 6+ | | 8* | 9 | 10 | 11 | | | | | 3 | 7 | | 14 | | | | | | |
| 27 | 24 | Kettering | 2–2 | 4100 | McGavin, Smith | 1 | 2 | 14 | 4 | 5 | 6 | | 8+ | 9 | 10 | 11 | | | | | 3 | 7* | | | 12 | | | | | |
| 28 | 7 Feb | Kidderminster | 2–2 | 1828 | Bennett, Smith | 1 | | | 4 | 5 | 6 | 7 | 8 | 9 | 10 | 11 | | | | | 3 | 2 | | | | | | | | |
| 29 | 11 | BOSTON | 1–0 | 3229 | McGavin | 1 | 14 | | 4 | 5 | 6 | 7 | 8 | 9* | 10 | 11 | | | | | 3 | 2+ | | | | 12 | | | | |
| 30 | 15 | Welling | 1–4 | 1837 | McDonough(pen) | 1 | 14 | | 4 | 5 | 6 | 7 | 8* | 9 | 10 | 11 | | | | | 3 | 2+ | | | | 12 | | | | |
| 31 | 28 | Altrincham | 2–1 | 905 | McDonough, McGavin | 1 | 2 | | 4 | 5 | | 7 | 14 | 9* | 10 | 11 | | | | | 3 | 6+ | | | 12 | 8 | | | | |
| 32 | 7 Mar | GATESHEAD | 2–0 | 2897 | Roberts, Masters | 1 | 2 | | 4 | 5 | | 7 | 14 | 9* | 10 | 11 | | | | | 3 | 6 | | | 12 | 8+ | | | | |
| 33 | 21 | NORTHWICH | 1–0 | 3218 | Smith | 1 | 2 | | 4 | 5 | 6 | 14 | 8+ | | 10 | 11 | | | | | 3 | 7* | | | | 12 | | | | |
| 34 | 24 | Bath | 0–0 | 1101 | | 1 | 2 | | 4 | 5 | 6 | | 14 | | 10 | 11 | | | | | 3 | 7 | | | 9 | 8 | | | | |
| 35 | 28 | KIDDERMINSTER | 3–0 | 5443 | Stewart, English, O.G. | 1 | 2 | | 4 | 5 | | | 14 | 9 | 10 | 11 | | | | | 3+ | 7 | | | 12 | 8 | 6 | | | |
| 36 | 14 Apr | SLOUGH | 4–0 | 3197 | Kinsella, Stewart, McDonough, Masters | 1 | 2 | | 4 | 5 | | | | 9 | 10 | 11 | | | | | 3 | 7 | | | | 8 | 6 | | | |
| 37 | 18 | TELFORD | 2–0 | 3964 | McDonough(2) | 1 | 2+ | | 4 | 5 | 6 | | 14 | 9 | 10* | 11 | | | | | 3 | | | | 12 | 8 | 7 | | | |
| 38 | 20 | MERHTYR | 2–0 | 4184 | Masters, Smith | 1 | 2 | | 4 | 5 | | | | 9 | 10 | 11 | | | | | 3 | 7 | | | 8 | | 6 | | | |
| 39 | 22 | Boston | 4–0 | 2305 | Masters, McGavin, McDonough (2)(1pen) | 1 | 2 | | 4 | 5 | 14 | | 12 | 9* | 10 | 11 | | | | | 3 | 7+ | | | 8 | | 6 | | | |
| 40 | 25 | Macclesfield | 4–4 | 886 | English(2), McDonough, O.G. | 1 | 2 | | 4 | 5 | | | 12 | 9 | 10* | 11 | | | | | 3 | 7 | | | 8 | | 6 | | | |
| 41 | 28 | KETTERING | 3–1 | 6303 | McDonough(2), McGavin | 1 | 2 | | 4+ | 5 | 14 | | 12 | 9 | 10* | 11 | | | | | 3 | 7 | | | 8 | | 6 | | | |
| 42 | 2 May | BARROW | 5–0 | 7193 | Masters(3), Smith, McDonough | 1 | 2 | | 4+ | 5 | 14 | | 10 | 9* | | 11 | | | | | 3 | 7 | | | 8* | 12 | 6 | | | |

* Changed name to Dart by deed poll during the season

# F.A.Cup

| | | | | | | | | | | | | | | | | | | | | | | | | | | | | | | | |
|---|---|---|---|---|---|---|---|---|---|---|---|---|---|---|---|---|---|---|---|---|---|---|---|---|---|---|---|---|---|---|---|
| 4/QR | 2 Nov | BURTON | 5–0 | 2147 | McDonough, Restarkk, Kinsella, McGavin(2) | 1 | 2 | | 4 | 5 | 6 | 7+ | 8 | 9* | 10 | 11 | | 3 | 14 | | | | 12 | | | | | | | |
| 1st | 16 | EXETER | 0–0 | 4965 | | 1 | 2 | 12 | 4 | 5 | 6 | 7 | 8 | 9 | 10 | 11* | | | | | | 3 | | | | | | | | |
| 1/R | 27 | Exeter | 0–0 | 4066 | Exeter won on penalties | 1 | 2 | 12 | 4 | 5 | | 7 | 8+ | 9 | 10 | 11 | 6* | | | | | 3 | 14 | | | | | | | |

# Bob Lord Trophy

(1st round – bye)

| | | | | | | | | | | | | | | | | | | | | | | | | | | | | | | | |
|---|---|---|---|---|---|---|---|---|---|---|---|---|---|---|---|---|---|---|---|---|---|---|---|---|---|---|---|---|---|---|---|
| 2nd | 8 Oct | KETTERING | 4–0 | 1289 | Kinsella(2), Collins, McGavin | 1 | 2 | 3 | 12 | 5 | | 7* | 8 | | 10 | 11 | | | 14 | | 5 | 4 | | | | | | | | 9+ |
| 3rd | 16 Dec | WYCOMBE | 2–6 | 919 | Restarick, McGavin | 1 | | 3 | | 6 | | | | 9* | 10 | | 7 | | 11 | 14 | 5+ | 2 | 8 | | | | | 12 | 4 | |

# F.A. Trophy

(1st round – bye)

| | | | | | | | | | | | | | | | | | | | | | | | | | | | | | | | |
|---|---|---|---|---|---|---|---|---|---|---|---|---|---|---|---|---|---|---|---|---|---|---|---|---|---|---|---|---|---|---|---|
| 2nd | 11 Jan | KINGSTONIAN | 2–2 | 2724 | English, Restarick | 1 | 2* | 14 | 12 | 5 | 6 | 7+ | 8 | | 10 | 11 | | | | | 3 | 4 | 9 | | | | | | | |
| 2/R | 14 | Kingstonian | 3–2 | 1642 | Bennett, Smith, McGavin | 1 | 2 | 12 | 4* | 5 | 6 | | 8 | | 10 | 11 | | | | | 3 | 7 | 9+ | 14 | | | | | | |
| 3rd | 1 Feb | Merthyr | 0–0 | 1211 | | 1 | 2 | | 4 | 5 | 6 | | | 9 | 10 | 11 | | | | | 3 | 7 | | | 8 | | | | | |
| 3/R | 4 | MERTHYR | 1–0 | 2746 | McDonough | 1 | | | 4 | 5 | 6 | 7 | 8 | 9 | 10 | 11 | | | | | 3 | 2 | | | | | | | | |
| 4th | 22 | MORECAMBE | 3–1 | 3296 | Stewart(2), McGavin | 1 | 2 | | 4 | 5 | | 7 | | 9 | 10 | 11 | | | | | 3* | 6 | | 14 | 12 | 8+ | | | | |
| 5th | 14 Mar | TELFORD | 4–0 | 3894 | McGavin, Bennett, Kinsella, Smith | 1 | 2 | | 4+ | 5 | 6 | 14 | 8 | 9* | 10 | 11 | | | | | 3 | 7 | | | | 12 | | | | |
| SF/1L | 4 Apr | MACCLESFIELD | 3–0 | 5443 | McDonough, English, Stewart | 1 | 2 | | 4 | 5 | | 14 | 12 | 9 | 10 | 11 | | | | | 3 | 6* | | | | 8 | 7+ | | | |
| SF/2L | 10 | Macclesfield | 1–1 | 1650 | Cook | 1 | 2 | | 4 | 5 | | | 14 | 9 | 10 | 11 | | | | | 3 | 7 | | | 12 | 8 | 6 | | | |
| F | 10 May | Witton (at Wemley) | 3–1 | 27806 | Masters, Smith, McGovin | 1 | 2 | | 4 | 5 | | | 12 | 9* | 10 | 11 | | | | | 3 | 7 | | | 8 | | 6 | | | |

COLCHESTER UNITED 1991–92 *Back row (left to right):* David Martin, Mike Masters, Shaun Elliott.
*Centre row:* Ian Phillips (Assistant Coach), Steve Foley (Youth Team/Assistant Coach), Paul Roberts, Paul Newell, Tony English, Scott Barrett, Martin Grainger, Roy McDonough (Player/Coach), Chris Toulson (Physiotherapist).
*Front row:* Gary Bennett, Nicky Smith, Eamonn Collins, Steve McGavin, Jason Cook, Steve Restarick, Warren Donald, Mark Kinsella.

## GM VAUXHALL CONFERENCE

| | | Home | | | | | Away | | | | | |
|---|---|---|---|---|---|---|---|---|---|---|---|---|
| | P | W | D | L | F | A | W | D | L | F | A | Pts |
| Colchester Utd | 42 | 19 | 1 | 1 | 57 | 11 | 9 | 9 | 3 | 41 | 29 | 94 |
| Wycombe W. | 42 | 18 | 1 | 2 | 49 | 13 | 12 | 3 | 6 | 35 | 22 | 94 |
| Kettering Town | 42 | 12 | 6 | 3 | 44 | 23 | 8 | 7 | 6 | 28 | 27 | 73 |
| Merthyr Tydfil | 42 | 14 | 4 | 3 | 40 | 24 | 4 | 10 | 7 | 19 | 32 | 68 |
| Farnborough T. | 42 | 8 | 7 | 6 | 36 | 27 | 10 | 5 | 6 | 32 | 26 | 66 |
| Telford Utd | 42 | 10 | 4 | 7 | 32 | 31 | 9 | 3 | 9 | 30 | 35 | 64 |
| Redbridge F. | 42 | 12 | 4 | 5 | 42 | 27 | 6 | 5 | 10 | 27 | 29 | 63 |
| Boston Utd | 42 | 10 | 4 | 7 | 40 | 35 | 8 | 5 | 8 | 31 | 31 | 63 |
| Bath City | 42 | 8 | 6 | 7 | 27 | 22 | 8 | 6 | 7 | 27 | 29 | 60 |
| Witton Albion | 42 | 11 | 6 | 4 | 41 | 26 | 5 | 4 | 12 | 22 | 34 | 58 |
| Northwich Vic | 42 | 10 | 4 | 7 | 40 | 25 | 6 | 2 | 13 | 23 | 33 | 54 |
| Welling United | 42 | 8 | 6 | 7 | 40 | 38 | 6 | 6 | 9 | 29 | 41 | 54 |
| Macclesfield T | 42 | 7 | 7 | 7 | 25 | 21 | 6 | 6 | 9 | 25 | 29 | 52 |
| Gateshead | 42 | 8 | 5 | 8 | 22 | 22 | 4 | 7 | 10 | 27 | 35 | 48 |
| Yeovil Town | 42 | 8 | 6 | 7 | 22 | 21 | 3 | 8 | 10 | 18 | 28 | 47 |
| Runcorn | 42 | 5 | 11 | 5 | 26 | 26 | 6 | 2 | 13 | 24 | 37 | 46 |
| Stafford Rgrs | 42 | 7 | 8 | 6 | 25 | 24 | 3 | 8 | 10 | 16 | 35 | 46 |
| Altrincham | 42 | 5 | 8 | 8 | 33 | 39 | 6 | 4 | 11 | 28 | 43 | 45 |
| Kidderminster | 42 | 8 | 6 | 7 | 35 | 32 | 4 | 3 | 14 | 21 | 45 | 45 |
| Slough Town | 42 | 7 | 3 | 11 | 26 | 39 | 6 | 3 | 12 | 30 | 43 | 45 |
| Cheltenham T | 42 | 8 | 5 | 8 | 28 | 35 | 2 | 8 | 11 | 28 | 47 | 43 |
| Barrow | 42 | 5 | 8 | 8 | 29 | 23 | 3 | 6 | 12 | 23 | 49 | 38 |

# SEASON 1992-93 Division Four

| No. | Date | Opposition | Res | Attend | Goalscorers | Newell | Donald | Roberts | Kinsella | English | Oxbrow | Devereux | Bennett | McDonough | Grainger | Smith | Abrahams | Phillips | Cook | Hazel | McGavin | Ball | Cawley | Green | Sorrell | Emberson | Betts | Martin | Hopkins | Flowers | Partner | Barber | Munson |
|---|---|---|---|---|---|---|---|---|---|---|---|---|---|---|---|---|---|---|---|---|---|---|---|---|---|---|---|---|---|---|---|---|---|
| 1 | 15 Aug | LINCOLN | 2-1 | 4131 | McDonough, Oxbrow | 1 | 2 | 3 | 4 | 5 | 6 | 7 | 8 | 9 | 10 | 11 | 12 | | | | | | | | | | | | | | | | |
| 2 | 21 | Barnet | 1-3 | 3600 | Kinsella | 1 | 2 | 3 | 4 | 5 | 6 | 7 | 8* | 9 | 10 | 11 | | 14 | | | | | | | | | | | | | | | |
| 3 | 29 | DARLINGTON | 0-3 | 3524 | | 1 | 14 | 3 | 4 | 5 | 6 | 2 | 8 | 9 | | 11 | | | 7* | 10 | | | | | | | | | | | | | |
| 4 | 1 Sep | SHREWSBURY | 0-2 | 3530 | | 1 | 2 | 3 | 4 | 5 | 6 | | 12 | 9* | | 11 | | | 7 | 8 | 10 | | | | | | | | | | | | |
| 5 | 5 | Bury | 2-3 | 2072 | Bennett, McDonough(pen) | 1 | 2 | 3 | 4 | 5* | 6 | | 8 | 9 | 14 | 11 | | | 7 | | 10 | | | | | | | | | | | | |
| 6 | 12 | WALSALL | 3-1 | 3218 | Bennett, Smith, McDonough(pen) | 1 | 2 | 3 | 4 | 5 | 6 | | 8 | 9 | 10 | 11 | | | 7 | | | | | | | | | | | | | | |
| 7 | 15 | Doncaster | 0-1 | 1719 | | 1 | 2 | 3 | 4 | 5 | 6 | | 8 | | 9 | 11 | | | 7 | | 10 | | | | | | | | | | | | |
| 8 | 19 | York | 0-2 | 3820 | | 1 | 2 | 3 | 4 | 5 | 6* | 12 | 8 | | 9 | 11 | | | 7 | | 10 | 14 | | | | | | | | | | | |
| 9 | 26 | CHESTERFIELD | 3-0 | 3436 | Bennett(2), Kinsella | 1 | | 3 | 4 | 5 | 6 | | 8 | | 2 | 11 | | | 7 | | 10 | 9 | | | | | | | | | | | |
| 10 | 10 Oct | Halifax | 4-2 | 2445 | Kinsella,Oxbrow, McDonough, Bennett | 1 | | 3 | 4 | | 6 | 12 | 8 | 9 | 2 | 11 | | | | | 10 | 7* | 5 | | | | | | | | | | |
| 11 | 16 | CREWE | 3-2 | 4524 | Bennett, McDonough, Oxbrow | 1 | | 3 | 4 | 12 | 6 | | 8 | 9 | 2 | 11 | | | 7* | | | 10 | 5 | | | | | | | | | | |
| 12 | 24 | Scunthorpe | 1-3 | 2473 | McGavin | 1 | | 3 | 4 | | 6 | 14 | 8 | 9 | 2 | 11 | | | 7* | | 10 | | 5 | | | | | | | | | | |
| 13 | 30 | WREXHAM | 2-4 | 4423 | Ball, Kinsella | 1 | | 3 | 4 | 6 | 12 | | 8 | 9 | 2 | 11 | | | 7* | | | 10 | 5 | | | | | | | | | | |
| 14 | 3 Nov | CARLISLE | 2-1 | 3263 | Roberts, Cawley | 1 | | 3 | 4 | 6 | | | 8* | 12 | 2 | 11 | | | 7 | | 10 | 9 | 5 | | | | | | | | | | |
| 15 | 7 | Cardiff | 1-3 | 5505 | Kinsella | | | 3 | 4 | 6 | | | 8 | 12* | | 11* | | | 2 | | 10 | 7 | 5 | 1 | 9 | | | | | | | | |
| 16 | 21 | ROCHDALE | 4-4 | 3172 | Cawley, Ball, Sorrell, McDonough | | | 3 | 4 | 6 | 14 | | 8* | 9 | | 11 | | | 12 | | 10 | 7 | 5 | 1 | 2 | | | | | | | | |
| 17 | 28 | Hereford | 1-3 | 1671 | Oxbrow | | 2 | 3 | | 6 | 14 | | 8 | 9 | | 11 | | | | | 10 | 7 | 5* | 1 | 4 | | | | | | | | |
| 18 | 11 Dec | TORQUAY | 2-0 | 2774 | McDonough, Smith | | | 3 | 4 | 6 | | | | 9 | 2 | 11 | | | 7 | | 10 | 14 | 5* | 1 | 8 | | | | | | | | |
| 19 | 18 | Gillingham | 1-0 | 2331 | McGavin | | | 3 | 4 | 6 | | | 8 | 9 | 2* | 11 | | | 7 | | 10 | | | | 12 | 1 | 5 | | | | | | |
| 20 | 26 | Northampton | 0-1 | 4861 | | | | 3 | 4 | 6 | | | 8 | 9* | 2 | 11 | 12 | | 7 | | 10 | | | | | 1 | 5 | | | | | | |
| 21 | 29 | SCARBOROUGH | 1-0 | 3640 | McGavin | | | 3 | 4 | 6 | | | 8 | 9 | 2 | 11 | | | 7 | | 10 | | | | | 1 | 5 | | | | | | |
| 22 | 2 Jan | Walsall | 3-1 | 3669 | Martin, McGavin, Cawley | | | 3 | 4 | | | | 8 | | 2 | 11 | | | 7 | | 10 | | 5 | | | 1 | 6 | 9 | | | | | |
| 23 | 8 | DONCASTER | 2-0 | 4402 | Grainger, McGavin | | | 3 | 4 | | | | 8 | | 2 | 11 | | | 7* | | 10 | 14 | 5 | | | 1 | 6 | 9 | | | | | |
| 24 | 16 | Chesterfield | 0-4 | 3016 | | | | 3 | 4 | | | | 8 | | 2 | 11 | | | 7 | | 10 | | 5 | | | 1 | 6 | 9 | | | | | |
| 25 | 22 | YORK | 0-0 | 4528 | | | | 3 | 4 | | | | 8 | | 2 | 11 | | | 7* | | 10 | 14 | 5 | | | 1 | 6 | 9 | | | | | |
| 26 | 29 | BARNET | 1-2 | 5609 | Bennett | | | 3 | 4 | | | | 8* | | | 11 | 12 | | 7 | | 10 | 2 | 5 | | | 1 | 6 | 9 | | | | | |
| 27 | 6 Feb | Lincoln | 1-1 | 3380 | Martin | | | 3 | 4 | 6 | | | 8 | | 2 | 11 | | | | | 10 | | 5 | | | 1 | 7 | 9 | | | | | |
| 28 | 13 | BURY | 0-0 | 3264 | | | | 3 | | 6 | | | 8 | | 2 | 11 | | | 14 | | 10 | 4 | 5* | | | 1 | 7 | 9 | | | | | |
| 29 | 20 | Shrewsbury | 3-4 | 2653 | Hopkins, Grainger(pen), McGavin | | | 3 | | 6 | | | | | 2 | 11 | 12 | | | | 10 | 4* | 5 | | | 1 | 7 | 9 | 8 | | | | |
| 30 | 26 | HALIFAX | 2-1 | 3007 | McGavin, Grainger | | | 3 | 4 | 6 | | | | 9 | 2 | 11 | 12 | | | | 10 | | 5 | | | 1 | 7 | | 8 | | | | |
| 31 | 12 Mar | CARDIFF | 2-4 | 4538 | McDonough(pen), McGavin | | | 3 | 4 | | | | 8 | 9 | | 11 | 12 | | 7 | | 10 | | | | | 1 | 2 | | 6 | 5* | 14* | | |
| 32 | 20 | Carlisle | 2-0 | 3003 | Cook, O.G. | | | 3 | 4 | | | | 8 | 9 | | 11 | 12 | | 7* | | 10 | | | | | | 2 | | 6 | 5 | | 1 | |
| 33 | 23 | HEREFORD | 3-1 | 3024 | O.G., McDonough, Abrahams | | | 3 | | 14 | | | 8 | 9 | 2 | 11 | 12 | | 7* | | 10 | | 5 | | | | 6 | | 4 | | | 1 | |
| 34 | 27 | Rochdale | 2-5 | 1783 | Smith, Abrahams | | | 3 | 4 | 8 | | | 12 | 9 | 2 | 11 | 10 | | | | | | 5 | | | | 6 | | 7* | | | 1 | |
| 35 | 6 Apr | Torquay | 2-2 | 2915 | McGavin, Ball | | | 3 | 4 | 6 | | | 12 | | 2 | 11 | 9 | | | | 10 | 7 | 5 | | | | | | 8 | | | 1 | |
| 36 | 13 | Scarborough | 1-0 | 1803 | Abrahams | | | 3 | 4 | 6 | | | | | | 11 | 9 | | 5 | | 10 | 7 | | | | | 2 | | 8 | | | 1 | |
| 37 | 16 | GILLINGHAM | 3-0 | 4695 | O.G., Smith, Abrahams | | | 3 | 4 | 6 | | | | | | 11 | 9 | | 5 | | 10 | 7 | | | | | 2 | | 8 | | | 1 | |
| 38 | 20 | NORTHAMPTON | 2-0 | 3519 | Ball(pen), Abrahams | | | 3 | 4 | 6 | | | 12 | | | 11 | 9 | | 5 | | 10 | 7* | | | | | 2 | | 8 | | | 1 | |
| 39 | 24 | Crewe | 1-7 | 3250 | English | | | 3 | 4 | 6 | | | 12 | | | 11 | 9 | | 5 | | 10* | 7 | | | | | 2 | | 8 | | | 1 | |
| 40 | 1 May | SCUNTHORPE | 1-0 | 3421 | Abrahams | | | 3 | 4 | 6 | | | | | 14 | 11 | 9 | | 5* | | 10 | 7 | | | | | 2 | | 8 | | | 1 | |
| 41 | 4 | Darlington | 0-1 | 2007 | | | | 3 | | 6 | | | | 12 | 2* | 11 | 9 | | 5 | | 10 | 7 | | | | | 4 | | 8 | | | 1 | |
| 42 | 8 | Wrexham | 3-4 | 9705 | O.G., Bennett, Kinsella | | | 3* | 4 | | | | 8 | | 5 | 11 | 9 | | | | 10 | 7 | 6 | | | | 2 | | | 14 | | | 1 |

# F.A.Cup

| | | | | | | | | | | | | | | | | | | | | | | | | | | | | | | | | | |
|---|---|---|---|---|---|---|---|---|---|---|---|---|---|---|---|---|---|---|---|---|---|---|---|---|---|---|---|---|---|---|---|---|---|
| 1st | 14 Nov | SLOUGH | 4-0 | 3848 | Sorrell, Bennett(2), Ball | | | 3 | 4 | 6 | 12 | | 8 | 9 | | 11 | | | | | 10 | 7 | 5 | 1 | 2 | | | | | | | | |
| 2nd | 5 Dec | GILLINGHAM | 1-1 | 5319 | McGavin | | | 3 | 4 | 6 | | | | 9 | 2 | 11 | | | 7 | | 10 | | 5 | 1 | 8 | | | | | | | | |
| 2nd/R | 16 | Gillingham | 2-3 | 4440 | Ball(2) | | | 3 | 4 | 6 | | | 12 | 9 | 2 | 11 | | | 7 | | 10 | 5 | | 1 | 8* | | 14 | | | | | | |

# Coca Cola (Football League) Cup

| | | | | | | | | | | | | | | | | | | | | | | | | | | | | | | | | | |
|---|---|---|---|---|---|---|---|---|---|---|---|---|---|---|---|---|---|---|---|---|---|---|---|---|---|---|---|---|---|---|---|---|---|
| 1/1L | 18 Aug | BRIGHTON | 1-1 | 3817 | English | 1 | 2 | 3 | 4 | 5 | 6 | 7 | 8 | 9 | 10 | 11 | | | | | | | | | | | | | | | | | |
| 1/2L | 26 | Brighton | 0-1 | 4125 | | 1 | 2* | 3 | 4 | 5 | 6 | | 8 | 9 | | 11 | 12 | | 7 | 10 | | | | | | | | | | | | | |

COLCHESTER UNITED 1992–93 *Back row (left to right):* Steve Foley (Youth Team Coach), Tony English (Captain), Martin Grainger, Nathan Munson, Steve McGavin, Paul Roberts, Roy McDonough (Manager).
*Centre row:* Chris Toulson (Physio), Robbie Deveraux, Nicky Smith, Julian Hazel, James Goodwin, Paul Abrahams, Eamon Mongan, Ian Phillips (Assistant Coach).
*Front row:* Gary Bennett, Warren Donald, Jason Cook, Mark Kinsella, Nicky Cropper.

# Advanced Subscribers

Gordon H. Parker, Colchester
Peter Powell, Colchester
Bob Dixey (Halstead)
Mike Thornton, Enfield, Romford
Keith Rowe
Ron Smith
John Chamley
Alan Chamley
Mark Chamley
Bernadette Chamley
Dave Johnson
Jeff Whitehead, Rowhedge
Pauline Harvey, Colchester
Mr.P.R.Bower,Copthorne,W.Sussex
Mark Whybrow, Colchester
Malcolm Slowgrove, West Bergholt
Andrew Twitchett
Bert Cardy, Richmond, Surrey
Alastair Riley, Wellington, Somerset
H.J. Green, Colchester
John R. Fothergill, Colchester
Andrew Bradshaw of Fordham
Peter R. Jones, Colchester
Chris Porcas, Tiptree Barsider
Lawrence Bloomfield, Colchester, Essex
Ken Newman, Lamarsh
David Hazell, Warwick
Brian Waller, Colchester
Keith Brandom, Great Tey
Geoff Harper - Colchester
Malcolm & Cicelie Smith, Gosfield
Jason Finch, Purleigh, Essex
Robert Simmons, Colchester
Fred Woods, Monkwick, Colchester
John Treleven
Dave McPherson, Colchester
J. Motson
David Earnshaw, Belper, Derbyshire
Raymond Shaw
T.R. Deeker

David Clow - Ardrossen
Hugh and Jeremy Fielden
Mr. K.P. Wood
J.A. Harris
Andrew Thomas, Sible Hedingham
Gary Bird, Sible Hedingham
David Keats, Thornton Heath
Moira and Frederick Furness
Alan Davies
Mr. D.M. Fuller
Terry Thompson, Colchester, Essex
Steven Petchey, Colchester
Terrence Wilde, Colchester, Essex
Stewart Fell
David Jowett
John Byrne
Graham Spackman
David Downs
L.A. Zammit
Fred Lee, Plymouth Argyle
Bernard John Lewis, Clacton
Mark Tyler
Peter Kirby, Maidstone
Philip H. Whitehead
Derek Hyde
Phil Hollow
M.J. Cripps
Geoffrey Wright
Willy Østby - Norway
Jonny Stokkeland, Kvinesdal, Norway
David Welham, Ardleigh, Essex
Mr. G. Haylock, Braintree
Terje Ovrebo, Norway
Duncan Watt
Andy Molden
Keith Wightman, Chelmsford
Coral & Paul, Bournemouth
Frank Wilkin
Paul Wilkin, Chelmsford
Ted Ketley, Colchester

Ann & Michael Crosby
Thora Spencer, Colchester
Steven Streeter, Colchester, Essex
Ian Spencer, Colchester
Richard Rose, Brentwood
Kevin Hayes, Glemsford, Suffolk
Andrew Bradford, Coggeshall, Essex
Peter Baxter
Peter Cogle
W.D. Phillips
A.H. Atkins, Toronto Canada
Peter Joyce, Longridge, Colchester
Gary Tuckwell, Safety Officer
Tony Bragg, Romford
Paul Dobson, Colchester, Essex
Vic Honer, Wickham Bishops
Karen Roberts, Witham, Essex
Rob Cross of Marks Tey
Robert Hadgraft
Martin Simons, Belgium
Lars-Olof Wendler, Sweden
Terry Frost
A.N. Other
Steve Emms
Mark Catchpole, Feering, Essex
Mr. T. Kershaw
S. Frost
Lloyd Smith, Sudbury, Suffolk
David Keyes, Tiptree
A.J. Austin, Stanway, Colchester
Chris Dowsett HRC
Michael Middleton, Colchester
Richard John Batterham, Stanway
Godfrey Kyte, Great Waldingfield
Ian Farthing, Lowestoft, Suffolk
Collins Family, Harwich
Marius Nieuwenhuis, West Bergholt
B.H. Standish
Harry Kay
Geoff Allman

Jonathan Hall
Gareth M. Davies, Holyhead
Geoff Toon, Colchester
Stephen Peacock, Colchester
Paul Kilvert, Hull, Yorkshire
Kevin Roberts, Colchester, Essex
Ian Ward, Lisbon, Portugal
Richard Stocken
Christopher Streeter, Colchester, Essex
Derek Pullen, Abingdon
H.R. Piper, Chelmsford, Essex
Andrew Cox, Wivenhoe
Stephen Garnham, Colchester
The Forsdike Family, Southampton
B.A. Dobson, Colchester
Glyn Appleby, Fordham, Colchester
Bryan Hicks, Walton
Peter Turner, Shakespeare Road
Joe Geddis, Colchester
Karen Duffield, Colchester
David Godfrey, York
David Kendall Edwards, Braintree
Ken Craig, Soham, Cambs.
Mike Clifford, Aldershot, Hants.
Frank Parry, Deal, Kent
Malc Hartley
Michael McConkey, Luton, Beds.
A. & J.A. Waterman
David Helliwell
Dave Smith
Mr. L. Burgess

Trevor Bailey, Capel, Suffolk
Andrew John Hurst
Graham Keeble, Colchester
Frank Owen, Colne Engaine
Gordon Poulter, Woolmer Green
David Todd, Harwich
Anthony Eves, Great Dunmow
From Thérèsa
Shaun Gould, Braintree
Mr. Noel Kearney
Chris Hooker, Ontario, Canada
Göran Schönhult, Sweden
Christer Svensson
Karen Ann Giblin
Andrew Anderson
Brian Tabner
Gordon Small
Bob Lilliman
Grahame & Jan Townrow
Tony Hesp, Marks Tey
Bob Searle, Westcliff
The Astle Family, Blackheath
Colin Jaggs, Roundhay, Leeds
Christopher Sell, Stansted, Essex
Glenn Speller, Thetford, Norfolk
Bob Ogden, Woodley, Berkshire
Mark Feist, Manchester
Jeremy Dimond, Aylesbury, Bucks.
Ian Hutley
Terry O'Connor, Chelmsford
Bernard Paul Willmott, Manningtree

Barry Bartlett, Prettygate, Colchester
David Amoss, St. Albans
Mike Gadbury, Weybridge, Surrey
Ed Carter, Colchester
Dale and Chris, Clubshop
Jon Minter, West Mersea
Paul Booker
Duncan Wyatt, Colchester, Essex
Russell Smith, Sudbury, Suffolk
Dennis Brian Allen, Copford
Peter Oldfield
Dennis Wood, Shoreham, Sussex
Jerry Everett
Nicola Newman, Colchester, Essex
Malcolm Root, Halstead, Essex
Kenneth E. Goody
David Lumb
Alan Hindley
John Draper – PNE Programmes
Vincent Taylor
Marcus Tinworth, Romford Close
Jolyon Everitt, Layer
Trond Isaksen, Norway
Clive Scoffin
Mr.R.G.Clarke, Witham, Essex
Mr. Pittock
Geoff Jackson, East Barnet
Joan Geddis, Shrub End
David and William Evans
Chris Phillips
Arran Matthews

## A SELECTION OF TITLES

**From**

# 'YORE PUBLICATIONS'
# 12 The Furrows, Harefield, Middx. UB9 6AT

**(Free lists issued 3 times per year. For your first list please send a S.A.E.)**

*REJECTED F.C. VOLUME 1 (Reprint) (By Dave Twydell)* The 2nd Edition of this popular book – now in hardback – this volume provides the comprehensive histories of: Aberdare Athletic, Ashington, Bootle, Bradford (Park Avenue), Burton (Swifts, Wanderers and United), Gateshead/South Shields, Glossop, Loughborough, Nelson, Stalybridge Celtic and Workington. The 288 well illustrated pages also contain the basic statistical details of each club. Price £12–95 plus £1–30 postage.

***REJECTED F.C. OF SCOTLAND – Vol. 1: Edinburgh and The South.*** *(By Dave Twydell)* The first of three volumes on the written and basic statistical details of the Scottish ex–League Clubs (Edinburgh City, Leith Athletic, St.Bernards, Armadale, Broxburn United, Bathgate, Peebles Rovers, Mid–Annandale, Nithsdale Wanderers and Solway Star). Price £12–95 Plus £1–30 Postage. **(Volume 2 – Glasgow and District.** Same price with another 11 Clubs' histories, including Third Lanark).

***'GONE BUT NOT FORGOTTEN – PART 2'*** *(By Dave Twydell)* The abbreviated histories of a variety of defunct non–League Clubs and Grounds; the old Hillingdon Borough, Wycombe's Loakes Park, Oswestry Town and Shirley Town are included in this edition (Part 1 is now sold out). A particular merit of these books is the high illustrative content, and with details for readers to track down the sites of the Grounds – 64 pages. Issued every 6 months Price £4–95 plus 45p postage

***PETERBOROUGH UNITED – The Official History of The Posh.*** *(By Andy Groom and Mick Robinson)* 273 x 202 m.m. hardback (with full colour dust jacket) containing 240 (high quality paper) pages. An extensive and well illustrated text section details the club's history from the earliest days. The statistical section contains the complete match and team details from the Club's formation in 1934. (Reprint) Price £14–95 plus £3–40 postage.

***AMBER IN THE BLOOD – History of Newport County:*** *(Tony Ambrosen).* The book tells the full written story of football in Newport from the pre–County days right up to the newly formed Newport AFC club. The text is well illustrtated, and a comprehensive statistical section provides all the results, attendances, goalscorers, etc. from 1912 to 1993 – the various Leagues and principal Cup competitions; additionally seasonal total players' appearances are included. A hardback book, containing 176 large pages is exceptional value at only £13–95 plus £2–60 postage.

***FOOTBALL LEAGUE – GROUNDS FOR A CHANGE*** *(By Dave Twydell).* A 424 page, A5 sized, Hardback book. A comprehensive study of all the Grounds on which the current Football League Clubs previously played. Every Club that has moved Grounds is included, with a 'Potted' history of each, plus 250 illustrations. Plenty of 'reading' material, as well as an interesting reference book. Price £13–95 Plus £1–70 Postage.

SPECIAL LIMITED EDITION
Reminiscences of Colchester Town Football Club

This Fascinating reprint of the 40 page booklet (referred to in the Colchester United history book) provides the history of Colchester Town Football Club (from 1873 to 1924).

Provides details of the Officials (including several photo's.), the players, the Grounds, etc.

Colchester Town
Football Club

Original copies are all but impossible to obtain now, but for a modest price you can now have your own copy.

**Price only £2–95**
**including U.K. post and packing.**

***THROUGH THE TURNSTILES** (by Brian Tabner)* This incredible book which provides the average attendance of every Football League Club, for every season from 1888/89 to 1991/92. (*'The best Football Book I have ever read. " At the bottom end of the price range for a quality book. "* – The Footballer Magazine) Well illustrated, and also relates the development of the game (angled towards attendances). Also details of the best supported 'away' teams, season ticket sales over the years, etc. Large format hardback and 208 packed pages. An excellent read at £13–95 plus £1–70 Postage

***COVENTRY CITY FOOTBALLERS (The Complete Who's Who)***
*By Martin & Paul O'Connor.* One of the most detailed books of its type. Every Football (and Southern) League player has been included – around 700. Seasonal appearances of every player, brief personal details, 'pen pictures', together with very detailed information on the movements of the players to other clubs. Plus: around 100 photo's of the Club's most memorable men, and information on the principal players from the pre–Southern League days. A hardback book with 224 large pages. £13–95 plus £2–60 postage.

***HISTORY OF THE LANCASHIRE FOOTBALL ASSOCIATION 1878–1928.*** A rare historical and fascinating hardback reprint (first published in 1928). Contains the history of the formative days of Lancashire football. Sections within the 288 pages include the early histories of about 20 Clubs (Manchester Utd., Wigan Borough, Rochdale, etc.), Lancashire Cup competitions, Biographies, etc. For those interested in the development of the game, this is a 'must', and you will definitely not be disappointed. Price £12–95 Plus £1–30 Postage.

***THE IRONSIDES. A Lifetime in the League***
***Who's Who of Newport County** (By Tony Ambrosen) ("Providing a hugely enjoyable read and a valuable reference book"* – S.Wales Argus). Every player who appeared for the Club in the Football League is given a potted football and personal history, plus lengthy sections on the players during the Club's three periods in non–League football and details of all the Managers and Trainers. Over 100 photographs, A5 size 224 page book. A 'must' for statisticians and others interested in this ex–League club. Price £8–95 Plus £1–00 Postage.

***MORE DEFUNCT F.C.*** (By Dave Twydell). A follow up to the successful 'Defunct F.C.' book (Now out of print). Detailed and well illustrated histories of defunct Clubs – *Bedford Avenue, Lovell's Athletic, Romford, Rugby Town, Slough Centre and West Stanley* – including basic statistics, 230 pages. Price £6–75 Plus £1 postage.

**Available from:**
**TRANS VIDEO PRODUCTIONS**
**Regent House, 16 Old Road, Linslade, Leighton Buzzard, Beds. LU7 7RD**
(Please add £1–00 P/P or obtainable from major video outlets)

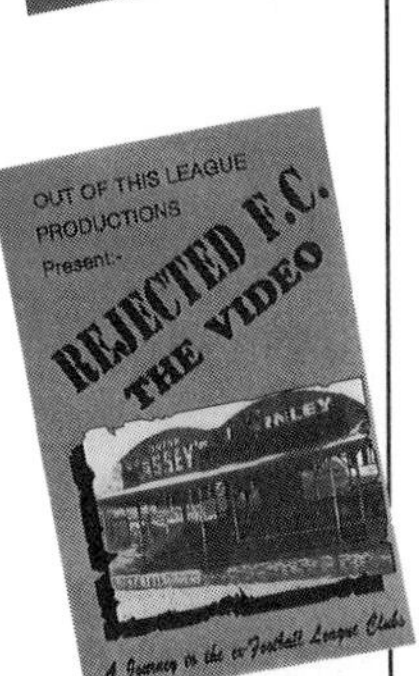


***REJECTED F.C. – The Video*** The video of the books (Rejected F.C. Volumes 1 and 2). Several hours of repeated entertainment. Includes extensive modern film shots, interviews with many personalities related to these teams, still shots to aid the telling of these Clubs' Histories... and an amazing collection of archive film (e.g. Ashington in 1924, pre–war New Brighton, Workington's last home League match, etc.). Every 'Rejected' club (from Accrington in 1888) is featured. Price £12–99 (incl. VAT), from major Video outlets.

***FOOTBALL PHOENIX*** – The sequel to 'Rejected F.C. – The Video'. The stories on film of the five post–war League Clubs who became defunct and have successfully reformed (Gateshead, Accrington Stanley, Bradford P.A., Newport County and Aldershot). Film clips include all the goals from County's last game, and the Carl Zeiss match, plus Aldershot's last League game, and footage from 1970 of the new Stanley. 80 minutes of excellent entertainment at only £10–99.

***YESTERDAY'S CIGARETTE CARD HEROES*** A video providing an insight of professional football in the 1930's to 1960's. A number of modern filmed interviews with famous players of 'yesteryear', including Tommy Lawton, Billy Wright, Roy Bentley, John Charles, etc. Their humourous stories, anecdotes, and other stories of their life in football. Includes cartoon strips illustrating their tales, archive action footage etc. 60 minutes of nostalgia! Price £10–99.

(Send a S.A.E. for full lists of Football and other specialist videos)